Handbook
on the
Aged
in the
United States

Handbook on the Aged in the United States

Edited by Erdman B. Palmore

GREENWOOD PRESS
Westport, Connecticut • London, England

Library of Congress Cataloging in Publication Data

Main entry under title:

Handbook on the aged in the United States.

  Bibliography: p.
  Includes index.
  1. Aged—United States—Handbooks, manuals, etc.
I. Palmore, Erdman Ballagh, 1930-
HQ1064.U5H23   1984   305.2'6'0973   84-4463
ISBN 0-313-23721-2 (lib. bdg.)

Library of Congress Catalog Card Number: 84-4463
ISBN: 0-313-23721-2

First published in 1984

Greenwood Press
A division of Congressional Information Service, Inc.
88 Post Road West
Westport, Connecticut 06881

Printed in the United States of America

10 9 8 7 6 5 4 3 2 1

To the millions of older Americans
whose rich diversity is
the basis for this handbook.

CONTENTS

FIGURES

TABLES

PREFACE

This handbook is the most comprehensive ever published on the aged in the United States. Each chapter is written by one or more recognized experts in their field. We are grateful to these contributors for the hard work and creative intelligence with which they have summarized the available information on the older Americans described in their chapters. Some present original research findings not previously published.

Most chapters include sections on various characteristics (demographic, psychological, and socioeconomic) of the category of older Americans under discussion; also covered are their history, special problems, special advantages, organizations and available services, research issues, references, and sources for additional information.

The handbook is divided into four main parts: Demographic Groups, Religious Groups, Ethnic Groups, and Groups Presenting Special Concerns. Within each part the various groups are treated in alphabetical order. There are also two appendices—one listing the major academic and research centers where more information may be obtained and another providing statistical tables about older Americans in general—and a general bibliography. The index provides handy reference to any topic or author.

Some explanation of the four main sections and the groups included in them may help clarify the organization of the handbook. "Demographic Groups" includes both traditional demographic groups and some groups that are not traditionally thought of as "demographic," such as famous aged and veterans. The latter fit here better than in the other sections.

"Religious Groups" includes chapters on the three main religious groups in the United States—Catholics, Jews, and Protestants. Other religious groups, such as Buddhists, Muslims, and Hindus, are not included because there are few elderly in the United States belonging to those groups and almost no information is available about them.

"Ethnic Groups" includes three groups that might be considered racial rather than ethnic—Asians, blacks, and Indians. They are included in this section because, broadly defined, "ethnic" means "of or relating to races or large groups of people classified according to common traits or customs" (*Webster's Collegiate Dictionary*).

"Groups Presenting Special Concerns" includes those whose particular circumstances warrant their being considered as a separate group. Some, such as the institutionalized and the mentally ill, require special care. Others, specifically criminals, present a problem to society, while still others, the victims of crime, are primarily victims of circumstance. Homosexuals, on the other hand, are differentiated by their life-style and sexual preference. In all of these groups, the elderly merit special concern.

We have attempted to write and organize the handbook in a way that will be interesting and useful not only to gerontologists and professionals working with older Americans, but to all adults concerned with their own aging or with the aged in the United States.

I wish to thank the editors of Greenwood Press for originating the idea for this handbook and for guiding it to a successful conclusion.

INTRODUCTION

ERDMAN B. PALMORE

The twenty-four chapters in this handbook deal with various groups of aged individuals in the United States. By way of introduction to the detailed discussions that follow, this chapter will review some of the basic facts and misconceptions about older Americans in general. More statistical information is presented in Appendix B.

Various studies have shown that a majority of Americans believe a number of negative stereotypes about the aged (for a review, see Palmore, 1982). Among the most frequent misconceptions are the following: the majority of the aged are sick or senile, useless, lonely and isolated; often bored, irritated, or angry; are usually unhappy or miserable; are set in their ways and unable to change; have more accidents than younger persons; are often victimized by criminals; are poverty stricken; and their situation is getting worse all the time.

In order to reduce such misconceptions we will review some of the basic facts about aging, both positive and negative. (Much of this material is based on Palmore, 1977; Palmore, 1981.*) We will group these facts into three categories: physical, mental, and socioeconomic. In each section we will first review some of the negative facts that show the real declines and problems of older Americans, and then review the more positive facts, which show that despite these declines and problems the majority are relatively healthy, useful, socially integrated, happy, and satisfied with life, and that their situation is generally improving over the years.

PHYSICAL FACTS

Lung vital capacity tends to decline in old age. Both lung vital capacity (the volume of air that can be forcibly expelled in one breath) and maximum breathing

*Adapted and reprinted by permission of *The Gerontologist*, Vol. 17, No. 4, August 1977, and Vol. 21, No. 4, August 1981.

capacity (the volume of air that can be moved in and out of the lungs in fifteen seconds) decline on the average from age 30 onward (Shock, 1962).

All five senses tend to decline in old age. Most studies agree that various aspects of vision, hearing, and touch tend to decline in old age. Some studies of taste and smell have not found a significant decline, but the best evidence indicates increases in taste and smell thresholds with age (Riley and Foner, 1968). Studies of structural atrophy in the tongue and nose with old age support the experimental evidence of decline in taste and smell (Birren, 1959).

Physical strength also tends to decline in old age. Studies of various kinds of muscular strength show declines in old age compared to young adulthood of 15 to 46 percent (Birren, 1959). More persons over 65 have chronic illnesses that limit their activity (43 percent) than younger persons (10 percent). The discrepancy is even greater for the percentage with chronic illnesses that limit their major activity: 37 percent of those over 65 compared to only 7 percent of those under 65 (National Center for Health Statistics, 1978).

On the other hand, older persons have fewer acute illnesses than younger persons: there are 102 acute illnesses per 100 persons over age 65 per year, compared to 230 for persons under 65 (National Center for Health Statistics, 1978). Thus, the higher rate of chronic illnesses among the aged is partially offset by the lower rate of acute illnesses. Furthermore, older persons have fewer injuries in the home than younger persons: 12.5 per 100 persons over 65 per year compared to 14 for persons under 65 (National Center for Health Statistics, 1978). The injury rate is especially high for children under 6: 26 per 100.

Drivers over age 65 also have fewer accidents per person than drivers under age 65. Older drivers have about the same accident rate per person as middle-aged drivers, but a much lower rate than drivers under age 30 (National Safety Council, 1976). Older drivers tend to drive fewer miles per year and apparently tend to compensate for any declines in perception and reaction speed by driving more carefully.

About 80 percent of the aged are healthy enough to engage in their normal activities. About 5 percent of those over age 65 are institutionalized, and another 15 percent among the noninstitutionalized say they are unable to engage in their major activity (such as work or housework) because of chronic conditions. This leaves 80 percent who are able to engage in their major activity (National Center for Health Statistics, 1974).

MENTAL FACTS

The reaction time of most old people tends to be slower than that of younger people. This is one of the best documented facts about the aged. It appears to be true regardless of the kind of reaction that is measured (Botwinick, 1967).

Old people usually take longer to learn something new. Experiments have consistently shown that older people take longer than younger people to learn new material (Botwinick, 1967). Studies of on-the-job trainees also show that older workers tend to take somewhat longer to learn new jobs (Riley and Foner, 1968). Yet, it is not impossible for most old people to learn new things. The studies cited above also show that most older persons can eventually learn new things about as well as younger persons, if given enough time and repetitions of the material to be learned.

The majority of old people are not senile (i.e., defect in memory, disoriented, or demented). Only about 2 or 3 percent of persons age 65 or over are institutionalized as a result of psychiatric illness (Busse and Pfeiffer, 1977). A series of eight community surveys found the prevalence of psychosis of all types to range from 4 to 8 percent (Riley and Foner, 1968). Thus, all the evidence indicates that less than 10 percent of the aged are disoriented or demented. It is more difficult to get accurate estimates of the proportion with defective memories, partly because of the different types of memory defects and partly because of different methods of measuring them. However, most studies agree that there is little or no decline with age in short-term memory storage capacity (using the digit span test). Four studies did find large age differences in free recall of words, but two of them found no age differences in recognition of words in a list (Woodruff and Birren, 1975). As for long-term memory, various community surveys have found less than 20 percent of the aged who cannot remember such things as the last president of the United States, their own correct age, birth date, telephone number, mother's maiden name, address, or the alphabet (Botwinick, 1967; Pfeiffer, 1975). Thus, it is clear that the majority of aged do not have serious memory defects.

The majority of old people are not set in their ways and unable to change. There is some evidence that older people tend to become more stable in their attitudes, but it is clear that most older people do change and adapt to the many major events that occur in old age, such as retirement, children leaving home, and serious illness. Their political and social attitudes also tend to shift with those of the rest of society, although at a somewhat slower rate than for younger people (Cutler and Kaufman, 1975; Glenn and Hefner, 1972).

The majority of older workers can work as effectively as younger workers. Despite declines in perception and reaction speed under laboratory conditions among the general aged population, studies of older workers (the 12 percent who are able to continue employment after age 65) under actual working conditions generally show that they perform as well, if not better, than younger workers on most measures. When speed of reaction is important, older workers sometimes produce at lower rates, but they are as accurate and steady in their work as younger workers. Consistency of output tends to increase by age, as older workers perform at steadier rates from week to week than do younger workers. In addition, older workers have less job turnover, fewer accidents, and less absenteeism than younger workers (Riley and Foner, 1968).

The majority of old people are seldom irritated or angry. The Kansas City Study found that over one-half of the aged said that they are never or hardly ever irritated, and this proportion increases to two-thirds at age 80 or over. About three-fourths said that they are never or hardly ever angry (Dean, 1962). The Duke Adaptation Study found that 90 percent of persons over age 65 said that they were not angry at any time during the past week.

The majority of old people report that they feel relatively happy or satisfied most of the time. Studies of happiness, morale, and life satisfaction either find no significant difference by age groups or find that about one-fifth to one-third of the aged score "low" on various happiness or morale scales (Riley and Foner, 1968). A national survey found that less than one-fourth of persons 65 or over reported, "This is the dreariest time of my life," while a majority said, "I am just as happy as when I was younger" (Harris, 1975).

SOCIOECONOMIC FACTS

The aged are more fearful of crime. In a nationally representative survey, 23 percent of those over 65 said that fear of crime was a "very serious problem" for them, compared to 15 percent of those aged 18 to 64 (Harris, 1975). Another national survey found that 51 percent of those 65 and over, compared to 41 percent of those under 65, answered yes to the question, "Is there any area right around here where you would be afraid to walk alone at night?" (Clemente and Kleinman, 1976). Especially high proportions of women, blacks, and metropolitan aged are fearful of crime. This greater fear of crime among the aged may be one reason their victimization rate is lower.

The aged actually have lower rates of criminal victimization than those under 65. Persons over 65 have substantially lower victimization rates in nearly all categories of personal crime: rape, robbery, assault, and personal theft (U.S. Department of Justice, 1977). The only category in which the victimization rate of older persons is even equal to that of younger persons is "personal larceny with contact" (which includes purse-snatching and pick-pocketing), and this category accounts for less than 3 percent of all personal crimes. When all personal crimes are added together, persons over 65 have a victimization rate that is less than one-fourth that of all persons over age 12 (31 per 1,000 compared to 128 per 1,000).

Medicare pays less than half of the medical expenses for the aged. In 1977, Medicare payments covered 44 percent of the personal health care expenditures of the aged (Gibson and Fisher, 1979). Medicaid covered an additional 17 percent (among the "medically indigent"), other public programs (such as those of the Veterans Administration) covered another 6 percent, and the remaining 33 percent was paid by private insurance or out of pocket.

Most medical practitioners tend to give low priority to the aged. A series of twelve empirical studies found that most medical students and doctors, nursing students and nurses, occupational therapy students, psychiatry clinic personnel, and social workers tend to believe the negative stereotypes about the aged and prefer to work with children or younger adults. Few specialize, or are interested in specializing, in geriatrics (Brown, 1967; Campbell, 1971; Coe, 1967; Cyrus-Lutz and Gaitz, 1972; Delora and Moses, 1969; Gale and Livseley, 1974; Garfinkel, 1975; Gunter, 1971; Miller, Lowenstein, and Winston, 1976; Mills, 1972; Spence and Feigenbaum, 1968).

About 1 percent more of the aged have incomes below the official poverty level than the rest of the population. In 1981, 15 percent of persons 65 or over had incomes below the official government poverty threshold ($4,359 for an individual and $5,498 for a couple over 65) compared to 14 percent for all persons (Pear, 1982). This is a decline from 35 percent of the aged in 1959. Even if the "near poor" are included, the total in or near poverty is only 25 percent.

The aged get approximately their proportionate share of the nation's income. In 1967 the aged's share of the nation's total personal income before taxes was about 10 percent, and they constituted slightly less than 10 percent of the total population (Bixby, 1970). In 1973 the aged received 11.2 percent of aggregate household money income before taxes, and they constituted 10.4 percent of the total population (U.S. Bureau of the Census, 1974). If taxes and transfer payments are taken into account, the aged receive more than their proportionate share of total personal income: in 1972 persons age 65 and over received 13.7 percent of total income after taxes were deducted and transfer payments added (Fried et al., 1973).

Social Security benefits automatically increase with inflation. Since 1975 Social Security benefits have been automatically increased whenever the Consumer Price Index (CPI) compiled by the Bureau of Labor Statistics for the first calendar quarter of a year exceeds by at least 3 percent the CPI for the first calendar quarter of the preceding year. The size of the benefit increase is determined by the actual percentage rise of the CPI during the quarters measured.

Supplemental Security Income (SSI) guarantees a minimum income for needy aged. In January 1974 the SSI program was established to provide a minimum monthly income for all persons over 65 with assets of less than a stated amount ($1,500 for an individual, $2,250 for a couple), excluding the value of a home, household goods, personal effects, an automobile, life insurance of less than $1,500, and property needed for self-support. In January 1981 persons over 65 could receive monthly SSI payments of up to $238 for an individual or $357 for a couple.

The majority of old people are not socially isolated and lonely. About two-thirds of the aged say that they are never or hardly ever lonely (Dean, 1962) or say that loneliness is not a serious problem (Harris, 1975). Most older persons have close relatives within easy visiting distance and contacts with them are relatively frequent (Binstock and Shanas, 1976). About half say they "spend a lot of time" socializing with friends (Harris, 1975). About three-fourths of the aged are members of a church or synagogue (Erskine, 1964), and about half attend services at least three times per month (*Catholic Digest*, 1966). Over half belong to other voluntary organizations (Hausknecht, 1962). Thus, between visits with relatives and friends and participation in church and other voluntary organizations, the majority of old people are far from socially isolated.

The majority of aged do not live alone. In 1975, for example, only 14.2 percent of men 65 or over lived alone, and 36 percent of women 65 or over lived alone (Siegel, 1976). The majority lived with their spouse (74 percent of men, 36 percent of women, 51 percent of the total 65 or over). The majority of old people report that they are seldom bored. Only 17 percent of persons 65 or over say that having "not enough to do to keep busy" is a "somewhat serious" or "very serious" problem (Harris, 1975). Another survey found that two-thirds of the aged said that they were never or hardly ever bored (Dean, 1962). The Duke Adaptation Study found that 87 percent of those 65 or over said that they were never bored in the past week.

Over three-fourths of old people are working or would like to have some kind of work to do (including housework and volunteer work). About 12 percent of persons 65 or over are employed; 21 percent are retired but say they would like to be employed; 17 percent work as housewives; 19 percent are not employed but do volunteer work; and another 9 percent are not employed and not doing volunteer work but would like to do volunteer work (Harris, 1975). These percentages account for 78 percent of the total.

Participation in voluntary organizations does not usually decline with age among healthy older persons. A number of recent nationwide surveys have shown that when the effects of socioeconomic differences and health are controlled, age bears little or no relationship to voluntary association participation in middle age or later life (Cutler, 1977). In longitudinal studies persons with either increased or stable participation far outnumbered those whose participation declined. However, declining health does tend to decrease participation.

The aged are the most law-abiding of all adult groups regardless of how this characteristic is measured. For example, persons over 65 have about one-tenth their expected arrest rate for all offenses (arrests of persons over 65 are 1.2 percent of the total arrests) and about one-twentieth their expected rate for felony offenses (those over 65 account for .5 percent of the total) (Federal Bureau of Investigation, 1974). Similarly, persons over 65 are incarcerated in prisons and jails at about one-tenth their expected rate (1.3 percent of all prisoners are 65 and older) (U.S. Bureau of the Census, 1973).

Fewer aged persons vote than do persons in middle-aged groups. Numerous cross-sectional studies have shown that voting participation increases with age from the twenties to the early sixties and then falls off after age 65 (Hudson and Binstock, 1976). A cross-national study found the same pattern in the United States, Austria, India, Japan, and Nigeria (Nie, Verba, and Kim, 1974). However, the lower voting participation of the aged is not due to aging processes, but to the larger proportions of the aged who are female and have less education (Glenn and Grimes, 1968; Houte and Knoke, 1975; Verba and Nie, 1972).

There are proportionately more older persons in public office than in the total population. This appears to be true of all public officials. In 44 percent of the years in which we have had a president, the president was over age 60, and in 14 percent the president was over age 65 ("Longevity," 1980). In 1975 21 percent of U.S. representatives and 39 percent of U.S. senators were 60 or over (U.S. Bureau of the Census, 1976) at a time when 15 percent of the total population was 60 or over. Older persons are also overrepresented among U.S. ambassadors, Supreme Court justices, cabinet members, and governors (Lehman, 1953; Schlesinger, 1966).

Older persons who disengage from active roles do not tend to be happier than those who remain active. On the contrary, most surveys and longitudinal studies have found that those who remain active tend to be happier than those who disengage, although some studies have found no relationship between activity and happiness. For example, several studies have found no overall relation between retirement and morale or life satisfaction (George and Maddox, 1977; Simpson and McKinney, 1966; Streib and Schneider, 1971). On the other hand, the Duke Second Longitudinal Study found small declines in life satisfaction and happiness after retirement (Palmore et al., 1979). A review of seventeen studies of activity and life satisfaction showed that most studies found significant positive relationships between more activity and greater life satisfaction, although a few of the relationships were not statistically significant (Larson, 1978).

When the last child leaves home, the majority of parents do not have serious problems adjusting to their "empty nest." Glenn (1975) concluded from his study that the last child leaving home does not typically have an enduring negative effect. Our longitudinal study also found no lasting negative effects of the last child leaving home, and instead found two significant positive effects: life satisfaction and happiness both increased significantly after the last child left home (Palmore et al., 1979).

The majority of persons past age 65 continue to have both interest in and capacity for sexual relations. Masters and Johnson (1966) found that the capacity for satisfying sexual relations continues into the decades of the seventies and eighties for healthy couples. The Duke Longitudinal Studies found that sex continues to play an important role in the lives of most men and the majority of women through the seventh decade of life (Palmore, 1974).

The health and socioeconomic status of older people (compared to younger people) in the year 2000 will probably be much higher than now. Measures of health, income, occupation, and education among older people are all rising in comparison to those of younger people. By the year 2000, the gaps between older and younger persons in these dimensions will probably be substantially smaller (Palmore, 1976).

Most old people are not pretty much alike. There appear to be at least as many individual differences between older people as there are at any age level; they are rich and poor, happy and sad, healthy and sick, of high and low intelligence, and so forth. In fact, some evidence indicates that as people age they tend to become less alike and more heterogeneous in many dimensions (Maddox and

Douglas, 1974). The belief that the elderly are all alike is one of the most widely held misconceptions about them. Many other negative misconceptions spring from this tendency to stereotype older Americans as one homogeneous mass. One of the main purposes of this handbook is to dispel this stereotype by showing how diverse older Americans really are. We hope it will become dramatically clear that not only are there dozens of markedly different types of older Americans, but that even within each category there is rich diversity.

REFERENCES

Binstock, R. H., and Shanas, E. (Eds.). *Handbook of aging and the social sciences.* Van Nostrand Reinhold, New York, 1976.

Birren, J. (Ed.). *Handbook of aging and the individual.* University of Chicago Press, Chicago, 1959.

Bixby, L. Income of people aged 65 and older. *Social Security Bulletin*, 1970, *33*, 3–34.

Blazer, D., and Palmore, E. Religion and aging in a longitudinal panel. *Gerontologist*, 1976, *16*, 82–85.

Botwinick, J. *Cognitive processes in maturity and old age.* Springer, New York, 1967.

Brotman, H. Advance data on income in 1975 with revisions of published data for 1974. U.S. Bureau of the Census, October 1976. Mimeo.

Brown, M. *Nurses' attitudes toward the aged and their care.* Annual report to the Gerontology Branch, U.S. Public Health Service. USGPO, Washington, D.C., 1967.

Busse, E., and Pfeiffer, E. (Eds.). *Behavior and adaptation in late life.* Little, Brown, Boston, 1977.

Campbell, M. Study of the attitudes of nursing personnel toward the geriatric patient. *Nursing Research*, 1971, *20*, 147–151.

Carver, R. Two dimensions of tests: Psychometric and edumetric. *American Psychologist*, 1974, *29*, 512–518.

Catholic Digest. Survey of religions in the U.S. *Catholic Digest*, 1966, *7*, 27.

Clemente, F., and Kleinman, M. Fear of crime among the aged. *Gerontologist*, 1976, *16*, 207–210.

Coe, R. Professional perspectives on the aged. *Gerontologist*, 1967, *7*, 114–119.

Current Population Survey. *Projections of the population of the U.S. by age and sex: 1975–2000.* U.S. Bureau of the Census, ser. P–25, no. 541. USGPO, Washington, D.C., 1975.

Cutler, S. Aging and voluntary associations participation. *Journal of Gerontology*, 1977, *32*, 470–479.

Cutler, S., and Kaufman, R. Cohort changes in political attitudes. *Public Opinion Quarterly*, 1975, *39*, 69–81.

Cyrus-Lutz, C., and Gaitz, C. Psychiatrists' attitudes toward the aged and aging. *Gerontologist*, 1972, *12*, 163–167.

Dean, L. Aging and decline of affect. *Journal of Gerontology*, 1962, *17*, 440–446.

Delora, J., and Moses, D. Specialty preferences and characteristics of nursing students in baccalaureate programs. *Nursing Research*, 1969, *18*, 137–144.

Erskine, H. The polls. *Public Opinion Quarterly*, 1964, *28*, 679.

Federal Bureau of Investigation. Uniform crime reports. USGPO, Washington, D.C., 1974.

Fried, E.; Rivlin, A.; Schultze, C.; and Teeters, N. *Setting national priorities*. Brookings Institute, Washington, D.C., 1973.

Gale, J., and Livseley, B. Attitudes toward geriatrics: A report of the King's survey. *Age and Aging*, 1974, *3*, 49–53.

Garfinkel, R. The reluctant therapist. *Gerontologist*, 1975, *15*, 136–137.

George, L., and Maddox, G. Subjective adaptation to loss of the work role. *Journal of Gerontology*, 1977, *32*, 456–462.

Gibson, R., and Fisher, C. Age differences in health care spending, fiscal year 1977. *Social Security Review*, 1979, *42*, 3–16.

Glenn, N. Psychological well-being in the post-parental stage. *Journal of Marriage and the Family*, 1975, *37*, 105–110.

Glenn, N., and Grimes, M. Aging, voting, and political interest. *American Sociological Review*, 1968, *33*, 563–575.

Glenn, N., and Hefner, T. Further evidence on aging and party identification. *Public Opinion Quarterly*, 1972, *36*, 31–47.

Golde, P., and Kogan, N. A sentence completion procedure for assessing attitudes toward old people. *Journal of Gerontology*, 1959, *14*, 355–363.

Gunter, L. Students' attitudes toward geriatric nursing. *Nursing Outlook*, 1971, *19*, 466–469.

Harris, L. *The myth and reality of aging in America*. National Council on the Aging, Washington, D.C., 1975.

Hausknecht, M. *The joiners*. Bedminster Press, New York, 1962.

Houte, M., and Knoke, D. Change in voting turnout, 1952–72. *Public Opinion Quarterly*, 1975, *39*, 52–68.

Hudson, R., and Binstock, R. Political systems and aging. In R. Binstock and E. Shanas (Eds.), *Handbook of aging and the social sciences*. Van Nostrand Reinhold, New York, 1976.

Kogan, N. Attitudes toward old people. *Journal of Abnormal Psychology*, 1961, *62*, 44–54.

Kossoris, M. Absenteeism and injury experience of older workers. *Monthly Labor Review*, 1948, *67*, 16–19.

Larson, R. Thirty years of research on the subjective well-being of older Americans. *Journal of Gerontology*, 1978, *33*, 109–129.

Lehman, H. *Age and achievement*. Princeton University Press, Princeton, N.J., 1953.

Longevity of presidents, vice-presidents, and unsuccessful candidates for the presidency. Metropolitan Statistical Bulletin, 1980, *61*, 2–8.

Maddox, G., and Douglas, E. Aging and individual differences. *Journal of Gerontology*, 1974, *29*, 555–563.

Mark, J. Comparative job performance by age. *Monthly Labor Review*, 1957, *80*, 1468–1471.

Masters, W., and Johnson, V. *Human sexual response*. Little, Brown, Boston, 1966.

Miller, D.; Lowenstein, R.; and Winston, R. Physician's attitudes toward the ill aged and nursing homes. *Journal of the American Geriatrics Society*, 1976, *24*, 498–505.

Mills, J. Attitudes of undergraduate students concerning geriatric patients. *American Journal of Occupational Therapy*, 1972, *26*, 200–203.

National Center for Health Statistics. *Health characteristics of persons with chronic activity limitation*. Ser. 10, no. 112. USGPO, Washington, D.C., 1974.

―――. *Current estimates from the health interview survey*. Ser. 10, no. 126, USGPO, Washington, D.C., 1978.

―――. *Monthly vital statistics report: Final mortality statistics, 1978*. Vol. 29, no. 6, supp. 2, USGPO, Washington, D.C., 1980.

National Safety Council. *Accident facts*. National Safety Council, Chicago, 1976.

Nie, N.; Verba, S.; and Kim, J. Political participation and the life cycle. *Comparative Politics*, 1974, *6*, 319–340.

Palmore, E. *Normal aging, vol. 2*. Duke University Press, Durham, N.C., 1974.

―――. The future status of the aged. *Gerontologist*, 1976, *16*, 297–302.

―――. Facts on aging: A short quiz. *Gerontologist*, 1977, *17*, 315–320.

―――. The facts on aging quiz: A review of findings. *Gerontologist*, 1980, *20*, 669–672.

―――. The facts on aging quiz: Part two. *Gerontologist*, 1981, *21*, 431–437.

―――. Attitudes toward the aged. *Research on Aging*, 1982, *4*, 333–348.

Palmore, E.; Cleveland, W.; Nowlin, J.; Ramm, D.; and Siegler, I. Stress and adaptation in later life. *Journal of Gerontology*, 1979, *34*, 841–851.

Pear, R. How poor are the elderly? *New York Times*, December 19, 1982, Sec. F, 4.

Pfeiffer, E. A short portable mental status questionnaire for the assessment of organic brain deficit in elderly patients. *Journal of the American Geriatrics Society*, 1975, *23*, 433–441.

Riley, M., and Foner, A. *Aging and Society. Volume 1: An inventory of research findings*. Russell Sage Foundation, New York, 1968.

Rossman, I. Anatomic and body composition changes with aging. In C. Finch and L. Hayflick (Eds.), *Handbook of the biology of aging*. Van Nostrand Reinhold, New York, 1977.

Schlesinger, J. *Ambition and politics*. Rand McNally, Chicago, 1966.

Shock, N. The physiology of aging. *Scientific American*, 1962, *206*, 100–110.

Siegel, J. Demographic aspects of aging and the older population in the U.S. *Current Population Reports*, ser. P–23, no. 59. USGPO, Washington, D.C., 1976.

Simpson, I., and McKinney, J. *Social aspects of aging*. Duke University Press, Durham, N.C., 1966.

Spence, D., and Feigenbaum, E. Medical students' attitudes toward the geriatric patient. *Journal of Gerontology*, 1968, *16*, 976–983.

Streib, G., and Schneider, C. *Retirement in American society*. Cornell University Press, Ithaca, N.Y., 1971.

Tuckman, J., and Lorge, I. The effects of institutionalization on attitudes toward old people. *Journal of Abnormal Psychology*, 1952, *47*, 337–345.

U.S. Bureau of the Census. *Persons in institutions and other group quarters*. Special Subject Report. USGPO, Washington, D.C., 1970.

―――. *Persons in institutions and other group quarters*. USGPO, Washington, D.C., 1973.

―――. *Money income in 1973 of families and persons in the U.S. Current Population Reports*, ser. P–60, no. 93. USGPO, Washington, D.C., 1974.

―――. *Statistical abstract of the United States*. USGPO, Washington, D.C., 1976.

―――. Social and economic characteristics of the older population: 1978. *Current Population Reports*, ser. P–23, no. 85. USGPO, Washington, D.C., 1979.

U.S. Department of Justice. *Criminal victimization in the U.S.* USGPO, Washington, D.C., 1977.

Verba, S., and Nie, N. *Participation in America.* Harper and Row, New York, 1972.

Williams, B. *Characteristics of the black elderly—1980.* Statistical Reports on Older Americans. Administration on Aging, USGPO, Washington, D.C., 1980.

Woodruff, D., and Birren, J. (Eds.). *Aging: Scientific perspectives and social issues.* Van Nostrand Reinhold, New York, 1975.

PART I

DEMOGRAPHIC GROUPS

1

CENTENARIANS

ROBERT E. PIERONI

HISTORICAL ACCOUNTS

Over 250 years ago, Benjamin Franklin informed the many readers of *Poor Richard's Almanack* that

on the 6th of this Month, 1711, died in England, Mrs. Jane Schrimshaw, aged 127 years; But England boasts some much longer livers. James Sands, of Horburn, in the County of Stafford, near Birmingham, lived 140 Years, and his Wife 120, in a perfect State of Health till the Day of their Deaths. He out-liv'd 5 Leases of 21 Years each, all made after his Marriage. Thomas Parr married his first Wife at 80 Years of Age, by whom he had one Child, and lived till he was something above 150. Henry Jenkins of the Parish of Bolton, in Yorkshire, died the 8th of this same Month, 1670, aged 169 Years. In these American Parts we have no such very old Men; not that the Climate is unhealthy, but because the present Inhabitants were not born soon enough (Franklin, 1976)

It is evident that Franklin, like nearly all his contemporaries, accepted without reservation the astounding ages attributed to certain purported centenarians. Indeed, in 1780 he predicted that the progress of science would develop the capacity to increase the human life span beyond 1,000 years (Ettinger, 1964).

Although claims for the existence of supercentenarians have been made since time immemorial, for the most part such claims remain unsubstantiated. As Comfort (1964a) has pointed out, they "depend largely on unsupported memory and tradition in a field where the emotional premiums of exaggeration are high."

The Shropshire farmer, Thomas Parr, noted by Franklin to have "lived till he was something above 150," is frequently mentioned as an example of an individual having lived to an extremely old age. Old Parr's tomb in Westminster Abbey records that he died at the age of 152 years, 9 months. After his death in 1635, his body was dissected by the famed William Harvey at the request of King Charles I. Harvey reported that Parr could have lived much longer if it were not for the excess food and alterations in his living habits which occurred when he was brought to London to live in the king's palace (Emerson, 1977).

Parr was supposedly summoned before the House of Commons for a misdemeanor committed at the age of 130. According to Legrand (Emerson, 1977), "Harvey is said to have been an eye witness to a coition successfully accomplished by Thomas Parr, at 140 years of age." It has been stated that until he was 130 years old, Parr was able to perform all the duties of a farmer, including threshing the wheat (Emerson, 1977).

In 1873 Thoms exposed the complete lack of documentation of Parr's claims for longevity (Comfort, 1964a; Thoms, 1879). As noted by Comfort (1964b), "It has been suggested that Old Parr's 'longevity' kept a life occupancy of a cottage going through three long-lived generations—father, son and grandson."

Historical claims of extreme old age among isolated tribes and populations are frequent. For example, Huang Ti (2697–2597 B.C.), writing in *The Yellow Emperor's Classic of Internal Medicine*, stated that "in ancient times the people lived (through the years) to be over a hundred years, and yet they remained active and did not become decrepit in their activities" (Veith, 1966).

According to the Bible, of the ten generations from Adam to Noah, Adam lived 930 years, Noah 950, and Methuselah, 969. The righteous Enoch suffered a premature death at age 365. The ten generations from Noah to Abraham did not fare as well age-wise as the antediluvian generations. However, we still find Shem living to 600 years, Sarah to 433, and Abraham to 175, and Moses succumbing at 120 years of age. King David, however, died at age 70 despite (or because of) the able and willing assistance of the maiden Abishag, who attempted to warm his body and breathe new life into the aging king (Brim, 1936; Milne and Milne, 1968).

RECENT ACCOUNTS

In 1970 *Medical World News* informed its readers of reports of individuals who were purported to be the oldest man and woman in the world. These were an Iranian male who claimed to be 190 years old and a Bolivian female 203 years of age. Although doubting the authenticity of these claimants, the medical report listed several factors which have been related to a long life. These include temperate climate, heredity, simple foods, lifelong physical labor, a rewarding family life, meaningful cultural traditions, humor, and a "strong nervous system." As will be seen, many of these key factors are frequently reported to be associated with the longevity of centenarians.

J.T. Freeman recently provided an interesting account of the famous Charlie Smith of Bartow, Florida, who died in 1979, purportedly at the age of 137. As noted by Freeman, "reasonable doubts of such tenure are in order in the absence of verification of the dates given for and by him, and more so in view of the common tendency particularly by nonagenarians to exaggerate age" (Freeman,

1982). Recently, the *American Association of Retired Persons (AARP) News Bulletin* ("One," 1982) described Arthur Reed of Oakland, California, who was seeking a job at the age of 122, as one of the nation's oldest individuals. The article quoted Reed as stating that he had been unemployed for six years. "I haven't got a job yet, but I'll get one soon," Reed said. "I'm not getting any younger, you know." Reed's Social Security records indicate that he was born on June 28, 1860. Norris McWhirter, editor and compiler of the *Guinness Book of World Records*, has pointed out that Social Security records have not always proved to be reliable, and he is actively investigating Reed's claim (McWhirter, 1982).

McWhirter feels that the greatest authenticated age to which any human ever survived was the 116th birthday that Shigechiyo Izumi of Japan celebrated on June 29, 1981. In Japan's first census, conducted in 1871, Izumi was recorded as being 6 years of age (McWhirter, 1982). In January 1981, Fannie Thomas died in this country at the age of 113 years, 273 days. She had survived slightly longer than Canada's famous centenarian, Pierre Joubert, who died in 1814 at the age of 113 years, 124 days (McWhirter, 1982).

Exceptional longevity has been claimed for individuals living in several areas of the world. These areas include the Caucasus region of the U.S.S.R., especially Abkhazia; the Hunza area of northern Pakistan; and the Vilcabamba region of southern Ecuador (Leaf, 1973, 1975; Davies, 1975). Ten years ago, Alexander Leaf in several interesting reports (1973, 1975) described these three population groups, which have been considered to be models of both longevity and fitness in old age. The populations of Abkhazia, Hunza, and Vilcabamba, which have frequently been reported to have unusual numbers of centenarians, all live in remote and mountainous regions (Leaf, 1973, 1975; Davies, 1975). Although the actual ages of the inhabitants are far from clearcut, and in many instances are exaggerated, Leaf and others (Leaf, 1973, 1975; Davies, 1975) have attributed their vigor to diet, exercise, and heredity, as well as psychological factors. The respect from their communities and their sense of being needed have been considered as contributing factors to the well-being and health of these older citizens.

One Soviet citizen claiming to be 117 years of age when interviewed by Leaf attributed his longevity to "active physical work and a moderate interest in alcohol and the ladies." Another, claiming to be 110 years of age, told Leaf that "if one is healthy, one is obliged to drink one liter of wine daily, and on holidays and weddings 17 to 20 tumblers are common!" Leaf pointed out that continuing interest in the opposite sex has frequently been regarded as essential for maintenance of vitality and vigor. A Vilcabamban, reportedly the oldest inhabitant of the region at 123 years of age, continued to drink, smoke, and flirt. He told his interviewer that "I can't see them too well anymore, but by feeling, I can tell if they are women or not." A U.S.S.R. centenarian who had married his seventh wife only three years before stated, "My first six wives were all wonderful women, but this present wife is an angry woman, and I have aged at least ten years since marrying her. If a man has a good and kind wife, he can easily live 100 years'' (Leaf, 1973, 1975).

AGE EXAGGERATION

According to McWhirter (1982), "No single subject is more obscured by vanity, deceit, falsehood, and deliberate fraud than the extremes of human longevity." Dublin, Lotka, and Spiegelman (1949) have noted that toward the end of life a tendency exists—either from ignorance or from pride—to overstate age. An elderly individual might exaggerate his or her age in order to gain the attention, prestige, or reverence that usually follows attainment of extreme old age (Rockstein and Sussman, 1979). A high correlation exists between the illiteracy rate of a region and the number of inhabitants who claim to be centenarians (McWhirter, 1982). Lack of adequate age documentation is common in areas claiming high percentages of centenarians. For example, in Hunza no written language exists at all, nor are there birth records (Medvedev, 1974). In some areas, families have used for later offspring the names of children dying in infancy without going to the trouble of correcting original birth records (Rockstein and Sussman, 1979). There is also the tendency for individuals, when estimating their ages, to round the ages off to higher, even numbers (Comfort, 1964b).

Mazess and Forman detected systematic age exaggeration after the age of 70 among Vilcabambans. They found that the ages claimed by centenarians were either unsubstantiated or incorrect (Mazess and Forman, 1979). Many Russian males are suspected of having assumed others' names and ages in order to avoid military conscription (Medvedev, 1974). Areas that claim high percentages of centenarians are able to derive economic rewards from tourism and political benefits from the favorable propaganda. Joseph Stalin, for example, who was born in Soviet Georgia, became, with increasing age, extremely interested in the reported longevity of his fellow Georgians. Local officials did their best to accommodate Stalin by "finding" more and more centenarians, and by accepting reports of extreme longevity without ample documentation (Medvedev, 1974). Medvedev has reviewed other factors associated with age exaggeration in the U.S.S.R. (1974).

The public should indeed be skeptical of claims for exceedingly long life spans. P.T. Barnum's admonition is as true today as when first uttered. Barnum himself had at one time exhibited an old black female named Joyce Heth who, it was claimed, was the 161-year-old nurse of George Washington. The public was fascinated with the many intriguing details Mrs. Heth supplied concerning our First Father's childhood. She turned out to be one of Barnum's star performers. Unfortunately for her many believers, her autopsy, as well as other evidence, indicated that Mrs. Heth could not have been older than 80 years of age. Additionally, it was revealed that she never had even seen Mt. Vernon.

She had been born in Brooklyn, N.Y., where she lived all her life (Cornell, 1973).

CENSUS DATA

The 1950 U.S. Census listed 4,475 centenarians—a ratio of nearly 3 centenarians per 100,000 inhabitants. As expected, many less-developed countries claimed much higher ratios of centenarians in their populations during this time (Acsadi and Nemeskeri, 1970). For example, the Dominican Republic claimed over 50 centenarians per 100,000 population, and Bolivia, 73. The Puerto Rican census listed 883 centenarians in a population of 2.2 million—a ratio of nearly 40 per 100,000 population. Of interest is that many developed countries claimed significantly lower ratios of centenarians than did the United States. In proportion to their populations, Australia, the United Kingdom, Denmark, France, and Sweden listed only about 20 percent as many centenarians as did the United States, and the percentages for Israel and Japan were 10 percent and 2.5 percent, respectively. It would be ironic if Japan, which currently lays claim to the highest mean life expectancy as well as to the oldest authenticated living centenarian, were to have only one-fortieth the ratio of centenarians as the United States It has been obvious for some time that U.S. census data in regard to centenari are far from accurate. Myers recently discussed the problem of age exaggeration in this country and illustrated how ages can be verified by using available census data (Myers, 1978).

In 1965 L. Haranghy discussed results of a nationwide study of Hungarian centenarians. The results are of general interest. Haranghy and colleagues noted that the number of listed centenarians had declined during the past century despite a constantly increasing life span. They also found that in surveys conducted at the turn of the century ludicrously lengthy life spans had been attributed to certain individuals. For example, a Hungarian male had reportedly lived to be 172 years old, and his wife, 164. Another male was listed as having attained the age of 185. Haranghy and co-workers discussed reasons for age exaggeration in previous surveys of centenarians in Hungary, and seriously questioned the validity of longevity data supplied by other nations. As they stated, "The declaration of age in national censuses is known to be incorrect in most countries. It is most characteristic that in socially and economically undeveloped countries the ratio of the centenarians to the total population is, according to the censuses, significantly higher than in the developed European countries" (Haranghy, 1965).

In the 1980 U.S. Census over 32,000 Americans were reported as being 100 years of age or older. This ratio of centenarians—1 of every 7,000, or about 14 for every 100,000 Americans—is over twice as great as was expected by demographic projections. It has been estimated that a subject born in the 1880s would be expected to have approximately 1 chance in 15,000 of surviving 100 years later. Among blacks in several southern states extremely high ratios of centenarians have been claimed. For example, 1 in 1,700 black females residing in Arkansas was purportedly a centenarian. The Census Bureau readily admits that significant overreporting of age exists and that census data are not as reliable as those collected by the Social Security Administration, which insists on proof of age before paying pensions. Additionally, a Census Bureau official stated that census computer programs used in the 1980 census were, in part, responsible for an apparent but nonexistent age bulge after age 99. This resulted from an editing procedure used to fill in gaps on census forms in which age had not been recorded. This error became significant only at age 100 or older ("Centenarian," 1982).

The Social Security Administration's data for 1980 indicated that 15,258 centenarians (11,132 females and 4,126 males) were on the rolls. This is in contrast to the 21,048 female and 11,146 male centenarians reported in the 1980 national census. Social Security figures indicate that, in proportion to the population, white females have more centenarians than any other group (1 in 9,677). This group is followed by black females (1 centenarian in 13,260), black males (1 in 18,854), and, in last place, white males (1 in 27,741) ("Centenarian," 1982).

Social Security beneficiaries aged 100 or more had risen from 5,300 in 1970 to over 15,000 in 1980, an increase of nearly 200 percent in just ten years, according to the Social Security Administration. The fact that a larger percentage of centenarians met minimum Social Security Administration earnings requirements during this time contributed to this dramatic increase.

ROLE OF HEREDITY

For many years, the standard, albeit ironic, advice for acquiring longevity has been to "pick long-lived parents." Anecdotal reports of remarkable longevity among parents of centenarians abound. The Pearls (1934), for example, in *The Ancestry of the Long-Lived*, stated that the ages of the six progenitors of one centenarian in their study totalled 599, that is, nearly 100 years each. Of interest is that two of the progenitors had reportedly died in accidents!

At the age of 87, Dr. Stephen Jewett, the noted American gerontologist and psychiatrist, published results of his interviews with seventy-nine individuals who ranged in age from 87 to 103. In discussing factors involved in the "longevity syndrome," Jewett underscored the importance of heredity as a determinant of an individual's life expectancy (Puner, 1979).

Numerous reports have likewise emphasized the importance of heredity in longevous individuals (Pearl and Pearl, 1934; Dublin, Lotka, and Spiegelman, 1949; Rockstein and Sussman, 1979; Murphy, 1978). A Duke University study (Palmore, 1982), however, revealed almost no correlation between a subject's longevity or predicted longevity and the ages when the mother and father died. Palmore interpreted these findings as suggesting that "the main effects of genetics on longevity occur at ages before sixty (when our subjects entered our study). That is, inherited diseases and other genetic imperfections probably relate to early death before age sixty. But for those who have survived sixty years, any residual genetic effects are washed out by the overwhelming weight of sixty years of environmental influence" (Palmore, 1982).

Murphy (1978) has recently critically reexamined some of the classic studies bearing on the relationship of heredity to human longevity. These include studies of genealogies, total populations, and twins. Murphy noted methodological problems in all of these earlier reports. He and his colleagues also reanalyzed the extensive survey on human longevity reported by the Pearls in 1934 (Pearl and Pearl, 1934). Murphy's results indicated that parental age does affect longevity, especially for sons. The maternal contribution to longevity was about twice that of the paternal contribution. He pointed out that although this familial component may be genetic, environmental factors may also have influenced the observed familial effects (Murphy, 1978).

It is obvious that the exact contributions of "nature" and "nurture" to human longevity remain unresolved. The evidence for the genetic contribution to longevity in animals is much stronger and more convincing than it is for man (Murphy, 1978). Most gerontologists, however, would have little difficulty accepting Korenchevsky's statement that "genetic factors predetermine the potential maximum span of life for every species, and to a certain extent the actual length of life for individuals within the species. Environmental factors, in their turn, may greatly affect the longevity; by various unfavourable influences they may considerably shorten the length of life" (Korenchevsky, 1961).

Nearly all studies of centenarians have indicated a greater proportion of females (Korenchevsky, 1961). The lower mortality of females has been noted in numerous other species in addition to humans (Comfort, 1964a). U.S. Census Bureau data for the first five decades of this century revealed in each decade a female to male centenarian ratio of about 1.5 to 1. An even higher female to male ratio was recorded in censuses conducted during this time in England and Wales (Korenchevsky, 1961). Post–World War II data submitted to the United Nations Statistical Office by thirty-five countries indicated that there were more female than male centenarians in thirty of the countries (Ascadi and Klinger, 1965). The 1980 data on centenarians from the Social Security Administration revealed a female to male ratio of 2.7 to 1, which was higher than that derived from the national census data, in which the ratio was less than 2 to 1 ("Centenarian," 1982).

LIFE EXPECTANCY

The Psalmist tells us that "the years of our life are three score and ten, or even, by reason of strength, fourscore" (Psalms 90:10). Currently, average life expectancy is approaching about 75 years. Even in the absence of premature death, Fries and Crapo (1981) estimate that the average death would occur at age 85. They estimate that 95 percent of all deaths would be found between the ages of 77 and 93, which is not far from the Psalmist's estimate.

We learn in Genesis 6:3 that "man also is flesh, yet his days shall be 120 years." Most gerontologists would accept this figure as the approximate upper limit of the human life span (Kent, 1980; Fries and Crapo, 1981; Comfort, 1964a). In 1912 Alexis Carrel hypothesized from his tissue culture experiments that neither senescence nor death is intrinsic to isolated cells (Duchesne, 1980). Fifty years later Leonard Hayflick contested these results and presented evidence that cultured human cells have a limited capacity to divide and therefore possess a finite life span (Duchesne, 1980). Based on fifty divisions exhibited by cultured human embryonic cells, Hayflick estimated that man's life span is in the range of 110 to 120 years (Kurtzman and Gordon, 1976).

There is considerable evidence that our bodies age and die according to the workings of an internal biological clock (Kent, 1982). Although most age-related diseases are degenerative in nature, age does not affect all organs and systems in a similar fashion. The biological ages of different organs are not uniform throughout the body. However, the aging process is associated with a gradual reduction in the reserve capacity of all organs of the body (Pieroni, 1980). In old age autopsies often do not provide conclusive causes of death (Kohn, 1982). This may result from a "total system failure" in subjects who have used up nearly all the reserves of multiple organs (Fries, 1982). Nevertheless, since the vast majority of the extreme aged have chronic medical problems, it is not surprising that centenarians harbor a variety of disease processes, many of which are readily evident on autopsy (Ishii and Sternby, 1978a, 1978b, 1978c). Three of the principal causes of death—cardiac disorders, cerebrovascular diseases, and malignancies—presently account for about 75 percent of all deaths in individuals age 85 and over (Rosenwaike et al., 1980). Cardiac disease alone is responsible for nearly 50 percent of all deaths in this age group (Rosenwaike et al., 1980), and autopsies of centenarians confirm the high prevalence of this disorder among the extreme aged (Ishii and Sternby, 1978a).

INCREASING LONGEVITY

Despite the increasing number of centenarians, it will still remain extremely rare for these individuals to survive beyond 110 years since this age is close to what is believed to be the maximum human life span (Fries and Crapo, 1981; Korenchevsky, 1961). As Kent (1980) has noted, "Recent gains in longevity have been confined to mean life span. . . . there have been no gains in maximum life span since the beginning of recorded time." The gains attained in life expectancy at birth, that is, average longevity, have been, however, most impressive. When Caesar was born, life expectancy was just 25 years; at the turn of the century Americans had an average longevity of 49 years (Rockstein and Sussman, 1979). Currently, life expectancy at birth has risen to nearly 75 years (Lowenstein and Schrier, 1982).

It is well recognized that the decreased mortality among infants and children is the most important factor contributing to increased human life expectancy

(Hershey, 1974). In those 70 and over, the longevity gain for men is not much more than a year over what it was at the turn of the century (Hershey, 1974). In recent years, however, a rather dramatic decline in the mortality of the extreme aged has been noted (Rosenwaike et al., 1980; Brody, 1982). Between 1966 and 1977 official U.S. statistics showed a more than 20 percent decrease in the mortality rate for Americans 85 years of age and older. This decline was not only greater than that shown by other adult age groups, but was considerably larger than earlier declines for the extreme aged (Rosenwaike et al., 1980). Reduction in deaths from cardiovascular disease has been especially noteworthy in the very old (Rosenwaike et al., 1980). The National Center for Health Statistics now estimates that in the year 2000, instead of an anticipated 3.3 million subjects aged 85 and over, there may be as many as 6.7 million (Rosenwaike et al., 1980; Brody, 1982).

PROLONGEVITY AND REJUVENATION ATTEMPTS

A variety of agents, including steroids and vitamin E, have been reported to be capable of modulating the *in vitro* life span of cultured cells (Florini and Adelman, 1981). Komarov (1982) has recently reviewed some of the means that have been reported to prolong life in experimental animals. Among these rejuvenating agents are drugs such as L-Dopa, vitamin B12, tetracycline, phenobarbital, and ATP. In addition, physical methods such as the use of magnetic fields, electrically charged drinking water, and low temperatures have also met with apparent success (Komarov, 1982).

It is of interest that, of the numerous methods that have been used throughout history in attempts to restore youth and prolong life span, many have involved sexual manipulations. These have included drinking milk from the breasts of young girls and sleeping with young virgins (Busse, 1973). Charles Edouard Brown-Séquard, the eminent French physician, attempted to reinvigorate himself, as well as his patients, by injecting extracts made from animal testicles (Emerson, 1977). In a classic communication to the French Society of Biology in 1889, he described what he considered the dramatically beneficial effects these extracts had produced on his 72-year-old body. He triumphantly announced, ''I have rejuvenated myself by 30 years and today I was able to pay a visit to my young wife!'' (Emerson, 1977).

Serge Voronoff, the Russian physician, was able to entice many elderly males to visit Paris in order to become rejuvenated by receiving grafts of monkey testicles. The Austrian scientist Eugen Steinach promised restoration of youth to any aged client who was willing to have his vas deferens ligated (Busse, 1973). As with other forms of sexual manipulation, there is no scientific evidence that longevity is affected by such measures.

Much continues to be written on methods that have been advocated to increase mean, and possibly maximum, human longevity (Prehoda, 1968; Mann, 1980; Pelletier, 1981; Emerson, 1977; Rosenfeld, 1976). Unfortunately, however, the

Fountain of Youth has yet to be found. The longevity-enhancing advice we get from centenarians themselves is often conflicting: "One of the two things that men who have lasted for a hundred years always say [is] either that they have drunk whiskey and smoked all their lives, or that neither tobacco nor spirits ever made the faintest appeal to them" (Auden and Kronenberger, 1962).

Woodruff (1977) and, most recently, Palmore (1982) have aptly reviewed the many factors that are considered important in helping us achieve our maximal potential life span. Surveys of centenarians (Lind, 1982; Baum, 1982) have, in general, tended to support earlier Duke University findings (Palmore, 1982) which suggest that "the most important ways to increase longevity are: (1) to maintain a useful and satisfactory role in society, (2) to maintain a positive view of life, (3) to maintain good physical functioning, and (4) to avoid smoking."

CHARACTERISTICS OF CENTENARIANS

Centenarians as a group have been the subject of numerous published reports in the past few decades. In addition to purely clinical and pathologic studies (Hubbard et al., 1976; Ishii and Sternby, 1978a, 1978b, 1978c), a variety of psychosocial analyses of centenarians have also appeared periodically in the literature (Karasawa et al., 1979; Benet, 1977; Poinsard, 1972).

In 1969 Lerner surveyed 267 centenarians receiving Social Security benefits in this country. He reported that longevity did not have much meaning or value for most of these individuals. Because of physical and/or psychological factors the centenarians had, in effect, "withdrawn from life and were simply existing." This bleak picture is in sharp contrast to that painted by others. Dr. Belle Boone Beard had conducted numerous interviews with centenarians and has extensive files on over 8,500 Americans claiming to be centenarians (Puner, 1979; "Americans," 1980). In her recent testimony before the House of Representatives' Select Committee on Aging ("Americans," 1980), Dr. Beard stated that "instead of old age inevitably bringing a picture of decrepitude, pain, loss of memory and usefulness, thousands of busy, interested, loving men and women over 100 show that old can be beautiful, that people in their second century can be happy, useful, contributing members of society."

Although the centenarians who joined Dr. Beard in giving testimony to Representative Claude Pepper and the Select Committee on Aging certainly could not be considered a random sample of Americans over 100, their statements shed light on the thinking of at least some centenarians ("Americans," 1980). Far from being "withdrawn" and "simply existing," these vibrant and outspoken individuals typified centenarians whom Beard referred to as being "no longer isolated individuals whom we call biological accidents or oddities," but among the "thousands of men and women 100 and over who are physically active and mentally alert" ("Americans," 1980).

Simone de Beauvoir (1972) reviewed several studies of centenarians living in different parts of the world. The French centenarians were described in the following terms: "Their minds were clear and their memories excellent. They were independent, even-tempered and sometimes gay; they had a lively sense of humor and they were very sociable. In the main, they behaved very differently from old people junior to them. Had they survived because of their exceptional physical and mental health or did their satisfaction in having lived so long give them their serenity?" In discussing the positive psychological and physical qualities of centenarians in other regions, including the United States and Cuba, de Beauvoir came to the conclusion that centenarians are "almost always quite exceptional beings" (de Beauvoir, 1972).

ACCOMPLISHMENTS

The accomplishments of elderly individuals, including centenarians, are frequent topics of discussion. Grandma Moses, for example, started to paint at age 76 and finished her famous "Christmas Eve" at age 100 (Schrier, 1982). When she died at age 101, scientist-writer Isaac Asimov queried, "How many living things that greeted the day and responded to the changing environment at the moment of [her] birth in 1860 were still doing so on the day of her death in 1961? The list is tiny" (Kurtzman and Gordon, 1976).

Michael Eugene Chevreul, one of the nineteenth century's most distinguished scientists, was instrumental in the development of the margarine and soap industries. Chevreul published works on theoretical physics at age 92 and lived to be 103 (de Beauvoir, 1972; Comfort, 1976).

Marion Jones of Scotland wrote her autobiography, *The Jottings of Julia*, at the age of 100. Shortly afterwards neighbors complained of noise arising from her apartment because of the large number of visitors. Miss Jones therefore decided to move to other quarters where she could entertain undisturbed (Glass, 1962).

About ten years ago, William J. Moore, an educator and the son of a slave, received considerable attention when he celebrated his 100th birthday in a hospital room, where he was recuperating from injuries he sustained during a tennis game. A former professional tennis player, Mr. Moore had seen no reason to abandon tennis because of his age or the fact that tennis no longer gave him his living (Puner, 1979).

It is obvious that, like the elderly in general, centenarians represent a heterogeneous population. It is also obvious that centenarians represent a sample of biologically superior survivors, coming as they do from a cohort in whom the mortality rate exceeds 99.9 percent. Not only are centenarians a "valuable historical resource," but they also comprise a growing and important component of our population ("Americans," 1980). Further concentrated, multidisciplinary research involving centenarians, their life-styles, physical and mental characteristics, and so on, may provide important clues toward how we might add years to our lives and, more important, life to our years.

REFERENCES

Ascadi, G., and Klinger, A. *Gerontological studies on Hungarian centenarians*. Akademiai Kiado, Budapest, 1965.

Ascadi, GY., and Nemeskeri, J. *History of human lifespan and mortality*. Akademiai Kiado, Budapest, 1970.

Americans over 100: Hearing before the Select Committee on Aging, House of Representatives, Ninety-Sixth Congress, First Session, November 14, 1979. USGPO, Washington, D.C., 1980.

Auden, W.H., and Kronenberger, L. *The Faber book of aphorisms*. Faber and Faber, London, 1962.

Baum, S. Review of Segerberg, O., *Living to be 100* (Charles Scribner's Sons, New York, 1982). *Gerontologist*, 1982, *22*, 461.

Benet, S. Life and stress among the centenarians of the Caucasus mountains. *Practical psychology for physicians*, 1977, *4*, 13–19.

Brim, C. *Medicine in the Bible*. Forben, New York, 1936.

Brody, J.A. Life expectancy and the health of older persons. *Journal of the American Geriatrics Society*, 1982, *30*, 681–683.

Busse, E.W. (Ed.). *Theory and therapeutics of aging*. Medcom, New York, 1973.

Centenarian count disclaimed. *The Patriot* (Harrisburg, Pa.), November 26, 1982, D5.

Comfort, A. *The biology of senescence*. Elsevier, North Holland, New York, 1964a.

————. *The process of ageing*. New American Library, New York, 1964b.

————. *A good age*. Crown, New York, 1976.

Cornell, J. *Fakes, frauds and phonies*. Scholastic Book Services, New York, 1973.

Davies, D. *The centenarians of the Andes*. Doubleday, New York, 1975.

de Beauvoir, S. *The coming of age*. G. P. Putnam's Sons, New York, 1972.

Dublin, L.I.; Lotka, A.J.; and Spiegelman, M. *Length of life: A study of the life table*. Ronald Press, 1949.

Duchesne, J. What is the living state? *Bulletin de la Classe des Sciences*, 1980, *66*, 300–306.

Emerson, G.M. (Ed.). *Benchmark papers in human physiology/11: Aging*. Dowden, Hutchinson and Ross, Stroudsburg, Pa., 1977.

Ettinger, R. *The prospect of immortality*. MacFadden Books, Garden City, N.Y., 1964.

Florini, J.R., and Adelman, R.C. *Handbook of biochemistry of aging*. CRC Press, Boca Raton, Fla., 1981.

Franklin, B. *Poor Richard's almanack*. Bonanza Books, New York, 1976.

Freeman, J.T. The old, old, very old Charlie Smith. *Gerontologist*, 1982, *22*, 532–536.

Fries, J.F. Genetic limits of life-span. *Physician and Patient*, 1982, *1*, 47–48.

Fries, J.F., and Crapo, L.M. *Vitality and aging*. W. H. Freeman, San Francisco, 1981.

Glass, J.C. *You can live to be 180*. Taplinger, 1962.

Haranghy, L. (Ed.). *Gerontological studies on Hungarian centenarians*. Akademiai Kiado, Budapest, 1965.

Hershey, D. *Lifespan and factors affecting it: Aging theories on gerontology*. Charles C. Thomas, Springfield, Ill., 1974.

The holy Bible, King James Version. American Bible Society, New York, 1972.

Hubbard, O.; Sunde, D.; and Goldensohn, E.S. The EEG in centenarians. *Electroencephalography and Clinical Neurophysiology*, 1976, *40*, 407–417.

Ishii, T., and Sternby, N.H. Pathology of centenarians. I. The cardiovascular system and lungs. *Journal of the American Geriatrics Society*, 1978a, *26*, 108–115.

————. Pathology of centenarians. II. Urogenital and digestive systems. *Journal of the American Geriatrics Society*, 1978b, *26*, 391–396.

————. Pathology of centenarians. III. Osseous system, malignant lesions, and causes of death. *Journal of the American Geriatrics Society*, 1978c, *26*, 529–533.

Karasawa, A.; Kawashima, K.; and Kasahara, H. Mental aging and its medico-psycho-social background in the very old Japanese. *Journal of Gerontology*, 1979, *34*, 680–686.

Kent, S. The evolution of longevity. *Geriatrics*, 1980, *35*, 98–104.

————. The biological aging clock. *Geriatrics*, 1982, *37*, 95–99.

Kohn, R.R. Cause of death in very old people. *Journal of the American Medical Association*, 1982, *247*, 2793–2797.

Komarov, L.V. Means of the life-prolongation. *Rejuvenation*, 1982, *10*, 46–48.

Korenchevsky, V. *Physiological and pathological ageing*. Hafner, New York, 1961.

Kurtzman, J., and Gordon, P. *No more dying*. Dell, New York, 1976.

Leaf, A. Every day is a gift when you are over 100. *National Geographic*, 1973, *143*, 93–119.

————. *Youth in old age*. McGraw-Hill, New York, 1975.

Lerner, J. The centenarians: Some findings and concepts regarding the aged. *Journal of the American Geriatrics Society*, 1969, *17*, 429–432.

Lind, S.D. Review of Pitskhelauri, G.Z., *The long-living of Soviet Georgia* (Human Sciences Press, New York, 1982). *Gerontologist*, 1982, *22*, 117–118.

Longevity. *Medical World News*, 1970, *11*, 48L.

Lowenstein, S.R., and Schrier, R.W. Social and political aspects of aging. In R.W. Schrier (Ed.), *Clinical internal medicine in the aged*. W.B. Saunders, Philadelphia, 1982.

McWhirter, N. *Guinness book of world records*. Bantam Books, New York, 1982.

Mann, J.A. *Secrets of life extension*. Bantam Books, New York, 1980.

Mazess, R.B., and Forman, S.H. Longevity and age exaggeration in Vilcabamba, Ecuador. *Journal of Gerontology*, 1979, *34*, 94–98.

Medvedev, Z.A. Caucasus and Altay longevity: A biological or social problem. *Gerontologist*, 1974, *6*, 381–387.

Milne, L.J., and Milne, M. *The ages of life: A new look at the effects of time on mankind and other living things*. Harcourt, Brace and World, 1968.

Murphy, E.A. Genetics of longevity in man. In E.L. Schneider (Ed.), *The genetics of aging*. Plenum Press, New York, 1978.

Myers, R.J. An investigation of the age of an alleged centenarian. *Demography*, 1978, *15*, 235–236.

One of nation's oldest seeks job at age 122. *American Association of Retired Persons News Bulletin*, 1982, *23*, 9.

Palmore, E.B. Predictors of the longevity difference: A 25–year follow-up. *Gerontologist*, 1982, *22*, 513–518.

Pearl, R., and Pearl, R. deW. *The ancestry of the long-lived*. Johns Hopkins University Press, Baltimore, 1934.

Pelletier, K.R. *Longevity: Fulfilling our biological potential*. Dell, New York, 1981.

Pieroni, R.E. *Famous teachings in modern medicine. Geriatrics, Part 1: General concepts*. Medcom, New York, 1980.

Poinsard, P.J. Geriatric psychiatry. *Pennsylvania Medicine*, 1972, *75*, 33–36.

Prehoda, R.W. *Extended youth: The promise of gerontology*. G.P. Putnam's Sons, New York, 1968.

Puner, M. *Vital maturity: Living Longer and Better*. Universe Books, New York, 1979.

Rockstein, M., and Sussman, M. *Biology of aging*. Wadsworth, Belmont, Calif., 1979.

Rosenfeld, A. *Prolongevity*. Knopf, New York, 1976.

Rosenwaike, I.; Yaffe, N.; and Sagi, P.C. The recent decline in mortality of the extreme aged: An analysis of statistical data. *American Journal of Public Health*, 1980, *70*, 1074–1080.

Schrier, R.W. (Ed.). *Clinical internal medicine in the aged*. W.B. Saunders, Philadelphia, 1982.

Thoms, W.J. *The longevity of man: Its facts and fictions*. Frederick Norgate, London, 1879.

Veith, Ilza. *The yellow emperor's classic of internal medicine*. University of California Press, Berkeley, 1966.

Woodruff, D. *Can you live to be 100?* New American Library, New York, 1977.

2

FAMOUS AGED

LUCILLE B. BEARON

Research for this chapter began with an informal poll: several friends and associates were asked to name some famous older people.[1] Faced with this spontaneous task, they could think of only a few names and their lists overlapped considerably. The names Ronald Reagan, Grandma Moses, George Burns, Colonel Sanders, and Santa Claus came up again and again.

It is not surprising that those polled would select these individuals as examples of famous older people. For each, their advanced age has been the focus of public controversy or attention. In 1980, Ronald Reagan's age (then 69) was a salient issue in his presidential campaign. Anna Mary ("Grandma") Moses became a legend for beginning a successful career as a painter at age 76 and continuing into her 100th year. George Burns, who won an Academy Award for acting at age 80, has in recent years based much of his comedy on his age (86 in 1983). The late Colonel Harlan Sanders (the late-in-life entrepreneur whose face beams from the logo of a popular fried chicken franchise) and Santa Claus both fit a physical stereotype of old age having memorable white hair and white beards.

It is noteworthy, though, that the respondents in this informal sample came up with so few additional examples of famous older people. In reality, there are hundreds of famous people aged 65 or over living and working in the United States today. Many of their names and faces garner instant recognition (see tables 2.1 and 2.2), but apparently the public does not think of them as "old." Most of these people developed their reputations from special achievements earlier in life but continue to work and to remain in the limelight. Because neither public controversy nor stereotypical attributes have called attention to their age, these famous older people tend to blend into the rest of the celebrity population; they may even be referred to as "ageless."

This chapter addresses three central questions: Who are the famous aged living in the United States today? What have they achieved in later life? What socio-

Table 2.1
Sixty-Three Celebrities Aged 65–74 (as of 1981)*

Name	Date of Birth	Occupation
Don Ameche	5/31/08	actor
Jim Backus	2/25/13	actor
Lucille Ball	8/06/11	actress
Ingrid Bergman**	8/29/15	actress
Milton Berle	7/12/08	actor
Victor Borge	1/03/09	comedian, pianist
Ernest Borgnine	1/24/17	actor
Lloyd Bridges	1/15/13	actor
Raymond Burr	5/21/17	actor
Kitty Carlisle Hart	9/13/17	arts administrator, former actress
Perry Como	5/18/12	singer
Norman Cousins	7/24/15	author, lecturer
Jacques Cousteau	6/11/10	marine explorer, film producer, writer
Buster Crabbe	2/07/08	actor, business executive
Bob Cummings	6/09/10	motion picture, stage, TV performer
Bette Davis	4/05/08	actress
Olivia de Havilland	7/01/16	actress
Phyllis Diller	7/17/17	actress, author
Buddy Ebsen	4/02/08	actor, dancer
Alice Faye	5/05/15	actress
Gerald Ford	7/04/13	former U.S. president
Glenn Ford	5/01/16	actor
Henry Ford	9/04/17	automobile manufacturing executive
Jackie Gleason	2/26/16	actor
Benny Goodman	5/30/09	orchestra conductor, clarinetist
Lorne Greene	2/12/15	actor
Alec Guinness	4/02/14	actor
Rex Harrison	3/05/08	actor
Lena Horne	6/30/17	singer
Burl Ives	6/14/09	singer, actor
Van Johnson	8/25/16	movie actor
Danny Kaye	1/18/13	actor, comedian, baseball executive
Ruby Keeler	8/25/10	actress
Gene Kelly	8/23/12	dancer, actor
Art Linkletter	7/17/12	radio and TV broadcaster
Fred MacMurray	8/30/08	actor
Karl Malden	3/22/14	actor
E. G. Marshall	6/18/10	actor
Dean Martin	6/17/17	actor
James Mason	5/15/09	actor
Ethel Merman	1/16/09	singer, actress
Ray Milland	1/03/08	motion picture actor, director

Table 2.1 *continued*

Name	Date of Birth	Occupation
Mitch Miller	7/04/11	musician
Robert Mitchum	8/06/17	actor
Harry Morgan	4/10/15	actor
Harriet Nelson	7/18/14	actress
David Niven	3/01/10	actor
Pat Nixon	3/16/12	former U.S. first lady
Richard Nixon	1/09/13	former U.S. president
Gregory Peck	4/05/16	actor
Vincent Price	5/27/11	actor
Anthony Quinn	4/21/15	actor, writer
Ronald Reagan	2/06/11	U.S. president
Buddy Rich	6/30/17	drummer
Artie Shaw	5/23/10	musician, writer
Dinah Shore	3/01/17	singer, TV talk-show hostess
Phil Silvers	5/11/12	actor
Red Skelton	7/18/13	comedian
James Stewart	5/20/08	actor
Danny Thomas	1/06/14	entertainer, TV producer
Orson Welles	5/06/15	actor, radio and theatrical producer
Jane Wyatt	8/12/12	actress
Jane Wyman	1/04/14	actress

*Names of celebrities were selected from *Family Weekly*, January 3, 1982–August 29, 1982. Information on dates of birth and occupation was drawn from *Who's Who in America 1982–83* or *The World Almanac and Book of Facts: 1983*.
**Died in 1982.

logical and psychological factors explain the success and status of this special group of older people? The nucleus of this chapter is a report of original research undertaken to gather some basic facts about this population.

FAMOUS AGED IN THE UNITED STATES: FACTS AND FIGURES

What does it mean to be "famous"? *Webster's Dictionary* (1981:821) states that "famous" could mean (1) much talked about, well known; (2) honored for achievement, celebrated; or (3) discreditably renowned, notorious. Each definition encompasses a somewhat different group of individuals.

According to the first definition, famous people are those who are widely known by the general public, regardless of whether their contributions to society are positive, negative, or insignificant. According to the second definition, famous people are those who are recognized by some segment of society for their

Table 2.2
Thirty-Two Celebrities Aged 75 or Over (as of 1981)*

Name	Date of Birth	Occupation
Fred Astaire	5/10/99	actor, dancer
Count Basie	8/21/04	composer, band leader
Eubie Blake***	2/07/83	musician
Ray Bolger	1/10/04	actor
George Burns	1/20/96	comedian
James Cagney	7/17/99	actor
Frank Capra	5/18/97	motion picture producer and director
Joseph Cotten	5/15/05	actor
Salvador Dali	5/11/04	artist
Henry Fonda**	5/16/05	actor
John Gielgud	4/14/04	actor, director
Jack Gilford	7/25/07	actor, comedian
Arthur Godfrey***	8/31/03	radio and TV entertainer
Cary Grant	1/18/04	actor
Lillian Hellman	6/20/07	playwright
Bob Hope	5/29/03	stage, radio, film and TV actor, comedian
John Huston	8/05/06	writer, motion picture director
Myrna Loy	8/02/05	actress
Raymond Massey	8/30/96	actor, director, producer
Laurence Olivier	5/22/07	actor
Norman Vincent Peale	5/31/98	clergyman
William Powell	7/29/92	actor
Dr. Seuss	3/02/04	author of children's books
Kate Smith	5/01/07	singer
Benjamin Spock	5/02/03	physician, educator
Barbara Stanwyck	7/16/07	actress
Gloria Swanson	3/27/99	actress
Rudy Vallee	7/28/01	orchestra leader
Johnny Weismuller	6/02/03	actor
Lawrence Welk	3/22/03	orchestra leader
Billy Wilder	6/22/06	motion picture writer, director, producer
Robert Young	2/22/07	actor

*Names of celebrities were selected from *Family Weekly*, January 3, 1982–August 29, 1982. Information on dates of birth and occupation was drawn from *Who's Who in America 1982–83* or *The World Almanac and Book of Facts: 1983*.
**Died in 1982.
***Died in 1983.

positive achievements. And, of course, with the third definition the famous would include a group of "infamous" individuals who have acquired a broad reputation for negative contributions to society.

In our technological age, being well known and much talked about are often the result of exposure in the mass media. People with considerable access to the mass media—actors, popular musicians, journalists, politicians, and athletes— are more likely to be widely known by the general public than are scientists or business executives. People in the public eye are often referred to as "celebrities."

Most of the celebrities discussed in this chapter gained public recognition through noteworthy achievements in their professions (and thus could qualify as famous under the second definition as well). It is possible, however, for people to become celebrities without appreciable talent, merely by garnering media attention. People can, for example, enter the public arena on the coattails of others, gain public attention by calculated association with public figures, or even become unwitting celebrities by chance involvement in news-making events that generate substantial attention (e.g., the Iranian hostage crisis). This kind of fame merely requires visibility and public interest.

On the other hand, some scientists, business executives, lawyers, architects, and other professionals and government officials could also be called famous. They are well known and honored by their colleagues for their noteworthy achievements even though they are, for the most part, not known to a broad general public. These people can be described as "high achievers." In this chapter, the word "famous" will refer to both those widely known and celebrated by the general public and those widely recognized by colleagues for their positive contributions in professional and community life.

The "famous aged," then, are simply those people 65 and over who are well known among the public or their peers. People can become famous at any age and stay famous long after the period of exemplary accomplishment or public attention by maintaining just enough visibility to assure recognition by succeeding generations of the public or newcomers to the profession. Thus, the group of famous aged could include (1) "early peakers" spending their later years retired and resting on their laurels or simply pursuing less public endeavors; (2) "steady strivers" who are continuing to build a reputation on a groundwork of significant achievements begun earlier; and (3) "late bloomers" making their greatest achievements or earning widespread recognition for the first time in later life.

A Description of the Famous Aged in the United States

Older people have distinguished themselves at all stages of American history. Even when the average life expectancy was significantly shorter, Benjamin Franklin helped write the Declaration of Independence at age 70 and served as Pennsylvania's chief executive at age 79. In World War I, 70–year–old Thomas Edison directed torpedo and submarine research; at 81 he was still patenting inventions. Books by Simone de Beauvoir (1972) and Alex Comfort (1976) provide many illustrations of the achievements of older people throughout history.[2] A search of books and relevant periodicals, however, failed to produce a comparable work on *contemporary* famous older Americans or to document the characteristics of this population.

The research presented here focused on generating lists of famous older people and statistics on their numbers and characteristics. Potential sources of data included reference works and periodicals containing lists of—and perhaps biographical information on—famous living Americans of all ages (for example, *Who's Who in America, Current Biography, The World Almanac and Book of Facts*, and popular magazines featuring celebrity profiles).

The first source chosen for this study was *Who's Who in America 1982–83* (1982) because it contains over 75,000 biographical sketches of accomplished people currently active in professional or community life.[3] An examination of a number of entries revealed that these people tend not to be "household names." The majority are in business, education, medicine, or law, and are high achievers in their respective fields. Although some celebrities are profiled in this work, they constitute a small subset of the biographees. A random sample of 500 names was drawn from this population.

Secondly, a list of names thought to be recognizable to the broad American public was assembled from the nationally syndicated tabloid *Family Weekly*. This publication is distributed to a mass readership as an insert in local Sunday newspapers. Each issue contains a list of approximately fifteen celebrities who have a birthday in the following week. Four hundred and thirty-nine celebrities were so acknowledged during the thirty-five-week period from January 3, 1982, through August 29, 1982.

Because of myths and negative stereotypes about older people, most people probably underestimate the number of older people in the ranks of the famous. In truth, the data showed that older people are overrepresented among the famous (regardless of whether "famous" is operationally defined in terms of public or professional recognition). People 65 and older constitute 15 percent of the adult population aged 18 and over, whereas they account for 23 percent ($N = 113$) of the sample drawn from *Who's Who in America* and for 22 percent ($N = 95$) of those featured in *Family Weekly*. Based on these estimates, *Who's Who in America* should contain about 16,500 examples of renowned and actively involved older people.

Most of the famous aged are from the group that could be called the "young-old" (cf. Neugarten, 1974), that is, under age 75. Among the older people in the *Who's Who in America* sample, roughly three-fourths were aged 65–74; in the *Family Weekly* sample two-thirds were under 75 (see table 2.3).[4] These figures are not surprising in light of the high mortality of people 75 and over, especially men (who constitute the majority of famous individuals). Nevertheless, the figures suggest that the population of the famous may contain more than 4,000 "old-old" people.

Although women outnumber men in the aged population at large by a ratio

Table 2.3
Age Distribution of Famous Aged in Two Samples

High Achievers (*Who's Who in America, 1982-83*)		
Age	*N*	*Percentage*
65-69	52	46.0
70-74	32	28.3
75-79	19	16.8
80-84	3	2.7
85-89	6	5.3
90 and older	1	1.0
Total	113	

Mean Age = 71.4

Selected Celebrities (*Family Weekly*)		
Age	*N*	*Percentage*
65-69	33	35.4
70-74	30	31.2
75-79	22	22.9
80-84	4	4.0
85-89	4	4.0
90 and older	2	2.1
Total	95	

Mean Age = 72.9

Percentages may not total 100 due to rounding.

of 3 to 2, men far outnumber women among famous older people. Less than 4 percent (N = 4) of the older biographees in *Who's Who in America* are women, although 21 percent (N = 20) of the older celebrities in *Family Weekly* are women. Women of all ages are underrepresented in *Who's Who in America* (they constitute an estimated 5 percent of the biographies)[5] because they are under-represented in the professions from which candidates for *Who's Who in America* are selected—law, business, medicine, and so on. The relatively greater proportion of women among the total celebrity population (33 percent)[6] can presumably be explained by the increased opportunities for women to be employed and recognized in the entertainment industry. The lower representation of women among the famous aged compared to younger ages reflects the limited labor force participation history of women in older cohorts.

The famous aged come from a variety of occupations. Among the biographees in *Who's Who in America*, 58 percent (N = 66) of the famous aged are in the professions (e.g., educators, physicians, lawyers, clergymen, scientists, architects), 11 percent (N = 12) are in the arts (e.g., writers, performing artists, entertainers, filmmakers), 24 percent ($N = 27$) are in business, administration, or politics, and 7 percent ($N = 8$) have significant involvement in two or more of these categories.[7] Most of the celebrities in *Family Weekly* are in the performing arts or the entertainment industry, although a small number ($N = 8$) are famous because of careers in politics, business, the clergy, and science.

Their claims to fame are as diverse as their occupations. Among the high achievers are a former secretary of agriculture, one of New York's top interior designers, and a chairman of a major league baseball club. Among the celebrities are the present and two former United States presidents, an award-winning author of children's books, an accomplished drummer, an explorer, and several Academy Award winners.

THE FAMOUS AGED IN LATER LIFE

All the available data point to the conclusion that most famous older people are famous because of something they did before the age of 65. But what are the famous aged doing in later life? Are they retired and simply resting on their laurels, are they continuing to build on their reputations, or are they reaching new peaks of achievement and public recognition?

Almost 2,300 individuals retired from their positions between the publication of the 1981 edition of *Who's Who in America* and the 1982 edition (which served as a data source for this research); it is not possible to determine what kinds of activities all these people are currently involved in. Most current biographees, however, would be called "steady strivers." Biographical sketches of ten randomly selected high achievers aged 75 and over provide some illustrations of the kinds of activities that such people engage in after age 65.[8] This sample includes a pediatrician who continues to practice medicine at age 76, a physician who serves as an associate dean in a medical school at age 78, a business executive who continues to serve as president of a corporation at age 78, an architect who continues his private practice at age 78, and a judge who continues to preside over a district court at age 79. Another member of the group published eight books between the ages of 65 and 77; yet another served as the United States' chief representative to a United Nations commission from the ages of 65 to 72. Several people hold (or have held in later life) offices or chair committees in local and national professional associations and serve on boards of corporations and universities.

Many celebrities aged 75 and over have continued active public careers well after the age of 65. Among those who remain fully involved in professional activities into their late seventies are actors Sir Laurence Olivier, 75, and Sir John Gielgud, 78, motion picture writers and directors John Huston and Billy Wilder, both 76, and comedian Bob Hope, 79. Musician and orchestra leader Count Basie continues to perform at age 78, and actors Robert Young, 75, and Arthur Godfrey, 79 (deceased in 1983), and clergyman Norman Vincent Peale, 84, have appeared in recent television commercials.

Some of the celebrities in the *Family Weekly* sample have developed new career interests in later life and have earned public attention for their efforts in this new field. While these people are not new to the limelight, they could be called "late bloomers" for their second careers. After a successful career as a pediatrician, world-famous author of *Baby and Child Care*, and college professor, Dr. Benjamin Spock retired at the age of 64 to become a political activist and candidate for elective office. Spock ran an unsuccessful campaign for president of the United States at age 69, and at age 79 continues to write and to make public appearances to express his views on nuclear weapons as well as on child care.

Silent screen and stage actress Gloria Swanson, 83, diversified her interests later in life to include sculpture and painting. At age 70, she returned to Broadway after a twenty-year hiatus to star in *Butterflies Are Free*. At age 80, she designed a new stamp for the United Nations Decade of Women and wrote a voluminous best-selling autobiography.

George Burns, 86, had an extremely successful career as a partner with his wife in the vaudeville, film, and television comedy team of Burns and Allen. After his wife's retirement when he was 62, he worked as a stand-up comic until, at the age of 79, he was offered a leading role in a motion picture. At age 80, Burns won an Academy Award for his acting in *The Sunshine Boys*, and since that time has starred in several other films that were well received by critics and public alike. His renewed popularity as a film star has paved the way for his increased visibility on television, where he appears as a frequent guest on talk and variety shows and in commercials.

Eubie Blake (deceased 1983) is another example of a high achiever whose celebrity increased as he aged into his eighties and beyond. Although well known in the black community for composing hundreds of songs and musical scores from 1899 through the 1940s, it was not until ragtime music was revived in the late 1960s that Blake, then in his eighties, received attention from a broader audience. Even though Blake had retired twenty years earlier, he was sought out as the elder statesman of ragtime. Consequently, in his late eighties he once again took on a full schedule of public appearances and piano concerts.

In 1978, when Blake was 95, an even larger segment of the public became aware of his accomplishments when a musical based on his life and work appeared on Broadway. At age 99, Blake rarely played piano in public but occasionally appeared in public for interviews or to accept awards.

EXPLAINING FAME AND CONTINUED ACHIEVEMENT IN LATER LIFE

Gerontologists have clearly documented that for many people old age offers more basic challenges than those of creative and public achievement. Those who must cope with such devitalizing problems as poor health, low income, inadequate housing, and social isolation have all they can do to survive; they hardly have enough resources to engage in activities that would make them stand out among their peers.

Even people with less traumatic later lives (the majority of older Americans) are unlikely to possess either the means or the motivation to attain substantial public recognition for their accomplishments. Many older people are forced by retirement policies or disabilities to abandon the lifelong work roles that provided their only avenue for self-expression and social recognition, and are excluded by age discrimination from assuming new work roles in màny fields. Many of today's older people are handicapped in pursuing new creative interests by a lack of education or are held back by negative socialization to old age, which has instilled such beliefs as "you can't teach old dogs new tricks." In addition, considerable research has shown that older people tend to have lower aspirations than younger people and to have less concern for social approval or recognition (cf. Maehr and Kleiber, 1981).

Yet the examples above illustrate that many famous older people continue to strive and take on new challenges in later life, earning them continued recognition from peers or the public. What are the structural factors and personal characteristics that enable these people to achieve in their later years?

Structural factors: Opportunity for Professional Involvement and Visibility

For the most part, famous people have opportunities and incentives in later life not readily available to most older people. Many can continue in professions where age—as a proxy for accumulated experience—is often viewed as an advantage (e.g., education, drama, music, politics). Palmore (1981) has observed, for example, that older people are overrepresented in public office and that, in 1975, 21 percent of U.S. representatives and 39 percent of U.S. senators were 60 and over compared to about 15 percent of the total population. His explanation (1982) is that it takes years to build the necessary broad base of public support and a viable political machine to elect a candidate to office. Thus, experience and seniority tend to make long-term incumbents attractive candidates for repeated election.

Some of these professions also offer the opportunity to maintain professional or public visibility while scaling down involvement through part-time or short-term employment. Retired educators, for example, can continue to earn the respect of their peers by taking advantage of increased leisure time to write books in their areas of expertise. Politicians can retire from elective office and still be honored and consulted as elder statesmen. Prominent musicians can teach master classes or give guest concerts as they choose. Actors can make occasional appearances in movies, or on television in cameo performances, commercials, or interview shows and stay in the public consciousness, even reaching younger audiences unfamiliar with their earlier careers.

The fact that many famous people continue to work and achieve in later life can be partially explained by their avoidance of incapacitating problems, their record of earlier success in a career, and their choice of a profession that allows them the opportunity to gain fame or recognition and to build on it in old age. On the other hand, most famous older people are in professions that should allow them adequate income to retire. Why is it, then, that many are motivated to take on new and ambitious challenges—and why do they succeed?

Personal Characteristics: Lifestyle and Attitude

Throughout biographies and interviews, the famous aged emerged as very special people. Their energy and enthusiasm appeared much greater than that of most people in middle age; their dedication to their professional lives appeared, in many cases, to be a labor of love. Their own words conveyed a philosophy of active resistance to the negative aspects of aging, an unwillingness to slow down or stagnate physically, mentally, or emotionally.

Many celebrities reported that they have rigorous physical exercise programs to help them keep up with their other activities. Dr. Benjamin Spock, 78, rows one and a half hours daily, and, according to one reporter (Filstrup, 1981), has the body and carriage of a fifty-year-old athlete. At age 76 dancer Ray Bolger reported that he did two hours of exercise daily, including acrobatics (Wixen, 1980). A recent article on New York State Arts Administrator Kitty Carlisle Hart, age 65, said that she exercises regularly, enjoying swimming, horseback riding, and most water sports ("Kitty," 1982). At 96 Eubie Blake reported that he did daily finger exercises to keep arthritis from affecting his piano playing (Rose, 1979).

Several stressed the belief that mental stimulation was very important to their well-being. Ray Bolger took up the study of languages so that he could read some great literary works in the original languages. At age 80, actress Gloria Swanson (1980) described the rewards of struggling to write her autobiography: "It made me use muscles in my head that I never used before and that is always thrilling." In his late nineties Eubie Blake was composing songs: "I still compose every time I get a new idea—and I still keep getting 'em" (Rose, 1979:160).

The attitudes of some of the famous aged were surprisingly future-oriented for people in later life; for example, both Lena Horne (65) and Ray Bolger (76) spoke in terms of their ambitions. Their attitudes about old age were in direct opposition to stereotypes and disbelievers who would have them slow down. Horne told an interviewer: "Psychologically something's pushing, pushing me. I seem to have this desire, this push to get it all neat and together. I'm aware of time, that's all.... I'm eager to stretch more, to put it all together" (Gillespie, 1981). She wants to defy old age with her high-energy performances; she hopes her audience will leave the theater saying, "How does that old broad do it?" ("Glamourous," 1981).

At age 76, Ray Bolger stated: "I believe age is so much more in the mind than in the body. The secret is in knowing 76 is just another number that young people often erroneously categorize as an age that is over the hill.'' He continued: ''I, myself, never expected to feel the way I do at this age. But I know now, that the age of maturity is not 21, 41 or even 61. It's when you reach the age of 70 and suddenly you realize you are still living, breathing, sexually active, enjoying life, doing things and, most important, you still have ambition to do more'' (Wixen, 1980).

THE FUTURE FAMOUS AGED

Demographers project that older people will become an increasingly large segment of the total population in the next few decades. With large numbers of people living longer, society will be forced to carve out more meaningful roles for them. If societal obstacles such as age discrimination, mandatory retirement, and earnings restrictions are removed and current trends toward lifelong learning and productivity are expanded, in the future older people may have increased motivation for self-actualization and public achievement. Thus, it may be more commonplace in the future to see an older person excelling in a given field of endeavor. Yet even with greater numbers of older people in the realm of the highly accomplished, there will still be only a small percentage who become famous.

ISSUES FOR FURTHER RESEARCH

So little is known about the famous aged that this subject provides a fertile area for theory and research. Additional basic descriptive information is needed, including more detailed and uniform information on the later-life activities of the famous aged. A valuable research project would be a systematic survey to collect data on life-style variables and attitudes among the famous aged which could then become the basis of comparative studies with other groups of older people. Longitudinal data could yield information on how these special older people cope with stressful life events and losses.

These data bases would enable gerontologists to determine in what ways the famous aged are different from the non-famous aged, and the extent to which later-life success is due to the presence of financial resources and other special opportunities. To the extent that famous older people rely on inner resources, gerontologists, writers, educators, and practitioners can draw upon this population for role models to inspire hope and motivation among aging Americans.

NOTES

1. I gratefully acknowledge the helpful and insightful suggestions that Dr. Erdman Palmore provided for developing and writing this chapter.

2. For two brief articles highlighting famous older people in world history, see ''Happy

Birthday, 1981," *People*, February 9, 1981, and "They defied old age...," *World Health*, 1982.

3. People become eligible for listing in *Who's Who in America* "by virtue of their positions and/or noteworthy achievements that have proved to be of significant value to society" (p. vi). They can be included on the basis of their incumbency in certain positions which the editors believe to be of significant responsibility and importance or on the basis of a career of significant achievement. (The editors note that in most cases attaining such responsible positions is contingent on great achievement.) People may be excluded from *Who's Who in America* after retirement from active participation in a career or public life. The editors state: "In large part, it is career development that determines inclusion or continuation" (p. vi).

4. The somewhat discrepant percentages reflect the fact that retired people (presumably an older group) are deleted from *Who's Who in America: 1982–83*, whereas they may remain listed among celebrities.

5. Based on the sample of 500 drawn from *Who's Who in America 1982–1983*.

6. Based on the sample of 439 drawn from *Family Weekly*.

7. This occupation distribution is somewhat different from that of the total sample of 500: fewer old people are in the categories of business, administration, and politics, reflecting the *Who's Who in America* policy of excluding people who formally retire from designated positions unless they continue developing their careers from a new position of responsibility and high achievement.

8. Individuals aged 75 and over were selected for this section because their accomplishments after the age of 65 were more ascertainable than were those of people who recently turned 65.

REFERENCES

Bloom, L.Z. *Doctor Spock: Biography of a conservative radical*. Bobbs-Merrill, Indianapolis, 1972.

Burns, G. *The third time around*. G.P. Putnam's Sons, New York, 1980.

Comfort, A. *A good age*. Crown Publishers, New York, 1976.

de Beauvoir, S. *The coming of age*. Warner, New York, 1972.

Filstrup, J.M. Dr. Benjamin Spock: What makes America's top baby doctor tick? *Fifty Plus*, November 1981, 20–24.

Kitty Carlisle Hart. *Current Biography*, 1982, *43*, 13–14.

Gillespie, M. Lena Horne finds her music, her daughter and herself. *Ms.*, 1981, *10*, 43.

A glamorous grandmother wants audiences to wonder: "How does the old broad do it?" *People*, December 28, 1981, *51*, 16, 26.

Happy birthday, Mr. President: A sample of great late bloomers proves life can begin at 70. *People*, 1981, *15*, 32–35.

Maehr, M.L., and Kleiber, D.A. The graying of achievement motivation. *American Psychologist*, 1981 *36*, 787–793.

Neugarten, B.L. Age groups in American society and the rise of the young-old. *Annals of American Academy*, 1974, 187–198.

Palmore, E.B. The facts on aging quiz: Part two. *Gerontologist*, 1981, *21*, 431–437.

———. Personal communication, December 1982.

Robisen, D. The top 25 Americans over 50: Our 1981 selection of the men and women who made the world a better place. *Fifty Plus*, 1981, *21*, 18.

Rose, A. *Eubie Blake*. Schirmer Books, New York, 1979.

Swanson, G. *Swanson on Swanson*. Random House, New York, 1980.

They defied old age.... *World Health*, February-March 1982, 36–37.

Webster's Third New International Dictionary. G & C Merriam, Springfield, Mass., 1981.

What in the world? *Family Weekly*, January 3, 1982–August 29, 1982.

Who's who in America: 1982–83, 42nd ed., vols. 1 and 2. Marquis Who's Who, Chicago, 1982.

Wixen, J. Bolger—76 and still dancing. *Modern Maturity*, April-May 1980, 83–84.

The World Almanac and Book of Facts: 1983. Newspaper Enterprise Association, New York, 1981.

3

GEOGRAPHIC GROUPS

TIM B. HEATON
WILLIAM B. CLIFFORD
CAROLINE HOPPE

Activities of the elderly, perhaps more than of any other adult age group, are bounded by their residential environment. Fortunately, the importance of residential settings has been recognized and those who take a geographical perspective have made significant contributions to social gerontology. Interest in geographical patterns has been heightened over the last decade by reversals in long-standing trends in population redistribution. Central cities, where concentrations of elderly are higher than average, are losing population. Since the young are more likely to leave than the elderly, these losses imply even greater concentrations of the elderly in these areas. At the same time, there has been a resurgence of growth in Sun Belt states and nonmetropolitan areas. In many instances, an influx of elderly residents has been the harbinger of more general growth in these areas (Fuguitt and Tordella, 1980). The impact of these trends on distribution of the elderly makes it all the more critical that we develop and refine models of elderly behavior that include a spatial component.

There are three general questions that guide this chapter. First, where are the elderly located and what processes underlie this distribution? Second, how do characteristics of the elderly vary geographically and what models might be used to explain this variation? Third, how well suited are various types of areas as residential environments for the elderly? In answering the first two questions emphasis will be placed on updating trends with recent census data and discussing analytic approaches for understanding these trends. In answering the third, we will review the literature regarding advantages and disadvantages of various residential settings.

GEOGRAPHIC DISTRIBUTION OF THE ELDERLY

A great deal of attention is given to the migration of older persons to such states as Florida and California; however, this migration accounts for only a small part of the total variation in the proportion of older persons among the geographic areas of the United States. Large movements of population have occurred within the lifetime of our present aging population that have affected the age structure of our states. Local variations in these movements have similarly affected the age structure of areas within states—metropolitan and nonmetropolitan counties and cities. Suburbanization has also influenced the age distribution within metropolitan areas; and the post–1970 turnaround migration has affected the age distribution within nonmetropolitan areas. Of course, the effects of these movements have occurred within the context of local variations in fertility and mortality.

State Variations, 1970–1980

Considerable variation exists in the degree of agedness among the states. The classification of agedness developed by Cowgill (1970) provides a helpful tool for assessing areal variation. Cowgill proposes that all populations in which less than 4 percent are age 65 and over be classified as "young." The second class, from 4.0 to 6.9 percent, is labeled "youthful." The class from 7.0 percent to 9.9 percent is called "mature," and the designation "aged" is given to populations with more than 10 percent 65 and over.

On the basis of this classification of the degree of agedness, we find that twenty-two states in 1970 and thirty-six states in 1980 were "aged" (see table 3.1). If we were to increase the lower limit of this class to 11.0 percent or more 65 and over, the class of states with the most aged would be reduced to eleven states in 1970 and to twenty-nine in 1980. At the other extreme, very few states have young or youthful populations, and the number classified as mature declined from twenty-five in 1970 to fourteen in 1980. Regardless of the cutoff employed, it is clear that the number of states classified as aged has increased.

Most aged states are concentrated in three separate sections of the country. The largest and most compact group in both 1970 and 1980 is located in the heart of the nation—Iowa, Arkansas, Nebraska, South Dakota, Missouri, and Kansas. Oklahoma was included in this list only in 1970. A second concentration of the aged is found in the northeastern states of Maine, Massachusetts, Rhode Island, and Pennsylvania. Massachusetts was the only state in this group to be included in both 1970 and 1980. The third area of concentration is the single state of Florida, which ranked number one in both periods. Other states that had relatively heavy concentrations of the elderly include the remaining states of the Northeast region and the states of the East North Central division with the exception of Michigan. The states of Kentucky, Mississippi, Oregon, and West Virginia also ranked high in both time periods.

At the other end of the continuum, with a very young population, is Alaska, with under 3 percent of its population 65 and over in 1970 and 1980. Not far behind are Hawaii and the southwestern states of Nevada and Utah. New Mexico was included in 1970, and Wyoming in 1980. Wyoming was the only state in

Table 3.1

Percentage of Population Aged 65 and Over, 1970 and 1980, and Decennial Change of Elderly Population, 1970 to 1980, for Regions, Divisions, and States and Rank of States by Percentage 65 and Over

Region, Division, and State	1970 % 65 and over	1980 % 65 and over	1970-1980 Change in % 65 and over	1970-1980 % Change in Numbers	Rank in 1970	Rank in 1980
United States	9.8	11.3	1.5	27.3	—	—
Northeast	10.6	12.3	1.7	17.3	—	—
New England	10.7	12.3	1.6	20.3	—	—
Connecticut	9.5	11.7	2.2	26.7	27	18
Massachusetts	11.1	12.7	1.6	14.8	10	10
Maine	11.5	12.5	1.0	23.6	9	11
New Hampshire	10.6	11.2	.6	31.9	19	28
Rhode Island	10.9	13.4	2.5	22.2	12	3
Vermont	10.6	11.4	.8	23.7	20	23
Middle Atlantic	10.5	12.4	1.9	16.3	—	—
New Jersey	9.7	11.7	2.0	23.9	26	19
New York	10.7	12.3	1.6	10.7	17	14
Pennsylvania	10.7	12.9	2.2	20.8	14	9
North Central	10.1	11.4	1.3	17.3	—	—
East North Central	9.4	10.8	1.4	18.4	—	—
Illinois	9.8	11.0	1.2	15.9	24	29
Indiana	9.5	10.7	1.2	19.0	28	32
Michigan	8.4	9.8	1.4	21.7	39	38
Ohio	9.3	10.8	1.5	17.8	32	30
Wisconsin	10.7	12.0	1.3	19.9	18	16

33

Table 3.1 continued

Region, Division, and State	1970 — % 65 and over	1980 — % 65 and over	1970-1980 — Change in % 65 and over	1970-1980 — % Change in Numbers	Rank in 1970	Rank in 1980
West North Central	11.7	12.8	1.1	15.2	—	—
Iowa	12.4	13.3	.9	11.0	2	4
Kansas	11.8	12.9	1.1	15.6	7	8
Minnesota	10.7	11.8	1.1	17.7	16	17
Missouri	11.9	13.2	1.3	15.7	6	5
Nebraska	12.3	13.1	.8	12.6	4	7
North Dakota	10.7	12.3	1.6	21.6	15	13
South Dakota	12.0	13.2	1.2	13.4	5	6
South	9.6	11.3	1.7	41.1	—	—
South Atlantic	9.5	11.8	2.3	49.5	—	—
Delaware	8.0	10.0	2.0	34.5	42	36
District of Columbia	9.3	11.6	2.3	6.1	33	20
Florida	14.5	17.3	2.8	71.3	1	1
Georgia	8.0	9.4	1.4	41.6	43	42
Maryland	7.6	9.4	1.8	32.2	45	43
North Carolina	8.1	10.2	2.1	46.4	41	34
South Carolina	7.3	9.2	1.9	51.3	46	44
Virginia	7.8	9.5	1.7	38.8	44	41
West Virginia	11.1	12.2	1.1	22.8	11	15
East South Central	9.9	11.3	1.4	31.2	—	—
Alabama	9.4	11.3	1.9	35.7	30	25
Kentucky	10.4	11.2	.8	21.9	21	27
Mississippi	10.0	11.5	1.5	30.8	22	22
Tennessee	9.7	11.3	1.6	34.8	25	26

34

West South Central	9.5	10.4	.9	34.8	—	—
Arkansas	12.3	13.7	1.4	32.0	3	2
Louisiana	8.4	9.6	1.2	32.5	40	40
Oklahoma	11.7	12.4	.7	25.9	8	12
Texas	8.8	9.6	.8	39.3	37	39
West						
Mountain	8.8	9.9	1.1	39.5	—	—
Arizona	9.1	11.3	2.2	90.7	34	24
Colorado	8.5	8.6	.1	32.1	38	46
Idaho	9.5	9.9	.4	39.8	29	37
Montana	9.9	10.7	.8	23.5	23	31
Nevada	6.3	8.2	1.9	113.6	49	47
New Mexico	6.9	8.9	2.0	65.6	48	45
Utah	7.3	7.5	.2	42.9	47	50
Wyoming	9.0	7.9	-1.1	23.6	35	48
Pacific	9.0	10.2	1.2	35.5	—	—
Alaska	2.3	2.9	.6	65.0	51	51
California	9.0	10.2	1.2	34.7	36	35
Hawaii	5.7	7.9	2.2	73.1	50	49
Oregon	10.8	11.5	.7	34.4	13	21
Washington	9.4	10.4	1.0	34.6	31	33

Source: U.S. Bureau of the Census, Census of Population and Housing 1970, and 1980 Summary Tape File 1.

the nation to register a decline in the percentage of population 65 and over during the decade (9.0 to 7.9 percent). It is also interesting to note that many of the southern and southwestern states had relatively low proportions of their populations 65 and over.

Historically, the states with high concentrations of the elderly are those from which there has been a consistent pattern of out-migration and in which the level of fertility has been moderate for the greatest part of the twentieth century. Those with low concentrations of elderly have been states with relatively heavy in-migration of young persons and high levels of fertility. However, these traditional patterns seem to be changing. That change is occurring is supported by the fact that many states that have shown the greatest increases in their aged population since 1970 are states with relatively low proportions of the aged. These states include Alaska, Arizona, Hawaii, New Mexico, Nevada, and South Carolina. In all of these states, the numbers of elderly increased by more than 50 percent from 1970 to 1980. Likewise, some of the states with the highest proportions of the elderly are those with the least increase during the decade. For instance, Iowa, Massachusetts, Nebraska, New York, and South Dakota had increases of less than 15 percent, compared with an average increase in the elderly population for the United States as a whole of 27 percent.

Of the four main geographic regions, the South had the highest rate of growth in the elderly population, followed by the West, Northwest, and North Central regions. Each of the geographic divisions of the North had total growth rates well below the national average for the nation as a whole. It is clear that the regions and divisions with the lowest concentration of elderly are the fastest growing, and vice versa.

Rural-Urban Differences

The preceding analysis of the distribution of the aged population reveals some of the gross variations and differences, but it does not shed light on the details of residential preference and migration. Since the historical trend in the United States has been toward urbanization, and since the position of the elderly in urban areas is somewhat different from that of the elderly in rural areas, the tradition of concern for rural-urban differences in the concentration of older persons has not lost its relevance.

Throughout much of our history, cities were the haven of the young, and rural areas, the source of young migrants to the cities, were left with high proportions of the elderly. This pattern has changed; in 1980, for the nation as a whole, urban areas had a slight margin over the rural population (see table 3.2). This represents a shift from 1970, when the urban population was slightly lower in the proportion of elderly persons (9.8 versus 10.1). There is also substantial variation within the broad categories of urban and rural. For instance, the rural population includes people who live on farms and in villages and small towns (i.e., places up to 2,500 population). The urban category is also heterogeneous,

Table 3.2
Percentage of Total Population Aged 65 and Over and Decennial Change of Elderly Population, 1970 to 1980, by Residence Areas for the United States

Residence areas	1970	1980	1970-1980	1970-1980
	% 65 and over	% 65 and over	Change in % 65 and over	% Change
Total	9.9	11.3	1.4	27.3
Urban				
Inside urbanized areas	9.8	11.4	1.6	30.2
	9.4	10.9	1.5	36.8l
Central cities	10.7	12.0	1.3	17.1
· Urban fringe	7.8	10.0	2.2	68.4
Outside urbanized areas	11.4	13.8	2.4	9.2
Places of 10,000 or more	10.8	12.9	2.1	-2.9
Places of 2,500 to 10,000	12.2	14.7	2.5	21.6
Rural				
Places 1,000 to 2,500	10.1	10.9	.8	19.6
	13.6	15.4	1.8	20.3
Other rural	9.6	10.3	.7	19.4

Source: U.S. Bureau of the Census, Census of Population and Housing 1970, and 1980 Summary Tape File 1.

including people who live in central cities, the suburbs, and in places outside urbanized areas with populations over 2,500.

Increasingly significant numbers of old people have been moving, at retirement, away from farms into small towns. This accounts for the fact that the populations of towns of 1,000 to 2,500 people contained the highest proportion of elderly people in both 1970 and 1980, 13.6 and 15.4 percent respectively. Moreover, this pattern appears to be more prevalent in the North Central region than in other parts of the country (see table 3.3). The lowest 1980 percentage, 10.0 percent, occurred in the urban fringe, that is, among the suburban population. This was also true in 1970. With the exception of central cities, the figures suggest that the proportion of the elderly population increases as the size of place declines. Despite the transformation of our society from a rural one to one that is dominantly urban, it is still true that the village or small town is to a considerable extent America's "old folks' home" in the relative sense (Smith, 1954). As an urban society, however, we must note that urbanized areas are where most of the total population and the elderly population live.

In this regard, the aged are more concentrated in the central cities of our urbanized areas than in the urban fringe (12.0 versus 10.0 percent in 1980). One explanation of this difference lies in the heavy migration of young adults from the central cities to the suburbs once they marry and have children. The population of the suburbs, then, is heavily weighted with young adults and their children and, consequently, the proportion of older persons is low. However, this somewhat oversimplified explanation is less applicable if the time perspective is broadened. The population of a suburb tends to age with the suburb (Sheldon, 1958).

Each of the residence categories had positive rates of decennial change in the elderly, with the single exception of places of 10,000 or more outside of urbanized areas (-2.9 percent). This represents something of an anomaly given the fact that the percentage of the population 65 and over in places of 10,000 or more increased from 10.8 percent in 1970 to 12.9 in 1980. The decline in the absolute number of elderly at the same time that they represent a greater proportional share of the population results from the out-migration of young persons.

The national pattern in the variation of the proportions of elderly persons by residence was also characteristic of each of the four regions (table 3.3). Although some minor variations existed, there was a slightly greater concentration of older persons in rural than in urban areas of the North Central Region. The West conformed to the pattern by size of largest place, but the overall proportion of elderly was less than the national average. The Northeast exhibited above average proportions in the urban categories and below average proportions in the rural categories, while the South most closely approximated the national pattern.

DEMOGRAPHIC COMPONENTS OF ELDERLY POPULATION CHANGE

On the surface, a demographic analysis of geographic differences in elderly population change is quite simple. People move in and out, they age, and they

Table 3.3
Percentage of Population Aged 65 and Over by Residence Areas for the United States and Regions, 1980

Residence areas	1980, % 65 and over				
	United States	Northeast	North Central	South	West
Total	11.3	12.4	11.4	11.3	9.9
Urban					
Inside urbanized areas	11.4	12.8	11.3	11.3	10.0
Central cities	10.9	12.6	10.5	10.6	9.8
Urban fringe	12.0	13.7	12.1	11.2	11.0
Outside urbanized areas	10.0	11.7	9.0	9.9	8.8
Places of 10,000 or more	13.8	14.8	14.5	14.1	11.4
Places of 2,500 to 10,000	12.9	14.8	13.4	13.0	10.7
	14.7	14.9	15.5	15.0	12.2
Rural					
Places 1,000 to 2,500	10.9	10.6	11.4	11.1	9.6
Other rural	15.4	14.2	17.5	15.3	12.2
	10.3	10.1	10.5	10.6	9.2

Source: U.S. Bureau of the Census, Census of Population and Housing 1970, and 1980 Summary Tape File 1.

die. There are two sources of entry—aging and in-migration—and two sources of exit—dying and out-migration. When the focus shifts from absolute size of the elderly population to relative size, the complexity of the analysis increases since behavior of the young must also be taken into account (Lichter et al., 1981). Fertility, mortality, migration of young and old, and size of the cohort in the transition from young to old, which in turn depends on past patterns of fertility, mortality, and migration, must all be included. Understanding redistribution of the elderly population depends on our ability to explain each of these sources of variation.

Fertility and Mortality

Let us assume a population that is closed to migration such that fertility, mortality, and aging are the only processes that need to be considered. A simplified model of historical changes in fertility and mortality patterns has been named the "demographic transition" (Davis, 1945; Notestein, 1945). Initially fertility and mortality are both high. First, mortality declines and the population experiences rapid growth. Then fertility decline follows and eventually equilibrium is again achieved. Corresponding to this transition in fertility, mortality, and size is an age-structure transition (Warnes, 1982). The fertility decline has by far the greatest impact on population aging and, in fact, mortality declines have actually produced a slightly younger population. As fertility declines the proportion of the population that is elderly increases, but the age-structure transition lags behind, since fertility effects must work up through the age structure. In the most developed societies change in age structure has been dramatic since the turn of the century (Clark and Spengler, 1980). In the United States only 4 percent of the population was 65 or older in 1900, increasing to over 11 percent in 1980, and the percentage is projected to go as high as 20 percent in the next sixty years (U.S. Bureau of the Census, 1979). If the fertility and mortality rates are stabilized, however, the age structure will eventually become fixed and invariant over time.

Most analyses of geographic differences in fertility and mortality have focused on urban-rural differences. Level of urbanization is negatively associated with fertility (Rice and Beegle, 1972), resulting in older populations in urban areas. Fertility effects may be slightly counterbalanced by higher mortality in urban areas (Smith and Zopf, 1970), which tends to create a younger population. There is a general feeling that as urban life-styles diffuse throughout the population geographic differences in fertility and mortality will dissipate, leaving migration as the major determinant of spatial variation in age structure.

Migration

Whenever our attention turns to units smaller than nations, migration cannot be ignored as an important component of change in age structures. Generally, the smaller the geographic unit of analysis, the greater will be the importance of migration. Moreover, there is no reason to believe that migration will achieve some equilibrium pattern in the future. Unlike fertility and mortality, the effects of migration are not expected to recede in the decades to come. Ebbs and flows of population movement will continue with changes in the cultural, economic, political, and social contexts within which migration occurs.

The major redistribution trends of the past century—from east to west, from country to city, and from core to periphery of cities—have been dominated by young migration. Even the current movement to nonmetropolitan areas that was initially observed for the elderly population is largely a result of what those under age 65 are doing (Heaton et al., 1981). Analysis of components of change in the elderly population at the county level indicates that young migration has a greater impact on age than do elderly migration, young natural increase, or aging in place (Heaton, 1983). A pattern of young out-migration has resulted in concentration of elderly populations in vast sections of the Midwest, in central cities, and in rural areas (Golant, 1979; Graff and Wiseman, 1978). Places that are left behind often house elderly nonmigrants.

In spite of the relative immobility of the elderly, however, elderly migration does have a dramatic impact in some areas. Since elderly migrants tend to come from a wide variety of origins but select among a comparably small number of destinations, we are much more likely to notice the growth in receiving areas than the losses (E.S. Lee, 1980b). That Arizona, Florida, the Ozarks, and northern Wisconsin are becoming retirement areas is more widely recognized than is the elderly movement out of much of the Northeast. In the 1970s this social impact on destinations was magnified by the tendency of elderly people to move from larger to smaller places. A small percentage decrease in the elderly population of a large city becomes a large percentage gain in small communities.

Elderly migration has been a popular subject for research over the last several years. We have moved well beyond simple recognition that models of migration developed for the general population, placing emphasis on economic incentives and job opportunities, are less applicable to the elderly. Trends in elderly migration patterns, comparisons of migrants and nonmigrants, areal correlates of elderly migration rates, and the impact of migration have all received attention (Longino and Jackson, 1980), but many questions still remain unanswered (Heaton, 1983).

Patterns of Elderly Population Change

Given the different processes that contribute to an older age structure, the percentage change in the elderly population by itself offers an incomplete description of population aging. To illustrate, two distinct analytic types of areas can be identified which are becoming older. In one type young people are moving out, and in the other old people are moving in. There is good reason to believe that these two community types would be very different socially and economically, but little empirical work has been done to determine how well these analytic types describe reality, much less to examine their social and economic differences.

The diverse patterns of age structure change are demonstrated in table 3.4. Based on rankings by change in percentage over age 65 between 1970 and 1980, groups of states are identified that had below average, average, or above average elderly change. States are further classified by whether their growth rates are above or below average. Of the states that experienced above average shifts in elderly population, a majority did so because both young and elderly growth rates were above average, but elderly rates were even higher than young rates. These states are concentrated along the South Atlantic seaboard and in the West. Other states in the Northeast grew older because elderly and young rates were below average but the elderly rates were relatively higher. Many Midwestern states are characterized by below average growth of both young and old and only moderate change in the percentage over age 65. In contrast, only in California, Georgia, and Tennessee did higher growth of young and old result in average gains in the percentage over age 65. Finally, several western states and Texas had below average elderly change because the young were growing at a relatively faster pace than the elderly, while a scattering of states in the West, New England, the Midwest, and the South had below average change resulting from slow growth for both young and old, but even lower rates for the elderly.

GEOGRAPHIC DIFFERENTIATION OF SOCIAL CHARACTERISTICS

Adaptation by the elderly to their environment is conditioned by health, resources, and other social characteristics. Such characteristics exhibit substantial spatial variation. There is evidence, for example, that both objective and subjective indicators of well-being are associated with the level of urbanization, but that the pattern of association is not necessarily consistent across types of indicators. Urbanization may be positively associated with income and health but negatively associated with life satisfaction (Lee and Lassey, 1980; Lawton, 1980a). Little attention, however, has been given to the role that patterns of aging play in influencing areal differences in social characteristics of the elderly. The elderly who remain behind are undoubtedly different from those who choose to move elsewhere. Areas with an older age structure resulting from out-migration of young people are different from areas to which old people are moving (Heaton, 1983). In this section, we examine characteristics of the elderly, comparing groups of states and levels of urbanization. As a source of data we utilized the March 1980 U.S. Bureau of the Census *Current Population Survey*.

Comparisons of socioeconomic characteristics of the elderly for the groups of states shown in table 3.4 demonstrate that classification by percentage growth alone obscures differences among states (table 3.5). The pattern of aging within each category of percentage change also makes a difference. States that are growing older because the young have low growth rates (column 6) have a low

Table 3.4

States Classified by Change in the Percentage over Age 65 and by Overall Growth Rate

States with Below Average Change in the Percentage Aged 65 and over		States with Average Change in the Percentage Aged 65 and over		States with Above Average Change in the Percentage Aged 65 and over	
Lo Growth	*Hi Growth*	*Lo Growth*	*Hi Growth*	*Lo Growth*	*Hi Growth*
Montana	Alaska	Kansas	California	Connecticut	Maryland
Wyoming	Oregon	Minnesota	Georgia	Rhode Island	Virginia
Colorado	Washington	Indiana	Tennessee	New York	Delaware
Maine	Idaho	Illinois		New Jersey	North Carolina
New Hampshire	Utah	North Dakota		Pennsylvania	South Carolina
Vermont	Texas	South Dakota		Washington, D.C.	Alabama
West Virginia		Wisconsin			Florida
Kentucky		Michigan			Nevada
Iowa		Ohio			New Mexico
Nebraska		Missouri			Arizona
Oklahoma		Arkansas			Hawaii
		Louisiana			
		Mississippi			

Table 3.5
Social Characteristics of the Elderly for State Groups

Social Characteristics		States with Below Average Change in the Percentage Aged 65 and over		States with Average Change in the Percentage Aged 65 and over		States with Above Average Change in the Percentage Aged 65 and over	
		Lo Growth	Hi Growth	Lo Growth	Hi Growth	Lo Growth	Hi Growth
Sex Ratio		.651	.802	.695	.677	.664	.749
% Currently Married:	Male	80.6	77.7	76.5	73.9	72.3	79.8
	Female	37.7	43.1	38.3	36.7	35.2	44.2
% Living Alone:	Male	14.5	13.7	18.3	17.8	23.8	18.9
	Female	11.6	12.1	15.2	15.9	19.8	18.1
% with $15,000+:	Male	30.1	31.1	29.5	33.4	35.1	32.4
	Female	21.6	22.5	21.4	25.6	27.2	26.8
% with 12+ Years of Education:	Male	40.2	46.2	37.2	46.9	38.6	42.5
	Female:	44.8	49.9	40.3	48.3	39.2	44.2

sex ratio, a below average marriage rate, an above average percentage living alone, and near average income and education. States with low overall growth and moderate elderly change (group 3) are near average in terms of sex ratio, marriage, and living alone, but have below average income and education. States with high overall growth and moderate elderly change (group 4) have below average marriage rates and above average income. States with below average percentage increases in the elderly are similar in terms of their low percentages of those living alone and receiving a low income, but they differ on marriage rates, sex ratios, and education.

Central cities have the most unbalanced family structure as indicated by the low percentages married, the high percentages living alone, and the low sex ratios (table 3.6). This pattern is more pronounced in central cities of large Standard Metropolitan Statistical Areas (SMSAs) than in smaller SMSAs. In terms of education and income, however, central cities do not deviate very far from the national average. In many respects suburbs, especially those in large SMSAs, are distinctive. Education and income are above average, the percentage married is above or near average, and the percentage living alone is below average. Nevertheless, there are clear differences between the suburbs in large and small SMSAs. Education and income attain their lowest values in nonmetropolitan areas, but the sex ratio and the percentage living alone are near the national average, and marriage rates are slightly above average. Farms are distinguished by the high ratio of males to females. It is the only category where males predominate. Living on a farm is associated with above average income, very high marriage rates of women, and low percentages living alone.

Comparisons across groups of states and level of urbanization clearly reaffirm that social characteristics of the elderly vary across space. This pattern of variation appears to be associated with patterns of aging. In areas with above average elderly growth, the elderly tend to be above average in income and education, and smaller percentages are living alone. The reverse seems to be true for areas with below average growth. It is impossible, however, to precisely identify the contribution that patterns of aging make to these differences in social characteristics. Many of the differences existed before 1970. Thus, patterns of aging need to be systematically compared with change in social characteristics. With the limited information we have presented so far, about all we can conclude is that spatial variation in social characteristics exists and that this variation shows some association with patterns of aging. In the following section we identify some approaches that might be utilized to further understand this association.

ANALYSIS OF GEOGRAPHIC DIVERSITY IN SOCIAL CHARACTERISTICS

Any serious attempt to explain spatial differences in social characteristics of the elderly must take into account the processes underlying the distribution of the elderly population. Although the lack of attention given to this subject leaves

Table 3.6
Social Characteristics of the Elderly by Level of Urbanization

Social Characteristics		Large SMSAs		Smaller SMSAs		Nonmetropolitan	Farm*
		Central City	Suburb	Central City	Suburb		
Sex Ratio		.657	.679	.622	.759	.696	1.186
% Currently Married:	Male	66.7	78.2	74.5	78.8	79.1	78.3
	Female	30.8	38.8	34.4	43.0	40.1	64.9
% Living Alone:	Male	20.1	11.8	17.4	14.3	13.5	10.0
	Female	45.6	38.0	44.9	36.9	42.3	19.0
% with $15,000 + Household Income:	Male	33.5	42.5	30.9	31.7	23.6	36.2
	Female	24.6	33.6	23.5	25.2	16.9	29.7
% with 12 + years of Education:	Male	41.5	49.5	43.2	44.6	32.5	31.0
	Female	41.6	46.8	43.1	46.1	37.7	43.8
% Retired:	Male	73.4	75.2	73.2	76.5	74.9	54.2

*Farms are not a distinct category exclusive of others. Here all farm residents are separated out for comparison whether they live in central cities, suburbs, or nonmetropolitan areas.

us with little in terms of a comprehensive theoretical approach, we are not altogether empty-handed. The notion of cohort succession (Riley et al., 1972) provides a useful starting point for considering the effects of aging in-place on composition of the elderly population. In addition, numerous studies of selective migration give important clues regarding the impact of in- and out-migration. In this section we briefly consider succession and selective migration as they relate to geographic differences in social characteristics of the elderly, and their potential usefulness is illustrated by an empirical analysis of change in the educational level of the elderly in central cities, suburbs, and nonmetropolitan areas.

Cohort Succession

The composition of the elderly population changes to the degree that new cohorts entering the elderly category differ from those who have already reached old age. Some important changes in cohort composition are documented by Uhlenberg (1979). For example, the proportion of the cohort surviving to age 65 is nearly twice as high for the 1930 birth cohort as for the 1870 birth cohort. Again comparing these two cohorts, there has been a decline in the percentage of foreign-born, the sex ratio, and the percentage of males in the labor force. Transformation of the elderly population reflects these changes.

Characteristics of cohorts are heavily influenced by the past history of events, and the influence of each event varies according to the age at which the event occurs. For example, educational attainment of people now entering old age was influenced by the Great Depression of the 1930s, occupational composition by World War II, family size by the baby boom, relationship to adult children by social movements of the 1960s, and income at retirement by policies established in the 1970s. The match between important events and age will be much different in the future. Thus, a sense of history is necessary to understand compositional change in the elderly population.

Selective Migration

In addition to the succession of cohorts, the net exchange of in- and out-migration alters the composition of the elderly population, and the degree of alteration depends on the magnitude and selectivity of in- and out-migration streams. Although our understanding of elderly migration is far from complete, substantial progress is being made in this area. At first glance, there appears to be some disagreement regarding the pattern of selectivity. On one side, elderly movement has been found to be associated with lower socioeconomic status (Goldscheider, 1966) and major life disruptions (Nelson and Winter, 1975). On the other hand, elderly migration seems to exhibit positive selectivity in terms of education, occupational prestige, and income similar to that of younger population (Chevan and Fischer, 1979). The apparent contradiction is resolved when local movers are compared with migrants; local movers tend to be negatively selected, while long-distance migrants are positively selected (Biggar, 1980).

Typologies of elderly migration derived from models of the decision-making process help to clarify the diversity of reasons for moving (Wiseman and Roseman, 1979). Classification depends on the mechanisms inducing migration, characteristics of migrants, and type of destination. Two very distinct types of migration can be identified: amenity and assistance. Amenity migration is characterized by search for a better location, a relatively high level of personal resources, and movement to a desirable location. In contrast, assistance moves are triggered by life disruption; they are often associated with lower resources; and destinations are selected that offer needed assistance. Either type can be long- or short-distance, but there appears to be a correspondence between amenity and long-distance migration and between assistance and short-distance migration.

Areas that are able to attract amenity migrants may experience improvements in socioeconomic status and other elderly characteristics. Nonmetropolitan areas are gaining family households as a result of the net migration exchange (Clifford et al., 1981), and they also benefit economically (Clifford et al., 1983). States that gain elderly migrants experience a decline in the average age of the elderly population since elderly immigrants to these states are younger than the elderly out-migrants (Rives and Serow, 1981), but the reverse is true for states with net out-migration of elderly. Areas that attract assistance-oriented migrants will undergo an increase in the age dependency burden. Thus, the impact of migration will depend on the types of moves that are occurring.

An Empirical Illustration

We have argued that spatial variation in composition of the elderly population results from spatial variation in cohort succession and from selective migration. Here we make a preliminary demonstration of the impact these two factors have had on levels of education of the elderly, comparing central cities, suburbs, and nonmetropolitan areas. Data for the analysis are taken from the March 1980 Current Population Survey. Those aged 60–64 are taken as the new cohort entering the elderly category. The impact of this new cohort is gauged by comparing education levels before and after this group is included in the total. The impact of migration is assessed by comparing the existing population with a hypothetical population where all migrants are subtracted from destinations and added to origins. This analysis is incomplete since the effects of mortality are not taken into consideration. More complete analysis would require longitudinal data.

Results of the analysis are shown in table 3.7. Both central cities and suburbs experience an appreciable gain in educational levels as a consequence of cohort succession. The high increase in suburbs is most likely a result of past in-migration of higher educational groups to suburbs. The lower increase in nonmetropolitan areas is attributable to lower educational attainment of nonmetro-

Table 3.7
Impact of Cohort Succession and Migration on the Percentage of Elderly with Twelve or More Years of Education

Population	Migration Included	New Cohort Included	Percentage of the Population with 12 or More Years of Education		
			Central Cities	*Suburbs*	*Nonmetropolitan*
Existing population age 65 and over	yes	no	16.7	19.8	15.9
Existing population age 60 and over	yes	yes	17.8	22.0	16.5
Estimate of population age 60, 5 years ago (Out-migrants are added and in-migrants are subtracted from population aged 65 and over)	no	no	16.7	20.5	15.3
Estimate of existing population without migration (Out-migrants are added and in-migrants are subtracted from population aged 60 and over)	no	yes	17.7	22.5	16.1
Average migration effect [(1−3) + (2−4)]/2			.1	−.6	.5
Average cohort effect [(2−1) + (4−3)]/2			1.1	2.1	.7

politan youth during the Great Depression in conjunction with selective out-migration of more educated persons thereafter. Migration had little impact on the educational levels of central cities, but it resulted in educational gains in nonmetropolitan areas at the expense of suburbs. This is consistent with our earlier suggestion that amenity-oriented migration to nonmetropolitan areas is positively selective of socioeconomic characteristics. Interestingly, each type of area has about equal gains in educational attainment resulting from different patterns of change.

RESIDENTIAL DIMENSIONS OF QUALITY OF LIFE

Primary determinants of successful aging include not only the older individual's socioeconomic status, condition of health, and level of activity, but also the environmental context in which the elderly person negotiates daily. In considering both the diversity of the elderly and the environmental settings in which they live, the ability of the aged to experience a satisfying, fulfilling existence depends, in large part, upon whether or not their needs are congruent with the offerings of their life space (Cantor, 1975). Life space constitutes not only the physical elements of the environmental landscape, but also the larger sociocultural context of institutions, individuals, societal norms and values, and the personal environment of family and friends. For the aged, the ability to optimize the advantages and endure the disadvantages becomes increasingly difficult with the advancement of years. As physical mobility and health decline, independent living arrangements become more difficult to maintain; there is a growing dependence on the part of the elderly for local services to provide for their medical, psychosocial, and physical needs. As a selectively vulnerable group, some are unable to interact successfully with their environment, be it urban, suburban, or rural in nature, without formal support measures. Despite the fact that the elderly, in general, are in fairly good functional health, tend to live with spouses or other kin, and have satisfactory contact with friends and family members, they must solve those problems associated with basic life support needs—housing, income, and health care. While such issues become unique to the individual, those who reside within the confines of a particular setting will share the common experience of making do with what resources that environment has to offer. Taking into account this interplay between individuals and their environment, we will examine the capacities of different residential settings to provide for and complement the needs of elderly residents. The following discussion will focus on four dimensions of residence: accessibility and availability of services, primary support networks, quality of housing, and life satisfaction.

Accessibility and Availability of Community Resources

In order for a particular residential setting to satisfy the needs of elderly dwellers and provide for successful aging, resources must be accessible to those who need them. Adequate mobility is critical to the well-being of the elderly; without appropriate means of transportation the senior citizen will be less able to utilize social services, engage socially with kin and friends, or take part in cultural activities at large. While a national commitment to the provision of improved transportation for the elderly has been in effect only in recent years, programs designed to meet the mobility needs of older Americans have not, as yet, succeeded in reflecting the diversity of life-styles, residential milieus, and social patterns of older users. As transportation may be considered the key ingredient to insuring an effective interchange between elderly individuals and their living environments, it is clear that a significant proportion are unable to negotiate their residential settings successfully (Stirner, 1978; Lawton et al., 1978).

Although the availability and structure of social services for the elderly have not been well researched, existing literature concludes that rural communities, compared to urban and planned retirement settings, are deficient in both availability and accessibility. Despite the attempts in the early 1970s to offset urban-rural differences in human services, significant discrepancies remain in terms of both delivery and availability. Although service provisions for the rural senior citizen have expanded, they are not on par with metropolitan systems (Taietz and Sande, 1979). Low population density, program location and staffing, and transportation costs are among the logistical issues that have presented obstacles to rural practitioners. Aged rural residents are also less apt to be aware of available programs. The problem is intensified by rural residents' perceptions of welfare; research has shown them to be more inclined to hold negative attitudes toward welfare than their urban counterparts. This, in turn, has led to reduced participation rates and, as a result, reduced federal outlays (Osgood, 1977). Failure to consider these issues has resulted in many rural programs being no more than "watered down versions of urban social service systems" (Coward, 1979).

Although urban areas characteristically provide extensive social services, accessibility remains the dominant area of concern even for those who reside in city cores. For example, in New York City, medical care is not proximate to many elderly dwellers. Those who cannot utilize public transit because of physical incapabilities are at a further disadvantage, making alternative methods of medical transportation a critical need (Cantor, 1975). In general, elderly persons use mass transit infrequently or not at all due to economic, physical, or operational reasons. As city resources are negatively correlated with distance from city cores, inner-city aged fare better when relying upon walking as a primary mode of transport. However, personal and/or service barriers serve to undermine the mobility of urban elderly, making for a diminished congruence between the older person's needs and transport systems (Carp, 1979).

While research has demonstrated that suburban elderly, as a group, have less need for social services, health-related services remain a major area of concern. The dispersed nature of suburban neighborhoods hinders accessibility. While the private car may be affordable to the average suburban resident, there are older persons who either are without the financial means or are physically incapable of driving (Carp, 1979). Thus, there is special need for home services, such as delivered meals and physician house calls, as well as more numerous and proximate senior centers (Gutowski, 1981).

The same situations hold true for those who reside in retirement communities where a car is, by and large, essential. In Sun Belt states, for example, public transportation is often inadequate except in major urban areas, such as Los Angeles, Miami, and Honolulu (Dickinson, 1978). Yet, planned retirement settings are generally proximate to community services. For example, most Sun Belt retirement communities offer the advantage of being located near medical facilities, but rural residents are without this logistical advantage (Dickinson, 1978). Although there is evidence that these residents have a potentially greater need for health services, they are underutilizers of other municipal services (Heintz, 1976). Planned communities for the older individual are designed to provide suitable "fits" between the individual and the living environment; they also provide supportive services for those elderly who not only have experienced loss of personal resources, but who will also experience increasing personal needs (Longino, 1981:15).

Primary Support Networks

In addition to an advantageous position with regard to mobility and accessibility of community resources, city cores may also provide other advantages. According to Aiello (1976), crowding has a positive effect on the perceived well-being of the elderly as it allows for maximum social contact. Proximity of peers, due to age concentration and status homogeneity, lends to the maintenance of friendship in old age (Rosow, 1970; Messer, 1967). As Cantor (1975) has shown regarding the elderly of New York City, close intergenerational relationships do take place in metropolitan areas. High population density "offers a large reservoir of persons living within the immediate vicinity from whom to draw on as intimates and friends" (p. 26). Others, however, have found social interaction to be positively related to small rather than large communities (Berardo, 1967; Youmans, 1967; Rosencranz et al., 1968; Schooler, 1975). According to Langford (1962), not only do smaller communities make for more proximate friends, but more frequent visiting takes place as well. Felton, Hinricksen, and Tsemberis (1981) and Lawton and Kleban (1971), however, have suggested that the urban elderly are more dissatisfied with their friendship networks despite the fact that frequent visiting occurs. For those urban elderly who do lack close friendship bonds, proximity of recreational and cultural activities allows a greater chance of engaging socially, if only to visit neighbors, shop, or attend church (Carp, 1975).

Family relationships, although not found to be correlated with the morale of the older individual, are important determinants to the general well-being of aged persons (E.S. Lee, 1980a). Kin may provide aid in service assistance, bureaucratic mediation, and emotional support. However, findings as to urban-rural patterns of family relationships remain contradictory. That familial bonds may be strong among aged urbanites was shown by Cantor (1975) among New York City's residents; ties of affection and assistance united aged parents and their offspring, and did so increasingly with the advancement of years. In Chicago, however, Lopata (1975) reported that aged residents, though not completely isolated, are not "strongly societally engaged." For many, familial relations were not reflective of a full support network; children and siblings of aged urbanites tended to operate independently.

There is little evidence to support the traditional assumption that rurality lends to well-integrated kin networks (Powers et al., 1979; Mirande, 1970). Rural elderly residents are more likely to live alone than among relatives, and have been found to experience more limited contact with family members than their urban counterparts (Bultena, 1969; Youmans, 1963). In Iowa, Bultena et al. (1971) found only 19 percent of the offspring of rural aged dwellers residing in the same community; 34 percent of the urban elderly's children did so. For Wisconsin, comparable figures were 26 percent and 51 percent (Bultena and Wood, 1969). As Mahoney (n.d.) has shown, children of aged urbanites are more likely either to share households or live nearby, perhaps because of out-migration of the young from rural areas and small towns. Although urban aged have more contact with children, there is evidence that offspring of rural elderly initiate visits to a greater extent than do those of urban dwellers (Youmans, 1963). This may be due to the relative economic and transportation deprivation of rural older persons and to the greater proximity of kin in urban areas.

In terms of intergenerational reciprocity, rural elderly appear to receive less aid from kin than do those living in metropolitan areas. They also have fewer savings and investments to fall back on in times of need (Auerbach, 1976). While Shanas's analysis of a national sample revealed three-fifths of rural aged receiving assistance of varying forms from kin (Shanas et al., 1968), Bultena et al. (1971) reported only two-fifths of older rural Iowans receiving regular aid from offspring and other sources, and Mahoney (n.d.) found similar results for elderly of rural Pennsylvania. For aged rural residents in need, assistance from friends and neighbors may serve to augment any lack of familial support; friendship patterns of help and exchange have been shown to be extensive in rural areas. Less kinship support and overall parent-child contact are offset by the ability of rural older persons to maintain close friendship ties; when in need, many have the assurance that there are good neighbors to call upon (Bultena et al., 1971; Hampe and Blevins, 1972). Neighborliness and friendship participation lend to the experience of greater social interaction among nonmetropolitan aged dwellers (Lozier and Althouse, 1974; Lawton et al. 1975). Although Bull and Aucoin (1975) and Harris et al. (1975) have reported no significant differences in subjective well-being between urban and rural older persons, rurality has been shown to lend higher measures of neighborhood satisfaction, family support, and overall happiness (Youmans, 1973, 1977). This may be due to the enhanced morale and self-regard which result when "significant others" provide support and security and help to minimize familial, social, and geographical isolation among aged residents of rural areas.

Planned retirement community residents share a similar experience of a general lack of support from kin. While elderly who move into these types of residential settings may be attracted to their service-enriched living environments, residents tend to have characteristics that merit the inherent secondary support sources of such environments. Many are older, widowed, childless, less healthy, and in need of instrumental support, especially when kinship assistance is lacking (Bultena and Wood, 1969; Longino, 1981). Although these residents do not seem to exhibit higher levels of social participation, motivation for moving into their respective communities has been shown to derive from network recruitment. Having friends or family members to retire with provides companionship among individuals of like backgrounds or interests. Many "find shelter from the gathering storms of late-life troubles, seeking a more manageable environment, more tailored and accessible services, and the warm companionship of those like themselves" (Longino, 1981:414).

Quality of Housing

Despite the fact that the housing of older persons is comparable to that of other age groups and is of relatively good quality, there is a subgroup that experiences structurally deficient housing. One-tenth of the elderly's housing falls into this category, and aged blacks, Hispanics, and rural aged are typically the most disadvantaged. Analysis of a 1973 Annual Housing Survey by the U.S.Bureau of the Census has revealed that the black aged, rural residents, and renters had greatest housing need (Lawton, 1980b). While urban elderly experience more negative neighborhood conditions, households of older rural residents exhibit more structural defects than those of the urban elderly. Struyk (1977) has shown that differences between rural and urban elderly households are greater than those between elderly and non-elderly households. Rural aged experience a substantially greater disadvantage in the quality of dwelling units, as they tend to reside in older, larger, and more structurally inadequate dwellings. In 1973, about 15 percent lacked complete plumbing, 8 percent did not have complete kitchen facilities, over half were without central heating, and almost 10 percent lacked running water (Struyk, 1977). Neighborhood conditions, however, proved to be more desirable than was the case for urban elderly. While structural deficiencies plagued 17 percent of older metropolitan residents, 30 percent of those living in rural areas inhabited dwellings that "other, more affluent segments of American society would shun" (Struyk, 197:138).

Although urban aged are most susceptible to adverse neighborhood conditions, civic renewal of older, commercial urban areas poses deleterious effects for elderly residents. Those who dwell in single-room occupancy accommodations are prime targets for relocation, the consequences of which hold minimal promise for those without familial alternatives and for those with restricted incomes. This is particularly true of the older male in poor health who lives alone, or for the aged of lower socioeconomic class (Felton, Lehmann, and Adler, 1981). Many elderly who confront urban renewal are long-term residents with social and economic attachments to their neighborhoods. For them, the personal cost of severing social ties or the problem of having to cope with increased living expenses once modern shopping malls replace old-time, cheaper establishments outweighs the physical advantages of environmental revitalization.

In contrast to rural and inner-city elderly, suburban older persons experience better housing conditions, the quality of housing being best in newly developed suburban areas. However, elderly residents of suburban areas have fewer housing options due to the predominance of single-family homes. As is the case with the older population in general, elderly suburban rental households appear to be at the greatest disadvantage. They face rising costs of living which leave but a small share of their income for other needs (Gutowski, 1981).

Planned for the housing needs of older persons, retirement communities provide not only a variety of housing arrangements, but quality housing as well. High levels of housing satisfaction in Sun Belt state communities, for example, reflect the fact that there is more housing available at lower cost. Favorable climatic conditions promote health and serve to reduce heating and insulation costs (Dickinson, 1978). In the main, retirement communities provide satisfying living environments for senior citizens; residents not only demonstrate high morale (Bultena and Wood, 1969), but also recommend these communities for peers (Sherman, 1972).

Life Satisfaction: Urban-Rural Comparison

Research into the role of the city in either alleviating or aggravating the problems faced by elderly residents has pointed out diverse personal and environmental characteristics that yield both pros and cons. Although the questions regarding urban viability are left unresolved, it is clear that some older urbanites are able to negotiate successfully, while the social and physical needs of others remain unmet (Berghorn et al., 1978; Erickson and Eckert, 1977; Cantor, 1975; Bourg, 1975; Lopata, 1975). As Carp (1975) has shown with regard to the elderly of San Antonio, Texas, despite the negative correlation between inner-city crime rates, poor housing, and crowding to indexes of life satisfaction, the city may be considered a viable environment. On balance, environmental attributes of "intense-cityness" or suburban location were shown to be associated with more active, autonomous, and satisfying use of time, space, and social network. Though generally less satisfied with neighborhood services, the suburban aged, compared to rural and central city elderly, appear more content with the quality of their communities (Gutowski, 1981; Gutowski and Field, 1979). Although suburban residence may not offer the amenities of metropolitan areas, suburbanites are apparently able to utilize available resources to attain a comparable satisfactory level of living (Tissue, 1981).

The unfavorable ranking given many objective characteristics in rural areas may be offset by other, more favorable, qualities of these settings. Youmans (1973; 1977) has found that rural elderly residents score as high or higher than their urban counterparts on measures of neighborhood satisfaction, family support, and overall happiness. Similarly, Hynson (1975) reported them to be more satisfied with their community, to express greater general happiness, and to have less fear of victimization than their urban counterparts. In contrast to the widely supported assumption that crime is, by and large, an urban problem, G. R. Lee (1982) asserts that despite the lower incidence of crime in rural areas, elderly dwellers evince just as high or higher levels of perceived risk. Moreover, Sauer and associates (1976), having reanalyzed Hynson's data, suggest that community size is not independently related to life satisfaction. Others report that there is no significant difference in subjective well-being between urban and rural older persons (Bull and Aucoin, 1975; Harris, 1975). However, as Liang and Warfel (1983) have pointed out, previous attempts to assess the relationship between life satisfaction and community type, in the main, have failed to differentiate indirect from direct effects, main effects from interaction effects. As their results indicate, urbanism does not have a direct effect on life satisfaction, although it does directly influence related determinants, such as objective and subjective social integration.

Such contradictory findings underscore the complexity of geographic variation in life satisfaction among the elderly. While perceived well-being may be higher among urban aged residents due to factors exclusive of neighborhood conditions, measures of subjective well-being among rural aged run counter to many objective dimensions of residence. Keeping in mind that we cannot make definitive statements regarding the viability of a particular residential setting for older Americans, it may be said that most elderly have been able to adapt to the environmental contexts in which they live; "older persons have maximized the congruence between their own needs and their environment. . . . They have come to know their communities—who the people are, where the resources are, and how to obtain satisfaction" (Lawton, 1980a:37).

CONCLUSION

Since the turn of the century we have experienced dramatic absolute and relative growth of the elderly population, and this growth will undoubtedly continue into the next century. Growth has been accompanied by geographic redistribution across regions and levels of urbanization. Spatial variation in relative size of the elderly population involves a complex set of interrelated factors including not only current and past patterns of elderly migration, but also temporal trends in young migration, fertility, and mortality. The geography of age differences is incomplete without reference to each of these factors, yet only modest progress has been made in documenting and quantifying the role that each plays in ongoing changes in age structure.

Not only are the elderly unevenly distributed, but there is also spatial variation in characteristics of the elderly. Change in this variation is also related to the processes underlying age distribution. Migration is selective and variation in characteristics of the cohorts entering old age reflect the impact of area-specific historical events. With the exception of literature on selective migration, we have made little progress in explaining spatial variation in characteristics of the elderly population.

Concern over the quality of life is evident in the body of literature that examines the advantages and disadvantages of various environmental settings for elderly residents. No single type of residence appears to be either ideal or entirely undesirable. Indeed, evaluation of environmental attributes is contingent on characteristics of the residents involved. Nevertheless, the lack of consistent findings from study to study is somewhat distressing and the low association between objective and subjective indicators does not provide a firm basis for policies aimed at improving residential environments.

In sum, we have limited understanding of the processes that underlie the spatial distribution of the elderly; the spatial variation in characteristics of the elderly; and the advantages and disadvantages of various residential environments. Clearly the emergence of the geography of aging was not a stillbirth, but whether it will pass from the insecurities and growing pains of youth into the maturation of adulthood remains to be seen.

REFERENCES

Aiello, J.R. Effects of episodic crowding: A developmental perspective. Paper presented at the Annual Meetings of the Eastern Psychological Association, New York, 1976.

Auerbach, A.J. The elderly in rural areas: Differences in urban areas and implications for practice. In L.H. Ginsberg (Ed.), *Social work in rural communities*. Council on Social Work Education, New York, 1976.

Berardo, F.M. *Social adaption to widowhood among a rural-urban aged population*. Bulletin 689, College of Agriculture, Washington State University, Pullman, Wash., 1967.

Berghorn, F.J.; Schafer,D.E.; Steere, G.H.; and Wiseman, R.F. *The urban elderly: A study in life satisfaction*. Universe Books, New York, 1978.

Biggar, J.C. Who moved among the elderly, 1965 to 1970: A comparison of types of older movers. *Research on Aging*, 1980, *2*, 73–91.

Bourg, C.J. Elderly in a southern metropolitan area. *Gerontologist*, 1975, *15*, 15–22.

Bull, C.N., and Aucoin, J.B. Voluntary association participation and life satisfaction: A replication note. *Journal of Gerontology*, 1975, *30*, 73–76.

Bultena, G.L. Rural-urban differences in the familial interaction of the aged. *Rural Sociology*, 1969, *34*, 5–15.

Bultena, G.L., and Wood, V. The American retirement community: Bane or blessing? *Journal of Gerontology*, 1969, *24*, 209–217.

Bultena, G.L.; Powers, E.; Falkman, P.; and Frederick, D. *Life after 70 in Iowa*. Sociology Report 95, Iowa State University, Ames, Iowa, 1971.

Cantor, M.H. Life space and the social support system of the inner city elderly of New York. *Gerontologist*, 1975, *15*, 23–27.

Carp, F.M. Life-style and location within the city. *Gerontologist*, 1975, *15*, 27–34.

————. Improving the functional quality of housing and environments for the elderly through transportation. In T.O. Byerts, S.C. Howell, and L.A. Pastalan (Eds.), *Environmental context of aging: Life-styles, environmental quality, and living arrangements*. Garland STPM Press, New York, 1979, 127–146.

Chevan, A., and Fischer, L.R. Retirement and interstate migration. *Social Forces*, 1979, *57*, 1365–1380.

Clark, R.L., and Spengler, J.J. *The Economics of individual and population aging*. Cambridge University Press, New York, 1980.

Clifford, W.B.; Heaton,T.B.; and Fuguitt, G.V. Residential mobility and living arrangements among the elderly: Changing patterns in metropolitan and nonmetropolitan areas. *International Journal of Aging and Human Development*, 1981, *16*, 139–156.

Clifford, W.B.; Heaton, T.B.; Voss, P.R.; and Fuguitt, G.V. The rural elderly in demographic perspective. In R.T. Coward and G.R. Lee (Eds.), *Every fourth elder: Aging in rural environments*. Springer, New York, 1983.

Coward, R.T. Planning community services for the rural elderly: Implications from research. *Gerontologist*, 1979, *19*, 275–282.

Cowgill, D.O. The demography of aging. In A.M. Hoffman (Ed.), *The daily needs and interests of older people*. Charles C Thomas, Springfield, Ill., 1970.

Davis, K. The world demographic transition. *Annals of the American Academy of Political and Social Science*, 1945, *273*, 1–11.

Dickinson, P.A. *Sunbelt retirement*. Sunrise Books/E.P. Dutton, New York, 1978.

Erickson, R.J., and Eckert, J.K. The elderly poor in downtown San Diego hotels. *Gerontologist*, 1977, *17*, 440–446.

Felton, B.J.; Hinricksen, G.A.; and Tsemberis, S. Urban-suburban differences in the predictors of morale among the aged. *Journal of Gerontology*, 1981, *36*, 214.

Felton, B.J.; Lehmann, S.; and Adler, A. Single-room occupancy hotels: Their viability as housing options for older citizens. In M.P. Lawton and S.L. Hoover (Eds.), *Community housing choices for older Americans*. Springer, New York, 1981, 109–122.

Fuguitt, G.V., and Tordella, S.J. Elderly net migration: The new trend of non-metropolitan population change. *Research on Aging*, 1980, *2*, 191–204.

Golant, S.M. *Location and environment of elderly population*. Wiley, New York, 1979.

Goldscheider, C. Differential residential mobility of the older population. *Journal of Gerontology*, 1966, *21*, 103–108.

Graff, T.O., and Wiseman, R.F. Changing concentrations of older Americans. *Geographical Review*, 1978, *68*, 379–393.

Gutowski, M. Housing-related needs of the suburban elderly. In M.P. Lawton and S.L. Hoover (Eds.), *Community housing choices for older Americans*. Springer, New York, 1981, 109–122.

Gutowski, M., and Field, T. *The graying of suburbia*. Urban Institute, 1979.

Hampe, G.D., and Blevins, A.L. *Survey of the aged for the state of Wyoming*. University of Wyoming, Laramie, Wyo., 1972.

Harris, L. *The myth and reality of aging in America.* National Council on the Aging, Washington, D.C., 1975.

Heaton, T.B. Geographical distribution of the elderly population: Recent trends. In M.W. Riley, B.B. Hess, and K. Bond (Eds.), *Aging in society: Selected reviews of recent research.* Lawrence Erlbaum Associates, 1983.

Heaton, T.B.; Clifford, W.B.; and Fuguitt, G.V. Temporal shifts in the determinants of young and elderly migration in nonmetropolitan areas. *Social Forces,* 1981, *60,* 41–60.

Heintz, K.M. *Retirement communities, for adults only.* Center for Urban Policy Research, New Brunswick, N.J., 1976.

Hynson, L.M. Rural-urban differences in satisfaction among the elderly. *Rural Sociology,* 1975, *40,* 64–66.

Langford, M. *Community aspects of housing for the aged.* Cornell University Center for Housing and Environmental Studies, Ithaca, N.Y., 1962.

Lawton, M.P. *Environment and aging.* Wadsworth, Belmont, Calif., 1980a.

Lawton, M.P. Housing the elderly: Residential quality and residential satisfaction. *Research on Aging,* 1980b, *1,* 309–327.

Lawton, M.P.; Brody, E.M.; and Turner-Massey, P. The relationships of environmental factors to changes in well-being. *Gerontologist,* 1978, *18,* 133–151.

Lawton, M.P., and Kleban, M.H. The aged resident of the inner city. *Gerontologist,* 1971, *11,* 277–283.

Lawton, M.P.; Nehemow, L.; and Teaff, J. Housing characteristics and the well-being of the elderly tenants in federally assisted housing. *Journal of Gerontology,* 1975, *30,* 601–607.

Lee, E.S. Aged migration: Impact on service delivery. *Research on Aging,* 1980a, 2, 243–254.

———. Migration of the aged. *Research on Aging,* 1980b, 2, 131–135.

Lee, G., and Lassey, M. Rural-urban differences among the elderly: Economic, social and subjective factors. *Journal of Social Issues,* 1980, *36,* 62–74.

Lee, G.R. Residential location and fear of crime among the elderly. *Rural Sociology,* 1982, *47,* 655–669.

Liang, J., and Warfel, B.L. Urbanism and life satisfaction among the aged. *Journal of Gerontology,* 1983, *38,* 97–106.

Lichter, D.T.; Fuguitt, G.V.; Heaton, T.B.; and Clifford, W.B. Components of change in residential concentration of the elderly population: 1950–1975. *Journal of Gerontology,* 1981, *36,* 480–489.

Longino, C.F., Jr. Retirement communities. In F.J. Berghorn, D.E. Schafer (Ed.), *The dynamics of aging.* Westview Press, Boulder, Colo., 1981, 391–418.

Longino, C.F., Jr., and Jackson, D.J. (Eds.). Migration and the aged. A special issue of *Research on Aging,* 1980, 2, no. 2.

Lopata, H.Z. Support systems of elderly urbanites: Chicago of the 1970s. *Gerontologist,* 1975, *15,* 35–41.

Lozier, J., and Althouse, R. Social enforcement of behavior toward elders in an Appalachian mountain settlement. *Gerontologist,* 1974, *14,* 69–80.

Mahoney, K.J. A national perspective on community differences in the interaction of the aged with their adult children. Faye McBeath Institute on Aging and Family Life, University of Wisconsin, Madison, n.d.

Messer, N. The possibility of an age concentrated environment becoming a normative system. *Gerontologist*, 1967, 7, 247–251.

Mirande, A.M. Extended kinship ties, friendship relations and community size: An exploratory inquiry. *Rural Sociology*, 1970, 35, 261–266.

Nelson, L., and Winter, M. Life disruption, independence, satisfaction, and the consideration of moving. *Gerontologist*, 1975, 15, 1960–1964.

Notestein, F.W. Population: The long view. In T.W. Schultz (Ed.), *Food for the World*, University of Chicago Press, Chicago, 1945, 36–57.

Osgood, M.H. Rural and urban attitudes toward welfare. *Social Work*, 1977, 22, 41–47.

Powers, E.A.; Keith, P.; and Goudy, W.J. Family relationships and friendships among the rural aged. In T.O. Byerts, S.C. Howell, and L.A. Pastlan (Eds.), *Environmental context of aging: Life-styles, environmental quality, and living arrangements*. Garland STPM Press, New York, 1979, 80–101.

Rice, R.R., and Beegle, J.A. *Differential fertility in a metropolitan society*. Rural Sociological Society Monograph Series, no. 1, West Virginia University, Morgantown, W.V., 1972.

Riley, M.W.; Johnson, M.; and Foner, A. *Aging and society. Volume 3: A sociology of age stratification*. Russell Sage Foundation, N.Y., 1972.

Rives, N.W., Jr., and Serow, W.J. Interstate migration of the elderly. *Research on Aging*, 1981, 3, 259–278.

Rosencranz, H.A.; Pihlblad, C.T.; and McNevin, T.E. *Social participation of older people in the small town*. Department of Sociology, University of Missouri, Columbia, 1968.

Rosow, I. Old people: Their friends and neighbors. *American Behavioral Scientist*, 1970, 14, 59–69.

Sauer, W.J.; Shehan, C.; and Boymel, C. Rural-urban differences in satisfaction among the elderly: A reconsideration. *Rural Sociology*, 1976, 41, 269–275.

Schooler, K.K. A comparison of rural and non-rural elderly on selected variables. In R.C. Atchley and T.O. Byerts (Eds.), *Environments and the rural aged*. Gerontological Society, Washington, D.C., 1975.

Shanas, E.; Townsend, P.; Wedderbum, D.; Friis, H.; Milhoj, P.; and Stehouwer, J. *Old people in three industrial societies*. Atherton Press, N.Y., 1968.

Sheldon, H.D. *The older population of the United States*. Wiley, N.Y., 1958.

Sherman, S.R. Satisfaction with retirement housing: Attitudes, recommendations and moves. *Aging and Human Development*, 1972, 3, 339–366.

Smith, T.L. The distribution and movements of the aged population. *Journal of Business*, 1954, 27, 108–118.

Smith, T.L., and Zopf, P.E., Jr. *Demography: Principles and method*. F.A. Davis, Philadelphia, 1970.

Stirner, F.W. The transportation needs of the elderly in a large urban environment. *Gerontologist*, 1978, 18, 207–211.

Struyk, R.J. The housing situation of elderly Americans. *Gerontologist*, 1977, 17, 131–139.

Taietz, P., and Sande, M. Rural-urban differences in the structure of services for the elderly in upstate New York counties. *Journal of Gerontology*, 1979, 34, 429–437.

Tissue, T. Old age, poverty, and the central city. In R. Kastenbaum (Ed.), *Old age on the new scene*. Springer, 1981, 181–198.

Uhlenberg, P. Demographic change and problems of the aged. In M.W. Riley (Ed.), *Aging from birth to death*. Westview Press, Boulder, Colo., 1979, 153–166.

U.S. Bureau of the Census. *Data from the annual housing survey*. Data Access Descriptions, no. 43, USGPO, Washington, D.C., 1979.

————. *Current Population Survey*. USGPO, Washington, D.C., 1980.

Warnes, A.M. (Ed.). *Geographical perspectives on the elderly*. Wiley, 1982.

Wiseman, R.F., and Roseman, C.C. A typology of elderly migration based on the decision-making process. *Economic Geography*, 1979, *55*, 324–337.

Youmans, E.G. *Aging patterns in a rural and an urban area of Kentucky*. Bulletin 681, Agricultural Experiment Station, Lexington, Ky., 1963.

————. *Older rural Americans*. University of Kentucky Press, Lexington, Ky., 1967.

————. Perspectives on the older American in a rural setting. In J.B. Cull and R.E. Hardy (Eds.), *The neglected older American*. Charles C Thomas, Springfield, Ill., 1973.

————. The rural aged. *Annals of the American Academy of Political and Social Science*, 1977, *429*, 81–90.

4

THE RETIRED

ERDMAN B. PALMORE

The retired constitute one of the most important categories of older persons, and certainly the largest category. Most older persons are retired. In 1981 only 4 percent of persons over age 65 were employed full-time (Harris, 1981). This means that there are about 26 million persons in the United States over 65 who are retired in the sense of not being employed full-time.

Retirement is also important because it affects the income, activities, and life-style of older persons. Furthermore, it is commonly believed that retirement tends to make people dissatisfied with life, impairs their health, and leads to premature death. There is little or no evidence to support these beliefs, but since they are so widely held, it is important to understand the evidence we do have.

On the societal level it is important because retirement rates affect the national labor supply, the employment opportunities of younger workers, and the amount of Social Security taxes necessary to provide retirement benefits. These societal effects lead to important policy questions regarding mandatory retirement, discrimination against older workers, and incentives for retirement or continued employment.

DEFINITIONS

Before we can describe the retired, we need to define who they are. There are a number of definitions of retirement, each of which may have value for some theoretical or methodological purpose. In this chapter we will use three basic definitions of retirement (Palmore et al., 1982).

1. *Objective Dichotomous*. In this definition a person is retired if employed less than 35 hours per week *and* receiving a retirement pension, either public or private. Under this definition, unemployed persons without pensions (such as homemakers) are not considered retired, and conversely, those working full-time are not considered retired even if they are getting retirement pensions.

2. *Objective Continuous.* This is based on the amount of employment: no employment means maximum retirement; part-time employment means partial retirement; and full-time employment means minimal retirement. A continuous measure such as this has the advantage of being appropriate for multiple regression analysis. About 86 percent of persons over 65 are in maximum retirement and another 10 percent are partially retired according to this measure (Harris, 1981).

3. *Subjective.* This is based on the person's own definition of retirement. If a person defines him/herself as retired, he/she is classified as retired regardless of amount of employment or pension receipt. About 79 percent of persons over 65 are retired according to this definition (Harris, 1981).

CHARACTERISTICS

Age

The characteristic most strongly related to retirement is age. The percentage of subjectively retired increases dramatically from 27 percent for those aged 55–64, to 77 percent for those 65–69, and to 80 percent for those aged 70 and over. (The percentages of those objectively retired show the same relationship.) If we exclude homemakers from the base, this increase is even more dramatic: 33 percent for those 55–64, 86 percent for those 65–69, 94 percent for those 70–79, and 97 percent for those 80 and over (Harris, 1981). On the other hand, because of the increased popularity of early retirement, over one-half of new retirees retire before age 65 (Bixby, 1976). However, the rate of early retirement has dropped somewhat during the recent recession and the median age at retirement has gone up from 63 in 1974 to 63.5 in 1981 (Harris, 1981).

Gender

Whether more men or women are retired depends on the definition used. According to the objective dichotomous definition, more men (93 percent) than women (73 percent) are retired because fewer women have been employed long enough to qualify for retirement benefits. Similarly, according to the subjective definition, more men (90 percent) than women (71 percent) consider themselves retired because 24 percent of the women over 65 consider themselves to be homemakers rather than retired. But according to the objective continuous measure, more women (98 percent) than men (94 percent) are fully or partially retired (Harris, 1981). If we exclude homemakers from the base and analyze only those with substantial work experience, then it is clear that women have a higher rate of retirement from employment than do men regardless of the definition.

Race

Similarly, whether more whites or blacks are retired depends on whether homemakers are included or not. If we compare total whites and blacks over 65, more blacks (88 percent) than whites (79 percent) are subjectively retired. But if we exclude homemakers (15 percent of whites, 6 percent of blacks) from the base, about equal proportions of whites and blacks with substantial work experience are retired (Harris, 1981).

Occupation

If we group retirees' previous occupations into three broad classes such as upper (professional, manager, official, proprietor), middle (clerical, sales, skilled, foreman, service), and lower (all others), we find that almost half were in the middle group and a little over a quarter each were in the upper and the lower groups (Harris, 1981). However, persons in the upper occupations are less likely to retire than those in the middle or lower groups because the upper occupations are more rewarding and are less frequently subject to mandatory retirement (Palmore et al., 1982).

Health

There are more sick and disabled persons among the retired than among those still employed over age 65, primarily because the retired includes all those who had to retire due to poor health. However, the vast majority of retirees feel that their health is not a serious problem. Only about one-fifth say that their health is a "very serious problem" (Harris, 1981).

PREDICTORS

What causes retirement? This is a difficult question to answer without controlled experiments, and these have never been done. We know what reasons retirees give for retiring, but these "reasons" are often only socially acceptable rationalizations for the real factors causing their retirement. However, we can analyze which characteristics predict retirement, and these predictors give us some insight into the factors leading to retirement (this section is based on Palmore et al., 1982).

In a series of analyses of the predictors of retirement in seven longitudinal studies, we found that the predictors vary markedly depending on how retirement is defined and measured. If the objective dichotomous or the subjective definitions are used among those 65 and over, then structural factors, such as occupation and job characteristics (for example, mandatory retirement rules, availability of pensions) that increase the incentives or necessity of retirement are the strongest predictors. Health and attitudes toward retirement are relatively unimportant. If the objective continuous measure is used, job characteristics are stronger predictors than all the other predictors combined.

In contrast, if we analyze early retirement (before age 65) or age at retirement, then subjective factors such as perceived health and attitude become more important. We interpret this to mean that subjective factors are more important in early retirement because it is less frequently encouraged or forced than retirement after age 65. At ages over 65 most workers are pressured to retire by mandatory retirement policies and expectations of employers, fellow workers, friends, and family. Therefore, only the few who are self-employed or in jobs not subject to mandatory retirement or employer pressures (structural factors) are able to continue much employment.

CONSEQUENCES

In another series of analyses of the seven longitudinal studies of retirement we found that the effects of retirement are less negative than generally believed (Palmore et al., 1984).

Income

It is widely believed that retirement sharply reduces income and forces many people into poverty. Our analysis found that while family incomes of retired men were about 35 percent lower than those of still-employed men, this difference is reduced by about half when differences in pre-retirement characteristics are controlled (such as pre-retirement income, age, education, and occupation). Thus, the retired men tended to have lower incomes *before* they retired due to their older age, lower education, and occupation. Retirement itself accounted for only about 1 percent of the variance in income after pre-retirement differences were controlled. Similarly, very few (about 3 percent) were forced into poverty as a result of retirement.

Health

A similar picture emerges from the analysis of health consequences. It is true that the retired tend to be in poorer health than those still employed (about 6 percent of the variance in health is explained by retirement status). But this difference is reduced by almost half when pre-retirement characteristics are taken into account. That is, the retired tended to be older and in poorer health *before* retirement. However, the question remains, does the remaining difference in health between retired and employed mean that retirement tends to cause health deterioration? We believe that it does not. We believe that there are two better explanations for this remaining association between retirement and poor health. First, we believe that although we attempted to control for pre-retirement levels of health, the health of some of those who later retired deteriorated between the time of the initial surveys and the time of retirement (which was often several years). Therefore, this deterioration in health *before retirement* caused the retirement, rather than the retirement causing the deterioration in health. This interpretation is supported by the fact that substantial proportions of retirees report *improved* health after retirement as a result of being freed from the stresses and pressures of their job. Secondly, we believe that retirees may be motivated to exaggerate their health limitations in order to justify their retirement, while those still employed may be motivated to minimize their health limitations in order to keep their jobs. A recent review of the research concludes that there is no clear evidence for adverse effects of retirement on health or longevity (Minkler, 1981).

Activity

There were few substantial effects of retirement on activities except for the reduction in hours employed (a result of the very definition of retirement) and modest increases in solitary activities, self-care activities, time spent with friends, non-employment work, and church attendance. Pre-retirement levels of activity were usually the strongest predictors of post-retirement activity. This means that those who were initially more active tended to be the ones who remained active later, regardless of whether retired or not.

Attitudes

Retirement also had little or no effect on most attitudes. The few statistically significant relationships between retirement and attitudes were not consistent within or between studies. There was no clear evidence in these studies for the common assumption that retirement tends to make people depressed or dissatisfied with life. Substantial proportions of retirees report *increases* in their happiness and life satisfaction as a result of their greater freedom to do what they want when they want to do it. All the surveys agree that the majority of retirees are satisfied with life. For example, two-thirds of the retirees in a national survey said that retired life was the same as or better than working life, with 40 percent saying it was better (Harris, 1981). Few are able and willing to go back to work (Harris, 1975). The few who are dissatisfied with life in retirement tend to be those with inadequate incomes or poor health. Thus, it appears that most dissatisfaction with life in retirement is due to dissatisfaction with income and health, rather than to dissatisfaction with retirement as such.

Early Retirement

However, we did find that early retirement had more negative consequences than retirement past age 65. This appears to be because a larger proportion of early retirees felt that they had to retire involuntarily because of poor health or lack of job opportunities, despite a greater loss of income.

In summary, these analyses show that (1) when pre-retirement characteristics are controlled, most of the supposed negative consequences of retirement are small or insignificant; but that (2) early retirement has more negative effects than later retirement.

REASONS FOR RETIREMENT

Involuntary

In 1981 over one-third (37 percent) of retirees said that they were forced to retire (Harris, 1981). Even more (45 percent) of those with lower incomes (below $5,000) and half of blacks said that they were forced to retire. Two-thirds of those forced to retire said that they had to retire because of disability or poor health. Only 7 percent of all retirees said that they had to retire because of their company's fixed retirement age. This is surprising since over 40 percent of workers are in companies that have mandatory retirement provisions (Clark et al., 1979). Apparently many retirees do not like to admit that they were forced to retire, or many choose to retire before they are forced to do so. Now that mandatory retirement before age 70 is illegal for most companies, the proportion of workers being forced to retire should decline further.

Predictors

In an analysis of the characteristics that predict involuntary retirement, among the men in the National Longitudinal Study we found that the strongest predictor was occupation: men in the lower occupations were substantially more likely to have been forced to retire. The second strongest predictor was health: men with health-related work limitations at the start of the study were more likely to have had to retire. The job characteristics and attitudes added little to the prediction equation.

Consequences

When analyzing the consequences of involuntary retirement, we found that there were important differences between those who had to retire because of poor health and those who had to retire because of mandatory retirement rules or other involuntary reasons. Those who had to retire because of poor health suffered substantially greater declines in living standards, life satisfaction, and leisure satisfaction than others. Those who had to retire for other involuntary reasons did have somewhat greater declines in living standards, life satisfaction, and leisure satisfaction than those who voluntarily retired, but these declines were relatively small (less than 1 percent of variance explained by retirement for other involuntary reasons).

Flexible Retirement

There are many arguments for flexible retirement policies based on ability and desire to continue working as an alternative to compulsory retirement at a fixed age (Palmore, 1972).

1. Compulsory retirement is by definition discrimination against an age category, contrary to the principle of equal employment opportunity.

2. Age, as the sole criterion for compulsory retirement, is not an accurate indicator of ability because of the wide variation in the abilities of aged persons.

3. Flexible retirement better utilizes the skills, experience, and productive potentials of older persons and thus increases our national production.

4. Flexible retirement increases the income of the aged and reduces the transfer payments necessary for income maintenance.

5. Flexible retirement reduces the resentment and animosity caused by compulsory retirement.

6. Flexible retirement makes possible a more gradual transition and easier adjustment to retirement.

The major arguments for compulsory retirement are administrative ease and reduction of unemployment. But using compulsory retirement to reduce unemployment is analogous to not allowing women or blacks to work in order to reduce the number of workers competing for jobs. There are other ways to reduce unemployment that do not involve discrimination against a category of workers.

HISTORY

Men

At the turn of the century only about one-third of the men over age 65 were retired (out of the labor force). The retirement rate increased rapidly during the depression of the 1930s and after passage in 1935 of the Social Security Act, so that by 1950 over half of the men 65 and older had retired (Brotman, 1982). Retirement has continued to increase by about 1 percent per year so that now about 90 percent of men 65 and older are retired. Early retirement (at ages before 65) was very rare at the turn of the century, but began to increase when men became eligible to get reduced Social Security retirement benefits at age 62. By 1960 19 percent of men aged 60–64 had retired (out of labor force); by 1970 early retirement increased to 25 percent; and by 1980 it had increased to 39 percent.

Women

Retirement among women shows a markedly different historical pattern from that of men. If one looks at labor force participation rates, most women past 65 (92 percent) were homemakers or retired at the turn of the century. This proportion has remained remarkably constant, dropping to a low of 89 percent in 1960, but returning to 92 percent by 1980. Apparently, the increasing proportion of women in the labor force has been balanced by the increasing popularity of retirement. Similarly, the proportion of homemakers or early retired (aged 60–64) has increased little between 1955 (71 percent) and 1980 (67 percent).

It remains to be seen what the long-term effects of the 1981 Age Discrimination in Employment Act will be on retirement rates. Although the act prohibits mandatory retirement before age 70, most estimates indicate that it may decrease retirement by only a few percentage points because most retirees are unable or unwilling to continue employment.

PROBLEMS

There are many widespread fears about retirement. A recent article titled "The First Step to the Cemetery" warned that retirement would be the "worst decision you have ever made," that retired people are "besieged by indifference, loneliness and uselessness" (Bernard, 1982). Many fear that if they retire they will soon drop into poverty, lose their minds, get sick, and die prematurely.

It is true that a generation or two ago many of these fears were based on fact. Before Social Security and pensions became common, a majority of retirees were poor, if not in poverty. At that time the majority probably were sick, senile, or disabled. Most retirees were close to death. But the facts have changed.

It is true that many retirees still face major problems, such as failing health, reduced income, and loss of purpose. But working people of all ages also have serious problems, and many of the so-called retirement problems are not necessary effects of retirement. Let us consider the facts on each of the major fears about retirement.

Poverty

Most retirees are not in poverty. Only about 18 percent of retirees over age 65 have incomes below the official government poverty levels (about $4,310 for a nonfarm individual and $5,690 for a nonfarm couple in 1982). This is only about 4 percentage points more than that for all Americans, so the chances of falling into poverty upon retirement are less than 4 in 100. It is true that most retirees do experience some reduction in income, but this is usually compensated for by some reduction in expenses and lower taxes. It is true that inflation can hurt those on fixed incomes, but retirees are at least partially protected from inflation by the automatic cost-of-living increases in their Social Security benefits.

Retirees are also protected from the ravages of unemployment since they do not have to continue employment.

Sickness and Death

Retirement does not increase mortality or illness. It is true that there are more sick among the retired than among the working, but this is probably because sickness causes retirement, not the other way around. Careful studies have shown that retirees from companies with mandatory retirement have no higher mortality rates than the rest of their age group. The vast majority (over three-fourths) of retirees are healthy enough to engage in their normal activities. Only one-fifth say that health is a "very serious problem" for them (Harris, 1981). The average retiree can expect to live about sixteen years after retirement.

Mental Illness

Most retirees are not mentally ill. Only about 5 to 10 percent are so psychiatrically impaired that they are unable to function normally. Many suffer from varying degrees of memory loss, but most find ways to compensate for this difficulty. Despite the temporary stresses of adjusting to retirement, there is no clear evidence that retirement tends to cause mental illness. Retirement can sometimes improve mental health.

Institutionalization

Most retirees do not end up in institutions. Only 5 percent of the aged are in a long-stay personal care institution such as a mental hospital or nursing home. Only about one-fourth of retirees end up in such institutions before death (Palmore, 1976).

Loneliness

Most retirees are not isolated or lonely. Retirees have about as many social and family contacts as non-retirees. Most retirees have close relatives within easy visiting distance and visits between them are relatively frequent. About three-fourths are members of a church or synagogue and about half attend services at least three times a month. Over half belong to other voluntary organizations. Only a small minority (about 12 percent) say that loneliness is a "very serious problem" for them (Harris, 1981).

Depression

Most retirees are not depressed in the clinical sense. Most retirees are satisfied with their retirement. Only about 3 percent of retirees are willing and able to work but cannot find work. Retirement increases happiness for some and decreases it for others, but it has no effect on happiness for the average retiree. The majority say, "I am just as happy as when I was younger," and "The things I do are as interesting to me as they ever were." Almost one-third say, "These are the best years of my life" (Harris, 1981).

Uselessness

Retirement need not mean the end of usefulness. About 17 percent of all retired men aged 62 to 70 work part-time. Many retire completely for a while and then go back to work, either full-time or part-time. About one-fifth do voluntary work and most continue to do useful work around the house or with hobbies.

ADVANTAGES

In contrast to the potential problems posed by retirement, there are several major advantages to retirement.

Freedom from Work

Some fortunate workers derive much satisfaction from their jobs. More workers find their work to be onerous, boring, unsatisfying, fatiguing, stressful, unhealthy, or even dangerous. For these workers, retirement is a blessed release from all the things about their jobs that they dislike.

Increased Leisure

Retirement means that all the time one spent earning a living can now be devoted to doing what one wants to do. The retiree is free to travel, pursue hobbies and crafts, develop skills, continue education, do volunteer work in the community, participate in church and club activities, visit friends and relatives, garden, improve the house and grounds, and even improve his or her health through more exercise and other preventive health practices. The retiree can maximize the variety of rewarding activities and can develop a flexible schedule so that she/he does as much or as little of these activities as desired, and when desired, rather than constraining them to the few leisure hours left after work.

Income Security

Retirement usually means some reduction in income, but this is at least partially offset by elimination of those expenses connected with the job (travel, clothes, lunches, etc.). Furthermore, most retirees enjoy a unique form of income security: a guaranteed income in the form of Social Security benefits and pensions which are not threatened by the possibility of demotion, pay cuts, layoffs, discharge, or disability. Only the rich have comparable income security.

PREPARATION FOR RETIREMENT

Several studies have shown that preparation for retirement programs can improve adjustment to retirement (Palmore, 1982). Yet few companies or institutions provide comprehensive retirement planning programs for their employees (O'Meara, 1977). Such programs should include both lectures (with audiovisual supplementation) and group discussion. This provides communication of useful information as well as group support, reduction of anxiety, and answering of personal concerns. Such programs have been found to be more effective than either approach by itself. Topics that should be covered in such programs include: attitudes toward retirement, company benefits and options, Social Security and Medicare, retirement budgets, legal aspects, physical and mental health, family relations, residence options, use of leisure, and increasing income after retirement.

The Duke Center for the Study of Aging has a coordinator's manual for companies or institutions wishing to offer such a program. The American Association of Retired Persons has a package and training program for coordinators of such programs. An individual who does not have access to such a program can use one of several good manuals to do his/her own retirement preparation (Otte, 1974; Sunshine, 1974).

Some of the most important steps in preparing for retirement are the following:

1. Inform yourself about retirement. Read some of the many pamphlets, articles, and books on retirement. Talk to retired people about their experience and advice. We spend about a fourth of our lives preparing for our working years. Surely a few years invested in preparing for retirement should pay off in better ability to avoid the dangers, solve the problems, and take advantage of the opportunities of retirement.

2. Develop a positive attitude toward retirement. Rid yourself of needless fears based on myths and stereotypes rather than the facts. Accent the positives (opportunities, advantages) and eliminate the negatives (limitations, dangers, fears). Persons with more positive attitudes usually adjust much better to retirement than those with negative attitudes.

3. Plan to keep active physically, mentally, and socially. Persons who remain active adjust much better than those who retire to the rocking chair. The body and mind and social skills need exercise all through life in order to remain healthy. This is especially true in retirement, when the temptations and expectations are usually to reduce activity.

4. Set new goals in life. When the goals of career and work are gone, something else must be put in their place or a person is likely to suffer from feelings of purposelessness, meaninglessness, and the resulting depression. New goals are an important source of motivation for the activity that is essential for continued health and happiness. Do not just retire *from* work; retire *to* take advantage of the many opportunities presented by retirement.

ORGANIZATIONS

Almost any of the many organizations for elders in our country could be considered as organizations for retired persons, since the retired constitute most of those over 65. We will list a few of the largest and most clearly focused on the retired.

American Association of Retired Persons
1901 K Street NW
Washington, DC 20006

Gray Panthers
3700 Chestnut Street
Philadelphia, PA 19104

National Council of Senior Citizens
1511 K Street NW
Washington, DC 20005

National Council on the Aging
1828 L Street NW, Suite 504
Washington, DC 20036

The following organizations or agencies are also good sources of information on retirement.

Administration on Aging
U.S. Department of Health and Human Services
Washington, DC 20201

The Gerontological Society of America
1835 K Street NW, Suite 305
Washington, DC 20006

National Institute on Aging
National Institutes of Health
Bethesda, MD 20205

Social Security Administration
Baltimore, MD 21235

In addition to numerous private programs for the retired, the following federal programs are of major importance.

Foster Grandparent Program
ACTION
806 Connecticut Avenue NW
Washington, DC 20525

Green Thumb
National Farmers Union
1012 14th Street NW
Washington, DC 20005

Retired Senior Volunteer Program
ACTION
806 Connecticut Avenue NW
Washington, DC 20525

Senior AIDES
National Council of Senior Citizens
1511 K Street NW
Washington, DC 20005

Senior Community Service Aides
1909 K Street NW
Washington, DC 20006

Senior Community Service Employment Program
1801 K Street NW, Suite 1021
Washington, DC 20006

Senior Community Service Program
National Council on the Aging
1511 K Street NW
Washington, DC 20005

Senior Environmental Employment Program
Administration on Aging
1909 K Street NW
Washington, DC 22049

Senior Opportunities and Services Program
Office of Economic Opportunity
1200 19th Street NW
Washington, DC 20506

Service Corps of Retired Executives
ACTION
806 Connecticut Avenue NW
Washington, DC 20525

Volunteers in Service to America
ACTION
806 Connecticut Avenue NW
Washington, DC 20525

RESEARCH ISSUES

Retirement is one of the most researched topics in gerontology. As a result, we know the basic parameters of retirement among men in general: the characteristics of men who retire, the causes and consequences of retirement among men, and differences between those who retire early and those who retire "on time." However, we know little about retirement among women, blacks, and lower income groups. What is needed now is research focused on these special groups. Also, we need to monitor changing patterns of retirement among all groups as economic and social conditions change, as fewer workers are forced to retire by mandatory retirement rules, and as the cohorts of retired persons become more healthy, more educated, and more financially secure.

One problem does remain in terms of the consequences of retirement: to what extent is the poorer health of retirees due to declining health prior to retirement, and to what extent is it due to retirement itself? As stated earlier, we assume that little or none of the retiree's poorer health is due to retirement itself, but the research needed to establish this conclusively has not been done. What is needed are comprehensive medical and functional examinations just prior to retirement and then some years after retirement, along with comparable examinations on a control group of non-retirees.

REFERENCES

Bernard, K. The first step to the cemetery. *Newsweek*, February 22, 1982, p. 15.

Bixby, L. Retirement patterns in the U.S. *Social Security Bulletin*, 1976, *36*, 3–19.

Brotman, H. Every ninth American. Falls Church, Va., 1982. Mimeo.

Clark, R.; Barker, D.; and Cantrell, R. Outlawing age discrimination. Report to Administration on Aging, 1979. Mimeo.

Harris, L. *The myth and reality of aging in America*. National Council on the Aging, Washington, D.C., 1975.

———. *Aging in the eighties*. National Council on the Aging, Washington, D.C., 1981.

Minkler, M. Research on the health effects of retirement. *Journal of Health and Social Behavior*, 1981, *22*, 117–130.

O'Meara, J. *Retirement: Rewards or rejection*. Conference Board, New York, 1977.

Otte, E. *Retirement rehearsal guidebook*. Pictorial, Indianapolis, 1974.

Palmore, E. Compulsory versus flexible retirement. *Gerontologist*, 1972, *12*, 343–348.

———. Total chance of institutionalization among the aged. *Gerontologist*, 1976, *16*, 504–507.

———. Preparation for retirement. In N. Osgood (Ed.), *Life after work*. Praeger, New York, 1982.

Palmore, E.; Fillenbaum, G.; and George, L. Consequences of retirement. *Journal of Gerontology*, 1984, *39*, 109–116.

Palmore, E.; George, L.; and Fillenbaum, G. Predictors of retirement. *Journal of Gerontology*, 1982, *37*, 732–742.

Sunshine, J. *How to enjoy your retirement*. American Management Association, New York, 1974.

5

SOCIOECONOMIC STRATA

GORDON F. STREIB

Social stratification refers to the fact that there are strata (layers or classes) that may be identified and demarcated in all human societies. These differentiate individuals and groups by their characteristics, privileges, status, esteem, and power. While socioeconomic position or social class is correlated with many aspects of behavior and attitudes (O'Rand, 1982), social classes in the United States are not genuine groups (Lenski, 1952). They are statistical categories or strata which demarcate various groupings of persons on the basis of income, occupation, education, or assets.

Social class is generally considered to be closely related to the occupational structure and how the positions in it are filled by members of society. However, at the end of the life cycle, older persons are at the end of the trajectory of their occupational histories. Most analysts of stratification ignore older persons, but since the elderly are an increasing proportion of the population, with those over 75 being the most rapidly growing segment, the social stratification of the elderly cannot be ignored. Moreover, with an increasing life expectancy, more older people will survive beyond age 65. When we turn to the later part of the life cycle, we need to consider social class from a different perspective than in the working years. In this chapter, we will discuss a number of perspectives relating to socioeconomic status: levels of income, net worth, structure of class, the frail elderly, and equity issues.

This analysis starts with a consideration of the American class structure as described by Eric Olin Wright and associates (1982). They assert that they are offering the first explicitly Marxian investigation of the American class structure based on empirical data. Their analysis rests upon the distinction between classes and occupations. From their Marxian perspective, occupational categories are not sufficient to understand class structure, for one must consider the class content of an occupation, namely, the control over investments, decision-making, other people's work, and also one's own work. Wright et al. report on their national

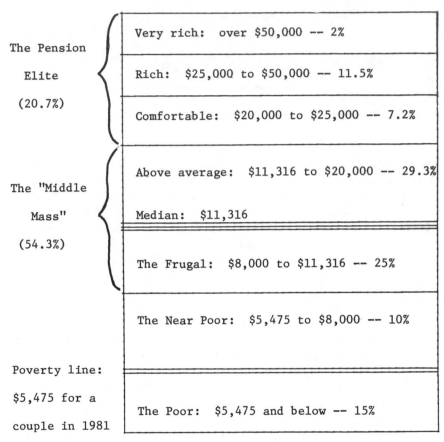

The Pension

Elite

(20.7%)

The "Middle

Mass"

(54.3%)

Poverty line:

$5,475 for a

couple in 1981

| Very rich: over $50,000 -- 2% |
| Rich: $25,000 to $50,000 -- 11.5% |
| Comfortable: $20,000 to $25,000 -- 7.2% |
| Above average: $11,316 to $20,000 -- 29.3% |
| Median: $11,316 |
| The Frugal: $8,000 to $11,316 -- 25% |
| The Near Poor: $5,475 to $8,000 -- 10% |
| The Poor: $5,475 and below -- 15% |

Adapted from H. Brotman, *Every Ninth American*, 1981, using U.S. Census data

Figure 5.1
Distribution of Income of the Elderly

survey of the U.S. working population and find that the working class is the largest class in the American class structure. They also observe that half of all locations in the class structure have a contradictory character, for "their class content is determined by more than one basic class. The American class structure cannot therefore be represented by any simple scheme of class polarization" (Wright et al., 1982:709).[1]

If Marxian sociologists report the absence of a polarized class structure among the younger population, it will be even more difficult to find polarization among the older population. Three factors complicate the evaluation of class position of the elderly: (1) most of them are retired, and therefore their relationship to the means of production is tenuous in comparison to those who are still in the labor force; (2) the health status of older individuals is correlated with consumption patterns and affects their socioeconomic position; and (3) the frail elderly and the institutionalized elderly constitute a special subclass within the older population. Their socioeconomic status, as dependent persons, has usually been neglected in studies of social stratification.

OLDER PERSONS IN THE LABOR FORCE

First, let us consider those older persons who have a direct relationship to the means of production because they are still working. Only a small percentage of the population over 65 years of age remains in the labor force. There has been a steady decline of the number of older men who continue to work. In 1950, 46 percent of older men were working, but in 1960, the proportion dropped to 33 percent, and in 1970, it was down to 27 percent. By 1975, only 20 percent of men 65 and over were working. The percentage of older women in the labor force has remained about the same for the last twenty-five years, at about 10 percent. Since 1975, it has been at 8.3 percent. With increasing age, there is a sharp decline in labor force participation, and by age 75 less than 2 percent are employed. Brotman (1981) notes that there is an increase in the proportion of employed workers in agriculture with advancing age, especially for men. These data tend to support the opinion of Wright (1979) that retirees occupy post-class positions. Let us turn to income as a way to analyze the class/age position of the elderly.

INCOME DISTRIBUTION OF THE ELDERLY

A second common measure of class or socioeconomic status is income. According to Brotman (1981), employing U.S. Census Bureau data, half of the almost 9 million families headed by an older person had incomes of less than $11,316 a year ($218 a week) as compared with $21,201 ($408 a week) for the 49.6 million families headed by a person under the age of 65 (see figure 5.1).

The generally lower income of the elderly is, of course, related to the fact that most of them are no longer working; in general, they have a 40 to 60 percent drop in income upon retirement.

Although a common stereotype is that the elderly are generally poor, in point of fact a substantial number have high incomes. For example, in 1979, over 7 percent of all older families had incomes between $20,000 and $25,000; another 11.5 percent had incomes between $25,000 and $50,000; and 182,000 families, or 2 percent, had incomes in excess of $50,000. Thus, some 20 percent of the older families in the United States had higher incomes than the median for younger families.

Perhaps the most vivid way to present the fact that a small number of the elderly have very high incomes is to consider the age of the very rich in the United States. The average age of millionaires in the United States is about 60 years and there is very little difference in the age of male and female millionaires. A study by *Fortune* magazine some years ago indicated that the very wealthiest persons in the United States—the centimillionaires—had an average age of 65 years (Louis, 1968).

We see the emergence of a new stratification system of older persons which can be divided into various strata, as shown in figure 5.1. At the top of the system are the pension elites—executives of large corporations who may receive pensions of $100,000 per year or more, plus a variety of fringe benefits, and perhaps other perquisites, such as stock options.

The next highest level of pension elites includes many military retirees, for officers can receive one-half pay after twenty years of service and three-fourths pay after thirty years of service. Many officers become "double dippers," and in Washington, D.C., there are thousands of retired officers with military pensions and high earnings as civilian workers. The average enlisted man retires at about 39 and lives an average of 33 years longer, during which time he can get another job, a second pension, and in most cases qualify for quite high Social Security benefits.

Senators, members of the House of Representatives, judges, and high-level civil service employees also have generous pensions and automatic cost-of-living increases. Sometimes by the adroit use of overtime pay to compute a higher average base pay government employees may have pensions that are higher than the salary they received while working.

Postal employees, state employees, and municipal employees, such as police and firefighters, are typical of the next layer of elite pensioners, and are labeled "comfortable," with incomes of $20,000 to $25,000. The average retired police officer and firefighter receive a pension 50 percent higher than other municipal workers of the same pay scale.

The next layer in figure 5.1, the "above average," includes the employees of large blue-chip companies and self-employed professionals. In 1981, the median retirement benefit for a $15,000 worker who retired was approximately $10,000, including Social Security, or two-thirds of pre-retirement earnings.

About 25 percent of the older population have incomes from $8,000 to the median ($11,316). We have labeled them "the frugal." These are the lower-middle-class white-collar or blue-collar persons. In many instances, they are home owners who have accumulated some savings. The major component of their net worth is the ownership of a home, usually free of debt.

The "middle mass" (Wilensky, 1961) is a concept that encompasses a variety of occupational and educational categories. It includes blue-collar persons who formerly worked in manual occupations and who may be at the top of the middle mass category, as well as professionals whose retirement income may place them toward the bottom of the category. The middle mass of older Americans constitutes those persons whose annual income ranges between $8,000 and $20,000. Almost 30 percent are above the median, from $11,316 to $20,000, and 25 percent are below the median, from $8,000 to $11,316.

The lowest 25 percent of the distribution, which is labeled the "near poor" and the "poor," are those persons who have had a lifetime in low-paying jobs, probably marked by periods of unemployment. Many of these persons have pursued what Wilensky (1961) called "disorderly careers." They have been employed in the peripheral economy, which will be discussed later.

An analysis of the pension scene indicates that there is a multiplicity of private and public pension plans. Their diversity must be understood in relation to the pressure and special interest groups that are involved in the particular industry, corporation, state or local government employment situation. For example, fire-fighters and police in practically every city in the United States have a pension scheme that is generous in its benefits, has early retirement privileges, and often has widow's benefits. The original impetus for these generous benefits was the accepted opinion that persons in these hazardous occupations need to be assured of financial security as they age. In the private sector, there have been corporations that have voluntarily established generous private pensions for employees—often to limit their mobility, to increase their loyalty, or to minimize unionization. Other private pensions stem from a completely different set of circumstances. Workers in highly unionized industries, such as automobiles, rubber, steel, and chemicals, often have excellent pension plans. In these industries, strong unions have gained generous benefits, sometimes through acrimonious bargaining and strikes. Some of the retirees in these industries are among the pension elites of the present scene.

In city, state, and federal government employment, generous pension plans often exist because the elected officials enact them into law, knowing that they probably will no longer be in office when the time comes for the benefits to be paid out (Morris, 1980; Rose and Peters, 1978). Therefore, it will be some future administration and legislature who will have to solve the problem of adequate funding. While a gesture is usually made in the direction of setting aside funds, they are often inadequate to meet the promises made by the present legislatures.

In summary, the multiplicity of pension plans in the United States is the result of the pressure and interest groups that operate in a free society for the benefit of their members. Generally speaking, their perspectives and attitudes toward pension plans are provincial and self-serving, and their main goal is to maximize the benefits for their constituency. They are not concerned with equity in the system at large.

Schulz emphasized that "looking at money income alone gives a distorted picture of the real situation" (Schulz, 1976a:21). He notes that there are three other factors that have an important impact on the economic status of elderly people. "First, there is the extent to which the income is actually available to meet current needs (what economists call *disposable income*). . . . Second, we need to assess the size, type, and distribution of assets held by older persons. And, finally, not all income is *money* income: sizable kinds of *in-kind* income are received by the elderly, improving their economic status" (Schulz, 1980:27).

It should also be noted that the income of the retired person "goes further" than the same income received by a working person. First, the retiree does not need to make payments into Social Security. In addition, the Social Security portion of his or her income is not taxed. For persons 65 and over, Medicare covers part of most medical expenses. Income taxes are lower, due to an additional exemption at age 65. Property taxes are reduced for the elderly in many cities. The costs of transportation to work are eliminated, in addition to the expense of parking fees, clothing for work, and lunches purchased outside the home. Many senior citizen discounts are offered (for example, for drugs and admission to theaters and concerts), and often reduced fare passes are available on public transportation, airlines, and so on. These financial advantages extend the dollar amount of income by 10 to 20 percent.

The use of current money income as a measure tends to overestimate the incidence of poverty, according to Moon (1977). She has shown that when current money income alone was used as an index, 40 percent of the sample fell below the poverty level ($2,000 in this survey). However, when a measure of economic welfare was employed, only 14 percent fell below the poverty level. The economic welfare index includes money income, annuities, in-kind transfers, taxes, and intra-family transfers. Schulz (1980:39, table 12) has pointed out that when all factors are considered, there is less poverty among the aged (over 65) than among the younger population. He has also noted (Schulz, 1976b) that the elderly receive 14 percent of the share of personal income but comprise 11 percent of the population. He adds the cautionary note that aggregate totals include persons over 65 still in the labor force.

In addition, data from a recent survey conducted for the National Council on the Aging by Louis Harris (1981) show that 22 percent of all age groups stated that "not having enough money to live on" is a very serious personal problem (N = 3452). However, only 17 percent of the over 65 category report that it is a very serious personal problem, compared to 23 percent of the population 18–54 years of age. It is a very serious personal problem for a much higher percentage of older blacks and Hispanics and for one-third of the older Americans with incomes under $5,000.

A more detailed analysis of the National Council on the Aging survey has been carried out by Sheppard and Mantovani (1982) in which they classified the retirees into three categories—"Well-Off" (41 percent); "Hard-Strapped" (35 percent); and "Intermediate" (24 percent)—on the basis of respondents' answers to two questions about income adequacy. Retirees were judging their own incomes' adequacy. Social Security played the predominant role in the income of the Hard-Strapped (almost three-quarters); on the other hand, less than half of the Well-Off (45 percent) reported that Social Security was a major source of income. Among the Well-Off, 37 percent reported investments and/or savings as a major income source, and among the Hard-Strapped only 8 percent mentioned these as major sources of household income.

PROPERTY AND NET WORTH

Closely related to income is the amount of property a person has accumulated. In addition to its material value, property also has symbolic qualities which often become accentuated in old age. An older person's home, furnishings, and possessions may be associated with a lifetime of values, feelings, and emotions.

In the United States, about 80 percent of elderly couples and 40 percent of elderly single persons live in an owned home (Schulz, 1980). Schulz also reports that 80 percent of the elderly homeowners own their homes free of debt. There is thus a sizable accumulation of assets, but most of it is not easily available for daily living expenses. Aside from assets in house property, Schulz estimates that about 70 percent of the aged families have assets valued at less than $10,000. The young-old are the group most well off in the elderly population.

Another component of stratification that is usually overlooked is net worth (assets minus debts). Henretta and Campbell (1978) have drawn attention to this significant measure of social status by the use of data on white males from the National Longitudinal Studies of the Labor Force. From the standpoint of stratification in later life, Henretta and Campbell show that as people age, consumption is increasingly affected by net worth. Within the age category they studied (50 to 64 years) there is an increase of assets with age. Among the important correlates of net worth are education, marital status, family size, and occupational status. Persons with less education, those who are unmarried or divorced or married with large families, and those having a low occupational status tend to have a lower net worth. Thus, net worth in late life represents the summation of one's educational attainments, occupation, career patterns, earnings, family composition, and consumption patterns.

HOW THE DUAL ECONOMY AFFECTS THE ELDERLY

How do we account for the income distribution and net worth of the elderly? One important factor is the dual economy explanation and the labor market segmentation that is associated with it (Averitt, 1968; Hodson and Kaufman,

1982). Economic outcomes in the post-work period are strongly influenced by whether a person has been employed in the core economy (also called the center, monopoly, or concentrated economy) or in the periphery.

The center economy, the heart of the industrial system, is composed of firms and organizations that are large in size and influence. Its organizations are corporate and bureaucratic; its production processes are vertically integrated through ownership and control of raw materials. The peripheral economy, in contrast, consists of small firms, often operated by a single individual or family. They provide essential goods and services and give employment to millions of citizens. The sales of these firms are more restricted than those in the center economy, and the market tends to be local; profits and earnings are commonly lower than for businesses in the core economy, and bankruptcy is more common.

What is the relevance of these facts to the stratification situation of older workers? The major consideration is whether an employee is covered by a pension plan and thus has an important source of income in addition to Social Security. In 1978, only about one-fourth of the retired population over 65 years of age received income from an employee pension (President's Commission on Pension Policy, 1981:26). Indeed, the Pension Commission has said that "the most serious problem facing our retirement system today is the lack of pension coverage among private sector workers." The lack of pension plans occurs primarily in the peripheral economy, in small businesses.

Ninety-three percent of the non-covered persons work in firms with fewer than 500 employees. The major reason that is given for the lack of pension coverage is the cost, for these firms operate in very competitive economic environments in which there are small profit margins.

The distinction between the center and peripheral sectors is also evidenced by the characteristics of the workers. Peripheral firms are more apt to employ women, minorities, and non-union workers; persons in these categories are less apt to receive pensions. A precise description of the way this manifests itself in pension coverage is shown by data on age category and industry in the President's Commission on Pension Policy report (1981). Almost three-fourths of the workers in manufacturing and mining are covered by a pension, while less than one-half of those in construction, 36 percent in services, and 19 percent in agriculture receive private pensions.

The greatest coverage, however, is in government service: in the federal government, 91 percent of the employees are covered by pensions, and in state and local government, 83 percent of the workers are covered. Among the analysts of the dual economy, there is disagreement as to how the government sector meshes into the theory of the dual economy. Some claim that government is integral to the center or core economy because of the close affiliation between core and government. Others challenge that interpretation and consider the government as a third sector of the economy.

The dual economy is important in its effect on retirement income, and hence on class position, status, and life-style, because workers in the core economy and in government service are far more likely to have a favorable economic situation in retirement than are workers in the periphery.

THE ELDERLY AND SOCIAL CLASSES

The general position outlined here is that social classes as polarized, self-conscious, adversarial groups are tenuous in the United States. This observation is particularly true for the elderly who comprise at least three ten-year age strata (cohorts). Their social characteristics are diverse, and they do not share a distinct culture. The lack of polarized classes does not mean that there are not gross discrepancies in income, wealth, style of life, and privileges. There is a vast and factual literature documenting the inequities in wealth and privilege in the United States (Davis, 1935; Harrop, 1980; Lundberg, 1968; Myers, 1907).

However, there is emerging in the United States a large middle class or "middle mass" who comprise professionals, white-collar workers, some skilled manual workers, and various kinds of technicians and mechanics (Gagliani, 1981; Hutber, 1976; Janowitz, 1978). Some writers are now arguing that a new form of class polarization is taking place within the middle class between the upper and lower strata (Johnson, 1982).

The lack of clearly demarcated classes does not mean that there is a lack of relationships that have class-like characteristics. But these relationships, it appears, have not brought about class awareness, class solidarity, and class actions for radical social change. Anthony Giddens (1973) has helped to conceptualize the situation by his use of the term "class structuration," which refers to the basis or process whereby classes are formed. Giddens (1973:105) points out that "the most important blank spots in the theory of class concern the processes whereby 'economic classes' become 'social classes,' and whereby, in turn, the latter are related to other social forms." Giddens has argued that strata have sharper boundaries than do classes. The boundaries between strata may be clearly defined and may be measured with some precision, as in the case of income.

What are the ways in which economic relationships are transformed into "noneconomic social structures," or classes? The principal method governing this structuration of class relationships is through mobility processes and mobility opportunities or chances. For the elderly, mobility chances are reduced or are nonexistent—a condition described by Giddens as "mobility closure." The closing off of mobility is related to the fact that most elderly are not in the labor force and that only a few elderly could take advantage of mobility chances because of their general reduction of strength, speed, and physical and functional capacity.

However, the discussion of class and age strata among the elderly must proceed beyond their participation in the labor market—because in the United States, the elderly are allocated considerable resources outside the market economy, namely by the political economy through government programs. This is shown by the fact that in 1981 the elderly received 36 percent of the total federal government expenditures in income security (U.S. Office of Management and Budget, 1980; Kutza, 1981). As Ball has emphasized (1978), the economic position of most of the elderly is locked into the benefit and welfare systems of postindustrial societies.

STATUS LOSS AND STATUS DISCREPANCY

Most investigators of stratification accept the multidimensional nature of stratification and have focused on a variety of observable indicators: income, occupation, education, property, ethnicity, and sex.[2] Surprisingly, age is not included in the array of variables.

Researchers on stratification in the latter part of the life cycle must recognize age and aging as strategic characteristics which are linked causally to other stratification indices and are primary reasons for downward mobility, or mobility closure, as it is called by Giddens (1973). In fact, much of the literature on retirement is actually a study of the differential loss of status and its consequences, or "status discrepancy." As used here, this term refers to the differential *loss* of status, in contrast to "status inconsistency," which refers to differential rankings on hierarchies at one point in time. Status discrepancy involves differential changes on different hierarchies over time, that is, as persons become older. In other words, there is a realization that in studying old age, one must acknowledge present rankings in relation to former positions on different hierarchies.

Status discrepancy is a useful concept in studying the stratification of the aged because it recognizes that older persons may experience changes in their ranking on one hierarchy but not on another. For example, most older people have a decline in income when they retire, but most do not experience downward movement in style of life. Most older people eventually relinquish their work role, but their educational attainment remains the same.

Status discrepancy also occurs because of the physical and mental decrements that are associated with the aging process of many people. The emergence of biological factors complicates the pattern of the usual indicators of stratification—income, education, work status, and ethnicity. The addition of the variable of health has significant effects on status, for no matter what high rank one reaches in income level, education, power, or style of life, if a person is mentally or physically disabled, his or her stratification position is altered significantly. The addition of this variable, so relevant at the end of life, adds a new dimension to status discrepancy.

In writing about socialization to old age, Rosow (1974) has said that the transition to late life in America has some distinctive configurations. Three of these have special relevance for stratification, namely, (1) a devalued position, (2) role discontinuity, and (3) status loss. He suggests that coping with these changes may involve new group structures and functions. His approach to status discrepancies is that socialization to new roles in old age can be facilitated by increased association with age peers. This means that older persons may adapt to status loss by having weakened ties with younger persons, and the elderly may concentrate in settings in which there is a higher proportion of the old. These conditions will enhance group supports, positive reference groups, insulation of members, and so on.

Research on social class and age strata in the latter part of the life cycle requires a shift in analytical perspective on the part of social scientists, who generally emphasize advancement, status attainment, and upward mobility as the norm. Instead of employing the same stratification rankings that apply to younger people, perhaps social scientists should develop new concepts and new ranking scales to measure the status of those beyond the working years. The study of the elderly requires a different perspective, focusing on status discrepancy and status loss.

THE FRAIL ELDERLY

Stratification in late life provides some unique phenomena for the analyst to interpret, which are the consequences of the aging process. Most elderly who live long enough become frail and to some degree dependent upon other persons (Streib, 1983). At any one point in time, approximately 5 percent of all elderly in the United States are institutionalized. However, it has been estimated that approximately 25 percent of the elderly will, at some time, become residents of nursing homes (Kastenbaum and Candy, 1973). Some will be there for only a short time and others will be there for periods of long duration. One way to classify the elderly is in terms of a spectrum of independence-dependence, as defined by a report of the U.S. Department of Health, Education and Welfare (1978).

Most Dependent	5% institutionalized
	6% non-institutionalized but vulnerable
Less Dependent	22% slightly dependent and in need of some support
Independent	67% self-sufficient

In other words, about one-third of the elderly population, somewhere between 8 million and 9 million persons, constitute the dependent segment of the elderly. The cost of institutionalizing the elderly varies in different communities and regions, from $12,000 to $24,000 or more a year. The overwhelming majority of these costs are paid from public monies. In other words, each of these individuals may make a larger claim against the gross national product than the typical American family of husband, wife, and two children, who now have a median income of around $21,000 a year.

To what stratification category do we assign those persons who are receiving substantial amounts of goods and services, far in excess of the typical family? There is no accepted conceptual scheme that enables one to bring these persons into the socioeconomic system of the elderly in general. Their general position in society is one that no one envies or aspires to. Most have few assets that they control—they have little or no personal income, their prestige and status are near the bottom of the social hierarchy, and their sense of self-worth and group identity is generally quite low. Their education, past occupation, and former style of life are largely irrelevant. This is truly a case of status discrepancy, in which a group receives a substantial economic subsidy and yet is considered low on most other ranking systems. Thus, when *income* statistics are presented for the elderly, there is no indication of the subsidy provided to the millions of dependent persons in this segment of the older population.

Another anomalous group consists of those whom the chart shows as slightly dependent and vulnerable. This category is more difficult to identify because they are not institutionalized and most are living in the community—some with family members, some in retirement facilities, and some in foster homes. In terms of subsidization of income, a considerable amount comes from public sources. If a person lives with family members, the family provides a considerable proportion of the shelter, food, and support services. If they are not in family situations, some kind of public subsidy often provides for their needs: Supplemental Security Income (SSI) payments, low rent subsidies, Meals-on-Wheels, and so on.

The report of the General Accounting Office (Comptroller General, 1979), based on a careful study in Cleveland, Ohio, reported that the average frail person living with relatives received services and help amounting to $2,729 a year. Thus, to merely report the income level of a frail older person may give little indication of his or her actual style of life or consumption of services. The intrusion of health status into the equation alters how the elderly are incorporated in a stratification system.

Another anomaly that complicates stratification for the dependent segment of the spectrum is the fact that there is often a needs test which must be met before one is eligible to receive public services. This means that, in some cases, the net worth and annual income of older people are reduced clandestinely by family or kin in order to insure eligibility. To our knowledge, there is no study of how extensive this practice is, and, indeed, it would be difficult to conduct objective social science research on this subject. However, one has the impression that considerable ingenuity is exercised by the elderly and their families in transferring assets to other persons. The assets no longer belong to the elderly persons themselves, and do not appear in any account of their net worth. This discussion of the stratification of the institutionalized and the vulnerable frail elderly shows how the analyst must take account of health status and its effects.

EQUITY

One of the compelling reasons to consider social class and age strata is because they involve fundamental issues of equity and social justice. The desire for social justice for older people has deep roots in the Western Judeo-Christian culture. When we speak of equity, we do not mean mere "legal equalness." We are referring to Radin's concept that equity also means "fairness combined with leniency and humanity" (Radin, 1948:126).

Ethical principles are often more difficult to carry out in a postindustrial society than in simpler societies and in earlier historical periods. The ethical principle of "just reward" takes on much greater complexity when the elderly comprise over 11 percent of the population and when their numbers are in the millions. The "honorable elders" are not one's own parents and close kin but comprise a vague mass of strangers. Noble ethical principles have to be translated into statutes and administrative regulations in order to bring about equity.

What is a just distribution of the resources of the society to its older population? In considering equity, one must first determine the criteria to assess it. There are four approaches: (1) The income of the person or group is compared to the level they attained at an earlier point in time. Economists, in discussing equity, use replacement of income as a measure. In retirement, what percentage of former income should people have? (2) Another way is to consider the elderly in relation to other age groupings. How do the elderly compare with the working segment? (3) Determination of relative deprivation is a third approach. Townsend (1979), for example, looks at how deprived the elderly are in comparison to the customary standard of living. (4) Finally, one can measure net worth. This involves a consideration of lifetime income, savings, debt, and net asset accumulation.

Another important equity issue is related to the marked differences in both pension opportunity and income levels resulting from the sector of the economy in which the individual worked. How does one justify the inequities in pension income levels of persons who did work of equal importance, requiring the same amount of training and skill, and who received the same wages? Yet after a lifetime of gainful employment, the two categories find themselves in vastly different economic situations. For example, one person might drive a truck for a city, state, or federal organization, or for a corporation in the center economy, and retire with a substantial pension and often Social Security in addition. Another person may spend his working life driving a truck for a small business in the peripheral economy and reach old age with only Social Security benefits.

The inequity demonstrated when people do the same work and yet receive vastly different benefits points up the necessity to consider the reward system in retirement and old age and to ask how such a system could be changed to reduce such differentials. Is it possible to equalize income in old age so that persons with equal skills and years of service get roughly equal rewards?

The equity issue becomes more nettlesome in relation to public policy because employees of federal, state, and local government receive their pensions primarily from general taxation. Although most of these plans involve employee contributions, in recent years the contributory portion is paid out rather quickly, within two or three years (Kleiler, 1978). This leads us to ask the question: "Will people who get no pensions (other than Social Security) continue to pay taxes willingly so that other people who may do the same kind of work are enabled to get generous pensions?

The issue of equity is of great interest because the discussion of stratification and social class often assumes the desirability of change. It is expected that changes will bring about an improvement over the status quo. But what are usually left unstated are the practical dilemmas of cost. Ethicists and advocates can invoke principles of equity readily, but are slow to consider the financial and political costs of implementing these principles. In short, someone gains and someone loses when an ethical principle of equity is promulgated and put into practice. The recent difficulty in attempting to put a curb on excessive increases in pensions for federal employees is an example of this problem.

Certainly, in developed capitalist societies, equity issues must be addressed in public policy discussions. American society is marked by wide ranges of privilege and power. However, as our analysis indicates, the simplistic notion that all of the aged are a deprived and underprivileged stratum will have to be revised.

NOTES

1. For another perspective on the Marxian and non-Marxian approaches to class theory see Korpi (1978). The literature on social stratification and the aged, on inequality, and on programs for improving the economic and social situation of the aged is growing rapidly. Among the works that are instructive and that offer different perspectives on some issues discussed in this chapter are (1) for Canada: Myles (1980, 1981); Tindale and Marshall (1980); (2) for Great Britain: Phillipson (1982); (3) for the United States: Estes (1979); Olson (1982).

2. This section is an abbreviated version of a discussion of status discrepancy to be published in a chapter on Social Stratification and Aging by G. F. Streib, in *Handbook of Aging and the Social Sciences*, 2nd ed. (1984).

REFERENCES

Averitt, R. T. *The dual economy: The dynamics of American industry structure*. Norton, New York, 1968.

Ball, R. M. *Social Security today and tomorrow*. Columbia University Press, New York, 1978.

Brotman, H. *Every ninth American*. Report prepared for the U.S. Senate, Special Committee on Aging. U.S. Department of Health, Education and Welfare, Washington, D.C., 1981.

Comptroller General of the United States. Report to the Chairman, Subcommittee on Human Services, House Select Committee on Aging (HRD-80-7). Washington, D.C., October 15, 1979.

Davis, J. *Capitalism and its culture*. Farrar and Rinehart, New York, 1935.

Estes, C. L. *The aging enterprise*. Jossey-Bass, San Francisco, 1979.

Gagliani, G. How many working classes? *American Journal of Sociology*, 1981, *87*, 259–285.

Giddens, Anthony. *The class structure of the advanced societies*. Barnes and Noble, New York, 1973.

Harris, L. *Aging in the eighties*. National Council on the Aging, Washington, D.C., 1981.

Harrop, D. *Paychecks: Who makes what?* Harper and Row, New York, 1980.

Henretta, J.C., and Campbell, R.T. Net worth as an aspect of status. *American Journal of Sociology*, 1978, *80*, 1204–1223.

Hodson, R., and Kaufman, R.L. Economic dualism: A critical review. *American Sociological Review*, 1982, *47*, 727–739.

Hutber, P. *The decline and fall of the middle class*. Associated Business Programmes, London, 1976.

Janowitz, M. *The last half-century: Societal change and politics in America*. University of Chicago Press, Chicago, 1978.

Johnson, D.L. *Class and social development: A new theory of the middle class*. Sage, Beverly Hills, Calif., 1982.

Kastenbaum, R., and Candy, S.E. The 4 percent fallacy: A methodological and empirical critique of extended care facility population statistics. *International Journal of Aging and Human Development*, 1973, *4*, 15–21.

Kleiler, F. *Can we afford early retirement?* Johns Hopkins University Press, Baltimore, 1978.

Korpi, W. *The working class in welfare capitalism*. Routledge and Kegan Paul, London, 1978.

Kutza, E.A. *The benefits of old age: Social welfare policy for the elderly*. University of Chicago Press, Chicago, 1981.

Lenski, G.E. American social classes: Statistical strata or social groups? *American Journal of Sociology*, 1952, *58*, 139–144.

Louis, A.M. America's centimillionaires. *Fortune*, 1968, *77*, 152–157.

Lundberg, F. *The rich and the super-rich*. Lyle Stuart, New York, 1968.

Moon, M. *The measurement of economic welfare*. Academic Press, New York, 1977.

Morris, C. *The cost of good intentions: New York City and the liberal experiment*. Norton, New York, 1980.

Myers, G. *History of the great American fortunes*. Random House, New York, 1907; repr. Modern Library, 1937.

Myles, J.F. The aged, the state and the structure of inequality. In J. Harp and J. Hofley (Eds.), *Structured inequality in Canada*. Prentice-Hall, Englewood Cliffs, N.J., 1980.

Myles, J.F. Income inequality and status maintenance: Concepts, methods, and measures. *Research on Aging*, 1981, *3*, 123–141.

Olson, L.K. *The political economy of aging: The state, private power and social welfare*. Columbia University Press, New York, 1982.

O'Rand, A. Socioeconomic status and poverty. In D. Mangen and W. Peterson (Eds.), *Research instruments in social gerontology. Volume 2: Social roles and social participation*. University of Minnesota Press, Minneapolis, 1982.

Phillipson, C. *Capitalism and the construction of old age*. Macmillan, London, 1982.

President's Commission on Pension Policy. *An interim report*. USGPO, Washington, D.C., 1980.

————. *Coming of age: Toward a national retirement policy.* USGPO, Washington, D.C., 1981.

Radin, M. *The law and you.* New American Library, New York, 1948.

Rose, R., and Peters, G. *Can government go bankrupt?* Basic Books, New York, 1978.

Rosow, I. *Socialization to old age.* University of California Press, Berkeley, Calif., 1974.

Schulz, J.H. *The economics of aging.* Wadsworth, Belmont, Calif., 1976a.

————. Income distribution and the aging. In R.H. Binstock and E. Shanas (Eds.), *Handbook of aging and the social sciences.* Van Nostrand Reinhold, New York, 1976b.

————. *The economics of aging.* 2nd ed. Wadsworth, Belmont, Calif., 1980.

Sheppard, H.L., and Mantovani, R.E. *Hard-strapped and well-off retirees: A study in perceived income adequacy.* National Council on the Aging, Washington, D.C., 1982.

Streib, G.F. The frail elderly: Research dilemmas and research opportunities. *Gerontologist*, 1983, *23*, 40–44.

————. Social stratification and aging. In R.H. Binstock and E. Shanas (Eds.), *Handbook of aging and the social sciences*, 2nd ed. Van Nostrand Reinhold, New York, 1984.

Tindale, J.A., and Marshall, V.W. A generational-conflict perspective for gerontology. In V.W. Marshall (Ed.), *Aging in Canada: Social perspectives.* Fitzhenry and Whiteside, Don Mills, Ont., 1980.

Townsend, P. *Poverty in the United Kingdom: A survey of household resources and standards of living.* University of California Press, Berkeley, Calif., 1979.

U.S. Department of Health, Education and Welfare. *Health: United States.* DHEW Pub. No. (PHS) 78-1232. USGPO, Washington, D.C., 1978.

U.S. Office of Management and Budget. *The budget of the United States Government, fiscal year 1981.* USGPO, Washington, D.C., 1980.

Wilensky, H.L. Orderly careers and social participation: The impact of work history on social integration in the middle mass. *American Sociological Review*, 1961, *26*, 521–539.

Wright, E.O. *Class, crisis and the state.* Verso Editions, London, 1979.

Wright, E.O.; Costello, C.; Hachen, D.; and Sprague, J. The American class structure. *American Sociological Review*, 1982, *47*, 709–726.

6

VETERANS

EDWIN B. HUTCHINS
JAMES L. FOZARD

The American veteran owes his or her special status in society to the simple fact that at some time in his life he or she served a tour of duty in one of the armed services. Whether in wartime or in peacetime, service in the armed forces is the defining characteristic of this large, mostly male population. Further defined by periods of national involvement in warfare, the population of veterans is not evenly distributed by age. The armed forces have expanded and contracted throughout our history, commanding the participation of various segments of the population at different times.

HISTORY

Beginning with the Revolutionary War, ten different wars have endowed over 42 million Americans with the status of veteran (table 6.1). A small number have earned veteran status during times of peace. Two-thirds of all veterans, or 29 million, are alive today and represent one of every eight Americans.

Most dramatic in cost to human life was the Civil War, when nearly a half million soldiers lost their lives. Largest in mobilization was World War II, when 16.5 million Americans donned a uniform; 406,000, or one in forty of these, died as the result of battle. Although the risks of dying as the result of battle have varied from one in six to less than one in a hundred, when morbidity data are added to mortality statistics, it becomes clear that under any circumstances membership in the armed forces during time of war could be costly to the participant. For those serving in World War II, one in fifteen was wounded or

The authors wish to thank the present and former Assistant Chief Medical Directors of the Office of Geriatrics and Extended Care, Dr. John H. Mather and Dr. Paul Haber, for their encouragement and support in the preparation of this chapter.

Table 6.1
Numbers Serving and Mortality Ratios for Periods of Military Service

Conflict	Period of Service[1]	Number Serving[1]	Deaths in Services[1]	Mortality as % of No. Serving	Wounds not Mortal[2]	Wounded as % of No. Serving[2]
American Revolution	1775-84	290,000	4,000	1.4	*	*
War of 1812	1812-15	287,000	2,000	0.7	*	*
Mexican War	1846-48	79,000	13,000	16.5	*	*
Indian Wars	1817-98	106,000	1,000	0.9	*	*
Civil War	1861-65	3,213,000	497,821	15.5	*	*
(Union)		(2,213,000)	(364,000)	(16.4)	282,000	12.7
(Confederate)		(1,000,000)	(133,821)	(13.4)	*	*
Spanish-American War	1898-1902	392,000	11,000	2.8	2,000	0.5
World War I	1917-18	4,744,000	116,516	2.5	204,000	4.3
World War II	1940-47	16,535,000	405,399	2.5	671,000	4.1
Korean Conflict	1950-55	6,807,000	54,246	0.8	103,000	1.5
Vietnam Era	1959-75	9,834,000	57,939	0.6	304,000	3.1
Total		42,287,000	1,162,921	2.8		

[1]Source: Veterans Administration.
[2]Source: The President's Commission on Veterans' Pensions, *Veterans' Benefits in the United States*, vol. 1, USGPO, Washington, D.C., 1956; and U.S. Department of Defense, unpublished data.
*Not available.

lost his life during this period. For the vast majority of veterans, service was at the very least an interruption in the regular flow of their life.

How the general society views enlisted persons has varied from peacetime to wartime and according to the popularity of the war. From the beginning the nation has treated the veteran with a certain partiality, although the actions of the government have often served its own purposes rather than the needs of the veteran. In 1776 the Continental Congress enacted legislation providing half-pay pensions for officers and servicemen disabled in the United States service. But the war was to go on for another eight years and the motive was primarily to entice enlistees (Dann, 1980).

By 1818 Congress moved to reward those who had served and sacrificed in the Continental Army, the naval service, and the marines, if they needed financial assistance. By the 1820s many Americans who had not served became romantics about the Revolution and gratitude was shown to the aging veterans who had served (Dann, 1980). From that time on Congress has periodically expressed this gratitude to the veteran in a series of benefits enacted through legislation. Since World War II over thirty separate pieces of legislation have elaborated the system of benefits with which the American veteran has been rewarded for the risks taken and the sacrifices made during times of national distress. Rarely does a session of Congress go by without added legislation benefiting the American veteran. This, then, is a defining factor that sets the veteran apart from the society in which he lives, and one of paramount significance for those who will be entering old age in the next few years.

If one looks across the various cohorts of veterans as defined by the periods of war, differences also are apparent by social class and race, and in the way these groups have been defined and viewed by society. During the Revolutionary War wealth could substitute for service. For example, Edward Elley, serving in the Continental Army, had money. He also "had a loving wife, and she vastly overpaid a substitute to replace him for the last month of his service" (Dann, 1980:234). While in present times money cannot buy a substitute, draft laws sometimes have been so cast as to allow exemptions for occupations essential to the war effort (e.g., farmer or munitions factory worker) or deferrals for those enrolled in college, the latter more frequently drawn from the middle and upper classes. Of all the periods of armed conflict, the one conscripting the largest number of men, 16,535,000, was World War II, and of all wars this one came closest to being classless. People came to the service from all walks of life and from all regions of the country, and were sent to all areas of the world.

THE AGING VETERAN

World War II veterans are of special interest because they represent a generation now reaching old age. Figure 6.1 graphically describes the contemporary distribution of American veterans by age and period of service. (See also table 6.2.) By 1990 the number of veterans 65 years of age and over will nearly

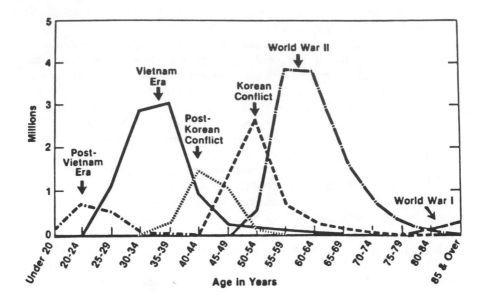

Source: Veteran Population, September 30, 1982, Office of Reports and Statistics, Research Division, Veterans Administration, December 1982.

Figure 6.1
The Aging Veteran Population. September 30, 1982

double from the present number of 4 million to well over 7.5 million veterans. By the turn of the century older veterans will number some 9 million. (See table 6.3 for specific data.)

For a sense of the role the veteran will play in the geriatric population at the turn of the century, one needs only to note that veterans presently constitute one-third of U.S. males over 65 years of age. By the year 2000 this proportion will be inverted and two of every three aging U.S. males will be veterans (figure 6.2). The great majority of these will be from World War II. Furthermore, the year 2000 will find a high proportion of these beyond the age of 75 (figures 6.3 and 6.4). At that time approximately 3.5 million veterans will be 75 to 84 years old; another half million will be in the 85 and over age range. While the veteran population is predominantly male, approximately one in fifty is female.

What then is special about this cohort and what of significance can be learned from study of the aging American veteran? Born in a country still emerging from its agrarian heritage, World War II veterans grew up during the Great Depression. As the country was drawn into a two-front war, these same men and women found themselves transported to all corners of the globe and cata-pulted upon their return into a full-blown industrialized society. Significant during the period of service from 1941 to 1945 was the disruption of normal civilian life and, for some, the stress of combat. Unlike the Vietnam serviceman, who

Table 6.2
Estimated Number of Veterans Living in the United States and Puerto Rico, by Age and Period of Service, September 30, 1982 (in thousands)

Age	Total Veterans	WAR VETERANS									Service between Korean Conflict and Vietnam Era Only
		Total^a	Vietnam Era		Korean Conflict		World War II^c	World War I	Post-Vietnam Era^d	
			Total^b	No Service in Korean Conflict	Total^bc	No Service in World War II				
All Ages	28,522†	24,262†	8,708	8,188	5,421	4,338	11,368	368	1,372	2,888
Under 20 years	9	—	—	—	—	—	—	—	9	—
20-24 years	735	12	12	12	—	—	—	—	723	—
25-29 years	1,718	1,162	1,162	1,162	—	—	—	—	556	—
30-34 years	2,890	2,818	2,818	2,818	—	—	—	—	72	—
35-39 years	3,364	3,084	3,084	3,084	10	—	—	—	11	269
40-44 years	2,465	951	944	941	10	10	—	—	1	1,511
45-49 years	2,538	1,527	260	137	1,390	1,390	—	—	*	1,011
50-54 years	3,326	3,241	215	23	2,781	2,624	594	—	—	85
55-59 years	4,133	4,125	115	7	703	274	3,844	—	—	8
60-64 years	3,838	3,836	65	3	336	28	3,805	—	—	2
65-69 years	1,917	1,917	27	1	136	11	1,905	—	—	—
70-74 years	836	836	6	*	46	1	835	—	—	—
75-79 years	301	301	*	*	14	*	301	—	—	—
80-84 years	149	149	—	—	4	—	74	75	—	—
85 years and over	303	303	—	—	1	—	10	293	—	—
Median age^e	50.8	54.0	35.6	35.2	52.4	51.5	61.6	87.3	24.7	43.9

Source: Veterans Administration.

Note: Excludes an estimated 127 (thousand) who served only between World War I and World War II, all of whom are 70 years of age or older, and 235 (thousand) who served only between World War II and the Korean Conflict, all of whom are 45-49 years of age. Also excluded are a small undetermined number of National Guard personnel or reservists who incurred service-connected disabilities while on an initial tour of active duty for training only.

^a Veterans who served in both World War II and the Korean Conflict, or in both the Korean Conflict and the Vietnam era.

^b Includes 520 (thousand) who served in both the Korean Conflict and the Vietnam era.

^c Includes 1,083 (thousand) who served in both World War II and the Korean Conflict.

^d Service only after May 7, 1975.

^e Computed from data by five-year age groups.

† There are also 58 living Spanish-American War veterans whose medium age is 102 years.

* Less than 0.5 (thousand).

Table 6.3
Actual and Projected Veteran Population for Selected Ages and Periods of
Service, FY 1981–2030
(in thousands)

End of Fiscal Year	Total Veteran Population	Veterans 65 Years and over	Veterans 75 Years and over	Vietnam Era Veterans	World War II Veterans
Actual					
1981	30,083	3,320	767	9,087	12,170
Projected					
1982	29,989	3,679	796	9,122	11,881
1983	29,882	4,127	834	9,145	11,582
1984	29,771	4,606	877	9,162	11,276
1985	29,646	5,154	940	9,176	10,957
1986	29,507	5,739	1,005	9,184	10,628
1987	29,362	6,277	1,097	9,189	10,290
1988	29,203	6,776	1,205	9,197	9,943
1989	29,034	7,250	1,347	9,198	9,588
1990	28,852	7,688	1,517	9,198	9,222
1991	28,658	8,036	1,723	9,195	8,853
1992	28,455	8,339	1,954	9,191	8,476
1993	28,238	8,531	2,246	9,182	8,092
1994	28,007	8,716	2,542	9,165	7,704
1995	27,769	8,906	2,883	9,132	7,310
2000	26,364	9,007	4,241	8,833	5,321
2005	24,745	8,332	4,564	8,347	3,459
2010	23,080	8,169	4,250	7,658	1,957
2015	21,537	8,644	3,684	6,748	935
2020	20,204	7,897	3,711	5,633	371
2025	19,081	7,013	4,146	4,360	128
2030	18,177	5,985	3,668	3,061	33

Source: Veterans Administration, Office of Reports and Statistics, Research Division, April 1982.

rotated into a combat zone to serve no more than a specified twelve-month
period, the World War II soldier was "in for the duration." This could and did
lead to a good deal of uncertainty about the future, especially if service was
with a frontline combat unit. Resultant anxiety symptoms and psychiatric cas-
ualties were in part caused by the service experience and in part simply aggravated
by it where the propensity for psychosomatic illness may already have existed.

The world would never be the same for their experience, nor would they.
While they may have been ready to go back to business as usual upon discharge
and while attitudinally they may not have been poised for social change, nevertheless they would experience it. Ultimately, these World War II American

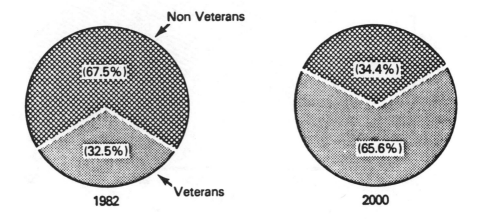

Source: Office of Reports and Statistics, Research Division, Veterans Administration, 1982.

Figure 6.2
Percentage of U.S. Males 65 and Over Who Are Veterans

veterans will significantly contribute to one of the most dramatic changes yet to come, the graying of America.

VETERANS' BENEFITS

Two factors affected the ease of reentry to civilian life. One was the high level of employment and the affluent economy that followed the war years. The other was the G.I. Bill, with its cornucopia of benefits serving to ease transition back into civilian status. Facilitating upward mobility were Veterans Administration mortgages and educational benefits.

It is ironic that for all of the costliness of fighting a war, the ultimate financial costs are yet to be borne following the cessation of hostilities. These come in the form of veterans' benefits. For the Civil War, veterans' benefits amounted to more than three times the cost of fighting the war. For the Spanish-American War, benefits were nearly six times the cost of battle. World War I benefits have more than surpassed the cost of fighting the war and will continue for some years to come. While expenditures for World War II veterans' benefits ($456 billion) have not exceeded the cost of battle ($1,603 billion), they too will continue for many years (*U.S. News and World Report*, October 25, 1982). The nature of these benefits is critical to an understanding of aging veterans as a

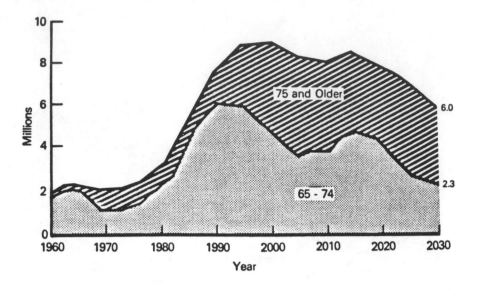

Source: Office of Reports and Statistics, Research Division, Veterans Administration, 1982.

Figure 6.3
Number of Veterans Age 65 and Over

special geriatric population. Significant were benefit programs in the areas of education, housing, insurance, compensation and pensions, and health care.

Two-thirds of the Veterans Administration annual budget, or approximately $15 billion, provides for the first five of these fixed-cost programs. Medical care accounts for 28 percent of the total Veterans Administration budget and potentially could be quite variable in cost. In 1982 the budget for the Department of Medicine and Surgery was $7 billion for all health care programs. In addition, by congressional mandate, veterans are given preference in federal employment. For every federal agency engaged in hiring an employee, veteran status is worth 5 points out of 100. If the veteran is disabled this is worth 10 points. While 98 percent of veterans are male and this preferential treatment in hiring could constitute an equity issue for women, for the most part the Veterans Administration does not have an adversarial relationship with its constituents, as do many regulatory agencies, serving instead as an advocate and service agency.

Housing Benefits

Most used of the benefits accorded the veteran has been the home loan program. Table 6.4 gives the experience for the World War II veteran in comparison to veterans in general. Those with experience in both World War II and the Korean

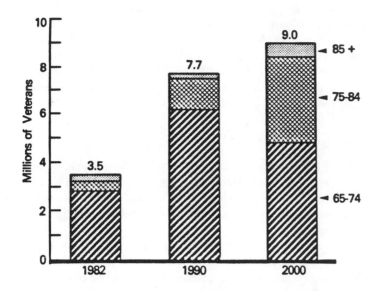

Source: Office of Reports and Statistics, Research Division, Veterans Administration, 1982.

Figure 6.4
Veterans Age 65 and Over, End of FY 1982 and Projected to 1990 and 2000

Table 6.4
Home Ownership by Veterans

	"How did you finance your first home?" Percent Responding to Each Category		
Method of Financing	WW II Veterans	WW II and Korea Veterans	All Veterans
VA Home Loan	36.5	44.9	34.7
Conventional Loan	33.6	32.1	37.7
Cash	10.7	5.1	6.6
Personal Loan	8.7	6.9	7.1
FIIA Loan	7.8	7.1	10.3
Land Contract	3.2	2.1	3.1
State Loan for Veterans	0.8	0.7	1.0
Farmers Home Loan	0.3	0.0	0.7
Other	0.9	2.7	1.0

Source: Veterans Administration, 1979 National Survey of Veterans.

conflict showed somewhat higher utilization of the program (44.9 percent) than did those with experience in just World War II (36.5 percent) or veterans in general (34.7 percent). For World War II veterans the Veterans Administration home loan was the method of financing most used in the purchase of their first home. Given that slightly less than two out of three indicated that they had been eligible for a Veterans Administration home loan at the time, this means that more than half of all those eligible for this benefit made use of it.

Educational Benefits

The G.I. Bill offered full support to veterans to advance their education, and 43 percent of all veterans have taken some advantage of this benefit. Of those who saw service in World War II, about 28 percent used some educational benefit (see table 6.5) and of these more than a million completed college under the auspices of the program.

The Federal Council on the Aging has projected the data on the educational attainment of tomorrow's elderly and notes that the next 30 years will see an increase in the educational attainment of the elderly. At present one of every six of our elderly has some college education (*Need*, 1981). For many World War II veterans, availability of educational benefits was instrumental in their attending college and the subsequent higher socioeconomic status they enjoyed due to their educational attainment.

Compensation and Pension Benefits

Compensation or pension benefits are generally used only by older veterans. However, utilization rates can be expected to increase over time. While the benefits given to veterans who fought in different wars are not directly comparable, changes over time can be inferred from inspection of table 6.6. A smaller percentage of World War I veterans reported receiving compensation in 1979 (5.8 percent) compared to the World War II cohort (9.6 percent). However, one out of three of the World War I survivors reported receiving a pension in 1979 compared to 5.4 percent of the World War II group. World War II veterans were proportionately more frequent users of these entitlements than were veterans in general.

Health Care Benefits

Veteran utilization of health care benefits is a more complex issue and one that for a variety of reasons has more dramatic implications for society in general. To understand these implications it is important to understand the development of the Veterans Administration health care delivery system since World War II. Paul Starr has described the character of the Veterans Administration hospital system at the time the World War II veteran was returning home.

Table 6.5
Educational Benefits Used by Veterans by Level of Educational Attainment before and after Use

Level of Educational Attainment	World War II Veterans				All Veterans			
	At Separation		By July 1978		At Separation		By July 1978	
	Number	%	Number	%	Number	%	Number	%
8 years or less	708,400	15.5	617,000	13.5	915,300	7.4	754,500	6.1
High School	2,980,000	65.2	1,919,600	42.0	8,473,200	68.5	4,762,300	38.5
College	882,100	19.3	2,033,900	44.5	2,981,100	24.1	6,852,800	55.4
Total Using Benefits	4,570,500	100.0	4,570,500	100.0	12,369,600	100.0	12,369,600	100.0
Total Veterans	16,535,000				28,522,000			
Percent of Total Veterans Using Benefits		27.6				43.4		

Source: Veterans Administration, 1979 National Survey of Veterans.

Table 6.6
World War I and World War II Veterans Receiving Compensation or Pension Compared with Estimated Total Veteran Population in 1979

Period of Service	Estimated Veterans Population	Receiving Compensation		Receiving Pension or Retirement		Total Receiving Compensation, Pension or Retirement	
		Number	*%*	*Number*	*%*	*Number*	*%*
WW I	594,000	34,217	5.8	196,626	33.1	230,843	38.9
WW II	12,674,000	1,217,522	9.6	681,493	5.4	1,899,015	15.0
Total, All Veterans	30,072,000	2,266,267	7.5	974,016	3.2	3,240,283	10.8

Source: Veterans Administration, 1979 Annual Report, Table 60, p. 160.

Table 6.7
Percentage of All Hospitalized Veterans Receiving Care in VA Hospitals by Service-Connected Disability, Age, Income, and Insurance

Category	Percent with VA Hospital Episodes	Number in Sample of Veterans Hospitalized in both VA and Non-VA Hospitals by Category
Service-connected Disability		
Yes	38.4	211
No	12.1	1,049
Age		
Under 45	11.2	373
45-64	18.6	678
65 and over	19.2	209
Income		
Under $10,000	29.3	527
Over $10,000	7.3	733
Insurance		
Yes	10.6	1,036
No	43.6	224
Total	16.5	1,260

Source: Adapted from William Frank Page, Why Veterans Choose Veterans Administration Hospitalization: A Multivariate Model. *Medical Care*, 1982, *20*, no. 3.

By World War II, the Veterans Administration, with ninety-one institutions, was already operating the largest hospital system in the country. However, corruption, low pay for medical staff, and the isolated location of many rural facilities gave Veterans Administration hospitals a dismal reputation. The new leaders of the agency after the war resolved to end its professional isolation as well as improve its physical plant. They decided to build new facilities in urban areas and, wherever possible, to establish close affiliations with medical schools. These affiliations involved the use of Veterans Administration hospitals for clinical research and training in the health professions. Medical school committees received the right to vote on appointments to the Veterans Administration medical staff. As a result, the revitalization of the Veterans Administration . . . funneled new resources to the medical schools and expanded their role in running American hospitals. (Geriatrics and Gerontology Advisory Committee, 1983)

Set up as a way to ensure oversight of the quality of care and as an inducement in the recruitment of physicians with sound professional credentials, the pattern of medical school affiliations served to deliver high-quality medical care to the one out of six American veterans who chose to use the system.

Those using the system are not, however, representative of the Veterans Administration population as a whole. In general, users of the system tend to be older, with lower incomes and without health insurance (table 6.7). As might be expected, those with service-connected disabilities are three times more likely to opt for care in a Veterans Administration hospital than those without such disabilities (Page, 1982).

VETERANS ADMINISTRATION TRAINING OF HEALTH CARE PROFESSIONALS

Following the changes instituted in 1947, most Veterans Administration hospitals were eventually integrated into modern academic medical centers through affiliations with more than 100 medical schools. In turn, the range and extent of education of health professionals supported by the Veterans Administration on a national level is extensive. Nearly 100,000 health professionals annually receive all or part of their training in a Veterans Administration facility. One-fourth of these 100,000 are medical house staff, one-fifth medical and dental students, and one-fourth nursing professionals. Of some 25,000 house staff training in Veterans Administration hospitals, 7,700 (or one of every six residents in training) receive their total salary from the Veterans Administration budget. In aggregate, half of all physicians practicing today received some portion of their training in a Veterans Administration hospital. During the course of these developments the veteran grew older, his life expectancy often extended by the care delivered in these Veterans Administration medical centers with their medical school affiliations. The success of the medical establishment in turning back the ravages of acute, usually infectious disease has increased average life expectancies dramatically for the veteran and the average American citizen alike. Noting this, the Geriatrics and Gerontology Advisory Committee, mandated by Congress to address the health care needs of older veterans, pointed out that

herein lies the dilemma. The natural processes of aging and chronic illness have superceded the onslaught of acute disease just at the time when a large number of veterans, the World War II cohort, are entering the upper age range. And the system that fostered this longevity is no longer fully appropriate to the needs of this constituency. Secondary and tertiary treatment facilities geared to respond to acute illness can no longer completely meet the needs of the World War II veteran as appropriately as they once did. The affiliation bond to medical education and the resultant intellectual and professional indebtedness incurred by the Veterans Administration hospital system should be reexamined. If the dilemma of chronic and long term care of the aging veteran by a short term acute care system is to be solved, the basic bond should be reestablished on revised and reordered bases. (Geriatrics and Gerontology Advisory Committee, 1983)

Generation of alternative models of care, accompanied by selective development of physical facilities and exemplary sites for the training of health manpower, represents an opportunity to better serve the aging veteran while at the same time preparing the next generation of health care professionals to serve the general society and its aging population. Continued maintenance of high-quality care in a mode appropriate to the changing needs of the aging population is heavily dependent on the responsiveness of the educational establishment and whether or not it can appropriately gear itself to the geriatric needs of the nation. The interest of the Veterans Administration in using its investment in the training of health professionals to address this task has been acknowledged by its administrator. Shortly after taking office as VA administrator, Harry N. Walters pointedly acknowledged the special role of the World War II veteran in what he termed the second challenge:

The Veterans Administration is committed to leadership and innovation in dealing with the second great challenge posed by the great cohort of veterans of World War II. Once it was the challenge of caring for that population's immediate needs in a way that would enhance the quality of their care and show leadership in accomplishing that goal. Today it is the challenge of the "graying of America", so large a proportion of which is the graying of the veteran. We have not been laggard in meeting this need, but rather are setting a course which will be as important to the rest of the nation as it is to veterans and their families. (Walters, 1983)

REFERENCES

Dann, John C. (Ed.). *The revolution remembered.* University of Chicago Press, Chicago, 1980.

Geriatrics and Gerontology Advisory Committee. *Health care of the aging veteran: A Report of the Geriatrics and Gerontology Advisory Committee,* USGPO, Washington, D.C., 1983.

The need for long term care: Information and issues. A chartbook of the Federal Council on the Aging. U.S. Department of Health and Human Services, Federal Council on the Aging, Office of Human Development Services, DHHS Publication No. (OHDS) 81-20704. Washington, D.C., 1981.

Page, William Frank. Why veterans choose Veterans Administration hospitalization: A multivariate model. *Medical Care,* 1982, *20,* no. 3.

U.S. News and World Report, October 25, 1982.

Walters, Harry N. Opening statement, Senate Appropriations HUD-Independent Agencies Subcommittee hearing on VA FY 1984 budget, March 10, 1983.

7

THE WIDOWED

HELENA Z. LOPATA

According to *Statistical Abstract of the United States*, (1981:38), there were 10,479,000 widows and 1,972,000 widowers in this country in 1980, a ratio of more than five to one. Widows form 12.8 percent of the female population, and 68 percent of women over 75 years of age are widows (see table 7.1). Less than a third of the widows are currently employed, but the figures are pulled down by the older women. On the other hand, 143,000 widows under 45 years of age and about 100,000 of those between ages 45 and 64 are not employed. One wonders how they support themselves since many do not have pre-adult children, which would make them eligible for Social Security. Widows tend to live alone, but the older the woman, the more apt she is to be living in a family and not the head of the household. Research has indicated that many lead lives restricted by inadequate social life, space, and support systems.[1] A very important fact about the widowed in America is their heterogeneity. The one thing they have in common is that they are no longer married due to the death of a spouse. In other respects they vary considerably.

Not surprisingly, the older the person the greater the probability that she or he will become widowed if she or he continues living. Few are so disabled that they need nursing home care and most have at least one relative nearby who provides support.

THE HISTORY OF WIDOWHOOD IN AMERICA

The social roles and support systems of people whose spouse dies vary by the society and community in which they live, where they are located in these social structures, and their personal resources. There is no consensus as to the status and life circumstances of widows in colonial America. Widowers did not present a social problem; their remarriage did not complicate the family line since it was patrilineal. Some observers claim that widows enjoyed high status and were in

Table 7.1
Marital Status of the Population by Sex and Age, 1980

SEX AND AGE	Total	Single	Married	Widowed	Divorced	PERCENT DISTRIBUTION				
						Total	Single	Married	Widowed	Divorced
Male	74,101	17,434	50,825	1,972	3,871	100.0	23.5	68.6	2.7	5.2
18-19 years	4,042	3,808	232	—	2	100.0	94.2	5.7	—	—
20-24 years	9,801	6,721	2,924	2	154	100.0	68.6	29.8	—	1.6
25-29 years	9,076	2,940	5,650	8	479	100.0	32.4	62.3	.1	5.3
30-34 years	8,270	1,298	6,310	11	651	100.0	15.7	76.3	.1	7.9
35-44 years	12,297	904	10,358	45	989	100.0	7.4	84.2	.4	8.0
45-54 years	10,962	699	9,347	176	740	100.0	6.4	85.3	1.6	6.8
55-64 years	9,870	565	8,414	397	495	100.0	5.7	85.2	4.0	5.0
65-74 years	6,549	357	5,346	557	290	100.0	5.5	81.6	8.5	4.4
75 years and over	3,234	142	2,244	776	71	100.0	4.4	69.4	24.0	2.2
Female	82,054	13,977	51,767	10,479	5,831	100.0	17.0	63.1	12.8	7.1
18-19 years	4,184	3,465	689	3	26	100.0	82.8	16.5	.1	.6
20-24 years	10,246	5,148	4,705	23	370	100.0	50.2	45.9	.2	3.6
25-29 years	9,357	1,947	6,584	33	792	100.0	20.8	70.4	.4	8.5
30-34 years	8,561	810	6,695	102	954	100.0	9.5	78.2	1.2	11.1
35-44 years	13,042	728	10,612	292	1,411	100.0	5.6	81.4	2.2	10.8
45-54 years	11,670	552	9,222	821	1,074	100.0	4.7	79.0	7.0	9.2
55-64 years	11,034	504	7,713	2,082	735	100.0	4.6	69.9	18.9	6.7
65-74 years	8,549	480	4,282	3,444	342	100.0	5.6	50.1	40.3	4.0
75 years and over	5,411	344	1,264	3,677	126	100.0	6.4	23.4	68.0	2.3

Source: U.S. Bureau of the Census, *Current Population Reports*, ser. P-20, no. 365.
Note: In thousands of persons 18 years old and over, except percent. As of March. Based on Current Population Survey, which includes members of Armed Forces living off post or with their families on post but excludes all other members of the Armed Forces. See *Historical Statistics, Colonial Times to 1970*, series A 160–171, for decennial census data.
— Represents zero or rounds to zero.

demand for marriage because of the shortage of women and because of their expertise in maintaining a household (Murstein, 1974). Others claim that this was not the case, and that widows had to maintain themselves through their own efforts, inheriting only part of the husband's estate without being given credit for contributing to it. Women lost all economic and political rights upon marriage, since English common law, brought over to this country, made the husband the representative of the marital unit. Widows, however, often inherited and ran businesses; until about the middle of the nineteenth century, women could be found in a variety of income- or goods-earning activities. The household was the major production unit, carried forth with the help of servants and apprentices. The farm or business needed the help of every member of the family of pro-creation. Husbands were replaced by hired hands if the widow could retain control over the source of livelihood.

The extreme economic dependence of the wife upon the earnings of the husband so evident for the past 150 years, though decreasing now, arose from a combination of very complex changes in American society. These included rapid industrialization and urbanization; the expansion of middle-class influence by the Victorian ideology of "true womanhood"; the pushing of women out of income-producing activities through protective legislation and the action of unions and guilds; and the introduction of childhood as a special stage of life requiring care and abstention from hard work (Aries, 1965; Lerner, 1969; Sicherman, 1975; Welter, 1966). The end result, combined with the decrease of support exchanges among the members of extended families, was often severe poverty for widows. The same phenomenon had occurred even earlier in England, giving rise to the series of Elizabethan laws attempting to control the problem (Burn, 1973). The United States inherited the attitudes toward the poor so typical of England. Children were taken away from many a widowed mother if the "charitable" organizations were convinced either that she was unable to care for them adequately if she worked for pay outside the home, or that she would subject them to poverty if she did not. Orphanages, workhouses, the shipping of half-orphans to farms, and similar systems were instituted in order to ensure that the children had a "decent" upbringing; the frequent assumption was that widows were somehow leading immoral lives and that a man was needed to discipline their children (Burn, 1973). Finally, "mothers' pensions" were instituted in most states after the 1909 White House Conference on the Care of Dependent Children, reflecting the growing belief that mothers make better caregivers than institutions or strangers and should have the funds to stay home full-time for this purpose. During the Great Depression few counties consistently provided such mothers' pensions; minority women seldom received them (Abbott, 1918; Brehm and Lopata, 1984; Leff, 1973). It was not until 1939, however, that the newly established Social Security Administration incorporated older widows and widowed mothers of dependent children into the system (Brehm and Lopata, forthcoming). They were freed from the means test by which Federal Aid to

Dependent Children determines who is worthy of financial help in cases in which the husband is absent for reasons other than death (Piven and Cloward, 1971).

In spite of the rise of women's employment outside the home during World War II and its gradual increase after a dip during the 1950s and 1960s, the "feminine mystique" so dramatically documented by Friedan (1963) kept most married women home until recent years. The typical life course of events included, for women, marriage at age 20, the birth of the first child at 22, the birth of the last child at 26, the beginning of the "shrinking circle" stage as the children left home, leaving the couple alone after the wife reached age 46 until the death of her husband (Duvall, 1967; Lopata, 1966). She remained a widow for an average of sixteen years.

In the meantime, American society has become increasingly volunteristic, in that social engagement—that is, entrance into social relations and social roles—requires individual initiative. Events such as the death of a husband or a friend, dispersion of the extended family and even of offspring, change in residence, the dropping of clubs and even the church connected with the deceased, and being dropped by married friends contribute to gradual disengagement on the part of people who do not have the personal resources to re-engage and create a new support network or restructure the prior one (Cumming and Henry, 1961). Personal resources required for re-engagement include money, health, self-confidence, and familiarity with the world outside of one's private territory. Unfortunately, many women socialized into "true womanhood" and functioning only in the private sphere of life do not have these personal resources to a sufficient degree to move into new life-styles upon widowhood, or after other life course changes. One of the major conclusions of a study of role modification of older widows conducted in metropolitan Chicago in the early 1970s is that the more education a woman has and the more middle-class a life-style she and her husband create when he is living, the more disorganized her life becomes when he dies; but, on the other hand, the more personal resources she has to rebuild her identity and life once the period of heavy grief is over (Lopata, 1973a, 1973b, 1979). Education is an extremely important background characteristic for both men and women and constitutes the main variable in predicting the life-style of the widow (Lopata, 1973b). It influences not only her capabilities, but also her choice of a husband, their life together, their income, and so forth. The higher-status woman has experienced greater disorganization of life and identity, at least in the recent past, because, as a couple, she and her husband are much more intertwined in each other's roles than are true working-class couples. They communicate more, belong together to social groups, have couple companionate friends, and do more with each other. The woman is also apt to be dependent upon her role as a wife, and being the wife of a specific man, for her identity and activities (see Berger and Kellner, 1970; Lopata, 1973c, 1975a, 1975b). Many of the older widows in metropolitan areas are relatively uneducated, products of ghetto or ethnic neighborhood schools, immigrants or the children of immigrants, and members of a variety of minorities (Lopata, 1971). But many older American widows do not fall into these categories and vary by social engagement focus, some being involved in jobs, others in voluntary work. Widows of all backgrounds can be engaged in multiple family and friendship roles.

PROBLEMS AND ADVANTAGES OF WIDOWHOOD

The problems associated with widowhood are apparent—the general population hearing about research in this area immediately become embarrassed and withdrawn. The main problem, labeled by Gorer (1967) the "pornography of death," and approached directly by Aries (1981), is, of course, death itself. Experiencing the death of an important other has been recognized as one of the most distressing events of life. There has been much scientific debate over the circumstances under which grief is more or less traumatic (Clayton et al., 1971; Gerber et al., 1975; Schoenberg et al., 1974). Anticipatory grief, or as Neugarten (1968) defines it, "rehearsal" for the death of the spouse, has been defined as a situation easing the trauma of that event. Others find that the longer the period of awareness of oncoming death and of care for an ill husband or wife, the harder the process of adjustment after the death finally takes place (Gerber et al., 1975). Gerber and associates (1975) thus disagree with Parkes (1964a, 1964b, 1975, 1976), who claims that sudden, unexpected, and untimely bereavement is hardest for the survivor. Glick, Weiss, and Parkes (1974) agree with Neugarten (1968) and most other researchers that "off time" widowhood presents unusual problems for the survivors, since their established support systems are organized around couples.

There are several problems involved in grief work: the sentiments the survivor experiences about the death, the responses of associates, and the need to recreate the self and life in the future. Most of the literature on grieving assigns it a life course with stages, and most people appear to be aware of such sequencing. This can of itself create problems as the survivor and those around him or her keep watching for "abnormal" tendencies to stay in a particular stage. Caine (1974) writes of having gone through the "crazies" at a certain point in her bereavement, making decisions that were irrational and feeling that she had lost control of herself. Depression is a frequent symptom of grief and leads to passivity vis-à-vis the environment and the self. My research indicates a second bad period after the initial grieving subsides, which occurs when the widow or widower finally realizes that no one can really help with the process and that the self must change. Identities of the past simply cannot be retained in the future; but many women who had depended upon the husband for a major source of self-image report a feeling of blankness as to their future selves (Lopata, 1973c, 1975b).

Associates of the past are often reported as avoiding the newly widowed. Many of the Chicago area women studied in the two projects summarized in *Widowhood in an American City* (Lopata, 1973a) and *Women as Widows: Support System* (Lopata, 1979) feel that they are dropped from the social life of their married friends. Friends themselves report that they tend to contact the widow for daytime activities only, reserving evenings when the husband is present for couple events. The widow hears of a dinner or party to which she has not been invited and this creates a feeling of rejection and tension in the relation. Going to public places with married couples also becomes awkward in terms of transportation and bills. Besides, couple companionate relations are built around "fun," and friends fear that the widowed will break down and cry or at least bring up the unpleasant topic of death.

Associated with the various sentiments surrounding grief is loneliness. A detailed analysis of the interviews with older widows indicated multidimensional forms of loneliness, felt together or at different times or by different women. Loneliness can be defined as a feeling of relative deprivation in which the person is unhappy with the type and degree of social interaction. Weiss (1973) has identified two major types of loneliness, social and emotional isolation. Women accustomed to the presence of a husband can miss him as a unique person, as a love object, and as someone who treated them as a love object. One woman explained that, although she often fought with her husband, at least he treated her as an important person with whom it was worth disagreeing, and no one does that now. Loneliness can be felt because no one else is present in the household; most of the women interviewed had never before lived alone. A husband was also the person around whom time and work were organized, and the widows experienced emptiness, much as do men insufficiently adjusted to retirement. In the case of middle-class women a whole life-style is often lost with the death of the husband: the clubs to which they belonged, the meetings the wife attended with him, the couple companionate evenings, the expenditure of money on leisure activities, and so forth. The widow usually experiences a drop in income, especially if the husband had been fully employed until his fatal illness or accident, as many were. There are women, of course, who benefit financially with widowhood because the husband drank or otherwise spent his earnings or was unable to bring in monies because of his illness. Social Security provides many women with the first steady income over which they have ever had control.

Regardless of how lonely widows feel at times, most become accustomed to living alone and refuse to move in with their married sons or daughters. In this American widows are unusual, compared to widows in other countries whose cultures insist on household sharing and do not allow a woman to live alone, or whose housing shortages prevent such independence. There are several reasons that American women choose to live alone. In the first place, they want control over their own territory, having everything where and how they want it, not having to share a bathroom or feel they are imposing on the space of others. Secondly, they know that there would be tension and even conflict if they moved in with a married child. As one respondent told me, her daughter, who lives in a "nice house" in New Orleans, said that the mother could move in with her family but that she "would have to keep [her] mouth closed." The mother exclaimed, "Now, what's the fun of living if you have to keep your mouth closed?'' Finally, many women explained that they had already worked as a housewife one time around, maintaining a home and a family, and did not want to do it again for someone else. The fear of being imposed upon, combined with other sentiments, prevents household sharing, even if the alternative is relative isolation and loneliness on occasion.

One solution to both financial and loneliness problems is a job, but many of these "displaced homemakers" have been out of the labor force for many years and are unable to find employment or lack the self-confidence necessary to pursue job training and job search (Steinhart, 1975, 1976). Unless the husband's illness is prolonged and requires her presence, employed wives tend to continue working outside of the home after the death. Widowers very seldom drop out of the labor force due to the wife's illness, so they work till retirement. In addition, widowers in retirement communities at least have plenty of company since there are so few of them compared to widows.

Childrearing can be a major problem for women widowed while the offspring are still young. Widows often report that the death of the father did not affect the children much because they were too young or already adult; but this appears to be a misjudgment, probably due to the inability of the mother to handle both her own and her offsprings' grief. Very few of the women in the samples studied sought professional care for themselves or their children during this traumatic time, and very few report that the helping professions offered assistance (see Lopata, 1980). Schools usually have no resources for such aid to children, although a number of researchers have tried to convince community leaders, including churches and schools, of the need to help people going through crises (Lopata, 1979). It is only when children get into trouble with community agencies that attention is drawn to their suffering.

One solution to the problems of widowhood is remarriage. Men tend to use this method more frequently than women, probably because there are so many women available, not only in their own age group but also in younger age groups, and our society does not discourage downward marriage in age for men as much as it does for women. On the other hand, many women report an unwillingness to remarry for several reasons. One is that they enjoy their independence and do not want to return to the dependent status of wife. Another reason is that they are aware of the statistics of the improbability of finding a new husband. A third reason is that they do not want to take care of an ill man again. Finally, many women idealize their late husband to the point of "sanctification" so that no living man can measure up to the dead one. Creating a sanctification scale, I found that those most apt to go to the extreme of claiming that the husband "had no irritating habits" are very elderly, white, ethnically identified, and less-educated women (Lopata, 1980). Very educated women tend not to use extreme sanctification, and poorer, especially black, women tend to hold many hostile feelings about their late husband. Sanctification accomplishes several functions for those widows who use it. In the first place, the process cleanses the husband of mortal weaknesses and negative sentiments. The spirit becomes benevolent and safely out of the way rather than in constant and often critical hovering. In addition, if such a saintly man married her, the widow must not be as unworthy as she often feels. In fact, for many women life with the husband was better than life without him, especially in retrospect, so he must have been pretty good. However, it does make it difficult for a widow who has idealized her late husband to find another man of equal stature. Hunt (1966) explains that divorced men shun widows because they feel that they cannot compete against the idealized late husband.

SUPPORT SYSTEMS

The support systems study of widows examined the in-flow and out-flow of ninety-five separate supports, defined as any object or action which the giver and/or the receiver defined as necessary or helpful in maintaining a style of life (Lopata, 1979:4). The supports were organized into four systems: economic, service, social, and emotional. Each respondent was first asked about her resources, parents, siblings, children, friends, and other relatives before the husband's fatal illness or accident and friends made since his death. These people were specifically identified throughout the interview, and each woman was given an opportunity to list up to three persons for each support.

Very few widows in our samples are involved in economic support exchanges, either as givers or as receivers of gifts of money or help in the payment of rent or mortgages, food, clothing, or bills. Those who are so involved list most frequently children and, in the case of gifts of money, grandchildren. Only one-eighth list giving money to others, and other kinds of support to others are listed even less frequently. Service supports received appear much more frequently. Over half of the women list someone as providing transportation and care during illness; around 40 percent list help with household repairs, shopping, and decision-making. The women are much less apt to see themselves as givers than as receivers of service supports, although 37 percent help people, mainly their children, during illness. Few have living parents, so they do not often enter the system, but it was a surprise to find out that the extended family of siblings, nieces and nephews, and grandchildren enter this system so infrequently. Assistance is provided on a sex-segregated basis. Sons help with house repairs, yard work, and car care. Daughters provide help with shopping and housekeeping. Very few widows provide or receive child care, and hardly any list car care or repairs and legal aid as support they provide others.

The social support system draws more people into the network. However, over half of the respondents claim never to go to public places or to play sports, cards, or games with anyone. Forty percent never entertain, although only 21 percent never visit. There is a strong possibility that the concept of entertaining has a formal or middle-class ring to it, while visiting is seen as an informal activity. Forty percent of the women state that they never travel out of town, 37 percent that they do not eat lunch with anyone, and 24 percent that they do not go to church. The most isolated appear to be the 8 percent who report that they do not celebrate holidays with anyone.

There are strong class variations as to the people with whom widows engage in these activities. Middle-class women tend to list friends, while working-class women list children or, in the case of going to church, list only themselves. Only 10 percent of the people listed as co-celebrants of holidays are siblings, but grandchildren account for 25 percent of the total listings. Friends are rarely mentioned in connection with holidays or travel out of town, or as partners in going to church.

The fourth and final system about which we asked was the emotional support system. Two series of questions were used to investigate this system. The first was labeled "sentiments" and included "Whom do you feel closest to?" "Whom do you most enjoy being with?" "To whom do you tell your problems?" "Who comforts you when you are depressed?" "Who makes you feel important?" "Who makes you angry most often?" and "To whom do you turn in time of crisis?" The next group of questions tapped "feeling states" by asking who most often makes the widow feel respected, useful, independent, accepted, self-sufficient, and secure. Table 7.2 summarizes the findings. Some very interesting distributions are revealed. For example, 63 percent of the women claim that no one makes them angry, a rather surprising finding. One-fifth of the women do not tell their problems to anyone or are not comforted. It is surprising that only 31 percent of the remarried women feel closest to their new husband, but over twice that number would turn to him in times of crisis. Siblings and other relatives are again largely absent from this system—and if widows do not think of them as providers of emotional supports, then they certainly cannot be as important as some of the literature on aging suggests. Friends, who appeared most often as people with whom the respondents engaged in social activities, are not as frequently seen as suppliers of emotional supports, a very interesting absence.

Numerous researchers have found that daughters are more active contributors to the support systems of the elderly than are sons. The same phenomenon was observed among Chicago-area widows. There were one-fourth more mentions of daughters than sons in the emotional support system. Only two of the supports drew more references to male than female children; sons are the people who most often make the mother angry and provide her with feelings of security (Lopata, 1979:198). Daughters also tend to live closer to the mother, but we do not yet know the process by which one child becomes more responsible for the care of the widow than do others. One of my respondents realized that she was not listing her sons very often in the support systems and explained that they live in Colorado. The question is, of course, why they live so far away. It is possible that our society gives sons greater freedom of movement away from parents than it gives daughters, but that is simply a hypothesis.

SUPPORT GROUPS

Few of the Chicago-area widows were affiliated with the self-help and religious groups designed to help people pass through a crisis. Some even complained

Table 7.2

Percentages of First and Total Listings of Present Husband, Children, and Self, and Total Listings of Other People Contributing to Emotional Support Systems of Chicago Area Widows

Emotional Supports "Now"	Number of First Listings	Number of Total Listings	Present Husband	Present Husband, Boyfriend 1st	Present Husband, Boyfriend Total	Children 1st	Children Total	Contributors—All Widows Self 1st	Self Total	Parents	Siblings	Other Relatives	Friends	Other People, Groups	No One
Sentiments															
Closest	82,044	144,277	31	4	3	65	60	2	1	3	10	9	10	2	2
Enjoy	80,706	145,463	43	7	4	53	52	0	0	2	8	13	16	3	5
Problems	81,664	112,996	54	5	4	37	42	7	6	2	9	4	12	5	21
Comfort	81,304	117,671	58	6	5	41	45	6	4	2	9	4	11	5	21
Important	79,630	128,246	53	8	5	52	57	6	4	2	4	7	9	4	12
Angry	80,320	89,275	15	2	2	18	22	1	1	0	3	4	2	9	63
Crisis	80,170	114,490	67	6	5	52	54	4	3	3	10	5	7	4	12
Feeling States															
Respected	81,035	144,162	40	5	4	54	52	7	4	2	4	7	12	13	4
Useful	80,459	126,334	40	5	4	46	50	16	11	2	4	2	7	9	13
Independent	79,819	97,652	31	2	2	13	20	61	50	0	4	2	3	7	7
Accepted	77,698	128,472	37	5	4	37	40	11	5	1	4	6	19	14	10
Self-Sufficient	78,953	100,142	35	3	3	14	21	61	49	1	4	3	6	5	10
Secure	79,883	111,801	59	6	5	28	36	40	30	1	4	7	4	9	10

Source: Helena Z. Lopata, *Women as Widows: Support Systems.* Elsevier, New York, 1979, p. 88.

that their priests, rabbis, or ministers did not offer support, except for officiating at the funeral. The Catholic women explained that the priest could not come to their home to help them grieve because "people would talk." Protestant women considered their ministers too busy taking care of whole families, but Jewish women most often expressed anger because they expected assistance with grief work (Lindeman, 1944; Glick et al., 1974). Some cities contain branches of the Catholic NAIM organization, which tries to help widows and widowers. It is mainly composed of widows, but the few widowers who are members receive a great deal of attention at social functions. Marriages are frequently reported in its newsletters. Harvard Medical School social scientists and psychiatrists studying younger widows and widowers encouraged Phyllis Silverman to start a widow-to-widow group in the Boston area (Silverman, 1976, 1972; Glick et al., 1974; Maddison, 1968). Since then, she has helped other communities organize similar groups. A Widow's Consultation Service operating with professional consultants and on a fee basis in New York could not survive, and the Boston group failed for years to get community funding, but there are several groups of a similar nature in many other places. Mental health specialists have become increasingly interested in the problems of widows, but Clayton and associates (1971) warn that grief should not be treated as an abnormal situation; rather, it should be dealt with as a necessary and normal process. Both the Harvard and the St. Louis research teams found that younger widows take the death of a spouse harder than do older widows, but that the self-help group's structure enables them to grieve and relive the past openly, which friends and relatives not going through grief often do not encourage. In addition, such groups often involve little cost, while psychiatrists and related professionals tend to be expensive. Widows often refuse professional help because they identify psychiatrists with serious mental illness and the related stigma. As stated before, few list such people as helpers following the husband's death or at the present time.

Some hospitals in larger cities that house many terminally ill patients have organized groups of relatives to assist them in the process, and an Institute of Thanatology periodically brings together researchers examining the consequences of death.

RESEARCH ISSUES

Although there has been increased interest in studying widowhood, there are many gaps in our knowledge and much need for more research. Widowers, who are fewer and who tend to be lost to researchers because they remarry soon, have been understudied, in spite of Berardo's (1968) warning that they have been neglected. Some comparative research has been done, but the data have not been published. More societies need to be studied so that we can better understand all the variables affecting the identities and support systems of widows and widowers. Much more information is needed on the process of grief work, which requires longitudinal rather than cross-sectional studies. This same method could be used to follow the whole support network through the illness and death of a member. Are there certain interactions among family members, for example, as death approaches and takes place, that can lead to "better" grief work? We often focus on the spouse only, rather than seeing the family or the immediate network as a functioning unit. The Glaser and Strauss (1965) research on the awareness of dying, in hospitals and among patients, should be extended to include families.

The inner dynamics of families going through crises are little known, and the process by which a child gets selected or selects the self as the main provider of support to the widow or widower needs examination. If we knew the characteristics that influence the process we could predict the direction of support flow. Personal resources such as age, health, education, location of residence, and so on, are important variables in influencing the re-engagement of widows and widowers, but more knowledge is needed on the interactions of these factors and the process by which a person who has experienced heavy grief finally pulls together a new life and identity. We also need to know the relative importance of other roles (such as that of employee or person involved in a career, voluntary association member, friend, etc.), in grief work and the restructuring of life.

All in all, our knowledge of widowhood has increased recently, thanks to a number of studies that followed the pioneering research done by Marris (1958) in London and Palmore et al. (1965) in America. However, the subject has been neglected in the past and we need to know more to understand both the changes that occur with the death of a spouse and the variables that influence voluntaristic change once the period of heavy grief is over. We can expect different patterns of life among widowed women in the future as the strong emphasis on women remaining in their "home domain" decreases and they become increasingly involved in public life. It is quite possible that the women whom we have examined in the 1970s simply form one or two transitional generations and that the better educated and socially involved women of the future will become very different widows. The heterogeneity can be expected to increase as women vary their entrance, exit, and sequencing of social roles (Lopata and Norr, 1979, 1980). More change is expected among women than among men, but this hypothesis should be tested through future research.

NOTE

1. The first study, summarized in *Widowhood in an American City* (Lopata, 1973a), involved a sample of 300 women aged 50 to 64 and 65 and over, drawn by the National Opinion Research Center of the University of Chicago. Focusing on role modification in the lives of urban women after they were widowed, the study was funded by a grant from the Administration on Aging, Department of Health, Education and Welfare (Grant AA-4-67-030-01A1) with the cooperation of Roosevelt University. Special thanks go to the members of the Midwest Council for Social Research on Aging and to Ethel Shanas,

Bernice Neugarten, and Robert Winch for their help in designing the basic interview schedule, and to the staff of the National Opinion Research Center for their cooperation at the different stages of work.

The support systems study, described in *Women as Widows: Support Systems* (Lopata, 1979), involved five different samples drawn by Social Security Administration statisticians from their lists. These included older widows receiving benefits because of their age; mothers of dependent children; women who used to be beneficiaries but whose children have grown; former widows who have remarried; and women who qualified only for the "lump sum" benefits to help defray funeral costs. When weighted by the ratios drawn, the sample represents 82,087 women.

The support systems study was funded through a contract with the Social Security Administration (#SSSA 71-3411), with the cooperation of Loyola University of Chicago. The interviews were conducted in 1974. I wish to thank Drs. Henry Brehm, Chief of the Research Grants and Contract Staff of the Social Security Administration, Nada Smolic Krkovic of the Institute of Social Work in Zagreb, Yugoslavia, and Adam Kurzynowski of the Szkola Glowna Planowania i Statystyki, Warsaw, Poland, for help with interview construction. Gloria Heinemann and other members of the University of Illinois Survey Research Laboratory conducted the interviewing and data reduction. The members of the Center for the Comparative Study of Social Roles of Loyola University of Chicago deserve special thanks, especially Deb Barnewolt, Monica Valasco, Sue Meyering, Terry Bauman, Gertrude Kim, and Frank Steinhart.

REFERENCES

Abbott, G. Mother's aid. *Women's Bureau, Monthly Newsletter*, 1918, 3rd issue, 282–285.

———. Recent trends in mothers' aid. *Social Service Review*, 1934, *8*, 191–209.

Aries, P. *Centuries of childhood*. Random House, Vintage Books, New York, 1965.

———. *The hour of our death*. Knopf, New York, 1981.

Atchley, R.C. Dimensions of widowhood in later life. *Gerontologist*, 1975, *15*, 176–178.

Bankoff, E. Widow groups as an alternative to informal social support. In M.A. Lieberman and L.D. Borman (Eds.), *Self-help groups for coping with crisis: Origins, members, processes and impact*. Jossey-Bass, San Francisco, 1979, 181–193.

Barrett, C. Review essay: Women in widowhood. *Signs*, 1977, *2*, 856–868.

Berardo, F.M. Widowhood status in the United States: Perspective on a neglected aspect of the family life-cycle. *Family Coordinator*, 1968, *17*, 191–203.

Berger, P., and Kellner, H. Marriage and the construction of reality: An exercise in the microsociology of knowledge. In H. Dreitzel (Ed.), *Patterns of communicative behavior*. Collier-Macmillan, London, 1970, 50–73.

Brehm, H., and Lopata, H.Z. *From social problems to federal policy: Widowhood*. Praeger, New York, 1984.

Burn, R. *The history of the poor laws with observations*. H. Woodfall and W. Straham, London, 1764; Repr. Augustus M. Kelley, Clifton, N.J., 1973.

Caine, L. *Widow*. Morrow, New York, 1974.

Clayton, P.J. Anticipatory grief and widowhood. *British Journal of Psychiatry*, January 1973a, *122*, 566.

————. The clinical morbidity of the first year of bereavement: A review. *Comprehensive Psychiatry*, 1973b, *14*, 151–157.

————. Mortality and morbidity in the first year of widowhood. *Archives of General Psychiatry*, 1974, *30*, 747–750.

Clayton, P.J.; Halikes, J.A.; and Mauriece, W.L. The bereavement of the widowed. *Diseases of the Nervous System*, 1971, *32*, 597–604.

Cumming, E., and Henry, W.E. *Growing old: The process of disengagement*. Basic Books, New York, 1961.

Duvall, E. *Human development*. 3rd ed. J.B. Lippincott, New York, 1967.

Freud, S. Mourning and melancholia. In J. Strachey (Ed.), *The standard edition of the complete psychological works of Sigmund Freud*, vol. 14. Hogarth Press, London, 1957.

Friedan, B. *The feminine mystique*. Norton, New York, 1963.

Gerber, I.; Rusalem, R.; Hannon, N.; Battin, D.; and Arkin, A. Anticipatory grief and aged widows and widowers. *Journal of Gerontology*, 1975, *30*, 225–229.

Glaser, B.G., and Strauss, A.L. *Awareness of dying*. Aldine, Chicago, 1965.

Glick, I.; Weiss, R.; and Parkes, C.M. *The first year of bereavement*. Wiley, New York, 1974.

Gorer, G. *Death, grief and mourning*. Doubleday, New York, 1967.

Hunt, M. *The world of the formerly married*. McGraw-Hill, New York, 1966.

Leff, M.H. Consensus for reform: The mother-pension movement in the progressive era. *Social Service Review*, 1973, *47*, 397–417.

Lerner, G. The lady and the mill girl: Changes in the status of women in the age of Jackson. *American Studies Journal*, 1969, *10*, 5–15.

Lindemann, E. Symptomatology and management of acute grief. *American Journal of Psychiatry*, 1944, *101*, 141–148.

Lopata, H.Z. The life cycle of the social role of housewife. *Sociology and Social Research*, 1966, *51*, 5–22.

————. Loneliness: Forms and components. *Social Problems*, 1969, *17*, 248–262.

————. Widows as a minority group. *Gerontologist*, 1971, *11*, 67–77.

————. *Widowhood in an American city*. Schenkman Publishing, General Learning Press, Cambridge, Mass., 1973a.

————. The effects of schooling on social contacts of urban women. *American Journal of Sociology*, 1973b, *79*, 604–619.

————. Self-identity in marriage and widowhood. *Sociological Quarterly*, 1973c, *14*, 407–418.

————. Couple-companionate relationships in marriage and widowhood. In N. Glazer-Malbin (Ed.), *Old families/new families*. Van Nostrand, New York, 1975a, 119–149.

————. Grief work and identity reconstruction. *Journal of Geriatric Psychiatry*, 1975b, *8*, 41–55.

————. Contributions of extended families to the support systems of metropolitan area widows: Limitation of the modified kin network. *Journal of Marriage and the Family*, 1978a, *40*, 355–364.

————. The absence of community resources in support systems of urban widows. *Family Coordinator*, 1978b, October, 383–388.

————. *Women as widows: Support systems*. Elsevier-North Holland, New York, 1979.

————. Widowhood and husband sanctification. *Journal of Marriage and the Family*, 1981, *43*, 439–450.

Lopata, H.Z., and Norr, K. Perceived job complexity by Chicago area women. Paper presented at the Annual Meeting of the American Sociological Association, Boston, 1979.

————. Changing commitments of American women to work and family roles. *Social Security Bulletin*, 1980, *43*, 3–14.

Lynch, J.J. *The broken heart: The medical consequences of loneliness*. Basic Books, New York, 1977.

Maddison, D. The relevance of conjugal bereavement to preventative psychiatry. *British Journal of Psychiatry*, 1968, *41*, 223–233.

Maddison, D., and Raphael, B. Conjugal bereavement and the social network. In B. Schoenberg, I. Gerber, A. Wiener, A. Kurscher, D. Peretz, and A.C. Carr (Eds.), *Bereavement: Its psychological aspects*. Columbia University Press, New York, 1968.

Maddison, D., and Walker, W.L. Factors affecting the outcome of conjugal bereavement. *British Journal of Psychiatry*, 1967, *113*, 1057–1067.

Mallan, L.B. Young widows and their children: A comparative report. *Social Security Bulletin*, 1975, *38*, 3–21.

Marris, P. *Widows and their families*. Routledge and Kegan Paul, London, 1958.

Morgan, L. A work in widowhood: A viable option. *Gerontologist*, 1981, *20*, 581–587.

Morgan, L.A. Economic change in mid-life widowhood: A longitudinal analysis. *Journal of Marriage and the Family*, 1981, *43*, 899–907.

Murstein, W.I. *Love, sex and marriage through the ages*. Springer, New York, 1974.

Neugarten, B. Adaptation and the life cycle. Paper presented at the FFRP Conference, Puerto Rico, June 1968.

Palmore, E.; Stanley, G.L.; and Cormier, R.H. *Widows with children under Social Security: The 1963 national survey of widows and children under OASDHI*. U.S. Department of Health, Education and Welfare, Social Security Administration Research Report no. 16, 1965.

Parkes, C.M. Grief as an illness. *New Society*, 1964a, April.

————. Effects of bereavement on physical and mental health: A study of the medical records of widows. *British Medical Journal*, 1964b, *2*, 274–279.

————. Unexpected and untimely bereavement: A statistical study of young Boston widows and widowers. In B. Schoenberg et al. (Eds.), *Bereavement: Its psychosocial aspects*. Columbia University Press, New York, 1975.

————. The broken heart. In E.S. Sneidman (Ed.), *Death: Current perspectives*. Mayfield, Palo Alto, Calif., 1976.

Piven, F.F., and Cloward, R.A. *Regulating the poor: The functions of public welfare*. Pantheon, New York, 1971.

Schoenberg, B.; Carr, A.; and Kutscher, A. *Anticipatory grief*. Columbia University Press, New York, 1974.

Sicherman, B. Review essay: American history. *Signs*, 1975, *1*, 461–485.

Silverman, P. Widowhood and preventive intervention. *Family Coordinator*, 1972, *21*, 95–102.

————. The widow-to-widow program: An experiment in preventive intervention. In E.S. Sneidman (Ed.), *Death: Current perspectives*. Mayfield, Palo Alto, Calif., 1976.

Silverman, P.; MacKenzie, D.; Pettipas, M.; and Welson, E. (Eds.), *Helping each other in widowhood*. Health Sciences Publishing, New York, 1974.

Steinhart, F. Labor force participation as a resource for support systems. In H.Z. Lopata, *Final report of support systems involving widows in American urban areas*. Social Security Administration, 1975.

———. An empirical test of the Sobol-Hoffman occupational engagement model. Paper presented at the Illinois Sociological Association Meetings, Chicago, 1976.

Treas, J., and VanHilst, A. Marriage and remarriage rates among older Americans. *Gerontologist*, 1976, *16*, 132–136.

U.S. Bureau of the Census. *Statistical abstract of the United States*. USGPO, Washington, D.C., 1981.

Weiss, R.S. *Loneliness: The experience of emotional and social isolation*. MIT Press, Cambridge, Mass., 1973.

Welter, B. The cult of true womanhood: 1820–1860. *American Quarterly*, 1966, *18*, 151–160.

8

WOMEN

ANGELA M. O'RAND

Women aged 65 and older comprise the fastest growing segment of the general population and the increasing majority among the aged. By age 75 they out-number men of their age by two to one in the general population and by a much greater ratio in the institutionalized population. They are more likely than their male counterparts to be living alone, impoverished, and not covered by private pension and/or health insurance programs. For these reasons, among others, an abundance of research, policy analysis, and program development with respect to older women has been undertaken over the past decade. Even the National Commission on Social Security Reform singled out this subgroup for special concern in its recommendations regarding major strategies for future reform (Social Security Administration, 1983).

It would be impossible to list all the valuable references on women within the limitations of this chapter. Indeed, a considerable amount of information on older women is presented in other chapters of this handbook and reveals the distinctive cross-section of women across demographic, cultural, and other special groups of the aged. However, a demographic and economic profile of older women in general will be presented here within a historical framework; it will focus on the important changes in women's work, health, and family lives over this century that have influenced the status of older women today and that point to changes in the status of this group to be expected and planned for in the future.

DEMOGRAPHIC PROFILE OF OLDER WOMEN

In 1979, there were 25 million persons in the United States born before 1915; approximately 60 percent of those in this group were women (U.S. Bureau of the Census, 1980a). This means that among those aged 65 or more there were 68 men for every 100 women. This ratio reflects a significant shift since 1930, when there were 100.4 males per 100 females in this group. Patterns of fertility, mortality, and migration over this century account for this change in sex ratio, which is expected to remain relatively stable through the turn of the century. By 2020 the ratio is projected to edge up only to 69.3 males per 100 women (U.S. Bureau of the Census, 1977).

More important changes associated with the elderly sex ratio will occur within the 65 and older age group. These will consist primarily of the increasing numerical majority of old-old women (aged 85 or more). In 1979, the direction of this pattern is clear. The sex ratios of age groups defined as 65 to 74, 75 to 84, and 85 and older were 77.0, 60.4, and 44.7 men per 100 women, respectively. Projections over the next four decades suggest that succeeding cohorts of elderly will continue this pattern, resulting in a large population of old-old women from the so-called baby-boom cohort (U.S. Bureau of the Census, 1977, 1980a).

The nonwhite elderly accounted for only about 9 percent of those 65 and older in 1979 and are not expected to exceed 11.5 percent by the turn of the century. The sex ratio for this group was 74.4, somewhat higher than for whites, but is not expected to change significantly over the next several decades (U.S. Bureau of the Census, 1977, 1980a).

Approximately 37 percent of women aged 65 or over in 1979 were married and living with spouses, while over half (52 percent) were widowed. Among the 85 and older subgroup, over three-fourths were widowed (U.S. Bureau of the Census, 1980b). The tendencies for women to live longer, to marry older men, and with increasing age to remain unmarried after widowhood make widowhood a largely female experience, with women accounting for 85 percent of all surviving spouses (Soldo, 1980; Lopata, 1979).

For elderly women in the 1980s widowhood is a phase of a marital history unlikely to have been interrupted by divorce (Ross and Sawhill, 1975). And while the prevalence of divorce among aged women is low (about 4 percent), long-term trends in divorce over this century have had an impact on all age groups of women. Succeeding cohorts of women have experienced higher probabilities of divorce (see table 8.1). However, each cohort has exhibited growing rates of separation and divorce with increasing age, and projections through 1990 reported in table 8.1 show a persistent though slowed rate of increase in this pattern. In short, today's older widow and tomorrow's older widow will probably represent very different family histories, and consequently very different economic and social statuses.

Divorce, separation, and widowhood combined have contributed to the extraordinary growth in the incidence of unrelated (or primary) individuals living alone and of female-headed families and households (Ross and Sawhill, 1975). Among women aged 65 to 74, approximately 36 percent live alone, while another 9 percent are heads of families, leaving about 46 percent living with their spouses. In the 75 and older group, these figures are 48 percent, 9 percent, and 20 percent, respectively (U.S. Bureau of the Census, 1980b). For older women this living

Table 8.1
Percentage Distribution of Marital Status for U.S. Women, 1975 Estimates and 1990 Projected Values

Ages	Never Married				Married Spouse Present				Divorced/Separated Spouse Absent				Widowed			
	1975	1980	1985	1990	1975	1980	1985	1990	1975	1980	1985	1990	1975	1980	1985	1990
15-19	89.2	90.0	90.0	90.0	9.8	8.8	8.7	8.6	0.9	1.2	1.3	1.4	0.0	0.0	0.0	0.0
20-24	44.0	51.0	54.6	54.6	50.0	42.0	38.2	37.8	5.8	6.9	7.1	7.5	0.2	0.1	0.1	0.1
25-29	16.0	20.0	25.5	28.4	71.4	64.1	58.1	54.8	12.0	15.4	16.0	16.4	0.5	0.4	0.4	0.4
30-34	8.2	9.8	12.1	15.2	77.8	72.0	68.2	64.6	13.1	17.4	18.9	19.4	0.9	0.8	0.8	0.8
35-39	5.4	6.2	7.2	8.5	79.6	74.4	71.7	69.4	13.3	17.8	19.6	20.6	1.7	1.6	1.6	1.5
40-44	3.6	5.4	6.1	6.8	85.0	80.4	78.5	77.0	9.0	11.9	13.2	13.9	2.4	2.3	2.2	2.2
45-49	4.4	3.9	5.5	6.1	77.8	73.9	70.9	69.3	12.1	16.5	18.0	19.1	5.7	5.7	5.6	5.6
50-54	4.7	5.1	4.6	6.1	76.8	73.2	72.2	70.2	9.3	12.5	14.0	14.7	9.2	9.1	9.2	9.0
55-59	5.3	4.8	5.2	4.0	70.9	68.2	66.6	66.1	8.6	11.6	12.9	13.8	15.3	15.3	15.3	15.4
60-64	6.5	6.0	5.6	6.0	62.3	60.4	59.7	58.5	6.4	8.6	9.6	10.3	24.8	25.0	25.1	25.0
65-69	6.6	7.0	6.5	6.2	51.4	48.9	48.2	47.7	6.6	8.9	9.9	10.6	35.4	35.2	35.4	35.5
70-74	7.9	6.9	7.2	6.8	39.8	38.6	37.7	37.4	4.8	6.5	7.3	7.8	47.5	48.0	47.8	48.0
75-79	8.2	7.9	6.9	7.2	24.8	23.4	23.0	22.5	4.3	5.8	6.5	7.0	62.7	62.9	63.5	63.3
80-84	8.1	8.2	7.9	5.9	15.1	13.6	13.1	12.8	4.1	5.6	6.2	6.7	72.7	72.6	72.9	73.6
85+	8.1	8.1	8.2	7.9	9.5	8.0	7.4	7.0	4.2	5.6	6.2	6.7	78.3	78.3	78.2	78.5

Source: George Masnick and Mary Jo Bane, *The Nation's Families 1960-1990*. Joint Center for Urban Studies of MIT and Harvard University, Cambridge, Mass., 1980, p. 154.

arrangement distribution is due to long- and short-term characteristics of their lives. Chief among the long-term causes is the low fertility of this cohort of aged women. These women had only half as many births per woman as the baby boom mothers who followed them. Filial resources are therefore more limited. On the other hand, short-term trends in the expansion of pension coverage and the extension of health care and in-kind transfers to support the elderly since the 1950s have made it possible, though not always easy, for older women to maintain alternative independent living arrangements (Masnick and Bane, 1980).

For older black women, living alone involves a greater chance of living in rented public housing; one-fifth of these women are located in such circumstances. Alternatively, however, most black families headed by older persons (about three-fourths) own their homes. In fact, extended family patterns that lead older black families headed by women to have children living with them or else to provide foster care of others further distinguish the living status of older black women from others in their age group (Faris, 1978). In many ways, older black women experience both the most isolated and the most integrated living arrangements.

The increasing tendency toward female-headed, single-parent families among younger cohorts of black women suggests that older black women may be better off today, in many respects, than in the future. Relatively high illegitimacy rates among teenagers and low remarriage rates after separation or divorce in these groups form the growing experience of succeeding cohorts of black women (Ross and Sawhill, 1975). These trends, coupled with the persistent tendency for black women to be employed in low-wage industries (i.e., service and retail trade), point to a permanent and growing subgroup of elderly poor.

ECONOMIC PROFILE OF OLDER WOMEN

Estimating the economic well-being of older populations is a complex process (O'Rand, 1982b). Current income alone is a fallible indicator of economic status in this group because of other resources, including assets, in-kind transfers, and family support systems available to the elderly, and because of lower patterns of consumption in every sphere except medical care. Also, across age subgroups of the elderly sources of income and costs of living vary. Still, among the poor or near-poor elderly, these other factors are less likely to be significant.

The average monthly Social Security benefit for a retired worker in 1979 was $287, and for a worker and wife, $489. These figures accounted for one-third of the income to aged units (either retired couples or retired workers alone) between 65 and 71 and for nearly half of the income of these units over age 72. The increased dependence by older groups on Old Age, Survivor, and Disability Insurance (OASDI) was accompanied by an increased dependence on assets as well (from 20 to 25 percent, respectively) and decreased dependence on all other sources (i.e., earnings, other pensions, etc.) (See Social Security Administration, 1982: 271–273).

When these figures are broken down by sex, the disadvantaged income status of older women becomes immediately apparent. The average monthly Social Security retirement benefit of women in 1979 was $244.50; and for women workers who retired early rather than at age 65 (about 79 percent of this group) the average was $232 per month (Social Security Administration, 1982: 113). The average benefit of black retired women in 1979 was $210 (Social Security Administration, 1982: 124). Finally, divorced wives of retired workers averaged $153 per month (p. 128).

The historical tendency is toward women's growing entitlement for Social Security based on their own earnings records (see table 8.2). Since 1960 women's retirement benefit eligibility based on their own records has grown by 13 percent to over 56 percent of all women beneficiaries aged 62 or more. This increase actually reflects an increase of over 200 percent in the number of retired women workers over this period. Meanwhile, women's beneficiary status based on husband's or children's earnings has dropped concomitantly, with beneficiaries entitled as wives showing the lowest increase in numbers in all groups (31 percent since 1960). Finally, entitlement as a parent to a child's earning record has dropped by 50 percent, reflecting the trend toward lower fertility and increasing dependence on the aged's own resources.

Older women retiring since 1960 are cohorts born largely before 1915 and almost entirely before 1920. The labor force participation histories of this group and succeeding cohorts are summarized in table 8.3. The figures for the cohort born between 1906 and 1910 are boxed in to emphasize the characteristic M-curve of labor participation of this group, which shows high rates of participation before the childbearing period, followed by a drop between ages 25 and 35, and a rise again until retirement age. Succeeding cohorts show increasingly higher rates of early labor participation and higher rates of attachment during the childbearing years. Accordingly, the trend toward women's increased entitlement to retirement benefits based on their own records is associated with the long-term trend toward labor force participation across their lives.

Once women retire they tend to remain out of the labor force, much as men do. This pattern is apparent in table 8.4, which tracks the labor force status patterns of a sample of men and women in the Longitudinal Retirement History Study of the Social Security Administration. By and large, men and women alike tend to follow orderly labor force status patterns, with continuous work followed by permanent withdrawal. About 75 percent of husbands, wives, and single women exhibit these orderly patterns (see patterns A through E in table 8.4). However, some do return to the work force after leaving, and the tendency is greater for women to return to work (see patterns M and O especially). The reasons cannot be analyzed exhaustively here. However, by and large, economic

Table 8.2
Number and Percentage of Women Beneficiaries Aged 62 and Over with Benefits in Current-Payment Status, by Type of Entitlement, 1960-1979
(Numbers in thousands)

		Basis of Entitlement						
		Own earnings record			Husband's or child's earnings record			
			Number entitled as—				Number entitled as—	
At End of Year	Total Number[a]	Percent of total	RETIRED WORKERS	DISABLED WORKERS	Percent of total	WIVES	WIDOWS	PARENTS
1960	6,619	43.3	2,845	21	56.7	2,174	1,546	33
1961	7,162	44.5	3,160	25	55.5	2,247	1,697	33
1962	7,806	45.2	3,494	32	54.8	2,388	1,858	34
1963	8,283	45.9	3,766	38	54.1	2,436	2,009	34
1964	8,710	46.6	4,011	45	53.4	2,463	2,157	34
1965	9,143	47.3	4,276	51	52.7	2,475	2,308	33
1966	9.711	48.2	4,624	61	51.8	2,504	2,490	32
1967	10,084	48.9	4,859	70	51.1	2,479	2,645	31
1968	10,524	49.3	5,111	78	50.7	2,521	2,784	30
1969	10,924	49.9	5,363	86	50.1	2,524	2,922	29
1970	11,374	50.6	5,661	92	49.4	2,546	3,048	27
1971	11,853	51.3	5,975	102	48.7	2,576	3,174	26
1972	12,379	52.0	6,325	115	48.0	2,613	3,301	25
1973	13,015	52.9	6,754	126	47.1	2,678	3,433	24
1974	13,539	53.7	7,126	144	46.3	2,701	3,546	22

1975	14,010	54.1	7,424	162	45.9	2,745	3,659	20
1976	14,489	54.7	7,744	182	45.3	2,781	3,763	19
1977	15,012	55.3	8,106	196	44.7	2,824	3,868	18
1978	15,452	55.9	8,430	202	44.1	2,844	2,960	16
1979	15,914	56.4	8,778	202	43.6	2,856	4,063	15
Percentage change, 1960-1979	140	—	209	862	—	31	162	−50

Source: B. Lingg, Women Social Security Beneficiaries Age 62 and Older, 1960-79. *Research and Statistics Notes*, no. 8. Social Security Administration, Washington, D.C., July 21, 1980, p. 4.

[a] Excludes special age-72 beneficiaries and adults receiving benefits because of childhood disability.

Table 8.3
Labor Force Participation Rates of Women, 1930–1970, by Age Group (Percentages)

Age Groups	1930	1940	1950	1960	1970
14 to 19	22.8	18.9	22.6	23.8	34.9
20 to 24	41.8	45.6	43.2	44.8	56.1
25 to 29		35.5	32.6	35.1	45.4
30 to 34	24.6	30.9	30.9	35.5	44.2
35 to 39		28.3	33.9	40.2	
40 to 44		26.0	36.2	45.3	50.3
45 to 49		23.7	34.8	47.4	53.0
50 to 54	18.0	21.2	30.8	45.8	52.0
55 to 59		18.5	25.9	39.7	47.4
60 to 64		14.8	20.5	29.5	36.1
65 and over	7.3	6.1	7.8	10.3	10.0
Total	23.6	25.8	29.9	35.7	41.4

Sources: U.S. Bureau of the Census. *Historical Statistics of the United States, Colonial Times to 1970.* House Document 93-78 (Part 1), USGPO, Washington, D.C., 1975. V. Oppenheimer, *The Female Labor Force in the United States.* Population Monograph Series, no. 5, University of California, Berkeley, 1970, p. 8.

need propels this group into the labor market to augment their incomes from earnings.

Sometimes earnings are even too low to provide minimum levels of economic well-being for elderly women. But for those who cannot work and do not have sufficient retirement incomes, other programs are available. Women account for three-fourths (73.1 percent) of all aged persons receiving Supplemental Security Income (SSI), that is, the federally administered program enacted in 1972 to assure a minimum level of income to each eligible aged or disabled person living in his/her own household. In 1979, this minimum amount of countable income from all sources was $208 for an individual and $312 for a couple. The predominance of aged women covered by the SSI program points even more clearly to the vulnerability of this group to poverty.

Poverty thresholds maintained by the Social Security Administration and the Bureau of Labor Statistics show that the rate of poverty among the elderly has declined to about 15 percent (U.S. Bureau of the Census, 1979c). The extension of the Social Security program to raise minimum income through the SSI, along with annual benefit increments tied to the Consumer Price Index, has largely accounted for this. Still, about one-sixth of all women over 65 and about one-third of unrelated (widowed, separated, or divorced) women over 65 fell below

Table 8.4
Transition Table: Labor Force Status Patterns 1969–1975 of
Men and Women in the RHS Study[a]

					Percent Following Pattern				
Labor Force Status Patterns:								All	Working
In = 1 Out = 0					All	All	Working	Single	Single
	1969	*1971*	*1973*	*1975*	*Husbands*[b]	*Wives*	*Wives*[c]	*Women*	*Women*[c]
A.	0	0	0	0	10.0	45.5	7.4	26.9	4.8
B.	1	0	0	0	11.1	6.2	13.1	9.2	13.4
C.	1	1	0	0	16.8	6.1	15.6	11.1	17.8
D.	1	1	1	0	13.7	4.6	12.0	8.9	14.8
E.	1	1	1	1	23.5	10.7	27.4	16.5	25.3
F.	0	1	1	1	.7	.6	.6	.5	.2
G.	1	1	0	1	6.7	2.7	6.3	4.0	6.2
H.	1	0	1	1	.9	.5	1.2	.6	.8
I.	0	1	0	0	.4	1.2	.9	.9	.8
J.	0	1	1	0	.2	0	0	.3	.3
K.	0	0	1	0	.2	.5	.3	.1	0
L.	0	0	1	1	.3	.9	.4	.3	.1
M.	0	0	0	1	4.9	15.6	3.1	12.2	2.6
N.	1	0	1	0	.5	.3	.7	.5	.5
O.	1	0	0	1	9.6	3.9	10.1	7.4	11.9
P.	0	1	0	1	.3	.5	.7	.2	.2
				(N)	(8,027)	(8,027)	(2,040)	(2,962)	(1,379)

[a]The longitudinal Retirement History Study (RHS) of the Social Security Administration is based on a panel of 11,153 men and unmarried women aged 58 to 63 in 1969 and followed biennially. Table is drawn from O'Rand (1982a).
[b]86 percent of male respondents are married.
[c]Working refers to attachment to the labor force prior to 1969. It is measured as having any earnings annually between 1964 and 1968, inclusively. All males and working males following this definition have essentially equivalent distributions across patterns.

the poverty threshold (U.S. Bureau of the Census, 1979c). Put another way, of all the older population estimated to be living below the poverty line, two out of three are women, and among these women 87 percent are not living with spouses (Orshansky, 1978).

The prevalence of poverty among older women is attributable in part to their greater dependence on Social Security for income maintenance. This situation stems from women's diverse patterns of household (family) and market work over their lifetimes (O'Rand and Henretta, 1982a, 1982b). Some women rarely enter or only briefly remain in the labor force over their lifetimes, while others who work may not do so continuously, may only work continuously after midlife, or else may work relatively continuously but change jobs (employers) frequently

(Jaffe and Ridley, 1976). These patterns of work are usually related to family roles that lead women to schedule their market work around childbearing, child-rearing, and husbands' job-related mobility. Marital dissolution from divorce or widowhood also influences women's work patterns (Masnick and Bane, 1980). Accordingly, women's opportunities to achieve eligibility for and/or higher benefit levels in private or government pensions are seriously limited. Whereas nearly half of older men in recent years have achieved final pension coverage from their longest jobs in the private sector, only 21 percent of older women have done so. And, among these two groups, women received approximately half the benefit incomes of men (U.S. Department of Labor, 1980a). Shorter work careers as a result of family roles account, in part, for this difference.

However, women's limited opportunities to vest successfully in retirement pensions are also influenced by the occupations and industries in which they work. The higher concentration of women in clerical, sales, and custodial jobs and in retail and service industrial sectors seriously depresses their chances of pension eligibility in spite of their work histories. The latter industries are characterized by poor pensions or no pensions (Kolodrubetz and Landay, 1973; Schulz et al., 1979). Firms in these industrial sectors tend to be small and non-unionized and to pay low wages with few fringe benefits. Accordingly, the coincidence of atypical work lives with limited pension opportunities creates a special double jeopardy for women's economic status at retirement.

HEALTH

At age 65 women can expect to live approximately eighteen years, or five years longer than men surviving to this age (U.S. Bureau of the Census, 1979c). Over that period they experience normal physiological changes associated with aging and varied morbidity and mortality patterns associated with race, work, and family histories, previous life-styles (including smoking and weight maintenance), and current social, psychological, and economic circumstances (Von Mering and O'Rand, 1981). Because of sex-related longevity, the chronic conditions of old age and the institutional arrangements (e.g., nursing homes and Medicaid) that exist to deal with them are largely the problems of old women, and particularly old-old women (U.S. Department of Health and Human Services, 1980).

Sex differences in both physiological and social behavioral illness patterns have long been observed across age groups (Verbrugge, 1976, 1979; Rossi, 1980). Among the elderly these differences are observable in patterns of mortality from leading causes of death, in health service utilization, and in the prevalence of selected chronic and stress-related disorders (Block et al., 1978:51–74). The three leading causes of death for both men and women—diseases of the heart, malignant neoplasms, and cerebrovascular diseases—have decidedly different trends. Death from heart disease has generally declined for women over the past two decades, although it still remains the major cause. An overall decrease in malignant neoplasms has been reported for women over the last two to three decades, although an increase since the mid-1960s is discernible among women under age 85. Breast cancer in the 65 to 74 age group and cancer of the colon in the over 75 age group are the primary death-causing forms of these diseases among women. Most recently, lung cancer has increased more rapidly in women. Finally, cerebrovascular disease as a cause of death has declined most rapidly (U.S. Department of Health and Human Services, 1982).

Other health indicators reveal that women over 65 experience more days of restricted activity and bed disability and more injuries annually than their male counterparts (U.S. Bureau of the Census, 1979c). Among older groups (over 75), the sex differences in these patterns become more dramatic and culminate in sex ratios of three to four females for every male over age 75 in selected full-care institutions (U.S. Department of Health and Human Services, 1980).

Most episodes of injury, restricted activity, and disability are associated with chronic disorders such as high blood pressure and osteoporosis and psychological or psychiatric problems associated with increased stress or depression (Block et al., 1978:51–74), rather than with the so-called killer diseases noted above. These episodes are not merely medical problems, but are also embedded in life-styles (e.g., nutrition, social isolation) and in the social distribution of health maintenance information and resources (Von Mering and O'Rand, 1981).

Finally, late life health status, like economic and living statuses, results in part from earlier life events. For women, patterns of childbirth are consequential for their health in old age. The scheduling of childbirth, for example, appears to have a strong association with cancer of the breast and other reproductive organs. As succeeding cohorts of women increasingly delay childbearing or forego it altogether, as trends in fertility and labor force participation suggest, the configuration of morbidity and mortality patterns among older women may shift accordingly. That is, the health of older women today and tomorrow cannot be separated from the content and contours of their lives across the domains of family and work (Rossi, 1980). Lifetime schedules of events in both domains bear upon normal physiological changes and probably affect actual disease patterns as well as coping mechanisms in response to these patterns.

ADJUSTMENT TO OLD AGE

A long tradition in gerontologic research has grappled with the question of how populations adjust to changing work, family, or age status (e.g., Neugarten, 1968, 1977; Atchley, 1976, 1982; Lowenthal et al., 1975; Schaie and Parham, 1976; O'Rand, 1983). By and large, this tradition has uncovered considerable heterogeneity in the response of different groups to both anticipated and unanticipated changes in their lives. In general, however, we know that predictable relationships exist between patterns of adjustment to old age and preparation for it. The latter, of course, is a function of lifetime opportunity structures in economic, familial, and social spheres. The variation in these structures between men and women and within each of these groups explains a large part of this adjustment.

Older women approach old age with fewer economic resources as individuals, but with more social-familial resources (Atchley, 1982). They retire for the same reasons as men—health and pension eligibility (O'Rand and Henretta, 1982a)—but tend to display more negative subjective responses to retirement. Typically, lower status, unmarried women exhibit this reaction. Women also appear to respond to stopping work at later ages with greater negative assessments of their health, even when functional assessments have been controlled for (O'Rand, 1983). But among older women, these negative subjective health evaluations are associated with lower economic status and fewer familial supports. Children tend to have a positive effect on women's adjustment, however, while they do not appear to influence men's (Atchley, 1976; O'Rand, 1983). Paradoxically, women's family roles negatively influence their work careers and earning capacities in earlier phases of their lives, but have positive returns to women in old age when noneconomic resources provided by children enhance women's lives.

Declining fertility patterns among women signal a significant future loss of resources for women in old age (Shanas, 1980; Treas, 1980). Some analysts have called for more "filial responsibility" in family policy relating to the elderly (Schorr, 1980), but such pleas are academic if demographic trends continue. Third-party roles in social supports for elderly women promise to continue as necessary features of policy toward the elderly of the future. Their appropriate development and application to older women's lives require continued attention.

PROBLEMS AND PROSPECTS

Recent research on women's retirement patterns has pointed to the disadvantaged pension status of women across industrial sectors, with older unmarried women at the threshold of retirement particularly at risk. While this is not a new discovery, what has become clear is that, despite the increasing lifetime work patterns of women, the pension system has viewed the "work career" in a fashion that ignores (1) the ways that women schedule and time their labor market behavior across the life cycle in response to family roles, and (2) the fact that marriages are economic partnerships.

The important features of women's work careers are as follows:

1. Diversity in scheduling of the work career, including such patterns as

a. Midlife career entry, that is, starting full-time work after childbearing is completed or after dissolution of marriage due to divorce, separation, or widowhood (O'Rand and Henretta, 1982a);

b. Intermittent entry into the work force scheduled around childbearing and family geographical mobility (Uhlenberg, 1974);

c. Frequent job changes (Jaffe and Ridley, 1976).

2. Tendency to be concentrated in only a few occupations such as those attached to sales, clerical, or domestic service work or limited to a few professions such as teaching and social service (Oppenheimer, 1970).

3. Tendency to be concentrated in only a few industries, particularly retail trade and personal services. These industries are characterized by high labor turnover, small firm size, lower wages and fringe benefits (including poor programs of pension coverage), and absence of unionization (Schulz et al., 1979).

These three factors are linked in the following way: "atypical" work career schedules (e.g., late entry or frequent job change) combined with location in lower paid jobs and less (pension) favorable industries produce a category of retirement-aged workers with special problems of economic dependency. These problems become particularly acute for those who are single (especially divorced) and without benefits from spouses' work. And since the latter are the fastest growing population subgroup, more options for their pension adequacy must be developed.

These labor market and work career patterns, in conjunction with long-term widowhood and divorce rates, have made the homemaker the subject of long overdue concern by the National Commission on Social Security Reform (Social Security Administration, 1983) and the Labor-Management Services Administration (U.S. Department of Labor, 1980b). The woman whose family role has led her to depend economically on her spouse can benefit from his private pension *only* if he is covered, does not die too soon, stays married to her, and/or is willing to reduce his benefit to provide her with a survivor annuity.

Social Security benefits based on different entitlement statuses are more readily available to married and unmarried women, but many "inequities and unintended results for women beneficiaries" persist (Social Security Administration, 1983:15). Homemakers have no individual eligibility and no credits of their own to add to employment credit. Divorced women can qualify for a 50 percent dependent benefit from their former spouse's account only if the marriage lasted ten years or more and only if the former spouse is actually retired. Finally, disability supports are unavailable to homemakers.

The concept of "earnings sharing" has surfaced often in recent years as an equitable solution to the problems of the homemaker and the female worker. Earnings sharing recognizes "marriage as an economic partnership with equal respect given to the division of labor chosen by each couple" (Social Security Administration, 1983:15). Each individual is accorded one-half of the total retirement credits earned by a couple during their marriage. Thus, both working and nonworking women would maintain continuous credits based on their share of the economic productivity of their marriages. As such, the problems of interrupted careers, sex differences in earnings, displaced homemakers, and uncovered disability are addressed in one solution.

Individual Retirement Plans (IRAs) represent another solution already implemented in the private sector. Since women are less likely to be covered by pension plans as individuals, whether or not they are employed, the opportunity to invest in long-term and tax-deferred retirement savings plans that continue in spite of job changes or intermittent work statuses is a direct approach to these problems. The adoption of this method of saving, however, is more likely to occur among higher-income individuals and couples with sufficient discretionary income (O'Rand and Henretta, 1982b).

RESEARCH ISSUES FOR THE FUTURE

The research agenda on older women has been formulated (Atchley, 1979; Trager, 1975; Treas, 1980; Schwab and Irelan, 1981). It includes several lines of inquiry into the diverse shapes of women's lives that lead to heterogeneous circumstances in their old age over succeeding time periods. The order and timing of work, family, and health events in women's lives are consequential for their opportunities in old age (Rossi, 1980). Women's lives are predictable yet highly variable (Lowenthal et al., 1975). The interaction of occupation and health is still unexamined for women. Furthermore, the multiple role that characterizes the working wife–mother is still unexamined in its effects on health and as a cause of stress-related symptoms. In short, the lifetime effects on women of pursuing different roles on different schedules are yet to be ascertained.

The influence of changing family size and family structure on cross-generational relationships should receive more attention (Schorr, 1980; Shanas, 1980). What are the prospects for filial responsibility toward elderly parents in a society characterized by declining fertility and the increased splintering of families by divorce? The present cohort of elderly, in many ways, are pioneers in new family life-styles and relationships for the future. But do we know enough about these new role models?

Prospective longevity and lifetime attachment to employment by women may bring women newfound authority in the workplace (Treas, 1980). Women will continue to live longer and increasingly healthier (i.e., less infirm) lives into the next century. Both retirement policy and women's vitality are already pushing retirement past age 65. The prospect of long work careers suggests increased occupational mobility by women in those firms and economic sectors with career ladders based on tenure and experience. Intermittent labor force status and sex discrimination have precluded this mobility in the past. Long-term trends, however, suggest a different scenario for the future. And assuming that public and private pension plans (1) institute needed reforms, and (2) achieve permanent and secure financial bases, married and unmarried women with and without sustained work lives in the future may face better lives in old age than estimates based on current population characteristics predict.

SOURCES FOR ADDITIONAL INFORMATION

Besides the selected references included in this chapter, additional sources of information on women are available from public and private organizations. The Bureau of the Census, the Department of Labor, and the Social Security Administration publish periodic reports that include information on elderly women. The Census Bureau's *Current Population Reports* offer annually updated estimates on women. Series P-23 of these reports presents special studies that include periodic reports focusing on the older population and on women; series P-20 presents monthly, midyear, and annual estimates and projections of the population for broad age, sex, and racial/ethnic groups; and series P-60 reports income and poverty data.

The Bureau of Labor Statistics and the Women's Bureau of the Department of Labor produce periodic special reports, short bulletins, and handbooks on women workers of all age groups. The Women's Bureau, in particular, has an archive listing references to books and other government publications and special collections on women in U.S. libraries.

The Social Security Administration publishes special reports on women, usually in the *Social Security Bulletin*. Its annual statistical supplement reports current poverty thresholds and benefit data on Old Age and Survivor Insurance (OASI), disability, Medicare, Medicaid, Supplemental Security Income, energy assistance, black lung disease, and public assistance.

Other government agencies issuing reports and testifying in behalf of the elderly include the Federal Council on Aging (created in 1973), the National Institute on Aging (1974), the Pension Benefit Guaranty Corporation (1974), the U.S. Commission on Civil Rights (which works in the area of age discrimination), and, in Congress, the Senate Special Committee on Aging and the House Select Committee on Aging. The latter has published a particularly valuable document of hearings before the Task Force on Social Security and Women of the Subcommittee on Retirement Income and Employment titled *Treatment of Women Under Social Security*. The four-volume transcript of the hearings spans the 1979–1981 period and includes a valuable set of statistics and statements from public and private groups in behalf of older women.

The National Retired Teachers Association and American Association of Retired People (NRTA/AARP) publishes fact sheets, journals, and guidelines for retirees and widows. The National Senior Citizens Law Center has case histories and reports on legal issues, including pension problems affecting older women. Other voluntary and service organizations active in testifying before Congress in behalf of older women and in disseminating information to women include the National Organization of Women, Women's Equity Action League, Federation of Business and Professional Women's Clubs, National Action Forum for Older Women, Women's Pension Project of the Pension Rights Center, Older Women's League, and the national network of Displaced Homemaker's Centers. Most libraries maintain directories of women's organizations, leaders, and locations in their reference sections.

REFERENCES

Atchley, R.C. Selected social and psychological differences between men and women in later life. *Journal of Gerontology*, 1976, *31*, 204–211.

―――. Issues in retirement research. *Gerontologist*, 1979, *19*, 44–54.

―――. The process of retirement: Comparing men and women. In M. Szinovacz (Ed.), *Women's retirement*, vol. 6, Sage Yearbooks in Women's Policy Studies. Sage, Beverly Hills, 1982, 153–168.

Block, M.R.; Davidson, J.L.; Grambs, J.D.; and Serock, K.E. *Uncharted territory: Issues and concerns of women over forty*. Center on Aging, University of Maryland, College Park, Md., 1978.

Faris, June B. (Ed.). Special issue of *Aging* on the black elderly. Administration on Aging, National Clearinghouse on Aging. USGPO, Washington, D.C., 1978.

Foner, A., and Schwab, K. *Aging and retirement*. Brooks/Cole, Monterey, Calif., 1981.

Grad, S., and Foster, K. *Income of the population 55 and older, 1976*. Social Security Administration, Staff Paper no. 35, USGPO, Washington, D.C., 1979.

Henretta, J.C., and O'Rand, A.M. Labor force participation of older married women. *Social Security Bulletin*, 1980, *43*, 10–16.

―――. Conjugal role structure and joint retirement. *Social Forces*, 1983, *63*, 504–520.

Jaffe, A.J., and Ridley, J.C. The extent of lifetime employment of women in the United States. *Industrial Gerontology*, 1976, *3*, 25–36.

Kolodrubetz, W.W., and Landay, D.M. Coverage and vesting of full-time employees under private retirement plans. *Social Security Bulletin*, 1973, *36*, 20–36.

Lingg, B. Women Social Security beneficiaries age 62 and older, 1960–79. *Research and Statistics Notes*, no. 8, Social Security Administration, Washington, D.C., July 21, 1980.

Lopata, H. *Women as widows*. Schenkman, Cambridge, Mass., 1979.

Lowenthal, M.F.; Thurnkev, M.; and Chiriboga, D. *Four stages of life: A comparative study of women and men facing transition*. Jossey-Bass, San Francisco, 1975.

McEaddy, B.J. Women in the labor force: The later years. *Monthly Labor Review*, 1975, *98*, 17–24.

Masnick, G., and Bane, M.J. *The nation's families: 1960–1990*. Joint Center for Urban Studies of MIT and Harvard University, Cambridge, Mass., 1980.

Neugarten, B. (Ed.). *Middle age and aging*. University of Chicago Press, Chicago, 1968.

―――. Personality and aging. In J.E. Biner and K.W. Schail (Eds.), *Handbook of the psychology of aging*. Van Nostrand Reinhold, New York, 1977.

Oppenheimer, V.K. *The female labor force in the United States: Demographic and economic factors governing its growth and changing composition*. Population Monograph Series, no. 5., University of California, Berkeley, 1970.

O'Rand, A.M. The determinants of retirement among older women. Final Report of Grant 02136 to the National Institute of Aging, Washington, D.C., 1982a.

———. Socioeconomic status and poverty. In D. Mangen and W.L. Peterson (Eds.), *Handbook of research instruments in gerontology*, vol. 2. University of Minnesota Press, Minneapolis, 1982b.

———. Loss of work role and subjective health assessment in later life among men and unmarried women. In A.C. Kerckhoff (Ed.), *Research in the sociology of education and socialization*, vol. 5. JAI Press, San Francisco, 1983.

O'Rand, A.M., and Henretta, J.C. Delayed work careers, industrial pension structure and early retirement among unmarried women. *American Sociological Review*, 1982a, *47*, 365–373.

———. Mid-life work history and retirement income. In M. Szinovacz (Ed.), *Women's Retirement*, vol. 6, Sage Yearbooks in Women's Policy Studies. Sage, Beverly Hills, 1982b.

Orshansky, M. Prepared statement before the House Select Committee on Aging. *Poverty among America's aged*. Hearing before the Select Committee on Aging, USGPO, Washington, D.C., 1978.

Ross, H., and Sawhill, I. *Time of transition: The growth of families headed by women*. Urban Institute, Washington, D.C., 1975.

Rossi, A.S. Life-span theories and women's lives. *Signs*, 1980, *6*, 4–35.

Schaie, K.W., and Parham, I.A. Stability of adult personality: Fact or fable? *Journal of Personality and Social Psychology*, 1976, *36*, 261–273.

Schorr, A.L. ''. . .Thy father and thy mother'': A second look at filial responsibility and family policy. Social Security Administration Publication 13-11953, USGPO, Washington, D.C., July 1980.

Schulz, J.H.; Leavitt, T.D.; Kelly, L. Private pensions fall short of preretirement income levels. *Monthly Labor Review*, 1979, *102*, 28–32.

Schwab, K., and Irelan, L.M. The Social Security Administration's retirement history study. In N.G. McCluskey and E.F. Borgatta (Eds.), *Aging and retirement: Prospects, planning and policy*. Sage, Beverly Hills, 1981, 15–29.

Shanas, E. Older people and their families: The new pioneers. *Journal of Marriage and the Family*, 1980, *42*, 9–15.

Social Security Administration. Annual statistical supplement, 1981. *Social Security Bulletin*, 1982, *45*.

———. Report of the National Commission on Social Security Reform. *Social Security Bulletin*, 1983, *46*, 3–28.

Soldo, B.J. America's elderly in the 1980's. *Population Bulletin*, 1980, *35*, 3–42.

Trager, N. (Ed.). *No longer young: The older woman in America*. Institute of Gerontology, University of Michigan-Wayne State University, Ann Arbor, 1975.

Treas, J. Women's employment and its implications for the economic status of the elderly of the future. In J. March, S. Keisler, V. Oppenheimer, and J.N. Morgan (Eds.), *The elderly of the future*. Academic Press, New York, 1980.

Uhlenberg, Peter. Cohort variations in the family life cycle experiences of U.S. females. *Journal of Marriage and the Family*, 1974, *36*, 284–294.

———. Older women: The growing challenge to design constructive roles. *Gerontologist*, 1979, *19*, 236–241.

U.S. Bureau of the Census. *Historical statistics of the United States, colonial times to 1970*. House document 93-78 (Part 1). USGPO, Washington, D.C., 1975.

———. Projections of the population of the United States: 1977 to 2050. *Current Population Reports*, ser. P-25, no. 704. USGPO, Washington, D.C., July 1977.

———. Characteristics of the population below the poverty level: 1977. *Current Population Reports*, ser. P-60, no. 119. USGPO, Washington, D.C., May 1979a.

———. The social and economic status of the black population in the United States: An historical view, 1790–1978. *Current Population Reports, Special Studies*, ser. P-23, no. 80. USGPO, Washington, D.C., June 1979b.

———. Social and economic characteristics of the older population. *Current Population Reports, Special Studies*, ser. P-23, no. 85. USGPO, Washington, D.C., August 1979c.

———. Estimates of the population of the United States, by age, race, and sex: 1976 to 1979. *Current Population Reports*, ser. P-25, no. 870. USGPO, Washington, D.C., January 1980a.

———. Marital status and living arrangements, March 1979. *Current Population Reports*, ser. P-20, no. 349. USGPO, Washington, D.C., March 1980b.

U.S. Department of Health and Human Services. Women and national health insurance: Where do we go from here? Report of the Secretary's Advisory Committee on the Rights and Responsibilities of Women. USGPO, Washington, D.C., 1980.

———. Changes in mortality among the elderly: U.S., 1940–1978. *Analytical Studies*, ser. 3, no. 22. PHS Pub. No. 82-1406. National Center for Health Statistics, Hyattsville, Md., March 1982.

U.S. Department of Labor. Women and private pension plans. Speech delivered by Helene A. Benson. USGPO, Washington, D.C., 1980a.

———. Perspectives on women: A databook. Bulletin 2080. Bureau of Labor Statistics. USGPO, Washington, D.C., 1980b.

Verbrugge, L. Females and illness: Recent trends in sex differences in the U.S. *Journal of Health and Social Behavior*, 1976, *17*, 387–403.

———. Female illness rates and illness behavior: Testing hypotheses about sex differences in health. *Women and Health*, 1979, *4*, 57–78.

Von Mering, O., and O'Rand, A.M. Aging, illness and the organization of health care: A sociocultural perspective. In C.L. Fry (Ed.), *Dimensions: Aging, culture and health*. Praeger, New York, 1981, 255–270.

PART II

RELIGIOUS GROUPS

9

CATHOLICS

CHARLES J. FAHEY
MARY ANN LEWIS

According to the latest national survey of the aged, 25 percent of persons over 65 are Catholics (Harris, 1981). This represents about 6,750,000 persons. According to the annual survey of the National Conference of Catholic Charities (1981), 565,000 elderly persons received services through its constituent agencies during that year. In 1981 there were 425,241 deaths of Catholics, most of whom were elderly (Official Catholic Directory, 1982).

These statistics show that the Catholic elderly are a major segment of the aged in the United States. Whatever affects the general aging population affects the Catholic aged, and any significant influence on aging among Catholics is likely to impact the general status of older Americans.

HISTORICAL PERSPECTIVE

While there were relatively few Catholics in the original thirteen colonies, they did exercise considerable leadership in the colony of Maryland. John Carroll of Carrolltown was one of the original signers of the Declaration of Independence. Students of the Revolution arc familiar with such Catholic figures as Lafayette, Pulaski, and Kosciuszko, who came from Europe to assist in the war against England.

In the early post-Revolutionary period, Catholics were found only in Maryland, Pennsylvania, New York, and Kentucky in any significant numbers. However, today's United States is more than the thirteen original colonies. Explorers and missionaries from France and Spain left their mark on our geography. A list of the oldest American cities reads like a litany. St. Augustine, Corpus Christi, San Antonio, Santa Fe, Los Angeles, San Francisco, St. Louis, and Sault Ste. Marie give evidence of their zeal and far-flung expeditions. It was not until the middle of the nineteenth century that millions of immigrants from Germany, Italy, France, and Ireland contributed to a rapid growth in the size of the Church.

It was during this period that many Catholic institutions were founded. George-town, founded in 1789, was joined by Boston College, Fordham, Villanova, Holy Cross, and a host of other colleges and universities. Today they number 237. It was also a time when many Catholic hospitals, homes for the aged, and orphanages were established, as well as numerous beneficial societies organized to address the cultural, economic, educational, and social needs of various immigrant groups. Most important, it was a period of growth in the number of parishes.

The "immigrant" period of the Catholic Church did not end with the advent of the twentieth century. Successive waves of political refugees from Hungary and Cuba have been joined by thousands of Southeast Asians, many of whom are Catholic. During the latter part of the twentieth century, millions of persons of Hispanic and often Catholic background have come from Mexico, Central America, and South America to seek a better life. Additionally, many have moved from Puerto Rico to the mainland. Today, a third of those identifying themselves as Catholic are of Hispanic background; of these, many cling to their cultural and linguistic roots.

SPECIAL PROBLEMS

Since Catholics represent such a significant part of the aged population in virtually every sector of our country, they share the opportunities and vulnerabilities of the general population. However, there are a number of elements that set Catholic elderly more or less apart from their fellow citizens, at least for purposes of analysis.

Vatican II and the events surrounding it have proved to be of enormous significance to the life of the Catholic Church worldwide. The Church in the United States is no exception. Even eighteen years after the final session of that gathering, its influence is still being felt. Older persons, in general, seem to have reacted well to the changes that came with the Council, although how comfortable they are with them seems to be in direct proportion to the amount of instruction they have received concerning the rationale for the various reforms. For some, however, modifications in liturgical practice and the general approach to spirituality have been seen as an impoverishment and greeted with anger and frustration.

Catholic congregations include many older persons. Changes in religious practice and decreased participation among the young and middle aged have exacerbated the trend occasioned by the decreased mortality in older age cohorts. The Church is graying faster than the population as a whole. Current trends in religious orders of men and women and the priesthood represent a special challenge to the Church. There is a disproportionately large number of older persons in these religious structures. The challenge is twofold: how does the Church minister to a growing congregation with fewer full-time personnel, and how will the Church respond to the needs of a large number of retired priests and sisters?

According to a study conducted by the Leadership Conferences of Men and Women Religious (1982), the median age of those in religious orders in the United States was 59 in 1982. There had been a rise of a year in this median age each of the previous three years. No reversal of this trend is in sight. Both the economics and the service implications of such a reality are severe.

A somewhat similar situation prevails in regard to diocesan priests. Though there has been no comparable study as to the exact age of such clergy, it is clear that this group is also aging without adequate replacement in younger cohorts. While this increase in the number of aged priests is somewhat less complicated since these priests work and live in a given geographic area (a diocese), the situation becomes more complex in that each diocesan priest has a responsibility for himself economically and socially in retirement.

Until the early 1970s priests and bishops retired only in instances of frailty. Today, in accord with the papal mandate contained in *Christus Dominus*, bishops must retire at 75. Each diocese sets its own rules about its priests. The prevailing practice is to have mandatory retirement at 75 and optional retirement at 70.

AGING AND CATHOLIC THEOLOGICAL TRADITION

While gerontologists are inclined to stress the positive aspects of the "third age," it is marked by a number of losses (Fahey, 1982). Loss of physical capacity, whether mild or severe, is nonetheless inevitable: it may be accompanied by memory and intellectual dysfunction, loss of loved ones, poverty, and greater social vulnerability. Death is the ultimate and greatest loss.

The Catholic Church has a pastoral approach that deals with these negative realities, placing them in a conceptual context of creation, sin, incarnation, redemption and resurrection. In addition to a theology that assists one in dealing with these difficult realities, there are a number of instrumental aids to help the individual cope with them. They range from a calendar that emphasizes the theme of redemption and eternal life, to sacramental and liturgical events that "celebrate" the victory of the individual over realities that might otherwise prove overwhelming.

The Church teaches that one's role or status is quite immaterial in the long-range view. It attaches value to a human being on the basis of humanness rather than on achievement, and provides its congregant with the opportunity to continue to participate in Church life on an intergenerational basis, offering substantial opportunity for service within its structures. It forwards a concept of "blessedness," which is rooted in love of neighbor and service to society. This is epitomized in the Beatitudes of the Sermon on the Mount.

Even death itself is faced continually in liturgy and viewed as a beginning rather than an end. Those facing death are afforded various forms of help and those who survive are offered a number of institutionalized ways of grieving and being supported by the Church.

Catholic theological tradition and ecclesial practice emphasize the necessity of good works for salvation. Similarly, they stress the concepts of justice and charity (Curran, 1982). In recent years, there has been growing concern about the moral and ethical implications of various aspects of society, whether they be culturally transmitted and sanctioned values or statutes, regulations, and public policy in general.

While there has been dispute about the meaning of the phrase "the Kingdom of God"—whether it be an internal reality alone or one involving the external world, or whether it refers only to the future or also to the here and now—there has been a rather consistent view that it is an ideal to strive for here and now by working for justice and peace, as well as a status to be achieved in the afterlife.

The Catholic social teaching emphasizes the necessity of caring not only for family members but also for strangers, not only through informal action, but also through public policy. The so-called welfare state finds a comfortable environment in Catholic social teaching.

The parish structure is an important societal vehicle both for congregants and, to an increasing degree, for neighborhoods as well. From an organizational perspective, the entire United States is covered by parishes. In turn, each parish is part of a diocese. Each parish and each diocese have similar characteristics, though they all have unique marks as well. These structures offer a means of nationwide communication and influence that is significant.

Parishes are conceptualized as "communities" to which people contribute and from which they draw. They are places of belonging on an intergenerational, age-irrelevant basis. The theology of the parish calls for it to be a community of faith in which people pray and learn together even as they meet one another's needs. To persons whose social relationships and identity may have become tenuous, such a place of belonging is an important asset. Particularly since Vatican II, the roles and functions in the Church open to lay persons have multiplied substantially. Virtually all of these are open to older persons and, indeed, are being filled by them.

In addition to this parish approach to aging, the Church has a number of extraparochial institutions and agencies to provide services and programs for older persons, particularly for those who are frail. These cover virtually all of the familiar ways society has developed to assist people in need of help. Generally such services are open to the whole community, not just to the Catholic population alone.

Catholic parishes play a major role in community organizations at the grass-roots level and have become much more deeply committed since Vatican II in ecumenical and interfaith efforts. There is a commitment, quite generally observed, to providing pastoral services to the homebound as well as to those in nursing homes and hospitals.

One of the most interesting and promising developments in the last decade has been the "parish outreach" program. The National Conference of Catholic Charities has encouraged its local constituents to put their professional skills to work in the parish structures. While there is a variety of models, most are geared to enhancing the parish's commitment and skill in humanitarian (i.e., service to individuals) and developmental (i.e., changing social structures) realms. In both areas elderly persons and their concerns have been a major focus. More than seventy dioceses have adopted this approach.

CHURCH STRUCTURE

The Catholic Church, hierarchical in nature, is simply but intensely organized. The basic Church unit is the parish. Each has a pastor (or, in some instances, co-pastors). Most parishes consist of people in a given geographical area. In a few instances, people of an ethnic group constitute a parish without regard to their place of residence.

A group of contiguous parishes constitutes a diocese headed by a bishop. These structures, as well as other external activities and elements of the Catholic Church, are prescribed by the Code of Canon Law. Its latest edition was promulgated in the spring of 1983. The diocese is the ultimate structure of the Church and it is joined with other dioceses by the unifying office of the Pope.

Since Vatican II, episcopal conferences (known in this country as the United States Catholic Conference and the National Conference of Catholic Bishops) have developed throughout the world. These represent the dioceses of a given country and function in regard to internal Church matters as well as in those areas where the Church interacts with society as a whole. The United States Catholic Conference generally attends to social affairs, both domestic and international, while the National Conference of Bishops deals with internal Church matters such as the sacramental and liturgical practice.

In recent years the United States Catholic Conference has become committed to aging matters through its Committee on Justice and Peace as well as through its Office of Domestic Affairs. The bishops issued a statement on aging, *Society and the Aged: Toward Reconciliation* (1976). The United States Catholic Conference played a major role in developing an organized Catholic presence at the 1981 White House Conference on Aging, at both local and national levels.

In addition to these official bodies, there are several voluntary national organizations that have significance to the field of aging. The National Conference of Catholic Charities (NCCC) represents the local Catholic Charities agencies, which are found in every part of the country. These agencies generally are rooted in a diocese, though some individual agencies are sponsored by religious orders. The National Conference of Catholic Charities serves as a means of communication, education, representation, and advocacy for its constituents. In 1963, occasioned by the 1961 White House Conference on Aging, the NCCC established a Commission on Aging, which is a rallying point for Catholic social service provided in the field of aging.

The Catholic Health Association is a national association representative of the many health institutions under Catholic auspices in the United States. Headquartered in St. Louis, it serves its constituents in a manner analogous to that of the NCCC. It has a council devoting itself to long-term care matters.

A major difference in Catholic health agencies, as contrasted with social services, is that most are sponsored by religious orders rather than dioceses. Religious orders are an important part of Church life, not only for those who are members, but also for society as a whole, since they provide so many health and social services to the community. Up until the 1960s religious communities focused their attention and efforts almost exclusively on corporate, institutional efforts such as hospitals, homes for the aged, schools, and residences. In more recent days, they have tended to shift their focus somewhat to more individualized activities. Religious men and women are to be found in a variety of traditional and nontraditional service and social action activities in every field, including that of the aging.

While most religious orders continue in service roles, others have chosen to become concerned with the structures of society and the movements and activities that influence them. Increasingly, religious communities have turned to using their corporate resources, both material and moral, for the service of those most vulnerable in society. For example, many religious communities are utilizing their property and other assets to house older persons.

Non-age-specific Catholic national organizations have begun to recognize aging as an issue and have identified it as an agenda item. The Knights of Columbus, the Daughters of Isabella, and the National Council of Catholic Women have initiated activities in the field of aging. Their efforts are of two categories: those that involve services to their own members (e.g., insurance and education programs) and those that involve the broader community (e.g., support of training programs to assist the frail elderly).

The Catholic community has extensive print media which serve it. Virtually every diocese has a newspaper. These are assisted by two national news services, one distinctively Catholic and the other more ecumenical in nature. Several national weeklies (*Our Sunday Visitor, National Catholic Reporter, National Catholic Register, The Wanderer*) and monthlies (*America, Thought*) appeal to people of all educational levels and political perspectives.

There is one Catholic organization that attempts to serve Catholics on an age-specific basis, the "Catholic Golden Age" movement. It has a monthly magazine and offers its members a variety of goods and services. It is analogous to the American Association of Retired Persons.

SERVICES

A wide variety of services is provided by the Catholic Church through various sponsorships for the elderly. These sponsorships include the local parish and the local diocese. In 1980, there were 18,829 parishes within 171 dioceses in the United States (*Official Catholic Directory*, 1981). While data on parish activities have not been computed, the National Conference of Catholic Charities (1981)

Table 9.1
Services to the Aging

Category	Number of Dioceses Responding	Percentage of Total Dioceses Responding	Number of Persons Served
Counseling	79	65.3	66,314
Foster Family Care	6	4.9	603
Group Home Care	10	8.3	1,049
Institutional Care	42	34.7	20,596
Homemaker Services	37	30.6	16,805
Day Care	19	15.7	31,721
Socialization Activities	56	46.3	242,063
Access Services	73	60.3	171,250
Emergency Shelter	17	14.0	2,147
Emergency Assistance	54	44.6	22,261

Source: National Conference of Catholic Charities Annual Survey, 1981, National Conference of Catholic Charities, Washington, D.C., 1982, p. 20.

disclosed that, of member organizations who responded to its 1980 annual survey, 109 dioceses reported that they provided services to 419,799 elderly persons. This figure represents 18.1 percent of all persons who received some type of assistance during that year. Table 9.1 gives the distribution of the services provided to the elderly.

The elderly are also served through the Catholic Health Association as well as through national volunteer organizations such as the National Council of Catholic Women and the St. Vincent De Paul Society. Additionally, congregations of religious men and women continue to serve the elderly through their institutions and social service agencies.

Under Church sponsorship, four types of housing are available to the elderly. There are over 5,000 apartment units for the elderly which provide optional dining services; adult foster care homes; over 6,000 beds in personal care facilities; and 446 nursing homes providing skilled and intermediate nursing care, with approximately 70,000 beds (United States Catholic Conference, 1983).

RESEARCH ISSUES

A number of Catholic research issues present themselves. Virtually any national research questions will perforce involve Catholics, and to a large extent the converse is valid as well. There are some issues specifically involving Catholics that should be addressed. They include the structure of the Catholic Church; value questions from a Catholic theological perspective; and issues concerning priests and religious.

The Catholic structure, particularly its parishes, dioceses, and national organizations, constitutes an important reality in the life of older Catholics. How these bodies serve the needs of older persons and how they might do so more effectively are matters of great importance. Fordham University's Third Age Center, with the support of the Robert Wood Johnson Foundation, currently is looking at one facet of this mosaic, that is, how these groups work together to assist the informal support systems of frail people. However, there are a number of other aspects of these same systems which should be analyzed as well.

The aging phenomenon of late twentieth century America is so massive as to constitute a new social reality. Ethical underpinnings of social relationships that served individuals, families, social structures, and public policy in the past are inadequate to deal with today's realities, to say nothing of tomorrow's.

The role of the family in a multigenerational society, the responsibility of an individual for his/her future with the reasonable expectancy of a prolonged life, the role of government in the lives of older persons, the extent and manner of intergenerational transfers both in private and public sectors are but a few of the issues that require analysis not only by economists, political scientists, and clinicians, but by ethicists and moralists as well.

Many issues arise out of the graying of full-time religious personnel. Addressing these matters is important to religious communities and to the Church in general, but also to the broad society since so many facets of the aging process of religious persons differ from those of their secular counterparts. Their single status, differing retirement pattern, rootedness in community, and religious values are of interest and may give clues as to how all might grow old more gracefully.

It should be noted that many research questions center around ethnic groups, as well as new and old migrants. Many of these persons and the cultures of which they are a part are closely connected with the Catholic Church. The special problems encountered by the aging members of ethnic groups constitute important social issues.

OTHER SOURCES OF INFORMATION

Catholic universities have been no quicker than their secular counterparts to address aging issues. In the past ten years, programs, activities, research projects, and individual scholars have begun to arise in such places as Georgetown, Catholic University, Notre Dame, St. Louis, Loyola of Chicago, and Fordham. The United States Catholic Conference, the National Conference of Catholic Charities, and the Catholic Health Association each has an identifiable structure or office to deal with aging issues. However, none has yet developed a primary leadership role, nor can a central resource for Catholic aging questions be identified.

EPILOGUE

An overview of Catholic elderly would be incomplete without a recognition of the importance of various societal events upon the Catholic effort in the field of aging. While the record of religious communities of men and women is illustrious in serving frail and vulnerable people, and while, for many, support has been given through the parish structure, a more deliberative, thoughtful, and concerted effort in this field has begun only recently. The sheer weight of numbers has been the single most significant factor in this movement, but there are other critical elements in this equation as well.

On the occasion of each of the White House Conferences on Aging, an ad hoc national group was established to assure the presence of a Catholic voice. In each instance the Catholic voice also became a Catholic "ear." Those who were organized to provide input were moved to organize the Church itself to be more effective in the field of aging. Out of each process the aging question has become more visible and the Catholic network and commitment more viable.

Similarly, in preparation for the 1982 World Assembly on Aging, the Holy See's mission to the United Nations undertook leadership to assure Catholic participation in that event. Opera Pia was founded to encourage Church efforts with the active aging. It convened Church leadership from throughout the world, with special emphasis on Third World countries. Regional meetings were held in Manila, Nairobi, Bogata, Castelgandalfo, and Toronto. In each instance, the agenda was designed to increase the Church's efforts in the field of aging. Both at the Vienna preliminary meetings of the nongovernmental organizations in March 1982 and at the World Assembly on Aging (United Nations, 1982) held in July and August of the same year, this Vatican/Opera Pia presence made important contributions to the documentation and to the Plan of Action itself.

The most significant aspect of this process was the increased involvement of the regional Bishop's Conference and the Vatican itself in aging issues. The opening session of the World Assembly offered the occasion for the most extensive papal message on aging in the history of the Catholic Church. The Catholic Church, like other churches, exists in and is influenced by society even as it influences it. On a variety of levels it is involved in the aging reality. As deep as that involvement is today, it is likely to increase in the future.

REFERENCES

Curran, Charles E. *American Catholic social ethics: Twentieth century approaches.* University of Notre Dame Press, Notre Dame, Ind., 1982.

Fahey, C.J. The Church and the third age. *America Magazine*, July 31, 1982.

Harris, L. *Aging in the eighties.* National Council on the Aging, Washington, D.C., 1981.

National Conference of Catholic Charities annual survey, 1981. National Conference of Catholic Charities, Washington, D.C., 1982.

National Conference of Catholic Charities Annual Survey—1980. National Conference of Catholic Charities, Washington, D.C., 1981.

The Official Catholic Directory. P.J. Kennedy and Sons, New York, 1981, 1982.

Society and the aged: Toward reconciliation. United States Catholic Conference, Washington, D.C., 1976.

Survey of retirement concerns of religious institutes in the United States. National Task Force on Religious Retirement Cases, National Conference of Catholic Bishops, Leadership Conference of Women Religious, Conference of Major Superiors of Men, Washington, D.C., March 1982.

United States Catholic Conference. Review of activities on behalf of the elderly within the Catholic Church in the United States, Washington, D.C., 1983.

World plan of action. United Nations World Assembly on Aging, Vienna, July 26–August 6, 1982.

10

JEWS

EVA KAHANA
BOAZ KAHANA

The focus of this chapter is on the background, characteristics, and life-styles of the Jewish elderly in the United States. Data will be presented on distinctive characteristics of these elderly as well as on commonalities that they share with other urban elderly and with elderly members of other ethnic groups who are also distinguished by immigrant status. The Jewish elderly comprise a growing proportion of the Jewish community. They currently represent 12.5 percent of the total Jewish population, which is about 2 percent greater than the proportion of aged in the general U.S. population. With increasing proportions of the very old, concerns for support and services to this group also merit attention.

Jews have been considered in sociological literature to constitute a religio-ethnic group (Gelfand and Olsen, 1979), denoting the fact that religion plays a highly significant role in the social organization of the everyday lives of members. In this sense ethnic Jews share similarities with ethnic Mormons but have been distinguished from other ethnic groups defined largely by national origin or language and only secondarily by religion (Watson, 1982).

Ethnic ascriptions classify a person in terms of his or her basic, most general identity as determined by his or her origin and background (Henry, 1976). Markers of ethnicity have been cited to include both shared symbols and ideologies as well as overt signs such as language or dress, and religious and voluntary organizations (Henry, 1976). Within this framework Jews are said to share a cultural style characterized by common religion, nationhood, and messianic hope (Katz, 1975). Furthermore, Jews also conform to Gordon's (1967) definition that ethnic groups are characterized by a shared feeling of peoplehood.

Rose (1965) has argued that a subculture among a segment of society is most likely to develop when members interact with each other significantly more often than they interact with persons in other categories. Research has shown that the Jewish elderly are most likely to form friendships and associations within their own ethnic group. Cohen (1982) found that 76 percent of Jewish aged report most of their friends to be Jewish. Such an identity as a subculture is further underscored when older persons have developed distinctive life-styles which contribute to a sense of group identity and consciousness. Myerhoff's (1980) studies of Los Angeles area Jewish elderly have stressed the salience of such a special group identity to the Jewish elderly.

Ethnic aged typically reside in large urban centers and comprise a significant segment of the elderly in urban areas. Often they also represent a disadvantaged group especially in need of services (Birren, 1969). Thus, research with urban aged is, almost by definition, research with minority group members. Whereas the aged in general have been identified as a minority that has been discriminated against and that holds a disadvantaged position in U.S. society, aged persons who are members of distinct ethnic groups have been considered to be minorities within minorities (Holzberg, 1982). The Jewish elderly may be legitimately considered as a minority within a minority, not only because they represent a distinct religio-ethnic group but also because many of these aged migrated to the U.S. to escape persecutions in their native lands. The vast majority of Jews emigrated from Europe to leave behind continued persecution or its threat and to free themselves of social constraints on their occupational and social mobility (Watson, 1982).

While other ethnic groups have shared "push-pull" migration factors, Jews faced considerable discrimination even after arrival in the United States in terms of jobs, housing, and educational opportunities, and were typically excluded from prevailing health and welfare supports of the larger society. They had to overcome prejudices in order to establish themselves in U.S. society and needed to institute special services to meet health and caretaking needs of elderly or disabled members of their ethnic group (Gelfand and Olsen, 1979).

JEWISH TRADITION AND IDENTIFICATION

The threat of Nazism and its materialization in the holocaust cast a lasting shadow on the lives of elderly and even middle-aged Jews in the 1980s. The vast majority have felt the personal threat of extinction as a people. For these elderly, personal survival is very closely tied in with the survival of the Jewish people.

To insure such a survival most of the Jewish elderly, regardless of personal level of religious practice, tend to venerate Jewish customs, culture, and traditions. They worry about assimilation of the younger generation, which is seen as a very direct threat to Jewish survival. They support and hold a strong belief in the state of Israel as the ultimate factor in insuring the continued existence of the Jewish people (Cohen, 1982).

Having undergone many actual or symbolic displacements and uprootings in their lives, the first-generation Jewish elderly in the United States seek to insure a sense of connectedness and continuity with their people through maintaining and affirming their common Jewish heritage (Myerhoff and Simic, 1978).

It cannot be assumed that every elderly Jew has a profound knowledge of the Jewish culture. Some rejected their Jewish identification, for varied reasons, after they arrived in the United States. However, anti-semitism, discrimination, and Hitlerism, counterbalanced by the revival of the Jewish state, contributed to their cultural re-identification. It is interesting to note that despite dire predictions of total assimilation and a general loss of interest in Jewish tradition among both younger and elderly Jews (Berger, 1966), there has been a general reawakening of interest in Jewish tradition and culture. This growing interest has paralleled the general revival of pride and interest in ethnic traditions that has been observed in the United States.

Generational differences in Jewish identification have frequently been suggested, indicating that elderly Jews are likely to be most identified with religious and ethnic tradition. Data from a national survey (Cohen, 1982) indicate, however, that in fact members of the middle generation (age 40–59) are more likely to observe traditional Jewish practices than are members of the oldest generation (i.e., those over age 60). The major decline in observance of traditions and Jewish identification appears between the middle and young generations. These data suggest that the elderly Jews of tomorrow are not likely to be significantly less identified with Judaism than are today's elders in spite of their greater level of acculturation to U.S. society.

SOURCES OF INFORMATION AND ORGANIZATION

The material presented in this chapter comes from diverse sources and is not limited to the published gerontological literature. Review of information on the Jewish aged presented some special challenges because of the paucity of published empirical data pertinent to life-styles and characteristics of the Jewish elderly. Paradoxically, a great deal of research focusing on older adults in the United States is based on studies of predominantly Jewish elderly. In part, this tendency has been due to the desire of Jewish service organizations to permit or sponsor social research. Research centers have been functioning in numerous Jewish-sponsored long-term care facilities, such as the Philadelphia Center, the Hebrew Rehabilitation Center (Roslindale, Massachusetts), and the Home for the Aged and Infirm Hebrews (New York City).

In view of the prevalence of gerontological research about the Jewish elderly, it is especially surprising that, typically, little or no reference is made to factors of ethnicity in reports of this work. One finds a close analogy here with the gerontological literature based on "incidentally female populations," which nevertheless provides little data on special characteristics, concerns, and problems of older women (Kahana and Kahana, 1983).

Sources of the published materials that provide information about elderly Jews include studies of intergenerational relationships and of the Jewish family, and studies in medical sociology and anthropology. The authors also refer to data from two of their own recent studies of Jewish elderly (Kahana and Kiyah, 1976; E. Kahana and B. Kahana, 1979).

Another important source of data comes from population surveys sponsored by various Jewish communities and welfare federations. Data on service programs and supports have also been located mostly within proceedings of conferences for Jewish communal organizations. We must note that the data obtained through these sources may be of variable quality. Furthermore, comparisons among diverse Jewish population surveys are difficult to make because of differences in timing of the surveys, instruments used, and classification schemes such as age breakdowns.

In order to describe the cultural and historical context for understanding values and life-styles of the U.S. elderly of today, a brief review of Jewish traditions regarding the aged will be presented, followed by a historical overview of Jewish aged in the U.S. today. Past and present characteristics of the elderly within the Jewish family are complemented by projections of future trends which are likely to influence social situations of tomorrow's Jewish elderly. Information is reviewed regarding diversity within the Jewish elderly population. Lastly, the authors focus on both community and institutional supports designed to serve the needs of the Jewish elderly.

RELIGIOUS AND HISTORICAL PERSPECTIVES

The Bible establishes the basic values portrayed in Judaism in relation to the aged. The aged were to be revered because they represent life's fulfillment and the wisdom of experience. Reverence for the old derives from one of the Ten Commandments, "Honor thy father and mother."[1] The term "elders" appears throughout the Bible and the Talmud (the code of Judaic-Babylonian law) to designate judges, sages, and leaders. Disrespect for the aged is said to be indicative of a corrupt generation. Respect for age was expressed in the directive "Thou shalt rise before the hoary head and honor the face of the old man." Accordingly, one should not sit in the seat of an old person, speak before he has spoken, or contradict him (Duckat, 1953). Despite the respect for the aged denoted in the Bible and the Talmud, old age is also described as a period of decline and frailty. "Upon the old man you make your yoke very heavy," or "He has shown no favor to the elders."

Values reflecting the importance of caring for older persons are also emphasized in the Old Testament. Concern with care of the aged is exemplified in the passage "Forsake not your parents in their old age." Nevertheless, specific directives regarding societal obligations to help the old do not appear in Jewish worship until the Middle Ages (Roth, 1972). Visits to the sick represent an important and commonly practiced form of Jewish charity or benevolence.

Community attention to special needs of the elderly was first stressed during the persecutions of Jews during the Middle Ages, when the family was no longer able to care sufficiently for the destitute elderly. In the seventeenth century the

Jewish community of Rome introduced the care of the aged as one of the divisions of its charitable activities. The first Jewish home for the aged on record was founded in Amsterdam in 1749. A special society for support of the aged was established in Hamburg in 1796, providing weekly assistance. The strong tradition for venerating and assisting the elderly serves as an important backdrop for understanding both the high levels of informal support and the extensive networks of formal support that have developed within the U.S. Jewish community to assist the elderly.

Historical Perspectives on Older Jews in the United States

In order to understand the special characteristics, life-styles, and attitudes of Jews that impact on their experiences as elderly persons and their treatment of the old, a brief overview of the history and background of the group is necessary.

The elderly Jews of today's United States have their historical roots in the Shtetl (small town) of Eastern Europe. The vast majority of Jews arriving in the United States with the immigration waves of the late nineteenth and early twentieth century shared a common life-style with the Shtetl in Central Europe. Here they lived in an essentially agrarian society and shared some characteristics with gentile peasant migrants. For the most part, however, Jews were segregated through discriminatory policies and practices into self-contained ghettos where they had relatively little interaction with other groups and were excluded from participation in the activities and governance of the broader community (Zborowsky and Herzog, 1952). Because of discrimination against Jews they were relegated to jobs unwanted by other segments of society and were frequently subjected to pogroms, that is, acts of violence and persecution. Because of restrictions on land ownership there were few status differentials among inhabitants of the Shtetl. Most lived their lives in poverty as marginal members of the larger society.

It has been suggested (Kutzik, 1967) that stratification in the Shtetl of Europe was based on factors such as engagement in philanthropic activities. Another important determinant of status was religious learning or scholarship (Howe, 1976).

Waves of Migration

Consideration of waves and patterns of migration is helpful for recognizing the great diversity of Jewish elderly in the United States. The successive waves of migration brought with them entrants from vastly different cultural backgrounds, languages, and ethnic traditions. The Jewish immigrants who arrived in the United States through the major waves of immigration in the late nineteenth and early twentieth century represent a majority of today's Jewish older adults.

The background of U.S. Jews must be viewed in the context of continuous immigration to the United States from early colonial times. There were about

25,000 Jews in the United States by 1880. The vast majority of elderly U.S. Jews arrived with the waves of immigration since the 1880s, and hence those elderly living today have a very high probability of being first-generation Americans. Between 1882 and 1924 Jewish immigration to the United States increased dramatically, yielding a Jewish population of 4.2 million by the end of that period. Restrictive quotas on U.S. immigration severely curtailed entry by Jews after 1924. There were some important small waves of immigration during the immediate pre–World War II period, primarily composed of German Jews escaping persecution. Only after the dramatic extinction of the Jews of Europe during the holocaust did the United States once again open its doors in 1944 to survivors of the holocaust. The Jewish population in the United States in 1977 was estimated to be 5.8 million (Goren, 1980). This represents a decline from 3.7 percent in 1937 to 2.7 percent in 1977.

There is historical evidence of close intergenerational family ties during the early periods in U.S. Jewish history. Thus, tombstones dating from this period indicate the typical inclusion of the elderly in the family plot. Many businesses were established as family businesses where the elderly could play important contributory roles. Many Jewish business establishments included the term "sons" in the name of the company, attesting to the intergenerational nature of the enterprise (Lederman, 1970).

Immigrant Background

Acculturation of Jews arriving with the succeeding waves of migration occurred at a different pace. Several factors entered into patterns of adjustment to life in the United States. The disparity between life in the United States and the country from which migrants originated played an important role. Thus, Jews from Germany and other Western European countries, who were largely middle-class, adjusted relatively quickly to the pace of life in the United States and continued to assume middle-class life-styles. Eastern European Jews who followed in the later waves of immigration had far greater barriers of life-style and social class to overcome. Many continued to live in or near poverty in sectarian communities, working as unskilled laborers or small tradesmen in largely immigrant neighborhoods. They frequently continued speaking Yiddish and associated only with others from within their own ethnic group (Myerhoff and Simic, 1978).

There are some special circumstances that must be considered in order to understand the elderly Jews of today who came to the United States as immigrants. Most of these immigrants left their own parents and grandparents behind in Europe when they arrived to the United States as children. Those who came as young adults frequently immigrated alone, parting from both their parents and grandparents. Many never resolved their guilt or conflict over "abandoning" their elders. For some the guilt was further punctuated by the great tragedy of the holocaust, wherein members of their family of orientation who had remained in Europe perished.

As Jews were transported from the world of the Shtetl in Europe to life in New York City, there were drastic alterations in life-style. There was a loosening of traditions, and changes occurred both in the structure and functioning of the Jewish family. Many Jews were quick to adopt the appearance and outlook of Americans and quickly shed their old-country attire, religious practices, and attitudes. Traditional respect for elders was bound to suffer in this environment. Elderly Jews had little training and few skills seen as functional by younger family members. They attempted to transmit values and attitudes, but in a specific sense their knowledge had become obsolete (Howe, 1976). Nevertheless, in spite of erosion in the role of elderly family members, the Jewish family continued to be close in comparison to other ethnic groups in the United States.

In the Jewish family women traditionally shared with men the task of supporting the family. In the Shtetl of Europe it was usual for women to combine the management of both a business and a home to enable the husband to devote most of his energies to the study of the Talmud. After immigration to the United States it was far less common for men to engage full-time in religious scholarship. Nevertheless, the expectation that women would assist in earning a livelihood for the family persisted. A much higher proportion of elderly Jewish women than women of other ethnic groups were gainfully employed after marriage (Krause, 1978). Among immigrant Jewish families there was far greater equality between husbands and wives than that prevailing in other ethnic immigrant families (Gordon, 1959).

Acculturation

Several factors have facilitated acculturation of Jews in U.S. society. Work has been found to facilitate mingling of diverse ethnic groups, learning of language, and acquiring customs of the new society (Krause, 1978). The great value placed on educational attainments within the Jewish culture also facilitated acculturation and upward mobility of younger members of Jewish families. The upward mobility of immigrant groups, and Jews in particular, through education has been axiomatic in U.S. society (Howe, 1976). It is noteworthy that in an ongoing project by the authors focusing on elderly survivors of the holocaust (Kahana, Kahana, and Harel, 1983), 82 percent of adult children of elderly survivors were found to be professionals. Yet the parents arrived in the United States after World War II with extremely limited financial and educational resources. Service in the army by many Jews during World War II also facilitated integration into U.S. society.

Even though individual members of the Jewish community increasingly acculturated to life in the United States, the Jewish community continued to serve as a focal point for services to the frail and elderly. The concept of sharing and community responsibility for needy Jews characterized Jewish settlements in the

United States from the early days. With increasing acculturation of immigrant families, needs for formal service delivery became more and more apparent.

The grandparents had a great deal of influence in early immigrant homes, keeping alive languages, religious practices, and customs brought from the Shtetl. After World War I many changes took place in the structure and composition of the immigrant family due to social and geographic mobility and changing values concomitant to acculturation. Older persons were often unable to live with children. In many instances they also opted for independent living. The extended family withered, being replaced by households that were increasingly nuclear in nature, with only parents and their young children living under one roof. The Social Security Act of 1935 and the development of pension plans also permitted sufficient economic independence for the elderly to live in their own homes. Although children continued to provide assistance to parents in times of crisis, older persons in need increasingly turned to community service organizations for more extended supports.

DEMOGRAPHIC CHARACTERISTICS OF ELDERLY JEWS IN THE UNITED STATES

The major source of information regarding the Jewish elderly at the present time is the National Jewish Population Study conducted in1970–1971 (Massarik and Chenkin, 1973). That study sought to provide data on a representative sample of the U.S. Jewish population. Data were obtained in every geographic region and from every community with a Jewish population of 30,000 or more. In addition, information was also obtained in proportional representation from medium-sized and small communities. A special outreach effort was also directed at Jews living in counties with very small Jewish populations. The survey included both Jews affiliated with the organized Jewish community and those considered unaffiliated or marginal Jews (Massarik and Chenkin, 1973). The limitations of this survey are the exclusion of institutionalized Jews and the fact that it is becoming increasingly dated.

More recent surveys of elderly Jews have been undertaken in numerous individual communities such as Seattle, Washington (Gortler, 1979); Little Rock, Arkansas (Krain, 1980); and Birmingham, Alabama (Katz et al., 1977). Of special interest is the Cleveland Jewish Community Survey of 1979 because it was conducted in a community that is fairly typical of urban centers within which the majority of today's U.S. aged reside.

Persons over the age of 65 comprised 11 percent of the national Jewish population in 1971, excluding those in institutions. Inclusion of the institutionalized aged was projected to yield a 12 percent figure.

Demographic analyses and projections indicate that the Jewish population in the United States is aging both in absolute and relative terms. Both the National Jewish Population Survey (Massarik and Chenkin, 1973) and the 1975 Gallup report, *Religion in America* (Johnson, 1976) furnish evidence that the average

age of the Jewish population today is higher than that of the general U.S. population. Thus, 43 percent of Jews are over age 50 versus 39 percent of general U.S. population. Furthermore, population statistics based on the youngest age cohorts point to a long-term acceleration of the aging trend within the U.S. Jewish population.

Demographic information currently available on the Jewish elderly suggests that they represent a higher proportion of the Jewish community than do elderly in the U.S. population as a whole (e.g., the Cleveland area Jewish aged surveyed in1980 comprise 14.3 percent of Jews, compared with 12.2 percent aged within the general Cleveland population). The Gallup Poll statistics also indicate Jews to be older than the rest of the population. The proportion of Jews over age 50 averaged eight percentage points higher than the rest of the population over five different age intervals. These age differentials are greater than those observed in the 1957 census or the 1971 National Jewish Population Survey.

The growing size of the elderly Jewish population is likely to lead to greater visibility as well as to increasing demands for services, especially by the oldest segment of the population, paralleling and even outpacing trends in the general U.S. population.

In the National Jewish Population Survey (Massarik and Chenken, 1973), women were found to exceed men (56 percent to 44 percent) in the 65 and over age group. These differences are based largely on the 65–79 age group, with the sex ratios being 50–50 in the 60–64 age group and 49 percent to 51 percent in favor of men in the 80 and over age groups. Of the family units headed by persons 65 years of age and older, 65 percent were found to be headed by men and 35 percent by women. This represents a great increase of households headed by women since 84 percent of all Jewish households are headed by men. Over 40 percent of households headed by persons over the age of 65 were single-person households. Only 7 percent of Jewish households were found to consist of three generations living together.

The percentage of foreign-born individuals was found to increase dramatically with each succeeding decade. Among those aged 65–69, 41 percent were foreign-born. The remainder in each age group was overwhelmingly first-generation. The percentage of those who were second- and third-generation ranged from 1 percent of the very oldest group to 3 percent in the 65–69 age category.

Dramatic differences in educational attainments were found between the 65 and older age group and the 50–64 age group. Thus, 71 percent of the older group (65 and over) did not go beyond high school compared to 48 percent in the 50–64 age group. Furthermore, twice as many individuals in the younger age category attained an undergraduate college degree or higher than in the older age grouping (50 percent versus 25 percent).

In terms of occupational characteristics among men, one-half of the 60–64 age group were managers or administrators, one-sixth were professional and technical workers, and one-eighth were sales workers. Among the 65–75 age group one-third were managers and administrators, with about one-fifth being professional-technical and sales workers. The majority of the women who had been gainfully employed were clerical workers.

Corresponding to secular changes between the young-old and old-old in terms of likelihood of being U.S.-born and in educational and occupational attainments, the young-old were also less likely to be members of a synagogue, observe Jewish dietary laws, or report their synagogue affiliation as Orthodox. There was one exception to this general trend, which was reflected in the lower rate of synagogue affiliation among the very old (70 and over) age group than among their younger cohorts. Fifty-one percent of those aged 60–69 belonged to a synagogue versus 33 percent of the 70 and older age group. This lack of affiliation, however, is not likely to be a reflection of lessened religiosity; rather, it is likely to be a result of the poorer economic situation and health among persons in the oldest age group (Kahana and Kiyah, 1976).

National statistics based on the 1971 study indicate that the elderly are the poorest segment of the U.S. Jewish population. Seventy-two percent of all Jewish households with incomes under $4,000 were headed by elderly persons. Furthermore, 44 percent of households headed by the elderly had incomes under $4,000. Data from three recent surveys of the Jewish community in Seattle (Gortler, 1979) indicate that when using figures adjusted for inflation there was no improvement in the proportion of elderly Jews whose incomes place them below the poverty level. It should be noted that in some smaller communities where Jewish population surveys have been conducted there appears to be less poverty among elderly Jews (Katz et al., 1977; Krain, 1980).

The 1980 Cleveland Survey represents a more in-depth approach to assessment of service needs and functional characteristics of elderly Jews; it utilized the Older Americans Resources and Services schedule (OARS) developed at Duke University. Since the OARS instrument has been utilized in several large-scale studies of U.S. elderly, this methodology permits, for the first time, a direct comparison between Jewish elderly and the aged in the general population (U.S. General Accounting Office, 1977).

The Cleveland Survey revealed an aged population of 14.3–15 percent in the Jewish community of about 80,000. The overall sex ratio in the Cleveland Survey was comparable to the figures obtained in the National Jewish Population Survey, with 55 percent of those sampled being female and 45 percent male. It is noteworthy that the 15 percent figure of elderly Jews for 1980 represents a 2.5 percent increase from the 1971 Jewish Population Survey.

Respondents of the Cleveland Population Survey were subdivided into three age groups, termed the Young-Old (age 65–69), the Old, (age 70–74), and the Aged (75 and older). Widowhood was the prevalent marital condition, with 60 percent of the Aged being widowed, compared to 24 percent for the Young-Old and 35 percent for the Old.

An individual's social network was shown to diminish with increasing age as portrayed by these three age groups. However, findings indicate that the stereotype of isolation and age applies only to a minority of older persons. Sources of help also change as one grows older. Within the Young-Old group the spouse was the chief helper, whereas in the Aged group the children were the chief source of help. Data also revealed a change in living arrangements, generally in the direction of home ownership to apartments as age increases. Age trends also reflected an increasing reliance on supports, that is, outside help in home management, with 30 percent of the Old-Old receiving outside help compared with only 11 percent of the Young-Old.

Consideration of independence in performing Activities of Daily Living (ADL) suggests that many older Jewish persons need help on a regular basis. Accordingly, 26 percent of the older Jewish population could not do housework without help; 14.8 percent could not shop without help; and 12 percent could not prepare their own meals without help.

In terms of social resources, marital status, contacts with friends and relatives, and availability of help during illness, 30 percent of the elderly were either moderately or severely impaired. In regard to economic resources, as indicated by past or present employment, value of dwelling, financial resources for emergencies, and medical insurance, 25 percent of the elderly were either severely or moderately impaired. Mental health, based on affect, judgment, ability to cope, and subjective appraisal of one's own mental health, was also substantially affected, with 20.9 percent of the elderly either severely or moderately impaired.

In examining the use of Jewish service agencies, it was found that the elderly make significant use of Jewish-sponsored community programs. The Jewish Community Center was the agency most widely utilized by respondents, followed by a Jewish-sponsored hospital.

Migration Patterns

The Jewish population of the United States has generally been concentrated in the Northeast. However, due to the absence of large-scale immigration and due to internal mobility, growing proportions now live in the South and West.

Goldstein (1982) analyzed migration patterns of Jews who were included in the 1971 population survey. He found that the highest mobility rates occurred among the older population. The greatest degree of lifetime international migration was observed in the 65 and older age group, with far less such movement found in younger age groups.

Although sex differences in mobility patterns of the general Jewish population were minimal, among the oldest age groups women portrayed far greater mobility than did men. Some of this mobility may be a function of relocation subsequent to widowhood. During the past five years, 2.8 percent of the elderly (men and women) moved internationally. Even larger proportions (9.5 percent of women and 5.9 percent of men) undertook interstate moves. Over one-third of widowed women age 65 and older undertook moves, with far fewer married women doing so. The married women tended to move within the same geographic region, while widows were more likely to make long-distance moves.

As younger members of the Jewish community continue their out-migration to the suburbs (Johnson, 1976), the less mobile elderly are increasingly left behind without cultural, commercial, or social services. Much of the long-distance migration by elderly Jews has been to Sun Belt locations, including southern Florida, Arizona, and southern California. This migration has led to the development of new, instantly aged Jewish communities.

The authors have recently completed a study of two unusual groups of Jewish elderly: those undertaking long-distance moves to Florida and to Israel. For some of the Jewish elderly such migration represents a continuation of a life-style of wandering. Thus, a significant proportion of those undertaking moves to Israel is comprised of elderly survivors of the holocaust who came to the United States subsequent to World War II. Florida-bound Jewish migrants are far more likely to be U.S.-born and generally have shown great residential stability throughout their lives (Kahana and Kahana, 1982). Consideration of adaptations of those adventurous elderly migrants provides some valuable insights into emerging life-styles among a segment of Jewish elderly and further underscores the diversity, ethnic identification, and values of this group.

An elderly person emigrating from the United States to Israel represents an interesting case study illustrating the search of some Jewish older persons for challenge and environmental change. The typical Israel-bound emigrant undertakes a move for ideological, if not idealistic, reasons. In contrast to retirees emigrating to Israel, the Florida-bound Jewish migrant is motivated less by ideological reasons and more by a desire to spend retirement years in a warm, tranquil environment. He or she wants to leave behind the heterogeneous milieu of city life and opts for an adult age-segregated environment.

There are some noteworthy similarities among elderly Jews who relocate to Israel and Florida. Risk-taking is a common feature of both these groups. They do not mind having to learn new behavior, adaptation, and life-styles. Both groups feel capable of emotionally investing themselves in their new environments and are willing to part with many of their lifelong neighbors and friends as well as family.

SHARED CHARACTERISTICS AND DIVERSITY AMONG JEWISH AGED

Even while focusing on the common cultural heritage, shared historical experiences, and demographic characteristics of elderly Jews, it is important to recognize that there are great intragroup differences among Jewish elderly. Generalizations about older Jews may enhance our understanding of this unique religio-ethnic group. Yet a closer examination of subethnic variation is necessary for a more accurate understanding of life-styles of older individuals or subgroups of elderly within the Jewish ethnic community.

Many foreign-born elderly never totally acculturated to life in the United States and continue to maintain marginal status. An in-depth anthropological study of immigrant Jews in the Los Angeles area supports this view (Myerhoff and Simic, 1978). In considering reminiscences or life review experiences of such aged it appeared that their patterns of migration have served to effectively cut them off from their childhood background. Such discontinuity is added to the gap between past and present experienced by all elderly due to the rapid cultural changes of the twentieth century (Cowgill and Holmes, 1972). Elderly respondents in Myerhoff and Simic's (1978) study frequently noted the cultural gap between themselves and their American-born children who became part of the mainstream culture. It has been suggested that such marginality may result in special emotional problems and even depression in late life (Linden, 1967). On the other hand, immigrant status has also been cited as resulting in enhanced social supports and integration (Weeks, 1981). In a study of leisure activities of elderly Jews, Guttmann (1973) found that Jews of immigrant background preferred leisure activities where they could express belongingness to the group, whereas American-born Jewish aged emphasized activities that expressed their individuality.

Religiosity and Denominational Differences

It has been argued that religiosity affects both the degree and type of adjustment that elderly Jews make to old age (Stambler, 1982). Recent sociological research has pointed to the importance of denominational preference, which influences value systems and interaction patterns of Jews (Lazerwitz and Harrison, 1979). Denominational preference is considered to be a particularly useful categorization because it simultaneously incorporates historical changes and value orientations.

Orthodox Jews comprise 11 percent of the U.S. Jewish population, Conservative Jews 42 percent, and Reform Jews 33 percent. Fourteen percent of adult Jews consider themselves to be unaffiliated. Orthodox Jews generally adhere to traditional religious practices and rituals and carry their value orientations over into all phases of their social lives. This includes dietary laws, Sabbath observance, daily prayers, and laws regarding family life. Conservative Jews accept modifications in religious practices based on their view of the demands of changing times, but generally value traditions even when they do not adhere to them in daily practice. Reform Judaism has emphasized an active effort to modernize and change the practices of traditional Judaism and emphasizes individual desires in choosing symbols of Jewish affiliation. Elderly Jews are found disproportionately in the more traditional branches of Judaism and are likely to adhere to tradition. Foreign-born Jews are also generally more traditional than their U.S.-born counterparts. Among third-generation Jews in the United States, 5 percent were found to be Orthodox, 28 percent Conservative, 40 percent Reform, and 27 percent unaffiliated (Lazerwitz and Harrison, 1979).

In a study of adjustment to old age by different religious groups, Orthodox Jews were found to portray more positive adjustment than non-religious Jews. Religious beliefs appeared to be positively related to good personal adjustment in old age. The role of faith and religion was especially positive in overcoming grief (Moberg, 1968).

Religiosity has been conceptualized as a multidimensional phenomenon in a study of religiosity among Jewish respondents representing different generational groups (Liebowitz, 1973). Interviews were conducted with 312 heads of households in an urban Jewish community. Findings revealed qualitative as well as quantitative differences in the direction of decreased religious identification on the part of younger generations.

In a study of religious practices among 6,911 adults in the Detroit area, Orbach (1961) found that Jewish males showed increased synagogue attendance with age. No similar increases were found for any other religious groups, with the exception of black Protestant males. Historical trends that have resulted in fewer Orthodox Jews among younger than older cohorts may be likely to contribute to these findings.

Urban Residence

The Jewish elderly live in predominantly urban areas, and consequently are subject to the stresses and problems of urban living faced by elderly of diverse ethnic groups. These special concerns include fear of crime, poor city services in inner-city areas, and out-migration of younger family members (Kahana, 1975). Service delivery to the Jewish elderly also reflects the special concerns and characteristics of urban services to the aged. Thus, staff recruitment and turnover represent special problems in institutional services (Kiyak and Kahana, 1978). Because of moves by younger members of the Jewish community to suburban areas, the locus of Jewish services is also typically moved to suburban Jewish population centers. The elderly are often left in central city areas that offer only minimal community services. Social contacts with members of the younger generation and informal social supports are also diminished for these elderly. Concern with neighborhood problems and fear of crime have been found to constitute an important concern and a source of uneasiness for urban elderly Jews even when they do not reside in high-crime areas (Kahana et al., 1977). A study of 115 elderly Jewish residents (Lawton and Cohen, 1974) in a high-crime, predominantly black slum in Philadelphia underscored the vulnerability of ethnic elderly in relation to the environment.

Occupation

Elderly Jews have been more likely than other ethnic elderly to be found in middle and upper occupational strata occupying managerial and professional roles. Retirement is hence likely to bring to this group greater relative status deprivation than that experienced by persons of working-class background. As the proportion of U.S.-born elderly is increasing with each successive cohort of older persons, the educational and former occupational status of the elderly is also expected to rise, further accentuating these trends.

It has been argued (Forman, 1979) that Max Weber's "work ethic" is deeply embedded in Jewish tradition. Due to Jewish social consciousness, work is an underlying drive based on the feeling of obligation to show the way to a better world. Strong endorsement of the work ethic is likely to lead to problems in retirement adjustment and to a devaluation of leisure versus work activities. Specific studies focusing on retirement adaptation of elderly Jews have not been located in the literature.

Results of a study of Jewish respondents of a Florida retirement community (Kahana et al., 1980) indicate high levels of involvement in volunteering, with about 40 percent of respondents being actively involved as volunteers. Social participation in clubs or formal organizations was also extensive for this group, with 61 percent reporting such involvement.

HEALTH AND MENTAL HEALTH: CHARACTERISTICS AND SERVICE UTILIZATION

A review of the incidence and prevalence of psychiatric and emotional disorders among Jews compared with other ethnic groups was conducted by Sanua (1981). Based on analyses of hospital admissions for mental disorders in New York State, the author found Jews to have low rates of psychoses of organic origin, alcoholism, and psychoses or disorders of advanced age. In contrast, Jews showed consistently higher rates than other religious-ethnic groups for manic-depressive psychoses and psychoneuroses. Jews were also found to be disproportionately treated in private hospitals as compared to state mental hospitals and also on an outpatient basis.

In a study of depression, Bart (1970) found rates of depression to be unusually high among middle-aged Jewish women in comparison to both black and white non-Jewish women of similar age. Rates of suicide in general are also lower among Jews than among the general U.S. population.

Rates of alcoholism and drug addiction have been found to be generally low in the Jewish population. Based on these data one would expect lower incidence of Korsakoff psychosis among the aged Jewish population. Studies suggest that ethnic identification and family cohesiveness are major factors responsible for lower addiction rates, since both of these factors were found to be largely absent among those Jews who were substance abusers.

Several studies from the field of medical sociology shed light on Jewish ethnic attitudes toward illness and help-seeking. Jewish patients are more likely than other ethnic groups to report health symptoms and to make use of medical facilities (Greenbaum, 1974). These findings would suggest that Jewish elderly should demonstrate high utilization of medical services. This expectation has been confirmed in a comparative study of Jewish and Polish elderly conducted by Kahana (1975).

The Aged in the Jewish Family

Sociological studies of Jewish families have not focused specifically on elderly family members. Nevertheless, they provide some of the most systematic data currently available on Jews in the United States and allow us to make inferences about intergenerational relations within the Jewish family.

Family solidarity has long been considered an important distinguishing feature of Jewish families (Farber et al., 1981). Religious tradition, coupled with historical factors including persecution and discrimination, has contributed to the traditional closeness of the Jewish family. Several empirical studies have lent support to this view (Landis, 1960; Winch et al., 1967). The Jewish approach to kinship has traditionally emphasized the importance of the extended family. Accordingly, Farber (1981) has found that among different religious groups in Arizona, Jews had the greatest contact with members of their extended family. Thus, 65 percent of Jews reported frequent contact with mothers-in-law compared with 35 percent of Catholics. Among different groups considered, adult Jews were found to maintain the most frequent contact with parents (90 percent having at least weekly contact), while those adhering to no religion had the least parental contact (50 percent). Jewish respondents in this study were also found to portray the closest bonds with their grandparents. One implication of greater familism is likely to be increased willingness to support elderly parents requiring assistance. In fact, a study by Wake and Sporakowski (1972) indicated that adult Jewish children were more willing to provide support to aged parents than were members of other religious groups.

Grandparenthood

Grandchildren provide opportunities to the older generation for a new and potentially important social role (B. Kahana and E. Kahana, 1979). This social role has special problems as well as special significance for the immigrant elderly, and in particular for the Jewish aged. Grandchildren may afford the aged a fulfillment of their own continuity and provide grandparents with opportunities to tell family history. The role of grandparents in Jewish life has also been one of the key factors in maintaining tradition and continuity of the family. Intergenerational influences tend to slow down the rate of change and introduce more stability, in families as well as in society.

In a series of case histories about Jewish grandmothers, Kramer and Masur (1976) note that because of the unusual and often dramatic life experiences of this generation of older Jewish women, they are little understood by their children or grandchildren and often share little in common with them.

In a study (Kahana and Coe, 1969) comparing Jewish grandparents living in a nonprofit home for the aged and Jewish grandparents living in the community, findings indicated significantly more frequent and more intense interaction with grandchildren for community than for institutionalized grandparents. Grandparenthood was evaluated as having great importance or salience by 79 percent of the community sample and 31 percent of the institutionalized aged. For the Jewish older person whose grandchildren have rejected some of the religious and ethnic values held dear by the older generation, grandparenting may present disappointment and a sense of discontinuity.

Recent Trends in Jewish Family Life

Several converging trends in Jewish family life in the United States are likely to have important implications for the status, roles, and support available to Jewish elderly. In recent decades, however, there have also been marked increases in Jewish divorce rates to the point where divorce rates for young Jewish couples approximate those in U.S. society at large (Gelfand and Olsen, 1979). Lower fertility among Jews is also likely to translate to a reduction in available social support from children for Jewish elderly when compared with their Catholic and Protestant counterparts.

Intermarriage has been far less common among older Jews than among younger Jews. Accordingly, 7 percent of all (ever married) Jewish couples had been intermarried; the rate of intermarriage was 14 percent among the under 35 age group. Older Jews whose children are intermarried may find less support for their own adherence to traditional life-styles or services. Furthermore, typically negative reactions by Jewish parents to intermarriage by their children are likely to translate into more limited, informal supports as they become more frail and in need of services.

The elderly Jewish person expects a great deal of support, attention, and care from children in accordance with the Jewish tradition of reverence for one's elders. When such care and regard are not forthcoming a great deal of relative deprivation is experienced.

Service Supports for the Jewish Elderly

Social processes that have resulted in a reduction in the availability of informal service supports for the U.S. elderly in general have also affected the Jewish community. Jewish agencies have responded to increasing needs and demands for services by the elderly segment of the population by diverse and innovative service programs. Many of these have been developed with assistance from federal programs, and programs have expanded beyond the traditional services offered through Jewish homes for the aged, family services, and community centers. This expansion came about both through diversification of program offerings by traditional service agencies and by involvement of additional agencies in the provision of services to the elderly.

Expansion of service programs for the elderly has resulted in some conflicts as lines of demarcation between agencies blur and as innovative programming may lead to interagency competition. Coordination of efforts among agencies has been the most difficult aspect of the development of services for older adults (Harel and Harel, 1978).

The community center has traditionally been an important locus of activity for American Jews in general and older adults in particular. Much of the involvement of elderly persons in community and senior centers has been in the form of contributory roles and active participation. More recently, senior center programs have also begun to serve the frail elderly.

The Jewish elderly have been found to affiliate with and participate extensively in Jewish communal organizations. Accordingly, close to 40 percent (more than three times the national average) report organizational memberships. The Jewish elderly also frequently serve as agency volunteers, assisting others primarily through Jewish communal agencies and organizations (Guttmann, 1979). These findings have been corroborated in a number of other investigations (Kahana, 1975; Bley, Goodman, Dye and Roth, 1972). Jewish elderly have been found to place a high value on helping and contributory roles (Midlarsky and Kahana, 1981). When joining senior centers for the first time, volunteer activities hold greatest attraction for elderly Jews (Bley et al., 1972).

A role of the Jewish senior center in the care of the impaired and even dying elderly has been recently advocated (Kaplan, 1982). Jewish community center summer camps have initiated programs to offer summer recreational experiences both to community and institutionalized older persons (Shapero, 1975). As the proportion of the very old is anticipated to increase in the future, one may also expect that programs of this type will be increasingly required to serve the growing segment of the vulnerable old-old population.

The synagogue is increasingly becoming an organization serving the older segments of the Jewish population (Schaalman, 1976). In some instances this new mission has been overtly and wholeheartedly endorsed, with the synagogue becoming a central community center and resource for the elderly (Balter, 1976). The far-reaching role of synagogues in serving Jewish elderly is also exemplified in synagogue-sponsored construction and management of apartment buildings for the elderly (Hersch, 1970).

Synagogue-based services allow for integration of ethnic and cultural symbols in program development. The impact of the ethnic reality on the life of the elderly Jew may be readily overlooked in a nonsectarian setting that has no commitment to Jewishness (Devore and Schlesing, 1981). Accordingly, in a survey of attitudes of ethnic aged toward service supports (Guttmann, 1979), 66 percent of all respondents (including Jews) preferred to have ethnic staff providing services.

Institutionalization and Elderly Jews

Institutionalization represents an unsettling life transition for older persons of all persuasions. For the Jewish elderly the process may be seen as especially traumatic because of the frequent belief that this life situation exemplifies the unwillingness of children to fulfill their responsibility of caring for their elders.

Institutionalization of an aged parent has been found to be a particularly important source of family strife and conflict within the Jewish family (Baum, Hyman, and Michel, 1976).

Wolk and Reingold (1975) in a study of institutionalized elderly Jews found that degree of acculturation was significantly related to adaptation in the institution. Their findings revealed that passive modes of coping with institutional life disproportionately characterized older immigrants who were least acculturated (e.g., not naturalized U.S. citizens). These passive elderly were at highest risk for deterioration and mortality subsequent to the first year of institutional living. Religious observance may represent a critical source of continuity into late life that is particularly important for older persons living in institutional facilities (Linzer, 1968). The absence of Jewish symbols is likely to further exacerbate the sense of isolation, loss, and alienation felt by many institutionalized older persons.

An anthropological analysis of life-styles of Jewish elderly of Sephardic origin living in an institutional setting has been provided by Hendel-Sebestyen (1979). In this study, role loss concomitant to aging and to institutionalization has been related to the acculturation of the Sephardic older Jew.

This study exemplifies the important role of ethnicity and the strength of the social norms of a minority culture which can, under some circumstances, dramatically alter the experiences of aged persons even in institutional settings. Cultural continuity thus can serve to protect the elderly from the normlessness and valuelessness of late life.

Institutional Care of the Jewish Aged

A portrayal of the administrative structure and functioning of institutional facilities under the sponsorship of Jewish organizations is provided by Shore (1982). The survey was conducted of 109 facilities with a 75 percent response rate. This number surpasses that reported in 1976, when there were 70 Jewish homes for the aged with 12,500 beds, serving 16,000 residents. The facilities ranged in size from 23 beds to 1,334 beds, with the majority having between 100 and 300 beds, but with 10 facilities having over 400 beds. Approximately 70 percent provide multiple levels of care. Two homes are licensed to operate a respite program and one home has a hospice program pending. The vast majority of these homes are filled to capacity (in excess of 80 percent are 96–100 percent full). Eligibility restrictions for would-be residents are age and geographic residence. These data indicate that the trend has also been away from homes for the aged catering to relatively well older persons to more medically oriented institutions. This change is due largely to the more advanced age and frail nature of current residents of homes for the aged.

Jewish-sponsored institutional facilities have been in the forefront of innovative program development in residential facilities for the elderly. It is not uncommon for such facilities to pioneer new treatment modalities, being willing to accept an element of risk which goes along with organizational innovation. A recent review of innovative programs in Jewish-sponsored congregate facilities was presented at the 1982 meeting of the Association of Jewish Homes for the Aged.

TRENDS FOR THE FUTURE

In projecting ahead to consider values, life-styles, and characteristics of the Jewish elderly of the future, complex demographic as well as cultural trends must be considered. Demographic information reviewed supports the notion of increasing assimilation of Jews and mobility patterns that are likely to further reduce interaction and mutual influences among generations. The great geographic mobility of Jewish families attests to the fact that the desire for independence, freedom, and economic advancement has become more highly prized than the preservation of close intergenerational ties (Heschel, 1974).

This diminished family cohesiveness has also been reflected in the greater tendency for elderly family members to migrate to the Sun Belt, away from children and grandchildren (E. Kahana and B. Kahana, 1979). The predisposition to migrate has been found to reflect a lack of "familism" (Winch et al., 1967). Furthermore, increasing demands for formal services, including institutional care, have been manifested within the Jewish community as families are less willing or able to provide informal support to frail elders (Harel and Harel, 1978).

Jewish families have been found to portray a great deal of diversity in lifestyles and orientation based on their degree of acculturation as represented by the number of generations they lived in the United States. Differences in values and orientations between Jewish elderly and elderly of other ethnic groups may be attenuated as second- and third-generation Jewish elderly become more integrated into American society. With elderly Jews of the future being more integrated into mainstream American culture and being better educated and more affluent than their counterparts decades earlier, one might anticipate a lessening of the importance of ethnic heritage. Such assimilation is likely to coincide with increased utilization of community-wide nonsectarian rather than ethnic-sponsored service programs.

Some researchers question the damage to kinship ties brought on by secular changes. Furthermore, there is evidence that at a time when many observers of the social scene lament the demise of the Jewish ethnic family, there appears to be a concomitant reawakening of interest in Jewish heritage and traditions (Selig-Kaufer, 1977).

In contrast to projections of diminishing Jewish identification by older persons of the next decades, data also point to a curious and tenacious maintenance of Jewish values by middle-aged Jews of today (Cohen, 1982). Accordingly, Jewish-sponsored community services are finding that utilization is growing rather than diminishing, and there appears to be a great upsurge of interest across Jewish communities in shared cultural symbols and history. The recent reawakening of interest in the holocaust and community-wide increases in support of Jewish day schools attest to this resurgence of ethnic identification within the Jewish community. Similarly, there is a return to tradition within Jewish denominations. Thus, while the proportion of Reform Jews is increasing, Reform temples are increasingly adopting more traditional rituals. Even Jewish-sponsored hospitals and chronic care institutions are willing to display more religious symbols and advocate observance of dietary laws and holidays (Shore, 1982).

The recent decline in federal support to services for the elderly and concomitant decentralization of service delivery are also likely to lead to increased private and sectarian initiative in provisions of service supports. Furthermore, one must be careful not to equate diminishing religious observance in successive generations of Jews with diminished ethnic and cultural identification. Thus, Myerhoff's (1980) study of ethnic Jews in Los Angeles underscored that even though many of the elderly Jews studied had never been religious even prior to immigrating to the United States, they all shared in venerating cultural and historical ties.

Social movements in the United States, including the emergence of black self-determination, have given impetus to pride and self-awareness among other minority groups, including the Jews (Shore, 1982). As descendents of families who were killed in the holocaust, most Jewish elderly symbolically identify as survivors. Continuity of their cultural tradition reinforces their comfort about their collective survival as a people.

A shared feeling of peoplehood thus becomes one of the most unique attributes of Jewish elderly. Findings of research on various aspects of life-styles and characteristics of this ethnic group have underscored noteworthy diversity. Yet in spite of religious, socioeconomic, and regional diversity, surprising commonalities in beliefs, value orientations, and identification are found, which further underscore the shared peoplehood of these elderly, forged through centuries of persecution and millennia of shared hopes for survival as a people.

NOTE

1. Specific Biblical citations for each of the passages noted here are provided in Roth (1972). They will be omitted in the text in order to facilitate clarity of presentation.

REFERENCES

Balter, S. The synogogue's service to the aged. *Sh'ma: A Journal of Jewish Responsibility*, 1976, *6*, 68–69.

Bart, P. Depression in middle aged women. *Transactions*, 1970, *8*, 69–74.

Baum, C.; Hyman, P.; and Michel, S. *The Jewish woman in America*. Dial Press, New York, 1976.

Berger, G. Cultural life of the aged Jew. *Journal of Jewish Communal Service*, 1966, *43*, 127–137.

Birren, J.E. The aged in cities. *Gerontologist*, 1969, *9*, 163–169.

Bley, N.; Goodman, M.; Dye, D.; and Roth, M. Senior adult group services: Are we hitting the mark? *Journal of Jewish Communal Service*, 1972, *49*, 150–156.

Cleveland Jewish Community Survey. *Older persons in the Cleveland Jewish community*, Report No. 1 of the Population Research Committee, Cleveland: Jewish Community Federation of Cleveland, June 1979.

Cohen, S.M. The American Jewish family today. *American Jewish Year Book*, 1982, *82*, 136–154.

Cowgill, D.O., and Holmes, L.D. (Eds.). *Aging and modernization*. Appleton-Century-Crofts, New York, 1972.

Devore, W., and Schlesing, E. *Ethnic sensitive social work practice*. Mosby, St. Louis, Mo., 1981.

Duckat, W. The attitude toward the aged in Rabbinic literature. *Jewish Social Service Quarterly*, 1953, *29*, 320–324.

Farber, B. *Conceptions of kinship*. Elsevier, New York, 1981.

Farber, B.; Mindel, C.H.; and Lazerwitz, B. The Jewish American family. In C.H. Mindel and R.W. Habenstein (Eds.), *Ethnic families in America: Patterns and variations*, 2nd ed. Elsevier, New York, 1981.

Forman, B. Attack on ageism: The Jewish stake in the work ethic. *Reconstructionist*, 1979, 17–23.

Gelfand, D.E., and Olsen, J. Aging in the Jewish family and the Mormon family. In D.E. Gelfand and A. Kutzik (Eds.), *Ethnicity and aging: Theory, research, and policy*. Springer, New York, 1979.

Goldstein, S. Population movement and redistribution among American Jews. *Jewish Journal of Sociology*, 1982, *14*, 4–23.

Gordon, A.I. *Jews in suburbia*. Beacon Press, Boston, 1959.

———. *The nature of conversion*. Beacon Press, Boston, 1967.

Goren, A.A. Jews. In S. Therstrom (Ed.), *Harvard encyclopedia of American ethnic groups*. Harvard University Press, Cambridge, Mass., 1980.

Gortler, J. The Jewish aged. Reprinted from *A study of the Jewish community in the greater Seattle area*. Jewish Community Federation of Seattle, Seattle, 1979.

Greenbaum, J. Medical and health orientations of American Jews, *Social Science and Medicine*, February 1974, *8*, 127–134.

Guttmann, D. Leisure-time activity interests of Jewish aged. *Gerontologist*, 1973, *13*, 219–223.

———. *Informal and formal support systems and their effect on the lives of the elderly in selected ethnic groups*. National Catholic School of Social Sciences, Catholic University of America, Washington, D.C., 1979.

Harel, Z., and Harel, B.B. Coordinated services for older adults in the Jewish community. *Journal of Jewish Communal Service*, 1978, *54*, 214–219.

Hendel-Sebestyen, G. Role diversity: Toward the development of community in a total institutional setting. *Anthropological Quarterly*, 1979, *52*, 19–28.

Henry, F. *Ethnicity in the Americas*. Mouton Publishers, Chicago, 1976.

Hersch, H. We are glad we are not young anymore. *The Jewish Digest*, 1970, *15*, 44–46.

Heschel, A.J. To grow in wisdom. In Union of American Hebrew Congregations, *Aging and retirement*. Union of American Hebrew Congregations, New York, 1974.

Holtzberg, C.S. Ethnicity and aging: Anthropological perspectives on more than just the minority elderly. *Gerontologist*, 1982, *22*, 249–257.

Howe, I. *World of our fathers*. Harcourt, Brace and Jovanovich, New York, 1976.

Isaacs, H. *American Jews in Israel*. John Day, New York, 1967.

Johnson, G.E. The aging of the Jewish community. *Sh'ma: A Journal of Jewish Responsibility*. 1976, *6*, 65–67.

Kahana, B., and Kahana, E. Grandparenthood from the perspective of the developing grandchild. *Developmental Psychology*, 1970, *3*, 98–105.

——. Changing roles of grandparents. Paper presented at the American Psychological Association Meetings, New York, 1979.

Kahana, B.; Kahana, E.; and Harel, Z. Perspectives on mental health of elderly survivors of the holocaust. Paper presented at Meetings of the Society for the Study of Social Problems, Detroit, August 1983.

Kahana, E., and Coe, R.M. Perceptions of grandparenthood by community and institutionalized aged. In *Proceedings of the 77th Annual Convention of the American Psychological Association*. Vol. 4. American Psychological Association, Washington, D.C., 1969.

Kahana, E., and Kahana, B. Voluntary relocation, adaptation and mental health of the aged. Progress report submitted to the National Institute for Mental Health, 1979.

——. Institutionalization of the aged woman: Bane or blessing? In M. Haug, M. Sheafor, and A. Ford (Eds.), *The physical and mental health of aged women*. Springer, New York, 1983.

——. Environmental continuity, discontinuity, futurity and adaptation of the aged. In G. Rowles and R. Ohta (Eds.), *Aging and milieu: Environmental perspectives on growing old*. Academic Press, New York, 1982.

Kahana, E.; Kahana, B.; Neale, V.; and Datwyler, M. Adaptive tasks, adaptive strategies and satisfaction following long distance moves. Paper presented at the 33rd Annual Scientific Meeting of the Gerontological Society, San Diego, Calif., November 1980.

Kahana, E., and Kiyah, A. Service needs of older women. In L. Troll and J. Israel (Eds.), *Looking ahead*. Prentice-Hall, Englewood Cliffs, N.J., 1976.

Kahana, E.; Liang, J.; Felton, B.; Fairchild, T.; and Harel, Z. Perspectives of aged on victimization, "ageism" and their problems in urban society. *Gerontologist*, 1977, *17*, 121–129.

Kaplan, F. The senior center and the dying. *Journal of Jewish Communal Services*. 1982, *58*, 123–132.

Katz, H.; Katz, L.; and Tropper, P. *The Jewish older population of Birmingham*. Jewish Community Center of Birmingham, Birmingham, Ala., 1977.

Katz, R.L. Jewish values and sociopsychological perspectives on aging. *Pastoral Psychology*, 1975, *24*, 135–150.

Kiyak, A., and Kahana, E. Development of an environmental preference scale for the elderly. Paper presented at the 11th International Congress of Gerontology, Tokyo, August 1978.

Krain, M.A. *To serve our seniors: A survey and needs assessment study of older Jewish populations of Little Rock, Arkansas*. Jewish Federation of Arkansas, Little Rock, 1980.

Kramer, S., and Masur, J. *Jewish grandmothers*. Beacon Press, New York, 1976.

Krause, C.A. *Grandmothers, mothers, daughters*. Institute on Pluralism and Group Identity, American Jewish Committee, New York, 1978.

Kutzik, A. The social basis of Jewish philanthropy. Ph.D. diss., Brandeis University, 1967.

Landis, J.T. Religiousness, family relationships, and family values in Protestant, Catholic and Jewish families. *Marriage and Family Living*, 1960, *22*, 341–347.

Lawton, M.P., and Cohen, J. Environment and well-being of elderly inner city residents. *Environmental Behavior*, 1974, *6*, 194–211.

Lazerwitz, B., and Harrison, M. American Jewish denominations: A social and religious profile. *American Sociological Review*, 1979, *44*, 656–666.

Lederman, S. The Jewish aged: Traditions and trends. In G.S. Rosenthal (Ed.), *The Jewish family in a changing world*. Thomas Yoseloff, New York, 1970.

Liebowitz, B. Age and religiosity in an urban ethnic community. *Gerontologist*, 1973, *13*, 65.

Linden, M. Emotional problems in aging. In N. Kuell (Ed.), *The psychodynamics of American Jewish life*. Twayne Publishers, New York, 1967.

Linzer, N. *The Jewish family*, Yeshiva University, New York, 1968.

Massarik, F., and Chenkin, A. United States' national Jewish population study: A first report. In *American Jewish Yearbook: 1973*, vol. 74, 264–306. Jewish Publication Society of America, Philadelphia, 1973.

Moberg, D.O. Religiosity in old age. In B. Neugarten (Ed.), *Middle age and aging*. University of Chicago Press, Chicago, 1968.

Myerhoff, B. Life history among the elderly: Performance, visibility and remembering. In K.W. Back (Ed.), *Life course: Integrative theories and exemplary populations*. American Association for the Advancement of Science Selected Symposium, No. 41. American Association for the Advancement of Science, Boulder, Colo., 1980.

Myerhoff, B.G., and Simic, A. (Eds.). *Life's career—Aging: Cultural variations in growing old*. Sage, Beverly Hills, 1978.

Orbach, H.L. Aging and religion: Church attendance in the Detroit metropolitan area. *Geriatrics*, 1961, *16*, 530–540.

Rose, A.M. The subculture of aging. In A.M. Rose and W.K. Petersen (Eds.), *Older people and their social world: The subculture of aging*. F.A. Davis, Philadelphia, 1965.

Roth, C. (Ed.). Age and the aged. *Encyclopedia Judaica*. Cater Publishing, Jerusalem, 1972.

Sanua, V. Psychopathology and social deviance among Jews. *Journal of Jewish Communal Service*, 1981, *58*, 1.

Schaalman, H. Serving the aging synagogue. *Sh'ma: A Journal of Jewish Responsibility*, 1976, *6*, 67–68.

Selig-Kaufer, M. A Jewish aging experience. *Dissertation Abstracts*, 1977, no. 16694.

Shapero, S.M. The vintage years. *Journal of Religion and Health*, 1975, *14*, 130–144.

Shore, H. *Directory of the North American Association of Jewish Homes and Housing for the Aging*. The Association, Dallas, 1982.

Stambler, M. Jewish ethnicity and aging. *Journal of Jewish Communal Service*, 1982, *58*, 336–342.

U.S. General Accounting Office. The well-being of older people in Cleveland, Ohio. USGPO, Washington, D.C., 1977.

Wake, S.B., and Sporakowski, M.J. An intergenerational comparison of attitudes toward the supporting of aged parents. *Journal of Marriage and the Family*, 1972, *34*, 42–48.

Watson, W.H. *Aging and social behavior: An introduction to social gerontology.* Wadsworth, Belmont, Calif., 1982.

Weeks, J. The role of family members and helping networks for older people. *Gerontologist*, 1981, *21*, 388–394.

Winch, R.F.; Greer, S.; and Blumberg, R.L. Ethnicity and extended familism in an upper middle-class suburb. *American Sociological Review*, 1967, *32*, 265–272.

Wolk, R.L., and Reingold, J. The course of life for old people. *Journal of the American Geriatrics Society*, 1975, *23*, 376–379.

Zborowski, M., and Herzog, E. *Life is with people: The culture of the Shtetl.* Schocken Books, New York, 1952.

11

PROTESTANTS

BARBARA P. PAYNE

Protestant churches' active concern about older people is not new. They have a long tradition of ministry to the aged, the widowed, and the sick. Protestants were facing the problems and challenge of the increase in the numbers of older persons twenty years before Congress enacted the Older Americans Act of 1965. The responses ranged from special programming to institutional care; from local church social action to denominational policy.

HISTORY

Among the earliest age-specific actions of Protestant churches was the establishment of homes for the aged. In 1939 a U.S. Department of Labor survey report listed 1,327 institutions for older people, of which 537 were church-sponsored. About two-thirds of the church homes (333) were Protestant (Lutheran, Methodist, Presbyterian, Episcopal). Although more numerous than the Jewish or Catholic homes, the Protestant homes were smaller. By 1954 the number of church homes had increased to 700 and was estimated to comprise 40 percent of the homes for the aged (Frakes, 1955:18–20; Maves, 1960; Maves and Cedarleaf, 1960).

Prior to the 1950s, church homes were about the only resource for poorer aged persons left alone, and there were long waiting lists. In response to this need, Protestant administrators initiated one of the early community care programs to serve older persons on a casework basis.

In 1948 the Federal Council of Churches of Christ (encompassing thirty-four Protestant and Eastern Orthodox groups) convened the first conference on church homes to address standards for operating homes and improving available facilities and services. This conference began a tradition of conferences and associations of church homes that is currently carried out through the American Association of Homes for the Aged and the Protestant Health and Welfare Assembly.

Although the number of church-sponsored homes continued to increase, the rapid growth of the for-profit homes (including nursing homes) beginning in the 1960s reduced the proportion of church-sponsored homes among U.S. institutions for the aged. Butler and Lewis (1977) estimated that religious institutions provide 44 percent of all nonprofit homes and 14 percent of all nursing homes.

Denominational Programs for Older People

Information about denominational and local church programming has always been difficult to obtain. No complete surveys or series of surveys provide basic information on the history of the various Protestant denominations and local church programs for older people. The major sources are the records and oral history of the many denominations; the research of Maves and Cedarleaf (1949); the journalistic survey of Protestant programs for the aged reported by Frakes (1955); Maves's study of "Aging, Religion and the Church" for the *Handbook of Social Gerontology* (1960); and the survey of programs under religious auspices by the National Interfaith Coalition (Cook, 1976).

Programming initiatives took place sometimes at the denominational (national) level, sometimes ecumenically with the Federal Council of Churches, and sometimes with government and other social agencies. Methodists, Presbyterians U.S.A., and Lutherans were early leaders in church programming for older members. A major development was the assignment of staff to be responsible for older adult work with members. In 1948 the Methodists gave high priority to aging and assigned the first national staff member to older adult work; others soon followed with either full-time staff or shared staff positions. Within ten years there were regional and state staff responsible for the development of older adult work in the local churches.

The National Lutheran Council was the first denomination to offer comprehensive consultation service in aging to help related agencies and local churches strengthen their programs, and to operate pilot centers for older people. In 1955 the American Lutheran Board for Christian Social Action adopted one of the first major denominational statements on church responsibility to the aged (Frakes, 1955:7–8).

Research

Maves and Cedarleaf (1949) conducted the first comprehensive study of the relationship of the Protestant churches to people over 60 years of age. Sponsored by the Federal Council of Churches and supported by a grant from the Arbuckle-Jameson Foundation of Pittsburgh and the Methodist Church, the two-year project (1946–1948) focused on group work and pastoral care in the local church and on an in-depth analysis of group work with older adults in thirteen local churches.

Other early research included Moberg's (1953–1965) studies of religiosity and adjustment to old age and the integration of older members in the congregation;

Orbach's (1961) analysis of data from the Detroit area project on age and faith; and Webber's (1954) study of Florida retirement communities documenting the early ecumenical Protestant services for migrant retirees.

Publications

Before 1965, church publications were the major means of informing the public and reporting research about aging. *Mature Years*, published by the Methodists (1954) and adopted by other denominations, was the first magazine for older people, predating the American Association of Retired Persons (AARP)'s *Modern Maturity*. Other early publications included pastoral aid books (Maves, 1951, 1954); special devotional materials (Emmons, 1953); Methodist, Presbyterian U.S.A., and Lutheran manuals and booklets for local church programming (Jacobs, 1957; Reisch, 1954; Stafford, 1953); and the *Christian Century*'s eight-article series on "Older People Confront the Church" (Frakes, 1955).

Training and Conferences

In 1955 the first National Conference on Churches and Social Welfare had a special section on the needs of an aging population. The denominations held national seminars and workshops to train ministers, state denominational staff, and lay members—including older lay members—to work with older people and to initiate special educational programs and services for older members in local churches. Many statewide and citywide interfaith conferences sponsored by Protestant councils of churches were held to stimulate interest in aging, share problems, and develop programs for the aged (Maves, 1960:716–717).

Local Church Programming

Historically, local Protestant churches assumed that their regular programming met the basic religious needs of older members. Prior to the 1960s churches were adapting their facilities to the special needs of older members by adding ramps, hearing aids, and so on, and by developing special programming. In a summary of existing information about these special programs for the 1960 *Handbook of Social Gerontology*, Maves listed (1) homebound programs; (2) Golden Age/Fellowship groups; (3) special education courses on aging; (4) transportation and home visitation programs; (5) utilization of church facilities for community programs on aging or for older people (pp. 721–723).

Many Protestant groups provided foster care placement of older people, homemaker services, and counseling (Johnson and Villaume, 1957:421–31). Some local church programs became national models for churches and community agencies in continuing education for older people, adult community centers, and day-care centers (Stough, 1965). The pre-1965 programs of the Protestant religious bodies were classic examples of programming developed by voluntary organizations becoming models for new government programs (Boorstin, 1973).

The period 1965–1980 was a relatively quiet one in the Protestant churches' response to aging. The churches cooperated with government and private agencies' programs and services for older people. Churches became sites for the Administration on Aging's congregate meal programs and provided volunteers for the meals on wheels programs. Many of the local chapters of the American Association of Retired Persons were located in local Protestant churches and supplemented church programming.

As an alternative to institutional care, the United Methodists in Kansas City, Missouri, developed an innovative ecumenical model of a local church program. In 1972 the Shepherd's Center was organized by older people and staff from twenty-one churches. They incorporated the experience and programs of churches and agencies over the past twenty years to attain their goal: to coordinate existing services and develop new services necessary to support older people in their own homes. Home-based and center-based programs and services were designed to maintain physical, social, and psychological functionality and to promote the personal growth of older persons. The center was operated and controlled by older people and based on volunteer services (Maves, 1982; Cole, 1981). The success of this venture received national attention from the media (e.g., the CBS documentary, "Volunteer to Live," 1977), gerontological organizations (National Council on the Aging [NCOA], AARP), and denominational leaders. The Mid-America Training Center was established with the cooperation of gerontologists at the University of Missouri, Kansas City, to respond to the national demand for information and training about the operation of Shepherd's Centers. Some forty Shepherd's Centers are operating throughout the United States, and the United Methodists have adopted the model as their non-institutional ministry to the elderly.

In the mid-1970s the denominations began to develop policy statements on aging, and the Presbyterian Church U.S.A. established a Center on Aging at the Presbyterian School of Christian Education. Protestant seminaries added curricula on aging; the National Interfaith Coalition provided an ecumenical organization to stimulate advocacy by the denominations and to prepare for participation in the White House Conferences of 1971 and 1981.

Cooperative Responses with Other Agencies

The Protestant sector participated in the first National Conference on Aging (1950) held by the U.S. Federal Security Agency and the first White House Conference on Aging (1960). Protestant leaders played an important role in the development of the policy statement on standards of care for older people in institutions for the National Welfare Assembly (1953, 1954).

The University of Florida's Institute of Gerontology devoted its eighth annual Southern Conference on Aging to "Organized Religion and the Older Person."

Protestant seminary faculty members delivered lectures and denominational leaders participated in this conference for church, government, private agency staff, and other professionals interested in aging. The published papers from the conference became major sources of information on churches and older people (Scudder, 1958). In 1965 the Administration on Aging (AOA) published case studies of four local Protestant church programs as examples of outstanding programs for the aged (Stough, 1965).

Increased interest and activity about aging is occurring among Protestants in the 1980s. Some examples are the Presbyterian Church U.S.A.'s continuation of the Panel Study on Ministry with Older Persons and their General Assembly's action setting 1983 as the "Year of the Older Person"; the Health and Welfare Division of the United Methodist Church's 1982 emphasis on the local churches' ministry with older persons; and plans by Episcopal churches for a Nationwide Teleconference on Ministry with the Elderly in the fall of 1983. These are but a few of the preparations Protestants are making at all levels of organization in response to the continued graying of their congregations.

CHARACTERISTICS

Demographic

Reliable social profiles of Protestant religious groups are difficult to obtain. The United States' constitutional provision for separation of church and state limits collection of data on religion by the government. Consequently, no data on religion have been collected by the Census Bureau since 1957. Information on all religious groups, including Protestants, comes from two principal sources: the denominations' annual reports, submitted to the National Council of Churches to be summarized in the *Yearbook of American and Canadian Churches*; and various public opinion polls, most of which do not have religion as a primary concern. The research organizations reporting data most frequently used by religious researchers are the Gallup Opinion Index (the American Institute of Public Opinion); the National Opinion Research Center (NORC); the Survey Research Center of the University of Michigan; and Louis Harris and Associates. Other sources are occasional research projects conducted by denominations. Social science researchers and gerontologists in particular rely more heavily on national opinion data than on the *Yearbook* or denominational studies. The data from the *Yearbook* must be used with caution, because church records are not always complete, usually pass through many hands, and go through many channels of church bureaucratic structure. Some churches, especially the smaller ones, do not keep records or do not report to the National Council of Churches. To compound the problem further, the definition of membership varies from denomination to denomination. Some Protestant groups count all baptized persons, including children, as members, but most include only "adults" 13 years of age and older as members (Jacquet, 1982:11). The most serious limitation for gerontologists is the omission of age distribution of the membership.

The national surveys use good sampling methods and maintain quality control over the interview process. But the size of the surveys are often too small for analysis of subgroups such as Protestants or specific denominations. The questions regularly asked by public opinion polls about religious preference do not tell us whether the respondent actually belongs to a church of his/her religious preference, nor do they allow for the variation within the main religious groups, such as Baptists, Methodists, Presbyterians, and so on.

The majority of older Americans are Protestants. Since 1957, the last year the U.S. Census Bureau reported age and religion (table 11.1), the proportion of older persons reported to be Protestant (70 percent) has remained remarkably constant. The 1975 Harris survey reported that 70 percent of those age 65 and over were Protestants, and the 1981 Gallup Poll reported that 66 percent of those 60 to 69 years of age and 71 percent of those 70 years of age and over were Protestants.

The pluralistic nature of American religion is particularly evident among Protestants. Most American denominations are Protestant: the 1982 *Yearbook* includes 218 religious bodies, of which 184 (84 percent) are Protestant. Unlike Catholic and Jewish bodies, Protestants are an internally pluralistic and autonomous collection of organizationally unrelated churches. The *Yearbook* reports 305,273 local Protestant churches with a membership of almost 73.5 million adults (Jacquet, 1982:242). The latest analysis of NORC data on the social characteristics of members of American religious groups found that the proportion of Protestant church members over 55 years of age ranged from 19 percent for Jehovah's Witnesses to 45 percent for Disciples (McKinney and Roof, 1982) (see table 11.2).

Among the Protestant members of all ages, there are more Baptists (19 percent) than Methodists (10 percent), Lutherans (6 percent), Presbyterians (4 percent), and Episcopalians (2 percent). On the basis of the NORC study, it can be estimated that the same rank order among denominations would hold for older members.

The NORC survey and the *Yearbook* data do not show the age composition of local churches. Some denominational leaders have informally reported urban churches with 50 to 90 percent of the membership over age 65. For example, in one metropolitan Atlanta neighborhood, the Baptist, United Presbyterian, and United Methodist churches are now mainly older adult churches. There are no systematic data on the numbers, denomination, and location of these older congregations, and no case studies have been done.

Gender

Most research reports more female than male Protestant members (Jacquet, 1962; "Religion," 1981). None of the national studies reported age, sex, and church preference. An exception was the Presbyterian Panel study of Ministry

Table 11.1
Religion Reported* by Age, United States, March 1957 (Percentage Distribution)

Religion	Total (Age 14 and over)	Ages 14-19	Ages 20-24	Ages 25-34	Ages 35-44	Ages 45-64	Ages 65 and over
Total	100.0	100.0	100.0	100.0	100.0	100.0	100.0
Protestant	66.2	66.8	65.0	64.8	64.5	66.6	70.0
White	57.4	56.2	54.3	55.1	55.8	58.7	63.7
Nonwhite	8.8	10.6	10.7	9.7	8.7	7.9	6.3
Roman Catholic	25.7	26.6	27.5	28.0	27.7	24.0	20.8
Jewish	3.2	2.5	2.4	2.8	3.2	4.0	3.4
Other Religion and Not Reported	2.2	2.0	2.1	1.8	2.1	2.5	2.8
No Religion	2.7	2.1	3.0	2.6	2.5	2.9	3.0

Source: U.S. Bureau of the Census, *Current Population Reports*, ser. P-20, no. 79, 1958, p. 7.
*In answer to the question: What is your religion?

Table 11.2
Protestant Church Membership by Age, 1980

	Sample N	Percentage Distribution by Age		
		18-34	*35-54*	*Over 55*
Total Sample	12,120			
Adventist	56	39	25	36
Assembly of God	72	31	38	31
Christian (Disciples)	117	30	26	45
Church of Christ	155	35	34	32
Church of God	88	33	35	32
Episcopal	322	29	34	37
Jehovah's Witness	66	52	29	19
Lutheran	962	31	34	34
Methodist	1,325	27	31	43
Nazarene	233	31	28	39
Northern Baptist	538	38	32	30
Northern Presbyterian	406	24	34	42
Other Evangelical	91	30	34	36
Other Pentecostal	233	44	32	24
Reformed	51	20	51	29
Southern Baptist	454	34	30	34
Southern Presbyterian	166	38	31	31
United Church of Christ	191	23	38	40
Black Protestant				
Methodist	259	32	30	37
Northern Baptist	362	40	32	28
Southern Baptist	454	36	30	34

Source: From *Yearbook of American and Canadian Churches, 1982*, edited by Constant H. Jacquet. Copyright © 1982 by The National Council of the Churches of Christ in the USA. Used by permission of the publisher, Abingdon Press.

with Older Adults that found 65 percent of the members age 65 and over to be women (Presbyterian Panel, 1980). The disproportionate number of women of all ages in the Protestant churches and of older women in the general population make it likely that there are substantially more older Protestant women than men.

Race

Most blacks of all ages are Protestant. Gallup (''Religion,'' 1979) reports that 92 percent of southern blacks and 76 percent of northern blacks are Protestant. The overwhelming majority (72 percent) of blacks in the NORC sample identify themselves as Baptists or Methodists. Seldom are blacks found in other Protestant groups in proportion to their numbers in the population. These proportions are probably true of aged blacks as well.

Socioeconomic

Socioeconomic rankings of the major Protestant groups provide some indication of the resources of the churches for programs and services for the elderly. Episcopalians and Presbyterians are usually ranked at the top of the social hierarchy, and Methodists, Lutherans, and Baptists are at the bottom (McKinney and Roof, 1982). More Protestants with high income (over $20,000) are members of the Episcopal, United Church of Christ, and Presbyterian congregations. Most liberal Protestants (Episcopalian, United Church of Christ, Presbyterian bodies) classify themselves as middle- or upper-class, while most conservative Protestants (Southern Baptist, Church of Christ, Assembly of God, Church of God, Pentacostal) perceive themselves as lower- or working-class. Aged Protestants probably follow the same socioeconomic rankings.

Older people support their churches with contributions, attendance, and service. Although there are no data on the income of old Protestants, there are occasional reports of their contributions to their churches. Gallup surveyed income contribution to churches and found that one person in six gives 10 percent or more (20 percent). Among older Southern Baptists four in ten gave 10 percent of their income ("Religion," 1981).

Protestants of all ages do not attend church as frequently as Catholics, but members over 50 years of age attend more frequently than other age groups ("Religion," 1981). Attendance past 50 years of age remains relatively stable until late old age, 75 years and older (Orbach, 1961).

Religiosity

Most older Protestants have "a great deal" of confidence in their church ("Religion," 1981:45) and they continue to hold a lifelong commitment to it (Campbell and Fukuyama, 1970:77–81; Payne and Mobley, 1978). Beliefs of the elderly (as of all ages) vary by denominational membership and range from conservative fundamentalist to liberal. Orthodoxy among older Protestants does not seem to increase with age but rather reflects cohort effects and lifelong patterns of religious faith and practice. The one exception identified by Stark (1968) is liberal Protestants, who develop stronger beliefs in immortality as they age. Traditional ritual practices are more important to older members than to younger ones (Stark, 1968; Campbell and Fukuyama, 1970; Payne and Mobley, 1978). Some studies report that the highest commitment to religious beliefs and religious knowledge occurs among the older members (Campbell and Fukuyama, 1970). Although orgnizational involvement may decrease for those over 70 years of age, private devotional activities increase.

Orbach's (1961) study of religiosity using the Detroit area data from 1951 to 1957 provides the only large sample of Protestants analyzed by age, race, sex, and religious attendance (table 11.3). He found a stable pattern of attendance until age 75 and older. Black females attend most frequently, and black males attend more frequently than white males at all ages. After 75 irregular attendance increases. If Stark's findings are correct, if may be assumed that private devotionalism increased for these older Detroiters.

Religious participation contributes to the personal adjustment of older Protestants, particularly if they held leadership positions in the past (Moberg, 1953; Gray and Moberg, 1977). Many continue to be informally consulted about church activities and maintain social roles and prestige within the church. Older members who continue to volunteer for church projects such as Shepherd's Centers maintain a high level of satisfaction with their church life and fill new prestigious roles that contribute to personal growth (Payne, 1977).

Religion is very important in the lives of low-income, inner-city, older black Protestants. Religiosity—participating in and commitment to the church, and personal devotions—contributes to adjustment in old age and happiness. Feelings of abandonment and loneliness are greater among those with low religiosity (Heisel and Faulkner, 1982). The significance of religion and religiosity carries over into institutional settings with frail blacks. Watson (1980) reports that elderly who attended church frequently before relocation to a nursing home continued to attend services until advanced old age (90 years of age and older).

Historically, Protestants have more individualistic patterns of religious belief and practice and are inclined to view misfortune and failure as caused by the individual's lack of responsibility (Maves, 1960:712). They also recognize the particular responsibility of the state in the social sphere and tend to support community and governmental institutions and policies that promote and protect human welfare (Robb, 1968).

PROTESTANT ATTITUDES AND POLICY

The centrality of the Bible is the Protestant Church's avowed basis of attitudes and policy about older people. Since the mid-1970s the major denominations' statements on aging contain an affirmation of the Biblical faith in the value and dignity of every woman or man regardless of age, and the commandment to honor and respect the elderly (Elder and McCracken, 1980; Payne 1980).

These policy statements affirm aging as a part of God's created order; recognize the elderly's need for assurance of God's continuing love; acknowledge older persons' potential for growth in a relationship with God and each other; recognize the church as God's instrument to accomplish these purposes; confirm the Biblical perspective of old age as life transformed, renewed, and filled with blessings and opportunities; and affirm that older people are to be respected, honored, and regarded as skilled resources for church lay ministry (Elder and McCracken, 1980).

Table 11.3

Age, Race, Sex, and Religious Attendance in the Detroit Area: Protestants

Age Group	Once a Week		Twice a Month		Once a Month		A Few Times a Year or Less		Never		No.	
	Male	Female	Male	Female	Male	Female	Male	Female	Male	Female	Male	Female
21-39 years:												
White	26.5	33.1	13.8	13.3	7.2	9.4	35.0	32.3	17.5	11.9	(610)	(753)
Negro	30.2	38.5	19.0	26.8	12.4	17.4	31.8	14.5	6.6	2.8	(242)	(317)
40-59 years:												
White	27.7	40.5	9.2	16.7	8.8	11.7	37.8	24.2	16.6	6.9	(524)	(538)
Negro	34.4	51.3	25.0	27.3	13.9	11.8	18.9	9.1	7.8	0.5	(180)	(187)
60-74 years:												
White	31.8	43.6	7.6	13.3	10.0	9.0	32.9	25.1	17.7	9.0	(170)	(211)
Negro	42.1	45.8	28.9	25.5	10.5	8.5	13.2	8.5	5.3	10.6	(38)	(47)
75 years and over:												
White	30.3	31.8	12.1	13.6	—	—	30.3	18.2	27.3	36.4	(33)	(44)
Negro	(1)*	(3)*	—	(4)*	(1)*	—	—	(2)*	(2)*	(1)*	(4)	(11)
TOTAL**												
White	27.7	37.0	11.1	14.5	8.0	11.4	35.7	28.1	17.5	10.5	(1340)	(1547)
Negro	32.8	43.3	22.0	27.0	12.7	14.5	25.2	12.4	7.3	2.8	(464)	(566)

Source: H. L. Orbach, "Age and Religious Participation in a Large Metropolitan Area: Detroit." Paper presented at the annual meeting of the Gerontological Society, Philadelphia, 1958. Reprinted from *Handbook on Social Gerontology* by Clark Tibbits (ed.) by permission of The University of Chicago Press. © 1960 by The University of Chicago. Published 1960.

*Number of cases.

**Total includes those for whom age was not ascertained.

Most of the denominations see the church as augmenting government programs. The distinctive role of the churches is "to advocate, plan and lead programs that contribute to the spiritual, physical, mental, emotional and social benefit of the aging; participate in ecumenical endeavors, and advocate for the cause and rights of the aging" (Elder and McCracken, 1980:8).

Attitudes of Clergy

Although Protestant parish clergy have extensive contact with older people and are in a position to influence attitudes toward older people, there is little systematic research on the attitudes of ministers toward older people. Moreover, most ministers receive little training in aging. The 1972 NRTA-AARP survey reported that only 24 of 126 theological seminaries had special courses to prepare students for ministry with older people. Since the late 1970s many courses in aging have been added to theological seminary training, but these offerings are electives.

Information about the attitudes of Protestant ministers toward older people indicates some ageism among the clergy. Moberg (1969) found that Protestant ministers evaluate older people more negatively than they evaluate young people or people in general. Longino and Kitson (1976) reported a less negative attitude and some ambiguity among Baptist ministers, who indicated that they enjoyed working with the elderly, but that compared to work with youth and younger adults, they found work with the elderly less enjoyable.

Most Presbyterian ministers in the Presbyterian Panel believe older peoples' opinions are valued in the church and should be included in all phases of the church's programs. They did, however, express a need for assistance in expanding their ministry to older adults. Specifically identified were understanding of the social, psychological, and spiritual needs of older adults; program models; and ideas and specific information for referral of older members to needed services.

Attitudes of Church Members

With the exception of the Presbyterian Panel Report, data on attitudes held by Protestants toward or about older people are almost nonexistent. Members participating in the Presbyterian National Panel study believed that older members receive equal or more consideration in church matters than younger adults, and that it is important to involve older people in every aspect of the church's program. The only negative view was the perception that older members suffered from inertia and that the church needed to do more to encourage their active involvement.

SPECIAL PROBLEMS

Problems unique to Protestantism are related to the voluntaristic and pluralistic nature of Protestant churches. Membership in the church is a voluntary "adult decision." Members are not limited to parish areas, but are free to attend the church of their choice. Consequently, "commuter" Protestants may pass a number of churches of their denomination on the way to church. Members move freely from one church to another, and among denominations. These voluntaristic practices may weaken the neighborhood linkages of support for older people, increase variations in the membership composition of the local churches, and contribute to the development of predominantly "young" or "old" congregations.

The pluralistic nature of Protestantism is evident in the proliferation of religious bodies (Jacquet, 1982) and in their uneven geographical distribution. Regional differences in access to a specific denomination and type of congregation affect access to familiar religious groups for relocated elderly Protestants.

Migration and relocation may cause older people to sever permanently their religious organizational support network or access to their regional type of church. There is more Snow Belt to Sun Belt migration than vice versa (Biggar et al., 1976). The conservative southern Protestants' perception of daily events is influenced by fundamentalist beliefs, a ritualism characterized by a conversion experience (being born again) and witnessing to this experience in the community. The older liberal northern Protestants may not adapt readily to this conservative southern church climate or may opt to do nothing on Sunday (Shortridge, 1977).

Migration and relocation are reported to increase the numbers of unchurched Protestants. California and Florida, with the highest immigration rates of older persons, also have the highest proportion of unchurched (California with 57 percent and Florida with 45 percent). A large proportion of the Protestant elderly migrants have opted to retire from church. Hale (1977) found that most elderly Protestant migrants to Florida were resistant to the high competition for their membership. Many felt that they had given a lifetime of faithful attendance elsewhere and just did not have the inclination or energy to start up again; instead, they fell back on the Protestant belief in personal religious autonomy.

For other older Protestants, health and family are factors affecting their church membership and participation. Relocating to be near family members or in a nursing home frequently separates older people from their churches. The extent of this problem is not known.

Problems related to the autonomy of the churches and cooperative planning are more a matter of speculation than research evidence. Other than the Shepherd's Center model and the National Interfaith Coalition on Aging's seminary training and advocacy projects, little is known about cooperative Protestant projects on behalf of older persons.

SPECIAL ADVANTAGES

There are few neighborhoods in the United States that do not have at least one of the Protestant churches. These churches reach more older people and a broader constituency of older people than do public senior centers. Since, as has already been noted, older Protestants have high confidence in their church programs, it is not surprising that older people are more likely to participate in church programs than senior centers (Harris, 1981). It is estimated that between 5 and 19 percent of older people participate in senior centers and other agency programs, but 61 percent participate regularly in church activities. Older Presbyterians support these estimates (Presbyterian Panel, 1980). They are more likely to be involved in organizations and activities for older people sponsored by the church than by secular groups. These church groups act as major support groups for older persons.

Many older people find their spiritual and social needs met through the organizations within the church, especially church school classes and women's groups or circles and opportunities for intergenerational relationships (Payne and Mobley, 1978; Presbyterian Panel, 1980).

Religious roles are retained when other social roles are being relinquished. There is no retirement age for church members. Church membership and religious roles provide social identity and continuity in the midst of change and loss of other social roles. Many older people assume new leadership or volunteer roles in the church that increase their involvement in the community (Payne, 1977).

Research on religion and death fears is limited and ambiguous. However, there is some evidence that older Protestants who participate regularly in the church indicate less fear of death (Martin and Wrightsman, 1970). There is little research on the support of ministers and members for dying older persons. Parish clergy are in a position, organizationally and geographically, to reach many older people with counsel and referrals for support services, and to educate all ages about the process of aging, the needs of older people, and their contribution to the church.

RESEARCH ISSUES

The major research issues revolve around the paucity of research and reliable statistical information on Protestant churches and older members. The *Yearbook* does not provide membership information by age or other significant social variables, and the national surveys do not systematically report their findings by age and religious preference.

Since the Maves and Cedarleaf study, there have been no comprehensive studies of Protestant churches and older people. At a time when the Protestant churches are graying at a faster rate than the general population, comprehensive research projects are needed: to plan for the baby boom cohorts moving into the over 65 age group; to determine how the decline in numbers of youth and the increase in the numbers of elderly, particularly women, will affect the organizational goals, programming, policy, and economic viability of Protestant churches and institutions; to determine the effects of retention of older workers upon the church staff/professional workers and upon the participation of the older members in the church.

Other issues include:

1. How do the differences in organizational structure, beliefs, and regional distribution of the many Protestant groups influence cooperative programming and the delivery of services for older people?

2. How do organizational structure, beliefs, policies, and activities affect the everyday life of older members? Do older members have equal access to leadership roles in the church or are they allocated by age?

3. Age integration versus age-specific programming is an issue for the churches as well as other social organizations. Case studies of different age models would contribute data for policy issues within and outside the churches.

4. It is not clear to what extent religiosity changes with age or what new patterns of religiosity are developed in response to the unique social, psychological, and physical events of late life.

The final issues are methodological. Most of the measures of religiosity and adjustment are from an earlier period (1950–1965). Retesting and revision of these measures for validity and reliability and the development of measures sensitive to specific current religious practice would increase gerontologists' understanding of the role of specific Protestant beliefs, rituals, and private practices in the aging process.

Most research about Protestants—organizational and individual members—is cross-sectional. It provides information on the age differences in behavior, but not on the effects of aging on members' religious beliefs and practice; nor does it document changes in church programs and organization due to the aging of the congregation. Cross-sequential studies and/or longitudinal studies using panel, survey, and case study design offer promise to resolve some of the research issues identified. Denominational studies such as the Presbyterian Panel Study, using standardized questions, are needed to identify Protestant denominational differences and for denominational planning.

RESOURCES

Thomas B. Robb, Director
Presbyterian Office on Aging
(Presbyterian U.S.A. and United Presbyterian U.S.A.)
341 Ponce de Leon Avenue
Atlanta, GA 30365

Lorraine Chiaventone, Executive Director
Episcopal Society for Ministry on Aging (ESMA)
RD #4, Box 146-A
Milford, NJ 08848

Charles Frazier—Section on Aging
Health and Welfare Ministries Division
Board of Global Ministries

The United Methodist Church
1200 Davis Street
Evanston, IL 60201

Horace L. Kerr
Senior Adult Ministries
Family Ministry Department
Baptist Sunday School Board
127 Ninth Avenue, North
Nashville, TN 37234

Thomas D. Cook, Executive Secretary
National Interfaith Coalition
298 Hull Street
Athens, GA 30601

Earl Kragnes, Senior Program Coordinator
NRTA-AARP
1909 K Street, NW
Washington, DC 20049

REFERENCES

Aging and the older adult: Social statements. The Lutheran Church in America, Division for Missions in North America, New York, 1978.

Biggar, J.C.; Longino, C.F.; and Flynn, C.B. Elderly interstate migration. *Research on Aging*, 1980, *11*, 217–232.

Boorstin, D. *The Americans: The democratic experience*. Random House, New York, 1973.

Butler, R.N., and Lewis, M. *Aging and mental health: Positive psychological approaches*, 2nd ed. Mosby, St. Louis, 1977.

Campbell, T.C., and Fukuyama, Y. *The fragmented layman*. Pilgrim Press, Philadelphia, 1970.

Cole, E.C. Lay ministries with older adults. In W.M. Clements (Ed.), *Ministry with the aging*. Harper and Row, New York, 1981, 250–265.

Cook, T.C. Aging and seminary training. In *The religious sector explores its mission in aging*. National Interfaith Coalition, Athens, Ga., 1976.

Elder, H.G., and McCracken, P.S. A preliminary analysis: Position/policy statements on aging of representative bodies in the U.S.A. Prepared for the National Interfaith Coalition on Aging for use in the National Symposium on Spiritual and Ethical Value System Concerns in the 1981 White House Conference on Aging, Erlanger, Ky., October 27–30, 1980.

Emmons, H. *The mature heart*. Abingdon Press, New York, 1953.

Frakes, M. *Older people confront the churches*. Christian Century Foundation, Chicago, 1955.

Gray, R.M., and Moberg, D.O. *The church and the older person*, rev. ed. Eerdman's, Grand Rapids, Mich., 1977.

Hale, J.R. *The unchurched: Who they are and why they stay away*. Harper and Row, San Francisco, 1977.

Harris, Louis. *The myth and reality of aging in America.* National Council on the Aging, Washington, D.C., 1975.

——. *Aging in the eighties: America in transition.* National Council on the Aging, Washington, D.C., 1981.

Heisel, M., and Faulkner, A.O. Religiosity in an older black population. *Gerontologist,* 1982, *22,* 354–358.

Jacquet, C.H. *Yearbook of American and Canadian churches.* Abingdon Press, Nashville, Tenn., 1982.

Jacobs, H.L. *Churches and their senior citizens.* Congregational Christian Conference of Iowa, Grinnell, Iowa, 1957.

Johnson, F.E., and Villaume, W.J. Protestant social services. In R.H. Kurtz (Ed.), *Social work yearbook.* National Association of Social Workers, New York, 1957, 421–431.

Longino, C.F., and Kitson, G.C. Parish clergy and the aged: Examining stereotypes. *Journal of Gerontology,* 1976, *31,* 340–345.

McKinney, W., and Roof, W.C. A social profile of American religious groups. In C.H. Jacquet, Jr. (Ed.), *The yearbook of American and Canadian churches,* Abingdon Press, Nashville, Tenn., 1982, 267–270.

Martin, D., and Wrightsman, L.S., Jr. The relationship between religious behavior and concern about death. *Journal of Social Psychology,* 1970, *65,* 317–323.

Maves, P.B. *The best is yet to be.* Westminster Press, Philadelphia, 1951.

——. The church and older people. *Pastoral Psychology,* 1954, *5,* 9–44.

——. Aging, religion and the church. In Clark Tibbitts (Ed.), *Handbook of social gerontology.* University of Chicago Press, Chicago, 1960.

——. More life in the golden years. In D.R. Shamblin (Ed.), *The interpreter.* United Methodist Communications, Nashville, Tenn., 1982, 26–27.

Maves, P.B., and Cedarleaf, J.L. *Older people and the church.* Abingdon-Cokesbury Press, New York, 1960.

Moberg, D.O. Church membership and personal adjustment in old age. *Journal of Gerontology,* 1953, *8,* 207–211.

Moberg, R.D. *The attitudes of ministers toward old people.* Ph.D. diss., Boston University Graduate School, Boston, 1969.

Orbach, H.L. Age and religious participation in a large metropolitan area: Detroit. Gerontological Society, Cleveland, 1961.

——. Aging and religion: A study of church attendance in the Detroit metropolitan area. *Geriatrics,* 1961, *16,* 530–540.

Palmore, E. United States of America. In E. Palmore (Ed.), *International handbook on aging.* Greenwood Press, Westport, Conn., 1980.

Payne, B.P. The older volunteer: Social role continuity and development. *Gerontologist,* 1977, *17,* 355–361.

——. Statement on aging. General Board of Global Ministries, United Methodist Church, Cincinnati, 1980.

——. Religiosity. In D.J. Mangen and W.A. Peterson (Eds.), *Social roles and social participation,* vol. 2. University of Minnesota Press, Minneapolis, 1982, 343–353.

Payne, B.P., and Mobley, C.M. Changes in the religious commitment of older Americans: Hints for future research. Paper presented to the Religious Research Association, Atlanta, October 1978.

Presbyterian Panel. The October 1980 questionnaire: Ministry with older adults in the United Presbyterian Church. United Presbyterian Church U.S.A., New York, 1980.

Reisch, H. *Ye visited me*. United Lutheran Church of America, New York, 1954.

Religion in America. Gallup Organization, Princeton, N.J., Research Center, 1979.

Religion in America. Gallup Organization, Princeton, N.J., Research Center, 1981.

Robb, T.B. *The bonus years: Foundations for ministry with older persons*. Judson Press, Valley Forge, Pa., 1968.

Scudder, E. *Organized religion and the older person*. Institute of Gerontology Series, vol. 8. University of Florida Press, Gainesville, Fla., 1958.

Shortridge, J.R. A new regionalism of American religion. *Journal for the Scientific Study of Religion* 1977, *16*, 1777.

Stark, R. Age and faith: A changing outlook on an old process. *Sociological Analysis*, 1968, *29*, 1–10.

Stafford, V. *Older adults in the church*. Methodist Church (General Board of Education), Nashville, Tenn., 1953.

Stough, A.B. *Brighter vistas: The story of four church programs for older adults*. U.S. Department of Health, Education and Welfare, Administration on Aging, Washington, D.C., 1965.

Watson, W.H. *Stress and old age*. Transaction Books, New Brunswick, N.J., 1980.

Webber, I.L. The organized social life of the retired: Two Florida communities. *American Journal of Sociology*, 1954, *59*, 340–346.

PART III

ETHNIC GROUPS

12

ASIANS

TOSHI KII

Substantial interest has been generated in the study of the Asian American elderly since the mid-1970s, primarily as the result of activities by minority advocacy groups. The Administration on Aging, established under the Older Americans Act of 1965, has been charged with the implementation of various programs in which priority attention has been given to meeting the needs of the low-income aged and the minority aged. Along with three other major minority groups—blacks, Spanish-speaking, and Native Americans—the Asian American elderly have become a target group to which federal funding has been directed by the Administration on Aging for needs assessment and feasibility studies of the delivery of social and health services to these groups and their utilization of these services.

Despite the recent interest in the Asian American elderly, substantive knowledge about them is still in a very primitive state. One reason for this lack of knowledge is that the major thrust of past research, except in a few cases, has been descriptive rather than analytical. Thus, we know something about the life-styles and problems experienced by, for example, Japanese American elderly or Chinese American elderly, but we know very little about how their ethnicity relates to the patterns of aging. If, indeed, ascriptive traits—such as race and ethnicity—and achieved status—such as education and income—are intertwined in determining one's life chances, self-image, perception toward external environments, and attitudes toward interpersonal relationships, to what extent do these variations derive from ethnic factors?

Another reason knowledge about the Asian American elderly as a whole is inadequate is the unevenness of information accumulated across the various Asian American ethnic groups. This is primarily due to the small size of the ethnic groups under study and the varied histories of their immigration to the United States. Thus, the relatively large groups within the Asian American community, such as Chinese Americans and Japanese Americans, whose immigration histories go back to the mid-nineteenth and early twentieth centuries, have been studied somewhat more than other, newer Asian Americans. Nonetheless, the tendency to present the elderly of only these groups, though it may be pragmatic from the researcher's standpoint, may have understated the diversity of Asian American elderly. Unlike other minority groups who have some common denominators with which members of the groups can identify, be they language, religion, or the majority-minority relationship, Asian Americans are so diverse from the religio-linguistic standpoint that it is quite plausible, even highly probable, that there is no such entity as the ''Asian American elderly.'' If variations among the elderly of various Asian American ethnic groups are greater than variations between each Asian ethnic elderly group and the majority elderly, or other minority groups, for that matter, one has to be extremely careful when making general statements about the Asian American elderly as such.

Although we know very little about the Asian American elderly, it is still possible to give some accounts based on past research. What follows is state-of-the-art knowledge with respect to the Asian American elderly.

DEMOGRAPHY OF ASIAN AMERICAN ELDERLY

One of the problems of studying the Asian American elderly is defining who Asian Americans are. The Census Bureau's classification is currently based on the geographical areas from which immigration to the United States has taken place. In addition, the Census Bureau combines Asian Americans with Pacific Islanders, who became Americans by virtue of territorial expansion and political annexation (the so-called Trust Territory of the Pacific) under the U.S. government. There are, all together, nineteen identifiable Asian and Pacific Islander ethnic groups—six Pacific Islander and thirteen Asian American. In the 1980 U.S. Census Asians and Pacific Islanders included nine groups which constituted 3.5 million people: Asian Indian, Chinese, Filipino, Guamanian, Hawaiian, Japanese, Korean, Vietnamese, and Samoan. Other groups are classified as ''others'' in the census tabulation. It has been variously reported in the media that there has been a tremendous increase in Asians and Pacific Islanders, from 1.5 million in 1970 to 3.5 million in 1980 (U.S. Bureau of the Census, 1981b). Most of the increase is due to immigration from Asia and the islands of the Pacific and to changes in the census classification, which in 1980 added four new groups, namely, Asian Indian, Guamanian, Samoan, and Vietnamese. Asian Indians, who numbered 362,000 in 1980, were classified under ''white'' in the 1970 census.

Although Asians and Pacific Islanders constituted less than 1.6 percent of the total U.S. population in 1980, there have been substantial changes among the major groups. The Japanese Americans, who had been the largest group until 1970, were surpassed by the Chinese and Filipinos in 1980. The most conspicuous increase was experienced by the Koreans, whose population by 1980 had shown more than a fivefold increase over 1970. Table 12.1 shows the total populations

Table 12.1
Numbers of Asians and Pacific Islanders in the United States and Percentages in Total U.S. Population in 1970 and 1980

	1970		1980	
	Number	*Percentage*	*Number*	*Percentage*
Chinese	435,062	0.2	806,027	0.4
Filipino	343,060	0.2	774,640	0.3
Japanese	591,290	0.3	700,747	0.3
Asian Indian	——	—	361,544	0.2
Korean	69,130	*	354,529	0.2
Vietnamese	——	—	261,714	0.1
Hawaiian	100,179	*	167,253	0.1
Samoan	——	—	42,050	*
Guamanian	——	—	32,132	*
Total	1,538,721	0.8	3,500,636	1.6

Source: U.S. Bureau of the Census, *1980 Census of Population*, Supplementary Reports (PC80-S1-3). U.S. Department of Commerce, Washington, D.C., July 1981, pp. 7–11.
* Negligible.
—— Not tabulated.

of the nine major Asian and Pacific Islander groups in 1980 and the five major groups in 1970 according to Census Bureau figures.

Unfortunately, at present the only information available on the age composition of different ethnic groups in 1980 is the proportion of those aged 65 and over, and the median age for Asian and Pacific Islanders as a whole. Table 12.2 shows these aging indices for the major racial and ethnic categories of the United States in 1980.

Asians and Pacific Islanders constitute a relatively young population as a whole. The primary reason for this has been increased immigration by young adult Chinese, Filipinos, Koreans, Asian Indians, and Vietnamese since 1965, when quota restrictions on immigration on the basis of race and nationality were legally eliminated. The Immigration and Naturalization Service reported that 1.5 million Asians were legally admitted during the 1970s. The relative youth of the group is also reflected in the proportion of Asians and Pacific Islanders who are 65 years old and over in the total U.S. population aged 65 and over. Although Asians and Pacific Islanders constituted approximately 1.6 percent of the U.S. population of 226.5 million in 1980, their elderly population aged 65 and over constituted only 0.83 percent (211,834 persons) of the total elderly in the United States (25.5 million). However, there are different degrees of aging among ethnic groups within Asians and Pacific Islanders. Table 12.3 shows the proportions

Table 12.2
Proportion of Population Aged 65 and Over and Median Age for White, Black, Asian and Pacific Islander, American Indian, and Hispanic Populations in 1980

	Proportion of People 65 and over (percentage)	Median Age
Whites	12.2	31.3
Blacks	7.9	24.9
Asians and Pacific Islanders	6.1	28.6
American Indians*	5.3	23.0
Hispanics	4.9	23.2
Total	11.3	30.0

Source: U.S. Bureau of the Census, *1980 Census of Population*, Supplementary Reports (PC80-S1-1). U.S. Department of Commerce, Washington, D.C., May 1981, pp. 1–3.
*Including Eskimos and Aleuts.

Table 12.3
Number and Proportion of People Aged 65 and Over among Japanese, Chinese, Filipino, Hawaiian, and Korean Populations in 1960 and 1970

	1960		1970	
	Number	*Percentage*	*Number*	*Percentage*
Japanese	29,235	6.0	47,303	8.0
Chinese	12,415	6.9	26,974	6.2
Filipinos	6,546	3.6	21,269	6.2
Hawaiians	——	—	4,007	4.0
Koreans	——	—	2,281	3.3

Sources: U.S. Bureau of the Census, *1980 Census of Population*, Supplementary Reports, (PC80-S1-3). U.S. Department of Commerce, Washington, D.C., July 1981, p. 10. Isao Horinouchi, "An Expanded Outline and Resource for Teaching a Course in Minority Aging: A Pacific/Asian Perspective," in George A. Sherman (Ed.), *Curriculum Guidelines in Minority Aging*. National Center on Black Aged, Washington, D.C., 1980, p. IV-30. Administration on Aging, *Aging*, Department of Health and Human Services, Washington, D.C., July-August 1981, p. 4.

of those aged 65 and over for the Asian American groups that are delineated in the 1960 and 1970 censuses.

With regard to geographical location, since almost 60 percent of the 3.5 million Asians and Pacific Islanders are located on the West Coast and in Hawaii (U.S. Bureau of the Census, 1980a), the majority of their elderly are presumed to be concentrated in these states. Thus, almost 62 percent of the Asians and Pacific Islander elderly aged 60 and over were estimated to reside in California, Hawaii, Washington, and the Trust Territory of the Pacific (Pacific/Asian Elderly Research Project, 1977a). Two other states where a large concentration of Asian Americans, and therefore of their elderly, are found are New York and Illinois. However, the degree of such concentration varied substantially from one group to another. In 1980, over 80 percent of Japanese, 69 percent of Filipinos, and 52 percent of Chinese resided in the West, including Hawaii, but only 40 percent of Koreans and Vietnamese and 20 percent of Asian Indians lived in the West (U.S. Bureau of the Census, 1981b). There has been a sizable increase in the percentage of Asians and Pacific Islanders residing in the South, from 7.4 percent in 1970 to 13.4 percent in 1980, most notably among Chinese, Filipinos, Koreans, Asian Indians, and Vietnamese, although Asians and Pacific Islanders constituted less than 0.6 percent of the total population of the southern states in 1980. The elderly of the Asians and Pacific Islanders reside in ethnic communities in large cities such as Honolulu, Los Angeles, San Francisco, New York, Chicago, Oakland, Boston, Seattle, Philadelphia, Denver, Washington, D.C., Stockton, California, Norfolk, Fresno, San Jose, and San Diego (Pacific/Asian Elderly Research Project, 1977a).

IMMIGRATION HISTORY

There are at least two reasons that a discussion of the history of Asian immigration to this country is relevant to the Asian American elderly. First, the majority of the contemporary elderly are still first-generation immigrants themselves since the history of Asian immigration to the United States is relatively recent. This has brought about a specific relationship to the larger society with regard to their life experiences, which include discrimination and prejudice, and regarding the scope of their perception of the community. Second, because the various ethnic groups have arrived at different times, they have developed ethnic enclaves, which not only have established a specific relationship with the larger society, but which also have created a stratification within the Asian American community.

There have been several major waves of Asian immigration to the United States since the mid-nineteenth century. The first wave arrived between the 1850s and the 1870s, when young male Chinese from the Canton province of China immigrated to the West Coast, mainly as construction laborers for the railroads and as gold miners. They came as sojourners intending to return to their homeland after earning enough money. But for the most part this did not happen. They were forced to take up low-paying, menial jobs and were pushed into ethnic enclaves known as Chinatowns. When the larger society began to perceive Chinese immigration as threatening, the Chinese Exclusion Act was legislated in 1882. It prohibited Chinese immigrants from bringing their wives and children to the United States as well as from obtaining certain jobs (Butler and Lewis, 1982).

The second wave came from the 1890s until roughly 1920, during which time young Japanese males came to Hawaii as sugar plantation workers and then to California as agricultural laborers. They came from primarily agricultural regions of Japan. The exception was students, who comprised about 20 percent of the Japanese in California in the early 1900s. Most of them worked as domestic servants (Kii, 1982). Like the Chinese immigrants in the earlier period, the Japanese also faced discrimination and hostile treatment from the larger society. An anti-Japanese movement was launched by the *San Francisco Chronicle* in 1905 with the support of the San Francisco labor unions (Daniels, 1962). The Asiatic Exclusion League, founded in the same year, promoted the idea of the impossibility of assimilation without injuring Americans because of the "low standard of civilization and religious prejudices" of the Japanese, not to mention their distinct racial characteristics (Daniels, 1962). There were numerous incidents of harassment of Japanese individuals and concerted boycotts against Japanese businesses, and the problem in California developed into an international problem between the Japanese and U.S. governments. This situation culminated in the Gentlemen's Agreement in 1908, under which no passports were issued by the Japanese government to Japanese citizens except to the parents, wives, and children of workers who were already in the United States. However, the anti-Japanese agitation persisted in California as the "picture bride" scheme brought Japanese women into the country to join Japanese men, a phenomenon that appeared immoral to Americans.

The fact that the Japanese population in California was increasing and spreading toward rural areas enabled the California legislature to enact the Alien Land Law in 1913, which restricted the purchase and leasing of land by Japanese. Eventually, the complete exclusion of Japanese from America was demanded by various groups. This demand culminated in the Asiatic Immigration Exclusion Act of 1924. For all practical purposes, Asian immigration was ended in 1924, except for Filipino laborers, who became a logical choice as a substitute source of labor in Hawaii and California in light of the exclusion of Japanese, and earlier, Chinese, immigration. The Philippine Islands became an American possession in 1898, and Filipinos were exempted from the Exclusion Act of 1924. There had been a small but steady immigration of farm laborers from the Philippine Islands since about 1915, which peaked in the late 1920s. But like their predecessors, Filipinos encountered discrimination. Anti-Filipino sentiments were at their height during the early 1930s, and the Tydings-McDuffie Act of 1934 limited Filipino immigration to fifty per year (Yu, 1980).

The third major wave of Asian immigration began after 1952, when the

McCarran-Walter Act allowed immigration from Asia on the basis of national quotas and eligibility for citizenship, but it was after 1965, when the previous quota system on the basis of race and nationality was repealed, that the surge of Asian immigration began to take hold. There has been a substantial increase in immigration, first among Mandaran-speaking Chinese via Hong Kong and Taiwan as political refugees fled from Communist China; second from the Philippines and Korea; and most recently from Indochina. In relative terms, Japanese immigration after 1952 has been negligible. As previously noted, the 1980 census showed that the population of Chinese Americans and Filipino Americans surpassed Japanese Americans, who constituted the largest Asian group in the 1970 census count.

One striking difference between the immigrants of the pre–Asiatic Immigration Exclusion Act of 1924 period and those after 1952 was in their occupational backgrounds. In the earlier period, the immigrants were unskilled and semiskilled (except for students), who for the most part were contract laborers in railroad construction, in the sugar plantations in Hawaii, and in agriculture in California. Since 1965, relatively large proportions of immigrants from various countries have been composed of professional and technical workers as well as political refugees who were educated and had white-collar occupations. One-third of the Filipino immigrants, for example, were professional workers, mostly medical technicians, in the late 1960s and 1970s (Yu, 1980). Among the Vietnamese refugees of 1975, the majority of household heads were engaged in white-collar jobs in their native countries and over 25 percent of them had college or postgraduate education (Skinner, 1980). In a study of the Korean blue-collar workers in the Chicago area, Kim and Hurh (1980) reported that the majority of adult immigrants had a college education and pursued white-collar occupations in Korea.

THE FAMILY

Myth has it that Asian American elders are well taken care of within the family because of the traditional values of familism, particularly with regard to respect and deference accorded to the elders of the family. This needs to be qualified. Reverence toward elders may have been a significant aspect of interpersonal relationships in the Oriental societies of the recent past, in which the major economic endeavors were agriculture and small business entrepreneurship, and the entire family or kin group was considered a basic unit of the work institution. In such a society it is reasonable to assume that the political power resided in the head of the family or the head of the kin group because he controlled the finances of the family business. Everybody else was a contributor to the family business, but all were economically dependent on the head. Both political and economic power provided the head of the family with a broad range of privileges and rights, which included management and distribution of the family inheritance, arranging marriages for children, and receiving support from children in one's old age. In turn, the obligations and responsibilities of the head of the family were to manage the family business and to provide economic security for family members. The major objective of the family was to survive economically, but this survival depended to a great extent on the efforts of earlier generations. Thus, the continuation of the family was essential if the family business was to be maintained. The deference and respect accorded to the elderly were the result of the indebtedness felt by subsequent generations as well as of the elderly's former political status as head of the family.

The contemporary Asian American elderly, the majority of whom are first-generation immigrants, broke away from the traditional work and family organizations when they were young and came to a completely new environment. Several factors contributed to the disruption of the traditional familism. One striking feature of the elderly among some Asian American ethnic groups is that their sex ratios are abnormal. As a point of reference, the overall sex ratio of Asian and Pacific Islander elderly showed 96 men to 100 women in 1980, whereas in the general elderly population the ratio was 68 men to 100 women. The sex ratio of elderly Chinese Americans in 1970 showed 131 men to every 100 women, and that of elderly Filipino Americans in 1960 showed 445 men to 100 women (Pacific/Asian Elderly Research Project, 1977a). These ratios are presumed to have been reduced substantially since then due to the greater longevity of women, and more significant, because more recent immigrants have been elderly women than elderly men. Nevertheless, these unusual sex ratios are reflected in current patterns of living arrangements and marriage among Asian Americans. In the case of Chinese elderly men, in 1970 over 26 percent lived alone, whereas only 16 percent of men in the general elderly population did. A larger proportion of Chinese elderly men had never married than was the case in the general elderly population, and many who had been married in China were without wives in the United States because of earlier restrictive immigration laws (Pacific/Asian Elderly Research Project, 1977a). In the case of Filipino elderly men, the abnormal sex ratio produced a high proportion of elderly men who remained single: 28.1 percent compared to 7.5 percent for men in the total elderly population in 1970 (Pacific/Asian Elderly Research Project, 1977a). There are two distinctive characteristics of the Filipino elderly who are married. One is that most are married to non-Filipino women (almost 50 percent), since Filipino women were not allowed to immigrate to the United States until recently. The other is that most are married to women who are considerably younger.

This unusual sex ratio did not appear among the Japanese or Korean American elderly. The sex ratio of Japanese elderly was 77 men to 100 women in 1970, only slightly higher than the ratio in the general elderly population. When the Gentlemen's Agreement of 1908 restricted Japanese immigration to the parents, wives, and children of Japanese laborers already in America, the improvised picture bride scheme enabled Japanese single men to find wives. Although this practice was partly responsible for the Asiatic Immigration Exclusion Act of 1924, it did create a less abnormal sex ratio among the Japanese elderly. The contemporary Japanese American elderly, both men and women, show patterns of marital status that are similar to those of the general elderly population in the United States. Korean American elderly actually show a slightly lower sex ratio than the general elderly population, 64 males per 100 females, which is a reflection of their more recent immigration. Immigration by young Koreans increased substantially during the 1970s, and they have been able to find work and establish their families in the United States and to send for their parents, grandparents, and other older relatives, many of whom have been women. Compared to other Asian American elderly, and indeed compared to the general elderly population, Korean American elderly are more likely to live in multi-generation households or in extended families. However, although their numbers are small, American-born Korean elderly and those who were among the early immigrants, most of whom reside in Hawaii and New York, showed high proportions of elderly women living alone (Pacific/Asian Elderly Research Project, 1977a).

It can be seen, therefore, that the history of immigration affected not only the traditional family system, but the formation of families as well. However, even those elderly who were able to establish a family were forced to adjust to new, emerging intergenerational relationships as their offspring became more and more acculturated in American society. Certainly, the traditional familism that they were accustomed to—the values they acquired during their formative years in their native countries with respect to supporting and caring for aging family members within the same household—encountered resistance from their children. This is not to suggest that the younger generations of Asian Americans have become disrespectful of or do not care about their elders. Rather, their newly acquired values and wider participation in American society enabled, and indeed often required, younger Asian Americans to break away from the traditional familism.

Occupational diversification between the generations contributed to this change to a great extent as the economic independence of children freed them from parental authority. Compared to the elderly themselves, their children are more highly educated and are engaged in more prestigious occupations. For example, younger adult Chinese have increasingly moved into professional and technical occupations. Over one-third of men and one-fourth of women were in these occupations in 1970, whereas the comparable figures in 1950 were only 6 percent for men and 11 percent for women (Huang, 1976). Younger adult Japanese Americans have the highest educational attainment of all Asian American groups, and well over one-third are in professional occupations.

What this means is that the process of intergenerational upward mobility invites a breakdown of the traditional family structure notwithstanding the more rooted cultural values of familism. It is true that if one looks at the existence of extended families in some of these ethnic populations, Asian American groups show higher proportions of such family arrangements than the national average. Eighteen percent of all Chinese families, 16 percent of all Japanese families, and 23 percent of Filipino American families are extended (Ignacio, 1976), while the national average was 12 percent in 1970. This, of course, does not point out the extent to which the elderly of Asian American groups live with a child's family. Data on living arrangements are scant, but the majority of Asian American elderly appear to live by themselves. Although the sample sizes are extremely small and the range of ages of the sample included those in their mid-fifties and older, the study carried out in the San Diego SMSA showed that 28 percent of the Chinese elderly, 53 percent of the Filipino elderly, and only a small proportion of the Japanese elderly lived with their children (Cheng, 1978; Peterson, 1978; Ishizuka, 1978). Increasingly, the extended family is becoming a rarity among aged Chinese Americans (Hsu, 1971), and, indeed, many elderly Chinese prefer living in ethnic communities, where they are familiar with the social world and can interact with people using Chinese tongues, to living with their children and the children's families, many of whom have moved to the suburbs or the outskirts of ethnic communities.

Acculturation and emerging structural assimilation into the larger society by the offspring's generation have contributed greatly to changes in intergenerational relationships. One of the more influential events that contributed to the acculturation process among the Japanese second generation (Nisei) was, ironically, life in the internment camps during World War II. Since the Nisei were given political power within the camps because they were able to communicate in English, the status of the Issei—the first-generation immigrants, who constitute part of the current Japanese aged—was greatly reduced, even though as heads of families the Issei had exercised authority over the Nisei before the evacuation. In a sense, internment camp life was a catalyst that allowed the Nisei to break away from the powerful intergenerational and vertical bondage which the Issei generation had imposed on them in the ethnic enclaves they lived in before the evacuation. After the evacuation ended, many Japanese Americans moved on to resettle in different parts of the country, where new skills and education as well as command of English provided the Nisei with much more opportunity in the larger community. This, in turn, redefined the relationship between the Issei and the Nisei. Thus, the contemporary Japanese American elderly are living in families whose structure has greatly changed. In adapting to the change by reducing their expectations, the Japanese American elderly appear to be minimizing the incongruity they might feel between the ideal and the reality. The expectation that the traditional filial piety will be observed is not found among the Japanese American elderly in a large Midwestern city (Osako, 1979). Most Japanese American elderly have also responded to the changing family with a fierce self-reliance. If assistance is absolutely required, the children can be relied on. Indeed, the elderly's relationship with their children appears to be maintained at a relatively high level in terms of frequency of visiting (Montero, 1979).

The process of acculturation and assimilation will further complicate the Chinese and Japanese family structure of the future. Increasingly, the younger generations are exercising exogamy, which the contemporary elderly have a difficult time understanding. Cultural homogeneity used to be the primary concern in uniting families, even to the extent that the partners came from the same province of the country. Now roughly 20 percent of young Chinese Americans and half of young Japanese Americans (the Sansei) are marrying members of out-groups (Yuan, 1980; Kikumura and Kitano, 1973). This is not only a sign of acculturation by the succeeding generations, but also a strong indication that these younger generations are able to flee from the authority of their parents in the matter of courtship and marriage. This is more an issue of the future elderly, but certainly it appears that they will face a different kind of adjustment and adaptation.

THE ETHNIC COMMUNITY

The history of Asian immigration to this country is relatively new. Like the earlier European immigrants, particularly those from eastern and southern European regions, Asian American immigrants suffered discrimination and prejudice. There is a common pattern in the history of immigration. New immigrants always suffer some form of discrimination from the indigenous population and even from earlier immigrants. This discriminatory behavior has been attributed to economic competition and the in-group and out-group conflict arising out of cultural-linguistic as well as religious differences (Simpson and Yinger, 1972). It appears that in the case of Asian immigration it was more than that. From the very onset of Asian immigration in the mid-nineteenth century, it was felt that people from Asia could never be assimilated into American society, culturally or otherwise. When the "melting pot" was celebrated as an American ideal at the turn of this century, immigrants from Asia, namely, the Chinese and Japanese, were never considered to be included in it. While Zangwill's 1908 Broadway play entitled *The Melting Pot* was an expression of American egalitarianism, "Chin-Chin Chinaman" and "Chink! Chink!" were songs in popular Broadway plays just a few years before (Huang, 1976). The visible racial characteristics of Asian Americans, as well as their language, customs, habits, and even clothing were reasons given for the supposed impossibility of their assimilation. These general prejudicial attitudes were codified by the government through the enactment of various restrictive and exclusionary acts during the latter nineteenth and early twentieth centuries. These legal restrictions were operative until 1952, when the McCarran-Walter Act conferred the right of naturalization on Asian immigrants and allowed a quota of 100 immigrants a year from Asian countries.

In 1965 the National Origins Act eliminated race, creed, and nationality as bases for immigration. Thus, the same quota that exists for European countries, 20,000, now applies to Asian countries as well, and discrimination from the legal standpoint has been eradicated.

Chinatowns, Little Tokyo, Japan Town, and Little Manila evolved out of the necessity for economic as well as psychoemotional survival of the earlier immigrants in the face of discrimination by the larger society. These ethnic enclaves continue to provide contemporary Asian American elderly with viable opportunities for social interaction, as the majority of them can communicate with others only in their native languages. Almost two-thirds of the Chinese elderly were foreign-born, and only 1.4 percent of them spoke English as their mother tongue in 1970 (Pacific/Asian Elderly Research Project, 1977a). The majority of Japanese elderly are also foreign-born, and less than 1 percent of them used English in 1970. Even among American-born Japanese elderly, only about 6 percent indicated that English was their mother tongue. Their social world, therefore, is almost exclusively limited to these ethnic enclaves, where they developed small retail businesses, service businesses, and entertainment outfits that catered to their own ethnic groups. These ethnic enclaves appear to be functioning well for the contemporary Asian American elderly, particularly the Chinese and Japanese, as places for social and leisure activities. These ethnic communities are also places where the Family and District Associations, the Japanese American Citizens League, and other organizations are actively involved in creating networks for the assistance of the elderly.

The Filipino community appears to lead a more fluid and less visible existence, at least to outsiders. While Japanese and Chinese immigrants formed associations on the basis of geographical origins in their native countries as well as kinship affiliations, the Filipino immigrants organized associations on the basis of common interests regardless of lineage or region of origin. At the same time, the Filipino immigrants were highly migratory and did not develop a merchant class which might have settled in specific urban areas of the country as the Chinese and Japanese first-generation immigrants did (Yu, 1980). And, indeed, a less restrictive, more individualistic orientation toward forming families, not to mention associations and organizations, enabled the Filipino immigrants, including elders, to marry outside of their group with high frequency, a further indication that they are less visible than other Asian Americans. The Korean community appears almost invisible to the outsider also, primarily because Korean immigration is relatively new. With the recent increases in the proportion of Korean immigrants who are educated and skilled in a trade, Korean Americans are building small but stable communities in various urban areas of the country. Language certainly is a major problem for the Korean elderly, as it is for all Asian American elderly. The development of a stable Korean community will provide some sort of psychoemotional stability to this newly emerging Asian American group if Chinese and Japanese experiences are any example. At this moment, the extended family structure is heavily relied on.

The role of ethnic communities is self-evident for the contemporary Asian American elderly. The origin of these communities, particularly for the Chinese and Japanese, may have been the result of a reaction to hostile encounters with the larger society. But it is a one-sided interpretation of the ethnic community if only positive aspects are looked at. As important as they are to the psychoemotional stability of various Asian American elderly, they have also perpetuated a clear demarcation of ethnic boundaries among the different groups. Since there exist distinct cultural-linguistic differences among Asian American elderly, and since their immigration histories are quite different, conflict, animosity, and prejudice exist between various Asian American ethnic groups. It appears that ethnic stratification systems exist among them. Indeed, the political conflicts in the Far East during the first half of the twentieth century have molded certain predispositions in the relationship among the Asian American ethnic groups in this country. The contemporary elderly from China, the Philippines, Japan, and Korea have experienced—directly or indirectly—a psychological incongruity arising out of the political relations among their native countries. In this sense, the Asian American ethnic communities can be looked at not only in terms of their relationships with the larger society, but also in terms of their relationships with each other. This is why it is quite difficult—if not, in fact, erroneous—to discuss the Asian American elderly as if they were an entity which could be monolithically understood.

SERVICE DELIVERY

A fair amount of research in the area of needs assessment and the extent of service utilization among Asian American elderly has been conducted (Pacific/ Asian Elderly Research Project, 1977b). Although some regional variations exist, the general evaluation on this issue is that the Asian American elderly underutilize available formal support systems. Whether this is a result of lack of effort on the part of service providers or the Asian American elderly's avoidance of them in preference of informal support networks has been a point of contention. The underutilization of service programs provided by state and federal agencies for the Asian American elderly has given many service providers, most of whom are non-Asian Americans, the idea that Asian Americans take care of their own elderly. But the previous discussions on the family and the ethnic community suggest that many Asian American elderly need a formal support system, but probably would not take the initiative in seeking assistance outside their ethnic communities because of their lack of English proficiency. The discriminatory immigration policies of the past also fostered in the contemporary Asian American elderly, particularly the Chinese and Japanese, a sense of distrust of government programs and a reluctance to deal with governmental bureaucracy.

Available social indicators show worse conditions among Asian American elderly than among the elderly in the general population. Poverty among all Asian American elderly is more extensive than it is among the general elderly. It has been estimated that 44 percent of Korean American, 28 percent of Chinese American, 25 percent of Filipino American, and 19 percent of Japanese American elderly were living in poverty in 1970 (Pacific/Asian Research Project, 1977a, 1977b). As might be expected, the majority of these elderly below the poverty level lived alone in 1970: 58 percent for the Chinese and Japanese and 63 percent for the Filipinos, as compared to 55 percent for the general elderly population under the poverty threshold. The median incomes of all ethnic groups of Asian

American elderly are considerably lower than that of the total elderly population despite the fact that a larger proportion of them participate in the labor force. The median income of Chinese elderly males was $805 less than that of the general male elderly population, and the median income of the Chinese elderly female was $333 less than that of the general female elderly population in 1970. For the Japanese American elderly, median income was $266 less for males and $128 less for females than the comparable figures for the general elderly population (Pacific/Asian Research Project, 1977a). The low incomes of the Asian American elderly are a reflection of the type of work they did while they were working, which was mostly in low-paying service, semi-skilled, and unskilled occupations. Often these occupations did not provide Social Security.

Health statistics for the Asian American elderly are almost nonexistent. In Hawaii and California life expectancies for the elderly Japanese and Chinese are longer than those for the white elderly population at ages 65 and over. Although no conclusive explanation has yet been provided for this differential mortality phenomenon among the aged of the different racial and ethnic groups, the same pattern is found among blacks vis-à-vis the white population. Carp and Kataoka (1976) reported that poor health was a major problem among the Chinese American elderly living in San Francisco's Chinatown, 30 percent of whom indicated that they were in poor health. Chinese American elderly show a higher degree of mental illness, perhaps because of their social and emotional isolation, and their suicide rate is three times as high as that of the general elderly population (Lyman, 1974).

Actual utilization of formal services by the Asian American elderly varies substantially from one ethnic group to another. Although the sample size was limited, a study by Salcido, Nakano, and Jue (1980) showed that Chinese American elderly used public programs least and that Filipino American elderly used such publicly available services as county hospitals, Social Security offices, and nutrition programs more frequently than Chinese, Japanese, and Korean American elderly. But community-based ethnic agencies were used extensively by these elderly of different ethnic origins, and even the use of other public agencies was greater when ethnic agency employees made special efforts to direct or escort them to these agencies. The majority of Chinese, Japanese, and Korean elderly preferred health care providers of their own ethnicity, but Filipino elderly did not show such a preference. It is also significant to note that in addition to the language and cultural barriers that are the source of underutilization of formal support systems, there seems to exist a sense of shame, particularly among Japanese American elderly, about the use of public services as a sign of dependence and inability to take care of themselves. In the San Diego study only a third of Japanese American elderly indicated that the government should be the institution responsible for meeting the needs of the elderly (Ishizuka, 1978). There is a tendency among Japanese American elderly, more than among other Asian American elderly, to rely on family and friends for assistance with personal problems (Salcido et al., 1980). In order to overcome barriers to service utilization it has been recommended to the Administration on Aging by the Pacific/Asian Elderly Research Project (1978) that the linkage between service delivery and effective use of service programs by the Asian American elderly consist of bilingual and bicultural personnel within the service program in addition to ethnic community intermediaries. It is worthwhile noting that the 1978 amendments to the Older Americans Act emphasized access to all existing services, including a requirement that area agencies on aging provide information and referral service in the appropriate language in areas where a large number of people speak a language other than English (Yip, 1981).

SUMMARY

Although knowledge about the Asian American elderly is still in a primitive stage, one can reasonably conclude that their current situation, both social and economic, has a great deal to do with the history of their immigration to the United States. Despite the general understanding that Asian Americans are more familistic in terms of caring for their elderly, the history of their immigration has forced many contemporary elderly to live outside of the normal family structure. Their occupational careers have not prepared them for comfortable retirement. Indeed, poverty is more rampant among them than among the elderly in the general population. Ethnic communities appear to be important lifelines for many of the Asian American elderly simply because of the language barriers they face and because of the discrimination and prejudice they have encountered in dealing with the larger society.

There exist substantial differences among the Asian American elderly of various ethnic origins. In this sense, each ethnic community has not only protected the elderly, at least in terms of their psychoemotional existence, from the larger community, but has also shielded them from other Asian ethnic communities. It is, therefore, entirely probable that each ethnic group has developed its own way of dealing with the elderly and its own mechanisms for adapting to the aging process. If differences indeed exist in adaptation to aging among the various Asian American ethnic groups—and there are ample indications that such differences exist, though no empirical data are available—what are the contributions of ethnicity to the aging process? The future Asian American elderly can be expected to show different patterns of aging by virtue of their broader acculturation into the larger society. Language and so-called cultural barriers will be minimal. It should then be possible to observe what influence, if any, strictly ethnic factors have on patterns of aging among Asian American elderly groups. Investigation of these factors is the major task facing the minority aging researcher in the future.

REFERENCES

Butler, R.N., and Lewis, M.I. *Aging and mental health*. Mosby, St. Louis, 1982.
Carp, F.M., and Kataoka, E. Health problems of the elderly of San Francisco's Chinatown. *Gerontologist*, 1976, *16*, 30–38.

Cheng, E. *The elder Chinese*. Campanile Press, San Diego, 1978.

Daniels, R. *The politics of prejudice*. University of California Press, Berkeley, 1962.

Hsu, F.L.K. *The challenge of the American dream: The Chinese in the United States*. Wadsworth, Belmont, Calif., 1971.

Huang, L.J. The Chinese American family. In C.H. Mindel and R.W. Habenstein (Eds.), *Ethnic families in America*. Elsevier, New York, 1976.

Ignacio, L.F. *Asian Americans and Pacific Islanders*. Pilipino Development Associations, San Jose, Calif., 1976.

Ishikawa, W. *Pacific Asian elderly*. Human Resources Corporation, San Francisco, 1978.

Ishizuka, K. *The elder Japanese*. Campanile Press, San Diego, 1978.

Kalish, R. and Yuen, S. Americans of East Asian ancestry: Aging and the aged. *Gerontologist*, 1971, *11*, 36–47.

Kalish, R. and Moriwaki, S. The world of the elderly Asian American. *Journal of Social Issues*, 1973, *29*, 187–209.

Kii, T. Japanese American elderly. In Nancy Osgood (Ed.), *Life after work*. Praeger, New York, 1982.

Kikumura, A., and Kitano, H.H. Interracial marriage: A picture of the Japanese American. *Journal of Social Issues*, 1973, *29*, 1–9.

Kim, K. and Hurh, W. Social and occupational assimilation of Korean immigrant workers in the U.S. *California Sociologist*, 1980, *3*, 125–142.

Lyman, S.M. *Chinese Americans*. Random House, New York, 1974.

Montero, D. Disengagement and aging among the Issei. In D.E. Gelfand and A.J. Kutzik (Eds.), *Ethnicity and aging*. Springer, New York, 1979.

Osako, M. Aging and family among Japanese Americans: The role of ethnic tradition in the adjustment to old age. *Gerontologist*, 1979, *19*, 448–455.

Pacific/Asian Elderly Research Project. *Census and baseline data: A detailed report*. Pacific/Asian Elderly Research Project, Los Angeles, 1977a.

———. *Existing research*. Pacific/Asian Elderly Research Project, Los Angeles, 1977b.

———. *Working paper: Preliminary framework for service delivery model building*. Pacific/Asian Elderly Research Project, Los Angeles, 1978.

Peterson, R. *The elder Pilipino*. Campanile Press, San Diego, 1978.

Salcido, R.M.; Nakano, C.; and Jue, S. The use of formal and informal health and welfare services of the Asian-American elderly: An exploratory study. *California Sociologist*, 1980, *3*, 213–229.

Simpson, G.E., and Yinger, J.M. *Racial and cultural minorities: An analysis of prejudice and discrimination*, 4th ed. Harper and Row, New York, 1972.

Skinner, K.A. Vietnamese in America: Diversity in adaptation. *California Sociologist*, 1980, *3*, 103–124.

U.S. Bureau of the Census. *1980 census of population: Race of the population by states*. PC80-S1-3, Supplementary Reports. U.S. Department of Commerce, Washington, D.C., May 1981a.

———. *1980 census of population: Race of the population by states*. PC80-S1-3, Supplementary Reports. U.S. Department of Commerce, Washington, D.C., July 1981b.

Yip, B. Accessibility to services for Pan-Asian elderly: Fact or fiction? In E.P. Stanford (Ed.), *Minority aging: Policy issues for the '80s*. Campanile Press, San Diego, 1981.

Yu, E.S.H. *Filipino migration and community organizations in the United States. California Sociologist*, 1980, *3*, 76–102.

Yuan, D.Y. Significant demographic characteristics in Chinese who intermarry in the United States. *California Sociologist*, 1980, *3*, 184–196.

13

BLACKS

RUTH L. GREENE
ILENE C. SIEGLER

In many ways the personal development, as well as the social, economic, and political participation of the present black elderly, has been defined and maintained by historical and contemporary social conditions to which blacks have had to respond and adapt. Because each cohort of the black elderly is exposed to different cultural practices and social and political conditions, cohort historical analysis can provide a useful context to analyze black aging by providing an awareness of the historical dimensions of the black experience in the United States and of how those dimensions influence personal life experiences throughout the life span. Table 13.1 helps focus our understanding of the relevant time periods.

COHORT HISTORICAL ANALYSIS

Wilson (1978) identified three major stages that blacks have experienced historically. The first stage includes the antebellum and post antebellum era. Stage two comprises the last quarter of the nineteenth century to about 1930, and is designated the period of industrial expansion. During these first two stages racial barriers were overt and systematic and were designed to eliminate blacks from economic, political, and social resources (Weinstein and Gatell, 1970; Marshall, 1967). The third period, extending from after World War II to the 1970s, showed a reduction of traditional racial conflict and an expansion of economic and social resources for blacks (Purcell and Cavanagh, 1972; Polaski and Marr, 1976). Historical data suggest that the black elderly aged 60 and above who developed, matured, and worked during the pre-industrial and industrial stages of race relations in the United States have experienced severe political, economic, and social subordination.

In the beginning of the nineteenth century blacks were prevented from voting through the use of the poll tax and literacy tests. Legal segregation was the norm

Table 13.1
Age of Various Cohorts in Different Years

	1900	1910	1920	1930	1940	1950	1960	1970	1980
Age of:				10	20	30	40	50	60
Cohort A (born 1920)									
Cohort B (born 1910)			10	20	30	40	50	60	70
Cohort C (born 1900)		10	20	30	40	50	60	70	80
Cohort D (born 1890)	10	20	30	40	50	60	70	80	90

Segregation Era   Civil Rights Era

and blacks were displaced from trades in which they specialized and relegated by employers, unions, and state laws to unskilled, strikebreaking, ''scab'' jobs. According to Wilson (1978:70),

Prior to the World War I period, very few blacks were employed in the nation's industrial plants. In the South, where before the Civil War blacks had successfully competed with whites in nearly every branch of industry, black labor had become restricted largely to agricultural work and to personal services. Organized white-worker resistance, reinforced by norms of racial exclusion that crystallized with the emergence of Jim Crow segregation, effectively prevented the free employment of black labor in industry.

During the 1920s and 1930s, the majority of blacks, those living in the South, suffered increasing unemployment as a result of the declining demand for farm labor due to mechanization, the devastation of the cotton crop by the boll weevil, and a reduced demand for cotton. The Great Depression was a particular hardship for black Americans. As Robert Weaver (1935: 200), former secretary of Housing and Urban Development, has observed:

Over half of the gainfully employed colored Americans are concentrated in domestic service and farming. The workers in these two pursuits are the most casual and unstable in the modern economic world. . . . The recent Depression has been extremely severe in its effects upon the South. The rural Negro—poor before the period of trade decline— was rendered even more needy after 1929. Many tenants found it impossible to obtain a contract for a crop, and scores of Negro farm owners lost their properties. . . . Thus, at the time of the announcement of the New Deal, there were many families without arrangements for a crop—and—an appreciable number without shelter.

There were moderate increases in economic and social participation by blacks during the early 1940s as more moved North for better opportunities. However, it was during the 1960s, as a result of the civil rights movement, expanded government policies and programs, increased educational opportunities, and efforts to reduce discrimination and segregation, that social, political, and economic resources opened up for black Americans. These gains, however, came too late to make an appreciable impact on the educational level or economic condition of the older cohort of the black elderly, but a larger number of the younger cohort of the older black adults have benefited. While prior to the 1960s almost all blacks suffered substantial economic, social, and educational subordination, current social and economic patterns show a mixed picture of more differentiation within the black population, with a prominent privileged middle class who have made advances in income, employment, and education, and an equally prominent underclass who are concentrated in lower-paying jobs.

Historically, changes in the social and economic structure and in racial conflict in the United States have had a profound effect on the life chances and personal experiences of black Americans. As socioeconomic trends and race relations change in America, they will have a great impact upon the social, economic, and psychological characteristics of the future black elderly.

SOCIAL AND ECONOMIC CHARACTERISTICS

Population

Current data from the U.S. Bureau of the Census show that the elderly population, the fastest growing age group in the United States, has increased to its highest proportion in history. In 1970, approximately 19 million Americans were 65 years of age and older. Currently, approximately 25 million adults, or over 11 percent of the population, are in this age group. Over the last decade, the elderly black population age 65 and over has had a larger increase than either the elderly white or the young black population (table 13.2). Blacks 65 years of age or older constituted approximately 8 percent of all older Americans.

The sex ratio of males to females in the elderly population, as shown in table 13.2, is low. Among blacks 65 and older, approximately 41 percent are males and 59 percent are females. Among whites the ratio is similar. In 1978, the geographic concentrations of the black elderly population differed from that of the white elderly population. Over half of the black population 60 and over was living in the South (see table 13.3).

Table 13.2

Distribution of Population Aged 65 and Over by Race and Sex, 1970 and 1980

Year, Sex, and Race	Total	65 and Over
		Number (in thousands)
1970, Total	203,235	19,972
Male	98,926	8,367
Female	104,309	11,605
White	178,098	18,272
Male	86,906	7,615
Female	91,192	10,657
Black	22,581	1,544
Male	10,749	669
Female	11,832	876
1980, Total	226,505	25,544
Male	110,032	10,303
Female	116,473	15,242
White	188,341	22,944
Male	91,670	9,220
Female	96,671	13,724
Black	26,488	2,060
Male	12,516	846
Female	13,972	1,214
	Percent Distribution	
1970, Total	100.0	9.8
1980, Total	100.0	11.3
1980 Male	100.0	9.4
1980 Female	100.0	13.1
1980 White	100.0	12.2
1980 Black	100.0	7.9

Source: U.S. Bureau of the Census, *Statistical Abstract of the United States*, USGPO, Washington, D.C., 1981.

Education

In 1970, nearly 30 percent of whites 65 and over had completed high school, as compared to 9 percent for older blacks. Over the decade, the high school graduation rates for blacks and whites have risen. As opportunities for school enrollment have increased, so has the educational attainment of blacks. However, by 1980, the proportion of whites who attended four years of high school was still substantially higher than that for blacks (See table 13.4).

Table 13.3
Percentage Distribution of Population Aged 65 and Over by Region, 1978

	Black		White
	Total	*65 and over*	*65 and over*
Total (in thousands)	24,710	1,930	20,316
Percent	100.00	100.00	100.00
Northeast	17.7	15.3	25.5
North Central	20.0	16.4	28.0
South	53.3	60.2	30.7
West	9.1	8.1	15.8

Source: U.S. Department of Health and Human Services, Characteristics of the black elderly. National Clearing House on Aging, Washington, D.C., 1980.

Table 13.4
Percentage Distribution of Population by Education Completed and Race, 1970 and 1980

	Black		White	
	55-65	*65 and over*	*55-65*	*65 and over*
1970				
Four years of high school	17.0	9.0	46.5	29.9
One year of college	6.3	4.4	18.2	13.3
Four years of college	3.8	2.0	9.1	6.7
1980				
Four years of high school	32.5	17.6	65.8	44.2
One year of college	10.3	6.5	25.1	18.4
Four years of college	4.3	3.5	12.8	9.0

Source: U.S. Bureau of the Census, Population profile of the United States. *Current Population Reports*, ser. P-20, no. 374. USGPO, Washington, D.C., 1982.

Table 13.5
Percentage Distribution of Population Aged 60 and Over by Employment Status, Sex, Age, and Race, 1979 and 1981

Sex and Employment Status	60-64 Black		60-64 White		65 and over Black		65 and over White	
	1979	1981	1979	1981	1979	1981	1979	1981
Male								
Percentage of total in labor force	58.8	52.8	63.3	59.3	21.9	16.8	20.6	18.6
Percentage of labor force unemployed	1.9	6.0	3.0	3.4	5.5	8.1	2.8	2.4
Female								
Percentage of total in labor force	37.2	37.6	33.6	32.1	11.9	9.3	7.9	7.9
Percentage of labor force unemployed	6.2	4.2	3.1	3.5	4.4	5.8	3.2	3.4

Source: U.S. Department of Labor, *Employment and Earnings.* USGPO, Washington, D.C., 1982.

Historically, blacks have lagged behind whites in school attendance. These differentials in school attendance between black age cohorts who attended high school during the 1930s and 1940s can be attributed to segregation practices and availability of schools for school-age black youth. There is evidence to show that as the younger-age black cohorts continue to complete higher levels of school enrollment we can expect high levels of educational attainment in the black elderly population, at least in the area of secondary education. Currently, 86.9 percent of the whites 25 to 34 years old have finished high school, as compared to 75.9 percent for blacks. While the number of black adults enrolled in college has doubled during the decade, only 11.7 percent of the black population 25 to 34 years old has completed college, as compared to 24.3 percent for whites. The differential in college completion will undoubtedly affect the income and occupational mobility of future older black adults.

Labor Force Participation, Poverty, and Income

Historically, the proportion of black women in the labor force has exceeded that of white women, yet their economic status does not reflect their sustained work history (Jones, 1983). Current trends in labor force participation of black and white females in the 55 to 59 age group show employment rates that are quite similar, but, as table 13.5 shows, the employment rate of black women

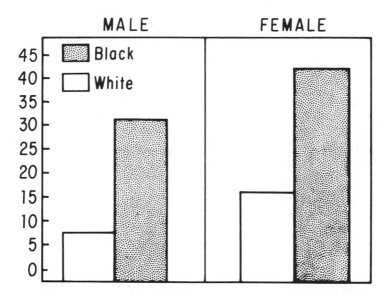

Source: U.S. Bureau of the Census, Characteristics of the population below the poverty level, *Current Population Reports*, p60, no. 133. USGPO, Washington, D.C., 1982.

Figure 13.1
Percentage of the Population Aged 65 and Over below the Poverty Level by Sex and Race, 1980

60 years or older, often heads of households, is still higher than that for white women. For these women, who in their younger years worked in occupations not covered by Social Security and who likewise receive little income from property and other assets, work is a necessity.

From 1979 to 1980, the labor force participation rate for older black and white men has declined. While black men at each age level experience considerably lower levels of labor force participation, the participation rates for blacks and whites at age 60 and over are comparable. In contrast, the unemployment rate for black men at age 60 is twice that of white men (table 13.5).

Currently, the poverty rate for blacks 65 and older is 31.1 percent, about three times the rate for whites (13.6 percent). A breakdown by sex of the 65 and over group shows that black women have the largest percentage below the poverty level, 35 percent of whom are heads of households (see figure 13.1). In 1980 the median income for black married couples 65 years of age and over was $7,350, compared to $12,340 for white married couples. Median income for nonmarried individuals showed the greatest disparity for black females (see figure 13.2). Current data on income distribution of the elderly indicate that white older adults are more likely than blacks to receive income from assets, pensions, and annuities, while the overwhelming majority of income for older black workers

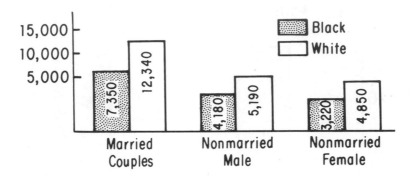

Source: U.S. Department of Health and Human Services, *Income of the population 55 and over, 1980*. No. 13-11871. Office of Research and Statistics, Social Security Administration, Office of Policy, Washington, D.C., January 1983.

Figure 13.2
Total Median Money Income of Population Aged 65 Years and Over by Marital Status, Sex, and Race, 1980

comes from earnings and Supplemental Security Income (Thompson, 1979; Davis-Wong, 1981).

Health and Mortality

Several measures have been used to assess the health status of the black elderly. These include mortality rates, clinical diagnoses from medical personnel, self-reports of health status, and behavioral indices which include measures of health limitations and disability. The findings generally indicate that elderly blacks experience higher mortality rates from chronic diseases and greater limitations of activities due to chronic conditions. As shown in the 1982 report of the health status of the United States from the U.S. Department of Health and Human Services (table 13.6), blacks have particularly high mortality rates in the circulatory disease categories. These findings are consistent with descriptive self-report data from a current nationally representative sample of black adults 55 and older who report moderate to high levels of physical health problems and high incidence of such chronic health diseases as hypertension, arthritis, and rheumatism (Chatters and Jackson, 1982).

The life expectancy at birth of black males and females in 1980 was 65.3 and

Table 13.6
Death Rates for Selected Causes of Death, 65 Years and Older, According to Race and Sex: United States, 1979

	Black		White	
	Male	*Female*	*Male*	*Female*
	Number (in thousands)			
Diseases of heart	1,723.2	1,136.6	1,724.9	781.0
Cerebrovascular diseases	449.4	366.6	250.5	180.6
Malignant neoplasms	1,298.1	626.6	1,065.4	587.7
Respiratory system	444.7	72.2	409.6	97.3
Motor vehicle accidents	39.6	10.5	29.1	13.8
Homicide and legal intervention	31.1	9.5	6.0	2.6
Suicide	12.9	2.6	33.5	7.9

Source: U.S. Department of Health and Human Services, *Health—United States, 1982.* DHHS Publication No. (PHS) 83-1232. USGPO, Washington, D.C., 1982.

74.0 respectively, as compared to 70.5 and 78.1 for whites (U.S. Department of Health and Human Services, 1982). Surprisingly, in spite of poverty and differential environmental hazards, black mortality rates are lower than those for whites past age 75 (Manton, 1982). Although a current explanation for this relative advantage of blacks at advanced age is that black and white populations have different rates of aging, we suspect that individual dynamics, which include coping strategies, may be an important influence. When one has lived with stress and few economic resources and assets throughout a lifetime, negative outcomes in late life may appear less serious, or one may have developed a reliable set of strategies for coping with transitions (Gatz et al., 1982).

Psychological Characteristics: Coping, Adaptation, and Mental Health

An area within the field of black aging that has received increased attention during the last few years is that of psychological aging. Psychological aging is defined as the ability on the part of the individual to adapt to the changing demands of his or her environment (Birren, 1977). The need for research into the relationship between psychological aging in the elderly and the impact of social and environmental factors on its progression is highlighted by several prevailing conditions.

First, until recently there has been little interest in understanding the relationship between stresses, life crises, coping strategies, behavioral responses, and the mental health of older people, and specific information on the adaptive strategies of the black aged is still limited.

Second, there is a critical lack of well-formulated theory which could offer guidelines for the development of research models to evaluate the mental health status of the black aged. Jackson (1980) states that there are two prevailing, but conflicting, theoretical positions concerning psychological aging in black adults: many theoreticians believe that race is the major determinant of psychological aging, while others assume that sex and socioeconomic factors play a major role in the differential effects of the aging process. The descriptive studies that have been conducted to assess the relationship of mental illness and such variables as age, race, and socioeconomic status have not been fully analyzed in the research literature on the black elderly (see Jackson, 1979). The incidence of poor mental health and the factors that influence its occurrence are not fully understood. One of the major problems in understanding the effects of variables on the indices of mental health is that there are so many definitions of mental health in the research literature and often these definitions are not adequately specified. Recent studies have questioned the adequacy of traditional models of mental health theory and practice for blacks and suggest that a broader perspective be employed that takes into consideration stress, coping, and adaptation as well as the environmental conditions that promote impaired mental health (Bell and Menta, 1981; Myers, 1982).

Some of the studies of mental health concerns of the black aged have focused on the effects of racism on mental health status and on the delivery of effective mental health resources to a majority of aged blacks (Carter, 1978; Poussant, 1983). These studies suggest that researchers take into consideration the environmental, economic, and cultural stresses that impinge on the elderly in the black community. Intervention strategies, in this context, involve changing those adverse conditions that lead to impaired mental health. Other researchers have measured the relationship of race and age to mental illness and have concluded that race is not an important predictor of mental illness when age, sex, and socioeconomic status are controlled (Dohrenwend and Dohrenwend, 1967).

Another body of literature focuses on the effect of culture and minority status on psychological well-being and mental health (Kent, 1971; Kobata et al., 1980). The emphasis of this research is on the diversity of and variation between racial groups. Kobata, Lockery, and Moriwaki (1980:458) have stated that when assessing the mental status of ethnic minority elderly, care must be taken to evaluate his "current problems, life situation, his social and personal world, his values and his life history." Current literature suggests that this minority status can have either positive or negative psychological outcomes. It has been suggested that blacks, because of their unique history, react differently in life crises. Jackson, Bacon, and Peterson (1977:178) argue that "because of societal barriers which perpetually confront blacks across the life span, the adjustment to aging, particularly psychologically, might be different and perhaps a relatively easier task in comparison to the adjustment of the white majority.''

One crucial omission in this stress and mental health model is the lack of clear delineation and specification of the coping strategies that have become systematized in the black elderly population. Coping strategies in this context have been defined by George (1980:30) as ''the covert and overt behaviors individuals use to prevent, alleviate, and respond to stressful situations.'' Little research has been conducted to examine the interrelationships among stressful life events within several event contexts. At present we know little about how life stresses differentially affect blacks and whites, or even men and women in the same racial group. We are still trying to find out what kind of coping strategies promote psychological well-being.

Future research should provide a better understanding of those factors that facilitate adaptive, successful coping and identify other circumstances that might precipitate impaired psychological well-being. In 1970, the President's Committee on Mental Health for the Elderly (U.S. Department of Health, Education and Welfare, 1979) reiterated what the demographic data had always shown. Blacks and other minorities, because of their life situation, were at high risk for mental health problems. Yet, we find an overwhelming number of these older adults who report that they are satisfied with their lives and are coping successfully with the transitions in later life.

Current research suggests that religion and strong family support systems are very important personal resources and strengths that black older adults use as they make adjustments in later life (Hill, 1972; Cantor et al., 1979; Bass et al., 1982; Carter, 1982; S. Taylor, 1982; Taylor et al., 1982). However, critics note that family functioning and structure and the importance attached to religion by older black adults may be more a function of socioeconomic status than race (Jackson, 1980; Seelback and Sauer, 1977). These studies are a salient example of the theoretical differences in the research literature on black aging.

RESEARCH ISSUES

Over the last decade there has been an extensive number of studies conducted to assess the effects of minority group status on the life situation and patterns of aging of older adults in the United States. In the literature on the black elderly at least three conceptual frameworks have emerged as guidelines for the development of research models: (1) double jeopardy, (2) social structure variations, and (3) age as equalizer. One theory, that of double jeopardy, states that black older adults have had special restrictions in opportunity and are more likely than whites to have lower incomes, poorer health, and less education, and are therefore quite different in their patterns of adjustment. A second position asserts that patterns of racial stratification and inequalities in the United States have changed in recent years and that the life chances of individual blacks are related to their economic class position rather than to their minority group status (Wilson, 1978).

Therefore, when social class is controlled, there is likely to be very little difference between whites and blacks. The third position suggests that the needs and problems of older adults are similar regardless of race. For these theorists, advancing age may equalize racial or social inequalities that existed earlier (Kent, 1971; Dowd and Bengtson, 1978).

These conceptual frameworks suggest multiple variables—social class, age, race, and sex—which together account for variant patterns in aging in black elderly. A comprehensive framework for studying the black elderly would view these variables as a dynamic system rather than as an aggregate of individual causal variables. Unfortunately, many studies have focused on too few variables or have viewed each variable as monolithic and static, thus overlooking the complexity of the issues.

A second criticism of existing studies of the black elderly, particularly those in the area of adaptation, is that too often the focus is on the impact of social interaction or socioeconomic variables on one specific outcome (i.e., life satisfaction, self-esteem, or employment status) and too little attention is given to the coping processes that the black elderly employ as they respond to their environment. Our own work in coping and adaptation shows that the differences that the black elderly display may be differences in style and expression—more a reflection of the process of adaptation than differences in outcome measures (Greene et al., 1982).

SPECIAL RESOURCES

We have not included a list of major organizations concerned with aging as addresses for these groups have been provided elsewhere in this volume. Two organizations are particularly active in the area of black aging:

National Urban League
500 East 62nd Street
New York, NY 10021

National Center on Black Aged
142K K Street NW
Suite 500
Washington, DC 20036

The references include a number of major references on black aged, in addition to those cited in the text.

REFERENCES

Bass, B.A.; Wyatt, G.E.; and Wyatt, B.J. (Eds.). *The Afro-american family: Assessment, research and treatment issues.* Grune and Stratton, New York, 1982.

Bell, C.C., and Menta, H. Misdiagnosis of black patients with manic depressive illness. *Journal of the National Medical Association*, 1981, *73*, 101–107.

Birren, J.E., and Renner, J. Research on the psychology of aging: Principles and experimentation. In J.E. Birren and K.W. Schaie (Eds.), *Handbook of the psychology of aging*. Van Nostrand Reinhold, New York, 1977.

Cantor, M.; Rosenthal, K.; and Wilker, L. Social and family relationships of black aged women in New York City. *Journal of Minority Aging*, 1979, *4*, 50–61.

Carter, A. Religion and the black elderly: The historical basis of social and psychological concerns. In R. Manuel (Ed.), *Minority aging: sociological and social psychological issues*. Greenwood Press, Westport, Conn., 1982.

Carter, J. The black aged: A strategy for future mental health services. *Journal of the American Geriatrics Society*, 1978, *26*, 553–556.

Chatters, L., and Jackson, J.S. Health and older blacks. *Quarterly Contact*, 1982, *5*, no. 2, 1–7.

Davis-Wong, D.A. Social Security and older blacks. *Urban Research Review*, 1981, *7*, no. 3, 1–11.

Dohrenwend, B.S., and Dohrenwend, B.P. *Class and race as status-related sources of stress*. Aldine Press, Chicago, 1967.

Dowd, J., and Bengtson, V. Aging in minority populations. *Journal of Gerontology*, 1978, *33*, 427–436.

Faulkner, O.; Heisel, M.A.; and Simms, P. Life strengths and life stresses: Explorations in the measurement of the mental health of the black aged. *American Journal of Orthopsychiatry*, 1975, *45*, 102–110.

Fischer, J. Negroes and whites and rates of mental illness: Reconsideration of a myth. *Psychiatry*, 1970, *32*, 428–446.

Gatz, M.; Gease, E.; Tyler, R.; and Moran, J. Psychosocial competence characteristics of black and white women: The constraining effects of "Triple Jeopardy." *Black Scholar*, January 1982, 5–12.

George, L. *Role transitions in later life*. Brooks-Cole, Monterey, Calif., 1980.

Greene, R.S.; Siegler, I.C.; and Gatz, M. *A qualitative analysis of racial differences in a study of coping*. Paper presented at the Annual Scientific Meeting of the Gerontological Society of America, Boston, November 1982.

Hill, R.B. *The strengths of black families*. Emerson Hall, New York, 1972.

———. *A demographic profile of the black elderly*. Aging, Nos. 287–288 (September-October 1978). U.S. Department of Health, Education, and Welfare, Administration on Aging.

Holzberg, C. Ethnicity and aging: Anthropological perspectives on more than just the minority elderly. *Gerontologist*, 1982, *22*, 249-251.

Jackson, J.J. Epidemiological aspects of mental illness among aged black women and men. *Journal of Minority Aging*, 1979, *4*, 76–87.

———. *Minorities and aging*. Wadsworth, Belmont, Calif., 1980.

Jackson, J.J.; Chatters, M.; and Neighbors, H.W. The mental health status of older black Americans. *Black Scholar*, 1982, 21–35.

Jackson, J.S.; Bacon, J.D.; and Peterson, J. Life satisfaction among black urban elderly. *Aging and Human Development*, 1977, *8*, 169–179.

Jones, B. The economic status of black women. In J.D. Williams (Ed.), *The state of black America, 1983*. National Urban League, New York, 1983.

Kent, D.P. The elderly in minority groups: Variant patterns of aging. *Gerontologist*, 1971, *11*, 26–29.

Kobata, F.S.; Lockery, S.A.; and Moriwaki, S. Minority issues in mental health and aging. In J.E. Birren and R. Sloane (Eds.), *Handbook of mental health and aging*. Prentice-Hall, Englewood Cliffs, N.J., 1980.

Manton, K. Temporal and age variation of United States black and white cause-specific mortality differentials: A study of the recent changes in the relative health status of the United States black population. *Gerontologist*, 1982, *22*, 170–179.

Marshall, R. *The Negro worker*. Random House, New York, 1967.

Myers, H.F. Stress, ethnicity and social class: A model for research with black populations. In E. Jones and S. Korchin (Eds.), *Minority mental health*. Praeger, New York, 1982.

Myers, J.K.; Lindenthal, J.J.; Pepper, M.P.; and Osrander, D.R. Life events and mental status: A longitudinal study. *Journal of Health and Social Behavior*, 1972, *12*, 398–415.

Northrup, H., and Rowan, R. *The Negro and employment opportunity: Problems and practices*. University of Michigan Press, Ann Arbor, 1965.

Nowlin, J.B. Geriatric health status: Influence of race and economic status. *Journal of Minority Aging*. 1979, *4*, 93–97.

Poloski, H.; and Marr, W. *The Negro almanac: A reference work on the Afro-American*. Bellwether Publishing, New York, 1976.

Poussant, A.L. The mental health status of blacks—1983. In J.D. Williams (Ed.), *The state of black America, 1983*. National Urban League, New York, 1983.

Purcell, T. and Cavanagh, G. *Blacks in the Industrial World: Issues for the Manager*. Free Press, New York, 1972.

Scott, J., and Gaitz, C.M. Ethnic and age differences in mental health measurements. *Diseases of the Nervous System*, 1975, *36*, 389–393.

See, J.J., and Miller, K.S. Mental health. In K.S. Miller and R.M. Greger (Eds.), *Comparative studies of blacks and whites in the United States*. Seminar Press, New York, 1973.

Seelbach, W., and Sauer, W. Filial responsibility expectations and morale among aged parents. *Gerontologist*, 1977, *17*, 492–499.

Taylor, R.J.; Jackson, J.S.; and Quick, A.D. The frequency of social support among black Americans. *Urban Research Review*, 1982, *8*, 50–60.

Taylor, S. Mental health and successful coping among aged black women. In R. Manuel (Ed.), *Minority aging: sociological and social psychological issues*. Greenwood Press, Westport, Conn., 1982.

Thompson, G.B. Black-white differences in private pensions: Findings from the Retirement History Study. *Social Security Bulletin*, 1979, *42*, no. 2, 15–22.

U.S. Bureau of the Census. Social and economic characteristics of the older population, 1978. *Current Population Reports*, ser. P-23, no. 85. USGPO, Washington, D.C., 1979.

———. *Statistical abstract of the United States: 1981*, 102nd ed. USGPO, Washington, D.C., 1981.

———. Characteristics of the population below the poverty level: 1980. *Current Population Reports*, ser. P-60. USGPO, Washington, D.C., 1982a.

———. Population profile of the United States: 1981. *Current Population Reports*, ser. P-20, no. 374. USGPO, Washington, D.C., 1982b.

U.S. Department of Health and Human Services. *Characteristics of the black elderly*. National Clearing House on Aging, Washington, D.C., 1980.

———. *Health—United States 1982*. DHHS Publication No. (PHS) 83-1232. USGPO,

Washington, D.C., December 1982.

———. *Income of the population 55 and over, 1980*. No. 13-11871. Office of Research and Statistics, Social Security Administration Office of Policy, Washington, D.C., January 1983.

U.S. Department of Health, Education and Welfare. *The reports of the President's Commission on Mental Health: Task Panel on the Elderly*. DHEW Publication No. (OHDS) 80-20960. USGPO, Washington, D.C., November 1979.

U.S. Department of Health, Education and Welfare, Public Health Service. *Health characteristics of minority groups, United States, 1976*. No. 27. Vital and Health Statistics of the National Center for Health Statistics, Washington, D.C., April 1978a.

———. *Health—United States: 1979*. DHEW Publication No. (PHS) 80-1232. Office of Health Research Statistics, and Technology, Washington, D.C., 1978b.

U.S. Department of Labor. Employment and earnings. USGPO, Washington, D.C., 1982.

Warheit, G.J.; Holzer, C.E.; and Arey, S.A. Race and mental illness: An epidemiological update. *Journal of Health and Social Behavior*, 1975, *16*, 243–256.

Weaver, R.C. The new deal and the Negro. *Opportunity—Journal of Negro Life*, 1935, *13*, no. 7, 1–10.

Weinstein, A., and Gatell, F., Jr. (Eds.). *The segregation era, 1863–1954*. Oxford University Press, New York, 1970.

Wilson, W.J. *The declining significance of race: Blacks and changing American institutions*. University of Chicago Press, Chicago, 1978.

14

EUROPEANS

BERTRAM J. COHLER

Much current discussion on aging in American society, including normative changes with age, as well as problems of social policy, has been based on findings regarding a particular generation or cohort of older persons, either those born in Europe, or the children of these European immigrants. Circumstances associated with life experiences in the Old World, such as traditional peasant life-styles, as well as those associated with immigration, leading to disruption in traditional ways of understanding self and place in the course of life, have affected the aging experience of older persons from European ethnic groups. Differences in circumstances, time, and mode of immigration, together with differences in patterns of settlement in the New World across specific ethnic groups, have further affected the experience of aging in the New World in ways that may not be as relevant for successive generations of better educated older Americans preserving ethnic ties in ways quite different either from the culture of the Old World, or the ethnic traditions of first- and second-generation members of European ethnic groups.

This chapter discusses aging from the perspective of the European-American experience, focusing primarily on three ethnic groups differing in time of immigration and mode of settlement in the United States: Irish, Italian, and Polish Americans. Ethnicity is understood in this chapter as referring to differences in value orientations or underlying cultural assumptions, leading to particular ways of perceiving and understanding experience, and specifying preferred alternatives for resolving such universal dilemmas as the relation of person and nature, or relations among persons (C. Kluckhohn, 1951; Kluckhohn and Strodtbeck, 1961). While there is only a limited range of solutions for such dilemmas, preferred rank order of solutions, together with associated rituals and beliefs, is important in organizing personal and collective experience, providing meaning for life and sense of identity (Weber, 1968; Devereux, 1975). Based on this view of culture, ethnicity may be defined as "maintenance of particular customs and beliefs, based on particular solutions for enduring human dilemmas, transmitted across generations, leading to a sense of distinctiveness or 'peoplehood' in a society which is historically and geographically separate, and which are not necessarily continuous with contemporary traditions within particular societies of origin.'' Even after several generations of residence in the United States, many persons descended from European peoples still identify with their European heritage (Greeley, 1971).

Two other aspects of this definition should be noted: (1) Experiences both of the immigrant and subsequent generations further affect ethnic traditions. Consistent with Wallace's (1956) discussion of culture change, persons faced with new traditions unlike their own often rely on familiar ways which, over time, become increasingly archaic and unlike those of the sending nation. These archaic and often stereotyped rituals and beliefs assist in maintaining positive morale among members of particular ethnic groups. (2) Immigration is often accompanied both by back-migration and return which, together with intermarriage, may further alter ethnic traditions across subsequent generations (Alba, 1982).

THE EUROPEAN PEASANT AND THE NEW WORLD

Over the course of more than 350 years, from the first settlements in the New World until the past two decades, the history of immigration to the United States has been largely that of the European peasant. More than two-thirds of all immigrants to the United States have come from rural Europe (Rubin, 1966; U.S. Bureau of the Census, 1975). Readable accounts of the history of European immigration to the United States have been provided by Handlin (1957), while discussions of specific ethnic groups are included in Thernstrom's (1980) encyclopedic volume. Most discussions of European immigration distinguish between two periods of European immigration, an "old immigration" of predominantly Northern Europeans between 1830 and 1870, and a "new immigration" of predominantly Eastern and Southern Europeans from about 1880 until World War I.

The so-called old and new immigrations reflect quite different historical participation in what Schooler (1976) has termed the "legacy of serfdom." As a consequence of this hierarchical social order, individual autonomy, self-direction, and initiative were discouraged: tenant farmers or serfs were expected to till and plow in common, as required by custom and the practices of individual lords. Across Europe, there was variation in the extent and duration of feudal social organization, from Scandinavia, where feudal ties were never established; to England and Ireland, where serfdom was abolished early in the seventeenth century; to Poland, Russia, and the eastern states of the German empire, where serfdom was gradually abolished during the early nineteenth century; and, finally, to Italy, particularly south of the Po River, where serfdom was formally abolished after the middle of the nineteenth century. This tradition continued, virtually unchanged, in southern Italy and Sicily until after the end of World War II (Banfield, 1958).

Schooler (1976) has demonstrated that persons from the old European immigration, especially members of the English, Irish, and Scandinavian ethnic groups, which are characterized by less extensive involvement with the legacy of serfdom, show more effective intellectual functioning, increased cognitive flexibility, and increased emphasis upon self rather than others as the perceived locus of actions, when contrasted with persons from the new Eastern and Southern European ethnic groups, which had prolonged contact with the legacy of serfdom. Indeed, Italian immigrants to the United States at the turn of the century came directly from the legacy of serfdom, while this form of social organization had ended in Poland a century earlier.

Variations in the legacy of serfdom as an influence upon patterns of settlement in the New World, as well as differences in adaptation to a new culture, provide useful means for understanding the history of ethnic groups in the United States, including differences in the use of social services among older persons from Northern and Southern European ethnic groups. The present discussion is focused primarily upon three Catholic ethnic groups—Irish, Polish, and Italian Americans—differing in extent of immersion in the legacy of serfdom, as well as in time of peak immigration to the United States. The Irish American group is characterized by membership in the old immigration and little participation in the legacy of serfdom, while Polish and Italian American immigrant groups, belonging to the new immigration, historically had participated more extensively in the feudal order.

The impact of the Anglo colonial tradition in the United States has been much greater than the actual number of immigrants involved. From the first Eastern Seaboard settlements until the beginning of the old immigration after 1830, there were only about 1 million English and Scotch-Irish settlers (Easterlin, 1980). At first, the old immigration presented little challenge to the Anglo-Protestant ethic (Weber, 1958), which emphasized the value of a rational, methodical way of life. However, by the 1850s establishment of the Catholic Church as a significant social and political force in American life hastened formation of ethnocentric social movements which advocated restoration of the eighteenth-century Protestant-colonial ideal. These movements, including the Know Nothing political party, the Social Darwinist movement under the leadership of William Sumner and Herbert Spencer, and, somewhat later, such fringe groups as the Ku Klux Klan, gathered increasing momentum over the second half of the nineteenth century, particularly after the onset of the new immigration, leading eventually to the restrictive immigration quotas imposed upon European immigration after World War I (Hofstadter, 1944; Jones, 1960).

The new immigration after 1880 was not only largely Catholic (with the exception of three and a quarter-million Eastern European and Russian Jews), but also largely illiterate. Easterlin (1980) reports that 54 percent of Southern Italians and 40 percent of Polish Catholics, as contrasted with only 2.6 percent of Irish immigrants, were unable to read and write. However, the traditional conformist and dependent mode of social organization of Eastern and Southern Europe provided a labor force with the value orientations appropriate for the development of a labor-intensive factory system, leading to the rapid industrialization of the United States by the beginning of the twentieth century (Gutman, 1977; Kohn, 1969).

Over the years between 1860 and 1914, nearly 4 million Southern Italian immigrants arrived in the United States (U.S. Bureau of the Census, 1975), 79 percent of whom arrived between 1900 and 1914. As a result of periodic repartitions of Poland during the nineteenth century, it is somewhat more difficult to determine the number of Polish immigrants. The U.S. Immigration and Naturalization Service recorded more than 150,000 Polish immigrants through 1899, but after the turn of the century the homeland of Polish immigrants was listed with the occupying nation for that region of the country. Lopata (1976) has reanalyzed data from the Immigration and Naturalization Service for the years following 1899, differentiating between Polish Catholics and Russian Jews living on the Polish-Russian border and immigrating to the United States over the same years as a consequence of the pogroms.

Recognizing that Lopata's figures are based on the self-reported peoplehood of immigrants, rather than on stated homeland of origin, more than a million and a half Polish immigrants arrived in the United States between 1900 and World War I. Catholic Poland ranks sixth among European sending nations (excluding England), following Germany with about five and a half million immigrants, Ireland with more than four and a third million immigrants, Italy with nearly four and a quarter million immigrants, Austria-Hungary with four million immigrants, and Russia with three and a quarter million (largely Jewish) immigrants.

The new immigration further added to the power of the Catholic Church as a major social and political force within American society. Furthermore, as contrasted with values of the old Irish immigration, the values of the new Catholic and Jewish immigrant groups could be less easily assimilated into American society. Emphasis on assimilation of the new immigrants to traditional American values was replaced by emphasis on cultural pluralism, stressing the importance of maintaining enduring differences in ancestry and traditions over time (Glazer and Moynihan, 1970).

AGING AND THE PEASANT FAMILY IN THE OLD AND NEW WORLD

Findings from ethnographic and empirical studies suggest that differences in the rank order for preferred solutions for basic human problems, the basis of cultural pluralism, continue in American society (Gordon, 1964). However, these differences may not be constant over time. Just as there are changes between the preferred rank order for solutions to universal dilemmas when contrasting the historic value orientations of given sending nations with those of European ethnic groups in America (Spiegel, 1971), there have also been changes in these solutions within particular ethnic groups in American society across generations or cohorts (Hansen, 1952; Gans, 1962; Cohler and Grunebaum, 1981). Cross-generational transmission of these value orientations is largely a function of pre-adult and adult socialization within the family (Mindel and Habenstein, 1976; Cohler and Grunebaum, 1981).

Immigration, which transforms culture into ethnicity, also leads to changes in social organization within the family which may be discontinuous between the Old and New World (Vecoli, 1972; Woehrer, 1982). Particularly within the Irish and Italian ethnic groups, the role of older parents in the family has shown dramatic reversals from the Old to the New World. Among Irish farm families of the West counties, although Social Security has lowered the retirement age (Streib, 1972), it is not uncommon for those offspring selected to run the family farm to be in their mid-forties, and still single, when the older parental couple retires from active management (Arensberg and Kimball, 1968; Fleetwood, 1980). From the early nineteenth century, the possibility that offspring could emigrate has relieved pressure on the older parental couple to relinquish control. Among Irish families in the United States, little of this traditional power of the parental generation may be observed; rapid social mobility (Greeley, 1974) and changes in helping patterns between urban families (Biddle, 1976) led to dramatic changes in the role of the older family member in the United States. Stated in terms of Kluckhohn and Strodtbeck's (1961) and Spiegel's (1971) discussion of variations in value orientations, the first-ranked preferred solution for relations among family members in the Irish family shifted from lineal in the Old World to individualistic in the New World, leading to reduced power exercised by the older parents.

Even more dramatic changes, leading to enhanced rather than reduced status for older persons, may be observed within the Italian family in the Old and New World. In contrast with Irish farm families, Italian peasants neither owned nor lived on their land. Rather, they lived along with other families in dense settlements known as agro-towns, working on rented plots often widely scattered in the district. Abject poverty across many generations enhanced suspiciousness of others, leading to what Banfield (1958) characterized as amoral familism, maximizing the gains of the nuclear family at the cost of ties to kindred. Older family members, less able to contribute to the household economy, have been regarded as a burden until the present time (Florea, 1980). Furthermore, there was danger that these older parents might inform siblings and other kindred of any good fortune, leading to demands for sharing and assistance which could soon deplete family resources. A similar impact of poverty upon family relations has been described in Stack's (1974) ethnographic study of black welfare families in the United States.

Clustered settlements led to especially rapid communication; as the first villagers emigrated, they sent back word of the opportunity in the New World, providing first-person testimony when returning for relatives. These first settlers from the agro-town provided ready access to housing and jobs, fostering a process of chain migration (McDonald and McDonald, 1964). Already familiar with urban life, Italian families immigrated to the larger cities of the Eastern Seaboard and the Midwest (Ward, 1971). Often, as a result of chain migration, several generations of relatives from the same family and village lived together in an apartment building, sharing resources and assistance and emphasizing interdependent family ties in a quite different manner from Old World family relations (Gans, 1962; Cohler and Grunebaum, 1981). These ethnic ghettos (Wirth, 1928), which were developed at least in part as a result of chain migration and which reflected the importance of ethnic traditions for continuing adjustment in the New World (Gans, 1962), rather than enduring simply as a consequence of residential segregation (Yancey et al., 1976), have been threatened by urban social changes, adversely affecting the morale of older residents of these ethnic communities.

Living in an industrial society, older persons could still make a contribution, both through participation in factory work and in caring for children and household so that younger family members could be free to work. The preferred solution for relations among family members changed from the more individualistic solution characteristic of Southern Italy to a collateral organization in the United States in which older family members were able to make significant contributions to the quality of family life, including transmission of beliefs and practices so important in the preservation of Old World customs in the United States (Gans, 1962; Bianco, 1974).

While immigration resulted in the dissolution of the traditional extended Irish farm family among Irish Americans and in the emergence of a modified extended family form among Italian Americans, immigration did little to change the social organization of the Polish family in the New World. Like the Irish peasant family, the Polish peasant had traditionally lived on a family farm rather than in urban settlements. However, language differences and differences in customs, including the tradition of serfdom, meant that immigration to the New World was much more difficult for the Polish peasant than for the Irish peasant. Over time, the Church parish emerged as a particularly salient force in immigration (Thomas and Znaniecki, 1918–1920; Lopata, 1976; Kantowicz, 1975). Reliance upon corporate decisions on the part of the parish, including the first decision to emigrate, led, over time, to reliance upon the Church and other civic organizations as the major source of support for new immigrants. Well-functioning voluntary associations, tied to the Church, continue to buffer members of the Polish community from many of the problems of the larger society (Sandberg, 1974; Lopata, 1976; Wrobel, 1979).

The position of the older Polish family member was little changed between the Old and New World. In a society in which all available land and possessions had long since been distributed, redistribution and accumulation of additional possessions could only be realized through marriage, emphasizing the importance placed upon collateral relations as the preferred solution for the dilemma of human relationships in the Old World, a preference that has been maintained in the New World (Lopata, 1976). In both the Old and New World, name and good reputation of older family members, as well as material goods accumulated over a lifetime by older family members, have provided an important source of status for younger family members. Since so much cultural transmission takes place through the parish, the role of older family members as a source of information about customs is less important within Polish families than within Italian families, where traditional suspicion of the Church, reinforced by traditional Irish American control of the Church, has been maintained in the New World.

ETHNICITY, PERSONALITY, AND AGING

Since the pioneering studies of national character by Abram Kardiner, Margaret Mead, and others, there has been much interest in the description of personality patterns of peoples. In their incisive review of national character studies, Inkeles and Levinson (1954) noted the difference between the concept of national character and that of modal or characteristic personality, a perspective also supported by Spiro's (1965) discussion of culturally constituted defense mechanisms. Originating in particular forms of childhood socialization as well as in continuing socialization across the course of adult lives (Brim, 1966; Cohler and Boxer, 1983), modal personality changes as a result of immigration in ways that parallel changes both in modes of social organization and in underlying values.

As Greeley and McCready (1975) have reported, reorganizing findings earlier presented by Kohn (1969), not only is there little support for hypothesized personality differences, but, more likely, findings may contradict those based on European sending nations. For example, with the exception of fatalism and cynicism, attitudes that Italian Americans are more likely than their Anglo counterparts to exhibit, modal personality patterns among Italian Americans were more similar than were those of Irish Americans to Anglo counterparts.

Comparisons of modal personality traits between Irish and Italian ethnic groups have been somewhat more successful. Findings from studies of Strodtbeck (1958), Spiegel (1971), Femminella and Quadagno (1976), and Cohler and Grunebaum (1981), reporting on differences in value orientations and socialization patterns across generations in Irish and Italian American families, and studies of personality and both physical and mental health across these two groups (Opler, 1959; Stein, 1971; Kohn, 1969; Cohler and Lieberman, 1977/1978) show that, compared with Italian Americans, Irish Americans are less impulsive, more concerned with future achievement as contrasted with present satisfactions, and more likely to express feelings of hostility inward, leading to increased feelings of depression, rather than outward onto the external world.

To date, little of this research has focused on personality changes across differing points in the adult life course, or on contrasting cohorts of older persons. Once again, as in other aspects of the study of ethnicity and aging, most comparisons of Italian and Irish middle-aged and older persons have been based on cohorts of older persons with little formal education, often born in the Old World, and suffering from the inevitable conflict in values between the Old and the New World (Wallace, 1956; Chance, 1965; Cohler and Lieberman, 1977/1978). Mostwin (1979) notes that older Polish respondents are particularly concerned that remembered traditions from the Old World be continued, especially fluency in Polish and perpetuation of the everyday services of the traditional Polish parish church.

Preservation of holiday rituals appears less salient in fostering morale on a day-to-day basis for these older immigrants than might be expected. Mostwin (1979) reports that morale among older (immigrant generation) ethnic respondents was largely determined by age and quality of leisure after retirement. Cohler and Lieberman (1977/1978, 1979, 1980), comparing older persons within Irish, Italian, and Polish ethnic groups (and considering effects due to generation of residence in the United States), report that all three first-generation ethnic groups, regardless of immersion in the legacy of serfdom in the homeland, maintain a suspicious stance toward the world, relying on defenses of externalization and projection in dealing with inner conflicts. Furthermore, Irish first-generation respondents report greater life satisfaction and fewer psychological symptoms than members of the two other ethnic groups, although membership in the Irish group is also associated with greater income and higher educational attainment, making it difficult to determine the extent to which these social background factors contribute to findings on life satisfaction.

Across second-generation Polish and Irish ethnic groups, intense concern is expressed regarding attainment of satisfying personal relationships and in realizing successful achievement in the larger world. Older second-generation Italian Americans continue to express the suspiciousness noted by several students of personality and ethnicity as a modal trait for this ethnic group (Greeley and McCready, 1975). In a later report, studying the mid-life transformation to increased interiority (Neugarten, 1979) among middle-aged men and women from these three ethnic groups, Cohler and Lieberman (1979) report that older first-generation Irish men show less change in the direction of an expected increase toward an interior and passive orientation to the world than men from the Italian and Polish groups.

AGING, ETHNICITY, AND DELIVERY OF SERVICES TO OLDER PERSONS

Many of the so-called sociopsychological changes believed to take place with aging, including problems in obtaining health and social services, have been based on study of a cohort of older foreign-born persons with little formal education and, as a result of early socialization in the legacy of serfdom, with problems both in being able to obtain and accept assistance. Findings from surveys of the population clearly document the changes in ethnic composition taking place in the cohort of persons over age 65.

Using a measure of mother tongue and birth either in the United States or abroad (relevant only for the new immigration), the median age of foreign-born Italian speakers, based on a survey of literacy (U.S. Bureau of the Census, 1969) was 63.6 years, while the median age for first-generation Polish speakers was over age 65 (63 percent of foreign-born Yiddish-speaking respondents were also over age 65). In contrast, only 6 percent of Italian speakers born in the United States and 7 percent of native-born Polish speakers were over age 65 (the median age for native-born Italian speakers was 45, while the median age for native-born Polish speakers was 47, and the median age for native-born Yiddish speakers was 50).

Using a measure of self-identification of ethnic origin or descent (U.S. Bureau of the Census, 1973), a similar picture emerges regarding the aging of European immigrant groups in the United States. Based on this self-report measure, persons identified with the Irish ethnic tradition comprised 8 percent of the population but 11 percent of persons over age 65, while persons identified with the Italian ethnic tradition comprised 4.3 percent of the population but 9 percent of persons over age 65, and persons identified with the Polish ethnic tradition comprised 2.5 percent of the population but 9.5 percent of persons over age 65. Considered separately by self-identified ethnicity and sex of respondent, 9.2 percent of Irish men, 8.7 percent of Italian men, and 8.2 percent of Polish men are over age 65, while 12.6 percent of Irish women, 9.3 percent of Italian women, and 10.7 percent of Polish women are over 65. The aging of the European ethnic groups is seen even more clearly among persons identified with the Russian-Jewish group, which comprises 1.1 percent of the population; 15.2 percent of these persons are over age 65, representing the European ethnic group with the largest number of older persons.

A third, and most recent, source of data, the 1979 current population survey of ancestry (U.S. Bureau of the Census, 1982), employed a question on ancestry in order to determine ethnic status. Using this self-report measure as a part of a survey of randomly selected households, 16 percent of persons of Irish and Italian ancestry were over age 65, as contrasted with 21 percent of Polish respondents (27 percent of Russian-Jewish respondents, the oldest of the ethnic groups, were over age 65). When considering mixed ancestry, the proportion of persons over age 65 dramatically drops for each of the three Catholic ethnic groups (1 percent for groups of mixed Irish and other ancestry, 9 percent for mixed Italian and other groups, and 4 percent for groups of mixed Polish and other ancestry). Figures reported separately for men and for women in these second- and later-generation groups are consistent with overall figures, although, as expected, lower proportions of men than of women over age 65 are reported for single ancestry groups and very small proportions of older men and women are reported within mixed ancestry groups.

As the last generation of older persons from the Old World is diminished through death, an era will end in which largely European-born elderly had required particular assistance in the use of health and social services. Figures from the 1970 census show that about one-third of all foreign-born persons in the United States were over age 65, and comprised about 15 percent of all persons over age 65; by 1975, only 25 percent of all foreign-born persons were over age 65, comprising 12 percent of all older persons, while Gelfand (1982) estimates that by the end of the 1980s the proportion of older persons who are foreign-born will drop to less than 5 percent. In 1970, an additional 16 percent of persons over age 65 were second-generation residents in the United States.

To date, much of what is known about psychological differences between age categories has been based on comparisons of younger generations to the generation of older persons from the new immigration, primarily those from the legacy of serfdom, leading to problems in distinguishing between cohort and aging (Botwinick, 1977; Neugarten, 1977; Palmore, 1978; Baltes et al., 1979). It is to be expected that older persons socialized from earliest childhood into the world view characterized by the legacy of serfdom would continue to express the ethnocentrism, discomfort with ambiguity, and difficulty in solving complex problems that characterize the legacy of serfdom (Schooler, 1976) as well as personality and cognitive changes often shown to be associated with aging.

Successive cohorts of older persons who are largely American-born and not socialized into the legacy of serfdom, and who are also better educated, are likely to demand more effective services and may be better health consumers than previous cohorts of older persons (Uhlenberg, 1977; Guttmann, 1979; Gelfand, 1982). Consistent with this prediction, Bengtson and Cutler (1976) report that, in 1972, only 30 percent of persons over age 65 had a high school education, but estimate that by the year 2020 more than 86 percent of older persons will be high school graduates. Such dramatic increases in the level of education will have implications for the level and quality of health and services to be provided for older persons across the next several generations.

To date, there has been little systematic documentation of changes in the use of health and social services across generations of European-born older persons and their aging children and grandchildren. It has been assumed that rapid social change, such as results from immigration and consequent "mazeway distortion," that is, distortion caused by the maze of U.S. social patterns (Wallace, 1956), may be associated with impaired mental health, increased psychophysiological symptoms, and lowered morale, leading to increased use of health and social services. Previous findings have suggested that the experience of immigration is not only stressful, but is also associated with lowered morale and increased psychiatric symptoms (and that these symptoms are a function of immigration rather than of preselection of otherwise less well adjusted persons) (Murphy, 1965; Malzberg, 1968; Cohler and Lieberman, 1977/1978).

Findings reported by Bengtson, Dowd, Smith, and Inkeles (1975) suggest that older persons may be particularly affected by social change since modernization is usually accompanied by devaluation of older persons. Such generalizations may be less useful when, as a result of social change such as immigration, the status of older persons is increased rather than decreased. Furthermore, as Hansen (1952) and Wallace (1956) have suggested, one effect of social change may be a "revitalization movement" in which there is increased emphasis on values understood by an ethnic group as traditional. Revitalization movements enhance the status of older persons, who become repositories of tradition regarding beliefs and rituals. At least in part, the social conflict experienced by immigrant groups in the United States, leading to increased reliance upon remembered traditions of the Old World as a means of coping with such conflict, has enhanced the status of older family members.

Across generations, continued emphasis upon the old ways has been important in buffering the effects of life strain as members of European ethnic groups have moved out beyond older neighborhoods, becoming part of the larger society. It may be for this reason that the third generation shows increased involvement in religion, as noted across a number of studies (Hansen, 1952; Greeley, 1974; Gelfand and Fandetti, 1980). Survey findings reported by Fandetti and Gelfand (1976) concerning urban-dwelling Italian and Polish American ethnic groups show that Italian Americans, particularly those within the third generation, were more likely than Polish Americans to believe in the importance of the family as the primary source of care and support for older persons. Furthermore, Italian Americans have traditionally been doubtful that the Church or other institutions could provide care for older persons equal to that provided by the family. Similar findings have been reported by Krause (1978) and by Cohler and Grunebaum (1981) on the basis of detailed interview and observational studies of Italian American families.

Gelfand and Fandetti (1980) report that suburban second-generation Italian Americans are much less willing to have older persons live in their households and tend to rely on the Church as a source of assistance to a greater extent than urban-living second-generation Italian Americans. Limitation in the ability of both husband and wife to work outside the home is cited as a major problem resulting from having older parents living in the same household.

Findings first reported by Thomas and Znaniecki (1918–1920) and, more recently, by Sandberg (1974), Kantowicz (1975), and Lopata (1976) suggest that Polish Americans have relied upon political institutions to a far greater extent than Italian Americans in solving problems, including care of older persons. Ironically, although the extended family was of greater significance in the daily life of the Polish peasant than of the Italian peasant, with immigration to the United States, Italian Americans developed a modified extended family (Litwak, 1965), available as a resource for older persons, while Polish Americans increasingly relied upon community rather than family as a source of support and assistance.

Older Italian American family members are particularly likely to provide assistance for a large social network of relatives and friends, many of whom come from families who lived together in the same village in the Old World, immigrating to the United States through chain migration. Suspicion of civic and formal organizations further increased expectations by family and friends for help and assistance by older family members within the Italian American ethnic group. The degree of interdependence expected from these older Italian American family members may seriously tax available time and energy (Femminella and Quadagno, 1976; Krause, 1978; Cohler and Lieberman, 1980; Cohler and Grunebaum, 1981).

While, in general, as Uhlenhuth and Paykel (1971) and Masuda and Holmes (1978) have shown, the number of reported stressful life events may decline with age, such findings fail to include the differing extent of immersion, across ethnic groups, in a network of family and friends, portrayed by Plath (1980) as consociates. The greater the involvement in a network of such consociates, the greater the number of demands for assistance and support experienced by older persons, and the greater the exposure to eruptive and hazardous or stressful life events, such as financial reversals, illness, and deaths, among consociates.

Demands upon the time of older persons may be so great that marked strain is experienced as a result of attempting to meet the competing demands of parent, spouse, and confidant; such strains may contribute to the lower level of morale reported within the group of older Italian respondents, as contrasted with the Polish and Irish ethnic groups (Cohler and Lieberman, 1980; Cohler, 1983). This description of older persons, especially within the Italian ethnic group, as still very actively engaged in caring for others, is in marked contrast with the stereotype of the older person in American society as merely the recipient, and not the provider, of assistance to the child and grandchild generation.

CONCLUSION

Social psychological study of older persons from European ethnic groups raises fundamental questions regarding the significance of ethnicity in American society, as well as of the problems in differentiating the effects of cohort and age in understanding personality and intellectual changes across the second half of life. Until the past two decades, the majority of immigrants to the United States have been from European countries and, particularly across the past half-century, from countries in which the legacy of serfdom was most entrenched. This mode of social organization, emphasizing passive compliance to authority and lack of initiative in decision-making in a highly stratified society, has had important implications not only for the manner in which these immigrants have become involved in American life, but also for a markedly ethnocentric and inflexible stance toward interpersonal relationships as these immigrants aged.

Now that cohorts of older persons include the better educated children, and even grandchildren, of these Eastern and Southern European immigrants, there are likely to be changes both in personality and in characteristic cognitive organization observed in later life, as well as in expectations regarding provision of health and social services. To date, there has been little study, across second and later generations, either of changing solutions for resolving basic human dilemmas, especially that regarding the organization of social relationships, or of the extent to which changes in the place of the older person in the family resulting from immigration from the Old to the New World will be maintained across successive generations. Preliminary evidence supports previous findings that Polish Americans, for whom the Church was an important institution in immigration, maintain reliance primarily upon voluntary and formal associations in providing services for older persons. Italian Americans, who have maintained their traditional suspiciousness of such institutions in the Old and the New World, continue, across the second and third generations, to rely primarily upon those modified extended ties first formed in the New World, and which were so important to the first generation in providing support and assistance for older family members.

Overall, while the peasant tradition represented by first-generation immigrants will change with increasing education and intermarriage, there is little evidence of a change in the importance of ethnicity in understanding personality, mental health, adjustment to aging, or family relations, among the descendants of either the old or the new European immigration. While, across generations, differences may be observed in preferred solutions for problems of social life, a sense of identity is preserved with others from the same traditional homeland in the Old World. Ethnicity is likely to continue as a significant force in American society; it is essential for those working with older persons to realize the salience of this dimension of social life in planning social and health interventions with older persons.

REFERENCES

Alba, R. The twilight of ethnicity among American Catholics of European ancestry. *Annals of the American Association of Political and Social Science*, 1982, no. 454, 86–97.

Arensberg, C., and Kimball, S. *Family and community in Ireland*, 2nd ed. Harvard University Press, Cambridge, Mass., 1968.

Baltes, P.; Cornelius, S.; and Nesselroade, J. Cohort effects in developmental psychology. In J. Nesselroade and P. Baltes (Eds.), *Longitudinal research in the study of behavior and development*. Academic Press, New York, 1979, 61–88.

Banfield, E. *The moral basis of a backward society*. Macmillan/Free Press, New York, 1958.

Bengtson, V., and Cutler, N. Generations and intergenerational relations: Perspectives on age groups and social change. In R.H. Binstock and E. Shanas (Eds.), *Handbook of aging and the social sciences*. Van Nostrand Reinhold, New York, 1976, 130–159.

Bengtson, V.; Dowd, J.; Smith, D.; and Inkeles, A. Modernization, modernity, and perceptions of aging: A cross-cultural study. *Journal of Gerontology*, 1975, *30*, 688–695.

Bianco, C. *The two Rosetos*. Indiana University Press, Bloomington, Ind., 1974.

Biddle, E. The American Catholic Irish family. In C. Mindel and R. Habenstein (Eds.), *Ethnic families in America*. Elsevier, New York, 1976, 98–124.

Botwinick, J. Intellectual abilities. In J.E. Birren and K.W. Schaie (Eds.), *Handbook of the psychology of aging*. Van Nostrand Reinhold, New York, 1977, 580–605.

Brim, O.G., Jr. Socialization through the life-cycle. In O.G. Brim, Jr., and W. Wheeler, *Socialization after childhood: Two essays*. Wiley, New York, 1966, 1–50.

Chance, N. Acculturation, self-identification, and personality adjustment. *American Anthropologist*, 1965, *67*, 372–393.

Cohler, B. Autonomy and interdependence in the family of adulthood: A psychological perspective. *Gerontologist*, 1983, *23*, 33–39.

Cohler, B., and Boxer, A. Morale, mental health, and aging. In C. Izzard and C. Malatesta (Eds.), *Affective processes in adulthood and aging*. Plenum, New York, 1983.

Cohler, B., and Grunebaum, H. *Mothers, grandmothers, and daughters*. Wiley, New York, 1981.

Cohler, B., and Lieberman, M. Ethnicity and personal adaptation. *International Journal of Group Tensions*, 1977/1978, *7*, 20–41.

———. Personality change across the second half of life: Findings from a study of Irish, Italian, and Polish-American men and women. In D. Gelfand and A. Kutzik (Eds.), *Ethnicity and aging: Theory, research and policy*. Springer, New York, 1979, 227–245.

———. Social relations and mental health. *Research on Aging*, 1980, *2*, 445–469.

Devereux, G. Ethnic identity: Its logical functions and its dysfunctions. In G. DeVos and L. Romanucci-Ross (Eds.), *Ethnic identity: Cultural continuities and change*. Mayfield Publishing, Palo Alto, Calif., 1975, 5–41.

Easterlin, R. Immigration: Economic and social characteristics. In S. Threnstrom (Ed.), *Harvard encyclopedia of American ethnic groups*. Harvard University Press, Cambridge, Mass., 1980, 476–486.

Fandetti, D., and Gelfand, D. Care of the aged: Attitudes of white ethnic families. *Gerontologist*, 1976, *16*, 544–549.

Femminella, F., and Quadagno, J. The Italian-American family. In C. Mindel and R. Habenstein (Eds.), *Ethnic families in America: Patterns and variations*. Elsevier, New York, 1976, 61–88.

Fleetwood, J. Ireland. In E. Palmore (Ed.), *International handbook on aging: Contemporary developments and research*. Greenwood Press, Westport, Conn., 1980, 194–207.

Florea, A. Italy. In E. Palmore (Ed.), *International handbook on aging: Contemporary developments and research*. Greenwood Press, Westport, Conn., 1980, 234–252.

Gans, H. *The urban villagers*. Free Press, New York, 1962.

Gelfand, D. *Aging: The ethnic factor*. Little, Brown, Boston, 1982.

Gelfand, D., and Fandetti, D. Suburban and urban white ethnics: Attitudes towards care of the aged. *Gerontologist*, 1980, *20*, 588–594.

Glazer, N., and Moynihan, D. *Beyond the melting pot*, 2nd ed. MIT Press, Cambridge, Mass., 1970.

Gordon, M. *Assimilation in American life: The role of race, religion, and ethnic origins*. Oxford University Press, New York, 1964.

Greeley, A. Ethnicity as an influence on behavior. In O. Feinstein (Ed.), *Ethnic groups in the city*. Heath Books, 1971, Lexington, Mass., 3–16.

————. *Ethnicity in the United States: A preliminary reconnaissance*. Wiley-Interscience, New York, 1974.

Greeley, A., and McCready, W. The transmission of cultural heritages: The case of the Irish and the Italians. In N. Glazer and D. Moynihan (Eds.), *Ethnicity: Theory and experience*. Harvard University Press, Cambridge, Mass., 1975, 209–235.

Gutman, H. *Work, culture, and society in industrializing America*. Random House/ Vintage Press, New York, 1977.

Guttmann, D. Use of informal and formal supports by white ethnic aged. In D. Gelfand and A. Kutzik (Eds.), *Ethnicity and aging: Theory, research and policy*. Springer, New York, 1979, 246–262.

Handlin, O. *Race and nationality in American life*. Little, Brown, Boston, 1957.

Hansen, M. *The Atlantic migration, 1607–1860*. Harvard University Press, Cambridge, Mass., 1940.

————. The third generation in America. *Commentary*, 1952, *14*, 492–500.

Hofstadter, R. *Social Darwinism in American thought, 1860–1915*. University of Pennsylvania Press, Philadelphia, 1944.

Inkeles, A., and Levinson, D. National character: The study of modal personality and sociocultural systems. In G. Lindzey (Ed.), *Handbook of social psychology*, vol. 2. Addison-Wesley, Reading, Mass., 1954, 977–1020.

Jones, M. *American immigration*. University of Chicago Press, Chicago, 1960.

Kantowicz, E. *Polish-American politics in Chicago*. University of Chicago Press, Chicago, 1975.

Kluckhohn, C. Values and value orientations. In T. Parsons (Ed.), *Toward a general theory of action*. Harvard University Press, 1951, Cambridge, Mass., 388–433.

Kluckhohn, F., and Strodtbeck, F. *Variations in value orientations*. Harper and Row, New York, 1961.

Kohn, M. *Class and conformity: A study in values*. Dorsey Press, Homewood, Ill., 1969.

Krause, C. *Women, ethnicity and mental health*. Institute on Pluralism and Group Identity of the American Jewish Committee, New York, 1978.

Litwak, E. Extended kin relationships in an industrial democratic society. In E. Shanas and G. Strieb (Eds.), *Social structure and the family*. Prentice-Hall, Englewood Cliffs, N.J., 1965.

Lopata, H. *Polish-Americans: Status competition in an ethnic community*. Prentice-Hall, Englewood Cliffs, N.J., 1976.

McDonald, J., and McDonald, L. Chain migration, ethnic neighborhood formation, and social networks. *Milbank Memorial Fund Quarterly*, 1964, *42*, 82–97.

Malzberg, B. *Migration in relation to mental disease*. Research Foundation for Mental Hygiene, Albany, N.Y., 1968.

Masuda, M., and Holmes, T. Life events: Perceptions and frequencies. *Psychosomatic Medicine*, 1978, *40*, 236–261.

Mindel, C., and Habenstein, R. (Eds.). *Ethnic families in America*. Elsevier, New York, 1976.

Mostwin, D. Emotional needs of elderly Americans of Central and Eastern European background. In D. Gelfand and A. Kutzik (Eds.), *Ethnicity and aging: Theory, research and policy*. Springer, New York, 1979, 263–276.

Murphy, H.B.M. Migration and the major mental diseases. In M.B. Kantor (Ed.), *Mobility and mental health*. Charles C. Thomas, Springfield, Ill., 1965, 5–29.

Neugarten, B. Personality and aging. In J.E. Birren and K.W. Schaie (Eds.), *Handbook of the psychology of aging*. Van Nostrand Reinhold, New York, 1977, 626–649.

———. Time, age, and the life cycle. *American Journal of Psychiatry*, 1979, *136*, 887–894.

Opler, M. Cultural differences in mental disorders: An Italian and Irish contrast in the schizophrenias. In M. Opler (Ed.), *Culture and mental health*. Macmillan, New York, 1959, 425–442.

Palmore, E. When can age, period and cohort be separated? *Social Forces*, 1978, *57*, 282–295.

Plath, D. Contours of consociation: Adult development as discourse. In P. Baltes and O.G. Brim, Jr. (Eds.), *Life-span development and behavior*, vol. 3. Academic Press, New York, 1980.

Rubin, E. The demography of immigration to the United States. *Annals of the American Academy of Political and Social Sciences*, 1966, no. 367, 15–22.

Sandberg, N. *Ethnic identity and assimilation: The Polish–American community*. Praeger, New York, 1974.

Schooler, C. Serfdom's legacy: An ethnic continuum. *American Journal of Sociology*, 1976, *81*, 1265–1286.

Spiegel, J. *Transactions: The interplay between individual, family and society*. Science House/Aronson, New York, 1971.

Spiro, M. Religious systems as culturally constituted defense mechanisms. In M. Spiro (Ed.), *Context and meaning in cultural anthropology*. Macmillan, New York, 1965, 100–113.

Stack, C. *All our kin: Strategies for survival in a black community*. Harper and Row, New York, 1974.

Stein, R.F. *Disturbed youth and ethnic family patterns*. State University of New York Press, Albany, N.Y., 1971.

Streib, G. Old age in Ireland: Demographic and sociological aspects. In D.O. Cowgill and L. Holmes (Eds.), *Aging and modernization*. Appleton-Century-Crofts, New York, 1972, 167–181.

Strodtbeck, F. Family interaction, values, and achievement. In D.C. McClelland, A. Baldwin, U. Bronfenbrenner, and F. Strodtbeck, *Talent and society: New perspectives in the identification of talent*. Van Nostrand, Princeton, N.J., 1958, 259–268.

Thernstrom, S. *Harvard encyclopedia of American ethnic groups*. Harvard University Press, Cambridge, Mass., 1980.

Thomas, W.I., and Znaniecki, F. *The Polish peasant in Europe and America*, 2 vols. Knopf, New York, 1918–1920.

Uhlenberg, P. Changing structure of the older population of the USA during the twentieth century. *Gerontologist*, 1977, *17*, 197–202.

Uhlenhuth, E., and Paykel, E. Symptom intensity and life-events. *Archives of General Psychiatry*, 1971, *25*, 340–347.

U.S. Bureau of the Census. Characteristics of the population by ethnic origin, November 1969. *Current Population Reports*, ser. P-20, no. 221. USGPO, Washington, D.C., 1971.

———. Characteristics of the population by ethnic origin, March 1972 and 1971. *Current Population Reports*, ser. P-20, no. 249. USGPO, Washington, D.C., 1973.

————. Social and economic characteristics of the older population, 1974. *Current Population Reports*, ser. P-23, no. 57. USGPO, Washington. D.C., 1975.

————. Ancestry and language in the United States, November 1979. *Current Population Reports*, ser. P-23, no. 116. USGPO, Washington, D.C., 1982.

Vecoli, R. European-Americans: From immigrants to ethnics. *International Migration Review*, 1972, *6*, 403–434.

Wallace, A.F.C. Revitalization movements. *American Anthropologist*, 1956, *58*, 264–281.

Ward, D. *Cities and immigrants: A geography of change in nineteenth century America*. Oxford University Press, New York, 1971.

Weber, M. *The Protestant ethic and the spirit of capitalism*, trans. T. Parsons. 1905; repr. Charles Scribner's Sons, New York, 1958.

————. Ethnic groups. In G. Roth and C. Wittick (Eds.), *Economy and society*. Bedminster Press, New York, 1968, 385–398.

Wirth, L. *The ghetto*. University of Chicago Press, Chicago, 1928.

Woehrer, C. The influence of ethnic families on intergenerational relationships and later life transitions. *Annals of the American Academy of Political and Social Science*, 1982, no. 464, 65–78.

Wrobel, P. *Our way: Family, parish, and neighborhood in a Polish-American community*. University of Notre Dame Press, Notre Dame, Ind., 1979.

Yancey, W.; Ericksen, E.; and Juliani, R. Emergent ethnicity: A review and formulation. *American Sociological Review*, 1976, *41*, 391–403.

15

HISPANICS

CARMELA G. LACAYO

The Hispanic presence in the United States predates that of the Europeans. This presence is still a major part of life in the Southwest, in Florida—indeed, throughout the United States—as the Hispanic population expands in numbers and in geographic areas. Many older Hispanics have been in the United States for generations; others have just arrived. The United States's proximity to Mexico, Central America, and the Caribbean helps to keep the Spanish language and Hispanic culture alive in this country.

The total U.S. population grew by about 11.5 percent between 1970 and 1980, from 203,211,926 to 226,594,825 persons. The total Hispanic population grew by a whopping 61 percent, from 9,072,602 in 1970 to 14, 605,883 in 1980 (U.S. Bureau of the Census, 1981). And the number of Hispanics aged 65 and over increased at an even greater rate, from 404,000 in 1970 to 708,800 in 1980, or 75 percent. This growth rate far exceeds the 25 percent growth rate for older whites and the 34 percent increase in the older black population between 1970 and 1980.

These figures make it clear that the Hispanic elderly are an increasingly significant part of the total older population in this country. Yet we know much less about older Hispanics than we do about older people from the dominant population groups. Most research data on the Hispanic elderly come from studies with limited geographic and topical scope. The first national needs assessment of the Hispanic elderly (Lacayo, 1980, hereafter called the Needs Assessment Study) yielded the primary baseline data on the status and needs of older Hispanics nationwide. The needs assessment respondents reported health as their main problem, followed by income and morale (or life satisfaction). The study also revealed that the Hispanic elderly use social services far less than their need for services indicates.

What will our society do to meet the needs of the burgeoning older Hispanic population? How will we respond to the problems that this group cites as their

primary difficulties? And how can we effectively use the rich cultural and ex-
periential resources of the Hispanic elderly? The heritage they bear and their life
experiences can be important sources of this country's cultural, economic, and
social vitality. Understanding the Hispanic elderly—their characteristics, special
problems and capabilities, and other aspects of their lives—is essential to answering these questions.

It has been said that communication is a matter of the mind, while understanding is a matter of the heart. This chapter intends to communicate knowledge
with the hope that a better understanding of the Hispanic elderly will result. As
a first step toward understanding, it is important to remember this: while older
Hispanics share a language and, to some extent, a history, they are a heterogeneous group that varies regionally and culturally.

CHARACTERISTICS

Demography

The Hispanic group in the United States is composed of several subgroups
who share a Spanish heritage. Figure 15.1 shows the constituencies that make
up the whole. Mexican Americans comprise about 60 percent of the Hispanic
group, with Puerto Ricans, other Spanish, and Cubans contributing smaller
numbers.

It is predicted that Hispanics will become the largest minority group in the
United States during the 1980s. Currently, Hispanics are the largest minority
group in California. Of the 14 million or more Hispanics in this country, approximately 4.9 percent are 65 years of age or more. This compares with 12.2
percent in the white population (U.S. Bureau of the Census, 1981). In other
words, the white population has two and one-half times the proportion of individuals age 65 and over as does the Hispanic group. Figures 15.2 and 15.3
illustrate the changing population pyramid for Hispanics in the United States
from 1970 to 1980. Both figures indicate the relative youthfulness of the total
Hispanic group. A different scale has been used for figure 15.3 (based on 1980
census data) because of the tremendous increase in numbers of Hispanics since
figure 15.2 (based on 1970 census data) was drawn. But the most noteworthy
change is the expansion of the upper half of the pyramid from 1970 to 1980.
The increase in old and nearly old Hispanics is causing the pyramid to lose its
Christmas-tree shape. The dramatic rise in the number of older Hispanics is not
just a future trend. It has already begun.

The 1980 census also reveals that the median age is 22.1 for Hispanics, 24.9
for blacks, and 31.3 for whites. From 1960 to 1980, the rate of increase of
median age has been highest among Hispanics. This is another indication that
the proportion of aged in the Hispanic group will sharply increase in the years
ahead. The cumulative effect of longer life expectancy, high fertility, and con-

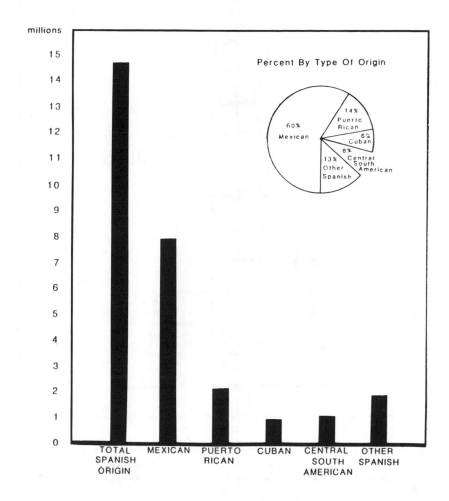

millions

Percent By Type Of Origin

60%
Mexican

14%
Puerto
Rican

6%
Cuban

8%
Central
South
American

13%
Other
Spanish

TOTAL SPANISH ORIGIN | MEXICAN | PUERTO RICAN | CUBAN | CENTRAL SOUTH AMERICAN | OTHER SPANISH

Figure 15.1
Persons of Spanish Origin in the United States, 1980 Census

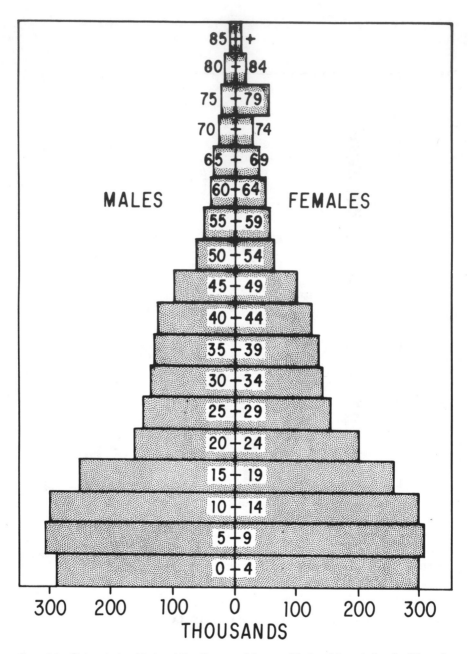

MALES   FEMALES

85 + +
80 + 84
75 + 79
70 + 74
65 + 69
60 + 64
55 + 59
50 + 54
45 + 49
40 + 44
35 + 39
30 + 34
25 + 29
20 + 24
15 + 19
10 + 14
5 + 9
0 + 4

300   200   100   0   100   200   300

THOUSANDS

Figure 15.2
Age Distribution of the Spanish Origin Population, 1970 Census

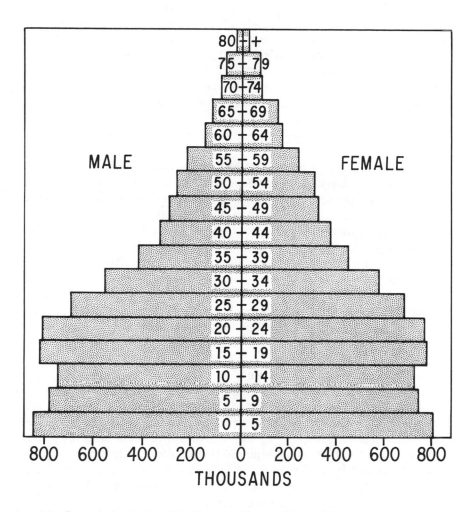

MALE   FEMALE

| 80 + + |
| 75 + 79 |
| 70 + 74 |
| 65 + 69 |
| 60 + 64 |
| 55 + 59 |
| 50 + 54 |
| 45 + 49 |
| 40 + 44 |
| 35 + 39 |
| 30 + 34 |
| 25 + 29 |
| 20 + 24 |
| 15 + 19 |
| 10 + 14 |
| 5 + 9 |
| 0 + 5 |

800 600 400 200 0 200 400 600 800

THOUSANDS

Figure 15.3
Age Distribution of the Spanish Origin Population, 1980 Census

tinued immigration indicates more substantial contributions by Hispanics to the aged group of the future.

In addition to population characteristics, older Hispanics differ in many other ways from the total elderly population. The following are but a few of the characteristics that illustrate this point.

Geographic Concentration

In 1980, over 60 percent of the Hispanic population resided in three states: California, Texas, and New York. Also, Spanish-origin persons comprised more than 10 percent of the total population for five states—New Mexico (36.6 percent), Texas (21 percent), California (19.2 percent), Arizona (16.2 percent), and Colorado (11.7 percent) (U.S. Bureau of the Census, 1981). Most Hispanics live in urban areas. And most of the fifty states have no significant concentration of Hispanics. Figure 15.4 gives a graphic portrayal of the concentrations of the Hispanics in the United States.

Language

The Spanish-speaking people, more than any other group, have tended to retain their native language. Aside from the desire to retain ethnic heritage, two main reasons are probably important: (1) proximity of the United States to Mexico and Latin America, and (2) the past exclusion of Hispanics from participation in the dominant society. Many older Hispanics find it difficult to communicate in English. In the Needs Assessment Study (Lacayo, 1980), interviews were conducted in the language chosen by the subject. An overwhelming 86 percent of the 1,803 respondents chose to be interviewed in Spanish. When asked the language they use most of the time, 93.8 percent of the older Cubans, 90.6 percent of the Puerto Ricans, 85.4 percent of the Mexican Americans, and 75.7 percent of the other Hispanics reported that they speak Spanish most of the time.

Education

Nearly 45 percent of aged Hispanics—or almost one out of every two elderly Spanish-origin persons—have completed less than five years of schooling. Almost two out of three aged Hispanics (66 percent) have not completed eight years of schooling. Older Mexican Americans are clearly among the most educationally deprived groups in our society. About five out of eight (64 percent) have less than a fifth-grade education. In sharp contrast, only 8 percent of non-Hispanic persons in the United States have less than five years of schooling. The median educational level for older Spanish-origin persons is 5.7 years, and just 3.1 years for aged Mexican Americans.

Housing

Table 15.1 shows the probability of being adequately housed by age, sex of head of household, and ethnicity. The person with the highest probability of

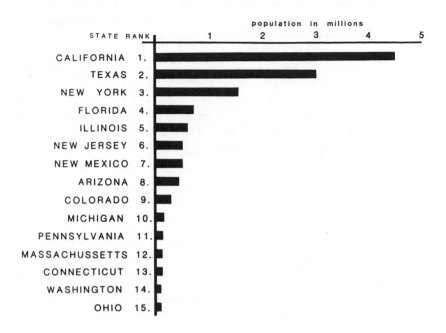

Figure 15.4
Spanish Origin Population in Selected States by Rank, 1980 Census

being inadequately housed is the male Hispanic who lives alone. He has only a .56 probability of living in adequate housing. The effects of race, ethnicity, and sex count far more than age alone as a determiner of poor housing. Income is directly related to each of these variables and is of final importance.

According to Bell and Zellman (1976), the quality of housing for Mexican Americans over 60 varies greatly by geographic region, but the incidence of substandard housing tends to be two or three times as great among Mexican Americans as among Anglos. Very few older Hispanics live in public housing, and few receive rent subsidies. Why? One reason is that many housing projects are high-rise accommodations complete with foyers through which one must pass in either entering or leaving the complex. These living arrangements are foreign to most older Hispanics.

Table 15.1
Probability of Being Adequately Housed

Sex of Head	Race/Ethnicity of Head	Household Size	Age of Household Head		
			65 and over	*30–64*	*Under 30*
Female	White	1 person	0.13	0.15	0.19
		2–5 persons	0.16	0.17	0.18
	Black	1 person	0.27	0.31	0.25
		2–5 persons	0.33	0.26	0.28
	Hispanic	1 person	0.18	0.30	0.27
		2–5 persons	0.24	0.24	0.29
Male	White	1 person	0.27	0.29	0.25
		2–5 persons	0.13	0.17	0.20
	Black	1 person	0.43	0.38	0.34
		2–5 persons	0.27	0.25	0.27
	Hispanic	1 person	0.56	0.37	0.40
		2–5 persons	0.21	0.25	0.23

Source: U.S. Department of Housing and Urban Development (1976).

Socioeconomic Factors

Income

Income levels are extremely low for aged Hispanics. In 1978, the median annual income was $3,812 for older Spanish-origin men and $2,455 for aged Hispanic women. About two-thirds (65 percent) of all older Spanish-origin men had annual incomes below $5,000. Approximately 90 percent of elderly Hispanic women had incomes below $5,000, including 33 percent with incomes under $2,000.

Older Hispanics are more than twice as likely to live in poverty as aged white persons. In 1980, almost 31 percent of all older Hispanics—or nearly one out of every three older Spanish-origin persons—lived in poverty. This compares to a 14 percent poverty rate among aged Anglos.

In 1980, the number in poverty increased by 32,000 for elderly Spanish-origin persons, from 147,000 in 1979 to 179,000. This represented the highest number of impoverished aged Hispanics since poverty statistics were first tabulated for the Spanish-origin population.

The poverty figures really represent only the tip of the iceberg for economically deprived aged Hispanics. Many more have incomes just barely above the poverty line or just hovering above the "near poverty" threshold. This threshold is 125 percent of the poverty level of $5,498 for two people in a family with an aged head of household (65 years old or more), and $4,359 for a single person aged 65 or older. In 1980, nearly 245,000 Spanish-origin persons 65 or older —or 42 percent of all aged Hispanics—were either poor or marginally poor. The net effect is that about three out of every seven older Spanish-origin persons either lived in poverty or so close to it that they had difficulty recognizing the difference. By contrast, 23 percent of Anglos aged 65 and older were marginally poor in 1980.

Low income also characterizes the total Hispanic population in this country. In 1980, the median income for Spanish-origin families was $14,717, compared to $21,904 for white families and $12,674 for black families.

Employment

Information on the employment status of elderly Hispanics is scarce. We do know that a greater percentage of older Hispanics have spent their lives in low-paying manual or service occupations than the majority of older persons in this country. These low-paying jobs keep many older Hispanics from accruing sufficient Social Security benefits to sustain them after retirement. Furthermore, very few older Hispanics have worked in jobs that offered private pension plans. As a result, older Hispanics participate in Social Security far less than the dominant older population.

Approximately one-fifth of all older Hispanics (except Puerto Ricans) are currently employed either full- or part-time. In the general population, 48 percent of the men and 23 percent of the women aged 55 or over are in the work force (U.S. Bureau of the Census, 1976). Two probable reasons for the lower percentage of Hispanics in the labor force beyond age 55 are (1) the large proportion of Hispanics who leave the work force because of ill health, and (2) the severe unemployment problem in this group. In the Needs Assessment Study (Lacayo, 1980), 9 percent of Hispanics aged 55 or over said that they were unemployed. And the scope of the unemployment problem is evident in this fact: unemployment soared by 59 percent for persons 55 or older in slightly more than one year—to 838,000 in October 1982, from 526,000 in August 1981, according to the Bureau of Labor statistics. This is a record high for older workers.

According to *Current Population Reports,* "Persons of Spanish Origin in the United States" (U.S. Bureau of the Census, 1976), about 57 percent of employed men of Spanish origin were in blue-collar jobs. One-half of the Hispanic women who are employed work in white-collar jobs, and one-third work in blue-collar jobs. Employment varies by Hispanic subgroup. For instance, 79 percent of Mexican American men work, compared to 67 percent of Puerto Rican men. Thirty-one percent of Puerto Rican women participate in the labor force, compared to 48 percent of Cuban women.

Occupation also varies by subgroup (U.S. Bureau of the Census, 1976). For example, more Puerto Rican men (24 percent) were employed in service occupations than Mexican American men (11 percent). According to Almquist

(1979), Cuban and Puerto Rican women are more apt to work in factories than are Anglo women. Older Hispanics in the Needs Assessment Study were asked to name the occupation in which they were engaged for most of their work life. Most were employed as operators, laborers, service workers, and housewives. Cubans have statistically higher percentages in the technical and professional occupations than either Puerto Ricans, Mexican Americans, or other Hispanics. Cubans also have a higher representation among sales and clerical occupations and are underrepresented among service workers and laborers.

Age is the reason for retiring most often given by members of all Hispanic subgroups. Among Cubans, 58.7 percent retired because of age. This figure compares with 51 percent of Mexican Americans and Puerto Ricans, and 50 percent of other Hispanics. The second most frequent reason given for retiring is poor health. More Mexican Americans (43 percent) retired because of poor health than any other subgroup. Puerto Ricans are least likely to retire because of poor health and most likely to retire because of lack of work.

Health

Little research has been done on the health of older Hispanics. Most of this research consists of case studies of limited geographic and informational scope. Health data from the first National Needs Assessment of the Hispanic elderly (Lacayo, 1980) show that:

1. The primary diseases among older Hispanics are arthritis, high blood pressure, and circulation problems. (Among older Mexican Americans, diabetes is the third most prevalent disease.)
2. The highest unattended medical care need is for dental services. Lack of money is the reason cited most often for not going to the dentist or the doctor.
3. Those who live alone have the most illnesses.
4. All older Hispanic subgroups use hospitals much less frequently than do other older Americans. In the general population aged 65 and over, 26.8 percent are hospitalized during any given year. But only 15 percent of Mexican Americans, 21 percent of Cubans, and 24 percent of Puerto Ricans and other Hispanics use hospitals at some time during the year. Insufficient funds and a fear or distrust of hospitals are the major reasons given for non-use in the face of need.

Other studies indicate a drastically lower life expectancy for Hispanics. One such study places the life expectancy for the Mexican American population at 56.7 years (Kurtz, 1970). Others have placed Hispanic life expectancy between 55 and 59 years of age.

Dowd and Bengtson (1978) found that 85 percent of Anglos aged 45–64 rated their health as good, while only 61 percent of Hispanics in the same age group said that they had good health. Additionally, larger proportions of Hispanics "feel old" than do Anglos. Hispanics are also much less likely than Anglos to express the expectation of living ten more years. For Anglos and Hispanics aged

63–65, 82 percent and 50 percent respectively expect to live ten more years. These results are not surprising when considered from a culturally sensitive perspective. Hispanics, despite their shorter life expectancy in chronological terms, do indeed live to be "old" in functional terms.

Family Structure and Living Arrangements

Many people think that most Hispanic elderly live in extended families—that "Hispanics take care of their own." But often this is not the case. Hispanic families do give significant social and emotional support to their elders. However, the low income and larger size of many Hispanic families keep these families from providing effective economic help for their older members.

Data from the Needs Assessment Study (Lacayo, 1980) indicate that only about 9.7 percent of the Hispanic elderly live in an extended family. Sixty percent live with their spouses only, while 30 percent live alone. And in a study of elderly Mexican Americans, Puerto Ricans, and Cubans, Bastida (1978) found that multigenerational households are infrequent and varied. Crouch (1972) found that older Mexican Americans reported less formal aid from family than from the church or government.

Studies by Korte (1978) and Laurel (1976) indicate that extended kin relationships are stronger among rural Hispanic elderly than among their urban counterparts. This suggests that urbanization may result in a lessening of ties between older Hispanics and their families.

Psychological Characteristics

Older Hispanics report that "mental health/life satisfaction" is their third most urgent problem, after health and income (Lacayo, 1980). No doubt their poor socioeconomic status is a major reason for this problem. Markides and Martin (1980) found that psychological distress was higher in their study's older Mexican American sample than in the Anglo sample. However, socioeconomic controls caused this relationship to disappear. Markides and Martin found it difficult to explain this finding, especially since they believe that Mexican Americans incur additional social stresses that do not affect the majority population. But these authors suggest that the family may function as a buffer to lower stress among Mexican Americans.

Other statistics confirm that the family is still an important source of social and emotional support for older Hispanics. Most Hispanic older people report that theirs is a "close family" and that they see their relatives and friends as often as they want, according to the first national study of chronic illness and support systems among the Hispanic elderly (Lacayo, 1980).

Religion is another principal factor in the well-being of the Hispanic elderly. In the Gallup Study (1978), 94.1 percent of the older Hispanics stated that religion is either very important or fairly important in their lives.

At the same time, many older Hispanics endure the sorrow of having some of their loved ones in a distant country, of not being able to communicate with their English-speaking grandchildren in this country, and of being part of a largely unwelcome minority. They may also suffer anxiety over their loved ones trapped in Latin and South American countries undergoing oppression and violence.

Some studies have sought to discover the frequency and sources of worry, and the helpers used in cases of stress, among older Hispanics. White (1981) found that 30 percent of the sample he investigated hardly ever worried about things, while 37 percent worried "fairly often." The sample was composed of both Mexican Americans and Anglos. The Needs Assessment Study (Lacayo, 1980) posed several questions regarding mental stress. When asked whether during the past year they had incurred a family problem that was difficult to handle alone, 19 percent of other Hispanics and 9 percent of Puerto Ricans answered affirmatively. Approximately one-third of those who reported problems handled the problems alone. When others were involved, relatives and friends were the ones most often mentioned, in that order. Friends were mentioned more than spouses as a source of help in family stress.

When asked whether they had been depressed during the past year, 56 percent of Cubans in the Needs Assessment Study responded affirmatively. This compares with 48 percent of other Hispanics, 45 percent of Puerto Ricans, and 35 percent of Mexican Americans. In terms of psychological well-being, the Hispanic elderly are survivors. Cultural values, traditions, and the Spanish language—the Hispanic heritage that they bear and impart to others—help the Hispanic elderly to endure despite severe hardship.

SPECIAL PROBLEMS

Elderly Hispanics share all the problems of the elderly in general: loss of physical vigor, feelings of dependency and uselessness, loneliness and isolation, thoughts of death and fear of dying, and a gradual lack of caring about themselves because of old age. All this is burden enough. But, in addition, many of the Hispanic elderly experience extreme poverty and all its consequences, such as inadequate housing and nutrition, and poor health care.

Not speaking English is another major problem for many Hispanic elderly. The language barrier means severe hardship for those older Hispanics who do not know about services available to them, or who cannot obtain needed services because the service personnel do not speak Spanish. The Needs Assessment Study (Lacayo, 1980) found that the neediest older Hispanics are the lowest users of services. Bilingual service providers, publications, and announcements are essential to solving this key problem.

SPECIAL ADVANTAGES

The Hispanic elderly in the United States straddle two cultures, two ways of life. Many of them have migrated to the United States and have experienced a continual adjustment to life here. Their history and heritage give the Hispanic elderly a unique perspective among older Americans.

The ability to share this unique perspective with younger Hispanics and with other Americans is a special advantage of the Hispanic elderly. The advantage really belongs to those of us privileged to learn about this perspective from older Hispanics themselves. Hispanic cultural values and traditions, the Spanish language, stories of overcoming hardship, of establishing a home, family, and friends in an (initially) unfamiliar society—all these are aspects of the unique legacy that the Hispanic elderly impart to us. ''Nuestras personas mayores son la herencia de nuestro pueblo''—the Hispanic elderly are surely our finest heritage.

ORGANIZATIONS AND PROGRAMS

The Asociación Nacional Pro Personas Mayores (National Association for Hispanic Elderly) is the principal national organization concerned with older Hispanics. It is a private, nonprofit corporation that seeks to make policymakers and the general public aware of the needs and status of the Hispanic elderly in the United States. The organization meets those needs through direct service programs, nationwide research, publication of media materials, and development of model projects. Headquartered in Los Angeles, the Asociación has regional offices in Miami and Washington, D.C.

Many local and regional agencies across the United States carry out programs by and for older Hispanics. The Asociación has published a national community service directory with names, addresses, and further details about these organizations.

RESEARCH ISSUES

Research on the Hispanic elderly is increasing, but the available information is still inadequate. National data are especially needed, since most information presently available is local in scope. The key research issues are those that affect most directly the Hispanic elderly's well-being—issues such as the use of social services, health, income, and morale/life satisfaction. Older Hispanics themselves name these topics as their main concerns.

Even when they know about, need, and are eligible for social services, the Hispanic elderly use services far less than the need warrants (Lacayo, 1980). Why? This may be the most important research question concerning older Hispanics. Answering it is a prerequisite to improving services to needy Hispanic elders. This issue can thus have a profound effect on older Hispanics' health, income, life satisfaction, and all other aspects of well-being.

Concerning health, more research is needed on chronological age versus functional age among the Hispanic elderly. Some data indicate that older Hispanics feel older and age sooner than their white counterparts. Their functional age outstrips their chronological age. Why is this so? In what ways do older Hispanics age sooner? What can be done about this phenomenon? Other health research areas that need study are how economic factors affect illness, and the formal and informal health and income supports used by older Hispanics. A recent study of chronic illness indictates that Hispanics aged 75 and over are no more chronically ill than Hispanics aged 55 to 74. What are the characteristics that set the "survivors" apart from the others?

Regarding income, research should focus on developing an income and employment profile of the Hispanic elderly, including their employment and income history; and on why eligible older Hispanics use Social Security benefits, other income supports, and other social services much less than their need for these supports suggests they should.

In the case of morale or life satisfaction, the extent and efficiency of emotional and social support rendered by family, friends, the church, and others warrant further study. How can these and other sources of support best be used in the future to improve older Hispanics' sense of well-being? This question presents another relevant research topic.

REFERENCES AND SOURCES FOR ADDITIONAL INFORMATION

References for this chapter follow. Some of the principal sources for further information on the Hispanic elderly are *A Research, Bibliographic, and Resource Guide on the Hispanic Elderly* (Asociación Nacional Pro Personas Mayores, Los Angeles, 1981); Center for Chicano Aged, Graduate School of Social Work of the University of Texas at Arlington; and publications of the San Diego State University Center on Aging.

REFERENCES

Almquist, E.M. *Minorities, gender, and work*. Lexington Books, D.C. Heath, Lexington, Mass., 1979

Asociación Nacional Pro Personas Mayores. *A research, bibliographic, and resource guide on the Hispanic elderly*. Los Angeles, 1981.

Bastida, E. Family structure and intergenerational exchange of the Hispanic American family. *Gerontologist*, 1978, *18*, 48–55.

Bell, D., and Zellman, G. *Issues in service delivery to ethnic elderly*. Rand Corporation, Santa Monica, Calif., 1976.

Crouch, B.M. Age and institutional support: Perceptions of older Mexican-Americans. *Journal of Gerontology*, 1972, *27*, 524–529.

Dowd, J.J., and Bengtson, V.L. Aging in minority populations: An examination of the double jeopardy hypothesis. *Journal of Gerontology*, 1978, *33*, 427–436.

Gallup Organization, Inc. *A Gallup study of religious and social attitudes of Hispanic Americans*. Gallup Organization, Princeton, N.J., 1978.

Korte, A.O. *Social interaction and morale of Spanish-speaking elderly*. Ph.D. diss., University of Denver, 1978.

Kurtz, S. (Ed.) In other Americas: Mexican-Americans. In *New York Times encyclopedia almanac*, Times Book and Educational Division, New York, 1970.

Lacayo, C.G. *A national study to assess the service needs of the Hispanic elderly*. Asociación Nacional Pro Personas Mayores, Los Angeles, 1980.

Laurel, N.F. An intergenerational comparison of attitude toward the support of aged parents: A study of Mexican-Americans in two South Texas communities. D.S.W. diss., University of Southern California, Los Angeles, 1976.

Markides, K., and Martin, H. Psychological distress among elderly Mexican-Americans and Anglos. *Ethnicity*, 1980, 7, 298–309.

U.S. Bureau of the Census. *Persons of Spanish origin in the United States: March, 1975*. USGPO, *Current Population Reports*. Washington, D.C., 1976.

———. Money, income, and poverty status of families in the United States: 1980. USGPO, Washington, D.C., 1981.

White, C.B. The inner city aged: San Antonio, 1980. Paper presented at the 34th Annual Meeting of the Gerontological Society of America, Toronto, November 1981.

16

INDIAN AND ALASKAN NATIVES

NATIONAL INDIAN COUNCIL ON AGING

There are about 50,000 Indians and Alaskan Natives age 65 or over in the United States. This makes them the smallest of the major ethnic/racial groups among the U.S. aged. However, their concentration in reservations and certain rural and urban areas, and their history first as "enemies" of the white man and then as "wards" of the government has created unique problems and opportunities. The following excerpts are taken from the first and only national survey of elderly Indians. Comparisons are made with a similar survey of all persons aged 60 or over in Cleveland, Ohio.

The first research effort ever undertaken to document the conditions of life of older Indian and Alaskan Native people nationwide was completed by the National Indian Council on Aging in 1980. The research examined in detail their economic and social resources, physical and mental health, capacity to perform the activities of daily living, housing conditions, transportation needs, and receipt of services.

MAJOR FINDINGS

Character of Life of Indian/Alaskan Native Elderly

The Indian/Alaskan Native elderly, especially those in a rural setting, tend to live in an extended family. Household size approaches three persons per household. Approximately half of all households consist of married couples and others such as children, grandchildren, and foster children. About 20–25% of the households have one or more foster children. In many cases the foster children are

Reprinted by permission from *American Indian Elderly: A National Profile*, National Indian Council on Aging, Albuquerque, N.M., 1981.

children of other relatives. Because of their strong family ties, Indian are less likely to socialize outside the family than are their counterparts in Cleveland. Interestingly, Indians and Alaskan elderly, even though they have close family ties, appear to be less trusting and less happy about their family relationships.

Compared to Cleveland elderly, Indian and Alaskan Native elderly are poor. More of them are employed than those in Cleveland, more are seeking work and they are less skilled than their counterparts. More than one-quarter (26.3%) have 0 to 4 years of education. Indians and Alaskan Natives are more likely to say they own their home, but many more are still paying mortgages, albeit the monthly payments are smaller. Housing stock is old and dilapidated. Twenty-six percent of the housing was built prior to 1939. There is considerable over-crowding too. Twenty-five percent of the respondents reported that bedrooms were occupied by three or more persons. Service outages of critical systems were also reported. Heat, water, and toilet outages were 20%, 24%, and 15% respectively. In Alaska 44% of all respondents claimed that they had heat outage during the preceding winter.

Indian and Alaskan Native elderly are more likely than Cleveland elderly to worry, feel less satisfied with life and have a perception that they are worse off financially.

Indian and Alaskan Native elderly have significant physical and mental health problems. Notably, they have the following problems to a greater extent than do those in Cleveland:

Tuberculosis

Diabetes

Liver Disease

Kidney Disease

Hearing Impairment

Sight Impairment

In the other health impairment areas Indians and Alaskan Natives are at least as impaired as those in Cleveland. Additionally, their perception of their physical health is poorer and they exhibit mental health problems (using the probably culture-bound 15 question OARS psychiatric evaluation as a measure) by a factor of two over the Cleveland sample (44% of the Indian/Alaskan sample answered five or more questions with responses indicating mental health impairment).

Character and Response of the Existing Service System

A network of comprehensive services for Indians and Alaskan Natives exists in most Indian controlled communities. The BIA [Bureau of Indian Affairs], IHS, and HUD [Department of Housing and Urban Development] provide most of the resources for this system. Indians are more likely to say they live in subsidized housing and receive health and nutrition services than their Cleveland counterparts. They tend to use the publicly provided services to a greater extent, mainly because there are no alternatives to care. Even though Indians are more apt to use the service system, they tend to use it less frequently than those in Cleveland use theirs. Part of the explanation of this behavior is that the extended family is called upon to provide services such as transportation, help in seeking employment and housing, checking and homemaker services. However, when asked, more Indians will state that more services are needed than are provided. One could conclude from this that:

There is a delivery system in place.

Families supplement the provision of service.

The extent to which needs are met is inadequate.

As a possible indication of the degree to which health service is underprovided, one notes that antibiotics are prescribed to about 15% of the Indian population whereas in Cleveland only 3% are receiving antibiotics. The question that one might ask is: "Are Indians coming in for one medical visit, being prescribed drugs, and not being followed up with additional visits to see if the medical problem is solved?"

(Table 16.1 lists several services received by Indians and Cleveland residents. This table highlights the degree to which some services are underprovided to Indians [transportation, coordination, employment, education] and some are overprovided, i.e., not wanted or felt to be needed when provided [checking, meal preparation, legal protective, personal care]). Given these findings it appears that services are being provided to Indians under the false assumption that they need the same services as the dominant society.

Comparison of Impairment Levels between Indian/Alaskan Native and Cleveland Elderly

The analysis of age versus impairment for the Indian and Cleveland elderly populations indicated that similarities exist between Cleveland's 65 and older population and (1) Indians/Alaskan Natives 55 and older and (2) rural Indians/Alaskan Natives 45 and older.

Number and Location of Indian/Alaskan Elderly Is Uncertain

This finding (or non-finding, if you will) came about when the sampling frame was being identified. Ideally, to accomplish a random sample requires a complete list from which sampling can be conducted. In the case of Indians living on reservations or Alaskans living in villages, relatively complete and accurate information about the age, name, and location of the elderly was readily available,

Table 16.1

Percent of Elderly Who Received and/or Wanted Services in Cleveland and among Indians/Alaskan Natives

Service Type	60+ Cleveland		60+ Indians	
	Rec'd.*	Wanted	Rec'd.*	Wanted
Public Transportation	4.9	21.1	14.5	36.9
Social/Recreation	26.0	32.0	47.5	42.0
Employment	0.7	2.6	6.8	8.6
Sheltered Employment	0.2	1.7	1.9	6.3
Education (Employment-Related)	0.4	2.5	2.5	12.0
Remedial Training	0.4	2.0	1.6	9.8
Mental Health Service	2.1	3.8	5.1	7.2
Psychotropic Drugs	19.5	20.1	11.7	11.7
Personal Care	11.9	9.1	11.3	9.8
Nursing Care	6.5	5.4	10.2	13.1
Physical Therapy	3.5	4.7	6.2	11.9
Continuous Supervision	8.8	6.9	11.8	14.1
Checking	49.1	32.3	50.5	39.1
Relocation/Placement	2.3	5.0	6.3	7.8
Homemaker	28.1	29.1	26.4	31.2
Meal Preparation	17.3	13.9	22.2	19.5
Legal/Protective	22.6	19.9	14.7	19.4
Coordination, Information, and Referral	11.3	15.5	36.3	46.9

Sources: Cleveland data are from the 1975 U.S. Government Accounting Office survey of elderly in Cleveland, Ohio. Indian data are from the 1980 survey of elderly Indians and Alaskan Natives.

*Services received within past six months.

because of the requirement by these communities to maintain tribal rolls for identification purposes. However, double counting persons on tribal rolls is a problem as back and forth migration is currently happening between reservations and urban centers of employment. The Indian elderly living in urban areas are most likely to be severely undercounted when one compares the list the Administration for Native Americans (ANA) maintains on its program recipients versus the "conventional wisdom" of program people in the field. Unless accurate population information is obtained, it will be impossible to determine the extent to which problems and needs of the Indian elderly exist in terms of the actual number of persons affected.

SPECIFIC FINDINGS

Computer runs were made yielding percentage responses for each salient variable (question) in the Indian/Alaskan data base. Results were compiled for

Table 16.2
Level of Impairment

| | Response Frequencies | | | | |
| | Indians and Alaskan Natives | | | Cleveland | Rural |
Response Categories*	45 +	55 +	60 +	60 +	45 +
Excellent CIS = 5-7	7.0	5.6	4.2	6.6	5.9
Good CIS = 8-10	24.6	23.2	22.6	21.3	24.4
Mildly Impaired					
CIS = 11-14	44.1	45.4	44.6	43.1	45.1
Moderately Impaired					
CIS = 15-18	15.8	16.6	18.0	21.2	16.0
Severely Impaired					
CIS = 19-21	6.9	6.5	7.8	6.1	6.9
Totally Impaired					
CIS = 22 +	2.1	2.6	3.0	1.6	1.6

*The "response categories" are our choice, based on some analysis of the demand for services by differently impaired subgroups. They have no standard definition in this case but are used for illustration only.
CIS = Cumulative Impairment Scale.

Indians and Alaskan Natives 45 and older, 55 and older, 60 and older, and for rural Indians 45 and older. These results were juxtaposed with the identical questions asked of the Cleveland sample so that comparisons between groups could be made.

The first three columns in table 16.2 are drawn from the Indian/Alaskan Native data base as a whole. Insofar as one of our major findings is that the rural/urban population split is not well known, the figures are unweighted and are simply the data base results.

The fourth column presents the comparable results from the Cleveland study. As noted previously, this data base significantly underrepresents the 60–64 year age group and the population includes non-whites at nearly three times the national average. Based on age/race analysis, the figures should be "worse" than what might be expected from a "true" 60 + national population data base. As a result the figures provide a conservative reference point.

The final column gives data for the 45 + "rural" (non-urban) American Indian/Alaskan Native population, which we contend is equivalent to the 60 + non-Indian population.

The first three columns, read from left to right, are indicative of the effects of age on the Indian population. Comparing the 60 + Indian data (column 3) with the Cleveland data (column 4) provides a reasonable basis for comparing the Indian and non-Indian "elderly" as currently defined. The 45 + Rural to Cleveland comparison should be used to validate our equivalent age hypothesis.

Note that the middle two categories (mild, moderate) tend to stay relatively

Table 16.3
Percentage Distribution of Elderly by Response Categories
on Five Functional Scales

	Response Frequencies				
	Indians and Alaskan Natives				Rural
	45 and	55 and	60 and	Cleveland	45 and
Response Categories	over	over	over	60 and over	over
Social					
Excellent/Good	74.2	73.2	70.6	67.2	75.2
Mild/Moderate	22.5	23.1	25.7	27.1	22.5
Severe/Total	3.2	3.7	3.8	5.6	2.2
Economic					
Excellent/Good	41.1	41.8	42.7	46.2	41.3
Mild/Moderate	49.3	49.3	47.9	51.4	490
Severe/Total	9.6	8.9	9.4	2.4	9.6
Mental Health					
Excellent/Good	74.7	73.3	70.7	65.2	72.7
Mild/Moderate	22.7	24.0	26.1	31.1	25.8
Severe/Total	2.6	2.7	3.2	4.5	1.4
Physical Health					
Excellent/Good	50.2	45.5	42.6	39.1	50.3
Mild/Moderate	43.8	47.5	49.5	54.9	43.6
Severe/Total	6.0	7.3	7.9	5.9	6.1
Activities of Daily Living					
Excellent/Good	65.8	60.7	57.3	61.4	62.4
Mild/Moderate	27.6	31.3	33.0	32.1	30.5
Severe/Total	6.6	8.0	9.7	6.6	7.2

Note that the pattern is generally consistent with the review of Cumulative Impairment Score, i.e., the general reduction in size of the excellent/good category with increasing age, and the increase in severe/total with age.

stable in size, while the first two (excellent, good) decrease with age and the last two (severely, totally) increase. Note also that while the 45 + Rural are not identical category by category, there are fewer "Excellent" than Cleveland and more "Severely Impaired," making the aggregate comparable, bearing in mind that the CIS, while numeric, is derived from ordinal scales (i.e., a rating of 3 is worse than 1, but not three times as "bad").

Consider the condensed chart (table 16.3) of Social, Economic, Mental Health, Physical Health, and Activities of Daily Living ratings. The "Social" ratings for the Indian population are generally "better" than for the non-Indian population, which we believe to be a relatively valid comparison based on the strength of the extended family. However, this generalization is qualified somewhat by the significantly different responses with regard to having someone to trust and feeling that someone can provide help for an extended period.

The "Economic" ratings are distinctly worse for the Indian population, as borne out by the detailed data on income, employment, and so forth. However, in comparing any data involving actual dollar values, it must be remembered that this survey was conducted in 1979–1980, while the Cleveland study was conducted in 1975. Significant inflation has occurred and the Cleveland distributions have not been corrected for inflation.

Generally speaking the Indian elderly work longer for less pay and have larger families to support. Not unexpectedly, they feel financially insecure and concerned about dealing with emergency situations. Virtually all of the differences between the Indian/non-Indian responses in this area are believed to be significant, and many of the differences are quite dramatic.

The "Mental Health" ratings are somewhat confusing. The overall "Mental Health" ratings (interviewers' judgement) indicate generally better mental health among Indians than among the Cleveland elderly. These ratings stand in sharp contrast to the detailed results of, for example, the application of the 15 item psychological test and the perception of the respondents themselves. Two issues need to be addressed in clarifying findings in this area: (1) are the Indian raters biased by their own cultural norms, and/or (2) is there culture bias in the standard questionnaire? The pervasive self-perception of poor mental health in this section is supported by the strong demand for mental health services in the services supplement, indicating that mental health is a problem for the Indian elderly despite the relatively favorable "scores" assigned by interviewers.

In "Physical Health" it can be observed that the ratings generally show a larger percentage of the Indian population in the Excellent/Good category, counterbalanced by a significantly larger population in the Severe/Totally Impaired category. The high incidence of specific diseases (such as Tuberculosis, Diabetes, Liver and Kidney Disorders, Eyesight, Hearing, and Drinking Problems), the demand for health aids, and a generally poor self-perception of health would tend to indicate another "rater bias" in regard to the Excellent/Good category.

The "Activities of Daily Living" scores would seem to support the same analysis as that given for Physical Health. ADL, dealing with the actual functional capacity of an individual to care for him- or herself, is a crucial measure of overall well-being. The detailed responses in this section show a consistently grim picture.

Analysis of Age versus Impairment

The allocation of national resources for serving the elderly is primarily defined by the geographic distribution of the elderly population, elderly being defined in terms of a specific chronological age.

The human problems toward which these programs are directed are not commonly shared by the group nominally defined as "the elderly," but vary considerably in scope, intensity, and time of occurrence. The use of a given chronological age as the basis for distributing resources and allowing service access is an administrative convenience which evades dealing with the issue of need, per se.

As evident in the foregoing review, the needs of the older Indian population are greater than those of the non-Indian population, both in severity and extent. Insofar as chronological age rather than need, per se, is the accepted factor currently in use for allocating resources, the question arises as to whether a different age criterion should be used for the Indian population in order to assume a more equitable distribution of resources. That is, if programs for the aged are generally directed at a population cohort having a certain set of characteristics, and a different cohort of Indians displays comparable characteristics, it would seem reasonable to alter the germaine administrative requirement to allow that comparable population to be served.

SUMMARY OF FINDINGS

The character of life for Indian and Alaskan Natives aged 45 and older is significantly different from that of the dominant population. Major differences between the Indian and non-Indian populations are evident throughout the data. These include such basic areas as relative income, education and employment levels, the importance of the extended family, and patterns of physical and mental health problems.

Impairment levels of Indians and Alaskan Natives 55 and older are comparable to non-Indian U.S. elderly 65 and older. Rural Indians and Alaskan Natives 45 and older are comparable to non-Indian elderly 65 and older.

The existing service system for Indian/Alaskan Native elderly falls short in satisfying needs for service. Although service delivery systems are in place in most Indian communities, it appears that services are being provided under the false assumption that the services delivered to the dominant society are also most suitable for the Indian community.

The exact number and location of Indian/Alaskan Natives 45 and older is not well documented, especially in urban areas. Unless accurate population information is obtained, it will be impossible to determine the extent to which problems and needs of the Indian elderly exist in terms of the actual number of persons affected.

PART IV

GROUPS PRESENTING SPECIAL CONCERNS

17

ADDICTS AND ALCOHOLICS

FRANK J. WHITTINGTON

Problems associated with the misuse of alcohol and other drugs among the elderly differ in at least one respect from most of the other problems that affect older people: they arise directly from an attempt on someone's part to help. That is, either a physician or an individual has misused a drug in an attempt to ease pain, cure disease, or reduce distress. Perhaps because of this peculiar characteristic, or perhaps because it is typically hidden from public and medical attention, alcohol and drug problems have not, until recently, received as much attention from researchers or clinicians as have other, more obvious concerns, such as economic insecurity, age discrimination, social isolation, and physical and mental illness.

In the last five years, however, books and articles have appeared in such numbers (see especially Gomberg, 1980; Judge and Caird, 1978; Kayne, 1978; Levenson, 1979; Mishara and Kastenbaum, 1980; Petersen et al., 1979b; Petersen and Whittington, 1982; Poe and Holloway, 1980) that it is no longer possible to label such problems "hidden." While much remains to be learned about the causes and consequences of such misuse as well as possible approaches to prevention and treatment, it is quite possible to describe the problem in some detail and to suggest some of the likely causes.

Accordingly, this chapter will summarize what is presently known about two groups of older persons who have drug problems—addicts and alcoholics. The first group—addicts—includes those individuals who are addicted to illegal drugs, primarily narcotics such as heroin or morphine, or to legal drugs that they obtain illegally. Some in this group are methadone addicts who have, for the most part, acquired this addiction as part of their treatment for addiction to illegal narcotic drugs. The second group includes those elderly persons who are addicted to alcohol or who experience problems from its use. These groups of older people have much the same types of problems with alcohol and narcotics that younger people do, but differ in important respects. A third group of drug misusers is without a doubt the largest and most diverse of the three. It includes older people who either misuse their legal, therapeutic drugs or who are the passive victims of the misuse of those drugs by others. While not within the purview of this chapter, this group and its problems are clearly important and worthy of attention. Interested readers are directed to one of the several recent books or review articles on this topic (Glantz et al., 1983; Levenson, 1979; Petersen, Whittington, and Beer, 1979; Petersen, Whittington, and Payne, 1979; Petersen and Whittington, 1982).

For the first two groups, data will be presented outlining the epidemiology of drug misuse, its known causes and apparent consequences, and (for alcoholics) current and suggested community responses to the problem. Due to space limitations, however, presentation of data on the use (as opposed to abuse) of these drugs, except in the broadest sense, will not be possible, nor will it be feasible to describe in any great detail either the findings regarding abuse or the studies from which they come. For these, the reader is referred either to the publications cited in the references or to any of the several lengthier reviews or bibliographies of this literature that are now available. (See especially Barnes et al., 1980; Glantz et al., 1983; Gomberg, 1980; Mishara and Kastenbaum, 1980.)

ADDICTS

While many legally prescribed drugs are potentially addicting, and some older persons have certainly become addicted to them in the course of their treatment, no reliable data on this group are known to exist. Therefore, this section will deal only with users of illegal drugs, the majority of whom are (or were) addicted to opiates, primarily heroin.

Comparatively little research has been done on the older abuser of illegal drugs, and what has been done shows quite clearly that such abuse involves mainly heroin and marijuana (Chambers, 1971; DuPont, 1976; Manheimer and Mellinger, 1969). Furthermore, all researchers in this area agree that use of illegal drugs by older people is relatively small compared to that of younger persons (Capel and Peppers, 1978; Capel and Stewart, 1971; DuPont, 1976; Pascarelli and Fischer, 1974; Peppers and Stover, 1979). For instance, DuPont (1976) has reported that only 2 percent of people over 50 have tried marijuana, while more than 50 percent of college-aged youth (18–21) have done so. In addition, Ball and Chambers's (1970) study of admissions to U.S. Public Health Service hospitals in Forth Worth, Texas, and Lexington, Kentucky, for treatment of opiate addiction revealed that 80 percent of such admissions were persons under 40, and that fewer than 4 percent were over 60. An even greater disparity was noted by Capel and Stewart (1971) in their study of addicts involved in a methadone maintenance treatment program for narcotics addicts in New Orleans. They found that only about 5 percent of the addicts in this program were over the age of 45.

However, there is also agreement among these writers on two other points:

(1) there are more older addicts—both in treatment and in the community but not being treated—than is popularly believed; and (2) the size of the older addict population is growing now, mainly as middle-aged addicts get older, and will undergo an explosive growth in the years to come.

It is clear that the general public has difficulty imagining an older person being involved with illegal drugs; it just does not fit the social stereotype of the apple-cheeked granny or even of the debilitated, isolated, lonely old man or woman. But most early researchers also expressed surprise at finding *any* older addicts among their study samples (Capel and Stewart, 1971; Capel et al., 1972; Pascarelli and Fischer, 1974). This surprise stemmed mainly from their initial acceptance of the conclusions of an even earlier study by Winick (1962) that seemed to show that addicts underwent a sort of "maturing-out" process in which they either gradually overcame their addiction through a sort of developmental process or simply became so debilitated after years of drug abuse that they could no longer carry on the life-style and so "burned out." Winick believed that drug abuse in the teens and early twenties was mainly caused by an inability to deal with the crucial developmental issues of those years, such as sexuality and career choice. He further reasoned that maturation—reaching the late thirties at least— might bring a kind of "emotional homeostasis" that would allow the addict to return to a drug-free life-style. This theory, coupled with the notion of addict burn-out, helped Winick to offer a plausible explanation for why so few addicts over 40 continued to be "known" to official government agencies.

However, O'Donnell (1969) investigated the addict "drop-out" phenomenon and offered firm evidence that calls the "mature-out" hypothesis into question, suggesting that the "disappearance" of older addicts may simply be a result of faulty research methods rather than a cessation of addiction. Such a position is given further support by Capel and Stewart (1971), Capel and Peppers (1978), and Pascarelli and Fischer (1974), who all found what they felt were significant proportions of addicts over 40 in the treatment programs they studied (ranging from 5 percent to 34 percent). In addition, Capel and his associates (1972) found thirty-eight addicts between ages 48 and 73 who were not in any treatment program but were, through a variety of adaptive techniques, apparently managing their habits without coming to official attention. All of these middle-aged and older addicts had neither matured out nor burned out of their addiction but had merely grown older along with it. It must be noted, however, that Pottieger and Inciardi (1982), in reviewing these data, conclude that many addicts probably do mature out of their addiction in some fashion and others probably do burn out. The key point here, though, is that many do not.

Moreover, all of these researchers agree that the number of elderly addicts has been increasing rapidly and that growth is likely to gain momentum over the next two decades. Capel and Peppers (1978), in particular, point out that, based on their 1976 follow-up study of the methadone clinic population initially interviewed by Capel and Stewart (1971) in 1969, the middle-aged and older cohorts have roughly doubled over a seven-year period, with the 45–59 age group increasing from 4.5 percent to 9.3 percent and the over 60 group moving from 0.5 percent to 1.2 percent. While these proportions are still relatively small, Capel and Peppers point out the greater tendency of older addicts to remain in treatment and suggest that "within the next ten years, . . . the number [of addicts] over 60 will have tripled or quadrupled its present size" (Capel and Peppers, 1978:397). This finding led Petersen, Whittington, and Beer (1979:18) to conclude: "If this prediction holds true and is replicated in each of the some 800 other such clinics across the country, then, even without considering the larger number of older addicts thought to be living in the community without institutional support, one can anticipate a national geriatric drug abuse problem of significant proportions."

ALCOHOLICS

There is significantly more published research on older alcoholics and problem drinkers than there is on older narcotics addicts. This is undoubtedly due to the fact that many more older persons use and abuse alcohol than abuse narcotic drugs, and, consequently, alcohol abuse among the elderly is both publicly and professionally perceived as the greater problem. Still, given the larger amount of attention devoted to it, surprisingly little is actually known about alcoholism and problem drinking in old age.

For example, we probably know more about drinking practices and the extent of *use* of alcohol among older people than we do about their drinking problems and the extent of their *abuse*. Nevertheless, as stated earlier, our discussion will be largely limited to a consideration of alcoholism and problem drinking. Specifically, after briefly defining the problem and discussing sources of information on alcohol abuse, we will present data on the frequency and extent of alcoholism/problem drinking among the elderly; outline general patterns of problem drinking behavior among the old; summarize what is known about the demographic, social, and psychological characteristics of older problem drinkers; and, finally, briefly mention some of the issues important in their treatment.

Certain problems plague all research on alcohol abuse, but two seem particularly troublesome in the older population. The first concerns the definition of alcoholism and the criteria to be used in its diagnosis. Schuckit and Pastor (1978) have identified three distinct traditions that have dominated this field of research, which they term the "addiction approach," the "socio-normative approach," and the "social problems approach." The addiction approach depends on the presence of either a physical or psychological compulsion to drink and judges this compulsion by the strength of withdrawal symptoms. Aside from other difficulties with applying this definition among younger people, there is a particular problem with using it with older persons because, as Schuckit and Pastor (1978:34) point out, "their reactions to alcohol consumption and withdrawal are even more variable than those of younger persons."

The second diagnostic tradition, the socio-normative approach, attempts to establish criteria for "normal," as opposed to "deviant," drinking habits and focuses in this attempt on the frequency and quantity of alcohol consumed. Obviously, norms governing drinking behavior vary widely by sex, race, ethnicity, and socioeconomic status, and we know so little about drinking patterns among older persons generally, and this older age cohort in particular, that establishing norms is difficult at best.

The final definitional approach focuses on the social problems that usually accompany alcohol abuse, such as inability to hold a job, marital difficulties, or legal problems. The ease of application of these diagnostic criteria has apparently been in large part responsible for the increasing popularity of the term "problem drinking" in place of the older label, "alcoholism." While an "alcoholic" might only be diagnosed by a physician, a problem drinker can be identified through normal social history interview techniques. It is, however, difficult to apply these criteria to many older people, whose employment, marriages, and even legal status may already have been disrupted by age-related events; the relative contribution of a pattern of heavy drinking to these problems is likely to be difficult to determine.

Another problem with research on drinking problems in old age is the "social desirability effect," the tendency of persons being interviewed to deny engaging in what they imagine to be socially undesirable behavior (heavy drinking) or to minimize its extent (Monk et al., 1977). This would seem to be particularly true for older people who are presently members of a cohort that seems to use alcohol far less than do other cohorts (Cahalan et al., 1969; Johnson and Goodrich, 1974; Knupfer and Room, 1964). Monk and his associates also suggest that older people may deny problem drinking because they tend to deny all problems as a psychological defense against the declines associated with old age.

Epidemiology

As already noted, data on alcoholism and problem drinking among the elderly are still rather limited, and there is so far little concurrence as to an actual prevalence. Schuckit and Miller (1976) have estimated that between 2 percent and 10 percent of the older population are alcoholic, and this range has been widely cited and accepted in the literature. However, since this percentage range translates into roughly 500,000 to 2.5 million older persons, it leaves open the question of an alcoholic diagnosis for some 2 million older people, which seems to be a very wide degree of uncertainty indeed. Nevertheless, data do exist from a limited number of community surveys, a somewhat larger number of studies of hospital and psychiatric treatment facility admissions and census data, and from analyses of various types of crime data, such as alcohol-related arrests and drunk driving. Data from each of these sources will be summarized.

Only three studies are known that have presented prevalence data on alcoholism or problem drinking of older people living in the community. The first was a survey carried out in New York City by Bailey, Haberman, and Alksne (1965) that asked their sample families whether they or any member of their family had ever had a problem because of too much drinking. This approach appears to fall within the social problems approach to diagnosis and would appear to be a rather broad definition; however, only 2.2 percent of the family members 65–74 years old were so identified, although this was roughly equal to the peak rate found in this sample (for 45- to 54-year-olds). It should also be noted that persons 75 and over were not included in the data reported. A similar approach was employed by James (1979) in her survey in Michigan, but the prevalence of alcohol problems found (7 percent) was significantly higher. Finally, a still higher rate was reported by Rathbone-McCuan and her associates (1976), who interviewed older persons living in a variety of community and institutional settings in Baltimore and found approximately 12 percent to manifest alcoholic symptoms. However, as Gomberg (1980) correctly points out, the rate was probably influenced unduly by the inclusion of nursing home and domiciliary settings because these are places where alcoholics tend to live. These data, then, coupled with Cahalan, Cisin and Crossley's (1969) finding that 6 percent of a national probability sample of persons 60 and over were heavy drinkers, would seem to indicate that the 2–10 percent range is essentially correct but that the actual proportion of elderly who are problem drinkers is still impossible to specify.

In the main, studies of hospitals and psychiatric facilities fail to define exactly how a diagnosis of alcoholism was made, but it is assumed that most probably followed generally the addiction approach. Also, these studies employed different definitions of the older age group (ranging from 50 and older to 65 and older), and some included both sexes, while others reported data for males only. In any case, studies of general hospital populations carried out between the late 1960s and mid-1970s reveal a wide variation of incidence rates. (Gomberg [1980] presents a very useful tabular summary of these findings.) While two studies of all newly admitted patients (Goldstein and Grant, 1974; Schuckit and Miller, 1976) reported rates of older alcoholics in the 15–20 percent range, others (Gomberg, 1980; McCusker et al., 1971) reported rates between 45 and 49 percent. (It should be noted, however, that the McCusker study included persons 50 and over in the "older" group.)

Similarly, studies of admissions to psychiatric hospitals and psychiatric wards of general hospitals reveal older alcoholics constituting between 15 percent and 44 percent of all admissions (Daniel, 1972; Gaitz and Baer, 1971; Rosin and Glatt, 1971; Simon et al., 1968; Whittier and Korenyi, 1961). A study by Zimberg (1974) of patients seen in a community mental health center during 1972 revealed that 17 percent had alcohol-related problems, and Schuckit presents data in two separate studies that show that 9 percent of the clients in alcohol treatment programs in the state of Washington were 60 and above (Schuckit, 1977) and that 16 percent of the female clients in one such program were 55 and older (Schuckit et al., 1978).

Based on these studies, it seems reasonable to conclude that many older alcoholics do receive treatment for their problem and that a substantial proportion of older persons under care in both general and psychiatric hospitals are there, at least in part, because of their alcohol problems. However, it is not possible, based on these data, to say whether older alcoholics are more or less likely to be identified than are younger ones or whether they are more or less likely to find their way into treatment.

One other source of data on the epidemiology of alcoholism among the elderly is that of arrests for public intoxication and reports on older men in Skid Row subcultures. Zax, Gardner, and Hart (1964) reported arrest data for public drunkenness in Rochester, New York, in 1961 showing older white males to have an arrest rate that was about two-thirds the peak rate of the sample (for 50- to 59-year-olds), but somewhat higher than that for white males under 40. Epstein, Mills, and Simon (1970) investigated the arrest records of older persons in San Francisco during a four-month period in 1967–1968 and found that a large majority (82 percent) were charged with public intoxication compared with only 46 percent of all adult arrests during this period.

Schichor and Kobrin (1978) used Uniform Crime Reports to study the criminal behavior trends of older persons (55 and older) between 1964 and 1974. They found that, at each of the three time periods studied, most of the misdemeanor arrests were for public drunkenness, but the proportion did decline over the eleven-year period from 61.7 percent to 46.3 percent. However, they also observed an almost exactly corresponding increase in the arrests of older persons for drunk driving (5.8 percent vs 19.4 percent). Schichor and Kobrin conclude that the police had reduced their commitment to the so-called revolving door criminal manner of dealing with public drunkenness and were more often relying on the noncriminal means of treatment and rehabilitation. It may also indicate that the older population is becoming generally healthier and is maintaining its ability to drive at later ages. This could be a sign that older people are becoming more like younger people in their vices as well as their virtues. Additional support for this view comes from Pottieger and Inciardi (1982), who conclude from their detailed review of studies of various types of "street populations" that the Skid Row subculture of largely older alcoholic men is changing in character and declining in size. In fact, they see an accumulation of social, economic, and legal changes working to alter the social environment of these men, "perhaps to the point that they become indistinguishable from alcoholics and other problem drinkers among the elderly conventional poor in our society" (1982:97).

Causes of Alcoholism in Old Age

As with many of the other issues surrounding this problem, so little research has been done that definite conclusions are hard to reach. To quote one group of authors in this area, "The causes of alcoholism in old age are not known" (Schuckit et al., 1978:406). In fact, one early researcher (Drew, 1968), observing the significant cohort differences in drinking behavior—with older age groups drinking less and showing much lower incidence of admission to alcohol treatment programs—concluded that alcoholism was a "self-limiting disease" and that alcoholics either burned out or matured out of their addiction much like narcotics addicts had been hypothesized to do (Winick, 1962). However, the reports by both clinicians and researchers of significant numbers of older alcoholics, many of whom had been problem drinkers for years, indicated that not all alcoholics were experiencing spontaneous remissions sometime in middle or early old age. In fact, there is now general agreement that at least two (and possibly three or more) types of elderly alcoholics exist, each with a distinct set of antecedents. "Early-onset" alcoholics are presumed to have begun drinking heavily at a younger age due to the same combination of disordered personality traits that is usually associated with alcoholism generally (Gomberg, 1980), while "late-onset" alcoholics are often reported to be simply reacting to depressing social events and losses such as retirement, widowhood, and failing health. In this view, the older alcoholic is attempting to adjust to change and is using alcohol to cope with the attendant stresses (Peck, 1979). Simon, Epstein, and Reynolds (1968), Rosin and Glatt (1971), and Zimberg (1974) all have reported that, in their samples of alcoholics in treatment, about two-thirds were early onset alcoholics and about one-third had developed a drinking problem in old age. On the other hand, Mishara and Kastenbaum (1980) have reviewed other studies that tend to show that an even higher percentage of older alcoholics are of long standing, and these authors conclude that relatively few drinking problems develop entirely after age 60. Borgatta, Montgomery, and Borgatta (1982) have demonstrated, moreover, that much of the writing and research on the issue of early- versus late-onset alcoholism is either flawed or suspect, and they argue that there exists no firm evidence of a significant late-onset alcoholic syndrome.

Other writers (Carruth et al., 1973; Gomberg, 1980) have described three types of older alcoholics. The first type, whom Gomberg labeled "the survivors," includes individuals whose alcoholism is long-standing and unremitting. These alcoholics have somehow managed to sustain a pattern of heavy drinking throughout life, though they probably reach old age in poor social and physical health. The second group includes persons who have experienced periodic bouts of alcohol abuse through their early and/or middle years but who were not necessarily recognized as alcoholic. In old age, however, they respond to life stresses by falling back on their former habit of using alcohol as a coping technique. These are referred to by Gomberg as "the intermittents." The third group, "reactive problem drinkers," is more or less equivalent to the late-onset alcoholics mentioned above. These are persons who have never had a particular problem with alcohol but develop one in old age as a coping response to age-related stress. The existence of this third group is doubted by Borgatta and his associates (1982).

A recent investigation by Dunham (1982) of lifetime patterns of drinking promises to form the basis for a further refinement of this typology. Dunham interviewed 310 older persons in Miami and asked them to recollect for him their drinking history. Roughly two-thirds of the sample (n = 210) were classified as lifelong abstainers. For the 100 drinkers in the sample Dunham was able to construct a typology of lifetime drinking patterns that included six distinct types: (1) rise and fall pattern (25 percent of the drinkers fell into this category), (2) rise and sustained pattern (28 percent), (3) light throughout life pattern (21 percent), (4) light with a late rise pattern (7 percent), (5) late starters pattern (11 percent), and (6) highly variable pattern (8 percent). While none of those categories was specified as alcoholic, it is clear from Dunham's descriptions that members of four of them—the "rise and sustained," "late risers," "late starters," and "highly variable" groups—had the potential to be problem drinkers. Interestingly, the division of these four types into two groups—early-onset of heavy drinking (patterns 2 and 6) and late-onset (patterns 4 and 5)—yields a two-thirds/ one-third division between the two (36 percent of the total sample vs. 18 percent) that is identical to those found by earlier investigators of early- and late-onset alcoholics. While Dunham's work is not descriptive of late life alcoholism, it is suggestive of the need for a further refinement of existing typologies.

Whatever their path, it is clear that some lifelong or periodic alcoholics do manage to grow old with their alcoholism, though the proportion who make it is far from clear. However, there is also abundant evidence that many alcoholics do not survive (Drew, 1968; Mayfield, 1974; Schmidt and deLint, 1972), and that many others stop drinking before old age (Cahalan et al., 1969; Glenn, 1981; Schuckit and Miller, 1976). Whether in response to treatment or through spontaneous cessation of problem drinking, as Glenn (1981:369) has ingeniously demonstrated through a cohort analysis of archival national opinion survey data, "something about biological, psychological, and/or social aging seems to tend to make drinkers stop drinking."

Characteristics of Older Alcoholics

It would be instructive to know something of the characteristics of older alcoholics, both as they compare with other older people who do not drink or who drink without problem, and in comparison with younger alcoholics. Unfortunately, except for a few notable studies, most available data simply describe the older alcoholic population. To even suggest comparisons such as those described above would require complicated and often unwarranted juxtapositions of data from different studies, and, to quote Borgatta and his associates (1982:400), commenting on a similar problem, "The temptation to speculate... is obvious, and it is resisted here." However, the following can be said about the characteristics of elderly alcoholics.

First, they appear to be predominantly male. Aside from Rosin and Glatt (1971), who found a predominance of females in their sample of elderly alcoholics in treatment, all other studies that have examined gender have found older males to outnumber females by ratios of from 2:1 (McCusker et al., 1971; Simon et al., 1968) to 5:1 (Rathbone-McCuan et al., 1976). Both Borgatta, Montgomery, and Borgatta (1982) and Smart and Liban (1982) found males significantly more likely to be heavy and/or problem drinkers than females, and Barnes (1979) reports that heavy drinking was ''almost non-existent'' among the older women in her New York State sample.

Only a study by Schuckit, Morrissey, and O'Leary (1978) allows for any comparison of older male and female alcoholics. (Although not reported here, both samples also allow comparison between older and younger groups while controlling for gender.) Compared to these older female alcoholics, the males appear to be slightly more racially diverse and more maritally stable (as expected in any older sample), to have a more antisocial history but a less extensive and varied history of drug use, and to be somewhat more likely to have experienced alcohol-related problems at work, with their marriage, with police, and with health. Except for suicide attempts, where women predominated, the men were also more likely to have had a history of psychiatric problems.

The racial characteristics of older alcoholics have been little studied. While Schuckit and his associates (1978) found the older (55 and over) alcoholics group to be white more often than the younger group (97 percent vs. 66 percent for women and 86 percent vs. 76 percent for men), and Dunham (1982) reported some ethnic differences in his six patterns of lifetime drinking, essentially nothing is known of the possible differences between older black and white alcoholics with respect to such variables as epidemiology, etiology, and result of the disease.

A number of studies have focused on various social characteristics of older alcoholics. Bailey, Haberman, and Alksne (1965) found the rate of alcoholism among widowed men (10.5 percent) to be about four times as great as for those who were married (2.5 percent) or single (2.9 percent). Another study, however (Rathbone-McCuan et al., 1976), found the typical older alcoholic to be divorced, separated, or never married. Schuckit, Morrissey, and O'Leary (1978) found that the older female alcoholics in their sample were more likely to be widowed (37 percent) than in any other marital status, though a relatively high proportion was separated or divorced (23 percent), and fully 57 percent were living alone. Half the males in their sample were married, but a large group (31 percent) was separated or divorced, and 32 percent lived by themselves.

With respect to employment status and income, the few findings are decidedly contradictory. For example, Smart and Liban (1982) found older problem drinkers to be less likely to be retired, but both Rathbone-McCuan and her associates (1976) and Borgatta and his co-workers (1982) found alcohol use and abuse related to unemployment. Likewise, the finding that older persons with higher income were more likely to drink (Borgatta et al., 1982) was offset by the observations that alcoholism is found in all income levels (Rathbone-McCuan et al., 1976) and that it is negatively associated with income (Smart and Liban, 1982).

Very little is known of the psychological characteristics of older problem drinkers. Beyond the observations that they are more likely than non-alcoholic elders to be depressed (Gomberg, 1980; Mishara and Kastenbaum, 1980; Zimberg, 1979) and socially alienated and lonely (Peck, 1979; Rathbone-McCuan et al., 1976; Rosin and Glatt, 1971; Schuckit et al., 1978; Zimberg, 1979), little reliable information exists. Mayfield (1974) asserts, but offers no evidence, that older alcoholics are less belligerent and less antisocial than younger alcoholics. Both Rosin and Glatt (1971) and Schuckit and his colleagues (1978) conclude from their research that older alcoholics are more socially stable than their younger counterparts and report less evidence of antisocial behavior or symptoms of psychiatric distress. Apfeldorf (1978) reviews literature on the personality traits of alcoholics and concludes that it should be possible to develop an alcoholic personality scale "to determine what components of personality persist through the lifespan and which components change" (p. 454).

Treatment of Older Alcoholics

It is a matter of some debate whether older alcoholics respond well to treatment and whether the outcome will be worth the effort involved (Gomberg, 1980). This is undoubtedly part of a larger concern on the part of many helping professionals over whether an investment of resources and time in *any* older client is justified given the (stereotyped) notion that the elderly are resistant to change, physically and mentally impaired, and would not be particularly socially valuable if they were to be restored. Mishara and Kastenbaum (1980) point out the "self-fulfilling prophecy" implications of such thinking. At any rate, neither doctors, aging programs, nor alcoholism treatment programs are usually equipped or anxious to deal effectively with older alcoholics (Gomberg, 1980; Kola et al., 1980; Zimberg, 1974). Nevertheless, a fair amount of research has now been done that points to the efficacy of treatment for older alcoholics and offers some guidance as to the best approaches to take.

The major problem in providing help to an elderly alcoholic seems to be getting him or her into treatment in the first place, and apparently the biggest roadblock to that effort is the alcoholic's own family (Droller, 1964; Mayfield, 1974; Rathbone-McCuan and Triegaardt, 1978). Droller (1964), in particular, suggests that many families create elaborate supporting routines in order to cover up the drinking of an older member and avoid public embarrassment. Other families simply deny that the problem exists, while still others have too few members or are too alienated from each other to be able to detect a drinking problem quickly. Of course, the older person may also deny the problem and delay seeking treatment. In fact, as Schuckit and Pastor (1978) point out, the help-seeking behavior of alcoholics is subject to the same social and psychological influences as that of people with cancer, arthritis, or the flu; some people are quick to self-diagnose and seek professional care at the first sign of aberrance, and others deny the problem and avoid such help.

Most research on treatment issues has focused on the relationship of age to the effectiveness of the therapy. One early study by Selzer and Holloway (1957) found no significant relationship between either the duration of alcohol use or of abuse and the alcoholic's prognosis in treatment. These authors also found that improvement during treatment was directly related to age, with the average age on admission to treatment of the improved group (49) exceeding by ten years that of the unimproved group (39). Later investigations also found that being at least 45 at the time of admission was associated with positive results over time (Bateman and Petersen, 1971, 1972; Wolff and Holland, 1964). Several other studies have focused more specifically on the treatment experience of elderly alcoholics and almost without exception these report that older alcoholics are very responsive to treatment (Droller, 1964; Pascarelli, 1974; Wilkinson, 1971; Zimberg, 1978) and that they are more likely than younger patients to complete the course of therapy (Linn, 1978; Schuckit, 1977). Older alcoholics seem to be particularly likely to respond when their drinking is of the late-onset variety that was likely to have arisen in reaction to age-related losses or stress (Cohen, 1975; Zimberg, 1978).

Experts appear to be divided on the treatment of choice for older alcoholics, but there is some agreement that various types of social therapies are helpful in many cases (Droller, 1964; Linn, 1978; Mishara and Kastenbaum, 1980; Rathbone-McCuan and Triegaardt, 1978; Zimberg, 1978). Family involvement, in particular, is thought to be crucial for the treatment of many older alcoholics for whom unsatisfactory family relationships may have been either a cause or a result of problem drinking (Rathbone-McCuan and Triegaardt, 1978). Other approaches, such as Alcoholics Anonymous, behavioral therapy, and drug treatment, each have advocates but few evaluation studies to demonstrate their effectiveness. There are, furthermore, many unique programs around the country that emphasize a particular variation of one of these approaches or a combination of them. Several of these programs, reviewed by Gomberg (1980) and Mishara and Kastenbaum (1980), appear to show promise.

SUMMARY

It is clear from this brief review of the literature pertinent to older drug addicts and older alcoholics that both groups are relatively small as "problem" groups go, even among the elderly. Nevertheless, older addicts and alcoholics do exist, both in treatment and living independently. Research supports the notion that, while some addicts probably burn out or mature out of their addiction, many do not, but rather grow old with it. Thus, it is anticipated that future cohorts of elderly addicts will continue to grow in size. Presently, little is known of the characteristics of these addicts, of the causes of their addiction, or of the factors differentially associated with addiction burn-out, mature-out, or adaptive management across the life span.

Older alcoholics constitute a much larger group than older addicts and are demonstrably the greater problem, though there is little agreement as to just how many elderly are affected. We do know that some alcoholics, like some addicts, appear to be able to begin their alcoholic careers early and carry them on into old age, while other elders seem to develop their drinking problems late in life, apparently as a coping response to some difficulty or loss experienced in old age. While debate continues over the relative likelihood of the early- and late-onset types of elderly alcoholic, it is clear that drinkers differ greatly in their patterns of drinking and problem drinking over a lifetime. Also apparent from research reports are the facts that older alcoholics tend to be male, white, unmarried, socially isolated, lonely, and depressed. While this social and psychological profile is not particularly surprising, older alcoholics are usually described as more socially stable than their younger counterparts. While getting older alcoholics to treatment or finding an appropriate program for them may be a problem, there is ample evidence that, once there, they do respond well, and often they do better than younger alcoholics. This seems especially true for older "stress-reactive" drinkers whose therapy involves social interaction and support from both family and peers, though many innovative programs exist that are proving helpful to the older alcoholic.

This review demonstrates both the known and the unknown: it conveys many important facts that describe and explain the characteristics and behavior of older addicts and alcoholics, but it also highlights the gaps in our knowledge. It is to these gaps that researchers must attend if more effective forms of treatment and prevention are to be discovered.

REFERENCES

Apfeldorf, M. The quantitative objective assessment of personality traits of alcoholics over the life span. *Addictive Diseases*, 1978, *3*, 449–456.

Bailey, M.B.; Haberman, P.W.; and Alksne, H. The epidemiology of alcoholism in an urban residential area. *Quarterly Journal of Studies on Alcohol*, 1965, *26*, 19–40.

Ball, J.C., and Chambers, C.D. (Eds.). *Epidemiology of opiate addiction in the United States*. Charles C Thomas, Springfield, Ill., 1970.

Barnes, G.M. Alcohol use among older persons: Findings from a western New York State general population survey. *Journal of the American Geriatrics Society*, 1979, *27*, 244–250.

Barnes, G.M.; Abel, E.L.; and Ernst, C.A. *Alcohol and the elderly: A comprehensive bibliography*. Greenwood Press, Westport, Conn., 1980.

Bateman, N.I., and Petersen, D.M. Variables related to outcome of treatment for hospitalized alcoholics. *International Journal of the Addictions*, 1971, *6*, 215–224.

———. Factors related to outcome of treatment for hospitalized white male and female alcoholics. *Journal of Drug Issues*, 1972, *2*, 66–74.

Borgatta, E.F.; Montgomery, R.J.Y.; and Borgatta, M.L. Alcohol use and abuse, life crisis events and the elderly. *Research on Aging*, 1982, *4*, 378–408.

Cahalan, D.; Cisin, I.H.; and Crossley, H.M. *American drinking practices*. Rutgers Center of Alcohol Studies, New Brunswick, N.J., 1969.

Capel, W.C.; Goldsmith, B.M.; Waddell, K.J.; and Stewart, G.T. The aging narcotic addict: An increasing problem for the next decades. *Journal of Gerontology*, 1972, *27*, 102–106.

Capel, W.C., and Peppers, L.G. The aging addict: A longitudinal study of known abusers. *Addictive Diseases*, 1978, *3*, 389–404.

Capel, W.C., and Stewart, G.T. The management of drug abuse in aging populations: New Orleans findings. *Journal of Drug Issues*, 1971, *1*, 114–121.

Carruth, B.; Williams, E.P.; Mysak, P.; and Boudreaux, L. *Alcoholism and problem drinking among older persons: Community care providers and the older problem drinker*. Rutgers Center for Alcohol Studies, New Brunswick, N.J., 1973.

Chambers, C.D. *An assessment of drug use in the general population*. New York State Narcotic Addiction Control Commission, New York, 1971.

Cohen, S. Drug abuse in the aging patient. *Journal of Studies on Alcohol*, 1975, *37*, 1455–1460.

Daniel, R.A. A five year study of 693 psychogeriatric admissions in Queensland. *Geriatrics*, 1972, *27*, 132–155.

Drew, L.R.H. Alcoholism as a self-limiting disease. *Quarterly Journal of Studies on Alcohol*, 1968, *29*, 956–967.

Droller, H. Some aspects of alcoholism in the elderly. *Lancet*, 1964, *2*, 137–139.

Dunham, R. Aging and changing patterns of alcohol abuse. In D.M. Petersen and F.J. Whittington (Eds.), *Drugs, alcohol and aging*. Kendall/Hunt, Dubuque, Iowa, 1982.

Dupont, R. Testimony before the Subcommittee on Aging and Subcommittee on Alcoholism and Narcotics of the United States Senate Committee on Labor and Public Welfare. Washington, D.C., June 1976.

Epstein, L.J.; Mills, C.; and Simon, A. Antisocial behavior of the elderly. *Comprehensive Psychiatry*, 1970, *11*, 36–42.

Gaitz, C.M., and Baer, P.E. Characteristics of elderly patients with alcoholism. *Archives of General Psychiatry*, 1971, *24*, 372–378.

Glantz, M.; Petersen, D.M.; and Whittington, F.J. (Eds.). *Drugs and the elderly adult*. National Institute on Drug Abuse, Washington, D.C., 1983.

Glenn, N.D. Age, birth cohorts, and drinking: An illustration of the hazards of inferring effects from cohort data. *Journal of Gerontology*, 1981, *36*, 362–369.

Goldstein, S., and Grant, A. The psychogeriatric patient in the hospital. *Canadian Medical Journal*, 1974, *111*, 329–332.

Gomberg, E.L. *Drinking and problem drinking among the elderly*. Institute of Gerontology, University of Michigan, Ann Arbor, 1980.

James, M. *Substance abuse among Michigan's senior citizens: Patterns of use and provider perspectives*. Michigan Office of Services to the Aging and Michigan Office of Substance Abuse Services, Lansing, 1979.

Johnson, L.A., and Goodrich, C.H. Use of alcohol by persons 65 years and over, Upper East Side of Manhattan. In National Institute of Alcohol Abuse and Alcoholism, *Alcohol and health*. USGPO, Washington, D.C., 1974.

Judge, T.G., and Caird, F.I. *Drug treatment of the elderly patient*. Pitman Medical, Kent, England, 1978.

Kayne, R.C. (Ed.). *Drugs and the elderly*, 2nd ed. University of Southern California Press, Los Angeles, 1978.

Knupfer, G., and Room, R. Age, sex, and social class as factors in amount of drinking in a metropolitan community. *Social Problems*, 1964, *12*, 224–240.

Kola, L.; Kosberg, J.; and Wegner-Burch, K. Perceptions of treatment responsibilities for the elderly alcoholic client. *Social Work in Health Care*, 1980, *6*, 69–77.

Levenson, A.J. (Ed.). *Neuropsychiatric side effects of drugs in the elderly*. Raven Press, New York, 1979.

Linn, M.W. Attrition of older alcoholics from treatment. *Addictive Diseases*, 1978, *3*, 437–447.

McCusker, J.; Cherubin, C.E.; and Zimberg, S. Prevalence of alcoholism in general municipal hospital population. *New York State Journal of Medicine*, 1971, *71*, 751–754.

Manheimer, D.I., and Mellinger, G.D. Marijuana use among urban adults. *Science*, 1969, *166*, 1544–1545.

Mayfield, D.G. Alcohol problems in the aging patient. In W.E. Fann and G.L. Maddox (Eds.), *Drug issues in geropsychiatry*. Williams and Wilkins, Baltimore, 1974.

Mishara, B.L., and Kastenbaum, R. *Alcohol and old age*. Grune and Stratton, New York, 1980.

Monk, A.; Cryns, A.; and Cabral, R. Alcohol consumption and alcoholism as a function of age. Paper presented at the Annual Meeting of the Gerontological Society, San Francisco, November 1977.

O'Donnell, J.A. *Narcotic addicts in Kentucky*. U.S. Public Health Service, Washington, D.C., 1969.

Pascarelli, E.F. Drug dependence: An age-old problem compounded by old age. *Geriatrics*, 1974, *29*, 109–115.

Pascarelli, E.F., and Fischer, W. Drug dependence in the elderly. *International Journal of Aging and Human Development*, 1974, *5*, 347–356.

Peck, D.G. Alcohol abuse and the elderly: Social control and conformity. *Journal of Drug Issues*, 1979, *9*, 63–72.

Peppers, L.G., and Stover, R.G. The elderly abuser: A challenge for the future. *Journal of Drug Issues*, 1979, *9*, 73–84.

Petersen, D.M., and Whittington, F.J. *Drugs, alcohol and aging*. Kendall/Hunt, Dubuque, Iowa, 1982.

Petersen, D.M.; Whittington, F.J.; and Beer, E.T. Drug use and misuse among the elderly. *Journal of Drug Issues*, 1979, *9*, 5–26.

Petersen, D.M.; Whittington, F.J.; and Payne, B.P. (Eds.). *Drugs and the elderly: Social and pharmacological issues*. Charles C Thomas, Springfield, Ill. 1979.

Poe, W.D., and Holloway, D.A. *Drugs and the aged*. McGraw Hill, New York, 1980.

Pottieger, A.E., and Inciardi, J.A. Aging on the street: Drug use and crime among older men. In D.M. Petersen and F.J. Whittington (Eds.), *Drugs, alcohol and aging*. Kendall/Hunt, Dubuque, Iowa, 1982.

Rathbone-McCuan, E.; Lohn, H.; Levensen, J.; and Hsu, J. *Community survey of aged alcoholics and problem drinkers*. National Institute on Alcohol Abuse and Alcoholism, Washington, D.C., 1976.

Rathbone-McCuan, E., and Triegaardt, J. The older alcoholic and the family. Paper presented at the National Alcoholism Forum, National Council on Alcoholism, St. Louis, 1978.

Rosin, A.J., and Glatt, M.M. Alcohol excess in the elderly. *Quarterly Journal of Studies on Alcohol*, 1971, *32*, 53–59.

Schmidt, W., and deLint, J. Causes of death of alcoholics. *Quarterly Journal of Studies on Alcohol*, 1972, *33*, 171–185.

Schuckit, M.A. Geriatric alcoholism and drug abuse. *Gerontologist*, 1977, *17*, 168–174.

Schuckit, M.A., and Miller, P.L. Alcoholism in elderly men. In F.A. Seixas and S.

Eggleston (Eds.), *Work in progress on alcoholism*. New York Academy of Sciences, New York, 1976.

Schuckit, M.A.; Morrissey, E.R.; and O'Leary, M.R. Alcohol problems in elderly men and women. *Addictive Diseases*, 1978, *3*, 405–416.

Schuckit, M.A., and Pastor, P.A. The elderly as a unique population: Alcoholism. *Alcoholism: Clinical and Experimental Research*, 1978, *2*, 31–38.

Selzer, M.D., and Holloway, W.H. A follow-up of alcoholics committed to a state hospital. *Quarterly Journal of Studies on Alcohol*, 1957, *18*, 98–120.

Shichor, D., and Kobrin, S. Note: Criminal behavior among the elderly. *Gerontologist*, 1978, *18*, 213–218.

Simon, A.; Epstein, L.J.; and Reynolds, L. Alcoholism in the geriatric mentally ill. *Geriatrics*, 1968, *23*, 125–131.

Smart, R.G., and Liban, C.B. Predictors of problem drinking among elderly, middle-aged and youthful drinkers. In D.M. Petersen and F.J. Whittington (Eds.), *Drugs, alcohol and aging*. Kendall/Hunt, Dubuque, Iowa, 1982.

Whittier, J.R., and Korenyi, C. Selected characteristics of aged patients: A study of mental hospital admissions. *Comprehensive Psychiatry*, 1961, *2*, 113–120.

Wilkinson, P. Alcoholism in the aged. *Journal of Geriatrics*, 1971, *34*, 59–64.

Winick, C. Maturing out of narcotic addiction. *Bulletin on Narcotics*, 1962, *14*, 1–7.

Wolff, S., and Holland, L. A questionnaire follow-up of alcoholic patients. *Quarterly Journal of Studies on Alcohol*, 1964, *25*, 108–118.

Zax, M.; Gardner, E.A.; and Hart, W.T. Public intoxication in Rochester: A survey of individuals charged during 1961. *Quarterly Journal of Studies on Alcohol*, 1964, *25*, 669–678.

Zimberg, S. The elderly alcoholic. *Gerontologist*, 1974, *14*, 221–224.

———. Treatment of the elderly alcoholic in the community and in an institutional setting. *Addictive Diseases*, 1978, *3*, 417–427.

———. Alcohol and the elderly. In D.M. Petersen, F.J. Whittington, and B.P. Payne (Eds.), *Drugs and the elderly: Social and pharmacological issues*. Charles C Thomas, Springfield, Ill., 1979.

18

CRIMINALS

RONALD H. ADAY

It has been suggested that the older prisoner comprises a unique category possessing special criminal and personal characteristics (Aday, 1976; Baier, 1961; Ham, 1976; Shichor and Kobrin, 1978). Some committed as adults for long terms have simply grown old in prison. Others have long histories of crime and a sequential career of institutional commitment. Yet others committed offenses relatively late in life and were sentenced to correctional institutions as older persons. In all instances, the aging offender often represents a special population in terms of criminal patterns and problems of individual adjustment to institutional life, posing special difficulties for the institution in regard to custody, medical care, rehabilitation, and eventual community reintegration.

In spite of his unique characteristics, problems, and status, the aging offender has been largely neglected by researchers. This situation may be attributed to several factors. Pollak (1941) mentioned that old criminals offer an ugly, sad picture resulting in less scientific appeal for researchers. It has also been suggested that most researchers and policymakers deem the crimes of youthful offenders as more serious and dangerous for the fabric of society than the crimes committed by old persons (Carlie, 1970). These past attitudes are rapidly shifting, however, as our elderly population grows in significance and as the criminal justice system encounters an increasingly higher proportion of arrests involving senior citizens. A greater interest is becoming evident as the media and those in policymaking positions are focusing more specifically on the elderly offender.

In response to this recent interest, this chapter will provide an identification of the types of crime that are generally associated with advancing age. Discussion will then focus on an analysis of the career crime patterns of the older offender. It is hoped that this overview will provide a greater understanding of the causality of crime during the latter stages of the life cycle. Finally, selected topics and problems associated with the institutional adjustment of the aging offender will be addressed.

Table 18.1

Percentage Distribution of Arrests for Violent Offenses among the 55 and Over Age Group, 1971, 1976, and 1981

	1971	1976	1981	% Increase
Murder	11.3	8.9	8.4	20
Forcible rape	2.3	3.2	4.6	71
Robbery	5.6	4.4	6.3	50
Aggravated assault	80.8	83.5	80.7	42
N	6,686	9,006	11,597	

Source: Federal Bureau of Investigation, Uniform Crime Reports, 1971, 1976, 1981.

THE INCIDENCE OF CRIME IN OLD AGE

The arrest statistics of the Uniform Crime Reports are often utilized as an important measure of criminal activity among the elderly (Barrett, 1972; Keller and Vedder, 1968; Shichor and Kobrin, 1978). Beginning in 1964 the Uniform Crime Reports presented age breakdowns at the upper age limits, thus permitting a more refined collection of arrest data by age (i.e., 50–54, 55–59, 60–64, and 65 and above). Shichor and Kobrin (1978) in their analysis of Uniform Crime Report statistics suggest that the designation of "elderly status" may be appropriately applied to the 55 and over age group. Previous studies indicate that the arrest data consistently indicate a sharp drop in the proportion of arrest in the 55–59 age category, with a leveling off of crime for those offenders over the age of 60 (Moberg, 1953; Pollak, 1941). It was concluded that this age group comprises a relatively homogeneous one with respect to the proportion of all arrests.

In all societies chronological age is considered to be important because it provides certain clues to the current phase of the individual's life cycle and, in turn, projects certain behavior expectations. It has been suggested that criminality is conditioned by age, with youth and young adulthood being the periods when criminality reaches its peak. As biological maturity is achieved, there is a pronounced decline, and with old age criminality virtually disappears for most offenses.

More specifically, in 1981, the Uniform Crime Reports indicated that only 4 percent of arrests made in the United States were of persons 55 years of age and older. Although there is an obvious decline in deviant behavior as persons grow older, a comparative analysis of Uniform Crime Reports based on five-year intervals from 1971 to 1981 reveals substantial percentage increases in criminal activity among those in the 55 and over category. During the eleven-year period, violent crimes increased as a whole approximately 42 percent. As table 18.1 indicates, the single most frequent arrest is that of aggravated assault. These

Table 18.2
Percentage Distribution of Arrests for Index Offenses against Property among the 55 and Over Age Group, 1971, 1976, and 1981

	1971	1976	1981	% Increase
Burglary	7.7	3.5	1.5	44
Larceny-Theft	89.0	95.0	92.0	61
Auto theft	3.3	1.5	5.5	30
N	18,318	38,758	45,861	

Source: Federal Bureau of Investigation, Uniform Crime Reports, 1971, 1976, 1981.

arrests constituted about 80 percent of the total arrests for crimes of violence among the 55 and over age group.

In crimes against property, arrests of the older offender have occurred most frequently in the general category of larceny-theft. As reported in table 18.2, this particular offense accounts for essentially all property offense arrests in this age group. Of note is the fact that while there is a slight decline in the proportion of arrests for burglary, total arrests increased 44 percent during the eleven-year period.

Other offenses generally classified as misdemeanors have proved important in establishing a profile of the elderly offender. Those reported here include sex offenses, drug abuse violations, gambling, drunkenness, driving under the influence, and disorderly conduct. While the highest proportion of arrests was made for drunkenness, table 18.3 shows a substantial decline (55 percent) over the eleven-year period. On the other hand, there is a significant increase in the proportion of arrests for driving under the influence. Perhaps these statistics indicate the shift toward more lenient police response to the alcoholism problem while enforcing more strictly the offense of drunken driving.

Table 18.3
Percentage Distribution of Arrests for Misdemeanor Offenses among the 55 and Over Age Group, 1971, 1976, and 1981

	1971	1976	1981	% Increase
Sex offenses	.8	1.4	1.6	33
Drug abuse violations	.4	.6	1.9	67
Gambling	4.2	3.5	2.5	−33
Drunkenness	71.1	57.8	43.3	−55
Driving under influence	15.0	29.5	39.0	41
Disorderly conduct	8.5	7.2	11.7	−1
N	341,001	255,916	246,190	

Source: Federal Bureau of Investigation, Uniform Crime Reports, 1971, 1976, 1981.

Due to the enormous problems of aging in a complex society, delinquency in the elderly population is difficult to determine and even more difficult to evaluate. While rates and crime vary with age, older offender characteristics and criminal motivation may also vary with specific populations, environmental conditions, and social policy. For example, Barrett (1972) has suggested that arresting officers have established more lenient policies with regard to the aging population, especially for offenses where the safety and rights of others are not involved. Only in areas of "hard crime," such as aggravated assault, homicide, burglary, narcotics law violation, and similar types of offenses, will the elderly as a rule be treated in the same way as younger persons. While arrest statistics are not precise and do not take into account data about conviction, they do provide a useful point of departure for establishing an overall profile of the elderly offender.

DEMOGRAPHIC CHARACTERISTICS

The verification of an accurate profile of the elderly inmate is a difficult task. Few systematic studies have provided the necessary comprehensive information for this segment of the prison population. While separate studies exist for several states, representative data on a national level have not yet been fully analyzed. Also contributing to the difficulty of determining a fair description of the elderly prisoner is the lack of a general consensus on what constitutes an "older or elderly" prisoner. Some studies report findings based on inmates 55 years of age and older, while other studies include only those elderly offenders beyond 60 or 65 years of age, respectively. Despite these limitations, crude generalizations can be drawn from previous studies in establishing an appropriate description of the elderly inmate.

As a whole, elderly inmates make up a small proportion of every prison system. Krajick (1979) reports that two separate prison surveys covering a total of thirty-six states show that about 1 percent of the prison population is 60 years of age or older. Goetting (1982) calculated from existing data that at the end of 1981 as many as 8,853 persons age 55 and older were imprisoned in state and federal prisons in the United States. This sum comprises approximately 2.3 percent of the total prison population.

In a recent comprehensive review of the literature from selected state data sources as well as several individual prison surveys, Goetting (1982) constructed what she termed an "ideal type" elderly inmate. Goetting was able to conclude that the typical elderly prisoner would more than likely be male, white, currently unmarried, and lacking a high school education. In addition, Panton (1976–1977) reported that the aged inmate functions at a lower level of intelligence than the non-aged inmate.

Aday (1979) also found that elderly prisoners were highly homogeneous concerning variables such as social class and occupation. Findings from a sample representing two state prisons, Arkansas and Oklahoma, demonstrated that, for the most part, elderly prisoners were unskilled laborers. Over 50 percent of the ninety-four male respondents sampled received no monthly income. For those claiming a monthly pension, $134 dollars was the reported median.

Understanding the health status of the elderly prisoner is a more perplexing endeavor. Special barriers contributing to this dilemma appear to be associated with the vast differences in prison populations and the divergent prison settings within which they reside. For example, Ham's (1980) study of aged and infirm male prison inmates focused on those inmates assigned to a "geriatric unit" due to a multitude of physical and mental disorders. Thus, such a specialized sample would not be representative of older inmates found in other more general prison environments.

In contrast to Ham's findings, Aday (1976) found that 25 percent of the elderly prisoners over the age of 55 reported no major health problems. Moreover, when asked to compare their health with the health of other aged inmates, responses were rather evenly distributed in the very good or average categories. Interestingly, only 9 percent of the elderly inmates housed in an integrated facility perceived themselves to be in poor health, compared to 16 percent of the sample taken from the "geriatric unit" who felt their health to be in a poor status. Wiltz (1973), in a general prison population, also found that the majority (66 percent) of his sample described their health as good or average. Thus, while these studies often mention the presence of ailments such as arthritis, respiratory diseases, heart disease, and diabetes, overall most elderly prisoners appear to be in fairly good health. This seems particularly true when the population being accessed is 55 years of age and over.

In summary, as Adams (1961) has stated, "health is a kind of variable upon which everything else depends." For the older prisoner, health may be a determining factor in his ability to maintain a normal work role as well as influencing participation in other social activities. In extreme cases, poor health may result in the older prisoner becoming more dependent on his immediate social environment.

CRIMINAL CHARACTERISTICS

The correctional history of the aged prisoner is a viable topic of analysis when developing an overall descriptive profile of this unique population. Numerous studies have delineated two distinctive types of elderly offenders. For example, in a pioneer paper on the older offender, Schroeder (1936) discovered that one group of elderly committed violent crimes such as murder and sex offenses. The offenders convicted of these crimes tended to be relatively free from early records of crime, and only 20 percent had been in prison before. In the second group, the criminal behavior tended to be a continuation of a pattern established at an earlier age. Of this group of older men convicted of the crimes of robbery, larceny, and burglary, 50 percent reported having had previous prison records.

Cromier and associates (1971) also reported significant differences between offenders who have no previous criminal record and those of the same age with a sometimes lengthy history of criminality. These differences were particularly evident in the types of criminal offenses committed and in the offenders' social values and personality. Cromier found that those individuals who started criminal activities early (ages 20 to 24) usually remained in the low socioeconomic stratum. While older first offenders were likely to be married, Cromier indicated that those in this subgroup were more likely to have committed homicide in a specific relationship (such as marriage) and to have committed sexual offenses during the libidinal crisis of middle age or later. Offenses against property proved to be the outstanding crime for those who started criminal activities before 25 years of age.

In a sample of ninety-four elderly prisoners over the age of 55, Aday (1976) found that 13 percent of the respondents reported having been arrested as juveniles. In addition, 58 percent of the older offenders were termed chronic or multi-offenders, illustrating an extended career of crime. However, one-half of the older inmates in this study were incarcerated for the first time after the age of 50. Of the crimes committed for the current period of incarceration, 67 percent were crimes of violence against another individual. A breakdown of crime distribution between those classified as chronic and first offenders revealed that murder and sex offenses were the most common for both groups. However, 80 percent of the first offenders were convicted of crimes of violence compared to 58 percent of those classified as multi-offenders.

Teller and Howell (1981) also dichotomize their sample of older prisoners into the first incarcerated and multi-recidivist. While the most frequent criminal activity among the two subgroups involved property crimes, first offenders were more likely to be sentenced for crimes against persons. In addition, first offenders reported that they committed their crimes in a spontaneous fashion and did not consider themselves as criminal. On the other hand, the multi-recidivists reported that they generally planned out their crimes and viewed themselves as criminals.

EXPLAINING CRIME IN OLD AGE

Numerous explanations exist as to why some elderly may continue careers of crime and why others commit their first offenses late in life. Shichor and Kobrin (1978) suggest that as the range of social interaction shrinks with advancing age interpersonal primary relationships become intense, with a resulting increase in opportunities for conflict. Similarly, Carlie (1970) stressed the older offender's mobility as being significant to the type of criminality in which he might engage. For example, persons committing crimes against property exhibited highest mobility, while those with the least degree of mobility committed crimes against persons.

Other precipitating factors have been associated with the biological changes due to aging. Rodstein (1975) contends that chronic brain syndrome may be associated with a loss of inhibitions, resulting in illegal sexual behavior such as exhibitionism, and in rigidity, suspiciousness, and quarrelsomeness, with consequent aggressiveness. Moreover, feelings of despair and undue dependence on family and social agencies may lead to violent aggressive acts against family members or close friends.

The presence of alcohol appears to be a contributing factor to the high incidence of violent crimes. Previous studies indicate that elderly inmates were likely to have been intoxicated at the time of their arrest (Aday, 1976; Krajick, 1979). Finally, Ham's (1976) investigation of aged male convicts in a Michigan prison discovered that all crimes of murder were committed by those involved in heavy drinking.

Those who had previously maintained a higher economic status may commit such crimes as fraud, forgery, tax evasion, and other white-collar offenses without perceiving them as immoral activities. In addition, economic insecurities—such as a loss of status as a bread-winner—resulting in acts of revenge against the business community before retirement may explain, in part, crimes committed in these white-collar categories (Rodstein, 1975).

In summary, Bergman and Amir (1973) stress that—as is true of criminality in youth—physical, personal, and environmental factors can explain the criminality of that minority of elderly who continue or become involved in deviant behavior late in life. Therefore, the general frustration of old age—poverty, alcohol abuse, loss of job and status, the boredom of retirement—sometimes coupled with long-time animosities, operate as determinants of criminal involvements of the elderly.

ADJUSTMENT TO PRISON LIFE

In recent years there has been an increasing interest in the general literature relating to the global effects of institutions. In general, the evidence accumulated over the past thirty years leaves little doubt that institutionalized populations exhibit differences from non-institutionalized populations. For example, in institutions people live communally, with a minimum of privacy, yet their relationships are extremely fragile. Many inmates subsist in a kind of defensive shell of isolation. Their mobility is restricted, and they have little access to a general society.

According to Lieberman (1968:343), "No matter what the particular characteristics of the population or the unique qualities of the total institution, the general thrust of empirical evidence emerging from many studies [suggests] that living in an institutional environment [has] noxious physical and psychological effects upon the individual whether young or old." Bergman and Amir (1973) support this notion when they describe aging prisoners as being frightened, ridiculed, depressed, anxious, and consequently dependent on the prison staff for protection. Similarly, Gillespie and Galliher (1972) describe their sample of older inmates in terms of bitterness and resentment: deprived of any future hope, they feel the full impact of the negative aspects of prison life. Likewise, Krajick

(1979) portrays elderly inmates as pathetic, and says that any reasonable person would have definite sympathy for the plight of old people in prison.

Conversely, other studies view prison as a possible refuge for the elderly inmate from the harsh elements of life on the outside. Reed and Glamser (1979) found prison life to be a positive experience as fifteen of nineteen subjects reported that they felt younger in prison. They conclude that older prisoners are not exposed to heavy labor or heavy drinking. They eat well, rest often, and have easy access to medical care.

In a similar fashion, Aday and Webster (1979) observe the prison setting as a sheltered environment conducive to institutional dependency for elderly inmates. The authors hypothesize that several variables may contribute significantly to the notion of the unique elderly prisoner becoming more dependency-prone due to the major events surrounding old age. For example, it was concluded that the length of incarceration will usually have a greater impact on role loss and interaction with those in the free community. If the social attachments outside prison decrease, this broken relationship may serve to make older prisoners more dependent on the institution, especially if they have no immediate family or friends on the outside to whom they can turn. High degrees of dependency were found among the unmarried, those first incarcerated at an early age, and those classified as multi-recidivist. Elderly prisoners with poor health, lack of family support, little or no income, and few employable skills may find prison to be a home away from home.

Likewise, Adams and Vedder (1961:179) addressed certain implications of institutional dependency regarding the final stages of imprisonment encountered by many older prisoners. In their words, "A long sentence may persist despite good prison conduct and parole may be denied reasonably because the prisoner has no family to whom he could go. Long confinement results in physical, intellectual, and emotional deterioration. . . . If society has little place for the older man in general, it has even less place for the elderly prisoner or exconvict."

Thus, prison life for the elderly prisoner can be viewed as a "seduction" process. The barrier to social interaction with society at large can be overpowering. For instance, Gaddis (1972), in "Home At Last: The Prison Habit," concluded that some process other than overt crime and punishment draws the criminal back behind bars. In a similar discussion, Jackson (1966) suggested that chronic convicts whose criminal and non-criminal careers outside of prison are marked by persistent failure often find prison to be the only place they can retire in some comfort.

In this regard, the inmate social system has principally viewed prisoner roles as alternative patterns of adjustment to a variety of deprivations imposed by total institutions. Therefore, for the older prisoner, imprisonment is a type of forced social disengagement from his customary social milieu. In this light, institutionalization can be perceived as a positive process as "prisonization" gives the older prisoner a new subculture, role, identity, and social group—which are vital for social and psychological well-being.

For example, Wiltz (1973) contrasts the social status of the non-institution-alized and the incarcerated elderly, attributing the exteme divergence in prestige to their different social environments. In non-institutionalized settings the elderly are rendered less valuable because the consequences of aging devalue them economically and socially. Their knowledge, skills, and ideas have become obsolete in a rapidly changing technological society. Conversely, the elderly prisoner does not experience the same sudden change in social status. In fact, in addition to maintaining a viable work role in the prison setting, many elderly receive a monthly pension, which places them at an economic advantage com-pared to other younger inmates (Goetting, 1982). Moreover, Wiltz (1973) further describes the inmate status hierarchy as one based partially on seniority, with the "lifers" being responsible for initiating norms and providing important lead-ership roles.

PARTICIPATION IN PRISON ACTIVITIES

Regardless of whether prison life will be perceived as a positive or negative experience, the elderly prisoner must, in some sense, structure time. Previous research indicates that activity in general, and interpersonal activity in particular, seem to be important for predicting an individual's sense of well-being in later years (Lemon et al., 1972). In brief, the activity model of aging maintains that substitutes are necessary to fill certain voids (i.e., work, friends, loved ones). Implicit here is the proposition that old age brings with it a decreasing number of roles for the older prisoner which may lead to a reorientation of attitudes and behavior to meet the requirements of the new situation.

Activities engaged in are usually determined by the older prisoner's physical and mental health as well as by the nature of the prison environment (i.e., minimum vs. maximum security, segregated vs. integrated), and opportunities available or utilized. For example, while educational programs are generally available in most prison settings, they typically are not conducive to participation by elderly inmates (Goetting, 1982). Although prison officials may discourage the elderly inmate from participating in formal education and vocational training programs, for the most part, older prisoners are uninterested in prison education (Bintz, 1974).

While some researchers find the imprisoned elderly joining organizations and taking an interest in politics (Reed and Glamser, 1979), others have found that higher age led to generally lower activity levels with few expectations (Jenson, 1977). Krajick (1979) further notes that "the older inmates are not as easy to motivate as the younger inmates. They need a lot of coaxing to get them involved. It would be good for them if we could do that, shake them out of their bore-dom. . . . There isn't much we have here that's of interest to them."

Social participation was also examined by Gillespie and Galliher (1972) with a special emphasis on the concept of anomie. The tests of participation in leisure time activities, association with other inmates, and the extent of boredom found

Table 18.4
Percentages Participating in Activities in Two Prison Environments

Activity	Geriatric Unit	Integrated Setting
Working	37	100
Watching TV	67	65
Religious activities	5	17
Checkers or dominoes	45	11
Gardening	2	—
Walking	17	7
Visiting friends and relatives	42	11
Fishing	10	—
Making jewelry	5	2
Craftwork or woodworking	12	11
Visiting other inmates	32	11
Visiting groups in community	22	—
Writing	5	7
Movies	—	5
Reading	45	37
Other activities	5	4

Note: Respondents were asked to select as many as five activities; therefore, the percentages far exceed 100 percent.

that inmates who have aged faster have fewer leisure time activities and fewer contacts, and see time pass less quickly.

Aday (1976) more thoroughly investigated the type and frequency of activities normally engaged in by older prisoners. Respondents were asked to "name the five most frequent things you do during the course of an ordinary week." Findings presented in table 18.4 indicate important differences between levels of activities found in a segregated, minimum security setting when compared to those in a segregated, maximum security prison. The findings do illustrate the fact that, when health permits, the older prisoner is typically involved in some type of work detail. Older prisoners at the maximum security prison were all able to work in some capacity. When health does not permit, however, other activities, when available, become more frequently engaged in; this appears to be the case for those housed in the segregated geriatric unit with a therapeutic focus.

SPECIAL PROGRAMS

While there has been a general increase in criminal activity among the elderly population, the fact remains that the elderly prisoner represents a very small proportion of the total prison population. The result is that the elderly criminal has consistently been relegated to a low-priority status within the prison environment as a whole. It is within this framework that the elderly inmate has been referred to as the "forgotten minority" (Krajick, 1979).

There has emerged in recent years, however, an awareness that special programs should be implemented to meet the needs of aged prisoners (Krajick, 1979; Wiegand and Burger, 1979–1980). In this sense, "special programs" usually constitute the distinctive treatment of the elderly prisoner housed in an age-segregated environment. Previous research supports the notion that participation in a specific group increases self-respect and increases capability to resume community life. Such age segregation provides the older prisoner with optimal opportunity for forming peer networks, while at the same time reducing vulnerability to violence.

Despite these arguments, Goetting (1983) noted in a national survey that forty-seven states and the federal prison system reported no formal special consideration for this category of prisoner. In these systems, the elderly, along with other inmates, are given housing and work assignments compatible with health and agility. In this regard, the elderly who are designated as infirm are granted special treatment. Goetting also reported that in some states (including Alabama, California, Georgia, Idaho, Michigan, Missouri, North Carolina, South Carolina, and Virginia) these facilities for the elderly infirm are referred to as special "geriatric" units. However, these units are merely medical or light-duty units which house infirm inmates, and the elderly are not selected out for special consideration.

According to Goetting (1983), only three states (Virginia, West Virginia, and Texas) reported the operation of special policies, programs, or facilities designed primarily to accommodate aged prisoners through standards based on chronological age or health status. For example, qualification for being admitted to West Virginia's fifty-bed open dormitory required a man to be at least 50 years of age, ambulatory, and mentally capable of independent living. It was reported that forty inmates reside at what has been termed the "Old Man's Colony." This number represents 71 percent of the total prison population age 50 and above.

Similarly, for Texas, the major determinant for special inmate treatment is health classification. Each inmate is assigned a medical classification (1–5) upon entry into the correctional system. All inmates 60 years of age and older are positioned in Medical Class 4 unless their health is critical enough for Class 5 placement. Inmates placed in these two medical classes are housed in separate facilities; they are restricted from field work and limited to light-duty jobs.

Likewise, Virginia reported a program designed for all inmates age 55 and older who were medically classified to exclude them from heavy work. In addition, Virginia operates the Aged Offender Program, which sanctions regularly scheduled monitored meetings focusing on specific concerns of the incarcerated elderly. This program normally accommodates sixty-two men over 50 years of age, representing approximately 13 percent of the total Virginia inmate population in that age category (Goetting, 1983).

In addition, Krajick (1979) provides comprehensive information on Project 60, a statewide private organization in Pennsylvania supplying services exclusively to elderly offenders. Project 60 was initiated to provide counseling and other services to approximately eighty-five inmates over the age of 60 in eight separate institutions. Moreover, Project 60 also reported working with an additional seventy inmates who were placed on parole. This program provides support services to aid the elderly prisoner in the initial parole process and, ultimately, in successful reentry into the community.

Conclusions drawn from the information provided here reflect the fact that few prison systems recognize the elderly prisoner in terms of chronological age and/or health status. However, the needs of the elderly in terms of health care, life cycle roles, friendships, and security remain, regardless of their immediate environment. In particular, many of the aged in our society are frustrated socially, economically, and psychologically and find difficulty in coping with changes over which they have no control. Thus, it has been suggested that due to the progressive deterioration and change of the bodily functions and sensory processes, older inmates need to be served by staff members who are familiar with the various components (physical, social, and psychological) of the aging process (Goetting, 1983). Whether the elderly offender's needs can be met more comprehensively in special facilities is a question which will need special attention as the elderly prison population increases over time.

RESEARCH ISSUES

Although the literature indicates that the older prisoner has unique characteristics and problems, there is a scarcity of research dealing with the general impact of imprisonment on the older prisoner. Of the few studies currently available on the subject, a number have significant methodological and theoretical limitations. The most frequent problem exhibited by previous research concerns sampling techniques. In addition to a lack of randomness, several important studies are based on extremely small samples, making it impossible to draw general conclusions from them.

Another shortcoming of studies of the older prisoner is that most are descriptive in nature and lack a basic theoretical orientation. In particular, few studies distinguish between the first offender and the multi-recidivist and the impact their crime careers have on adjustment to prison life. This appears to be an area worthy of attention, especially for those responsible for implementing programs designed to combat recidivism or related probation problems.

Due to the inherent problems presented by extreme differences in data sources and prison environments, a national survey of a random sample of inmates would remove some of the major research gaps that currently exist. A comprehensive profile would provide valuable information about the personal background and criminal history of the elderly inmate. In particular, comprehensive data would provide the opportunity for additional comparisons with non-prisoners as well as with prisoners from different age categories.

Moreover, due to the complexities of growing old in prison, there appears to be a need for further explorations focusing on single dimensions of crime causality and prison adjustment. For example, what are the differences in the types of crimes and the nature of punishment for crime between the aged and younger individuals? To what degree does the life history of the young criminal advancing into old age impact on the career of crime? How do we accurately explain the etiology of crime appearing for the first time late in life? What are the effects of social class, family relations, social frustrations, and cultural background on the nature of crime committed by the aged? Answers to these questions, among others, would serve to reduce the current gaps in knowledge concerning the elderly offender.

Finally, research appropriateness and the impact such research has on social policy is an important area of concern. The question of special policies, programs, and facilities for elderly inmates poses a true dilemma, and deserves recognition both among those interested in the well-being of the elderly and among those interested in prison policy. Despite the increasing accommodations being made for at least some elderly prisoners, they are still, for the most part, "forgotten people." For example, as the proportion of the elderly in the general population has increased, so has research into the problems of the aged and programs geared toward the elderly. However, research and programs targeted for the elderly criminal have not kept pace with this movement. With the continued increase in criminal activity among the elderly population as a whole, learning more about the determinants of crime in old age, and about institutional adjustment, recidivism, and parole, seems important.

The field of gerontology can contribute significantly to this endeavor. Professionals in the field can provide a greater awareness and understanding of the problems associated with the overall process of aging. For only through the context of a heightened understanding of aging in general can the problems of criminality, prison adjustment, and community reentry of the aged be fully addressed.

REFERENCES

Adams, M.E., and Vedder, C. Age and crime: Medical and sociological characteristics of prisoners over 50. *Journal of Geriatrics*, 1961, *16*, 177–180.

Aday, R.H. Institutional dependency: A theory of aging in prison. Ph.D. diss., Oklahoma State University, 1976.

———. Toward the development of a therapeutic program for older prisoners. *Offender Rehabilitation*, 1977, *4*, 343–348.

Aday, R.H., and Webster, E. Aging in prison: The development of a preliminary model. *Offender Rehabilitation*, 1979, *3*, 271–282.

Baier, G.F. The aged inmate. *American Journal of Corrections*, 1961, *21*, 4–16.

Barrett, J.H. Aging and delinquency. In *Gerontological psychology*. Charles C Thomas, Springfield, Ill., 1972.

Bergman, S., and Amir, M. Crime and delinquency among the aged in Israel. *Geriatrics*, 1973, *28*, 149–157.

Bintz, M.T. Recreation for the older population in correctional institutions. *Therapeutic Recreation Journal*, 1974 *8*, 88.

Carlie, M.K. The older arrestee: Crime in the later years of life. Ph.D. diss., Washington University, St. Louis, 1970.

Cromier, B.M., et al. Behavior and aging: Offenders aged 40 and over. *Laval Medical*, 1971, *42*, 15–21.

Federal Bureau of Investigation. Uniform crime reports. USGPO, Washington, D.C., 1971, 1976, 1981.

Gaddis, T.E. Home at last: The prison habit. *The Nation*, 1972, *214*, 719–721.

Gillespie, M.W. and Galliher, J.F. Age, anomie, and the inmate's definition of aging in prison: An exploratory study. In Donald P. Kent et al. (Eds.), *Research planning and action for the elderly*, Behavioral Publications, New York, 1972.

Goetting, A. The elderly in prison: Issues and perspectives. Manuscript, Western Kentucky University, 1982.

———. The elderly in prison: Programs and facilities. In D.J. Newman et al. (Eds.), *Elderly criminals*. Oelgeschaler, Gunn and Hain, Cambridge, England, 1983.

Ham, J.N. The forgotten minority: An exploration of long-term institutionalized aged and aging male prison inmates. Ph.D. diss., University of Michigan, 1976.

———. Aged and infirm male prison inmates. *Aging*, July-August 1980, DHHS Pub. No. (OHD) (AOA) 79-20949.

Hays, D.S., and Wisotsky, M. The aged offender: A review of the literature and two current studies from the New York State Division of Parole. *American Geriatrics Society*, 1969, *17*, 1064–1073.

Jackson, B. Who goes to prison: Caste and careerism in crime. *Atlantic Monthly*, 1966, *1*, 52–57.

Jenson, G.F. Age and rule-breaking in prison: A test of socio-cultural interpretations. *Criminology*, 1977, *14*, 555–568.

Keller, O.J., and Vedder, C.B. The crimes that older persons commit. *Gerontologist*, 1968, *8*, 43–50.

Krajick, K. Growing old in prison. *Corrections Magazine*, 1979, *5*, 32–46.

Lemon, B.; Bengston, V.; and Peterson, J. An exploration of the activity theory of aging: Activity types and life satisfaction among in-movers to a retirement community. *Journal of Gerontology*, 1972, *24*, 511–523.

Lieberman, M.; Prock, V.; and Tobin, S. Psychological effects of institutionalization. *Journal of Gerontology*, 1968, *23*, 243–253.

Moberg, D.O. Old age and crime. *Journal of Criminal Law, Criminology and Police Science*, 1953, *41*, 764–776.

Panton, J. Personality characteristics of aged inmates within a state prison population. *Offender Rehabilitation*, Winter 1976–1977, *2*, 203–208.

Pollak, O. The criminality of old age. *Journal of Criminal Psychopathology*, 1941, *3*, 213–235.

Reed, M., and Glamser, F. Aging in a total institution: The case of older prisoners.

Gerontologist, 1979, *19*, 354–360.

Rodstein, M. Crime and the aged. *Journal of the American Medical Association*, 1975, *234*, 639.

Schroeder, P.L. Criminal behavior in the later period of life. *American Journal of Psychiatry*, 1936, *92*, 915–928.

Shichor, D., and Kobrin, S. Note: Criminal behavior among the elderly. *Gerontologist*, 1978, *18*, 213–218.

Silfen, P. Adaption of the older prisoner in Israel. *International Journal of Offender Therapy and Comparative Criminology*, 1977, *21*, 57–65.

Teller, F.E., and Howell, R.J. The older prisoner: Criminal and psychological characteristics. *Criminology*, 1981, *18*, 549–555.

Wiegand, N.D., and Burger, J.C. The elderly offender and parole. *Prison Journal*, Autumn-Winter 1979–1980, *59*, 49–60.

Wiltz, C. The aged prisoner: A case study of age and aging in prison. Master's thesis, Kansas State University, Manhattan, Kans., 1973.

Wooden, W., and Parker, J. Aged men in a prison environment: Life satisfaction and coping strategies. Paper presented at the Annual Meetings of the National Gerontological Society, San Diego, 1980.

19

THE DISABLED

DONALD W. CALHOUN
AARON LIPMAN

A presentation of the current state of knowledge about the disabled elderly must begin with the fact that relatively little research has been focused on people who are old *and* have physical handicaps. Beyond uttering the usual sociological cliché that more study is needed, we will infer and extrapolate from the considerable research that is available on both the old and the disabled. A starting point is the fact that, clinically, disability is a function of the aging process in two ways.

PREVALENCE, SEVERITY, AND AGE

1. As we get older, the *prevalence* of disabling conditions is greater. An example is the statistic that 97 percent of the population over 60 have some degree of osteoarthritis. Tactile sensitivity declines after the fifties. The number of taste buds is greatly decreased after 60. The incidence of colorectal cancer rises steadily up to age 80. Breast cancer in women has its highest incidence after 85. Hypertensive heart disease rises till age 90. "All elderly people living in the United States have atherosclerosis of greater or lesser severity." Hip fractures in women due to bone decalcification (osteoporosis) rise 250 percent between ages 50 and 64 and double again over age 75. "Osteoporosis is so common in the elderly woman that it is more unusual to find normal bone than it is to find osteoporotic bone." Men between 50 and 80 lose bone density at 5 percent per decade. Glucose tolerance decreases with age. The incidence of diabetes is 2 per 1,000 population under age 25, 8.0 from 25 to 44, 20 from 45 to 54, 44 from 55 to 64, and 64 from 65 to 74. "The aged kidney is half a kidney." The incidence of large gastric ulcers peaks between 50 and 60. Mild clinical protein deficiency, with fatigue, slow healing, and lowered resistance to infection, is common in the aged. (Most of these incidence data are from Cowdry's "The Care of the Geriatric Patient," 1976.)

2. As we age, the *severity* of whatever impairments we have tends to increase. A dramatic example is the discovery, made about 1980, of deterioration in the condition of survivors of the last great polio epidemic of the 1950s: some ambulatory patients were regressing to wheelchairs, and some patients who had been breathing quite satisfactorily on their own were forced to return to iron lungs. The situation was severe enough to call for the convocation of an International Conference on Respiratory Rehabilitation and Post-Polio Aging in Chicago in 1981 as part of the International Year of Disabled Persons (Laurie, 1980).

What these two propositions mean will be made clearer by defining disability. The variety of disabilities is indicated by the guidelines issued by the Office for Civil Rights of the Department of Health, Education and Welfare (HEW) (now the Department of Health and Human Services [HHS]), telling who is protected against discrimination under Section 504 of the 1973 Rehabilitation Act ("Programs," 1976:29561). These guidelines begin by telling us that "Handicapped person means any person who (i) has a physical or mental impairment which substantially limits one or more major life activities, (ii) has a record of such an impairment, or (iii) is regarded as having such an impairment." An example of (i) would be blindness or epilepsy, of (ii) a history of heart disease or cancer, of (iii) a facial disfigurement that offends others, or a limp that is not physically disabling, but leads others, or oneself, to see one as a "cripple."

Physical impairment includes "any physiological disorder or condition, cosmetic disfigurement, or anatomical loss affecting one or more of the following body systems: neurological; musculoskeletal; special sense organs; respiratory, including speech organs; cardiovascular; reproductive; digestive; genito-urinary; hemic and lymphatic; skin; and endocrine." Mental impairment embraces "any mental or psychological disorder, such as mental retardation, organic brain syndrome, emotional or mental illness, and specific learning disabilities." HEW further specifies "such conditions and diseases as orthopedic, visual, speech, and hearing impairments, cerebral palsy, epilepsy, muscular dystrophy, multiple sclerosis, mental retardation, emotional illness, and...drug and alcohol addiction." The "major life functions" that may be impaired by these physical and mental impairments include "caring for one's self, performing mental tasks, walking, seeing, hearing, speaking, breathing, learning, and working."

Metropolitan Dade County, Florida, Nondiscrimination Ordinance 75-46, which does not include mental disability, further defines physical handicap as "any stabilized physical disability, infirmity, malformation, or disfigurement which is caused by bodily injury, birth defect, or illness." The ordinance specifies "epilepsy, any degree of paralysis, amputation, lack of physical coordination, blindness or visual impediment, deafness or hearing impediment, muteness or speech impediment, or physical reliance on a seeing-eye dog, wheelchair or other remedial appliance or device, or illness without reasonable medical prognosis for recovery."

The Social Security Administration, in a 1972 survey of disability entitled

Disability Survey 72, listed nine groups of impairments. They are, from highest to lowest in terms of their frequency in the severely disabled population: musculoskeletal, cardiovascular, mental, respiratory, digestive, endocrine, neoplasm, urogenital, and neurological.

The HHS definition of disability distinguishes disabilities that objectively exist, or have existed, from those that are believed to exist. This suggests that disability in either younger or older people lies in part in the attitudes of others, which are usually shared by the "disabled" peron. Erving Goffman has emphasized the ways in which minorities and other deviant groups, including the physically disabled, are stigmatized so that their members are disqualified from full social acceptance. "By definition. . .we believe the person with a stigma is not quite human. On this assumption we exercise varieties of discrimination through which we effectively, if often unthinkingly, reduce his life chances" (Goffman, 1963:5). When one has a visible handicap people focus their attention in conversation— even in spite of themselves—on the disability rather than on the content of what the person is saying. This process leads many people with an impairment to suffer what Goffman calls "alienation from interaction"—they are too self-conscious about their physical appearance to be able to concentrate upon what they, and the other person, are trying to say. Some students of the subject would say that the real disability lies not in the physical impairment, but in the "spoiled identity" that arises from such stigmatization. Age, like handicap, is occasion for stigmatizing a person, so that the disabled elderly suffer a doubly spoiled identity. For example, a lecherous youngster may be seen as an attractive stud, but a lecher of 75 is a "dirty old man." Let him be sightless as well and he becomes a "dirty blind old man," target for all the fears and repulsions that have traditionally been aroused by the unsighted.

Roger Barker, an experienced student of the psychology of disability, saw the question of physical impairment and stigmatization in a different perspective. "The fact that the physically disabled individual has to face is that in some respects he is an inferior person." He compared the disabled person with the victim of religious or racial prejudice, whose "reality situation involves only social rejection. . . .The underprivileged status of the disabled person is due, on the one hand, to his own physical defects and, on the other hand, to the negative attitudes of the normal majority with whom he must live. . . .No amount of optimistic talk can remove the fact that, other things being equal, a physically disabled person is relatively ineffective in a social world devised for physically normal persons" (Barker, 1948:32, 35). A person with defective legs, said Barker, may learn to operate a sewing machine but will lack the flexibility to operate two automatic machines, moving from one to the other. In a fire such a person may be a liability to self and others. In 1983, with an awareness of possibilities for the disabled that we lacked in 1948, we might give less weight to the bottom line of physical impairment and more to the element of stigma and prejudice than did Barker.

Since the Social Security study is primarily concerned with work disability,

Table 19.1
Age and Disability (per Thousand Population), 1972

Age	Total Disability	Occupationally Disabled	Secondary Work Limitations
20-34	22	16	33
35-44	49	23	36
45-54	86	51	53
55-64	185	56	48

Source: Social Security Administration, *Disability Survey 72: Disabled and Nondisabled Adults.* U.S. Department of Health and Human Services, Office of Policy, Office of Research and Statistics, Research Report No. 56, USGPO, Washington, D.C., April 1981, p. 7.

it does not include data beyond the traditional retirement age of 65. It does make our initial clinical propositions specific in ways which may, with qualifications, be extrapolated for the population past 65. "The prevalence of chronic conditions in the adult population increased markedly with age.... The prevalence of disability also rose with age, but the increase was much steeper (Social Security Administration, 1981:52). The disabled made up 8 percent of the population under 45, 19 percent of those 45–54, and 29 percent of those 55–64 (p. 55). Table 19.1 shows the distribution by age groups of three levels of disability: total disability, occupational disability, and secondary work limitations. Another summary showed that 3 percent of the 1972 working population under age 45 was "severely disabled," as were 9 percent of the 45–54 age group and 18 percent of those over 55 (p. 53).

The likelihood of disability is increased in those who have multiple impairments, and these are related to the aging process.

Five percent of the population reporting one condition was severely disabled; ten times that proportion was severely disabled among persons with four or more conditions.... Moreover, four times as many of the currently disabled aged 55-64 as of those aged 20-34 had four or more conditions. For the severely disabled, about half of those aged 45-64 had four or more conditions; less than 5 percent of the nondisabled in that age group reported that they had at least four chronic conditions. (Social Security Administration, 1981:60)

Another significant indicator of the relationship between aging and disability was the finding that the percentage of disability attributed to accidents decreased with age, dropping slightly after 45 and more rapidly after 55. "Obviously, the decline after age 45 in the importance of accidents as a cause of chronic impairment also reflects the fact that chronic, degenerative disease begins to occur more frequently after middle age" (Social Security Administration, 1981:61–62).

Among the different types of impairment analyzed in the Social Security study, there were differences in the effect of aging. Among the disabled, the prevalence of cardiovascular conditions between ages 55 and 64 was almost seven times the prevalence under age 45. For endocrine disorders, it was over six times as high. But for neurological impairments, it was less than twice as high (Social Security Administration, 1981: 54).

In the severely disabled group, for different disorders there was also a sharp difference in the ratio between the amount of the disability rate at higher ages attributable to wider prevalence of the condition, and the amount due to increasing severity of the condition. Analysis of variance showed 75 percent of the higher disability rate of people over 55 with musculoskeletal disorders to be due to increasing severity. The same figure held for cardiovascular impairments. But for neurological ailments the figure was only 13 percent (Social Security Administration, 1981:56). Colloquially speaking, with neurological disorders the main thing is that with age more people join the club, whereas with musculoskeletal and cardiovascular impairments those already in the club get worse.

In citing incidence data, we must remember that they indicate tendencies to which not all (or even most) of the disabled elderly fall victim. Although "one of the best documented changes that occurs with increasing age is the slowing of response time,. . . the effects of loss of speed in the elderly can be minimized by habits of exercise, opportunities for practice, and motivational patterns. Furthermore,. . . many of the aged can perform more rapidly than some of the young" (Storandt, 1976:323). The majority of people over 65 report their health as excellent or good, and only a minority are limited in their ability to move about freely. Since good health is such an important resource in maintaining independence and autonomy in old age, we cannot judge the severity of the problem by numbers alone.

The clinical impact of aging on disability gives rise to the social and social psychological ramifications that are the main theme of this chapter. We shall discuss this topic in terms of specific functions that are impaired in the disabled, and the specific problems of social interaction to which they are likely to lead when aggravated by age.

IMPAIRMENT OF FUNCTION

Disability, at whatever age, tends to limit a person's physical interaction with the environment. One may be handicapped in walking, using stairs or inclines, standing for long periods, sitting for long periods, stooping, crouching or kneeling, lifting or carrying weights, reading, and handling or fingering. The Social Security study found that 94 percent of recipients of disability benefits and 87 percent of a group of severely disabled people who were not receiving benefits were limited in one or more of these activities. Seventy-nine percent of the disability beneficiaries and 57 percent of the nonbeneficiaries had five or more limitations (Social Security Administration, 1981:206). Of persons classified as "totally disabled," 89 percent were impaired in physical movement, 29 percent in sensory ability, and 16 percent in personal self-care (p. 224). On the age axis, the study reported that in the general population "the proportion of persons with some limitation increased significantly in middle age: 35 percent of persons aged 45–54 and 64 percent of those 55–64 reported a limitation compared with 18 percent of those under 35" (p. 69). Another study of physical performance found limitation escalating further among "senior citizens": whereas only 20 percent of those 65–74 had substantial limitations in such activities as walking, climbing, and bending, 42 percent of individuals 75 and over were so encumbered (Nagi, 1976).

Such impairment of basic physical relationships to the environment undermines independent personal identity. "The ability of an individual to remain ambulatory may be the only dividing line between institutionalization and remaining an active member of a community and society" (Helfand, 1976:310). The mechanics of walking are thus critical. Walking is a process of repeatedly falling forward and then "catching" one's weight with the lumbar back. A painful lumbar region, due to age and/or specific disability, may make this impossible. Short of institutionalization, loss of independence may involve the need for physical help in using public transportation, getting about out of doors, or simply getting out of the house—or out of bed. A 1978 sample study from the general population over 65 showed 44 percent experiencing difficulty in walking stairs, 13 percent in getting about the house, 14 percent in washing and bathing, and 36 percent in cutting toenails (Shanas, 1978: Table 2-3). The Social Security report delineated dramatically the upward curve of physical dependence with age: "Persons 55 years of age and older reported they needed help with personal care about seven times as frequently as those aged 20–34 and twice as frequently as those aged 45–54" (Social Security Administration, 1981:70).

IMPAIRMENT, ISOLATION, AND DEPENDENCE

The total impact of this physical dependency must be seen in the light of simple socioeconomic facts. "In contrast with the nondisabled, the disabled population tended to be older, poorer, less educated, more likely to be divorced, separated or widowed, and more likely to be black. . . . Little education and low income interacting together (and exacerbated by old age) tend. . .to characterize the disabled population in the United States" (Social Security Administration, 1981:1). One disabled person in ten lives alone. Among severely disabled older women, the figure is 22 percent. Disabled workers who are employed are concentrated in the lowest-status and lowest-paying occupations. They constitute 10 percent of all workers, but make up one-sixth of the force of laborers, farm workers, and service workers. When the Social Security disability survey was conducted, the average wage of severely disabled workers was approximately one-third that of the nondisabled workers (pp. 23–24). The question that arises is, Who cooks the meals and cuts the toenails for these isolated and poverty-stricken people? The answer is suggested by Shanas's report on who performs the heavy household tasks that 32 percent of whites and 62 percent of blacks over 65 perform with difficulty or not at all: spouse, paid helper, child (presumably adult) in household, child not in household, or nobody. For one-fifth of the blacks, the helper reported is "none" (Shanas, 1978: Table 4-5).

What we have said so far touches on the marital and sexual situation of the disabled elderly. If needed help of any kind is provided by a "paid helper," who pays? "For those disabled persons without a spouse, or if the spouse is unable to work," says the Social Security report, "options for financial adjustments within the family structure become minimal" (Social Security Administration, 1981:1). For the general population, 51 percent of white women over 65 and 64 percent of black women are widowed (the comparable figures for men are 13 and 20 percent) (Shanas, 1978: Table 1-6). Moreover, "the disabled person's spouse is more likely to have died than the spouse of the nondisabled individual" (p. 12). Even at age 35, the percentage married is lower for disabled than for nondisabled persons. One-third of severely disabled people are unmarried, as compared with one-fifth of the nondisabled.

What is the quality of life of the 10 percent of disabled persons who live alone, and of the one in five severely disabled women who do so? We have little direct statistical evidence on the isolated elderly disabled, but Shanas's data on the population over 65 may throw some light. One can find evidence here to support either of two polar interpretations: the view of the Social Security report that the extended family is no longer a source of support for either the disabled or nondisabled elderly (Social Security Administration, 1981:291); or Shanas's position that most elderly people tend to maintain close relationships and that the modified extended family, facilitated by transportation and communications technology, is now the effective family unit (Shanas, 1979). Let us look at the evidence from Shanas's data for each viewpoint.

On the negative side, Shanas lists four hypotheses that undergird the idea of alienation of the elderly:

(1) Because of the geographic mobility of the population of the U. S. most old people who have children live at great distances from their children; (2) Because of the alienation of old people from their children, most older parents rarely see their children; (3) Because of the predominance of the nuclear family in the U. S., most old people rarely see their siblings or other relatives; (4) Because of the existence and availability of large human service bureaucracies, families are no longer important as a source of care for older people. (Shanas, 1979:6)

Some of Shanas's data partially support the alienation hypothesis. Twenty-three percent of white persons and 25 percent of blacks over 65 who were not living with children had no family contacts the week before they were interviewed. Sixteen percent of blacks over 75 who lived alone had had no human contact the previous Sunday. Thirty-nine percent of whites and 42 percent of blacks over 65 who had no living children had seen no sibling or other relative in the past week. Not surprisingly, 46 percent of black unmarried women over 75 reported themselves as "often or sometimes lonely."

Evidence for a brighter view: It is not the physical pattern of living but the emotional bond that is crucial. A functional extended family need not live together as a household. "Intimacy at a distance" may prevent alienation of the old. Shanas's data give much evidence that such intimacy does exist: 29 percent of the over-65 whites who lived alone and 34 percent of the blacks had been visited by a neighbor the previous day. Forty-one percent of the whites and 42 percent of the blacks who did not live with a child had a surviving child within ten minutes' distance. Sixteen percent of whites and 29 percent of blacks received regular or occasional financial help from children. Forty-seven percent of all over-65 persons had within the past month taken care of a great-grandchild, kept one overnight, given the child money gifts, or made it presents.

On balance, Shanas has here and elsewhere supported her conclusion: "In contemporary American society, old people are not rejected by their families nor are they alienated from their children. . . . The truly isolated old person, despite his or her prominence in the media, is a rarity in the United States" (Shanas, 1979:3–4).

It must be stressed that Shanas's data are for a sample of the general population, and that the disabled elderly are less mobile. For example, if a surviving child is within ten minutes, whose ten minutes is it—the child's or the elderly parent's? It makes a big difference if the parent is disabled.

SEXUALITY, HEALTH MAINTENANCE, AND NUTRITION

Age, disability, widowhood, and negative cultural attitudes may add to alienation and aloneness by impairing sexuality. Specific disabilities pose problems: although quadriplegics can very often erect and ejaculate satisfactorily, pelvic and other paralysis makes intercourse difficult or impossible for spinal-cord injured males.

Disability impairs the capacity of the elderly for taking care of their health needs, including nutrition. Shanas found a number of reasons why older people may fail to get the needed help of a physician (Shanas, 1978: Table 3-4). Money was given as a reason by 32 percent of white and 47 percent of blacks. Fear was another reason, interestingly cited more often by men than by women, both black and white (19 percent of black men). Problems of transportation (obviously magnified among the disabled) were given as a reason more often by women of both races (17 percent of white and 10 percent of black women). Lack of confidence in doctors ("Doctors can't help") appeared more often with blacks than with whites. "General procrastination" was the reason for not seeing a doctor cited by 26 percent of whites and 18 percent of blacks. This may have reflected a general sense of hopelessness, lack of organization, and dependence.

All of these barriers may be aggravated when the older person is disabled. Although physician's fees generally mount with the age of the patient, they are higher for the severely disabled at all ages (Social Security Administration, 1981:114). People classified as "totally disabled" spend three times the average amount for medical care, especially hospitalization (p. 103). The severely disabled are the group least likely to have their own resources to pay medical bills (p. 117).

The German pun "Man ist was er isst" (one is what one eats) reflects the importance of nutrition. Also, the activity of eating and the conversation that accompanies it are among the few pleasures remaining to many older persons. These are impaired physiologically when age or disability reduces the efficiency of jaws, teeth, salivary glands, and mucous membranes. They are also impaired when aged disabled people living alone cook for themselves, often with limited refrigeration and poor cooking and storage facilities. When to these are added loss of appetite and loss of energy due to protein deficiency, the path of least resistance is junk foods—packaged, processed, easily prepared, high in carbohydrates, and devoid of the vitamins and minerals especially necessary for the metabolism of the elderly. These conditions make vitamin supplements a necessity for geriatric patients.

INSTITUTIONS AND ALTERNATIVES

Isolated and dependent elderly may soon face the issue of independence versus institutionalization. Like most other dilemmas confronted by the disabled elderly, this is a physiological-sociological problem. Only 5 percent of the population over 65 live in institutions. Elderly people generally prefer the privacy and independence of home. Some 65-year-olds actually live with their parents. Sternberg, discussing the obstacles to rehabilitative therapy with the elderly disabled in 1976, listed (1) the deteriorating effects of disabling disease on general health; (2) the typical combination of multiple impairments; (3) the lessened tolerance for physical effort; (4) the slowing of the learning process with age; and (5) confinement in a custodial unit (Sternberg, 1976:403). Adams and Sindell suggest that "loss of caretakers rather than physical deterioration precipitates nursing home placement" (1968:5). (We might suggest that this is a matter of emphasis rather than an either-or proposition: caretakers would not be needed or missed were it not for physical deterioration.) Lieberman reported in 1969 that "institutionalized aged are consistently found to be worse off than aged persons living in the community" (Lieberman, 1969:330). Institutional mortality rates for the first year of confinement, especially for men, are higher than in the community. They get higher for different types of institutions in the following order, from lowest to highest: homes for the aged; nursing homes; state hospitals. Two of the main reasons for mortality may be the stress of moving and the stress of confinement in a total institution. Added to this is the fact that "the expectation of long, painful, terminal care may be self-fulfilling" (Wessen, 1964:7).

Research on the impact of environmental change on mortality in the elderly, especially the handicapped elderly, has been contradictory. A study by Borup, Galligo, and Heffernan (1979) reported that 75 percent of previous studies had concluded that environmental change does not increase mortality. The Borup study, using an experimental group of Utah elderly relocated from legally closed nursing homes and a control group who were not relocated, found that "those patients experiencing relocation had a significantly lower mortality rate than those who did not undergo a change in their environment." However, this may be because the relocated patients were younger. For the specifically disabled elderly, Kral and associates (1968) reported that they were more vulnerable after change in environment. The later (1979) Borup research reported no significant mortality difference between handicapped and nonhandicapped patients after relocation.

If our goal for the disabled elderly is that described as the fundamental concern of the occupational therapist, "the development and maintenance of the individual's capacity to perform those tasks and roles essential to productive living throughout the life span" (Leimer, 1976), we will applaud, as an alternative to institutionalization, the supplementation of home living by professional homemakers, home health aides, community health nurses, and community health and recreational centers.

Realization that the elderly have varying degrees of need has given rise to an approach aimed at providing services on a continuum of care. At one end of the continuum is the dependent older person who may have a problem but who does not require extensive assistance. Further along the continuum are elderly people with some problems that can produce functional impairment. Increasing levels of dependence follow, ultimately ending with elderly people classified as fully dependent and requiring long-term intensive and full-time assistance.

It is not a question of whether one service is better than another. The question is whether one service is more appropriate than another for an older person with specific needs. Unfortunately, we often lack needed services or facilities, with the result that if an older person cannot take care of himself at home the only alternative is institutionalization.

Independence and dignity for the disabled elderly will require that we resume the long-term trends toward more enlightened public policy that have been reversed in recent years. The rise of urban industrialism in the nineteenth century brought recognition that industrial accidents are not usually a matter for individual blame, but a statistically predictable fact of the industrial process. This concept of "liability without fault" resulted in workman's compensation laws, first in Europe and eventually in the United States. The same socioeconomic forces brought a realization that in an urban-industrial society aging is a natural fact of life with which the individual or family may be powerless to cope. Thus again, first in Europe and later here, we established Social Security for the aged. Humanistic goals for the elderly disabled will require public supplementation of individual and family income and more community health and recreational services. Although this will require federal funding where community and individual resources are inadequate, the goals of freedom and dignity for the disabled call for local control and participation by those who are served.

REFERENCES

Adams, M., and Sindell, M.G. Tenacity of the social network in maintaining aged disabled in the community. Paper presented to the Gerontological Society, Denver, November, 1968.

Barker, R. The social psychology of physical disability. *Journal of Social Issues*, 1948, *4*, 28–35.

Borup, J.H.; Galligo, D.T.; and Heffernan, P.G. Relocation and its effects on mortality. *Gerontologist*, 1979, *19*, 135–140.

Goffman, E. *Stigma: Notes on the management of spoiled identity*. Prentice-Hall, Englewood Cliffs, N.J., 1963.

Helfand, A.E. Care of the foot. In *Cowdry's "The care of the geriatric patient,"* 5th ed., ed. Franz U. Sternberg, Mosby, St. Louis, 1976.

Kral, V.A.; Grad, B.; and Berenson, D. Some reactions resulting from the relocation of an aged population. *Canadian Psychiatric Association Journal*, 1968, *13*, 201–209.

Laurie, G. (Ed.). Respiratory rehabilitation and post-polio aging problems. Symposium in *Rehabilitation Gazette*, 1980, *23*, 1–10.

Leimer, S.J. Occupational therapy. In *Cowdry's "The care of the geriatric patient,"* 5th ed., ed. Franz U. Sternberg. Mosby, St. Louis, 1976.

Lieberman, M. Institutionalization of the aged. *Journal of Gerontology*, 1969, *24*, 330–340.

Nagi, S. An epidemiology of disability among adults in the United States. *Milbank Memorial Fund Quarterly*, Fall 1976, *54*, 350–370.

Programs and activities receiving or benefiting from federal financial assistance: Nondiscrimination on the basis of handicap. Department of Health, Education and Welfare, Office of the Secretary. *Federal Register*, July 17, 1976, *41*, 33822–3.

Shanas, E. Report to the Administration on Aging on a national survey of aging, 1978.

———. Social myth as hypothesis: The case of family relations of old people. *Gerontologist*, 1979, *19*, 3–9.

Social Security Administration. *Disability survey 72: Disabled and nondisabled adults*. U.S. Department of Health and Human Services, Office of Policy, Office of Research and Statistics, Research Report No. 56, USGPO, Washington, D.C., April 1981.

Sternberg, Franz U. (Ed.). *Cowdry's "The care of the geriatric patient,"* 5th ed. Mosby, St. Louis, 1976.

Storandt, M. Psychologic aspects. In *Cowdry's "The care of the geriatric patient,"* 5th ed., ed. Franz U. Sternberg. Mosby, St. Louis, 1976.

Wessen, A.F. Some sociological aspects of long-term care. Part 2. *Gerontologist*, 1964, *4*, 7–14.

20

HOMOSEXUALS

AARON LIPMAN

For years gerontologists have been explaining that the elderly are not a monolithic category of homogeneous people, all of whom fall into a set of predictable patterns. Similarly, homosexuals constitute a great variety of people who vary in life-styles, self-concept, gender, and many other ways. Bringing these two broad categories together in a discussion of "elderly homosexuals" does not simplify the problem of reviewing their characteristics and roles in society. If anything, it makes discussion more complicated.

The present chapter reviews a number of important issues and factors that must be considered in developing an understanding of elderly homosexual people. It does this by providing a review of major research findings on topics that range from the meanings of homosexuality for various segments of the population through stereotypes, personality characteristics, social support systems, legal problems, life satisfaction, gender differences, and responses to stigmatization. As will be seen, this is a difficult area of research, but a picture of the elderly homosexual is beginning to emerge.

THE MEANINGS OF HOMOSEXUALITY

A homosexual has been defined as one "who is motivated in adult life by a definite preferential erotic attraction to members of the same sex and who usually (but not necessarily) engages in overt sexual relations with them" (Marmor, 1980:5). This definition provides a useful point of departure because it recognizes that feelings are different from behavior—one can be celibate and still be a homosexual.

The labels used by various segments of society often reveal the meanings that they attach to homosexuality. Many heterosexual people use pejorative terms, which focus attention on the deviant aspects of homosexuality as seen from traditional perspectives. Homosexuals themselves, however, prefer labels such as "gay," "lesbian," or "homophile," since these terms refer to their entire life-style, "a way of being in the world which only incidentally involves sexual activity with persons of the same sex. From their point of view this makes sense since they spend much more of their time at work or with friends or on household chores than in explicitly sexual contexts" (Bell and Weinberg, 1978:115). These authors point out that even the term "homosexual" is rejected by many homosexual men and women, since it literally defines them in terms of their sexuality alone.

There appears to be some consensus among social scientists regarding the definition of a homosexual in terms of activities other than narrowly sexual ones (Adelman, 1980; Bell and Weinberg, 1978; Raphael, 1974; Warren, 1974). It is maintained that defining someone as a homosexual simply describes that person's sexual orientation, whereas a "gay" identity implies not only sexual preference, but affiliation with the entire gay community in a sociocultural sense. On the other hand, many lesbians feel that the word "gay" is inappropriate for them because of this identity as part of a male life-style community; it ignores many of their needs and priorities and would better be used exclusively for males (Adelman, 1980; Kimmel, 1977a).

Even on an exclusively sexual basis, categorizing humans in terms of sexual preference and sexual orientation must be highly qualified, since the majority of male and female homosexuals have had heterosexual sex at least once in their lifetimes (Bell and Weinberg, 1978).

Historically, in our society homosexuality has been interpreted as deviant behavior. The historical antecedents of this interpretation are both religious (homosexuality was a sin) and legal (homosexuality was a crime). In the twentieth century a new dimension was added: the medical model defined homosexuality as a sickness—a psychopathological state or mental illness (Dank, 1971). Today, all of these meanings are changing. For example, in 1973 the American Psychiatric Association made its momentous resolution that "homosexuality per se cannot be classified as a mental disorder," reflecting a significant change in attitude, although the legal prohibition against certain sexual acts still exists.

Many of these far-reaching changes in the meaning of homosexuality came as a concomitant of the societal emphasis on cultural pluralism and the rights of ethnic minorities. Increasingly, members of the homosexual population in America view and present themselves not as deviant, but as an oppressed minority group. "The homosexual community drew on the examples of ethnic minorities, who shared their experience of centuries of psychological as well as social oppression, to encourage its members in 'coming' out with a proud self-image" (Humphrys, 1979:137). This new meaning raised consciousness among homosexuals. The subsequent proliferation of organizations became a means of identifying with a homosexual group. Many homosexual leaders felt that these changes lent respectability to their activities and increased the sense of community and cohesion for its members. In addition, the new meaning acted as a barrier to social isolation by permitting meeting places and communication for individuals who shared their life-style. Participation in these organizations created shared activities and satisfied the social and sexual needs of many of their members.

Because of these changing meanings, particularly during the past decade, male and female homosexuals have become increasingly visible, more open in their disclosure of their sexual orientation, and more assured and assertive when confronting discrimination (Adelman, 1980). On a formal level, they have organized to attain both community and political support. In the professions, for example, in 1975 the Association of Gay Psychologists and the American Psychological Association Task Force on the Status of Lesbian and Gay Male Psychologists were instrumental in getting the American Psychological Association to add a clause to its nondiscrimination policy specifying that there should be no discrimination on the basis of sexual orientation.

The terms "coming out," "gay liberation," and "raised consciousness" are all familiar to students of recent history. Whether an individual has "come out" and identified himself with the gay community or has remained "in the closet" will certainly influence his style of life as an aged individual. Most recent studies of homosexuals are based on those individuals who have "come out" and/or identified themselves with a gay life-style. Martin and Lyon (1979:135–136) point out, however, that "gays of advanced age today are likely to have been closeted throughout their lives. . . . Many are still afraid to come out, even though they are retired and need no longer fear the loss of a job." Whether the proportion of older gays who have come out is representative of their numbers in the homosexual population remains questionable. This complicates the scientific study of older homosexuals and our ability to draw generalizable conclusions regarding their numbers, attitudes, and activities.

While there is a growing body of literature attempting to define and draw meaningful scientific generalizations regarding homosexuality, and a large amount of research on the elderly, comparatively little work has been done on elderly homosexuals. However, the process of aging among homosexuals, in addition to responding to such demographic determinants as socioeconomic status, gender, and education level, is affected by societal attitudes toward their sexual preference and life-style. And we have reason to suspect that this group is larger than is commonly estimated.

STUDIES OF HOMOSEXUALS

Even though data on the scope and characteristics of elderly homosexuals are sorely needed, they are not easily obtained. Empirical studies of aging homosexuals have been conspicuously incomplete and nonrepresentative. The category is largely an invisible and anonymous one. Extrapolating from the most reliable estimates that between 5 and 10 percent of the general population are homosexual (Melville, 1982), the proportion of the aged who are homosexuals is probably as high or higher than the proportion of the aged who are nursing home residents.

There can be only estimates of the incidence of homosexuality, since for many older individuals it has been and remains a hidden type of behavior. Obviously, this is because of its perception as deviant. Humphrys, for example, in his book *Tearoom Trade* (1970), found that over half of his sample of people using public restrooms for homosexual sex kept their activities secret because they were heterosexually married.

Nowhere has there been a study of a national representative sample of homosexuals. In most investigations the samples used have been extremely small, and many studies have been based on specific geographic regions. When mailed questionnaires have been used, the response rate has been low. These extremely small samples have precluded complex analysis of the data collected and have limited generalizations about aging homosexuals. Rarely have control groups been used, so that we have no data on how aging homosexuals in a particular study would compare with aging heterosexuals, or even with homosexuals who have not "come out." Sampling methods overlook those who do not admit homosexuality to others; belong to no gay organizations; and do not go to tea rooms, bars, or baths. Since it is impossible to identify all the individuals in the population under study, it is impossible to sample them properly.

Finally, all the studies on homosexuality have been cross-sectional rather than longitudinal. As a consequence, the historical or period effect and cohort effect have confounded both estimates and reported behavior of homosexuals. For example, "Will young adults today, whose exploration of alternative lifestyles is much greater than was the exploration of today's older persons in their youth, continue such innovative behavior into old age?" (Dressel and Avant, 1978). "The analysis of the separate effects of age, period, and cohort is one of a class of problems for which the effects of the different variables are confounded with one another" (Rodgers, 1982:774).

It was Kinsey (1948:639) who pointed out still another complicating factor in any attempts to study homosexuality. Kinsey thought of homosexuality and heterosexuality not as two separate categories, but as a continuum from exclusively heterosexual to exclusively homosexual. He contended that people "do not represent two discrete populations, heterosexual and homosexual. . . . only the human mind invents categories and tries to force facts into separate pigeonholes. The living world is a continuum in each and every one of its aspects." In addition to variations along this continuum, there are also cases where older individuals have reportedly changed from exclusively homosexual to exclusively heterosexual activity, and vice versa (Christenson and Johnson, 1973).

Kinsey (1948) found that 37 percent of the males and 13 percent of the females in his studies had had at least some homosexual experience. Only 1 percent of the females were exclusively homosexual, and about 2 or 3 percent of the males. Thus, the proportion of males who were *exclusively* homosexual was about three times greater than that of females, and even among those who were predominantly but not exclusively homosexuals, the proportion of males was about three times greater than that of females. Sixty-three percent of the males and 87 percent of the females were exclusively heterosexual.

Kinsey's researchers were instructed to guess whether a respondent was homosexual or not, before asking any questions about homosexuality. The researchers were able to guess correctly in only 15 percent of the cases (Tripp, 1975). When asked, "Do you feel that most people can tell that you are gay?" 72 percent of Almvig's (1982) respondents believed that most people could not. It has been found that only a small proportion of homosexuals conform to the effeminate male or "butch" female stereotype, or consistently play either active or passive corresponding roles (Almvig, 1982).

The final difficulty that has acted as a formidable barrier to research has been reported on by the Task Group on Homosexuality established by the American Sociological Association, in response to a Sociologists' Gay Caucus resolution in 1978. They concluded (*ASA Footnotes*, 1982:1) that "the fear of stigma diverts sociologists, heterosexual and homosexual alike, from doing research on homosexuality. . . . colleagues may assume that persons doing research on homosexuality are themselves gay or lesbian—a risk that only the bravest or most foolhardy are likely to run." Activist gay and lesbian social scientists are attempting to ameliorate this situation by pressing their professional associations to investigate and publicize this state of affairs. In addition, they are conducting scholarly research on the topic in order to help fill some of the void in this area.

Stereotypes versus Reality

In the past, as the term itself implies, there was a tendency to lump homosexuals together as a group and to believe that their life experiences were similar because they shared a preferential attraction for members of the same sex. The state of research on the elderly homosexual is reminiscent of the early stages of gerontological research itself, where one of the first jobs consisted of debunking the stereotypes of the majority of elderly people as institutionalized, poverty-stricken, isolated, depressed, and in poor health. The next phases involved dividing "the elderly" into discrete, recognizable, component subgroups and finding differences among them that often depended more on gender, income, health, and so on, than on age itself.

In a similar manner, a number of researchers (Bell and Weinberg, 1978; Francher and Henkin, 1973; Friend, 1980; Kelly, 1974, 1977; Laner, 1978; Levitt and Klassen, 1974; Minnigerode, 1976; Minnigerode and Adelman, 1978; Raphael and Robinson, 1980; Weinberg and Williams, 1974) have addressed the question of the correctness of the stereotype of the older gay male or lesbian and have found it to be unsubstantiated. Kelly (1977:329) presents the following composite picture of the stereotypic view of the aged male homosexual as a pathetic figure:

He no longer goes to bars, having lost his physical attractiveness and his sexual appeal to the young men he craves. He is oversexed, but his sex life is very unsatisfactory. He has been unable to form a lasting relationship with a sexual partner, and he is seldom active sexually anymore. When he does have sex it is usually in a "tearoom" (public toilet). He has disengaged from the gay world and his acquaintances in it. He is retreating further and further into the "closet"—fearful of disclosure of his "perversion." Most of his assoications now are increasingly with heterosexuals. In a bizarre and deviant world centered around age, he is labeled "an old queen," as he has become quite effeminate.

Friend (1980:245) also refers to "the popular view of the older gay male as lonely, maladjusted, and living marginally to the institutions of society." And Minnigerode (1976:273) adds that "folk wisdom suggests accelerated aging in homosexual men."

Raphael and Robinson (1980:225, 216), in their in-depth study of lesbians whose ages ranged from 50 to 73, referred to the stereotype that lesbians, "because of weak or absent family ties, spent their later years friendless, lonely, and with low opinions of themselves"; they also referred to the "myth of a sexual and emotional desert for lesbians in old age."

The popular stereotype of the aging homosexual, then, has been a very negative one, picturing him as lonely, sexually frustrated, appearing older than his years, abandoned by friends and society, and, in all, a pathetic figure. It is not surprising that homosexuals, being socialized in our society, share many of its attitudes, values, and opinions regarding aging homosexuals, that is, share the stereotype. "It is a tenet of social psychology that we appropriate the image of ourselves that others project" (Humphrys, 1979:40).

According to a number of researchers, however, the reality differs radically from this negative stereotype. In contrast to his composite stereotype, Kelly (1980:186) presents the following composite of the "real" older gay man:

Thus, the aging men in this study bear little resemblance to the stereotyped composite image circulating in society at large. In contrast to the mythical man, the "composite" older man in the study group does not frequent tearooms but occasionally goes out to bars, particularly those that serve his peer group. The extent of his participation in the gay world is moderate but based largely on his individual desires. He has many gay friends and fewer heterosexual friends. His sex life is quite satisfactory and he desires sexual contact with adult men, especially those near his own age, but he is not currently involved in an exclusive relationship. He does not consider himself effeminate, nor does he like to define himself in terms of gay age-labels, but he remembers the terms that were commonly applied to "old gays" when he was younger.

In his study of forty-three homosexuals ranging in age from 32 to 76, Friend (1980:245) found that the older gay men in his study were "well adjusted and content with their lifestyle." Although Weinberg and Williams found that their older male respondents attended homosexual bars and clubs less frequently, they also refuted the folk image of the old homosexual as being depressed and lonely. They found no age-related differences in anxiety, loneliness, depression, or self-acceptance. In some respects, in fact, they suggested that the older homosexual males in their study expressed a greater sense of well-being than did the young males. They concluded that their older respondents worried less about exposure of their homosexuality and had more stable self-concepts. Raphael and Robinson (1980) found the same to be true in their study of aging lesbians. And contrary to the stereotype as well, Minnigerode (1976) found no evidence of accelerated aging in homosexual males, while Laner (1978) affirms that lesbians do not experience accelerated aging as early as do heterosexual women, nor does the age of their partners appear to be as important. Most of the recent studies, then, refute the earlier-held notion that the older homosexual is a lonely, rejected, pathetic figure.

Homosexuals in Primary Groups

One phenomenon that emerged in a number of studies for both older males and females was the existence of extended friendship groups which appear to function as surrogate families. Family ties and children are two sources of emotional support for most older people. Because the stigma of homosexuality often causes estrangement from other family members, and since many lesbians never marry or have children, Wolf (1978) has asserted that lesbians form close friendships, which take the place of these familial supports in their old age. Raphael and Robinson (1980) consider the development of these strong friendship ties, which are composed primarily of other older lesbians, to be an adaptation to aging on the part of the older lesbian; these friendship supports help her to survive in the absence of the kinship networks relied upon by most older people in the heterosexual society, and further help her to cope with what is still, for most lesbians, a hostile environment. The single most important factor in determining the quality and existence of kinship support is the reaction of family members to "coming out." "Those lesbians who did not come out with family members or who came out and received continuing negative family responses...had weak or totally absent kinship ties which they replaced with friendship networks" (Raphael and Robinson, 1981:16).

This same phenomenon of friendship support networks has been reported in the literature for older gay men as well. Faced by rejection and the loss of family support when they come out, these men form strong friendship ties with their peers, who take the place of their families. Bell and Weinberg (1978) reported that not only do homosexual men have many more close friends than do their heterosexual counterparts, but that these friends also function as their surrogate families, both in everyday exchanges and on holidays, birthdays, and similar times usually celebrated within a family context. Francher and Henkin (1973) had previously reported the existence of a close friendship network among older gay males. Friend (1980) reports this same phenomenon, but believes that instead of replacing lost family support, it merely reinforces those family supports that are there. Whether these friends replace or merely reinforce the family, most recent studies have described aging homosexuals, both male and female, as having more friends, on the average, than do their heterosexual counterparts.

Personality and Self-Image

In addition to these friendship networks, Almvig (1982), Berger (1982), Francher and Henkin (1973), and Kimmel (1979) indicate that both gays and lesbians have an awareness of being responsible for themselves in old age, rather than relying on family or offspring; they have also developed self-reliance and independence through performing both traditional male and female tasks during their lifetimes, and many have already lived alone successfully. They thus have fewer discontinuities in life than aging heterosexuals, who might have had children leaving home, or relied on support from family that was not forthcoming, and who might have been confined to traditional gender roles in performing everyday tasks, which would necessitate their learning new tasks when they had to live alone for the first time in their lives (Kimmel, 1977b, 1979–1980). In the words of one elderly homosexual: "The preparation for old age is much better among gays than it is among heterosexuals. Because you've always been that way—you haven't expected anyone to take care of you except yourself. You've cut yourself off from Mama and Poppa and you have no children to look to, and you'd bloody well better take care of yourself" (Kimmel, 1979–1980:144).

Francher and Henkin (1973:673) concluded that the homosexual male experienced a life crisis centering around his sexual identity; adjustment to this identity results in a different order of aging from that experienced by his heterosexual counterpart. The authors suggest that "a life style wherein family responsibilities are absent may not present to the homosexual the same sense of traumatic loss so commonly felt by heterosexual men. In addition, we suggest that a self-interested and narcissistic life pattern may offer supplementary supports for coping with the problems of role loss, declining sexuality, and 'disengagement.' "

Legal Difficulties in Homosexual Life

One of the difficulties faced by older gays and lesbians is the absence of a well-developed legal infrastructure giving them rights as couples (Fenwick, 1978; Harry, 1979). Since they cannot legally be recognized as married in any state in the United States, they are not defined as kin, and when one partner is hospitalized, institutionalized, or dies, the other partner faces problems that a heterosexual partner would not. Intensive care units in hospitals, for example, limit a critically ill person's visitors to "family," which often effectively shuts out a gay or lesbian person's long-term partner, but allows in family members (Berger, 1982). In addition to lack of bereavement counseling (Berger, 1982; Dulaney and Kelly, 1982), Pogoncheff (1979) has indicated that nursing care in hospitals can be adversely affected if personnel are aware of an individual's homosexuality. Family members may legally intervene to arrange an ill or dying gay person's affairs, whereas that individual's partner may not. Widows' benefits, such as Social Security, workman's compensation, and certain pension plans, are not available to survivors of homosexual long-term relationships. "Legal and inheritance problems are often especially significant, both in planning one's estate and in the surviving lover's actual inheritance of the intended property" (Kimmel, 1978: 127). However, in San Francisco recently, the city awarded survivor's benefits to a homosexual whose partner was killed, and proposed an ordinance which would give unmarried partners of all city employees—regardless of their sexual preferences—the same health and other spousal benefits (*Newsweek*, December 13, 1982:74). In addition, a New York appeals court ruled recently that a gay man of 32 could adopt his partner, aged 43, as his son, in order to qualify as "family" so that they could continue to occupy their New York apartment when it became a cooperative. The court said that "the best definition of a family is a continuing relationship of love and care, and an assumption of responsibility for some other person" (*Miami Herald*, July 9, 1982:12A). These may be precedent-setting decisions that might more positively affect the legal status of elderly homosexuals in the future.

Correlates of Life Satisfaction

Just as the aging heterosexual's life satisfaction depends to a great extent on his adjustment as a youth and his life-style and support system, so does that of the aging homosexual. Bell and Weinberg, in their definitive study, *Homosexualities* (1978), found five different life-styles which appeared to correlate with the individual's life satisfaction. They found that the "Close Coupled" resembled marriages and involved a strong emotional commitment on the part of both partners. Both the men and the women were the happiest of all life-style groups. Twenty-eight percent of lesbians and 10 percent of gay men were living as Close Couples. Eighteen percent of males and 17 percent of females lived in "Open Couples"; there was less commitment, and both members had clandestine outside affairs. These were not as well adjusted as the Close Couples, but compared with heterosexual respondents in their activities and psychological states. "Functionals" (15 percent of males and 10 percent of females) were compared to "swinging singles"; they lived alone and had a large number of sexual partners. They were sociable and their adjustment was second only to the Close Coupled. "Dysfunctionals" (12 percent of males, 5 percent of females) resembled the Functionals in that they lived alone and had many sexual partners. However, they were prone to psychological, social, and sexual problems, and found it difficult to form intimate relationships. The "Asexuals" (16 percent of males and 11 percent of females) lived alone and had infrequent sexual contacts; their most prominent characteristic was their lack of involvement with others. These categories appear to be of some value; future research on the aged homosexual might utilize these typologies in place of the more conventional categories of "married," "single," and so on. However, this categorization should not over-shadow the major factors in life satisfaction—the acceptance of self as a homo-sexual and a benign societal response to this disclosure.

Gender Differences

Life-style, self-concept, and support systems, then, appear to be important variables in differentiating between older homosexuals; gender is another. Both male and female homosexuals have usually been raised as heterosexuals and socialized as youngsters into the traditional male and female roles. A number of investigators have theorized that some of the differences in sexual patterns as well as life-style of both the young and the elderly are based on these gender differences. Thus, in Bell and Weinberg's study (1978), 75 percent of white males reported having had more than 100 different sexual partners over their lifetimes, whereas 2 percent of the white women reported these frequencies. Close to half of the males (43 percent) had had 500 partners, compared to none for females; 28 percent of male homosexuals reported 1,000 partners or more. Furthermore, of the Close Coupled studied, there were almost three times as many women as men represented. Raphael and Robinson (1981:16) stated that, for lesbians, "serial monogamy was the dominant life pattern." Minnigerode and Adelman (1978), in comparing elderly homosexual women and men, found that, throughout their lives, sex had a higher priority for men than for women. The males frequently viewed their homosexuality in terms of sexual activity, whereas the women viewed it in terms of interpersonal relationships. In fact, one writer claims that the use of sex as a casual recreational activity is so central to the male homosexual experience, that "love relationships are likely to survive only if they are sexually non-exclusive" (Suppe, 1981:77).

These statistics can be explained by the divergent gender socialization that existed in our society at the time these older people were socialized. The sexual script for males, both heterosexual and homosexual, was to view sex as recreation and conquest; it could be separated from emotional and affectional commitments. While male heterosexuals have had the same script, they interacted with women who had been socialized to view sex in the context of an emotional relationship involving love, commitment, and faithfulness; these acted as a constraint on their sexual activity in terms of number of partners. The male homosexual has had no such constraints. Lesbians, on the other hand, engage in a minimal amount of cruising, one-night stands, and sexual encounters in public places (Fleming and Washburne, 1977); are generally not promiscuous; and focus more on long-term emotional relationships (Riddle and Morin, 1977; Sage, 1975). In fact, the value a woman places on intimate relations appears to be similar whether her partner is male or female. Almvig (1982:93) states that

because lesbians are first raised as little girls to be heterosexual women, roles are defined as nurturing and tasks are defined as taking care of the family no matter what happens.

The longevity of a relationship is ingrained as a supreme value. It is no wonder that once a lesbian relationship is firm, both women, who have been reared according to similar cultural values, work to keep the relationship together until the death of a spouse or until unreasonable constraints are put on the relationship.

It appears that gender differences exert a greater influence on a relationship than does sexual orientation. As mentioned previously, in seeking for new terminology many lesbians reject being referred to as part of the gay community because they perceive many differences between homosexual men and women as a group. Adelman (1980) quotes an anonymous article by a lesbian who avers that gay men oppress women as much as do straight men; there are still male and female concerns to be dealt with in differentiating homosexuals. The preferred terminology as reflected in recent literature appears to be "gay" for males and "lesbian" for females.

THE CONSEQUENCES OF STIGMATIZATION

A major problem unique to the elderly homosexual is a result of stigmatization of homosexuality by the society; this has made the homosexual highly vulnerable to discrimination. Goffman (1963:5) has defined the sociological features found in stigma as follows: "An individual who might have been received easily in ordinary social intercourse possesses a trait that can obtrude itself upon attention and turn those of us whom he meets away from him, breaking the claim that his other attributes have on us." The public's continuing bias against homosexuals can be seen in a recent poll (National Opinion Research Center, 1982) where 70 percent of the respondents regarded sex between the same sexed persons as "always wrong." In another survey of public attitudes, Levitt and Klassen (1974) indicated that over two-thirds of the respondents would prohibit the employment of homosexuals as medical doctors and government officials, while over three-quarters believed that they should not be allowed to work as judges, teachers, or ministers. In a more recent survey of sociologists, the overwhelming majority (63 percent) of chairpersons and heads of sociology departments reported that "hiring a known homosexual would produce serious problems or that it just could not be done" (ASA Footnotes, 1982:1); 84 percent reported this in regard to hiring gay rights' activitists. Kimmel (1979:152) has spoken of the "life-long pattern of secrecy, hiding, covering-up and leading a double life that characterizes some older gay persons. This involves not only the perception of vulnerability, but also an internalization of the social stigma about homosexuals." Kimmel (1979:151) has singled out the themes of secrecy, anger, and vulnerability "to special threats of exposure, loss of job, social stigma, arrest or physical violence" as being significant for all gays. For older gays they are even more important, he believes, since they have suffered more oppression, and for a longer period of time, than have their younger counterparts.

An important consequence of stigmatization has been the rise of self-help organizations. Older homosexuals who were active before gay liberation had two national organizations that were not age-specific to which they might relate—the Mattachine Society and later the Daughters of Bilitis. In recent years a number of self-help organizations for older homosexuals have been reported, none of which is yet national in scope. Among the local ones that are presently functioning are the Society for Senior Gay and Lesbian Citizens, with offices in Hollywood and Los Angeles; the G4O Plus Club in San Francisco; Slightly Older Lesbians in Berkeley; and Senior Action in a Gay Environment, with headquarters in New York City. There is a National Association of Lesbian and Gay Gerontologists in San Francisco. In addition to studying the whole range of subjects dealing with the elderly, a number of its members are currently conducting research on elderly lesbians and gays. They have rendered an important service in publishing an updated bibliography on lesbian and gay aging (Catalano et al., 1982).

CONCLUSIONS

Regardless of one's personal orientations toward homosexuality, or of the acceptance or rejection of homosexuality that exists in the society at a given moment, it is important to codify and present whatever knowledge we currently have concerning the aging homosexual. By doing so we expand our substantive knowledge and dispel some of our own stereotypes, and do the same for the population at large. We also perform this function for the elderly homosexuals, who as participants in their culture have internalized many of the negative stereotypes and images shared by society at large. In addition, Kimmel (1977a, 1978, 1979–1980) has suggested that young homosexuals of both sexes seldom have role models whom they can emulate in the same way as young heterosexuals have parents and grandparents to whose life-styles they can relate. As Kimmel has pointed out, since young homosexuals do not have aging homosexuals with whom to identify, they tend to fear old age, incorporating the same myths about aging and the same stereotypes about the aged homosexual as does the general public, thus giving them a doubly negative view of their eventual destiny.

While our contemporary data base is relatively rudimentary in terms of well-validated research based on rigorous methodology, a picture begins to emerge concerning elderly homosexuals. While it is not definitive, this overview incorporates our present day knowledge and allows us to draw a few tentative conclusions. For the elderly homosexual, it appears that socialization processes for males and females supersede questions of sexual preference; gender differences remain pronounced among elderly lesbians and gays. Being creatures of their culture also accounts for the homosexuals' internalization of negative values concerning themselves as homosexuals, as well as older persons; they see their own old age as a case of double jeopardy. Research on gay and lesbian elderly dispels this myth, with reports of friendship support systems and surrogate families. Life-style also appears to be an important determinant of adjustment, just as it is for heterosexuals. Of the five life-styles described by Bell and Weinberg

(1978), those who lived as Close Couples showed the highest level of happiness and adjustment; one might speculate that these would in turn make the best adjusted elderly homosexuals. A major problem faced by elderly homosexuals all through their lives is that of stigmatization and consequent discrimination.

Attitudes toward homosexuality have undergone a great deal of liberalization in recent years. There are still many elderly homosexuals who have not come out; their numbers are impossible to estimate. However, there is a heightened awareness of homosexuals' needs and rights, both among homosexuals and among the greater society. In major cities, age-graded organizations exist which are designed to respond to those needs—from the need to meet others of their own age in a benign community-center type of environment which might be common to all elderly, to the need to allow the partner of a gay nursing home resident visiting rights usually denied anyone but family members. Eventually, we hope to be able to describe fully which aspects of the aging process for the elderly homosexual are functions of his or her choice of life-style, and which are concomitants of aging for everyone whose life chances they share.

ORGANIZATIONS FOR SENIOR GAYS AND LESBIANS

G Forty Plus
P.O. Box 6741
San Francisco, CA 94101

The National Association of Lesbian and Gay Gerontologists
1290 Sutter Street, Suite 8
San Francisco, CA 94109

National Gay Task Force
80 Fifth Avenue
New York, NY 10011

Senior Action in a Gay Environment
208 West 13th Street
New York, NY 10011

Slightly Older Lesbians
2329 San Pablo Avenue
Berkeley, CA 94701

The Society for Senior Gay and Lesbian Citizens
    (also known as Project Rainbow)
255 S. Hill Street
Los Angeles, CA 90012
    and
1213 N. Highland Avenue 201
Hollywood, CA 90028

For an extensive list of homosexual organizations, you may write for a copy of GaYellow Pages, published by Renaissance House, Box 292 Village Station, New York, N.Y. 10014.

REFERENCES

Adelman, M.R. Adjustment to aging and styles of being gay: A study of elderly gay men and lesbians. Ph.D. diss., Wright Institute, Berkeley, Calif., 1980.

Almvig, G. The invisible minority: Aging and lesbians. Master's thesis, New School for Social Research, New York, 1982.

ASA Footnotes, 10 December 1982, 1.

Bell, A.P., and Weinberg, M.A. *Homosexualities: A study of diversity among men and women.* Simon and Schuster, New York, 1978.

Berger, R. The unseen minority: Older gays and lesbians. *Social Work*, 1982, *27*, 236–242.

Catalano, D.J.; Raphael, S.M.; and Robinson, M.K. *Bibliography: Lesbian and gay aging.* National Association of Lesbian and Gay Gerontologists, San Francisco, 1982.

Christenson, V., and Johnson, A.B. Sexual patterns in a group of older never married women. *Journal of Geriatric Psychiatry*, 1973, *6*, 80–89.

Dank, B. Coming out in the gay world. *Psychiatry*, 1971, *34*, 180–197.

Dressel, P., and Avant, R. Neogamy and older persons. *Alternative Lifestyles*, February 1978, 13–36.

Dulaney, D., and Kelly, J. Improving services to gay and lesbian clients. *Social Work*, 1982, *27*, 178–183.

Fenwick, R.D. *The advocate guide to gay health.* Dutton, New York, 1978.

Fleming, J.B., and Washburne, C.K. *For better, for worse.* Charles Scribner's Sons, New York, 1977.

Francher, J.S., and Henkin, J. The menopausal queen: Adjustment to aging and the male homosexual. *American Journal of Orthopsychiatry*, 1973, *43*, 670–674.

Friend, R.A. Gaying: Adjustment and the older gay male. *Alternative Lifestyles*, 1980, *3*, 231–248.

Goffman, E. *Stigma: Notes on the management of spoiled identity.* Prentice-Hall, Englewood Cliffs, N.J., 1963.

Harry, J. The marital liaisons of gay men. *Family Coordinator*, October 1979, 622–629.

Humphrys, L. *Tearoom trade: Impersonal sex in public places.* Aldine, Chicago, 1970.

———. Exodus and identity: The emerging gay culture. In M.P. Levine (Ed.), *Gay men: The sociology of male homosexuality.* Harper and Row, New York, 1979.

Kelly, J.J. *Brothers and brothers: The gay man's adaptation to aging.* Ph.D. diss., Brandeis University, Waltham, Mass., 1974.

———. The aging male homosexual: Myth and reality. *Gerontologist*, 1977, *17*, 328–332.

———. Homosexuality and aging. In J. Marmor (Ed.), *Multiple roots of homosexual behavior.* Basic Books, New York, 1980.

Kimmel, D.C. Patterns of aging among gay men. *Christopher Street*, January 1977a, 28–31.

———. Psychotherapy and the older gay man. *Journal of Psychotherapy: Theory, Research and Practice*, 1977b, *14*, 386–393.

————. Adult development and aging: A gay perspective. *Journal of Social Issues*, 1978, *34*, 113–130.

————. Adjustments to aging among gay men. In B. Berzon and R. Leighton (Eds.), *Positively gay*. Celestial Arts, Millbrae, Calif., 1979.

————. Life-history interviews of aging gay men. *International Journal of Aging and Human Development*, 1979–1980, *10*, 239–248.

Kinsey, A.C.; Pomeroy, W.B.; and Martin, C.E *Sexual behavior in the human male*. W.B. Saunders, Philadelphia, 1948.

Laner, M.R. Growing older male: Heterosexual and homosexual. *Gerontologist*, 1978, *18*, 496–501.

Levitt, E., and Klassen, A. Public attitudes toward homosexuality: Part of the 1970 national survey by the Institute for Sex Research. *Journal of Homosexuality*, 1974, *1*, 29–43.

Marmor, J. Overview: The multiple roots of homosexual behavior. In J. Marmor (Ed.), *Homosexual Behavior: A Modern Reappraisal*. Basic Books, New York, 1980.

Martin, D., and Lyon, P. The older lesbian. In B. Berzon and R. Leighton (Eds.), *Positively gay*. Celestial Arts, Millbrae, Calif., 1979.

Melville, K. *Marriage and family today*. Random House, New York, 1982.

Miami Herald, July 9, 1982.

Miller, B. Gay fathers and their children. *Family Coordinator*, October 1979, 544–552.

Minnigerode, F. Age status labeling in homosexual men. *Journal of Homosexuality*, 1976, *1*, 273–276.

Minnigerode, F.A., and Adelman, M.A. Elderly homosexual women and men: Report on a pilot study. *Family Coordinator*, 1978, *27*, 451–456.

National Opinion Research Center (NORC). *General social surveys, 1972–1982: Cumulative codebook*. NORC, University of Chicago, 1982.

Newsweek, December 13, 1982, 74.

Pogoncheff, E. The gay patient: What not to do. *RN Magazine*, April 1979, 46–49.

Raphael, S. Coming out: The emergence of the lesbian movement. Ph.D. diss., Case Western Reserve University, Cleveland, Ohio, 1974.

Raphael, S., and Robinson, M. The older lesbian: Love relationships and friendship patterns. *Alternative Lifestyles*, 1980, *3*, 207–229.

————. Lesbians and gay men in later life. *Generations*, 1981, *6*, 19–21.

Riddle, D., and Morin, S. Removing the stigma: Data from individuals. *American Psychological Association Monitor*, November, 1977.

Rodgers, W.L. Estimable functions of age, period, and cohort effects. *American Sociological Review*, 1982, *7*, 774–787.

Sage, W. Inside the colossal closet. *Human Behavior*, August 1975, 16–23.

Suppe, F. The Bell and Weinberg study: Future priorities for research on homosexuality. *Journal of Homosexuality*, 1981, *6*, 69–97.

Tripp, C.A. *The homosexual matrix*. McGraw–Hill, New York, 1975.

Warren, C. *Identity and community in the gay world*. Wiley, New York, 1974.

Weinberg, M.A., and Williams, C.T. *Male homosexuals: Their problems and adaptation*. Oxford University Press, New York, 1974.

Wolf, D.G. Close friendship patterns of older lesbians. Paper presented at the American Gerontological Society Meeting, Dallas, November 1978.

21

THE INSTITUTIONALIZED

LINDA K. GEORGE

For many of us, the terms "nursing home" and "long-term care facility" bring to mind images of frail, dependent older people. There is a lot of truth to this perception: the vast majority of institutional residents in our society are age 65 and older and are in poor physical or mental health. A note of caution is necessary, however. Although most institutionalized adults are age 65 or older, only a small proportion of older adults are in institutions. For example, in 1977 (the most recent year for which detailed information is available), only 4.8 percent of Americans age 65 and older were residents of long-term care facilities (National Center for Health Statistics [hereafter cited as NCHS], 1979). Furthermore, some of those in retirement and rest homes are not frail or disabled, but choose to live there for companionship, freedom from household chores, and so forth.

This chapter begins with an overview of the institutionalized population, including rates of institutionalization. The next topic reviewed is the history of institutional care for the elderly in the United States. Other topics considered include descriptions of the types of institutions in which older people reside; characteristics of the institutional population; predictors of institutionalization; effects of institutionalization; and policy issues associated with institutional care.

THE NUMBERS GAME

It has been said that statistics are an excellent tool for use in making falsehoods appear as facts. Although this is an unfortunate statement in that scientists routinely use statistics to present information in a convenient and comprehensible manner, it is true that statistics can be misleading unless they are presented and interpreted carefully. Information about the institutionalized elderly illustrates both the confusions and clarifications involved in the use of statistics.

As noted above, almost 5 percent of the older population reside in long-term care facilities. Although this is a true statement, it does not provide the full picture with regard to the probability that an older person will enter a long-term care facility sometime during later life. Although the amount of time that older people reside in nursing homes and long-term care facilities varies widely, there is a great deal of movement in and out of institutions. Each year, more than 1 million older persons are discharged from long-term care institutions, almost evenly divided among discharges to the community, transfers to other health facilities, and deaths (NCHS, 1979). The statistic that about 5 percent of the elderly are in institutions is a cross-sectional snapshot of the institutional population that inevitably misses the implications of the substantial movement in and out of long-term care facilities.

Two kinds of studies have helped to supplement cross-sectional snapshots of the institutionalized population. In one type of study, a group of older persons is followed longitudinally (or over time). It then is possible to see how many of the original group enter long-term facilities during the study. Palmore (1976) performed such a study and reports that about 20 percent of the elderly become institutionalized for at least a short period of time. Another type of study is based on examination of the death certificates of older adults from a specific geographical area. Because death certificates include information about place of death, it is possible to see what proportion of deaths occur in long-term care facilities. Available studies using this approach estimate that 20–28 percent of all deaths of older people occur in long-term care facilities (Ingram and Barry, 1977; Kastenbaum and Candy, 1973). Together, then, these two types of studies suggest that at least 20–28 percent of the older population are institutionalized some time during later life and that long-term facilities often are the older person's last residence.

NURSING HOMES IN HISTORICAL CONTEXT

Nursing homes are relatively new social innovations. Until the late 1930s and early 1940s, there were few nursing homes in the United States. The care of dependent elderly people was provided by families, with the exception of a few very isolated older persons who were relegated to the back wards of state and county institutions. As well as being an instrumental force in the development of retirement as we now know it, the Social Security Act of 1935 provided states with matching funds for the development of nursing homes and other facilities for the needy elderly. These beginning efforts in long-term care by the federal government were escalated during the 1950s with the initiation of Old Age Assistance (OAA) programs and during the 1960s with the Kerr-Mills amendments to the Social Security Act (Hickey, 1980).

Unquestionably, however, the largest impetus to the nursing home industry in this society was the enactment of Medicare and Medicaid in 1965. Medicare and Medicaid are Titles XVIII and XIX of the Social Security Act, respectively. Medicare operates as a health insurance program for people age 65 and older, providing universal hospital coverage and voluntary supplemental medical insurance. Like the private health insurance plans typical for younger people, Medicare includes limits on the types and amounts of services received and requires coinsurance and deductibles from recipients. In spite of the substantial benefits that Medicare has brought to older people, it covers only about 45 percent of the medical expenses sustained by the older population. Medicare includes stringent requirements concerning reimbursement for institutional care, including the requirement that hospitalization precede admission to a long-term care facility; limits upon the amount of institutional care that will be reimbursed; and limits upon the types of services reimbursed. Moreover, long-term care facilities must obtain licenses certifying them for Medicare reimbursement. The licensing requirements cover features such as safety and medical equipment, standards of sanitation, meal preparation standards, and staffing patterns.

Medicaid is a comprehensive health care reimbursement program for the poor of all ages. Low income and the absence of other financial resources are the cornerstones of Medicaid eligibility. Medicaid pays for a larger range of services than Medicare and does not include the time limits, coinsurance, and deductibles characteristic of Medicare. Medicaid is funded jointly by federal and state funds; consequently, there are some variations from state to state in eligibility requirements and the services provided. Like Medicare, Medicaid reimbursement for institutional care is limited to those facilities that have been certified as meeting the requirements for Medicaid reimbursement.

As might be expected, the enactment of Medicare and Medicaid dramatically increased the utilization of nursing homes and other long-term care facilities. The growth of the nursing home industry has been further fueled by the steady growth of the older population.

TYPES OF INSTITUTIONS

The U.S. Bureau of the Census defines ''institutions'' as group quarters housing six or more residents and providing congregate meals. It is important to realize that the term ''long-term care institution'' subsumes a variety of types of institutions with differing characteristics, populations, and costs. The specific types of institutions that have evolved largely reflect the types of care that Medicare and Medicaid are willing to reimburse. The terms used to describe the various types of long-term care facilities vary somewhat from state to state, although the essential characteristics are quite similar across all geographic regions. For our purposes here, we will use the terms most closely identified with federal reimbursement policies.

Skilled nursing facilities (SNFs) provide the most intensive level of medical care available in long-term facilities. The services provided by SNFs include twenty-four hour nursing service, a formal treatment plan for each patient, and supervised dietary and medical care. It is assumed that skilled nursing care typically will be of short-term duration, provided during convalescence from an illness episode. This assumption is translated into limited time coverage of skilled nursing care under Medicare. In fact, however, many older people have long-term needs for intensive nursing/medical care. In such cases, when Medicare benefits are exhausted, patients must either pay for their skilled nursing care or else meet the eligibility requirements for Medicaid reimbursement.

Intermediate care facilities (ICFs) provide less intense medical care than SNFs. In essence, ICFs provide a combination of nursing and personal care services. Intermediate care often is viewed as a long-term arrangement for those older persons who suffer chronic impairments precluding independent living in the community. Medicare does not cover the costs of intermediate care; conse-quently, most intermediate care is paid for via Medicaid and patients' personal resources. As one would expect, however, intermediate care is considerably less expensive than skilled nursing care.

Domiciliary care homes (often called retirement homes or rest homes) provide primarily custodial care for residents, but also provide limited personal care services. Nursing and medical services are not provided in domiciliary care homes. Such facilities are highly appropriate residential settings for those older persons with stable chronic impairments in functional ability, but who do not require supervised medical or nursing assistance. Domiciliary homes should not be confused with boarding homes or rooming houses. The latter provide neither custodial care nor personal care services. Because domiciliary care homes are not oriented toward the management or treatment of medical problems, they are not covered by Medicare and Medicaid reimbursement policies, although some state and local programs will pay for domiciliary care received by needy clients. Domiciliary care is less expensive than either skilled or intermediate care.

It should be noted that a long-term care facility may offer multiple levels of care. For example, the same institution may offer both intermediate and skilled nursing care. Medicare certification rules concerning levels of care were liber-alized in the 1972 amendments to the Social Security Act. Since the enactment of those amendments, the number of long-term facilities offering multiple levels of care has increased dramatically. There is no question that the liberalization of these rules has resulted in improved quality of care for older institutional residents. Residents of many homes now can remain in the same facility as their conditions improve or deteriorate; whereas they previously would have had to be transferred to other facilities in order to obtain different levels of care.

Public mental hospitals are a final type of long-term care facility that merits discussion. Historically, public mental hospitals have been repositories for large numbers of impaired older persons. In some cases, the older residents of such institutions were long-term patients who had entered the institutions as children or young adults and had grown old in the mental hospitals. In other cases, the older residents were recent admissions who were placed in the facilities because of mental (and even physical) illnesses that developed during later life. Two historical events have resulted in a significantly smaller number of older residents in public mental hospitals.

First, and in a rather gradual manner, the establishment of Medicare and

Medicaid, as well as the concomitant growth in the number of available nursing home beds, resulted in fewer new admissions of older persons to mental hospitals. Prior to the availability of nursing homes, state mental hospitals often provided the only available institutional beds for impaired older adults who could no longer live independently in the community.

Second, and in a more dramatic manner, the deinstitutionalization movement of the late 1960s and early 1970s resulted in the mass discharge of large numbers of long-term residents of public mental hospitals. Many of those discharged were impaired older adults. Although the deinstitutionalization movement was intended as a method of permitting larger numbers of impaired persons to reside in the community (with the aid of appropriate social services), the effects of this trend were not uniformly positive. Many former mental patients have been unable to obtain the integrated social services needed to permit stable community lifestyles. There now is considerable evidence that the deinstitutionalized older population has largely been absorbed into ICFs and domiciliary care homes (Sherwood and Mor, 1980). Although such residential settings can provide custodial and personal care services, most of these institutions do not provide mental health services. Consequently, many deinstitutionalized elderly do not receive the types of services most relevant to their impairments. At any rate, public mental hospitals currently house less than 1 percent of the institutionalized elderly—and few older persons are in such facilities on a long-term basis.

The remainder of this chapter addresses the characteristics of persons in long-term care facilities exclusive of public mental hospitals. In terms of the types of institutions in which the institutionalized population resides, recent data suggest that about 19 percent are in SNFs, about 24 percent reside in facilities offering both skilled and intermediate care, about 32 percent are in ICFs, and about 25 percent are in domiciliary care homes (NCHS, 1979).

CHARACTERISTICS OF THE INSTITUTIONALIZED AGED

Most of the information presented below was obtained from the 1977 National Nursing Home Survey, conducted by the National Center for Health Statistics (NCHS, 1979). NCHS conducts these national surveys on a periodic basis and the information generated is invaluable for understanding the characteristics of the institutionalized population. The 1977 survey covered 1,303,100 nursing home residents in 18,900 long-term care facilities.

Age

The vast majority of institutionalized persons are older adults (86.4 percent are age 65 and older). Furthermore, the risk of institutionalization increases sharply after age 65. As previously noted, 4.8 percent of the population age 65 and older are residents of long-term care facilities. The comparable percentage for the 75 and older population is 10.3 percent, and 21.6 percent of the population age 85 and older are residents of institutions. Thus, rates of institutionalization increase sharply with advancing age.

Sex

The vast majority of institutional residents (about 71 percent) are women. Several factors contribute to this sex differential. First, women live longer, on average, than men. In the United States in general, there are only 72 men per 100 women in the over 65 population. Thus, there are simply many more women than men at advanced ages. Second, although women live longer than men, they are nonetheless more likely to suffer multiple chronic conditions that put them at greater risk of institutionalization (General Accounting Office, 1977). Third, and most important, women are much more likely to be unmarried than are older men. Absence of a spouse or other caretaker is a major factor leading to institutionalization.

Marital Status

Marital status is closely related to the likelihood of institutionalization, with the unmarried especially likely to be placed in a long-term care facility. In 1977, only 11.9 percent of the nursing home population were married, compared to 57.6 percent of the U.S. population age 65 and older. In contrast, 62.3 percent were widowed, 6.7 percent were divorced or separated, and 19.1 percent had never married. The widowed comprise the majority of the institutional population. Because women typically outlive their husbands, these marital status differences help to explain the gender differences among the institutionalized aged.

Race

The vast majority of institutional residents (92.2 percent) are white, compared to 84 percent of the general U.S. population. Only 6.2 percent are black; 1.1 percent are Hispanic; and less than half a percent each are Native American (American Indian or Eskimo) or of Asian origin. This underrepresentation of minority groups among the institutionalized is difficult to understand. Certainly they do not reflect differences in the health and functioning of older ethnic group members. Indeed, available evidence suggests that minority group members are, on average, more impaired than older whites (General Accounting Office, 1977; 1979). Although it is certainly true that minority elderly tend to have significantly lower incomes and economic resources than older whites, these differences do not seem to adequately explain the differences in rates of institutionalization. Medicare, and especially Medicaid, have provided sufficient resources that economically deprived older adults typically can obtain institutional care. Instead, the differences in rates of institutionalization appear to reflect subcultural differences in the willingness to institutionalize older persons and discrimination against minority aged. Older members of minority groups are more likely to remain in the community, cared for by family members and other social support groups, regardless of their level of impairment (Eribes and Bradley-Rawls, 1978). Part of the reason for the underrepresentation of minority groups in long-term care facilities is discrimination in admission policies—either official or unofficial.

Primary Diagnosis

Most residents of long-term care facilities suffer one or more chronic illnesses that severely impair their ability to care for themselves. The National Nursing Home Survey obtains information about the primary diagnosis of long-term care residents. In 1977, 39.7 percent of the nursing home population had a primary diagnosis of circulatory system disease (including congestive heart failure, arteriosclerosis, hypertension, stroke, heart attack, and ischemic heart disease). An additional 20.4 percent had a primary diagnosis of mental disorder (including senile psychosis, other psychoses, chronic brain syndromes, senility without psychosis, mental retardation, and alcoholism). The remaining one-third of the long-term care residents had a variety of other primary diagnoses, including arthritis and rheumatism, diseases of the nervous system, bone fractures, cancer, and diseases of the respiratory and digestive systems. Although information about primary diagnosis is important, it must be interpreted with caution. The vast majority of nursing home residents suffer multiple illnesses; thus, primary diagnosis represents only part of the medical burden experienced by institutional residents.

Functional Status

Functional status refers to the individual's ability to perform activities that are essential to independent living and self-care. Most of us take our ability to perform activities such as bathing, dressing, and eating for granted. Very few institutional residents can make such assumptions. The 1977 National Nursing Home Survey indicates the following levels of functional impairment for various activities of daily living: 36.3 percent of the nursing home population required assistance in bathing; 69.4 percent required assistance in dressing; 52.5 percent required assistance in using the toilet; 66.1 percent could walk only with assistance or were bedfast; 45.3 percent could not control their bladders or bowels; and 32.6 percent required assistance in eating. As these statistics indicate, the majority of institutional residents are highly impaired in terms of activities of daily living. Although a portion of these functional limitations are temporary or reversible, the majority represent long-term functional impairments.

The available information about diagnoses, multiple chronic conditions, and functional limitations makes an important point. The vast majority of institutional residents are incapable of independent living in the community. The common stereotype of older people being relegated to institutions simply because they are old is not supported by available data about the characteristics of nursing home residents. Although there probably are individuals in institutions who are potentially capable of living in less restricted environments, such cases are relatively rare.

PREDICTORS OF INSTITUTIONALIZATION

Common sense, as well as various social science theories, suggests that the best predictor of institutionalization should be health status. That is, in an equitable health care system, one would hope that the best predictor of nursing home utilization would be need for such service-rich environments. As we already have seen, the vast majority of nursing home residents are in fact medically and functionally impaired. On the basis of such information, it is tempting to assume that health status and medical need are indeed the best predictors of institutionalization. There is another factor, however, that needs to be taken into account. Available evidence suggests that for every impaired older person residing in a long-term care facility, there are at least two—and perhaps as many as five— equally impaired older persons who are residing in the community (Duke Center for the Study of Aging, 1978; General Accounting Office, 1979). Given this situation, it is obvious that poor physical health and medical need do not, by themselves, constitute a sufficient explanation for institutionalization. The question of interest thus becomes, What are the factors that predict who among the impaired elderly enters a long-term care facility?

Before addressing that question, it is important to distinguish among three groups of long-term care residents. The members of one group suffer relatively temporary conditions and are discharged from the long-term care facility as their health and functional status improve. Examples of such situations include after-hospital care and recovery from a fractured hip. In a recent analysis of the National Nursing Home Survey, Liu and Manton report that 46 percent of the 1976 admissions to long-term care facilities were discharged by the end of the year (1983). Another group of long-term care residents comprises those who enter long-term care facilities in very serious condition and who die shortly after admission. A minority, but a significant minority, of nursing home admissions fall into this category. Indeed, in one study, 14 percent of the admissions to a nursing home died within 24 hours (Ingram and Barry, 1977). One of the reasons that seriously ill older persons are transferred from hospitals to nursing homes is that Medicare places stringent limitations on the amount of coverage for inpatient hospitalization. Once an individual has exhausted his or her Medicare hospital benefits, there is great pressure to move the individual to a nursing home or other facility as quickly as possible. The third group of nursing home residents comprises those that enter long-term care facilities with one or more chronic conditions and who stay there for long periods of time.

Cross-sectional studies pose inherent limitations in terms of understanding length of stay. Although such studies can obtain information about the duration of time between admission and the survey, the ultimate length of stay cannot be determined. The National Nursing Home Survey is cross-sectional. In that survey, nursing home residents exhibited the following distribution of length of stay: 14.5 percent had been in long-term care facilities for less than three months; 21.9 percent had been residents for three to eleven months; 32.8 percent had been residents for one to three years; and 30.8 percent had been residents for more than three years. Another method of assessing distributions of length of stay in institutions is to examine discharges. In this way, one can observe the total duration of residence for a group of patients who have completed their stays. In 1977, 1,117,500 patients were discharged from nursing homes (NCHS, 1979). Of those discharges, about 35 percent of the residents had died, about 36 percent were transferred to other health facilities, and about 29 percent were discharged to the community. Also interesting, of the discharges due to death of the patient, fully 25 percent died within one month of admission. These figures document the three types of nursing home residents previously described: short-term convalescent patients who are discharged to the community, short-term seriously ill patients who die shortly after admission, and a larger long-term resident population.

The predictors of the two short-term patient groups are relatively clear and straightforward. For the short-term convalescent group, admission to a long-term care facility is predicted by an acute care episode requiring temporary nursing care and supervision. For the short-term group that dies shortly after admission, the nursing home serves as a facility where seriously ill older persons can receive terminal nursing care. It is the long-term residents that require careful scrutiny in terms of the predictors of institutionalization. It is this group that lives in institutions while a larger number of equally impaired older adults manages to maintain community living. Thus, it is the long-term residents for whom the predictors of institutionalization require further clarification.

There now is considerable evidence that the factor that best distinguishes long-term nursing home residents from equally impaired older community residents is the absence of a caretaker or social support network among the institutionalized. Impaired older adults are able to remain in the community if there are caretakers available to provide nursing, personal care, and custodial services. In the absence of such caretakers, independent living is precluded and the impaired older adult must be placed in an institutional environment where nursing, personal care, and custodial services can be obtained from paid personnel. This difference in the availability of social support also helps to explain many of the demographic characteristics associated with institutionalization. Old age, and especially advanced ages, are associated with both decreased availability of social support and increased risk of institutionalization. At advanced ages, widowhood is more likely, thus precluding caretaking from one's spouse, and one's children are themselves likely to be old and, perhaps, physically impaired. Older women are especially likely to be widowed and to find themselves without caretakers. Thus, although physical illness and impairment constitute a major factor associated with institutionalization, social support is the key factor determining which of the impaired elderly enter long-term care facilities.

THE EFFECTS OF INSTITUTIONALIZATION

It is very difficult to determine the effects of institutionalization upon older people. First, in order to examine the impact of institutionalization, one must examine individuals before and after they enter the long-term care facility in order to observe the changes that occur during the institutionalization process. Second, one must compare those people who become institutionalized with community residents who are similar to those who enter long-term care facilities. Since most community residents are in better health than those persons who are admitted to nursing homes it would not be fair to compare typical community-dwelling elderly with nursing home residents. Rather, we want to compare older people who are alike in every way except where they live. This kind of comparison is very difficult to achieve and no previous studies include such comparisons. The few longitudinal studies available, however, will be briefly reviewed.

Morris (1975) examined changes in morale over a one-year period among older persons who had been admitted to a nursing home. The results indicated that morale typically increased over the one-year period. Morris also examined the relationship between morale and the appropriateness of the institutional placement (as judged by clinical raters). Those persons who had been placed in an environment that provided appropriate services experienced increases in morale; this pattern was not true for the smaller number of individuals who were judged to have inappropriate institutional placements. This study is quite limited in that only one dimension of well-being is examined and we lack information about residents' levels of morale prior to institutionalization. This study is important, however, in that it demonstrates that appropriateness of placement is an important variable in the effects of institutionalization upon well-being.

The works of Lieberman and Tobin (Lieberman, 1975; Tobin and Lieberman, 1976) constitute the major available longitudinal examination of the impact of institutionalization upon well-being. In order to isolate the effects of institutionalization itself, three samples were measured over time: (1) a relocation sample that was measured before (while on a waiting list) and after admission to a nursing home; (2) an institutional sample of persons who had been in nursing homes for one to three years; and (3) a community sample of older persons who remained in the community throughout the course of the study. Five dimensions of well-being—physical health, cognitive functioning, emotional states, affective responsiveness, and self-perception—were measured at three times thought to be important for the relocation sample: prior to institutionalization, two months after relocation, and one year after relocation. The other two groups were measured at comparable times.

The most important finding of Tobin and Lieberman's study is that prior to institutionalization, the relocation sample resembled the institutional sample more than the community sample. Tobin and Lieberman suggest that the low levels of well-being among institutionalized persons exist prior to entering a long-term care facility and reflect the events that lead to institutionalization (health deterioration or loss of social support) rather than the effects of institutionalization. Tobin and Lieberman also found that the effects of relocation from a community to an institution are most acute during the initial stages of institutionalization. During the first few months, interviews with recently admitted nursing home residents indicated increased preoccupation with feelings of loss and reports of relocation-related problems such as lack of privacy and conflicts with roommates.

Many long-term residents also experience relocation from one nursing home to another. Data from the 1977 National Nursing Home Survey indicate that 13.7 percent of all live discharges from long-term care facilities are actually transfers to other nursing homes (NCHS, 1979). Two longitudinal studies have examined the effects of relocation from one long-term facility to another. Bourestom and Tars (1974) examined the effects of relocation from one nursing home to another on mortality rates and health. The study included three samples: (1) a radical-change sample of individuals who were moved to a larger facility in another community; (2) a moderate-change sample of individuals who were moved to a new building in the same facility; and (3) a control sample of individuals who were not relocated. Data were collected one month prior to relocation of the first two groups and at four occasions during the year after relocation. At six months after relocation, differences in mortality rates were dramatic: 26 percent of the control group had died, compared to 37 percent of the moderate-change group and 43 percent of the radical-change group. Higher death rates also were observed among members of the radical-change group prior to relocation, suggesting anticipatory stress. Self-perceptions of health also decreased dramatically after relocation for the radical-change group. This study makes a unique contribution to the literature in that the findings strongly suggest that the degree of change resulting from relocation is directly related to the probability of negative impact on well-being.

Borup and his associates conducted a longitudinal study that compared older institutional residents who were forced to relocate to other nursing homes to a group of institutional residents who did not relocate (Borup et al., 1979; 1980). The two groups were compared in terms of self-rated health, hypochondria, stamina, functional abilities, hygiene, and mortality. In contrast to Bourestom and Tars, Borup and associates found no negative effects as a result of relocation—and, indeed, found modest positive effects resulting from relocation. Such contradictory findings reinforce a point made by Bourestom and Pastalan (1981): future research should focus upon identification of the conditions under which, and the types of older persons for whom, relocation from one institution to another results in positive and negative effects.

A definitive study of the effects of institutionalization has not yet been performed. Although there are a limited number of longitudinal studies, there has not been a longitudinal study in which impaired older community residents are monitored over time—during which some participants enter long-term care institutions and the others remain in the community. Application of this research design would add greatly to available knowledge about the predictors and effects of institutionalization.

ORGANIZATIONS

There are a number of national organizations that can provide useful information about nursing homes and other long-term care institutions. These organizations have materials that are available upon request. Organizations of potential interest include:

American Association of Homes for the Aging
Suite 770
1050 17th Street, NW
Washington, DC 20036

American College of Nursing Home Administrators
4650 East-West Highway
Washington, DC 20014

American Health Care Association
1200 15th Street, NW
Washington, DC 20005

National Council of Health Care Services
Suite 402
1200 15th Street, NW
Washington, DC 20005

Although these national organizations can provide useful information about the general services available in institutional settings, it often is useful to have information available about a more specific geographic area. In most areas, councils on aging and area agencies on aging can provide information about locally available services. In many areas, these agencies have developed guides to local nursing homes. If institutional placement is being considered, it is recommended that both national and local information be obtained.

The financing of institutional care typically is an important issue. Medicare benefits are detailed in the *Medicare Handbook*, published by the Social Security Administration and available at all local Social Security offices. This handbook, which is updated every year in order to reflect current policies, is an invaluable resource for people who are covered by Medicare. The handbook also is a potentially important resource for planning for later life; younger people are encouraged to become acquainted with Medicare regulations also. Medicaid regulations vary somewhat from state to state; therefore, there is no single information source regarding eligibility requirements and benefits. Local departments of social services are the best source for information about Medicaid.

POLICY AND RESEARCH ISSUES

Long-term care is a high-priority area in several federal agencies, including the Health Care Financing Administration, the National Center for Health Statistics, the Administration on Aging, the National Institute on Aging, and the National Institute of Mental Health. These agencies have varying responsibilities for long-term care, ranging from basic research concerning the causes and consequences of institutionalization, to evaluation of the effectiveness of various service delivery strategies, to administration of Medicare and Medicaid. The reasons for a policy emphasis upon long-term care go far beyond administrative and programmatic responsibilities, however. As our population ages, public investments in institutional care will continue to escalate dramatically. Serious questions have been raised about whether we, as a society, will be able or willing to make the investment required to provide long-term care services to those that need them. The financing of institutional care is a major challenge that will become even more critical during the next fifty years.

Concerns about the cost of long-term care should be balanced by concerns about its quality. Institutional care—or at least the portion of institutional care that is financed by Medicare and Medicaid—already is subject to extensive federal regulation. Nonetheless, there are serious questions about the quality of care actually provided to impaired older adults. Current federal regulations primarily cover issues such as staffing patterns, equipment inventories, and sanitation and safety standards. These issues are important, but do not guarantee quality of care. Smoke alarms and oxygen tanks do not ensure that institutional staff provide quality medical care or a living environment that is as comfortable as desirable. Much more attention needs to be devoted to defining, measuring, and monitoring quality of care in long-term care institutions.

The term "long-term care" has evolved, in recent years, from an emphasis upon purely institutional care to the broad range of services that should be available to impaired older adults in both institutional and community settings. Using this broader definition of long-term care, the provision of homemaker services, nutrition programs, congregate housing, and visiting nurse services are all part of long-term care. This broader definition is useful. Impaired older adults are found both in institutions and in the community—and, as we have seen, equally impaired older persons are found in both settings. In order to best provide appropriate services to the entire impaired older population, a continuum of long-term care services is needed, and institutions are only one component of this service continuum.

The broadened definition of long-term care raises several important policy issues. Much work needs to be done to determine the kinds and levels of impairments that can be served best in community settings and those that can most appropriately be treated in institutional settings. Financing issues are part of this effort. Some impaired older persons (especially the least impaired) probably can be served more cost-effectively in the community, while others (those with the most severe impairments) can be served with a better cost-benefit ratio in institutions. If the continuum of care notion is to be successfully implemented, reimbursement regulations will have to be altered substantially from current practices. Under current regulations, for example, it is impossible to use Medicare for most community services (such as nutritional programs and homemaker services) without prior hospitalization or for extended periods of time. Indeed, current Medicare regulations are commonly recognized as providing incentives for institutional rather than community-based care (Hickey, 1980).

Using the expanded definition of long-term care, family caregiving also becomes an appropriate area of inquiry. We already know that there are at least two equally impaired older adults living in the community for every impaired institutional resident and that family caregiving is the major resource that permits impaired older adults to remain in the community. Family caregiving is both economically and socially attractive. Current research suggests that families provide 80 percent of the value of services received by older impaired community residents while federal programs pay nearly 80 percent of the costs for institutional care (General Accounting Office, 1979). Family caregiving thus translates into a direct savings for public programs. Family caregiving is socially attractive in that the life quality of older adults is enhanced by community residence—and more older people report fearing institutionalization than death (Harris, 1975).

In spite of the social benefits that accrue from family caregiving, recent evidence compellingly documents the fact that caregiving can be a burdensome and taxing task for family members. Common problems associated with family caregiving include financial burden, increased physical health problems, difficulties managing both caregiving and employment, emotional discomfort including feelings of guilt and depression, and interference with social and recreational activities (Zarit et al., 1980). Part of a long-term care service continuum should be programs to lessen caregiver burden and to enhance caregiver effectiveness. Examples of such services, which are now largely unavailable, include respite care for family caregivers, educational programs to teach caregivers appropriate management techniques for the chronic problems suffered by their older relatives, and tax incentives for families that provide assistance to impaired older relatives (Sussman, 1976).

The process by which public policy and services for the older population are authorized, designed, and implemented is complex. At the most basic level, publicly supported services are political phenomena. They are influenced by government officials, bureaucratic administrators, lobbyists, and other special interest groups. Established social service programs typically reflect the political compromises required to assemble sufficient support for policy adoption, regardless of whether the compromises contribute to or detract from the effectiveness, efficiency, and rationality of those programs (Binstock and Levin, 1976; Lakoff, 1976).

Where, in this complex political process, is the potential contribution of research? Under ideal circumstances, research contributes to policy development and implementation in a number of ways. First, all social intervention rests on a conceptualization of what the world is like and what can be done to alter its less desirable qualities (Estes and Freeman, 1976). Since social scientists systematically observe and study the social world, the information they gather is useful to those groups who authorize and design service programs. Social scientists also often evaluate the impact of social interventions by applying their theories and measurement skills to the task of determining whether programs have accomplished their stated goals.

Institutionalization and long-term care merit considerable research effort. Financing of long-term care, quality of care, achieving a balance between institutional and community-based services, enhancing family caregiver abilities and effectiveness—all of these are important policy issues in the area of long-term care. They also, however, comprise an important agenda for future research. Such effort will help us to understand the process of institutionalization, its impact upon older people, and, perhaps most important, can help in the design and implementation of appropriate services for impaired older adults.

REFERENCES

Binstock, R.H., and Levin, M.A. The political dilemmas of intervention policies. In R.H. Binstock and E. Shanas (Eds.), *Handbook of aging and the social sciences*. Van Nostrand Reinhold, New York, 1976.

Borup, J.H.; Gallego, D.T.; and Heffernan, P.G. Relocation and its effect on mortality. *Gerontologist*, 1979, *19*, 135–140.

———. Relocation: Its effect on health, functioning, and mortality. *Gerontologist*, 1980, *20*, 468–479.

Bourestom, N., and Pastalan, L. The effects of relocation on the elderly: A reply to Borup, J.H., Gallego, D.T., and Heffernan, P.G. *Gerontologist*, 1981, *21*, 4–7.

Bourestom, N., and Tars, S. Alterations in life patterns following nursing home relocation. *Gerontologist*, 1974, *14*, 506–509.

Duke Center for the Study of Aging and Human Development. *Multidimensional functional assessment: The OARS methodology*, 2nd ed. Center for the Study of Aging and Human Development, Durham, N.C., 1978.

Eribes, R.A., and Bradley-Rawls, M. The underutilization of nursing home facilities by Mexican-American elderly in the Southwest. *Gerontologist*, 1978, *18*, 363–371.

Estes, C.L., and Freeman, H.C. Strategies of design and research for intervention. In R.H. Binstock and E. Shanas (Eds.), *Handbook of aging and the social sciences*. Van Nostrand Reinhold, New York, 1976.

General Accounting Office. *The well-being of older people in Cleveland, Ohio*. General Accounting Office, Washington, D.C., 1977.

————. *Conditions of older people: National information system needed*. General Accounting Office, Washington, D.C., 1979.

Harris, L. *The myth and reality of aging in America*. National Council on the Aging, Washington, D.C., 1975.

Hickey, T. *Health and aging*. Brooks/Cole, Monterey, Calif., 1980.

Ingram, D.K., and Barry, J.R. National statistics on deaths in nursing homes: Interpretations and implications. *Gerontologist*, 1977, *17*, 303–308.

Kastenbaum, R.S., and Candy, S. The 4% fallacy: A methodological and empirical critique of extended care facility program statistics. *International Journal of Aging and Human Development*, 1973, *4*, 15–21.

Lakoff, S.A. The future of social intervention. In R.H. Binstock and E. Shanas (Eds.), *Handbook of aging and the social sciences*. Van Nostrand Reinhold, New York, 1976.

Lieberman, M.A. Adaptive processes in late life. In N. Datan and L.H. Ginsberg (Eds.), *Life-span developmental psychology: Normative life crises*. Academic Press, New York, 1975.

Liu, K., and Manton, K.G. The characteristics and utilization pattern of an admission cohort of nursing home patients. *Gerontologist*, 1983, *23*, 92–98.

Morris, J.N. Changes in morale experienced by elderly institutional applicants along the institutional path. *Gerontologist*, 1975, *15*, 345–349.

National Center for Health Statistics. The National Nursing Home Survey: 1977 summary for the United States. *Vital and Health Statistics*, ser.13, no. 43. USGPO, Washington, D.C., 1979.

Palmore, E. Total chance of institutionalization among the aged. *Gerontologist*, 1976, *16*, 504–507.

Sherwood, S., and Mor, V. Mental health institutions and the elderly. In J.E. Birren and R.B. Sloane (Eds.), *Handbook of mental health and aging*. Prentice-Hall, Englewood Cliffs, N.J., 1980.

Sussman, M.B. The family life of older people. In R.H. Binstock and E. Shanas (Eds.), *Handbook of aging and the social sciences*. Van Nostrand Reinhold, New York, 1976.

Tobin, S.S., and Lieberman, M.A. *Last home for the aged*. Jossey-Bass, San Francisco, 1976.

Zarit, S.H.; Reever, K.E.; and Bach-Peterson, J. Relatives of the impaired elderly: Correlates of feelings of burden. *Gerontologist*, 1980, *20*, 649–655.

22

THE MENTALLY ILL

ERDMAN B. PALMORE

The mentally ill are one of the largest problem groups among the aged. The proportion of aged with severe psychiatric impairments is estimated to be between 5 percent and 10 percent, and those with mild to moderate impairments between 10 percent and 40 percent (Busse and Blazer, 1980). This translates into about 2 million aged with severe impairment and up to another 11 million with mild to moderate impairments. The proper care and treatment of such a massive group is clearly one of the major problems of our society and our health care system. For example, it has been estimated that if only the aged mentally ill *in institutions* (over 600,000 persons) were given each week a minimum of one hour of treatment from a psychiatrist, it would require more psychiatrists than are in practice today (Busse and Blazer, 1980).

CHARACTERISTICS

There is probably no more mental illness among the aged than among younger age groups in our population. Some studies have found that the rate of psychiatric impairment increases with age (Bremer, 1951; Essen-Moller et al., 1956; Kay et al., 1964; Lowenthal and Berkman, 1967; Nielsen, 1962; New York State Department of Mental Hygiene, 1961). However, several of these studies have found that the prevalence of neurosis and schizophrenia declines with age, while the prevalence of psychosomatic complaints and organic brain syndrome increases. Thus, the aged mentally ill, in comparison with younger mentally ill, are more likely to have psychosomatic or organic brain impairments and less likely to have neurotic or schizophrenic impairments.

Most of these studies have also found more mental illness among aged women than among aged men. A few studies have found little or no differences between men and women in rates of mental illness. The usually higher rates of mental illness among women (at all ages) may be due to some genetic difference in susceptibility between men and women, or to greater psychosocial stress among women; or to the methods of identifying cases of mental illness (women may be more willing to admit psychiatric symptoms); or to a combination of all three explanations. However, aged men have more brain syndromes from alcoholism and nemosyphilis (Larson et al., 1963).

Some studies have found that married persons have lower rates of mental illness than the single or widowed, but these have usually been based on hospitalization rates rather than community surveys (Birren and Sloane, 1980). Since married persons are less often hospitalized than others, the hospital population does not accurately reflect the community. One community survey (Bellin and Hardt, 1958) found no significant differences among marital statuses in rates of mental disorder, once age, health, and socioeconomic status were held constant. Furthermore, there is the problem of causal order: even if married persons have less mental illness, is it because marriage protects against mental illness, or is it because the mentally ill are less likely to marry and stay married?

Almost nothing is known about possible differences between races or ethnic groups in rates of mental illness among the aged, but the few studies that have compared white and black aged have found no significant differences (Busse and Blazer, 1980).

As for the different types of mental illness among the aged, estimated rates vary considerably from study to study because of different diagnostic criteria and possibly because of the different samples studied. However, the community studies tend to agree that the most common types are neuroses and personality disorders. Organic mental disease is usually next in frequency, while schizophrenia, paranoid and affective psychosis are least frequent. Studies of the aged *in institutions* in the United States tend to agree that the most common diagnosis is organic mental disorder, while the second most common diagnosis is schizophrenic or paranoid psychosis (Redick et al., 1973; Teeter et al., 1976; Lowenthal and Berkman, 1967). These differences between community studies and institutional studies indicate that the aged with neuroses and personality disorders are less likely to be institutionalized than those with organic, schizophrenic, or paranoid psychoses.

As for socioeconomic status, all community studies of mental illness among the aged have found higher rates of mental illness among lower-status persons (Leighton et al., 1963; Srole et al., 1962; New York State Department of Mental Hygiene, 1961; Roth and Kay, 1962; Lowenthal and Berkman, 1967). For example, Lowenthal and Berkman found that the psychiatric impairment rate was twice as high among those with less than eight years of schooling than among those with four or more years of college. Similarly, those with annual incomes under $1,500 had four times the psychiatric impairment rate of those with over $5,000.

There are two main explanations for this strong and consistent relationship between lower socioeconomic status and more mental illness: heredity and environment. The heredity explanation states that persons in the lower statuses tend to inherit more genetic weaknesses which predispose them to mental illness. The environmental explanation states that persons in the lower statuses are subject to more stresses from their environment which cause their mental illnesses. A third explanation, the "drift" theory, states that those persons who have a tendency toward mental illness (whether because of heredity or early environment) tend to "drift" downward in the socioeconomic system, while more healthy individuals tend to rise, thereby causing an accumulation of mental illness in the lower statuses. There is evidence to support all three explanations, and all three probably explain part of the association.

All studies also agree that one of the most common characteristics of the aged mentally ill is physical illness (Kay et al., 1964; Lowenthal and Berkman, 1967; New York State Department of Mental Hygiene, 1961). Those with organic brain syndrome also have substantially higher mortality rates (Helgason, 1973; Nielsen et al., 1977). This association between mental and physical illness may be because physical illness tends to cause mental illness, or vice versa, or both forms of illness may be the result of greater stress or inferior constitutions.

HISTORY

The history of mental illness among the aged parallels that of mental illness in general, with one important exception. In pre-modern times mental illness was usually assumed to be caused by devils or evil spirits which took possession of a person's mind and body. With the growth of scientific knowledge these devil theories were gradually replaced by theories that postulated that mental illness is caused by specific lesions or diseases in the central nervous system, or by genetic deficiencies, or by emotional stresses which cause the central nervous system to malfunction. However, it is still widely assumed that mental illness among the aged (or "senility") usually is caused by inevitable and normal processes of aging. While it is probably true that certain types of mental illness among the aged (Alzheimer's disease or primary degenerative dementia) is caused by age-related changes in the brain, many and probably a majority of the mentally ill aged have disorders that are not caused by normal aging processes (Birren and Sloan, 1980). There are many aged today who are thought of as "senile" (and therefore hopeless cases) who, if they were younger, would probably be thought of as simply eccentric, neurotic, depressed, or even schizophrenic. Thus, for many of the aged mentally ill, the old "devil theory" has been replaced by an equally unscientific "senility theory."

Until the end of the eighteenth century, the mentally ill were usually confined in prison-like institutions called workhouses along with criminals, paupers, and the unemployed of all ages, and there was little differences in the way they were all treated. It was only in the early 1800s that most states started separate insane asylums in order to protect the mentally ill from dangerous stresses of the community or workhouses, and to attempt their rehabilitation, or at least to treat them humanely. However, until recently many older persons were put into such asylums or mental hospitals not because they were dangerously ill, but primarily because they had no other home and no one else would care for them.

In 1963 the Community Mental Health and Mental Retardation Centers Bill was passed as part of a movement to "deinstitutionalize" those mentally ill who are not dangerous to themselves or others and who cannot benefit from confinement in an institution. This movement has had two effects. On the one hand, millions were returned to the community who did not need institutionalization. On the other, millions of impaired older persons were dumped into inferior nursing homes or rooming houses with few or no community services to help them cope with community living. The result has been a multiplication of many problems in the affected neighborhoods and among the mentally ill who were dumped and largely left to fend for themselves. This was especially true of the aged mentally ill because they constituted a disproportionate share of those deinstitutionalized and because they faced special age-related problems of adapting to the community.

SPECIAL PROBLEMS

The aged mentally ill share with other mentally ill a stigma that is difficult to erase. Even in our "enlightened" age, many people share feelings of fear and revulsion of the mentally ill which they do not have of the physically ill. A person with a broken leg is often viewed more sympathetically and positively than a person with a neurosis or psychosis. This difference in attitude is probably rooted in a number of assumptions. One assumption is that people should not be blamed for their physical illness (even though their life-style or carelessness may well have caused it); while the mentally ill are often held responsible (their illness was caused by "immoral behavior" or a "weakness in character" or "lack of self-discipline"). Another assumption is that modern medicine can cure most physical illnesses but cannot cure most mental illnesses. Once a person has had a mental illness, he or she is marked for life and viewed suspiciously thereafter by family and friends as well as by employers, the police, and other persons in authority. Another assumption is that the mentally ill are more dangerous than the physically ill: one need not fear someone with a broken leg, but one had better watch out for "crazy people" because one never knows how they might harm one.

This stigma becomes a case of "double jeopardy" when it is applied to an old person, because being old in our society is often considered to be another stigma. Thus, ageism is a special problem for the aged mentally ill because ageism assumes that most older people are useless, worthless, helpless, hopeless, unpleasant, sick, and ugly. Such prejudices result in discriminatory behavior against the aged, which tends to fulfill the prophecy by making old people useless, helpless, hopeless, and so on. Such ageism increases stress for older people, which may increase mental illness among the aged.

Another special problem is that mental illness among the aged is often not recognized (but assumed to be "normal aging") and therefore not treated, so that the afflicted person simply suffers in silence or continues to deteriorate until it is too late for effective intervention. Even if mental illness is recognized, often it is assumed that nothing can be done about it and so no therapy is attempted. Sometimes this assumption is justified, but often it is not. The more we learn about mental illness among the aged, the more we find we can treat it effectively.

Another special problem is the shortage of mental health workers willing and able to treat the aged. Geriatric units of mental hospitals and nursing homes suffer from chronic staffing problems that are even more severe than in other treatment facilities. Numerous studies have shown that mental health professionals and paraprofessionals tend to prefer to work with younger patients (Butler and Lewis, 1982). This is another reflection of the ageism that pervades our society. Furthermore, those who are willing to work with older patients often have no special training in treating geriatric patients.

A final problem is that mental illness among the aged is often compounded by physical illness and disabilities. We have noted that mental and physical illnesses are often closely associated, especially among the aged. This means that effective treatment of mental illness among the aged tends to be more complex and difficult than at other ages.

MITIGATING FACTORS

However, there are a few advantages that the aged mentally ill enjoy compared to the younger mentally ill. For one thing, the aged are covered by Medicare, which pays for about 40 percent of their total health care costs. Without these benefits, their treatment would be even less adequate and more of a burden to the aged and their families than it is now.

Second, the aged mentally ill are not usually expected to earn a living when and if they recover. Among younger persons, the pressure to earn a living (despite the stigma of mental illness) often produces stress which interferes with recovery. The aged are usually considered rehabilitated if they can just care for themselves.

Third, the aged usually have a lifetime of achievement behind them to support their self-esteem and overall life satisfaction. Often younger persons have not had time to achieve much before they become mentally ill.

TREATMENT

There has been considerable growth in recent years in the theory and practice of treating the aged mentally ill (Butler and Lewis, 1982). This growth has several new emphases: the importance of restoring patients to active lives as well as rehabilitating them in the community; the potentiality of reversibility, both in functional disorders and in some of the organic disorders; prevention as well as therapeutic efforts; and comprehensive evaluations in order to deal with the usually complex set of problems presented by older patients.

There has also developed recently greater interest in inherent changes that can be expected as the individual progresses through the life cycle. This includes a new interest in the psychology of old age and in gero-psychiatry. There are exciting recent developments occurring in the neurosciences that are likely to make great contributions to understanding human behavior and to the treatment of mental disorders. An example is the catecholamine hypothesis of affective disorders, which suggests that the functional turnover of catecholamines is increased at specific central synapses in mania and is decreased in depression (Butler and Lewis, 1982). Drugs have been developed to increase or decrease the action of catecholamines.

Because of the shortage of psychiatrists to treat mentally ill aged, several other kinds of specialists are becoming more involved. Nurses, social workers, psychologists, pastoral counselors, paraprofessionals, and members of newly emerging specialties are doing much of the work traditionally thought of as "psychiatry" in treating the aged (Butler and Lewis, 1982). In addition, more than 1,500 psychiatrists now identify themselves as having a primary interest in older patients. More than 400 of these joined the American Association for Geriatric Psychiatry in its first year of existence (1978). In 1979 the American Psychiatric Association showed a commitment to the problems of aging by establishing a Council on Aging.

Yet despite this growing interest and the increasing number of practitioners treating the mentally ill aged, only a small proportion get the treatment they need. Various studies have shown that relatively few of the patients in outpatient treatment (from 2 to 4 percent) are over age 65 (Busse and Blazer, 1980). In the OARS Durham Community Survey only 1 percent of the aged were receiving any counseling or psychotherapy from any source, although 10 percent perceived the need for such services. As for inpatient treatment, only 5 percent of all admissions to the major psychiatric care services in the United States are age 65 or over (Birren and Sloane, 1980). This is probably less than a third of those needing such treatment.

Why do so few of the mentally ill aged get treatment? There are four major barriers to adequate treatment of mentally ill aged: attitudes of the aged, attitudes of professionals, transportation, and finances. The characteristics and attitudes of the aged themselves constitute major obstacles to adequate treatment. The aged have substantially less education on the average than younger people, and this education was acquired in an earlier era when less was known about health and psychiatry. Thus, many aged are ignorant about many mental symptoms that a more informed person might recognize as serious enough to require examination, if not treatment. The elderly may simply dismiss these symptoms as signs of aging that do not warrant treatment.

Even when the aged recognize that a symptom indicates the need for some treatment, they are less likely to seek professional help. They are more likely to listen to lay advice, quacks, or old wives' tales or to use patent medicines or nostrums. This may result from ignorance about the value of professional treatment; fear of psychiatrists and the uncomfortable, expensive treatment they may prescribe; or fear of mental hospitals and the greater fear of being labeled mentally ill.

Many mental health professionals are less interested in treating the aged than in treating younger people and may even avoid the aged because their care seems to be less rewarding psychologically and financially (Butler and Lewis, 1982). The Group for the Advancement of Psychiatry has listed some of the major reasons for negative staff attitudes toward treating older persons (1971).

1. The aged stimulate the therapist's fears about his own age.
2. The aged arouse the therapist's conflicts about his relationship with parental figures.
3. The therapist believes he has nothing useful to offer older people because he believes they cannot change their behavior or that their problems are all due to untreatable organic brain diseases.
4. The therapist believes that his psychodynamic skills will be wasted if he works with the aged, since they are near death and not really deserving of attention.
5. The patient might die while in treatment, which could challenge the therapist's sense of importance.
6. The therapist's colleagues may be contemptuous of his efforts on behalf of aged patients.

Thus, even when older persons recognize their symptoms as needing treatment and decide to seek professional care, they may be discouraged by the resistance and subtle ageism of mental health professionals.

A third barrier to adequate treatment is the various transportation difficulties that many aged face. A combination of circumstances may make transportation difficulties particularly formidable to older persons. As younger people tend to move from rural areas toward the city and from the older, deteriorating sections of the city to the suburbs, the aged are likely to be left behind and become concentrated in rural areas and older sections of the cities. Unfortunately, these are the very areas in which psychiatrists and mental health facilities usually are scarce. Thus, the aged may have to travel great distances to reach psychiatric service, yet they are the least mobile and have the greatest difficulty with transportation because of their condition and lack of private cars.

The fourth and probably most formidable barrier is financial. Mental health care is expensive, especially when psychotherapists, private nurses, and hospitalization are involved. Such care is far beyond the means of most older people (Butler and Lewis, 1982). Public care is sometimes adequate, but is usually far from satisfactory. Medicare, while it has reduced the dependence of older patients on family support or charity, has not managed to provide adequate mental health care for the majority of elders needing it. Medicare pays only about 40 percent of the average older person's health expenses. The deductibles, coinsurance provisions, limitations on amount of service, and services not covered by Medicare still leave substantial and often insurmountable financial barriers. Medical coverage for psychiatric disorders is unrealistically limited and was inserted in Medicare legislation as a kind of afterthought. There is a 190-day lifetime limit on treatment in mental hospitals, and the patient must pay 50 percent of outpatient services from a physician. There is also an annual limit of $250 on outpatient care. Social workers, psychologists, and other mental health personnel are not appropriately covered on an outpatient basis. Contrary to sound psychiatric practice, Medicare promotes hospitalization rather than care in the community (Social Security Administration, 1971). As a result, thousands of older patients with psychiatric problems are receiving no care or only routine custodial care in a nursing home.

Needed Treatment

What kinds of treatment are needed by the mentally ill aged? We do not have space to describe all the possible therapies and services that may be needed, but we will list the major ones and comment on their potential usefulness.*

Diagnostic Evaluation. The purpose of the mental health diagnostic evaluation is to examine the problems of the older person in order to decide what is wrong and what can be done to alleviate these problems. The evaluation should be based on historical data from the person's past; current medical, psychiatric, and social examinations; and the evaluator's personal interactions with the individual. The conditions required for a good evaluation include the establishment of rapport, assurance of confidentiality, a private and quiet setting, sufficient time for an unhurried examination, clarification of the purpose of the evaluation, and as comprehensive a set of examinations as is feasible and appropriate. A diagnostic evaluation is recommended before any treatment or services is begun.

Physician Services. Physicians should be on call for emergency home visits on a twenty-four-hour basis and for ongoing medical evaluation and management of patients. Psychiatrists should be involved in the treatment of most mental illness, especially if there is an organic component to the illness or if drug therapy is involved.

Nursing Services. These include services of registered nurses (RNs), especially those of public health nurses and psychiatric nurses; licensed practical nurses (LPNs); and home health aides. Public health nurses are RNs (and sometimes LPNs) who work for tax-supported city or county health departments. The Visiting Nurse Association is a voluntary organization supported by private donations which also provides nursing services similar to the public health nurse services. Psychiatric nurses are RNs who specialize in mental health care. LPNs work under the supervision of RNs and perform many of the same nursing services. Home health aides also provide simple nursing care. The main problem with these nurses and aides is that there are far too few to meet the needs of many mentally ill aged.

*This section on treatment is based on data from Butler and Lewis, 1982.

Homemakers. These paraprofessionals provide various homemaking services to people with short-term or long-term physical or emotional illness. Anything directly connected with an individual's care can be part of their work: light cooking, cleaning the patient's room, and washing clothes, as well as simple nursing services. Again, the number of homemakers and home health aides in the United States is a small fraction of the estimated need.

Physical, Occupational, and Speech Therapists. The physical therapist should be responsible for physical rehabilitation following accidents or illnesses, and should be responsible for any equipment and appliances necessary for rehabilitation. The services of the physical therapist include exercise and massage. The occupational therapists seek to teach, restore, and maintain the occupational performance skills, behaviors, and attitudes crucial to independent and healthy functioning. Speech therapists are those who specialize in restoring or correcting speaking abilities.

Social Services. These are the economic and social supports that are not strictly medical or psychiatric. In the past, social service has been rendered mainly by social workers, but this is no longer true. Clergy, police officers, nurses, government officials, volunteers, paraprofessionals, homemakers, and home health aides often render social services. The types of social services available for mentally ill aged include information and referral; financial support; help with personal needs, including companions, telephones, shopping, transportation, grooming, and pets; family respite service to give the family time off from caring for the aged person; home safety; friendly visiting and outside contact; recreation; education; employment; religious support; and housing. These services can be of great importance in the prevention of mental illness and in its treatment.

Outpatient Care. This refers to the medical and psychiatric treatment given to people who live in the community rather than in institutions. It can be provided by hospital outpatient clinics, neighborhood health centers, family agencies, day hospitals, and day-care centers.

Multipurpose Senior Centers. These centers can provide a wide range of services both inside the facilities and outside. Their purpose is to provide a center for comprehensive services and to avoid the duplication and confusion between various agencies that would otherwise occur.

Protective Services. These provide the needed management for those aged who are so mentally deteriorated or disturbed that they cannot manage their affairs in their own best interest and who have no relatives or friends able and willing to manage their affairs.

Institutionalization. Mental health workers usually seek to maintain the mentally ill at home as long as it is feasible and appropriate. Improved community services would make it feasible and appropriate to maintain many more aged in their homes than is now done. However, there are many cases in which it is not possible or advisable to care for the person at home, and short- or long-term institutional care is required. The various kinds of institutional care available include: emergency shelter when sudden problems arise or when time is needed for appropriate evaluation and decision; acute hospitalization for stays up to about three months; chronic hospitalization for organic brain damage or other chronic conditions; foster care for persons with little need for nursing or medical care; nursing homes, including profit and nonprofit homes, skilled nursing facilities, and intermediate care facilities; and homes for the aged, which are voluntary nonprofit institutions, often with nursing home components.

Psychotherapy. This includes individual and group psychotherapy; family therapy; behavioral modification; and biofeedback, which uses electronic monitoring devices to teach patients to control selected behaviors. In the past, such therapies were rarely offered to older patients because it was thought that they would not be as responsive or benefit as much as younger persons. Recent research and theory have revised that view so that psychotherapy is being offered with highly beneficial results to many aged patients.

Environmental Therapy. This is basically the reduction of ageism in the environment, which causes so much mental illness and makes recovery from it so difficult. It includes developing awareness of ageism and reducing age denial; promotion of federal legislation and policies to reduce ageism, such as the Age Discrimination Act and the Older Americans Act; mobilization of community resources to help the aged; registration drives to register all those eligible for various income and service programs so that they can in fact receive benefits; self-care and self-help programs; increasing employment opportunities; advocacy for the aged; legal services; and consultations for agencies, homes, and other organizations on how to improve administration and staff services.

Drug Therapy. This includes the use of antianxiety drugs, antidepressants, antimanic drugs, and antipsychotic drugs. These drugs can be of great value in the treatment of anxiety, severe agitation, depression, and psychosis. However, they should not be the sole form of treatment given to any mentally ill person. When possible, other approaches to the amelioration of symptoms should be tried first. If drugs are found to be necessary they should be administered only as one component of an organized treatment plan. The physician prescribing the drugs should be aware of the different dosages appropriate and the different reactions possible among the aged as compared to younger persons.

Electroshock Therapy. If antidepressants and psychotherapy are contra-indicated or do not produce the desired results, electroshock therapy (EST) may be indicated in severe, refractory depression. However, EST should be administered only after comprehensive evaluations, and only with full patient consent and under carefully controlled conditions including the use of preshock sedation and muscle relaxants to avoid fractures.

ORGANIZATIONS

Appendix A provides names and addresses of academic and research centers on aging. The following list includes those organizations particularly concerned with the aged mentally ill.

Administration on Aging
HHS North Building
330 Independence Ave. SW
Washington, DC 20201

Alzheimer's Disease and Related Disorders Association
32 Broadway
New York, NY 10004

Alzheimer Disease Association
31 Meadow Park Ave.
Columbus, OH 43209

Alzheimer Disease Society
Wollin Associates, 560 Sylvan Ave.
Englewood Cliffs, NJ 07632

Alzheimer Support, Information, and Service Team
c/o University of Washington, RP-10
Seattle, WA 98195

American Association for Geriatric Psychiatry
230 N. Michigan Ave., Suite 2400
Chicago, IL 60601

American Association of Homes for the Aging
1050 17th St. NW, Suite 770
Washington, DC 20036

American Geriatrics Society
10 Columbus Circle
New York, NY 10019

American Psychiatric Association, Council on Aging
1700 18th St. NW
Washington, DC 20009

American Psychological Association, Division of Adult Development and Aging
1200 17th St. NW
Washington, DC 20036

American Public Health Association, Section of Gerontological Health
1015 18th St. NW
Washington, DC 20036

Association for Alzheimer's and Related Disease
5000 W. 109th St.
Bloomington, MN 55437

Center for the Study of the Mental Health of the Aging, National Institute of
Mental Health
Rockville, MD 20857

Chronic Organic Brain Syndrome Society
17th Floor, Allegheny Bldg.
429 Forbes Ave.
Pittsburg, PA 15219

Council of Home Health Agencies and Community Health Services
National League for Nursing
10 Columbus Circle
New York, NY 10019

Gerontology Society of America
1411 K St. NW, Suite 300
Washington, DC 20005

Group for the Advancement of Psychiatry, Inc., Committee on Aging
c/o Mental Health Materials Center
419 Park Ave. S.
New York, NY 10016

Home Health Services Association
407 N. St. NW
Washington, DC 20024

International Federation on Aging
1909 K St. NW
Washington, DC 20006

National Association of Home Health Agencies
426 C St. NE
Washington, DC 20002

National Association of Social Workers
1425 H St. NW
Washington, DC 20005

National Citizens' Coalition for Nursing Home Reform
1424 16th St. NW, Suite 204
Washington, DC 20036

National Council of Health Care Services
1200 15th St. NW, Suite 402
Washington, DC 20005

National Council of Homemaker–Home Health Aide Services
67 Irving Place
New York, NY 10003

National Council of Senior Citizens
1511 K St. NW
Washington, DC 20005

National Council on the Aging
1828 L St. NW, Suite 504
Washington, DC 20036

National Geriatrics Society
212 W. Wisconsin Ave.
Milwaukee, WI 53203

National Institute on Aging
National Institutes of Health
Bethesda, MD 20205

Southern Gerontological Society
c/o E.B. Palmore
Box 3003, Duke Medical Center
Durham, NC 27710

Western Gerontological Society
833 Market St., Room 1114
San Francisco, CA 94114

RESEARCH ISSUES

There are several types of research on mental illness among the aged that have begun to produce promising results. Many of these, however, are so limited by the small numbers of persons studied, by unrepresentative subjects, by the limited variables studied, or by other methodological problems, that it is difficult to reach definite conclusions or generalize to larger groups from these studies. Because of this, much more research in the following areas is needed to effectively prevent and treat mental illness among the aged.

1. *Community-based studies of the incidence and prevalence of mental illness among the aged.* Much of our knowledge about mental illness among the aged is limited to studies of institutionalized populations, which we know do not represent the larger number of non-institutionalized mentally ill aged. Estimates of incidence and prevalence, based on the limited community studies done so far, vary widely because of differing methods and criteria. The estimates vary even more widely when specific types of mental illness are concerned. We need more large-scale studies using comprehensive, reliable, valid, and comparable methods to resolve these discrepancies between the existing studies.

2. *Longitudinal studies of mental illness among the aged.* These are needed to determine the antecedents (causes) and the consequences of mental illness. Most of our theories about the causes and consequences of mental illness among the aged are based on cross-sectional studies at one point in time. We need longitudinal studies, with repeated measures on the same individuals over time, to determine what factors cause mental illness and what are the results of mental illness. Such studies are important both for the prevention and the treatment of mental illness.

3. *Longitudinal studies of institutionalization.* These are needed to determine the antecedents and consequences of institutionalizing mentally ill aged. Most studies in the area of institutionalization are either cross-sectional or do not include a comparable control group, so we know little about what factors lead to institutionalization, and even less about how institutionalization helps or harms the patient. It is probable that

institutionalization helps some in some ways and hurts some in other ways. Since the numbers of aged institutionalized and the costs of institutionalization are growing markedly, there is a particularly urgent need for research in this area.

4. *Studies of the effectiveness of various treatments.* These would include studies of the effectiveness (cost-benefit analyses) of all the treatment methods listed in the section on treatment above; especially needed are studies which assess the effectiveness of psychotropic drugs, various types of psychotherapy, and social services. Many of the drug studies have not examined possible differential effects on older persons. Many of the studies of psychotherapy have not used older subjects because of the assumption that psychotherapy would not be effective with older persons. Studies of the effectiveness of social services in preventing mental illness among the aged are especially promising because effective prevention would reduce the need for any kind of treatment. "An ounce of prevention is worth a pound of cure" is probably as true of mental illness among the aged as of any other type of illness.

5. *Development and testing of methods for reducing ageism.* Since ageism, in its many forms of prejudice and discrimination against older persons, is one of the most important stresses that contribute to mental illness, effective methods for reducing ageism would be one of the most important means of preventing mental illness. Existing legislation and educational programs may be helping to reduce ageism, but much research is needed to find out which methods or combinations of methods are most cost-effective and practical. If we can eliminate ageism in the United States, we will have gone a long way toward drastically reducing mental illness among the aged, as well as creating an environment in which most of us could look forward to our later years as truly "golden years."

REFERENCES

Bellin, S., and Hardt, R. Marital status and mental disorders among the aged. *American Sociological Review*, 1958, *23*, 155–162.

Birren, J., and Sloane, R. (Eds.). *Handbook of mental health and aging*. Prentice-Hall, Englewood Cliffs, N.J., 1980.

Bremer, J. A social psychiatric investigation of a small community in northern Norway. *Acta Psychiatrica et Neurologica Scandinavica Supplementum* 62. Ejnar Munksgaard, Copenhagen, 1951.

Busse, E., and Blazer, D. (Eds.). *Handbook of geriatric psychiatry*. Van Nostrand Reinhold, New York, 1980.

Butler, R., and Lewis, M. *Aging and mental illness*. Mosby, St. Louis, 1982.

Essen-Moller, E.; Larsson, H.; Vooenberg, C.; and White, G. Individual traits and morbidity in a Swedish rural population. *Acta Psychiatrica et Neurologica Scandinavica Supplementum* 100. Ejnar Munksgaard, Copenhagen, 1956.

Group for the Advancement of Psychiatry, Committee on Aging. *The aged and community mental health*, vol. 8, ser. 81, Washington, D.C., November 1971.

Helgason, T. Epidemiology of mental disorders in Iceland. *Excerpta Medica International Congress Series No. 274*, 350–357, Excerpta Medica, Amsterdam, 1973.

Kay, D.; Beamish, P.; and Roth, M. Old age mental disorders in Newcastle-upon-Tyne. *British Journal of Psychiatry*, 1964, *110*, 146–158, 668–682.

Larsson, T.; Suogren, T.; and Jacobson, G. Senile dementia. *Acta psychiatrica et Neurologica Scandinavica Supplementum* 167. Ejnar Munksgaard, Copenhagen, 1963.

Leighton, D.; Harding, J.; Macklin, D.; MacMillan, A.; and Leighton, A. *The character of danger*. Basic Books, New York, 1963.

Lowenthal, M., and Berkman, P. *Aging and mental disorder in San Francisco*. Jossey-Bass, San Francisco, 1967.

New York State Department of Mental Hygiene. *Mental health survey of older people*. State Hospital Press, New York, 1961.

Nielsen, J. Geronto-psychiatric period-prevalence investigation in a geographically delimited population. *Acta Psychiatrica et Neurologica Scandinavica*, 1962, *38*, 307–330.

Nielsen, J.; Homma, A.; and Bjorn-Henriksen, T. Follow-up 15 years after a geronto-psychiatric prevalence study. *Journal of Gerontology*, 1977, *32*, 554–561.

Palmore, E. The social factors in aging. In E. Busse and D. Blazer, *Handbook of geriatric psychiatry*. Van Nostrand Reinhold, New York, 1980.

Redick, R.; Kramer, M.; and Taube, C. Epidemiology of mental illness and utilization of psychiatric facilities among older persons. In E. Busse and E. Pfeiffer (Eds.), *Mental illness in later life*. American Psychiatric Association, Washington, D.C., 1973, 199–222.

Roth, M., and Kay, D. Social, medical and personality factors associated with vulnerability to psychiatric breakdown in old age. *Gerontologica Clinica*, 1962, *4*, 147–160.

Social Security Administration. *Financing mental health care under Medicare and Medicaid*. Research Report No. 37. USGPO, Washington, D.C., 1971.

Srole, L.; Langner, T.; Michael, S.; Opler, M.; and Rennie, T. *Mental health in the metropolis*. McGraw-Hill, New York, 1962.

Teeter, R.; Garetz, S.; Miller, W.; and Hailand, W. Psychiatric disturbances of aged patients in skilled nursing homes. *American Journal of Psychiatry*, 1976, *133*, 1430.

23

SUICIDES

NANCY J. OSGOOD

In approximately the third century B.C., the well-known Roman stoic Seneca delivered the following discourse on suicide in old age:

> For this reason, but for this alone, life is not an evil—that no one is obliged to live.... If life pleases you, live. If not, you have a right to return whence you came. I will not relinquish old age if it leaves my better part intact. But if it begins to shake my mind, if it destroys its faculties one by one, if it leaves me not life but breath, I will depart from the putrid or tottering edifice. I will not escape by death from disease so long as it may be healed, and leaves my mind unimpaired. I will not raise my hand against myself on account of pain, for so to die is to be conquered. But if I know that I must suffer without hope of relief, I will depart, not through fear of the pain itself, but because it prevents all for which I would live. (Lecky, 1869:217–220)

Through the centuries suicide has generally been philosophically condoned as more appropriate for the old, especially those who are physically ill or suffering intense pain, than for members of any other age group.

The purpose of this chapter is to examine suicide among the elderly in the United States. An analysis and discussion of relevant statistics and research will be presented to highlight the extent and the dimensions of suicide in this country. Theoretical explanations and conceptual models to explain and interpret findings from a wide variety of studies will be offered, as well as suggestions for the recognition and possible prevention of suicide among the aged.

THE AGE FACTOR IN SUICIDE

Suicide rates for different age groups suggest that suicide in the United States and in most other industrialized countries for which data are available is clearly

The author wishes to thank Dr. Arthur Bigot and Dr. John McIntosh for helpful information and valuable insights provided during the writing of this chapter.

more frequent among older than among younger persons (Atchley, 1980; Sainsbury, 1962; Dublin, 1963; Niccolini, 1973; Maris, 1969a; McIntosh et al., 1981; Weiss, 1968).

Although, as McIntosh et al. (1981) point out, the oft-cited statement that the aged comprise 10 percent of the population but commit 25 percent of the suicides exaggerates the case, the relationship between age and suicide is essentially accurate. According to these researchers, who based their finding on U.S. Census Bureau figures from 1978 and official statistics compiled by the National Center for Health Statistics in 1976, those 65 and over made up 10.7 percent of the U.S. population and committed 17 percent of the suicides. Miller (1976), who analyzed 1975 data from the National Center for Health Statistics, noted that more than 100,000 persons 60 and over kill themselves each year. Data from that year revealed that those 60 and over represented 18.5 percent of the U.S. population but committed 23 percent of all suicides (Miller, 1979). It is clear that more older people kill themselves than do younger people.

Most elderly who attempt suicide are deadly serious about killing themselves. Unlike younger individuals, the elderly seldom attempt suicide as a cry for help or a means by which to get attention (Miller, 1979). According to Sendbuehler and Goldstein (1977), the ratio of completed suicides to attempts for the elderly is approximately 8:1. Several studies confirm that elderly persons almost always succeed in killing themselves and rarely make attempts that fail (Grollman, 1971; Resnick and Cantor, 1970; Gardner et al., 1964; Kreitman, 1977). The elderly more often use lethal means and have less recuperative powers, two possible explanations for the higher percentage of successful suicides in this age group (Batchelor and Napier, 1953; Benson and Brodie, 1975; Dublin, 1963; O'Neal et al., 1956).

Dramatic as these figures are, they underestimate the frequency of suicide among the aged. As Miller (1979), McIntosh et al. (1981), Osgood (1982), and others have noted, many suicides among the aged are not recognized and/or reported as suicides. The elderly can easily take overdoses of drugs, mix drugs, fail to take life-sustaining drugs, starve themselves, drink excessively, or have fatal "accidents."

DEMOGRAPHIC FACTORS IN ELDERLY SUICIDE

Suicide is indeed more prevalent among the elderly; however, certain segments of the elderly population are more likely to commit suicide than others. More specifically, elderly white males are the most vulnerable. This section reviews major findings from previous studies that have examined the role of sex, race, marital status, social class and occupation, and living environment in suicide among the elderly.

Sex

In all age groups suicide rates are significantly higher for males than females (Dublin, 1963; Bromley, 1966; Durkheim, 1951). So pronounced is this trend that Dublin (1963) referred to suicide as a "masculine type of behavior." The disparity of male and female suicide rates is more pronounced for the elderly than for any other age group.

Suicide among the elderly has consistently proven to be more prevalent among males (Miller, 1978; Birren, 1964; Bock, 1972; Botwinick, 1973; Maris, 1969a, 1969b; Kimmel, 1974; Sendbuehler and Goldstein, 1977; Atchley, 1980). White males over 65 have a suicide rate four times the national average, whereas white females over 65 have a rate twice the national average (Sendbuehler and Goldstein, 1977; Resnick and Cantor, 1970). The elderly male suicide rate in this country was 26.5 per 100,000 in 1978, a dramatically high rate relative to the suicide rate for the United States as a whole, which has remained between 9 and 13 per 100,000 since World War II (U.S. Bureau of the Census, 1980; see also Miller, 1979:3).

The elderly white male suicide rate is significantly higher than the elderly white female rate. Overall the ratio is roughly 3:1 (Niccolini, 1973). The suicide rate for white females reaches a peak in mid-life and then declines, whereas the male suicide rate continues to increase through the eighth decade of life (Miller, 1979; Breed and Huffine, 1979; Bromley, 1966; Sainsbury, 1962; Kaplan, 1979). The ratio of male to female suicides in the 65–69 age group is about 4:1, but by 85 the ratio is about 12:1 (Miller, 1979; Kastenbaum, 1972; Rachlis, 1970; Weiss, 1968). This disparity in rates has also been found for almost all European countries except Norway and Finland (Kastenbaum, 1972; Atchley, 1980; Sainsbury, 1968; Dublin, 1963).

Race

Elderly suicide rates for nonwhites are considerably lower than for whites (Miller, 1979; Busse and Pfeiffer, 1969; McIntosh and Santos, 1981; Niccolini, 1973). The ratio of elderly white to elderly nonwhite suicides in the later age groups is approximately 3:1 (Niccolini, 1973).

The trend for whites is an increase in suicides through the last stages of the life cycle. By contrast, minority suicide rates peak between 25 and 30 years of age and then decline through the later stages of the life cycle (McIntosh and Santos, 1981; Resnick and Cantor, 1970). Resnick and Cantor (1970) found suicide rates for blacks and whites to be roughly equal until age 35, when the rate for whites becomes two to three times higher.

There is great diversity among racial groups incorporated in the nonwhite category (Breed and Huffine, 1979; McIntosh and Santos, 1981). For instance, suicide rates of Chinese Americans are higher than those of whites at all ages; however, those of American Indians are higher only in youth (Kramer et al.,

1972). Data on specific minority groups are sparse; however, those data that are available suggest that each group displays its own characteristic age pattern of suicide (McIntosh and Santos, 1981). McIntosh and Santos (1981) found that suicide rates are highest among the old for Chinese, Japanese, and Filipino Americans. By contrast, suicide among elderly blacks and Native Americans is rare.

Marital Status

Nonmarried persons at all ages are more likely to commit suicide than are married persons (Breed and Huffine, 1979; Durkheim, 1951; Kastenbaum, 1972). Studies consistently reveal that the widowed elderly are particularly vulnerable to suicide (Gardner et al., 1964; MacMahon and Pugh, 1965; Kopell, 1977; Payne, 1975; Gubrium, 1974; Gibbs, 1965; Maris, 1969a, 1969b; Resnick and Cantor, 1970; Miller, 1978). In particular, elderly widowers represent the most "at risk" group for suicide (Berardo, 1967, 1968, 1970; Bock and Webber, 1972; Townsend, 1968).

Social Class and Occupation

In his classic study, *Le Suicide: Etude de Sociologie*, Durkheim (1897; translated as *Suicide*, 1951) described suicide as mainly an upper-class phenomenon, suggesting that, unlike their fellows in lower socioeconomic classes, members of the upper class have fewer external restraints and controls on their behavior, resulting in higher rates of suicide. Since Durkheim's original work a body of literature on the relationship between social class and suicide has developed. Although some studies have found suicide most prevalent among members of the upper class, most of the studies reveal higher rates of suicide for members of the lower socioeconomic classes, including elderly members of the lower classes (Bock and Webber, 1972; Gardner et al., 1964; Breed, 1963; Sainsbury, 1963; Stengel, 1964; Weiss, 1968; Maris, 1967, 1969a).

Occupation has been used as a major indicator of social class position in the United States. Most studies confirm that suicide rates are highest among those in low-status occupations (Dublin, 1963; Dublin and Bunzel, 1933; Powell, 1958; Maris, 1967; Sainsbury, 1968).

Previous research has also confirmed a direct relationship between downward social mobility, occasioned by job loss or "occupational skidding," and suicide (Breed, 1963; Gardner et al., 1964; Maris, 1967, 1969a; Batchelor, 1957). Retirement in our society may be viewed as age-specific occupational skidding. Numerous researchers have implied a relationship between retirement and suicide (Maris, 1969a; Batchelor, 1957; Breed and Huffine, 1979; Butler, 1975; Farberow and Moriwaki, 1975; Kopell, 1977; Miller, 1979; Sainsbury, 1962, 1968; Wolff, 1971).

Living Environments

Environment has a major effect on human behavior. Suicide rates are highest for those elderly living in urban areas, particularly lower-class, inner-city neighborhoods experiencing social disorganization (Sainsbury, 1963; Cavan, 1928; Schmid, 1953; Gardner et al., 1964; Henry and Short, 1954).

Another important predictor of suicide in the aged is isolation, desolation, or loneliness. The negative effect of social isolation has been identified as a key variable in elderly suicides (Townsend, 1968; Gubrium, 1974; Shanas et al., 1968; Tunstall, 1966; Sainsbury, 1963). Elderly male widowers are particularly isolated geographically, socially, and emotionally, and as a result are even more vulnerable to suicide (Bock, 1972; Bock and Webber, 1972; Berardo, 1970; Maris, 1969a).

THEORETICAL EXPLANATIONS AND CONCEPTUAL MODELS

The Cultural Context

Cowgill and Holmes (1972) developed a cross-societal theory of aging demonstrating a strong relationship between level of modernization in society (based on level of technology, degree of urbanization, rate of social change, and degree of Westernization) and status of the aged. They concluded that in Western technologically advanced societies the aged are devalued and hold less power, status, and economic control than in less advanced societies. Their theory gained further support from Palmore and Manton's (1974) cross-cultural study in thirty-one countries, which demonstrated that the status of the aged is lower in more modernized countries. Suicide rates of the aged are highest in urban, industrialized countries, such as the United States (Quinney, 1965).

Rosow (1967) argues that the relative position of the aged in any society is governed by six institutional factors: (1) their ownership of property and control over the opportunities of the young; (2) their command of strategic knowledge and skills; (3) strong religiosity and sacred traditions; (4) strong kinship and extended family bonds in a communal or Gemeinschaft-type of social organization; (5) a low productivity economy; and (6) high mutual dependence and reciprocal aid among members (p. 9). In American society, according to Rosow, the aged suffer a loss of status position on all these institutional dimensions.

American society highly values youth and beauty, productivity, progress, speed, and independence. In his classic study of American society, Robin Williams (1970) concluded that occupational success is not just one life goal among others in American society, but is *the* outstanding trait of American culture. Mizruchi's work (1964) further confirms the emphasis on work and success in our society. Retired from participation in the occupational role, the elderly may suffer a severe loss of status, role, and power in our society, as well as loss of income.

The elderly in this country are often viewed as useless, dependent, nonproductive, a burden to be borne by younger members of the society. They are "over the hill, down the drain, out to pasture, fading fast" (Butler, 1975:2). They are often the victims of ageism or negative stereotyping. Images of aging found in books, cartoons, well-known jokes and sayings, and the media present a picture of the elderly as sexless and senile, grumpy and cranky, rigid and conservative in their values and thinking, wrinkled and toothless. As Lillian Troll suggests, the stereotype of the elderly woman in this country portrays her as "poor," "dumb," and "ugly" (Troll, 1977). The elderly in this country are advised to buy cream to cover up "those ugly age spots and wrinkles," to join health and figure spas, and to try all sorts of diets to "keep that youthful figure." Hair dyes to "get rid of that ugly gray," dentures and tooth polish to "recapture that youthful smile," and tonics and pills to "feel young and look young again" are also available. If all these remedies fail to transform an old face and figure into a young one, the multibillion dollar cosmetic business in the United States surely can perform the miracle.

In our youth-oriented, production-minded society the aged are devalued. Their skills become obsolete in the face of rapid technological change. Their wisdom and experience, gained from years of living, is not valued by many in the next generations who confront a different world from the one in which their parents and grandparents lived.

How do the elderly view themselves in such a culture? Presumably, when all of the diets and pills and creams and cosmetics fail, the elderly are forced to see themselves as old. Indeed, many accept the negative cultural images, and consequently their self-esteem and self-concept suffer.

The Sociological Perspective

Although earlier writers had reported a relationship between suicide rates and various variables, the first well-known sociological study of suicide was conducted in 1897 by Emile Durkheim. Durkheim's *Suicide* has exerted a major influence on sociology as a discipline and has served as a blueprint for later sociological studies of suicide in particular. In his work, Durkheim, influenced by the earlier work of Morselli (1882) and others, attempted to demonstrate that suicide cannot be explained by psychological or biological factors alone. Durkheim held that the nature and extent of man's involvement in society is a decisive factor in suicide and that various social factors, over which the individual has little or no control, are important in understanding the variations in suicide rates. As he noted:

First of all, it can be said that, as collective force is one of the obstacles best calculated to restrain suicide, its weakening involves a development of suicide. When society is strongly integrated, it holds individuals under its control, considers them at its service and thus forbids them to dispose willfully of themselves. . . . There is, in short, in a cohesive and animated society, a constant interchange of ideas and feelings from all to each and each to all, something like a mutual moral support, which instead of throwing the individual on his own resources, leads him to share in the collective energy and supports his own when exhausted. (Pp. 209–210)

In other words, the nature and extent of one's involvement in society constitute an important determining influence on one's vulnerability to suicide.

Durkheim sought explanations for variation in the suicide rate in terms of the degree to which man is integrated into the society and the extent to which his conduct is regulated (Durkheim, 1951). He derived two major propositions, namely (1) that the suicide rate varies inversely with the degree of integration of the group; and (2) that the suicide rate varies inversely with the degree of normative regulation.

Regarding the former, suicide varies with the strength of bonds between the person and the groups with which he is affiliated. Thus, not only is the person more vulnerable to suicide if he is too weakly integrated into groups that provide meaning and control over his life, but excessive integration also increases proclivity to suicide.

What Durkheim called integration has something to do with a person's social ties to the larger group, with his level of meaningful interaction with other members of the larger social group, with his degree of social "belongingness." Persons who are deeply and intimately involved with others in various social groups should, therefore, be low suicide risks. Durkheim consequently found the unmarried to have the highest rate of suicide. He identified the type of suicide that results from lack of integration as "egoistic": the stronger the forces throwing the individual onto his own resources, the greater the likelihood of egoistic suicide, according to Durkheim. The type of suicide resulting from overintegration, which was best demonstrated by the kamikaze pilots in World War II, Durkheim termed "altruistic."

In his writings Durkheim stressed the importance of integration into particular groups: family, religious, political, and occupational. In a close-knit society to which the individual is tied, the community shoulders some of the problems of the member, provides guidelines for action and sanctions for deviance, and offers a source of mutual support.

Regarding the second proposition, Durkheim's theory states that under certain conditions the regulative systems of society may be described as being in an abnormal state. This proposition has received the greatest amount of attention in the social sciences because it underlies the theory of anomie. In short, internal social dislocations resulting from social changes increase the probabilities that people will take their own lives. Suicide rates are, thus, abnormally high during periods of sudden prosperity as well as during periods of sudden economic depression because an abnormal number of society's members are thrust out of their usual roles, statuses, and societal contexts. Anomic suicide reflects a weakening of the social controls that help regulate the morally mandated aspirations of society's members and the morally mandated means by which these aspirations may be attained (Mizruchi, 1964). When society fails to regulate the behavior of its members, according to Durkheim, passions run wild, desires are unlimited, and there are no norms specifying appropriate behavior. The result of such a state of normlessness is that man is forced to make his own life choices, regulate his own behavior, and find his own way. The person finding himself in such a position is provided no clear-cut set of rules. No specific set of expectations of what behavior is appropriate exists. The subjective component of such a situation leaves the individual with nowhere to go. Suicide resulting from the overregulation of human behavior was labeled "fatalistic"; however, Durkheim gave few examples of this type of suicide in his work.

Durkheim classified suicide among the aged as "egoistic." He postulated that suicide increases with age because society as a moral force begins to recede from the person, in terms of both his goals and his commitments, as he ages and withdraws from various roles and positions. The older individual is less integrated into and less dependent upon society.

Building on the early work of Durkheim, Irving Rosow (1967) suggests that the elderly tend to be less integrated into society due to (1) their removal and withdrawal from certain organizational contexts and associated roles, which weakens their ties to mediating structures, such as work, voluntary associations, and similar organizations; and (2) the contraction of their intimate social world, which results from relocation, incapacitation, and death of friends and peers. In comparison to other age groups, the elderly belong to fewer formal and informal social groups and also have fewer friendships (Rosow, 1967; Blau, 1973).

Not only are the elderly more likely to commit egoistic suicide because of their lack of integration into formal and informal social groups; they are also more likely to commit anomic suicide as well. As Rosow (1973) and Neugarten (1968) point out, our culture does not provide older members with definitions and meaningful norms, so the older person is left to structure the "aged role" himself with no clear prescriptions as to the appropriate behavior, a condition referred to by Durkheim as "anomie."

In his book Durkheim reported that suicide varied by age and gender. Most notable was the markedly high ratio of suicides of men compared to women: 3:1. His classic explanation for the greater proportion of suicides among widowers, as compared to widows, is that men derive more from marriage than women.

Durkheim recognized that participation in the family represented one of the most important ties among society's members. He suggested that the state of marriage and membership in a family integrate members by exerting a regulative force on them and by acting as a stimulant to intensive interpersonal relations that draw members into firm and meaningful union, thus providing some degree of immunity against suicide. Durkheim explained higher rates of suicide among the widowed as due to "domestic anomie," that is, a deregulation of behavior resulting from the death of a spouse. He also viewed widowhood as a force that weakened the familial integration of individuals. Thus, the suicide of the widowed may be referred to as both anomic and egoistic. Berardo (1968, 1970) similarly describes widowhood as vague and unstructured, lacking any clear guidelines for behavior and lacking supportive interaction with friends, kin, and co-workers. Two other followers of Durkheim, Henry and Short (1954), explain suicide in terms of the weakening of the relational system constituted by marriage; and Bock (1972:72) points out, "Marriage not only integrates the individual into a close and meaningful association but also regulates him by requiring him to take the other person into account in activities and decisions."

The elderly male widower is the most vulnerable to suicide and likely to be the most socially isolated (Berardo, 1967, 1968, 1970; Maris, 1969a; Gubrium, 1974; Bock and Webber, 1972; Bock, 1972). He has fewer relatives and kin living nearby, participates less with family and friends, and is less involved in formal organizations and the community. As Berardo points out, widowhood is difficult because of the lack of clear-cut expectations; this is felt more acutely by the widowed male who, unlike the female, is often unfamiliar with domestic and other roles not associated with formal occupation. Coupled with this is the fact that females have traditionally maintained kin and friendship networks.

Durkheim considered the occupational group, endowed with political status, to be particularly cohesive and to constitute the richest channel for a common life. He advocated reintegration in modern industrial society through intermediate occupational groups. Powell (1970) also notes that the male is primarily integrated into American society through the occupational role.

Aged white males in America suffer the most severe status loss of any group. Maris (1969a), Breed (1963), and Powell (1970) have all related the high suicide rates of elderly white males to the severe loss of status, power, money, and role relationships formerly provided by participation in work. By comparison, women generally, and males among the minorities, two groups that traditionally have held lower-status positions in our society, have less to lose upon retirement than white males and thus tend to display lower rates of suicide than white males.

A related sociological position, derived from the symbolic interactionists' perspective, is role theory (Lopata, 1973; Blau, 1973). Symbolic interactionists posit that individuals derive an identity and sense of the self through interaction with significant others in the performance of social roles in groups. Some sources of identity are more important than others, that is, some relationships, such as marriage, involve "significant others." According to Everett C. Hughes, some roles are associated with "master status" and have a greater impact on the self and identity than others. The occupational role is a "master status" in our society, particularly for males.

Loss of social roles, according to this perspective, results in a loss of identity and subsequent loss of esteem, lowered self-concept, and a sense of meaninglessness in life. From this perspective widowhood and retirement are viewed as major losses of social roles, which place the individual outside his normal group of patterned associations, which formerly served to locate incumbents in a matrix of other roles and provide a sense of identity and meaning.

Psychological Perspectives

Although he primarily emphasized social forces as causes of suicide, Durkheim recognized and noted the intimate connection between losses in the social realm and those in the psychological one. In *Suicide* he wrote that egoism is said to be accompanied by "collective currents of depression and disillusionment," and by "miserable weariness and sad depression" (1951:214, 225).

Freud, however, is recognized as the father of psychological explanations of suicide. In his early work Freud (1917) contended that loss of a loved one results in feelings of abandonment and rejection, which may swell into anger directed against the lost loved one. Loss results in a particular state of mind in the individual. In an attempt to kill the memory of the lost loved one, suicide may result. In his later works Freud (1948) postulated the existence within each human being of a death instinct (Thanatos) which, in the case of suicidal intent, may overcome the life instinct (Eros).

Influenced by Freud's earlier work, several psychological explanations of suicide have focused on the concepts of loss and depression as they affect the state of mind of the individual and perhaps induce suicide. Loss of loved ones, physical health and faculties, job, status, power and income, personal possessions, social roles, self-esteem, and self-confidence contribute to depression in the aged. Depression has been identified as a major factor in elderly suicide (Gardner et al., 1964; Barraclough et al., 1974; Bennett, 1973; Benson and Brodie, 1975; O'Neal et al., 1956; Batchelor and Napier, 1953; Butler and Lewis, 1973). Batchelor (1955) noted that at least 80 percent of all suicidal old people are depressed. In another statement Batchelor went so far as to suggest that "all suicidal old people . . . are depressed" (1955:291).

Two major factors have been recognized as contributing to depression and suicide among the aged: helplessness and hopelessness. Bibring (1953) developed a theory that depression is an ego state where the feeling of helplessness is the basic underlying dynamic. Seligman (1975, 1976) defines helplessness as a state in which individuals experience an inability to control significant life events and suggests that it is the core of all depression. The aged are the most susceptible to helplessness, according to Seligman, because they have experienced the greatest loss of control. Shultz (1976) similarly argues that loss of job, income, physical health, work, and childrearing roles results in increased helplessness and depression in the aged. Applebaum (1963) and Stengel (1964) have also identified the basic feeling of helplessness as a factor in suicide.

Karl Menninger (1938), who has exerted a major influence on the study of depression and suicide in the aged, postulated that suicide results from three wishes: the wish to kill, the wish to be killed, and the wish to die. He characterized suicides of the elderly as a result of the wish to die. In emphasizing the wish to die as the major motive in elderly suicide, Menninger identified hopelessness as a major contributing factor. Farber (1968) similarly conceived of suicide among the aged as a desperate response to hopeless, intolerable life situations when he wrote, "Suicide occurs when there appears to be no available path that will lead to a tolerable existence. . . . It is when the life interest is one of despairing hopelessness that suicide occurs" (p. 17). Farber defines hope as the relationship between a sense of personal competence and life-threatening events. Hopelessness has also been identified in numerous other studies as a motive in elderly suicide (Beck et al., 1975; Perlin and Schmidt, 1975; Schneidman and Farberow, 1957; Maris, 1981; Breed, 1967; Sullivan, 1956).

In the elderly, depression often manifests itself in specific somatic complaints, including changes in eating and sleeping patterns, fatigue, increased heart rate, headaches and muscle pains, constipation, and other concerns with bodily functions (Zeamore and Eames, 1979). According to Zung (1980), depressed elderly persons are "anxious, preoccupied with physical symptoms, fatigued, withdrawn, retarded, apathetic, inert, disinterested in their surroundings, and lacking in drive." Numerous other studies have shown that apathy, withdrawal, and functional slowness are common symptoms of depression in the elderly.

The Stress Model in Suicide

Selye (1956) and others later defined stress as physical stimuli and emotional factors which place a strain on the homeostatic system. Stress has since been defined by Lazarus (1966) as the degree of imbalance between the demands of a life event or group of life events placed on the individual and his ability to cope with those demands. Holmes and Rahe (1967) have similarly defined stress from a life events perspective. Their forty-two-item checklist of stressful life events remains one of the most popular instruments used to measure stress. A stressor has been defined in the literature as anything which implies a threat to the organism. External stressors include events such as widowhood, retirement, or relocation, whereas internal stressors refer to changes in bodily or mental function, or disease within the organism.

According to Marv Miller (1979:25), "Whether an older person is able to resolve a suicidal crisis or succumbs to self-inflicted death is very much a function of the ability to cope with stress." Late life represents a period of multiple stresses at a time when the organism is least able to deal with stress. Impaired ability to cope with stress has been noted as a major characteristic of the aging process by Eisdorfer and Wilkie (1977), Jarvick (1975), and Welford (1962). Failing health and chronic disease, impaired eyesight, hearing, and cognitive functioning, as well as poorer recuperative powers, are all sources of stress in late life. Such stress may further consist of loss of income, status, and power; loss of social roles in work, family, and the community; loss of family, friends, and loved ones; loss of mobility and independence; loss of home and personal possessions; isolation through physical disability; and a variety of other losses. Rosow (1973) suggests that loss of social roles and function, which accompanies the aging process in this country, introduces stress because role loss excludes the aged from participation in work, family, and other social groups. Ageism and negative cultural images have also been noted as a source of stress in late life (Lehr, 1977; Loether, 1975; Payne, 1975).

Stress has been demonstrated to have a negative effect on physical health (Holmes and Rahe, 1967; Dohrenwend and Dohrenwend, 1974; Holmes and Masuda, 1974; Rabkin and Streuning, 1976) and mental health (Lowenthal and Haven, 1968; Payne, 1975) and to precipitate suicide (Paykel et al., 1975).

The available body of literature on stress and aging identifies various factors that mediate the effects of stress. Personal resources (health and income), social supports (family, friends, formal and informal group memberships), personality characteristics (ego defenses, flexibility), and coping strategies (fight, flight, freeze) determine, in large part, whether the aging individual effectively withstands stress or succumbs to mental or physical breakdown, death, or suicide.

In a recent study Elwell and Maltbie-Crannell (1981) found that income and health and the social support of family and friends significantly lessened the negative impact of stress on their elderly subjects, particularly elderly males. They also discovered a strong direct negative relationship between role loss and personal resources and social support available (i.e., those who had lost more social roles had less money, poorer health, and fewer relations with family and friends). Similarly, Palmore et al. (1978) in their large-scale Duke studies concluded that stressful life events, such as retirement, per se do not cause specific problems for the aged; however, those elderly with few psychological, personal, and social resources who suffer many losses in a short period of time are particularly vulnerable to break down. Numerous researchers have similarly noted the importance of personal and social resources in mediating the negative effects of stress (Pearlin and Schooler, 1978; Hale and Lebowitz, 1974; Janis, 1974).

Many students of stress have focused on personality characteristics and coping strategies as they mediate the negative impact of stress. Elderly individuals with better verbal skills, higher intelligence, a better memory, higher morale, better self-concept, a sense of mastery or control over life, well-developed psychological defenses, and flexible personalities fare better when confronted by the multiple stresses of aging. McIntosh et al. (1981), Rosow (1973), Miller (1979), and others have all emphasized the importance of stress as a predictor of suicide among the elderly. Rosow suggests that people can be placed on a continuum. On the one end are persons who have very high tolerance to stress and unusual flexibility and resilience, having personalities which allow them to adjust to strain. On the other are persons with low tolerance for strain, limited personality resources, and rigid, ineffective modes of responding to crises.

According to Birren and Renner (1977), personality intervenes in four ways: some people create or seek stress, others avoid or minimize it. These are behavioral tendencies. Internally, once confronted with stress, some amplify the stress, others dampen it. Atchley (1976) and George (1980) have both noted the importance of one characteristic, which they refer to as "flexibility," in facilitating successful adaptation to retirement and other events characteristic of late life. An ability to adjust to new circumstances, to change patterns of thinking or behavior, if necessary, and to take life as it comes characterizes the flexible individual, who can successfully cope with stress.

Miller (1979) and McIntosh et al. (1981) point out that coping strategies that can be relied upon in late life are developed early in life and practiced and refined throughout adolescence and mid-life. Three late life coping strategies described in the literature are: renewed assault on goals established earlier in life; psychological and social denial (Weisman, 1972; Weisman and Hackett, 1967); and "freeze," an adaptive response described by Jarvick and Russell (1977) in which the elderly play dead and shift their mind into neutral. Lazarus (1966, 1975; Lazarus et al., 1974) has noted the importance of cognitive processes in coping. He discusses two components of cognitive appraisal: primary, in which the individual evaluates the person/environment transaction to determine if the event is stressful or not and to what extent; and secondary, in which the individual evaluates coping resources and options available. Obviously, impaired sight, hearing, or memory and other cognitive impairments negatively affect the elderly's ability to cope with stress and thus avoid suicide.

SUMMARY AND CONCLUSIONS

Available statistics clearly demonstrate that the elderly are more prone to commit suicide than other age groups in the United States. Furthermore, certain groups of elderly are more at risk than others. Males, the unmarried, whites, those in lower socioeconomic classes and low-status occupations or who have experienced "occupational skidding," and the lonely and isolated in urban areas are the most susceptible to suicide.

Various explanations have been offered for the disproportionately higher rates of suicide among the aged, particularly white widowed males. Explanations have focused on multiple losses suffered by the elderly (physical, emotional, mental, financial, personal, and social) as they precipitate depression, a causal factor in elderly suicide. The stress model identifies loss and depression as factors that impact on vulnerability to stress, ability to cope with stress, and suicide in the elderly. Finally, viewed in a larger cultural context, suicide is more characteristic of the aged in Westernized, urbanized, industrialized societies than in pre-industrialized or developing countries.

It should be clear that there are many interrelated factors that predict suicide in the elderly. As Barter (1969:9) previously noted with respect to the etiology of elderly suicide, "A precipitating cause may be less obvious and the suicide may appear to be a reaction to a total life situation more than any single event." Figure 23.1 presents a hypothetical representation of the relationship between

Figure 23.1
Theoretical Model of Aging and Suicide

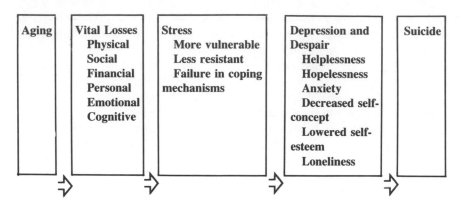

aging and suicide. It is not an empirically established causal model, but rather a suggested direction of possible relationships to be tested in the future. The multiple losses of aging render the elderly more vulnerable to stress, while at the same time depleting their resistance to stress and their coping mechanisms. Faced with multiple stresses and decreased ability to cope, the elderly are often left helpless to alter their life situations. The resulting sense of despair and hopelessness produces a lowering of self-concept and self-esteem in the helpless elderly. The situation of many elderly is "like a closed room in which one is subjected to excruciating and relentless emotional and physical pain, a room in which the one door leading out is labeled SUICIDE" (Maris, 1981:315).

We as a society and as gerontologists have a responsibility to our elderly members to recognize and identify those particularly susceptible to suicide. Most of the elderly who commit suicide are depressed. Physicians, practicing gerontologists, ministers, social workers, family, and friends should learn to recognize the symptoms of depression in the aged. Loss of appetite, change in mood, sadness, change in sleep pattern, and increased somatic complaints should be especially noted. The majority of elderly who commit suicide also give verbal or behavioral clues before they take their own lives. Sensitivity to the needs and feelings of the aged is crucial.

We also have a responsibility to provide meaningful new social roles, or at least to allow our aged to continue to perform the roles they have engaged in all their lives. Finally, an important aspect in suicide prevention is education about the aging process, myths and realities of old age, and problems and stresses of late life. Such education is necessary if we are ever to truly value our aged as worthwhile, contributing citizens and to erase the myths and stereotypes surrounding aging in this country.

In the final analysis, perhaps nothing short of a cultural revolution, in which old age comes to be viewed once again as a valued status in our society, rather than as a cursed disease or burden, will significantly reduce the number of elderly suicides in this country.

REFERENCES

Applebaum, S.A. The problem solving aspect of suicide. *Journal of Projective Techniques*, 1963, *27*, 259–268.

Atchley, R.C. *The sociology of retirement*. Wiley, New York, 1976.

————. Aging and suicide: Reflections on the quality of life. In S.G. Haynes, M. Feinkib, J.A. Ross, and L. Stallones (Eds.), *Epidemiology of aging*. NIH Publication No. 8-969, U.S. Department of Health and Human Services, July 1980, 158.

Barraclough, B.; Bunch, J.; Nelson, B.; and Sainsbury, P. A hundred cases of suicide: Clinical aspects. *British Journal of Psychiatry*, 1974, *125*, 355–373.

Barter, J.T. Self destructive behavior in adolescents and adults: Similarities and differences. In U.S. Department of Health, Education and Welfare, *Suicide among the American Indians: Two workshops*. PHS Publication No. 1903, USGPO, Washington, D.C., 1969, 7–10.

Batchelor, I.R.C. Management and prognosis of suicidal attempts in old age. *Geriatrics*, 1955, *10*, 291–293.

————. Suicide in old age. In E. Schneidman and N. Farberow (Eds.), *Clues to suicide*. McGraw-Hill, New York, 1957.

Batchelor, I.R.C., and Napier, M. Attempted suicide in old age. *British Medical Journal*, 1953, *2*, 1186–1190.

Beck, A.T., and Rush, A.J. A cognitive model of anxiety formation and anxiety resolution. In G. Sarason and C.D. Spielberger (Eds.), *Anxiety and stress*, vol. 2. Wiley, New York, 1975.

Bennett, A.E. Psychiatric management of geriatric depressive disorders. *Diseases of the Nervous System*, 1973, *34*, 222–225.

Benson, R., and Brodie, D. Suicide by overdoses of medicines among the aged. *Journal of the American Geriatrics Society*, 1975, *23*, 304–308.

Berardo, F.M. Social adaptation to widowhood among a rural-urban aged population. Washington Agricultural Experiment Station Bulletin 689, USGPO, Washington, D.C., December 1967.

————. Widowhood status in the United States: Perspectives on a neglected aspect of the family life cycle. *Family Coordinator*, 1968, *17*, 191–203.

————. Survivorship and social isolation: The case of the aged widower. *Family Coordinator*, 1970, *19*, 11–25.

Bibring, E. The mechanism of depression. In P. Greenacre (Ed.), *Affective disorders*. International Universities Press, New York, 1953.

Birren, J. *Relations of development and aging*. Charles C. Thomas, Springfield, Ill., 1964.

Birren, J.E., and Renner, V.J. Health behavior and aging. Paper presented at the Conference of the Institut de la Vie, Vichy, France, April 1977.

Blau, Z.S. *Old age in a changing society*. New Viewpoints, New York, 1973.

Bock, E.W. Aging and suicide. *Family Coordinator*, 1972, *21*, 71–79.

Bock, E.W., and Webber, I. Suicide among the elderly. *Journal of Marriage and the Family*, 1972, *34*, 24–31.

Botwinick, J. *Aging and behavior*. Springer, New York, 1973.

Breed, W. Occupational mobility and suicide among white males. *American Sociological Review*, 1963, *28*, 179–188.

———. Suicide and loss in social interaction. In E.S. Schneidman (Ed.), *Essays in self destruction*. Science House, New York, 1967.

Breed, W., and Huffine, C. Sex differences in suicide among older white Americans: A role and developmental approach. In O.J. Kaplan (Ed.), *Psychopathology of aging*. Academic Press, New York, 1979.

Bromley, D.B. *The psychology of human aging*. Penguin, Baltimore, 1966.

Busse, E.W., and Pfeiffer, E. *Behavior and adaptation in late life*. Little, Brown, Boston, 1969.

Butler, R.N. *Why survive? Being old in America*. Harper and Row, New York, 1975.

Butler, R.N., and Lewis, M.I. *Aging and mental health: Positive psychological approaches*, 2nd ed. Mosby, St. Louis, 1973.

Cavan, R.S. *Suicide*. Russell and Russell, New York, 1928.

Cowgill, D.O., and Holmes, L.D. (Eds.). *Aging and modernization*. Appleton-Century-Crofts, New York, 1972.

Dohrenwend, B., and Dohrenwend, B. (Eds.), *Stressful life events: Their nature and effects*. Wiley, New York, 1974.

Dublin, L. *Suicide*. Ronald Press, New York, 1963.

Dublin, L., and Bunzel, B. *To be or not to be*. Harrison, Smith and Robert Haas, New York, 1933.

Durkheim, E. *Suicide: A study in sociology*. Free Press, New York, 1951.

Eisdorfer, C., and Wilkie, F. Stress, disease, aging, and behavior. In J.E. Birren and K.W. Schaie (Eds.), *Handbook of the psychology of aging*. Van Nostrand Reinhold, New York, 1977.

Elwell, F., and Maltbie-Crannell, A.D. The impact of role loss upon coping resources and life satisfaction of the elderly. *Journal of Gerontology*, 1981, *36*, 223–232.

Farber, M.L. *Theory of suicide*. Funk and Wagnalls, New York, 1968.

Farberow, N., and Moriwaki, S. Self-destructive crises in the older person. *Gerontologist*, 1975, *15*, 333–337.

Freud, S. *Mourning and melancholia. Collected papers IV*. 1917; repr. Hogarth Press, London, 1948.

Gardner, E.A.; Bahn, A.K.; and Mack, M. Suicide and psychiatric care in the aging. *Archives of General Psychiatry*, 1964, *10*, 547–553.

George, L.K. *Role transitions in later life*. Brooks/Cole, Monterey, Calif., 1980.

Gibbs, J.P. (Ed.). *Suicide*. Russell and Russell, New York, 1965.

Grollman, E. *Suicide: Prevention, intervention, and postvention*. Beacon Press, Boston, 1971.

Gubrium, J.F. Marital desolation and the evaluation of everyday life in old age. *Journal of Marriage and the Family*, 1974, *36*, 107–113.

Hale, S., and Lebowitz, B.D. Stress, isolation, and psychiatric impairment among the urban elderly. Paper presented at the 27th Annual Meeting of the Gerontological Society of America, Portland, Ore., 1974.

Henry, A., and Short, J.F. *Suicide and homicide*. Free Press, Glencoe, Ill., 1954.

Holmes, T., and Masuda, M. Life changes and illness susceptibility. In B. Dohrenwend and B. Dohrenwend (Eds.), *Stressful life events*. Wiley, New York, 1974.

Holmes, T.H., and Rahe, R.H. The social readjustment scale. *Journal of Psychosomatic Research*, 1967, *11*, 213–218.

Janis, I. Vigilance and decision-making in personal crisis. In G.V. Coelho, D.A. Hamburg, and J.E. Adams (Eds.), *Coping and adaptation*. Basic Books, New York, 1974.

Jarvick, L.E. Thoughts on the psychobiology of aging. *American Psychologist*, 1975, *30*, 576–583.

Jarvick, L.E., and Russell, D. Anxiety, aging, and the third emergency reaction. *Journal of Gerontology*, 1977, *34*, 197–200.

Johnson, B.D. Durkheim's one cause of suicide. *American Sociological Review*, 1965, *30*, 875–886.

Kaplan, O.J. (Ed.). *Psychopathology of aging*. Academic Press, New York, 1979.

Kastenbaum, R., and Aisenberg, R. *The psychology of death*. Springer, New York, 1972.

Kimmel, D. *Adulthood and aging*. Wiley, New York, 1974.

Kopell, B.S. Treating the suicidal patient. *Geriatrics*, 1977, *32*, 65–67.

Kramer, M.; Pollack, E.S.; Redick, R.W.; and Locke, B.Z. *Mental disorders/ suicide*. Harvard University Press, Cambridge, Mass., 1972.

Kreitman, N. *Parasuicide*. Wiley, New York, 1977.

Lazarus, R.S. *Psychological stress and the coping process*. McGraw-Hill, New York, 1966.

————. Psychological stress and coping in adaptation and illness. In S.M. Weiss (Ed.), *Proceedings of the National Heart and Lung Institute Working Conference on Health Behavior*. U.S. Department of Health, Education and Welfare, Publ. No. 76-868, USGPO, Washington, D.C., May 1975.

Lazarus, R.S.; Averill, J.R.; and Opton, E.M., Jr. The psychology of coping: Issues of research and assessment. In G.V. Coelho, D.A. Hamburg, and J.E. Adams (Eds.), *Coping and adaptation*. Basic Books, New York, 1974.

Lecky, W.E.H. *History of European morals from Augustus to Charlemagne*, 2 vols. D. Appleton, New York, 1869.

Lehr, U. Stereotypes of aging and age norms. In J.E. Birren and K.W. Schaie (Eds.), *Handbook of the psychology of aging*. Van Nostrand Reinhold, New York, 1977.

Loether, H.J. *Problems of aging: Sociological and social psychological perspectives*, 2nd ed. Dickenson Publishing, Belmont, Calif., 1975.

Lopata, H.Z. Self-identity in marriage and widowhood. *Sociological Quarterly*, 1973, *14*, 407–418.

Lowenthal, M., and Haven, C. Interaction and adaptation: Intimacy as a critical variable. In B. Neugarten (Ed.), *Middle age and aging*. University of Chicago Press, Chicago, 1968.

McIntosh, J.L.; Hubbard, R.W.; and Santos, J.F. Suicide among the elderly: A review of issues with case studies. *Journal of Gerontology*, 1981, *4*, 63–74.

McIntosh, J.L., and Santos, J.F. Suicide among minority elderly: A preliminary investigation. *Suicide and Life Threatening Behavior*, 1981, *11*, 151–166.

MacMahon, B., and Pugh, T. Suicide in the widowed. *American Journal of Epidemiology*, 1965, *81*, 23–31.

Maris, R.W. Suicide, status, and mobility in Chicago. *Social Forces*, 1967, *46*, 246–256.

———. *Social forces in urban suicide*. Dorsey Press, New York, 1969a.

———. The sociology of suicide prevention: Policy implications of differences between suicidal patients and completed suicides. *Social Problems*, 1969b, *17*, 133–149.

———. *Pathways to suicide: A survey of self-destructive behavior*. Johns Hopkins University Press, Baltimore, 1981.

Menninger, K. *Man against himself*. Harcourt, Brace and World, New York, 1938.

Miller, M. Suicide among older men. Ph.D. diss., University of Michigan, Ann Arbor, 1976.

———. Toward a profile of the older white male suicide. *Gerontologist*, 1978, *18*. 80–82.

———. *Suicide after sixty: The final alternative*. Springer, New York, 1979.

Mizruchi, E.H. *Success and opportunity*. Free Press, Glencoe, Ill., 1964.

Morselli, E. *Suicide: An essay on comparative moral statistics*. D. Appleton, New York, 1882.

Neugarten, B. (Ed.). *Middle age and aging*. University of Chicago Press, Chicago, 1968.

Niccolini, R. Reading the signals for suicidal risk. *Geriatrics*, 1973, *28*, 71–72.

O'Neal, P.; Robins, E.; and Schmidt, E.H. A psychiatric study of attempted suicide in persons over sixty years of age. *Archives of Neurological Psychiatry*, 1956, *75*, 275–284.

Osgood, N.J. Suicide in the elderly: Are we heeding the warnings? *Postgraduate Medicine*, 1982, *72*, 84–88.

Palmore, E.; Cleveland, W.P.; Nowlin, J.B.; Ramm, D.; and Siegler, I. Stress and adaptation in later life. *Journal of Gerontology*, 1978, *34*, 841–851.

Palmore, E., and Manton, K. Modernization and status of the aged: International correlations. *Journal of Gerontology*, 1974, *29*, 205–210.

Paykel, E.S.; Prusoff, B.A.; and Myers, J.K. Suicide attempts and recent life events. *Archives of General Psychiatry*, 1975, *32*, 327–333.

Payne, E.C. Depression and suicide. In J.G. Howells (Ed.), *Modern perspectives in the psychiatry of old age*. Brunner/Mazel, New York, 1975.

Pearlin, I.I., and Schooler, C. The structure of coping. *Journal of Health and Social Behavior*, 1978, *19*, 2–21.

Peck, R. Psychological developments in the second half of life. In J.E. Anderson (Ed.), *Psychological aspects of aging*. American Psychological Association, Washington, D.C., 1956.

Perlin, S., and Schmidt, C.W., Jr. Psychiatry. In S. Perlin (Ed.), *A handbook for the study of suicide*. Oxford University Press, New York, 1975.

Powell, E.H. Occupation status and suicide. *American Journal of Sociology*, 1958, *23*, 131–139.

———. *The design of discord*. Oxford University Press, New York, 1970.

Quinney, R. Suicide, homicide, and economic development. *Social Forces*, 1965, *43*, 401–408.

Rabkin, S.G., and Streuning, E.L. Life events, stress and illness. *Science*, 1976, *194*, 1013–1020.

Rachlis, D. Suicide and loss adjustment in the aging. *Bulletin of Suicidology*, 1970, *10*, 23–26.

Resnik, H.L.P., and Cantor, J. Suicide and aging. *Journal of the American Geriatrics Society*, 1970, *18*, 152–158.

Rockwell, D., and O'Brien, W. Physicians' knowledge and attitudes about suicide. *Journal of the American Medical Association*, 1973, *225*, 1347–1349.

Rosow, I. *Social integration of the aged.* Free Press, New York, 1967.

———. The social context of the aging self. *Gerontologist*, 1973, *12*, 82–87.

Sainsbury, P. Suicide in later life. *Gerontologica Clinica*, 1962, *4*, 161–170.

———. Social and epidemiological aspects of suicide with special reference to the aged. In R.H. Williams (Ed.), *Processes of aging: Social and psychological perspectives.* Atherton Press, New York, 1963.

———. Suicide and depression. In A. Cooper and A. Walk (Eds.), Recent developments in affective disorders. *British Journal of Psychiatry* (Special Publication), 1968, *2*, 1–13.

Schmid, C.F. Suicide in Minneapolis. *American Journal of Sociology*, 1953, *39*, 30–48.

Schneidman, E., and Farberow, N. *Clues to suicide.* McGraw-Hill, New York, 1957.

Schultz, R. Effects of control and predictability on the physical and psychological well-being of the institutionalized aged. *Journal of Personality and Social Psychology*, 1976, *33*, 563–573.

Seligman, M.E.P. *Helplessness.* W.H. Freeman, San Francisco, 1975.

———. Learned helplessness and depression in animals and men. In J.T. Spence, R.C. Carsen, and J.W. Thibaut (Eds.), *Behavioral approaches to therapy.* General Learning Press, Morristown, N.J., 1976.

Selye, H. *The stress of life.* McGraw-Hill, New York, 1956.

Sendbuehler, J.M., and Goldstein, S. Attempted suicide among the aged. *Journal of the American Geriatrics Society*, 1977, *25*, 245–248.

Shanas, E.; Townsend, P.; Wedderburn, D.; Friis, H.; Milhof, P.; and Stehouwer, G. *Old people in three industrial societies.* Atherton Press, New York, 1968.

Stengel, E. *Suicide and attempted suicide.* Penguin, Baltimore, 1964.

Sullivan, H.S. *The collected works of Henry Stack Sullivan.* Norton, New York, 1956.

Townsend, P. Isolation, desolation, and loneliness. In E. Shanas, P. Townsend, D. Wedderburn, H. Friis, P. Milhof, and G. Stehouwer (Eds.), *Old people in three industrial societies.* Atherton Press, New York, 1968.

Troll, L.; Israel, J.; and Israel, K. *Looking ahead: A woman's guide to the problems and joys of growing older.* Prentice-Hall, Englewood Cliffs, N.J., 1977.

Tunstall, J. *Old and alone.* Routledge and Kegan Paul, London, 1966.

U.S. Bureau of the Census, *Statistical abstract of the United States, 1980.* USGPO, Washington, D.C., 1980.

Weisman, A.D. Common fallacies about dying patients. In A.D. Weisman (Ed.), *Dying and denying: A psychiatric study of terminality.* Behavioral Publications, New York, 1972.

Weisman, A.D., and Hackett, Th.P. Denial as a social act. In S. Levin and R.T. Kahana (Eds.), *Psychodynamic studies on aging.* International Universities Press, New York, 1967.

Weiss, J.M.A. Suicide in the aged. In H.L.P. Resnik (Ed.), *Suicidal behaviors: Diagnosis and management.* Little, Brown, Boston, 1968.

Welford, A.T. On changes of performance with age. *Lancet*, 1962, *1*, 335–339.

Williams, R.M., Jr. *American society.* Knopf, New York, 1970.

Wolff, K. The treatment of the depressed and suicidal geriatric patient. *Geriatrics*, 1971, *26*, 65–69.

Zeamore, R., and Eames, N. Psychic and somatic symptoms of depression among young adults, institutionalized aged, and noninstitutionalized aged. *Journal of Gerontology*, 1979, *34*, 716–722.

Zung, W. Affective disorders. In E. Busse and D. Blazer (Eds.), *Handbook of geriatric psychiatry*. Van Nostrand Reinhold, New York, 1980.

24

VICTIMS OF CRIME

PRUE GERRY
BARBARA P. PAYNE

Crime is not a new national issue, but how it affects the elderly is a relatively new area of study for gerontologists and criminologists. Although criminologists Block and Geis first pointed out the risk potential of the elderly to criminal victimization in 1962, it was not until the 1970s that awareness of the differential impact of crime on the elderly became sufficient to receive attention from policymakers, advocacy groups, and researchers (Cook and Cook, 1976; Cunningham, 1976; Ragan, 1977).

HISTORY: CRIMES AGAINST THE ELDERLY

For a decade, public attention to the victimization of the elderly was channeled into political and programmatic actions by those concerned about the welfare of the elderly. The 1971 White House Conference on Aging recommended that policies to protect the elderly be given high priority. The emphasis was carried over to the 1981 White House Conference on Aging. The president called attention to the plight of the elderly as special victims of crime in 1975 (Ford, 1975). Numerous congressional committees of the House and Senate held hearings on the victimization of the elderly (U.S. House of Representatives, Select Committee on Aging, 1981a; ibid., 1981b). The National Retired Teachers Association/American Association of Retired Persons (NRTA/AARP) developed a crime prevention program for its elderly members. The journal *Police Chief* devoted two issues to the criminal victimization of the elderly (Adkins, 1977; Pope and Feyerheim, 1976), and the Administration on Aging's (AOA) house publication, *Aging*, devoted an issue and carried a feature article on crimes against the elderly as a national crisis (Goldsmith and Thomas, 1974). National magazines carried feature stories on the impact of victimization on the elderly (*Time*, November 29, 1976; *Newsweek*, July 12, 1976). In 1975, the Administration on Aging supported a National Conference on Crimes Against the

Elderly in Washington. All this activity created the popular assumption that crimes against the person were higher for the elderly than for the general population.

When researchers began to investigate the problem and test assumptions about the victimization of the elderly, they found not only contradictory evidence, but strongly ensconced stereotypes about crime among the elderly, as well as a new problem, the elders' fear of crime. In fact, low actual victimization rates occurred together with high rates of fear, creating a fear-victimization paradox (Linquist and Duke, 1982). Research efforts to resolve or explain this paradox continue to dominate the research literature on crime among the elderly.

The most commonly held stereotype was that crime affects the elderly much more than other age groups (Ragan, 1977). The Harris surveys (1975, 1981), conducted for the National Council on the Aging, found that most Americans, including older people, believed that crime and the fear of crime are major problems and handicaps of old age. Older people consistently ranked crime and the fear of crime along with inflation as the most serious problems affecting their activities and life-style.

CHARACTERISTICS

Demography: Extent of Victimization

The basis for determining the extent of criminal victimization of the elderly has been to calculate victimization rates by age and type of offense. The major sources of data for analysis of the extent of victimization are local crime statistics; the FBI's Uniform Crime Reports; the U.S. Census Bureau's crime panel surveys for the Law Enforcement Assistance Administration (U.S. Department of Justice, 1975; Cook and Cook, 1976); the National Opinion Research Center's General Social Surveys; and community studies, such as the Boston study (Conklin, 1976), the Midwest Research Institute's Kansas City study (Cunningham, 1976), and the Los Angeles study (Ragan, 1977). Evidence from age-specific victimization studies based on these data showed that the commonly held beliefs about the extent of crime against the elderly and the fears of elders were unwarranted. People 65 years of age and older were less likely to be victimized in all major crime categories than younger persons, with the exception of personal larceny (purse-snatching and pocket-picking) and fraud (flimflam, medical, insurance, and consumer schemes).

The age pattern of victimization continued to hold for 1980 crime statistics and national surveys. Table 24.1 presents the rate of personal victimization by age and type of offense. As in other age groups, the most frequent crime against the elderly was personal larceny without contact. Another recent study on criminal victimization by the U.S. Department of Justice (1981) reported that the violent crime rate against persons between the ages of 12 and 25 was eleven times higher than for persons 65 and over. An average of the victims of personal

Table 24.1

Estimated Rate of Personal Victimization and Type of Victimization by Age of Victim and Type of Victimization, United States, 1979 (rate per 100,000 persons 12 years of age or older)

Type of Victimization	12 to 15	16 to 19	20 to 24	25 to 34	35 to 49	50 to 64	65 or older
Base	14,915,853	16,407,828	19,971,034	34,797,027	36,170,363	32,452,041	23,528,860
Rape and attempted rape	133	316	261	126	55	11	4
Robbery	940	1,037	1,212	602	508	346	247
Robbery with injury	238	383	437	217	147	132	103
Serious assault	110	219	260	129	84	51	30
Minor assault	128	164	177	88	63	81	72
Robbery without injury	337	405	515	227	246	171	85
Attempted robbery without injury	315	249	260	158	115	42	59
Assault	4,266	5,666	5,727	3,656	1,563	674	340
Aggravated assault	1,325	2,081	2,222	1,349	598	231	108
With injury	565	651	779	445	179	80	29
Attempted assault with weapon	760	1,430	1,443	904	419	151	78
Simple assault	2,941	3,585	3,505	2,307	965	443	232
With injury	848	1,002	939	583	243	53	39
Attempted assault with weapon	2,093	2,583	2,566	1,723	722	391	194

Table **24.1** *continued*

Type of Victimization	25 to 15	16 to 19	20 to 24	25 to 34	35 to 49	50 to 64	65 or older
Personal larceny with contact	291	270	429	279	210	250	353
Purse snatching	23	84	101	76	35	68	90
Attempted purse snatching	0	8	0	15	21	47	74
Pocket picking	268	177	329	189	154	135	190
Personal larceny without contact	13,898	14,343	14,406	10,491	7,866	5,041	1,811

Source: U.S. Department of Justice, *Sourcebook of Criminal Justice Statistics*, Bureau of Justice Statistics, Washington, D.C., 1981, p. 253. Categories may not sum to total because of rounding.

crimes from 1973 to 1980 showed that people 65 years of age or older were victims at a rate of 7.6 per 1,000 compared to 37.1 per 1,000 for those under 65. The number of rapes was too small to yield statistically reliable data. But for some nonviolent offenses, such as purse-snatching and pocket-picking, elders were as likely to be victimized as younger persons.

Clearly, from these studies, victimization rates among the elderly are low; however, between 1973 and 1978 criminal victimization of the elderly increased by over 13 percent while the total increased only 9 percent. Several gerontologists (Goldsmith and Goldsmith, 1976; Malinchak, 1980) warned that assumptions based on crime statistics and aggregate data may be misleading and/or lead to an oversimplification of the crime problem of the elderly. When crimes against the elderly are viewed as a part of the general crime configuration, the unique pattern of elder victimization and its differential impact on them are obscured (Lawton, 1981; Antunes et al., 1977). Furthermore, these age-specific victimization rate studies fail to distinguish between the actual victimization, exposure to crime, and perceived threat of crime.

Types of Crime

None of the crime rate studies supported the popular stereotype that the elderly were special because they were victimized more frequently than others. Quite the reverse was found. On the basis of rates, younger people were the special victims (Cook and Cook, 1976).

In an effort to determine what is special about elderly victimization, Antunes et al. (1977) used the LEAA data to examine the mix of victimization experienced within each age category. They found a strikingly different pattern between age categories of crimes classified as violent (rape and assault) and predatory (robbery and personal larceny combined). Table 24.2 shows that violent crimes accounted for 29.6 percent of crimes against the elderly, and predatory crimes for 70.4 percent. The reverse pattern was found for all other age groups, 12 to 50 years of age.

Rape, fraud, and abuse have been selected as emerging new forms of victimization of older people.

Rape

Most crime reports have shown that the rape of older people was too low to be included in the crime rates. As a result, older women rape victims are not likely to be included in rape studies. This omission may also reflect the general disbelief that older women are targets for rape. Some local studies using multiple sources of data found a higher incidence of rape than that indicated by the national statistics and interpreted it as a serious and significant crime among the elderly. For example, the Midwest Research Institute's study of serious crimes committed against persons over 60 years of age reported five cases of rape, one involving an 84-year-old victim of multiple rape (Cunningham, 1976). In 1981,

Table 24.2
Distribution of Victims by Type of Crime within Age Categories

	12-16	17-20	21-26	27-32	33-39	40-49	50-64	65 and over
Type of Crime								
Assault	74.8	73.3	70.8	72.2	71.4	65.6	50.2	28.1
Robbery	17.4	15.7	16.9	16.3	19.2	22.3	27.0	39.1
Personal larceny	5.0	7.2	7.3	9.2	7.1	10.9	21.9	31.3
Rape	2.8	3.8	5.0	2.3	2.3	1.2	.9	1.5
Violent crime (Rape and assault combined)	77.6	77.1	75.8	74.5	73.7	66.8	51.1	29.6
Predatory crime (Robbery and personal larceny combined)	22.4	22.9	24.2	25.5	26.3	33.2	48.9	70.4
(N)	(1,155)	(973)	(1,075)	(567)	(369)	(463)	(473)	(236)

Source: G. E. Antunes et al., ''Patterns of Personal Crime against the Elderly,'' *Gerontologist*, 1977, 17, 323 (Secondary Analysis, LEAA Surveys–1973, 1974).

the Kansas City police and the Rape Crisis Center recorded seventeen cases of rape of women over the age of 65 in the same four-block neighborhood. Injuries ranged from bruises and broken bones to stroke, coma, and death (*Kansas City Star*, October 13, 1981).

Aside from these studies and occasional single cases or media accounts, we found no systematic or published research on the differential impact of rape on older people. However, limited evidence suggested age differences in the physical and social-psychological effects of sexual assault on the older woman (Cunningham, 1976; Davis, 1979). Physical changes such as loss of vision, hearing, muscular power, and agility increase susceptibility to attack and weaken self-defense; weakening of the female genitals and skeletal system increases the probability of severe injuries and a longer recovery period. The social-psychological effects on aged victims may include greater psychological trauma than for younger women due to violation of their conservative sex norms; age differences between the victim and the offender; heightened feelings of powerlessness and guilt, fearfulness, and anxiety; and ageism—no one will believe them (Gerry, 1983).

In a 1982 research survey on older women rape victims, Gerry investigated the differential impact of rape among women known to the Atlanta Rape Crisis Center over a twelve-month period. Out of 200 mailed questionnaires, 80 were completed (40 percent) and 46 (23 percent) were returned labeled ''moved,'' "refused," or "deceased." The 80 subjects ranged in age from 20 to 95 years of age. Gerry (1983) reported significant age differentials among the women rape victims in the following areas:

1. Altered life style: Older women moved more often within or out of the city; had others move in with them; changed their phone number; took extra security precautions; obtained weapons; installed security devices.

2. Somatic distress: Older women more often had increased headaches; weight change; greater intake of alcohol. Older women shared with all age groups of victims increased sleeping difficulties and nervousness; decreased interest in sex; increase in digestive problems.

3. Psychological distress: Older women reported a higher level of fear and anxiety than younger age groups; greater increases in hostility/aggression and anger than younger women; less difficulty with socializing after rape than younger women; and less feelings of isolation. All ages had increased fearfulness; older women experienced more hallucinations, paranoia, and more crying spells. Although all had difficulty with memory, concentration, and decision making, older women had more difficulty.

4. Mortality: Increased mortality occurred only among the older women: 7 percent died within a 12 month period after the rape.

Fraud

Violent and predatory crimes are not the only forms of criminal victimization of the elderly. Elders are especially vulnerable to frauds, con games, and swindles that rob them of life savings and even subsistence (Goldsmith and Goldsmith, 1976:2; Geis, 1976:12). Although all adults are subject to frauds and related crimes, the list of frauds perpetrated against and designed for the elderly is a long and varied one (Goldsmith and Goldsmith, 1976:2). Since the 1960s, medical quackery, insurance and land swindles, pyramid sales, and a variety of consumer frauds have been documented as types of fraud disproportionately affecting older people. Some of the schemes were designed specifically to entrap older people. These include the following:

1. The pigeon drop involves the elder's encounter with a younger adult (usually a woman), who has found a suitcase or wallet with a huge amount of money in it. The con artist offers to split the money if the older person will put up some "good faith" cash in order to get in on the deal. When the older person provides the deposit, the suitcase or wallet is given over to the older person for safekeeping. The con artist never returns and the wallet or suitcase is found to contain a few real dollars on either end of a wad of phony money.

2. The bank examiner swindle. The older person, usually an older woman living alone, receives a telephone call and is told there is someone embezzling money at her bank and the bank needs her help to catch the thief. She is asked to withdraw cash from her account. After she does this, the bank supposedly sends a messenger to pick up

her money so that the serial numbers can be checked. Of course, the messenger is not from the bank and the thief gets away.

3. Insurance fraud. Older people are sold nonexistent insurance protection or insurance that will not meet their needs or expectations.

4. Medical quackery. Treatments for chronic illness and pain that are worthless.

5. Bereavement schemes. A grieving person receives a Bible ordered just before the death of his/her spouse; a bill for $50 is enclosed, which far exceeds the worth of the item.

6. Consumer frauds on exercise programs, dancing lessons, securities and commodities, credit deceptions, etc.

7. Phony charitable solicitation frauds which play on the desire of older people to be of help.

8. Pencil-whip the mark scheme. The con artist promises a combination of home improvements and debt consolidation. When the contract is signed, it is turned over to a finance company and the con artist disappears. (Goldsmith and Goldsmith, 1976)

Most research and other data on frauds against the elderly come from congressional hearings, the media, selected reports of the FBI, and local law enforcement agencies. Despite the lack of systematic evidence, most researchers conservatively estimate that older persons, especially the frailest of the frail, are more likely than younger persons to be the victims of con artist and bunco types of fraud. The New York Police reported 5,000 con game complaints by elders and a loss of $5 million in 1976 (Hahn, 1976:46). In a study of bunco victims in Los Angeles and San Francisco, Younger (1976) reported that 90 percent of the bunco (swindling by misrepresentation) victims were women over 65 years of age. Consumer frauds involving health insurance and medical plans, mail order, and work at home offers were also disproportionately represented among Younger's cases. Medical quackery and health-related schemes were estimated as a $50 million a year business. The most common schemes included cures for cancer, arthritis, baldness, obesity, and methods for restoration of youthful vigor. In the California study, elders were the victims in seven out of every ten cases of medical fraud coming to the attention of the state's criminal justice system.

A recent fraud case illustrates the unique threat of insurance fraud schemes to older people—especially the frail ones. In 1982 the FBI cracked a highly organized phony insurance business operative over the past twelve years in a number of states. The victims, all in their eighties, thought they were purchasing supplementary Medicaid/Medicare health insurance. The potential victims were culled from membership lists of senior citizens' organizations. The number of victims is hard to determine because many do not know they were victims or have died without knowing (Vardeman and Parker, 1982).

Elder Abuse: Institutional and Domestic

Elders may be abused by caretakers in institutions such as nursing homes, hospitals, and day-care centers and by family or household members. More is known about institutional abuse than about domestic abuse of older people.

Offenses related to institutional abuse of the elderly surfaced in the 1970s and were the subject of congressional investigations. In the 1980s, attention has shifted to boarding house abuse as the institutional focus of local, state, and federal investigation (U.S. House of Representatives, Select Committee on Aging, 1981b).

Forms of institutional abuse include the willful infliction of physical pain or injury, beating, overmedication, inadequate nutrition, and unsanitary conditions; psychological abuse that causes mental anguish, for example, scolding, excessive criticism, loss of rights of a patient; social abuse, including isolation, inadequate social space, unnecessary restriction of social interaction, and loss of property; and administrative abuse through fraudulent practices such as pharmaceutical kick-backs, unnecessary or excessive medical treatment, and failure to deliver contracted services. Institutional offenses are classified as assault, theft, fraud, and violation of licensure regulations.

Although elder abuse as a form of domestic violence has been suspected for a long time, it only began to receive systematic attention in the late 1970s (Steinmetz, 1978). The major sources of information on domestic victimization of elders are the studies of Block and Sinnott (1979); Douglass, Hickey, and Noel (1979); O'Malley et al. (1979); Hickey and Douglass (1981); and hearings held by the U.S. House of Representatives' Select Committee on Aging (1981a).

Elder abuse victims most often reside with their adult children who psychologically, socially and/or physically mistreat them. Labeled by the English "Granny Bashing" or "Gramslamming," elder abuse has been defined by O'Malley et al. (1979) as a form of family violence characterized by "the willful infliction of physical pain, injury, or debilitating mental anguish, unreasonable confinement, or willful deprivation by a caretaker of services which are necessary to maintain mental and physical health."

The general consensus is that there are five major types of abuse: physical abuse, psychological abuse, financial abuse, social neglect, and violation of rights.

1. Physical abuse includes "malnutrition, injuries such as bruises, welts, sprains, dislocations, abrasions, or lacerations (Block and Sinnott, 1979); withholding of personal and medical care; and a lack of supervision (Lau and Kosberg, 1979).

2. Psychological abuse includes verbal abuse, (i.e., scolding or excessive criticizing); coercion (e.g., forcing an elder to change his residence against his wishes); and "infantilization" or the failure to treat the parent as an adult and making decisions for the older adult as if he/she were an infant (Block and Sinnott, 1979; Douglass et al., 1979).

3. Financial abuse comprises monetary or material theft and misuse (Lau and Kosberg, 1979).

4. Neglect may be active or passive. Active neglect includes withholding medicine, food, or help when it is necessary for the well-being of the elder. Passive neglect includes ignoring or isolating the elder (Douglass et al., 1979).

5. Violation of rights includes taking an elder's property without due process of law; having him/her declared incompetent and committed to a mental institution without due process of law (U.S. House of Representatives, Select Committee on Aging, 1981a; Lau and Kosberg, 1979); and change of residence or environment against his/her will.

The underreporting of such abuse by the elderly themselves and by neighbors, friends, and professionals makes it difficult to determine the extent of such abuse. The victim's physical or psychological condition and his fear of more abuse, including threat of being sent to a nursing home, contributes to the underreporting. The reluctance or inability of older people to report abuse by family members has led researchers to label elder abuse "the hidden crime of the 1980s." Nevertheless, available survey data show that one in ten elderly persons living with a family member has been subjected to some form of abuse (Koch, 1980).

The profile of the elderly abuse victim emerging from the studies is that of a female, over 75 years of age, Protestant, middle-class, living with the abuser, or a relative of the abuser, who has a mental or physical disability (O'Malley et al., 1979; Block and Sinnott, 1979). Thus, the victim is like the average aged person.

The profile of the abuser (Block and Sinnott, 1979) is that of a white female, who is a relative, most often a child, of the victim. The abuser is often a repeater and abuses because of psychological problems. Most abusers suffer from some form of stress such as alcohol or drug addiction, a long-term medical complaint, or financial difficulties (O'Malley et al., 1979). Most research has shown that the abuser views the high level of physical or emotional care or financial assistance expected by the elderly as a major source of stress, leading to abusive behavior.

Five major causes of abusive behavior directed at elders, as reported by Hickey and Douglass (1981) and Steinmetz (1981), include:

1. Dependency and vulnerability of the elders.

2. Retaliation and role reversal.

3. Negative environment over a long period of time; limitation of life space.

4. Tyranny of the older person; elder abuse of the adult family member.

5. Family stress and lack of coping strength.

Care of the elderly by families is expected to increase as our older population increases. This care may place excessive physical, emotional, and financial demands on the family, resulting in an increase of elder abuse (O'Rourke, 1981). As a result of the research findings between 1978 and 1981 and the 1981 House Select Committee hearing, the Administration on Aging supported projects to raise community awareness of the problem of elder abuse and to make reporting of cases easier. Therefore, researchers speculate that reported incidents of elder abuse and arrests for crimes associated with elder abuse can be expected to increase.

Socioeconomic

Other variables related to crimes against the elderly reported by researchers were: location of the crime; characteristics of the offender; residence (place and type); and sex of the victim. Research placed the location of most violent crimes on public streets or in public places. But *all* crimes against the elderly (violent and predatory) took place in or near their homes. Public places for older victims were found to be doorways and halls of residences, elevators, or commercial places near their homes, contrasted to commercial places, bars, and cultural and recreation events for younger age groups. If the elders resided in a high-crime area, the streets and public parts of the residence were the dangerous public places for them (Antunes et al., 1977; Cunningham, 1976; Lawton and Yaffee, 1980). Elderly victims were more likely than younger ones to be victims of residential robberies or purse-snatching because most older people were not working (Antunes et al., 1977; Conklin, 1976). Most predatory crimes took place when victims were alone; and elders were more likely to be alone than younger persons (Conklin, 1976; Cunningham, 1976).

The offender was most likely to be a young (mostly teenage) black, who worked with accomplices and used force on the elderly victims, who were usually white and female (Conklin, 1976).

Since predatory crimes take place in or near the elderly's homes, many re-searchers reason that the incidence of violent crimes is lower for older people. They tend to avoid the public places where the risk of victimization is higher, or they are often accompanied by one or more persons (Antunes et al., 1977; Lawton and Yaffee, 1980; Linquist and Duke, 1982).

Differences in victimization experienced by males and females are not great except for personal larceny without contact. Table 24.3 shows that the 1979 victimization rate for males was higher for larceny without contact (22.7) than for females (18.9), while the rate for larceny with contact was slightly higher for females (4.0) than males (2.9). Males were victims of violent crimes (7.1) more often than females (5.0).

Psychological

Although older people are less likely to be victimized by crime, they fear crime much more than the general population (Adams and Smith, 1976; Antunes

Table 24.3
Personal Crimes: Victimization Rate (per Thousand Population) for Persons Aged 65 and Over by Sex and Type of Crime, 1979

Sex	Number of Persons in the Group	Crimes of Violence	Rape	Robbery			Assault			Crimes of theft	Personal Larceny	
				Total	With Injury	Without Injury	Total	Aggravated	Simple		With Contact	Without Contact
Male	9,689,000	7.1	10.0	3.4	1.1	2.3	3.8	1.3	2.5	25.6	2.9	22.7
Female	13,844,000	5.0	0.1[a]	1.8	1.0	0.8	3.1	0.9	2.2	18.9	4.0	14.9

Source: U.S. Department of Justice, *Sourcebook of Criminal Justice Statistics*, Bureau of Justice Statistics, Washington, D.C., 1981, p. 254.

[a] Rate, based on zero or on about ten or fewer sample cases, is statistically unreliable.

Table 24.4
Fear of Criminal Victimization by Age, United States, 1980 (Percentages)

	Level of concrete fear		Level of formless fear	
Age	High	Moderate to Low	High	Moderate to Low
18 to 29 years	49	51	36	64
30 to 39 years	46	54	30	70
40 to 49 years	34	66	34	66
50 to 59 years	40	60	41	59
60 years and older	33	67	43	57

Source: Adapted by U.S. Department of Justice, *Sourcebook of Criminal Justice Statistics*, Bureau of Justice Statistics, Washington, D.C., 1981, p. 183, from the Figgie Report on Fear of Crime, *America Afraid* A-T-O, Willoughby, Ohio, 1980, pp. 32-34, 42-44, 49, 51, 54.

et al., 1977; Clemente and Kleiman, 1976; Harris, 1975, 1981; Sundeen and Mathieu, 1976). Since 1965, data from National Opinion Research Center surveys have consistently reported that the elderly are more fearful of crime than any other age groups (Adams and Smith, 1976). Fear is believed to lead to self-imposed "house arrest," limited activity, and reduced life satisfaction (Conklin, 1976). Fear of crime has become more of a problem than crime itself (*Atlanta Constitution*, April 5, 1982; Linquist and Duke, 1982). It is clear that fear among the elderly is real and pervasive. The significance of the fear is not whether it is warranted or not, but the effect it has on older people (Clemente and Kleiman, 1976; Goldsmith and Thomas, 1974; Lawton and Yaffee, 1980; Malinchak, 1980).

Table 24.4 shows the results of the 1981 Figgie Report on the fear of crime in America adapted by the U.S. Department of Justice. Persons 60 years of age and older rated lower on the concrete fear index (worrying specifically about being the victim of criminal assault, mugging, knifing, or armed robbery) but higher on the formless fear index (nonspecific worry about safety in one's home, neighborhood, and the larger community) than any other age group.

The fear of crime is not only higher among the elderly in general, but most research (e.g., Clemente and Kleiman, 1976; Erskine, 1974; Furstenberg, 1971; Gubrium, 1974; Lawton and Yaffee, 1980; Lebowitz, 1975; Newman, 1976) has shown that it is especially high among certain types of elderly. Fear is higher among:

1. Elders living in the center city than among those living in the suburbs.

2. Urban elders than rural elders.

3. Older blacks than older whites.

4. Older women than older men; however, older men express more fear of crime than younger men.

5. Those in age-heterogeneous public housing than in age-homogeneous housing.

6. Older victims than non-victims.

7. Lower-income elders (under $7,000) than those with higher incomes (over $7,000).

8. Elders living in high-crime areas than those in low-crime areas.

9. Elders living alone than those living with family or in institutions.

The Social Context and Consequences

Gubrium (1974) theorized that safe neighborhoods and residences, along with an extensive network of mutually supportive age peers, would decrease victimization. Lawton and Yaffee (1980) found that fear of crime among elderly public housing residents ($N = 662$) of housing sites ($N + 53$) in thirty-eight communities was significantly lower than among residents of age-mixed housing. Despite their locations in high-crime areas, the elderly housing environments provided better than average physical security and formal and informal protection mechanisms for the tenants when they were outside the building.

Cook et al. (1978) investigated the physical and economic consequences of crime in an attempt to demonstrate that the fear of crime among the elderly was unwarranted. Based on analysis of 1973–1974 LEAA data, they found that as far as physical injury was concerned, elders were less likely to be attacked or to be injured when attacked; however, when attacked they suffered more internal injuries; lost consciousness more often; suffered more cuts (but fewer broken bones); and lost teeth more than other assault victims. The medical care cost was a considerably larger portion of their income than for younger adult victims (Cook et al., 1978:345–346). They reported the economic consequences for elder victims of larceny to be the same or less severe than for other adults, but the same or more severe than for other adults when adjusted for differences in monthly income.

Research evidence may demonstrate that the elder's fear is unwarranted, but it does not necessarily follow that the elder's fear will decrease. Cook and Cook (1976) speculated that the continued fear of crime among the elderly is media-created and fed with anecdotal data. It is more likely to be a period effect and reflects the increase in crime in American society since 1960. It could be speculated further that elders are overexposed to media reports about crime and overreact to the victimization accounts they hear from their peers. Social programs to reduce the incidence of victimization and to allay the fears of the elderly have been found to actually increase the fear of highly safety-conscious older persons (Norton and Courlander, 1982).

Linquist and Duke (1982) sought to resolve the paradox of low victimization and high fear of crime among the elderly by reconceptualizing the issue. They applied the ''at risk'' concept to victimization data from the San Antonio law enforcement data. The high-risk age group were those with social and economic activity, who were out of the home in commercial and recreational places, and out late at night. The elderly were a low "at risk" group, which accounted for the low victimization rates. Linquist and Duke interpreted the low victimization rates of the elderly as high given their low "at risk" level, which helps to explain their seemingly unwarranted fears.

ORGANIZATIONS AND PROGRAMS

Through the efforts of the International Association of Chiefs of Police, most local law enforcement agencies have a crime prevention program for the elderly or a special unit to assist older people. These programs vary from special units like the New York City Bronx Robbery Unit that investigates robberies against the elderly to educational programs for older people, telephone and escort services, and cooperative projects with senior citizen organizations (for additional information on the police program, see Malinchak, 1980).

The Area Agencies on Aging located in every community provide local information on crime prevention programs for the elderly and support special projects to raise community awareness of the problem and support for the elderly.

The American Association of Retired Persons' (AARP) Criminal Justice Services have a senior coordinator and staff specialists to work nationwide with older persons' groups, law enforcement officers, and public administrators to promote understanding of the kinds of crime most often committed against older people, to reduce the risk of victimization, and to develop effective law enforcement measures. Their slide tape programs are available and free to organizations and community agencies. The senior coordinator and staff work closely with governmental agencies at all levels and with Congress on issues of victimization. AARP's research foundation, the Andrus Foundation, has supported research on crime and aging.

Other agencies that provide some services are the Department of Housing and Human Development, the Farmers Home Administration, and state consumer protection departments.

In 1981, several university criminal justice departments and gerontology institutes initiated an annual elderly offender conference on problems unique to the elder offender and the impact of the growing number of older offenders/ prisoners on the criminal justice system.

The limited number of special programs and organizations specifically concerned with crime against the elderly reflects the underdevelopment of this area in gerontology.

RESEARCH ISSUES

Gerontological research on victimization of the elderly in the 1970s raised basic methodological issues that are familiar to criminologists: the reliability of aggregate data based on local law enforcement records; and the age categories used in analysis. FBI uniform crime statistics rely on records of local law enforcement agencies. Since many of these agencies do not collect data on the age of the victim, the reports cannot adequately reflect the extent of criminal victimization of older people. A related and equally serious issue is the lack of consistency in age categories used to define the older victim or offender and to determine rates of victimization by age. Some studies and statistical reports used 45 years of age and older (Shichor and Kobrin, 1978); some used age 60 and over (U.S. Department of Justice, 1981) and others used age 65 years and over (U.S. Department of Justice, 1975). None of the studies used age 75 and over. To collapse the younger age categories downward (age 65 and under) mixes populations usually separated in gerontological research to explain age differences in behavior, that is, those in the work force from those not in the work force. To collapse the older age category upward to include all people age 65 and over fails to distinguish differences between the young-old and the old-old in physical vulnerability and "at risk" of victimization.

Another methodological issue is the limitations of the cross-sectional method in the study of age differences in victimization and criminal behavior. The fallacy of this method has been demonstrated by Palmore to be the assumption that cross-sectional age-group differences are due to aging, when in fact they are "composed of both aging effects and cohort differences. . . . observed age-group differences in a cross-sectional study may be all or partly the result of cohort differences rather than aging effects" (Palmore, 1981:5). This raises the question that the cross-sectional method cannot answer: Are the low crime rates and high fear of crime among persons aged 65 and over due to cohort differences rather than aging effects? Antunes et al. (1977) tried a within age category analysis, but the category was composed of several age cohorts and data were limited to one point in time. The solution to many of the issues generated by previous research on crime and the elderly might be found by using a cross-sequential model which combines cross-sectional and longitudinal methods (Palmore, 1978). This would make it possible to report age (actual age and physical/psychological status), period (environmental), and cohort (peer) effects on criminal victimization and fear of the crime.

New issues and unresolved issues from previous research relate to the following questions: (1) Do major events in later life (retirement, widowhood, illness, moving, physical and psychological vulnerability) increase the risk of older people to victimization? (2) Do these events affect the trauma of victimization? (3) Do age composition and type of residence affect the level of fear of victimization among older people?

Age and Vulnerability

Antunes et al. demonstrated from a within age category analysis that violent (serious) crimes were a larger proportion of offenses against the elderly than crime rates would indicate, that is to say the serious crime rate for the elderly is much lower, .2 (Antunes et al., 1977:322), when the analysis is between age categories than when the analysis is within an age category, 29.6. Linquist and Duke's (1982) findings indicated that developing measures of "at risk" for different groups redefines the actual risk and perceived fear of victimization among older people. They speculate that life-style differences of older people change the type of risk but do not decrease it. The age changes affecting life-style and risk were retirement, widowhood, household composition, physical and psychological changes, and changes in dependence. At this point in time, research to resolve these issues of vulnerability and risk is tentative and speculative.

Environments

Lawton and Yaffee's (1980) findings on the effects of age-homogeneous and age-heterogeneous housing on risk and perceived fear of victimization raise questions about the effects of the environment of non-public housing in different types of neighborhoods on real and perceived fear of victimization. We know more about age-homogeneous residents of public and private housing than about older residents of other types of housing.

Demographic Changes and Research Issues

Events of the 1980s and projected changes in the age composition of American society are raising additional issues for future research. What period effect will the graying of the baby boom generation have on crimes among older people? Will the next cohorts of older people be less vulnerable or more at risk than current cohorts of older people? Will life-style differences of the baby boom generation affect the rate of victimization and the fear of crime?

It is obvious that much more research is needed to explain the age differences in real and perceived victimization of older people. It is also obvious that cross-sequential studies utilizing more appropriate age categories and within cohort analysis are needed in future research. Perhaps one of the most important implications of our review of the research is that the problem of crime and the elderly involves more than victimization rate studies. It encompasses the entire criminal justice system, including judges, law enforcement officers, prison systems, and older offenders. More research is needed on all parts of the system in order to plan for the safety and well-being of the elderly of the future.

REFERENCES

Adams, M.E., and Vedder, C.B. Age and crime. *Geriatrics*, 1961, *16*, 177–181.

Adams, R., and Smith, T. Fear of neighborhood. National Opinion Research Center Report on Social Change Project, no. 127. National Opinion Research Center, Chicago, 1976.

Adkins, O. Crime prevention: Huntington's answer. *Police Chief*, December 1977.

Antunes, G.E.; Cook, F.L.; Cook, T.D.; and Shogun, W.D. Patterns of personal crime against the elderly. *Gerontologist*, 1977, *17*, 321–327.

Block, H.A., and Geis, G. *Man, crime and society*. Random House, New York, 1962.

Block, M.R., and Sinnott, J.D. (Eds.). Methodology and results. In *The battered elder syndrome: An exploratory study*. University of Maryland, College Park, 1979.

Clemente, F., and Kleiman, M.B. Fear of crime among the aged. *Gerontologist*, 1976, *16*, 207–211.

Conklin, J.E. Robbery, the elderly, and fear: An urban problem in search of a solution. In J. Goldsmith and S. Goldsmith (Eds.), *Crime and the elderly*. D.C. Heath, Lexington, Mass., 1976, 99–111.

Cook, F.L., and Cook, T.D. Evaluating the rhetoric of crisis: A case study of criminal victimization of the elderly. *Social Service Review*, 1976, *50*, 641–642.

Cook, F.L.; Skogan, W.G.; Cook, T.D.; and Antunes, G.E. Criminal victimization of the elderly: The physical and economic consequences. *Gerontologist*, 1978, *18*, 338–349.

Cunningham, C.L. Pattern and effect of crime against the aging: The Kansas City Study. In J. Goldsmith and S. Goldsmith (Eds.), *Crime and the elderly*. D.C. Heath, Lexington, Mass., 1976.

Davis, J., and Brody, E.M. *Rape and older women: A guide to prevention and protection*. U.S. Department of Health, Education and Welfare, National Institute of Mental Health, Washington, D.C., 1979.

Douglass, R.L.; Hickey, T.; and Noel, C. *A study of the maltreatment of the elder and other vulnerable adults*. University of Michigan, Ann Arbor, 1979.

The elderly: Prisoners of fear. *Time*, November 29, 1976, 21–22.

Erskine, H. The polls: Fear of violence and crime. *Public Opinion Quarterly*, 1974, *38*, 131–145.

Federal Bureau of Investigation. Uniform crime reports. Washington, D.C., 1964–1974.

Foorlick, J., and Howard, L. Inside the Burger Court. *Newsweek*, July 12, 1976, 101–102.

Ford, G.R., President. Crime message to Congress. Office of the White House Press Secretary, Washington, D.C., June 19, 1975.

Furstenberg, F.J. Public reaction to crime on the streets. *American Scholar*, 1971, *51*, 601–610.

Geis, G. Defrauding the elderly. In J. Goldsmith and S. Goldsmith (Eds.), *Crime and the elderly*. D.C. Heath, Lexington, Mass., 1976, 7–9.

Gerry, D.P. The effects of rape on three age groups of women: A comparison study. Paper presented to the Southern Gerontological Association, Atlanta, April 1983.

Goldsmith, J., and Goldsmith, S. *Crime and the elderly*. D.C. Heath, Lexington, Mass., 1976.

Goldsmith, J., and Thomas, N.E. Crimes against the elderly: A continuing national crisis. *Aging*, June-July 1974.

Gubrium, J.F. Victimization in old age. *Crime and Delinquency*, 1974, *20*, 245–250.

Hahn, P.H. *Crime against the elderly: A study in victimology*. Davis Publishing, Santa Cruz, Calif., 1976.

Harris, L. The myth and reality of aging. National Council on the Aging, Washington, D.C., 1975.

———. Aging in the eighties: America in transition. National Council on the Aging, Washington, D.C., 1981.

Hickey, T., and Douglass, R.L. Neglect and abuse of older family members: Professionals' perspectives and case experiences. *Gerontologist*, 1981, *21*, 171–176.

Koch, L., and Koch, J. Parent abuse: A new plague. *Parade*, January 27, 1980.

Lau, E.E., and Kosberg, J.I. Abuse of the elderly by informal-care providers. *Aging*, September/October, 1979.

Lawton, M.P. Homogeneity and heterogeneity in housing for the elderly. In M.P. Lawton, R.J. Newcomer, and T.O. Byerts (Eds.), *Community planning for an aging society*. Dowden, Hutchinson, and Ross, Stroudsburg, Pa., 1977.

———. Crime, victimization, and the fortitude of the aged. *Aged Care and Services Review*, January 1981.

Lawton, M.P., Nahemow, L.; and Teaff, J. Housing characteristics and the well-being of elderly tenants in federally assisted housing. *Journal of Gerontology*, 1975, *30*, 601–607.

Lawton, M.P., and Yaffee, S. Victimization and fear of crime in elderly public housing tenants. *Journal of Gerontology*, 1980, *35*, 768–779.

Lebowitz, B.D. Age and fearfulness: Personal and situational factors. *Journal of Gerontology*, 1975, *30*, 696–700.

Linquist, J.H., and Duke, J.M. The elderly victim at risk. *Criminology*, 1982, *20*, 1–10.

Malinchak, A.A. *Crime and gerontology*. Prentice-Hall, Englewood Cliffs, N.J., 1980.

Newman, O. Defensible space. In J. Goldsmith and S. Goldsmith (Eds.), *Crime and the elderly*. D.C. Heath, Lexington, Mass., 1976.

Norton, L., and Courlander, M. Fear of crime among the elderly: The role of crime prevention programs. *Gerontologist*, 1982, *22*, 388–394.

O'Malley, H.; Segars, H.; Perez, R.; Mitchell, V.; and Kneupfel, G.M. *Elder abuse in Massachusetts: A survey of professionals and para-professionals*. Legal Research and Services for the Elderly, Boston, 1979.

O'Rourke, M. *Elder abuse: The state of the art*. Legal Research and Services for the Elderly, Boston, 1981.

Palmore, E. When can age, period, and cohort be separated? *Social Forces*, 1978, *57*, 282–295.

———. *Social patterns in normal aging: Findings from the Duke Longitudinal Study*. Duke University Press, Durham, N.C., 1981.

Pope, C.E., and Feyerheim, W. A review of recent trends: Effects of crime on the elderly. *Police Chief*, February 1976, 29–32.

Ragan, P.K. Crimes against the elderly: Some interviews with blacks, Mexican-Americans, and whites. In M.A. Rafai, *Justice in older America*. D.C. Heath, Lexington, Mass., 1977, 25–36.

Steinmetz, S.K. Battered parents. *Society*, July/August 1978.

———. Elder abuse. *Aging*, January/February 1981.

Sundeen, R.A., and Mathieu, J.T. Urban elderly environments of fear. In J. Goldsmith and S. Goldsmith (Eds.), *Crime and the elderly*. D.C. Heath, Lexington, Mass., 1976, 51–66.

U.S. Department of Justice. *Criminal victimization surveys in thirteen American cities*. USGPO, Washington, D.C., 1975.

———. *Sourcebook of criminal justice statistics*, Bureau of Justice Statistics, Washington, D.C., 1981.

U.S. House of Representatives. Select Committee on Aging. *Elder abuse: Examination of a hidden problem*. U.S. House of Representatives, Select Committee on Aging, USGPO, Washington, D.C., April 3, 1981a.

————. *Fraud and abuse in homes*. USGPO, Washington, D.C., June 25, 1981b.

Vardeman, J., and Parker, D. FBI enters probe of insurance swindle. *Atlanta Constitution*, October 13, 1982.

Younger, E.J. The California experience in crime prevention programs with senior citizens. In J. Goldsmith and S. Goldsmith (Eds.), *Crime and the elderly*. D.C. Heath, Lexington, Mass., 1976, 159–169.

SOURCES FOR ADDITIONAL INFORMATION

American Association of Retired Persons
Andrus Foundation
1909 K Street, NW
Washington, DC 20049

National Council of Senior Citizens
1511 K Street, NW
Washington, DC 20005

National Council on the Aging
1829 L Street, NW
Washington, DC 20036

U.S. Senate Special Committee on Aging
G-233 Senate Office Building
Washington, DC 20510

For local information contact the State Office on Aging, Area Agency for Aging, or County Council on Aging.

APPENDIX A

ACADEMIC AND RESEARCH CENTERS ON AGING

The following is a list (in alphabetical order by college or university) of the major academic and research centers on aging in the United States. Most offer courses, short-term education or training, research, and special opportunities for older adults. More information may be obtained on these and other centers from the *National directory of education programs in gerontology*, E. Sullivan (ed.), published by the Association for Gerontology in Higher Education, 600 Maryland Ave. SW, West Wing Suite 204, Washington, DC 20024.

Institute for Life-Span Development and Gerontology
The University of Akron
Akron, OH 44325

Center for the Study of Aging
University of Alabama
P.O. Box 966
University, AL 35486

Center for Aging
University of Alabama in Birmingham
University Station
Birmingham, AL 35294

Department of Sociology, Anthropology, and Gerontology
University of Arkansas at Little Rock
Little Rock, AR 72204

Institute of Gerontology
Ball State University
Muncie, IN 47306

Graduate Program in Gerontology
Baylor University
Waco, TX 76798

Program in Economics and Politics of Aging
Heller School
Brandeis University
Waltham, MA 02254

Center for the Study of Aging
Division of Human and Community Services
College of Health Sciences
University of Bridgeport
Bridgeport, CT 06601

Center on Aging and Health
Case Western Reserve University
Cleveland, OH 44106

Center for the Study of Pre-Retirement and Aging
The Catholic University of America
Washington, DC 20064

Gerontology Program and Center
The University of Connecticut
Storrs, CT 06268

Institute of Gerontology
University of Denver
2142 S. High
Denver, CO 80208

Institute of Gerontology
College of Education and Human Ecology
University of the District of Columbia
1100 Harvard Street, NW, Room 114
Washington, DC 20009

Center for the Study of Aging and Human Development
Box 3003
Duke University Medical Center
Durham, NC 27710

Gerontology Center
University of Evansville
P.O. Box 329
Evansville, IN 47702

Center for Gerontological Studies
3357 GPA, University of Florida
Gainesville, FL 32611

Multidisciplinary Center on Gerontology
Florida State University
Tallahassee, FL 32306

Third Age Center
Fordham University
113 West 60th Street
New York, NY 10023

Gerontology Center
University of Georgia
Athens, GA 30602

Gerontology Center
Georgia State University
University Plaza
Atlanta, GA 30303

I.U. Center on Aging
HPER 140-142
Indiana University
Bloomington, IN 47405

Center on Aging
Fairchild Hall, Room One
Kansas State University
Manhattan, KS 66506

Gerontology Center
Kean College of New Jersey
James Townley House
Union, NJ 07083

Gerontology Center
Kent State University
Kent, OH 44242

Gerontology Center
University of Louisville
Louisville, KY 40292

Gerontology Department
Madonna College
36600 Schoolcraft Road
Livonia, MI 48150

Center on Aging
Room 1120, Francis Scott Key Hall
University of Maryland
College Park, MD 20742

University of Massachusetts Center on Aging
University of Massachusetts Medical Center
55 Lake Avenue North
Worcester, MA 01605

Center for Life Cycle Studies
Memphis State University
Memphis, TN 38152

Center on Aging
University of Miami
P.O. Box 248092
Coral Gables, FL 33124

Scripps Foundation Gerontology Center
Miami University
Oxford, OH 45056

Institute of Gerontology
The University of Michigan
300 North Ingalls Street
Ann Arbor, MI 48109

All-University Center on Aging
University of Minnesota
304 Walter Library
117 Pleasant Street SE
Minneapolis, MN 55455

Gerontology Department and Institute of Gerontology
Molloy College
1000 Hempstead Avenue
Rockville Centre, NY 11570

Institute of Gerontology
State University of New York at Albany
Albany, NY 12222

Center for the Study of Aging
State University of New York at Buffalo
Buffalo, NY 14214

Center for the Study of Aging and Dying
State University of New York
College at New Paltz
New Paltz, NY 12561

Division of Gerontology
New York University Medical Center
New York, NY 10016

Gerontology Center
Norfolk State University
Norfolk, VA 23504

Center on Aging
4011 Bon Aire Drive
Northeast Louisiana University
700 University Avenue
Monroe, LA 71209

Center for Studies in Aging
North Texas State University
P.O. Box 13438, NT Station
Denton, TX 76203

Gerontology Center
University of Oklahoma
OU Health Sciences Center
627 N.E. 15th
Oklahoma City, OK 73190

Center for Gerontology
University of Oregon
1627 Agate Street
Eugene, OR 97403

Center on Human Development
S-110 Henderson Human Development
The Pennsylvania State University
University Park, PA 16802

Long-Term Care Gerontology Center
University of Pittsburgh
Pittsburgh, PA 15260

The Center on Aging
Presbyterian School of Christian Education
1205 Palmyra Avenue
Richmond, VA 23227

Gerontology Center
Rhode Island College
600 Mt. Pleasant Avenue
Providence, RI 02908

Institute on Aging
Rutgers University
4 Huntington Street
New Brunswick, NJ 08903

University Center on Aging
San Diego State University
San Diego, CA 92182-0273

Center for Education in Gerontology
University of Santa Clara
Santa Clara, CA 95053

Leonard Davis School of Gerontology
Ethel Percy Andrus Gerontology Center
University of Southern California
University Park
Los Angeles, CA 90007

Department of Gerontology
College of Sociology and Behavioral Science
University of South Florida
Tampa, FL 33620

Center for Gerontological Studies
Southwest Missouri State University
Springfield, MO 65802

All-University Gerontology Center
Syracuse University
Brockway Hall
Syracuse, NY 13210

Institute on Aging
Temple University
1601 North Broad Street
Philadelphia, PA 19122

Gerontology Services Administration
University of Texas Health Science Center
5323 Harry Hines Boulevard
Dallas, TX 75235

Institute of Gerontology
Utica College of Syracuse University
Utica, NY 13502

Center on Aging
Virginia Commonwealth University
Box 228, MCV Station
Richmond, VA 23298

Center of Gerontology
Virginia Polytechnic Institute and State University
Blacksburg, VA 24061

Institute on Aging
Long-Term Care Gerontology Center
University of Washington, RD-34
Seattle, WA 98195

Department of Psychology
Box 1125
Washington University
St. Louis, MO 63130

Institute of Gerontology
Wayne State University
Detroit, MI 48202

Gerontology Center
Gerontology 1208
Weber State College
Ogden, UT 84408

Gerontology Center
West Virginia University
Morgantown, WV 26506

University Gerontology Center
Wichita State University, Box 121
Wichita, KS 67208

Institute on Aging and Adult Life
University of Wisconsin
425 Henry Mall
Madison, WI 53706

Yeshiva University Gerontological Institute
55 Fifth Avenue
New York, NY 10003

APPENDIX **B**

STATISTICAL
TABLES

The following tables give historical and current information on the basic demographic and health characteristics of older Americans as a whole.

Table B.1 shows that Americans over age 65 have been growing older as a group since the turn of the century. That is, there has been a steady decrease in the proportions of those aged 65 to 74 and a steady increase in the proportions of those over age 80.

Table B.2 shows that the proportion of the total U.S. population age 65 and over has also increased steadily since the turn of the century and will probably continue to increase until it reaches a peak around the year 2030.

Table B.3 shows that the sex ratio (number of males per 100 females) has decreased among older Americans at a faster rate than among the rest of the population. This means that there are fewer older men compared to older women as time goes on, and this is especially true in the oldest groups. This is because the greater longevity of women has a cumulative and greater impact on the oldest age groups.

Table B.4 shows that most older men are married, while the majority of older women are widowed. This is because women tend to live longer than men and because men tend to marry women younger than themselves. As a result, more older women than men live alone or are institutionalized (table B.5).

Table B.6 shows that white females tend to live longer than any other sex-race group and have almost eighteen years left to live on the average after they reach age 65. Men, in contrast, have about thirteen years left after age 65. However, life expectancy has been steadily increasing for all categories.

Table B.7 shows that older Americans do not rate their health as being as good as younger persons, but about two-thirds still rate their health as good or excellent. Whites and upper-income categories have more rating their health as excellent than others.

Table B.8 shows that the majority of older Americans report no limitation on their activity; 83 percent say they are able to carry on their major activity, even though they may be limited in the amount or kind of activity.

Similarly, table B.9 shows that almost 83 percent report no limitation on their mobility and only 5 percent report that they are confined to their house.

Table B.1
Percentage Distribution of the Population 65 Years Old and Over by Age, 1900–1975
(Estimates and projections as of July 1)

AGE	1900	1930	1950	1960	1970	1975
65 years and over	100.0	100.0	100.0	100.0	100.0	100.0
65 to 69 years	42.3	41.7	40.7	37.7	35.0	36.2
70 to 74 years	28.7	29.3	27.8	28.6	27.2	25.8
75 to 79 years	} 29.0 }	} 29.0 }	17.4	18.5	19.2	17.9
80 to 84 years			14.1	9.6	11.5	11.8
85 years and over				5.6	7.1	8.4

Source: U.S. Bureau of the Census, *Current Population Reports*, ser. P-25, nos. 311, 321, 519, 614, 601.

Table B.2
Percentage of the Total Population Aged 65 and Over, 1900–2050

Year (July 1)	Percent	Year (July 1)	Percent
1900	4.1	1980	11.0
1910	4.3	1990	11.7
1920	4.6	2000	11.7
1930	5.4	2010	11.9
1940	6.8	2020	14.6
1950	8.1	2030	17.0
1960	9.2	2040	16.1
1970	9.8	2050	16.1
1975	10.5		

Source: U.S. Bureau of the Census, *Current Population Reports*, Special Studies, ser. P-23, no. 59, May 1976, p. 9.

Table B.3
Sex Ratios for Broad Age Groups, 1900–2010
(Males per 100 females)

Age	1900	1930	1960	1970	1975	Projections 1980	1990	2000	2010
All ages[a]	104.4	102.5	97.8	95.8	95.3	94.9	94.6	94.5	94.4
65 to 74 years	104.5	104.1	86.7	77.7	76.8	75.8	75.4	76.3	77.0
75 to 84 years	(NA)	(NA)	77.4	65.9	61.5	59.8	58.1	57.4	57.9
85 years and over	(NA)	(NA)	63.8	53.2	48.5	44.1	39.9	38.5	37.8
65 years and over	102.0	100.4	82.6	72.0	69.3	67.9	66.1	64.9	65.5
75 years and over	96.3	91.8	75.0	63.3	58.4	56.0	53.7	52.5	51.8

Source: U.S. Bureau of the Census, *Current Population Reports*, ser. P-23, no. 59, 1976, p. 13.
[a]Figures for 1980-2010 are based on the U.S. Census Bureau's Series II projections. For an explanation of this series, see U.S. Bureau of the Census, *Current Population Reports*, ser. P-25, no. 601, 1975, p. 7.
(NA) = Not Available.

Table B.4
Distribution of the Older Population by Marital Status by Age and Sex, 1975

Marital Status	Male 65 to 74 years	75 years and over	65 years and over	Female 65 to 74 years	75 years and over	65 years and over
Percent, total	100.0	100.0	100.0	100.0	100.0	100.0
Single	4.3	5.5	4.7	5.8	5.8	5.8
Married	83.9	70.0	79.3	49.0	23.4	39.1
Spouse present	81.8	68.2	77.3	47.3	22.3	37.6
Spouse absent	2.0	1.8	2.0	1.8	1.1	1.5
Widowed	8.8	23.3	13.6	41.9	69.4	52.5
Divorced	3.1	1.2	2.5	3.3	1.5	2.6

Source: U.S. Bureau of the Census, *Current Population Reports*, ser. P-20, nos. 33, 105, 255, 287; and ser. P-25, no. 607.

Table B.5
Living Arrangements of Men and Women Aged 65 and Over, 1975
(By Percent)

Male			Female		
		65-74 YEARS			
Family	*Alone*	*Institutionalized*	*Family*	*Alone*	*Institutionalized*
85	12.1	2.9	64.6	32.9	2.5
		OVER 75 YEARS			
74.5	18.2	7.4	49.4	40.6	10.0

Source: U.S. Bureau of the Census, *Current Population Reports*, Special Studies, ser. P-23, no. 59, May 1976, p. 48.

Table B.6
Selected Life Table Values by Age, Race, and Sex, United States, 1974

	Total	**White**		**All Others**	
		Male	*Female*	*Male*	*Female*
Expectation of life (additional years) at age					
65	15.5	13.4	17.6	13.4	16.8
Median age at death	75.8	72.5	80.2	66.4	74.2
Life expectancy at birth					
1900	47.3	46.6	48.7	32.5	33.5
1960	69.7	67.4	74.1	61.1	66.3
1970	70.9	68.0	75.6	61.3	69.4
1974	71.9	68.9	76.6	62.9	71.3
Percent of population reaching age 65					
1900-1902	40.9	39.2	43.8	19.0	22.0
1974	73.8	68.5	82.7	52.9	69.9
Death rates (1975) per 1,000 population					
all ages	9.0	10.2	7.9	10.1	6.8
55-64	15.0	19.7	9.4	28.6	16.5
65-74	32.2	44.0	21.7	50.1	31.8
75-84	74.5	97.3	60.8	88.1	62.2
85 and over	152.1	184.2	146.4	116.5	88.8

Source: U.S. Department of Health, Education and Welfare, Public Health Service, Health Resources Administration, National Center for Health Statistics, *Vital Statistics of the U.S.*, 1974, vol. 2, section 5, "Life Tables"; and *Monthly Vital Statistics Report*, "Provisional Statistics, Annual Summary for the U.S., 1975, Births, Deaths, Marriages, Divorces."

Table B.7

**Self-Assessment of Health Status by Age for Selected Demographic Characteristics, 1973
(Percentages)**

	Total			Excellent			Good			Fair			Poor		
	17-44	45-64	65+	17-44	45-64	65+	17-44	45-64	65+	17-44	45-64	65+	17-44	45-64	65+
Total	100	100	100	52	35	29	39	42	39	7	16	22	1	6	9
Sex															
Male	100	100	100	57	38	31	35	40	38	6	15	21	1	6	10
Female	100	100	100	48	33	28	42	44	40	8	18	23	2	6	9
Race															
White	100	100	100	54	36	30	38	42	40	6	15	22	1	6	8
All other	100	100	100	38	24	20	45	39	33	13	26	28	3	10	18
Family Income															
Under $5,000	100	100	100	40	18	25	42	35	38	13	28	25	4	18	11
$5,000-$9,999	100	100	100	48	29	31	42	44	39	9	20	22	2	6	7
$10,000-$14,999	100	100	100	54	37	36	39	45	38	6	14	18	1	4	8
$15,000 and over	100	100	100	62	47	39	34	42	41	4	9	15	1	2	4

Source: National Center for Health Statistics, *Health United States*, 1975, pp. 437, 439, 551, using Health Interview Survey data.

Table B.8
Chronic Activity by Age and Sex, United States, 1974
(Percentages)

Sex and age	Total Population	With No Limitation of Activity	With Limitation of Activity				
			Total	Limited but not in major activity[a]	Limited in amount or kind of major activity[a]	Unable to carry on major activity[a]
Both sexes							
All ages	100.0	85.9	14.1	3.5	7.3	3.3	
65 years and over	100.0	54.1	45.9	6.6	22.1	17.1	
Male							
All ages	100.0	85.7	14.3	3.6	5.6	5.1	
65 years and over	100.0	50.3	49.7	4.8	15.0	29.8	
Female							
All ages	100.0	86.0	14.0	3.5	8.8	1.7	
65 years and over	100.0	56.9	43.1	7.8	27.2	8.2	

Source: National Center for Health Statistics, *Vital and Health Statistics*, ser. 10, no. 112, 1976, "Health Characteristics of Persons with Chronic Activity Limitations."

[a]Major activity refers to ability to work, keep house, or engage in school or preschool activities.

Table B.9
Percentage of Persons with Mobility Limitation According to Selected Demographic Characteristics, United States, 1972 (By Age)

Demographic Characteristic	With Limitation of Mobility											
	Total			Confined to the house			Need help in getting around			Have trouble getting around alone		
	17-44	45-64	65+	17-44	45-64	65+	17-44	45-64	65+	17-44	45-64	65+
Total[a]	.9	4.8	17.6	.3	1.3	5.2	.3	1.1	6.7	.5	2.4	5.8
Sex												
Male	1.0	5.0	16.2	.2	1.2	4.9	.2	1.2	6.0	.5	2.6	5.4
Female	.9	4.6	18.6	.1	1.4	5.3	.2	1.0	7.2	.4	2.3	6.1
Color												
White	.9	4.4	17.0	.2	1.2	4.9	.3	1.0	6.5	.4	2.2	5.6
All other	1.5	8.6	23.7	.4	2.7	7.7	b	1.6	8.3	.7	4.3	7.7
Family Income												
Under $5,000	2.5	12.9	20.2	.7	4.1	6.0	.6	2.7	7.5	1.1	6.1	6.7
$5,000-$9,999	.9	4.8	14.7	b	1.1	4.2	b	1.2	5.2	.5	2.5	5.2
$10,000-$14,000	.6	2.8	14.9	b	.6	4.3	.2	.6	6.2	.3	1.5	4.5
$15,000 and over	.4	1.5	14.9	b	b	3.7	b	.4	7.2	.2	.9	4.0

Source: National Center for Health Statistics, *Health United States 1975*, pp. 495, 497, 563, using Health Interview Survey data.

[a]Includes unknown income.

[b]Figure does not meet NCHS standards of reliability or precision.

BIBLIOGRAPHY

No handbook on older Americans as comprehensive as this one has been previously published. However, there are numerous texts and handbooks on various aspects of aging which may be useful to the interested reader. A few of the more recent and prominent ones are listed below, in alphabetical order by author's last name.

Achenbaum, W. *Shades of grey: Old age, American values, and federal policies since 1920*. Little, Brown, Boston, 1983.

Atchley, R. *The social forces in later life*. 3rd ed. Wadsworth, Belmont, Calif., 1980.

Barrow, G.M., and Smith, P.A. *Aging, ageism, and society*. West, St. Paul, Minn., 1979.

Binstock, R.H., and Shanas, E. (Eds.). *Handbook of aging and the social sciences*. Van Nostrand Reinhold, New York, 1976.

Birren, J.E., and Schaie, K.W. (Eds.). *Handbook of the psychology of aging*. Van Nostrand Reinhold, New York, 1977.

Busse, E., and Blazer, D. (Eds.). *Handbook of geriatric psychiatry*. Van Nostrand Reinhold, New York, 1980.

Busse, E.W., and Pfeiffer, E. (Eds.). *Behavior and adaptation in late life*. 2nd ed. Little, Brown, Boston, 1977.

Cowgill, D.O., and Holmes, L.D. (Eds.). *Aging and modernization*. Appleton-Century-Crofts, New York, 1972.

Finch, C.F., and Hayflick, L. *Handbook of the biology of aging*. Van Nostrand Reinhold, New York, 1977.

Harris, C.S. *Fact book on aging: A profile of America's older population*. National Council on the Aging, Washington, D.C., 1978.

Harris, L. *Aging in the eighties*. National Council on the Aging, Washington, D.C., 1981.

Haynes, S.G.; Feinleib, M.; Ross, J.A.; and Stallones, L. *Epidemiology of aging*. National Institutes of Health, Washington, D.C., 1980.

Hendricks, J., and Hendricks, C.D. *Aging in mass society: Myths and realities*. 2nd ed. Winthrop, Cambridge, Mass., 1981.

Jackson, J.J. *Minorities and aging*. Wadsworth, Belmont, Calif., 1980.

Kalish, R.A. *The later years: Social applications of gerontology*. Brooks/Cole, Monterey, Calif., 1977.

Kart, G.S., and Manard, B.B. (Eds.). *Aging in America: Readings in social gerontology*. Alfred Publishing, New York, 1976.

Levin, J., and Levin, W. *Ageism: Prejudice and discrimination against the elderly*. Wadsworth, Belmont, Calif., 1980.

Palmore, E. *International handbook on aging: Contemporary developments and research*. Greenwood Press, Westport, Conn., 1980.

———. *Social patterns in normal aging: Findings from the Duke Longitudinal Studies*. Duke University Press, Durham, N.C., 1981.

Riley, M.W., and Foner, A. *Aging and society. Volume 1: An inventory of research findings*. Russell Sage Foundation, New York, 1968.

Riley, M.W.; Johnson, M.E.; and Foner, A. *Aging and society. Volume 3: A sociology of age stratification*. Russell Sage Foundation, New York, 1972.

Riley, M.W.; Riley, J.W., Jr.; and Johnson, M.E. *Aging and society. Volume 2: Aging and the professions*. Russell Sage Foundation, New York, 1969.

Schulz, J.H. *The economics of aging*. 2nd ed. Wadsworth, Belmont, Calif., 1980.

Wantz, M.S., and Gay, J.E. *The aging process: A health perspective*. Winthrop, Cambridge, Mass., 1981.

The most prominent American journals on aging and their publishers are:

Aging
Administration on Aging
HHS North Building
330 Independence Ave. SW
Washington, DC 20201

The Gerontologist
Gerontological Society of America
1411 K St. NW, Suite 300
Washington, DC 20005

International Journal of Aging and Human Development
Baywood Publishing Co.
120 Marine St.
Farmingdale, NY 11735

The Journal of Gerontology
Gerontological Society of America
1411 K St. NW, Suite 300
Washington, DC 20005

Research on Aging
Sage Publications
275 S. Beverly Dr.
Beverly Hills, CA 90212

AUTHOR INDEX

SUBJECT INDEX

CONTRIBUTORS

Ronald H. Aday, Ph.D., Gerontology Program Coordinator, Middle Tennessee State University

Lucille B. Bearon, Ph.D., Department of Sociology, Norfolk State University

Donald W. Calhoun, Ph.D., Department of Sociology, University of Miami

William B. Clifford, Ph.D., Department of Sociology, North Carolina State University

Bertram J. Cohler, Ph.D., Committee on Human Development, The University of Chicago

Msgr. Charles J. Fahey, Director, The Third Age Center, Fordham University

James L. Fozard, Ph.D., Office of Extended Care, Veterans Administration Central Office

Linda K. George, Ph.D., Center for the Study of Aging and Human Development, Duke University Medical Center

Prue Gerry, Ph.D., Gerontology Center, Georgia State University

Ruth L. Greene, Ph.D., Department of Psychology, Johnson C. Smith University

Tim B. Heaton, Ph.D., Family and Demographic Research Institute, Brigham Young University

Caroline Hoppe, Ph.D., Department of History, University of Southern California

Edwin B. Hutchins, Ph.D., Director, Center for Research on Health Professions Education, University of Pennsylvania

Boaz Kahana, Ph.D., Oakland University

Eva Kahana, Ph.D., Director, Elderly Care Research Center, Wayne State University

Toshi Kii, Ph.D., Department of Sociology, Georgia State University

Carmela G. Lacayo, President, National Association for Hispanic Elderly

Mary Ann Lewis, Ph.D., The Third Age Center, Fordham University

Aaron Lipman, Ph.D., Department of Sociology, University of Miami

Helena Z. Lopata, Ph.D., Center for the Comparative Study of Social Roles, Loyola University

National Indian Council on Aging, Albuquerque, N.M.

Angela M. O'Rand, Department of Sociology, Duke University

Nancy J. Osgood, Ph.D., Medical College of Virginia, Virginia Commonwealth University

Erdman B. Palmore, Ph.D., Center for the Study of Aging and Human Development, Duke University Medical Center

Barbara P. Payne, Ph.D., Director, Gerontology Center, Georgia State University

Robert E. Pieroni, M.D., College of Community Health Sciences, The University of Alabama

Ilene C. Siegler, Ph.D., Center for the Study of Aging and Human Development, Duke University Medical Center

Gordon F. Streib, Ph.D., Department of Sociology, University of Florida

Frank J. Whittington, Ph.D., Department of Sociology, Georgia State University

About the Editor

ERDMAN B. PALMORE is Professor of Medical Sociology and Senior Fellow in the Duke Center for the Study of Aging and Human Development. He is the author of *International Handbook on Aging* (Greenwood Press, 1980), *Social Patterns in Normal Aging,* and *Normal Aging I* and *II.*